Politics and Government
in Germany, 1944–1994
Basic Documents

Politics and Government in Germany, 1944–1994
Basic Documents

Edited by Carl-Christoph Schweitzer,
Detlev Karsten, Robert Spencer,
R. Taylor Cole†, Donald Kommers,
Anthony Nicholls

Berghahn Books
Providence • Oxford

First published in 1995 by

Berghahn Books

Editorial offices:
165 Taber Avenue, Providence, RI 02906, USA
Bush House, Merewood Avenue, Oxford, OX3 8EF, UK

Library of Congress Cataloging-in-Publication Data
Politics and government in Germany, 1944–1994 : basic documents /
    edited by Carl-Christoph Schweitzer ... [et al..].
        p.   cm.
    Rev. ed. of: Politics and government in the Federal Republic of
Germany.   1984.
    Includes bibliographical references and index.
    ISBN 1-57181-854-5   1-57181-855-3 (pbk.)
        1. Germany--Constitutional history--Sources.   2. Germany--Politics
and government--1945- --Sources.   3. Germany--Foreign
relations--1945- --Sources..   4. Germany--History--Unification, 1990-
-Sources.   I. Schweitzer, Carl-Christoph.   II. Politics and
government in the Federal Republic of Germany.
KK4443.6.P65   1995
343.43'029--dc20   94-25228
[344.30229]   CIP

British Library Cataloguing in Publication Data

A catalogue record for this book is available from the British Library.

Printed in the USA by Edwards Brothers, Inc., Ann Arbor MI on acid-free paper.

Contents

6   Defence Policy and the Armed Forces

1976—*Doc. 5c:* The employers' criticisms of co-determination at board level, 1977—*Doc. 5d:* The Trade Union view of co-determination, 1978—*Doc. 5e:* The Federal Constitutional Court's judgment on the Co-determination Act, 1979—*Doc. 6:* Foreign workers as a challenge to policy, 1993—*Doc. 7:* Treaty on the establishment of a monetary, economic and social union, 18 May 1990—*Doc. 8:* The Treuhandanstalt, n.d.—*Doc. 9:* Restitution before compensation, 23 September 1990—*Doc. 10:* Financial transfers required, 1993

Preface to the First Edition

Interest in the Federal Republic has been growing throughout the Anglo-Saxon world, stimulated by the leading role that country is now playing in Western Europe, as well as by its undoubted political and economic achievements. There are many introductory accounts of the history and politics of the Federal Republic available, but the documentary basis needed to complement such explanatory books is lacking. We have tried to set out the documents in such a way that each section—be it on the Bundestag, the Federal Constitutional Court or the political parties, for example—can be read as a self-contained unit, with its own explanatory introduction and editorial comments; the book has been designed to serve both as a description of the Federal system and as a source book for students; inevitably this has meant selection, but no key point has been omitted. The editors of this volume have all had experience of teaching German politics in Anglo-Saxon universities and have themselves felt the need for a book of this kind. We hope that many teachers of political science, recent history, German studies and international relations will find it of substantial assistance in the preparation of courses and also of use as a means of stimulating interest in the subject among those students motivated to carry out further research.

The documents printed in this volume are taken from original German sources. Where a suitable English translation already existed, we have utilised and acknowledged this. These translations have not been amended, even in the few instances where this might have increased the clarity of the text or where the same German terminology has been translated by differing terms in separate instances. In the majority of cases, however, translations were commissioned by the editors. The source is normally given in German, unless translation of the title makes it more comprehensible for English-speaking readers. We ourselves have used the English translations of German terms wherever possible, but some words are in such common use—Bundestag (Federal Parliament) or Länder (Federal states) for example—that we have kept these in German. In addition a Glossary of terms and abbreviations is provided.

We would like to express our heartfelt thanks to the many institutions which have assisted us and without which this volume could not have been produced, particularly to the Presse- und Informationsamt der Bundesregierung in Bonn, which provided *inter alia* funds for translations, the Robert-Bosch-Stiftung in Stuttgart, which generously financed editorial sessions, and the President of Duke University, North Carolina, who so kindly hosted one of those sessions. Each contributor bears the responsibility for his own chapters; the whole volume was coordinated by C.C. Schweitzer, who provided the original concept.

Summer 1983   Carl-Christoph Schweitzer, Detlev Karsten (Bonn)
Robert Spencer (Toronto)
R. Taylor Cole (Durham)
Donald Kommers (Notre Dame)
Anthony Nicholls (Oxford)

Preface to the Second Edition

The success of the first edition, published in 1984, showed that there was a pressing need for a collection of basic documents in English dealing with the politics and government of the Federal Republic. The 1984 edition dealt exclusively with West Germany. As a result of the revolutionary developments beginning in 1989—the dissolution of the Warsaw Pact, the end of the Cold War, and the collapse of the Soviet Union—a new and enlarged Germany has again arrived on the international scene. Unification influenced legal, cultural, economic, and political aspects of German society, and at the same time the resurgence of ethnic and tribal conflict in the former communist states of Central and Eastern Europe played an important part in reshaping the newly united Germany's role in Europe and the world.

Largely as a result of these historic events which dated the original collection, and at the urging of colleagues and of our publisher, Dr Marion Berghahn of Berghahn Books, we have updated and reorganized the text. The second edition also includes two entirely new chapters dealing with the former German Democratic Republic and with the process of German unification.

We have also changed the sequence of chapters. The chapters on domestic policy and political institutions now follow those which deal with the origins of the Federal Republic and of the German Democratic Republic, foreign policy, Berlin, the two Germanies up to 1989 and German reunification. This new sequence reflects the fact that many aspects of domestic policy, constitutional change, and institutional reform were responses to the achievement of unification. In addition, the two chapters on federalism have been reduced to a single chapter.

Finally, the editor's wish to express their admiration and affection for R. Taylor Cole, a co-editor of the first edition. A Professor Emeritus of Political Science at Duke University, he was a former President of the American Political Science Association and a distinguished authority on German government and politics. At an early stage in planning the first edition we met at his home in Durham. With his death in 1991 we lost a dear friend and respected colleague. We remember him not only for his serene advice and sound judgement, but also for his unfailing kindness and generosity. We proudly dedicate this second edition to his memory.

The aim of this book is to make available to those English-speaking readers interested in present day Germany major source materials relating to the Federal Republic's political system. While some of the problems dealt with have already been documented in English elsewhere, we have kept the chapters fairly short, hoping, however, to provide the reader with an up-to-date overview in more convenient form than would otherwise be available. The literature listed at the end of the volume should be helpful for further study. Some relevant statistics and figures are provided as supporting evidence to points made in the main chapters. The book describes the political system in Bonn as it is in 1994, just after the latest Bundestag election of 16 October, although it does not neglect the appropriate historical background to the various parts of that system.

December 1994

Introduction

The Federal Republic of Germany is not the first parliamentary democracy in German history, but so far it has been the most successful one. Analysts have often drawn comparisons between the Federal Republic and its antecedent, the Weimar Republic of 1919–33. Both Republics were able to invoke traditions of liberal thought and local self-government going back over several centuries; in particular, the 1848 revolutions in Germany had witnessed a widespread enthusiasm for parliamentary rule and political freedom. Both the Weimar Republic and the Federal Republic were burdened with the legacy of military defeat, which brought with it serious economic and social consequences. Here, however, similarities between the two German parliamentary democracies came to an end. In the case of the Federal Republic, there was, in addition, the hateful memory of Nazi rule and the prospect of national dismemberment. These difficulties will be referred to in the first, historical, chapter of this book. In any case, some forty-five years after the Federal Republic was established we are able with justice to echo the words of one early observer and claim that 'Bonn is not Weimar'.

The stability and vitality exhibited by the Federal Republic has been remarkable. It should not be forgotten, of course, that the Western Allied powers avoided many of the more crass errors of 1918–19. For example, they took responsibility for the administration of Germany after defeat and did not subject the new German democracy to an apparently eternal reparations burden. However, we are more concerned here with the extent to which the German founding fathers of the Federal Republic consciously learned from the mistakes of the past to establish a more secure democratic system.

This 'historical dimension' explains why a number of constitutional precautions were taken against a possible repetition of the abuses in Weimar, not to mention the Third Reich. The rights of individuals, of associations and of political parties had to be more carefully protected. The Basic Law *(Grundgesetz)* of 1949 was carefully framed to meet such dangers. It is not least through such provisions in the Basic Law, as examined in Chapter 11, that the resurgence of anti-democratic forces, whether of the Right or the Left has, since 1949, been effectively prevented.

Just as important as political stability has been economic growth. This particularly successful aspect of the Federal Republic's history can be attributed partly to the consistent policy of 'Social Market Economy', which is examined in Chapter 14.

In economic as well as political matters, the letter of the law is of central importance. This is a very significant characteristic of the political system of Germany, and it will be reflected in almost every chapter of this volume. To an extent which may surprise Anglo-Saxon readers, the founders of the Federal Republic, successive legislators and, above all, the judges in the Federal Constitutional Court have relied upon the power of legal provisions to ensure the proper functioning of many important elements in the country's political system. This applies, for example, to the democratic administration of political parties, the observance of democratic principles in the armed forces and the safeguards which are designed to protect the parliamentary system in time of national emergency. In presenting their analysis of that system through the documents, the editors of this volume are aware how risky it is to equate constitutional theory—or the letter of the law—with what actually happens in day-to-day politics. Where it seems appropriate, therefore, they attempt to point out discrepancies between theory and practice in the working of the system.

Bearing this particular problem in mind, a political scientist or historian might then ask: what is the overall *systemic framework* within which the political actors of Germany operate? As in other Western democratic systems, one might distinguish between three different levels of activity which reinforce and complement each other. The first is the *governmental* level, comprising the three classic powers of the executive, the legislature and the judiciary. It is at this level that decision-making takes place, and here that policies are carried out and evaluated. Secondly there is an *intermediary* level of interest groups, most of which exert pressure on the governmental level—a characteristic common to all pluralist societies. Lastly there is the *primary* level, the grass roots of the system, made up of the mass of active citizens who have attained voting age. According to the democratic theory on which the Federal Republic was based, the indivisible sovereignty of the state rests at this level. This is expressed very clearly in Article 20 of the Basic Law: 'All state authority emanates from the people'. It goes on to state that the people exercise that authority 'by means of elections and voting and by specific legislative, executive and judicial organs'.[1] This sentence leaves no doubt that the German political System is based on the idea of 'representative' rather than 'direct' democracy.[2]

So far as the political parties are concerned—as treated in Chapter 8 of this volume—they can be seen as straddling all three levels through grass roots membership, representation of particular interests and participation in government or opposition. Germany is unusual in that the political parties are actually recognised in the constitution itself—i.e. in Article 21 of the Basic Law. Without political parties there could be no parliament in Germany; so far there has not been one single member of the Bundestag elected independently of a political party. Without the support of one or more political parties no chancellor can obtain power and maintain his cabinet in office. The German system is basically one of party government.

When surveying the governmental level of the German system, we can see that the classic division of powers between the executive and the legislative branches is more a theoretical than a practical distinction. In this, the situation in Bonn is similar to that in the capitals of other Western parliamentary democracies. The reason for this is that under normal circumstances there is an identity of interest between the government and the majority which supports it in parliament (described in Chapter 7). It is, therefore, difficult to decide 'who controls whom'.

It is certainly not possible to speak of a *de facto* supremacy of parliament in such systems. In the German context the 'chancellor in Parliament' is supreme, so long as he can muster a majority. It was in this connection that the term 'chancellor democracy' has been coined to describe the German system; it was first applied to Konrad Adenauer's remarkable period of office from 1949 to 1963. The constitution deliberately strengthened the chancellor's position by comparison with his predecessors in the Weimar Republic; in particular it was made impossible for the Bundestag to eject him from office unless it simultaneously voted for a new chancellor in the so-called 'constructive' vote of no-confidence. In the first thirty-three years of the Federal Republic's history such a vote was only moved twice, and it only succeeded on one occasion, when Chancellor Helmut Schmidt was replaced by Helmut Kohl in October 1982.

Within the government the chancellor has a very strong position, as will be shown in Chapter 9. He possesses the right to lay down the general policy guidelines and wields the ultimate executive power.

That is not in the hands of the Federal President, who for the most part exercises his duties in an office concerned with what Bagehot termed the 'dignified parts', but with no real authority.

However, the concept of the separation of powers in the Federal Republic has survived better than the relationship between legislature and executive on the one hand and the judiciary on the other. In particular, the Federal Constitutional Court has played a very important role in controlling both legislative bodies and government activity. Chapters 10 and 12 provide striking illustrations of these functions. In a number of significant cases the Constitutional Court has effectively checked the power of both the Federal government and the Bundestag.

There is another restraint on central government. This is a phenomenon sometimes described as 'vertical' separation of powers: the federal structure of the German Republic. The states—or Länder— of Germany participate in the central legislative process through the second chamber, the Bundesrat.

Although the answer to the question 'who governs?' might seem to be 'the chancellor', this would be an over-simplification. The chancellor and his cabinet, not to mention the political parties, can come under pressure from the intermediary level, the interest groups, and also from the mass media, which sometimes seem to act as an interest group or even independent power factor. This issue will be the subject of Chapter 13, which aims to demonstrate the considerable influence of pressure groups on the decision-making process on all levels.

In Germany, as in other industrialised societies, there seems to be a danger that pressures on the legislature and the executive authorities by special interest groups undermine a government's capacity to rule effectively. A resulting sense of impotence can have a demoralizing effect on the political system. 'Ungovernability' *(Unregierbarkeit)* is perceived as a problem. This is especially true when there are conflicting priorities at stake, such as the desire to protect the environment, on the one hand, and the need for increased energy supplies on the other, or the requirements of the defence budget as against the costs of the welfare state. Governments often find it difficult to steer a straight course when buffeted by pressures from different directions and they are particularly sensitive to such influences when elections are pending. Since German governments have to contend with Land elections as well as Federal ones, their position is especially difficult. These matters are touched on in this volume in the chapters relating to political parties and pressure groups (8 and 13).

One relatively new phenomenon in German politics has been the emergence of so-called 'citizens' initiative groups' *(Bürgerinitiativen)*.

Originally concerned with specific local issues, such as housing or environmental protection, they are now building an alternative type of political grouping to the conventional Bundestag parties. Styling themselves as the Green movement they are currently threatening to replace the liberal party (FDP) as the third political force between the Christian Democrats and the Social Democrats throughout Germany. The strength of this movement should not be exaggerated. Nevertheless, it is possible to detect in it a shift of opinion amongst part of the electorate—the third level of the system mentioned above—and the emergence of a new political culture. This seems to owe a good deal to the younger and academically trained section of the population, which is consciously trying to develop a form of grass-roots democracy *(Basisdemokratie)* hitherto almost absent from the German political tradition.

In the Bundestag election of 16 October 1994, the CDU-FDP coalition government of Helmut Kohl suffered losses but secured sufficient seats to ensure a working majority and thus continuity in government policy. The SPD under Rudolf Scharping won increased support but failed to secure sufficient seats to enable it to form a government with the Bündnis 90-The Greens. Features of the election apart from the victory of Chancellor Kohl, who a few months earlier appeared doomed to defeat, included the survival of the liberal FDP and increased support for the Bündnis 90-The Greens as well as for the PDS, the successor party to the communist SED in the former GDR. The right-wing Republican party secured only 1.9 per cent of the vote and thus failed to obtain representation in the Bundestag.

Notes

1. Translated passages of the Basic Law here and throughout the volume are quoted from the official translation by the Press and Information Office of the Federal Government, Bonn, 1981, with the exceptions stipulated in various chapters concerning amendments which came into force in September/October 1994. Only such amendments, however, were inserted or quoted that were deemed to be of special interest to the reader.
   Unless otherwise stated, translations of documents were commissioned by the authors.
2. By amendment to the Basic Law the following Art. 20a was newly inserted in September 1994: 'The state shall, bearing in mind also its responsibility for future generations, preserve the natural fundamental structures for living by legislation and in accordance with law and justice through its executive and judicial organs within the constitutional order.'

1
The Origins of the Federal Republic of Germany, 1944–1949

Robert Spencer

For forty years, until the tumultuous events of 1989/90, the Federal Republic of Germany celebrated its birthday on 23 May, the date in 1949 on which the Parliamentary Council *(Parlamentarische Rat)*, meeting in Bonn, formally approved its constitution *(Grundgesetz)*. * A provisional creation, the new state formed in the zones occupied in 1945 by the three Western Powers, it was intended to last, as the final article of the constitution decreed, only until 'a constitution adopted by a free decision of the German people comes into force'.[1] The Federal Republic had both German and non-German origins.[2] It was a product of the Second World War, at whose end unconditional surrender and the resulting absence of any central government in Germany had led to the unprecedented assumption by the four leading Allied powers of 'supreme authority with respect to Germany, including all the powers possessed by the German Government, the High Command, and any state, municipal, or local government or authority'.[3] It was also even more directly a product of the Cold War, as East-West differences frustrated the four-power cooperation envisaged in the original post-surrender arrangements. But while Germany was a highly important object of international politics after 1945, the Federal Republic also owed to German initiatives and reflected German traditions, which merged with Allied (and especially American) policies directed towards the 'eventual reconstruction of German political life on a democratic basis'.[4] The extent to which the Federal Republic was the result of the policies of the Western Allies and the extent to which it was the consequence of the endeavours of the Germans themselves is still the subject of academic debate.[5]

Given the wartime occupation agreements between the Allied powers, this outcome was largely unforeseen. True, as late as the

* *Notes for this chapter begin on p. 26.*

Crimea (Yalta) conference in February 1945, Britain, the United States, and the USSR had indeed included among their objectives the 'dismemberment of Germany as they deem requisite for future peace and security'.[6] But they quickly abandoned this policy. At the final wartime meeting at Berlin (Potsdam) in the summer of 1945 they agreed that 'for the time being, no central German government shall be established', but also that during the period of occupation 'Germany shall be treated as a single economic unit'. In addition they envisaged the creation of 'certain essential central German administrative departments' headed by German 'under secretaries', to deal with such matters as finance, trade, transport, communications, and industry.'[7] But determined French opposition to any step which appeared to threaten the revival of a centralized German power prevented their creation.[8] After 1945, the fissiparous tendencies in the occupation arrangements agreed to in the London-based European Advisory Commission in 1944–45 (Doc.1), and the bitter East-West disagreements especially over reparations which, it was agreed at Yalta, 'Germany must pay in kind' to cover Allied losses,[9] together with the resulting dispute over economic policies in occupied Germany, led to the progressive hardening of zonal borders into frontiers dividing differing social and political systems. Within four and a half years of the German surrender, hostile governments had emerged in East and West, as the self-proclaimed German Democratic Republic (DDR/GDR) came into existence on 7 October 1949 in the Soviet zone of occupation with its capital in the Soviet sector of Berlin (see also Ch.3). It was no accident that the decisive steps towards the creation of the Federal Republic in the three Western zones of occupation took place during the total blockade by Soviet forces of land and water routes connecting the Western sectors of Berlin with the Western zones, which for eleven months left only the vital air links intact (Doc.2).

At the beginning the victorious powers had viewed the purpose of the occupation not to liberate but to control a defeated enemy nation, and at the start they discouraged 'fraternization' with German officials and the population, stressed denazification and demilitarization, and emphasized the paramountcy of Allied control.[10] Two years later a new policy decreed that 'there should arise in Germany as rapidly as possible a form of political organization and a manner of political life which, resting on a substantial basis of economic well-being, will lead to tranquillity within Germany and will contribute to the spirit of peace among nations'.[11] And well before that date, the American zone had been merged with the British in the interest of German economic recovery and, confronted with the failure to secure agreement on institutional and political reconstruction on a Germany-wide basis, conscious efforts had begun to recreate German administrative, political and institutional life at the local and regional level.

While the Federal Republic also owed its origins to German efforts, and it reflected German traditions dating back to the Weimar Republic and to the ill-fated attempts to establish a national Germany on a liberal-democratic basis in 1848, the occupation arrangements had paid scant attention to the old Länder boundaries. In the American zone of occupation, Land Bavaria with its capital in Munich was still intact. By September 1945 fragments of Hesse and the old Prussian province of Hesse-Nassau had been reorganized into the new Länder of Württemberg-Baden and Greater Hesse. The northern exclave Bremen became a fourth Land. In the British zone, Lower Saxony, Hamburg, and Schleswig-Holstein became Länder in their own right, while a new Land was created, North Rhine-Westphalia, with its capital in Düsseldorf. Developments in the French zone lagged in view of French designs for annexation or economic exploitation. Baden and Württemberg-Hohenzollern were left as separate Länder. The Saar and a part of the Rhine province of the Palatinate were separated, and the remainder of the French zone organized as Rhineland-Palatinate with its centre in Mainz.[12] In the Soviet zone Brandenburg, Saxony, and Thuringia were left untouched, but Pomerania, cut in half by the Polish 'occupation', was joined to Mecklenburg, and Anhalt and the Prussian province of Saxony formed a new Land. Land governments were set up in which effective Soviet control was 'democratically disguised'[13] (see also Ch.3).

In the interests of effective administration, which was beyond the capacity of the occupation forces, the American and British military governors appointed as a temporary measure a hierarchy of German officials culminating in the formation of a Länder Council (*Länderrat*) composed of minister-presidents who, as General Lucius D. Clay, the United States Deputy Governor, reminded them, were asked to undertake a difficult transitional responsibility because of their 'known anti-Nazi past and ... liberal views'.[14] The Western allies were anxious to encourage German participation through elections on a democratic basis. From the very first months of the occupation the Germans took advantage of this policy to recreate German political life. Three major political forces soon emerged. The Social Democrats (SPD), the only party to vote against Hitler's Enabling Act in March 1933, emerged as a powerful force in the West following the tragic enforced fusion of its eastern wing with the communists in 1946. The current of traditional German liberalism revived in the Free Democratic Party (FDP). And the new political force of Christian Democracy emerged in the Christian Democratic Union (CDU) and its Bavarian sister party, the Christian Social Union (CSU), in the tradition of the old Centre Party, but no longer exclusively Catholic (Doc.3; see also Ch.8). At the same time German politicians played a key role in the evolution of new institutions (and especially of the Land constitutions) authorized and encouraged by the Occupation Powers.[15] The pace at which the Germans regained control over their own destiny was speeded up as Western frustrations over disagreements with the Soviet Union increased. After the Foreign Ministers failed to reach agreement on an all-German solution at the Moscow conference in March-April 1947, the Germans launched their own (but abortive) attempt to stave off the looming division of their country by holding a conference in Munich, in June 1947, of minister-presidents from all the German Länder, east as well as west (Doc.4).

As the East-West breach became manifest in 1948, Marshall Plan aid, coupled with the, at first controversial but in the outcome highly successful, Social Market Economy (see also Ch.14) introduced into the combined American and British zones in the summer of 1948 by Ludwig Erhard (Doc.5), together with the currency reform of June 1948, provided the basis on which the West Germans could move along the road towards recovery and prosperity and underlined the need for the parallel political reconstruction. The decisive step in this process was the London conference of the three Western powers and the Benelux states. In a series of meetings extending from February to June 1948 it agreed on the establishment of a West German state, on measures towards Western European integration, on the creation of the International Authority under which the Ruhr industrial area would be controlled by the Occupation Powers, and on a Military Security Board to allay the fears of Germany's neighbours.[16] In accordance with the London decisions the military governors assembled the minister-presidents of the Länder in Frankfurt and authorized them to convene a constituent assembly to draft a constitution. The sixty-five members of what (to spare German sensitivities) became known as the Parliamentary Council comprised delegates chosen by the Länder legislatures. The distribution of the parties (twenty-seven each from the CDU/CSU and SPD, five FDP and the remaining six from three smaller parties including two from the revived Communist party) explains the narrowness of decisions on most issues, although the mood of the Council was for the most part conciliatory and pervaded by a willingness to make compromises.[17] When the Council met for the first time on 1 September it elected

Konrad Adenauer, a former Centre Party politician in the Weimar Republic and long-time mayor of Cologne, as president, with vice-presidents from the SPD and the FDP. The distinguished professor of constitutional law, Carlo Schmid, was chosen chairman of the Main Committee. A draft, based on the document prepared by a meeting of the minister-presidents at Herrenchiemsee in August, was completed by 1 November 1948.

The document which, in deference to German wishes, the occupation powers eventually agreed should be termed a Basic Law, was conservative in tone. While anxious to erect barriers against any new threat of dictatorship, the members of the Parliamentary Council were also concerned to avoid the errors of 'over-democratization' which were widely believed to have contributed to the fate of the Weimar Republic.[18] Discussions, especially on 'financial federalism', continued throughout the winter, when the intervention of the military governors, who were concerned at the degree of centralization in the constitutional draft, led to further debate and compromise in Bonn and prolonged the process to the early summer.

The revised Basic Law was finally adopted by the Parliamentary Council on 8 May 1949, four years to the day after Germany's surrender of the Third Reich. Approval by the military governors, with some significant reservations, followed on 12 May (Doc.6), and the Occupation Statute, outlining the powers reserved to the Western Powers, came into effect on the same day. The Basic Law was approved by the Land assemblies and ratified by the Parliamentary Council in a formal ceremony on 23 May (Doc.7).

The elections to the Federal Republic's first Bundestag which followed on 14 August 1949 foreshadowed the political pattern which was to persist for the succeeding decades. Despite a widespread belief that, as in much of the rest of Europe, the disturbed state of the old continent after the collapse of the Third Reich meant that the time was ripe for a turn to the left, the Christian Democratic Union and its Bavarian wing, the Christian Social Union, emerged as the strongest party, with a narrow majority over its principal rival, the Social Democratic Party (31.0 per cent of the popular vote against 29.2 per cent). On 12 September Professor Theodor Heuss, a respected historian and publicist who had been active in German politics before 1933, was elected federal president (Doc.8). Three days later, Dr Adenauer, who had played a leading role in the construction of the CDU (see also Ch.8), was elected federal chancellor by the narrowest of possible margins—one vote, presumably his own. Lacking an overall majority for his own party, he formed a coalition with the Free Democrats and the small, conservative German Party, the first of the successive coalitions which have conducted the government of the Federal Republic since 1949 (Doc.9). Given his age (he was seventy-three in 1949), few could have expected that Konrad Adenauer would remain chancellor and dominate the German political scene for a further fourteen years, or that the period of CDU dominance in the chancellery would endure until 1969.

The other German state which was to merge with the Federal Republic in 1990 came into being in a very different fashion. Following the early development of a German administrative structure for their zone, the Soviets led the way in making political parties of key importance (see also Chs.3 and 8). A group of Moscow-trained, German Communists under the leadership of Walter Ulbricht had arrived in Bruchmühle, just east of Berlin, on 30 April 1945, the day of Hitler's suicide. On 11 June, one day after Soviet Order No.2 authorized the formation of 'anti-fascist parties' and 'free trade unions', the revived Communist Party of Germany (KPD) emerged (Doc.10). In April 1946 it was directed by the Soviet Military Administration into a merger through which it absorbed the SPD (which was henceforth banned from the Soviet Zone). The new Socialist Unity Party of Germany (SED) (see also Ch.3) became the instrument of Soviet policy (Doc.11). On 6 December 1947, as the differences between the victorious allies widened, the SED organized demonstrations in Berlin to demand the formation of a 'German People's Congress for Unity and Peace'(Doc.12). Designed as a pre-parliament (*Vorparlament*), it led a vociferous propaganda attack against the West. In March 1948 a second 'People's Congress' established a four-hundred strong 'German People's Council' which, in October, approved in principle a provisional constitution providing for a bicameral legislature and every ostensible feature of parliamentary democracy (Doc.13). Endorsed by the 'People's Council' in March 1949, it was the basis of the regime which came into being on 7 October of the same year, with Wilhelm Pieck, a pre-1933 Communist as President, Otto Grotewohl, the former leader of the SPD in the Soviet Zone, as Prime Minister, and Walter Ulbricht as one of the Deputy Prime Ministers. The People's Council was simply proclaimed as the Provisional Chamber of the new regime (Doc.14). In the first elections, postponed to October 1950, even Nazi totalitarian records were shattered: of the 98.539 per cent of the electorate which voted, 99.719 per cent cast their votes in favour of the single list of candidates presented by the 'National Front' of all parties which had been proclaimed in advance of the poll by Walter Ulbricht. As the SED party chief and in 1960, after the death of Wilhelm Pieck, as Chairman of the State Council, he was to remain the most powerful figure in the East-German hierarchy until he was toppled in May 1971 (see also Ch.3).

The first two documents which follow constitute the basic wartime agreements for the four-power occupation of Germany within its 1937 frontiers (exclusive of the Königsberg area whose annexation to the Soviet Union was approved at Potsdam, and the remaining territories east of the Oder-Neisse line which were placed under Polish administration pending a final peace treaty). The third, enacted two years later, sealed the fate of Prussia.

Document 1a

PROTOCOL BETWEEN THE GOVERNMENTS OF THE UNITED KINGDOM, THE UNITED STATES OF AMERICA, AND THE UNION OF SOVIET SOCIALIST REPUBLICS, AND THE PROVISIONAL GOVERNMENT OF THE FRENCH REPUBLIC ON THE ZONES OF OCCUPATION IN GERMANY AND THE ADMINISTRATION OF 'GREATER BERLIN', 12 SEPTEMBER 1944, AS AMENDED BY THE AGREEMENTS OF 14 NOVEMBER 1944 AND 26 JULY 1945

Source: Selected Documents on Germany and the Question of Berlin, 1944–1961, London, HMSO, 1961, Cmnd. 1552, 27–30, 35–6, 45–8

The Governments of the United Kingdom of Great Britain and Northern Ireland, the United States of America, and the Union of Soviet Socialist Republics and the Provisional Government of the French Republic, have reached the following agreement with regard to the execution of Article 11 of the Instrument of Unconditional Surrender of Germany:

1. Germany, within her frontiers as they were on the 31st December 1937, will, for the purposes of occupation, be divided into four zones, one of which will be allotted to each of the four Powers, and a special Berlin area, which will be under joint occupation by the four Powers.
2. The boundaries of the four zones and of the Berlin area, and the allocation of the four zones as between the U.K., the U.S.A., the U.S.S.R. and the Provisional Government of the French Republic will be as follows:

Eastern Zone ...
The territory of Germany (including the province of East Prussia) situated to the East of a line drawn from the point on Lübeck Bay where the frontiers of Schleswig-Holstein and Mecklenburg meet ... will be occupied by armed forces of the U.S.S.R., with the exception of the Berlin area, for which a special system of occupation is provided below.

...

North-Western (United Kingdom) Zone ...
The territory of Germany situated to the west of the line defined in the description of the Eastern (Soviet) Zone, ... will be occupied by the armed forces of the United Kingdom.

...

South-Western (United States) Zone ...
The territory of Germany situated to the south and east of a line commencing at the junction of the frontiers of Saxony, Bavaria and Czechoslovakia and extending westwards along the northern frontier of Bavaria to ... where the latter meets the Austro-German frontier will be occupied by armed forces of the United States of America.
For the purpose of facilitating communications between the South-Western Zone and the sea, the Commander-in-Chief of the United States forces in the South-Western Zone will
(a) exercise such control of the ports of Bremen and Bremerhaven and the necessary staging areas in the vicinity thereof as may be agreed hereafter ...

...

Western (French) Zone ...
The territory of Germany, situated to the south and west of a line commencing at the junction of the frontiers of Belgium and of the Prussian Regierungsbezirke of Trier and Aachen and extending eastward along the northern frontier of the Prussian Regierungsbezirk of Trier ... to the point where the eastern frontier of the district of Lindau meets the Austro-German frontier will be occupied by armed forces of the French Republic.

...

Berlin Area ...
The Berlin area (by which expression is understood the territory of 'Greater Berlin' as defined by the Law of the 27th April 1920) will be jointly occupied by armed forces of the U.K., U.S.A., and U.S.S.R., and the French Republic assigned by the respective Commanders-in-Chief. For this purpose the territory of 'Greater Berlin' will be divided into the following four parts ... [19]
(3) The occupying forces in each of the zones into which Germany is divided will be under a Commander-in-Chief designated by the Government of the country whose forces occupy that zone.

...

(5) An Inter-Allied Governing Authority (Kommandatura) consisting of four Commandants, appointed by their respective Commanders-in-Chief, will be established to direct jointly the administration of the 'Greater Berlin' Area.

Document 1b

STATEMENT BY THE GOVERNMENTS OF THE UNITED KINGDOM, THE UNITED STATES OF AMERICA, THE UNION OF SOVIET SOCIALIST REPUBLICS AND THE PROVISIONAL

GOVERNMENT OF THE FRENCH REPUBLIC ON CONTROL
MACHINERY IN GERMANY, 5 JUNE 1945

*Source: Selected Documents on Germany and the Question of Berlin,
1944–1961,* London, HMSO, 1961, Cmnd. 1552, 43–4

(1) In the period when Germany is carrying out the basic requirements of
unconditional surrender, supreme authority in Germany will be exercised,
on instructions from their Governments, by the British, United States,
Soviet and French Commanders-in-Chief, each in his own zone of occupation, and also jointly, in matters affecting Germany as a whole. The four
Commanders-in-Chief will together constitute the Control Council. Each
Commander-in-Chief will be assisted by a Political Adviser.

(2) The Control Council, whose decisions shall be unanimous, will ensure
appropriate uniformity of action by the Commanders-in-Chief in their
respective zones of occupation and will reach agreed decisions on the chief
questions affecting Germany as a whole.

(3) Under the Control Council, there will be a permanent Co-ordinating
Committee composed of one representative of each of the four Comman-
ders-in-Chief, and a Control Staff organised in the following Divisions
(which are subject to adjustment in the light of experience):
Military; Naval; Air; Transport; Political; Economic; Finance; Reparation,
Deliveries and Restitution; Internal Affairs and Communications; Legal;
Prisoners of War and Displaced Persons; Man-power.

...

(7) The administration of the 'Greater Berlin' area will be directed by an
Inter Allied Governing Authority, which will operate under the general
direction of the Control Council, and will consist of four Commandants,
each of whom will serve in rotation as Chief Commandant ...

(8) The arrangements outlined above will operate during the period of
occupation following German surrender, when Germany is carrying out
the basic requirements of unconditional surrender. Arrangements for the
subsequent period will be the subject of a separate agreement.

Document 1c

CONTROL COUNCIL LAW NO.46: ABOLITION OF THE STATE
OF PRUSSIA 25 FEBRUARY 1947

Source: Control Council, Official Gazette, No.14, 31 March 1947, 262

The Prussian State which from early days has been a bearer of mili-
tarism and reaction in Germany has de facto ceased to exist.

Guided by the interest of preservation of peace and security of
peoples and with the desire to assure further reconstruction of the
political life of Germany on a democratic basis, the Control Council
enacts as follows:

Article I

The Prussian State together with its central government and all its agencies is abolished.

Article II

Territories which were part of the Prussian State and which are at present under the supreme authority of the Control Council will receive the status of Länder or will be absorbed into Länder ....

In the wartime agreements no firm arrangements were made for water and land connections between Berlin and the Western Zones. The postwar arrangements for air corridors and a four-power Berlin Air Safety Centre, however, made possible the 1948–49 air lift during which the people of West Berlin, led by Germans such as the ex-Communist, Ernst Reuter, whose election as Governing Mayor had been vetoed on Russian insistence, rallied to the Western side.

Document 2a

CONTROL COUNCIL APPROVAL OF AIR CORRIDORS, 30 NOVEMBER 1945

Source: Documents on Berlin, 1943–1963, Munich, 1963, 37ff.

...

(110) Proposed Air Routes for Inter-Zonal Flights
The Meeting had before them CONL/P (45) 63.
Marshal Zhukov recalled that the Coordinating Committee had approved the establishing of three air corridors, namely, Berlin-Hamburg, Berlin-Bückeburg and Berlin-Frankfurt-on-Main.
Field Marshal Montgomery expressed the hope that in due course the question of establishing the remaining air corridors would be settled satisfactorily.
General Koenig approved the paper in principle and shared the opinion of Field Marshal Montgomery.
Marshal Zhukov expressed himself confident that in due course the other air corridors would be opened ...

The Meeting
(110)
(a) approved the establishment of three air corridors from Berlin to the Western zones as defined in CONL/P (45) 63;

(b) agreed to refer proposal of the Soviet delegation on the placing of air-fields at the disposal of the Soviet authorities or the setting up of Soviet ground crews in the Western zones to the Air Directorate for study.

Document 2b

SPEECH OF ERNST REUTER TO AN SPD RALLY, 24 JUNE 1948

Source: Berlin. *Quellen und Dokumente, 1945–51*, (2. Halbband), Berlin, n.d., 1468–9

... At our large demonstration in front of our Reichstag building on 18 March I said: After the 1948 Prague incident the entire world posed the question: Whose turn will it be next? Finland maybe or even Berlin? The Berlin popula tion gave its answer clearly and distinctly. We shall apply all the means at our disposal and repel to our utmost the claim to power which wants to turn us into slaves and helots for a political party. We lived under such slavery in Adolf Hitler's empire. We have had enough of that. We do not want a recurrence ...

We know precisely that we are an unarmed, conquered and basically defenceless nation. Our strength does not lie in the outer strength, this was taken from us. The protection from which we outwardly benefit, for instance by our police force, is more than questionable. Our strength really only lies in the fact that we defend with all means the freedom of our people, their right to self-assertion and self-government ...

There are always people who at critical moments start to talk about how one must come to terms with reality, with facts, with things and conditions. For example, people thought they were insulting me by saying I was the personification of a lack of discernment of actual conditions. Here, too, we Germans have collected enough bitter experiences. We know this way as well. Everyone who came to terms with the actual conditions in 1933 was also prepared to make peace with Hitler. There were enough excuses. People always wanted to prevent something worse. In the end Germany lay in ruins. We had not only lost our freedom but we were also retarded for a generation, condemned to a beggar's existence.

Today we are basically dealing with the same problem. Today, too, Berlin can only exist, Germany can only exist, if it learns to fight for its freedom, for its right and for its self-assertion and does not sell its birthright ...

In spite of the assumption of supreme authority by the governments of the United Kingdom, the United States, the USSR, and the Provisional Government of the French Republic following the unconditional surrender of the German High Command on 8 May 1945, within a few months the formation of political parties was authorized in all four zones of occupation.

Document 3

THE EMERGENCE OF GERMAN POLITICAL PARTIES AFTER
1945; DIRECTIVE BY THE BRITISH MILITARY GOVERNMENT
CONCERNING THE FORMATION OF POLITICAL PARTIES, 15
SEPTEMBER 1945

Source: Ossip K. Flechtheim, ed., *Dokumente zur parteipolitischen Entwicklung in Deutschland*, I, Berlin, 1962, 109–12

In order to encourage the development of a democratic spirit in Germany
and prepare free elections for a date yet to be appointed, the following directives are issued herewith:

Art. 1. Formation of Political Parties

(1) Political parties can be formed in a district (Kreis) according to the directives contained herein.

(2) The military government can allow parties which have been formed
according to these directives to unite with one another in larger areas,
thereby dispensing with certain rules and conditions.

(3) Membership in political parties must be voluntary.

Art. 2. Method of Application

(4) Every person or group of persons who has the wish to form a political
party for a Kreis can apply to the military government for permission to form
such a party.

...

(6) Notification of permission, whether to form a party or unite already
established ones, will be delivered to the applicants by the military government. This permission (in future to be called military government permission) will be issued in writing and will contain the rules and conditions
according to which the political party is to be formed or according to which
already established parties can be united. Neither the formation nor the
union of political parties can take effect before the military government permission is granted.

(7) The grant of a military government permission according to this regulation does not include the right to hold political meetings without a permission according to Regulation No. 10 or to organize public processions
without a permission according to Regulation No. 11.

...

ALL-GERMAN MEETING OF MINISTER-PRESIDENTS, MUNICH,
5–7 JUNE 1947

The collapse of any hopes of four-power agreement over Germany at the
Moscow conference of Foreign Ministers (March-April 1947) and the continuing serious economic situation (which inspired the Americans to launch the
Marshall Plan in June) encouraged the Western powers to place greater
emphasis on reconstruction, economic and political. The threat which this
involved of the division of Germany along the line dividing the Soviet zone

from those of the Western powers persuaded the German minister-presidents to launch an initiative of their own, ostensibly to grapple with economic issues but in fact constituting a last-ditch effort to proceed on a four-zonal basis.

Document 4a

INVITATION OF THE MINISTER-PRESIDENT OF BAVARIA, EHARD, TO A CONFERENCE OF MINISTER-PRESIDENTS OF ALL FOUR OCCUPATION ZONES, 7 MAY 1947

Source: Akten zur Vorgeschichte der Bundesrepublik Deutschland, 1945–1949, II, Munich, 1979, 424–5

In the name of the Bavarian government I hereby invite the minister-presidents of all Länder [States] of the four occupation zones to a conference in Munich. I propose as a date Friday the 6th and Saturday the 7th of June. Terms of reference of the conference should be an exploration of measures to be proposed by the responsible minister-presidents to the allied military governments with the aim of preventing the German people from sliding down further into a hopeless economic and political chaos. The Germans are no longer physically and psychologically in a position to come to grips with another winter of hunger and cold in the midst of destroyed cities on the verge of an economic collapse and in political despair. Together, therefore, we must do our best to give the German people a new hope for a gradual improvement of their overall situation. Conscious of this duty towards the Bavarian people and towards the whole German people the Bavarian government proposes to pave the way, through such a conference, for the cooperation of all Länder in Germany on the basis of an economic unity today and a political merger in the future.

The Bavarian government hopes that the minister-presidents of the Länder in all four zones will participate in these deliberations and thereby give evidence of their belief in the unifying ties comprising all parts of Germany as well as their determination to construct together a new state in whatever form ...

Document 4b

FINAL STATEMENT OF MINISTER-PRESIDENT EHARD, 7 JUNE 1947

Source: Akten zur Vorgeschichte der Bundesrepublik Deutschland, 1945–1949, II, Munich, 1979, 586–7

...

Not for us alone, but for the community of all nations we want to strive to the best of our ability. We consider the exclusion of the German people from an active participation in international life especially tragic and disastrous because we are convinced that all basic problems confronting Europe and the world today can be solved if there is good will. This applies equally to the elementary question of reconstructing Germany as a state and to the problems of security, of the delimitation of frontiers, of the overall economy and even of reparations.

However, a German question cannot be solved without Germany. If others are prepared to listen to us, then we will be able to point at least to outlines of a solution to all problems. This I say with great earnestness. Fate and history have placed the German people in the midst of Europe. It cannot well be the meaning of history that we, the Germans, should constitute the line of division in Europe, its main point of dispute, an arena of terrible strife between East and West. We do not want to separate, we want to bring Europe together. We want to be in the midst of that Europe, a sanctuary of peace and security, of justice and humanity ....

Document 4c

REPORT OF THE GENERAL SECRETARY OF THE LÄNDERRAT, ERICH ROSSMAN, TO LT. COL. WINNING, US REGIONAL GOVERNING COORDINATION OFFICE, 9 JUNE 1947
Source: Akten zur Vorgeschichte der Bundesrepublik Deutschland, 1945–1949, II, Munich, 1979, 589–92

...

On the basis of the impressions I got during my stay in the Eastern zone of occupation I had advised the Bavarian government most urgently to stick to their basic approach that only problems connected with the economic impasse of the German people should be dealt with at the Munich conference, that no topic should be ostensibly placed on the agenda which would, by the nature of things, be very problematic, since that could easily result in a breakdown of the whole conference ...

The question as to whether they (the minister-presidents of the Eastern zone) would attend, remained open until June 4th. Surprisingly they then actually arrived in Munich on June 5th ... Although I myself as well as Minister President Ehard had ... requested that proposals should be put forward for the agenda (in advance), no such cooperation was entered into. Whether they took up this position purposely from the beginning or only with the intention of thereby underlining more forcefully the importance attached to the one demand actually put forward at the conference itself, cannot be determined with any certainty ...

The minister-presidents of the Western zones had hoped that joint efforts of the minister-presidents of all zones in those fields where the immediate needs are greatest would enable them to achieve more and more unanimity in their overall approach to the larger political issues and in the end bridge the differences of opinion existing in regard to those issues today. The walk-out of the minister presidents of the Russian zone has destroyed all such hopes. This occurrence has clearly demonstrated the fact that the time does not yet seem to have come when Germany as a whole can put on record a common stance vis-à-vis the occupying powers. However, the conference of Munich has shown most impressively that the will to achieve (national) unity again is very much alive ...

Ludwig Erhard, who had directed the Frankfurt Economic Council of the combined United States-British Zones since 1 January 1947, launched the West German 'economic miracle' by abandoning the controls which he believed were paralysing German recovery and taking full advantage of the inclusion of the Western zones in the Marshall Plan (European Recovery Plan).

Document 5

LUDWIG ERHARD ON THE SOCIAL MARKET ECONOMY, 22 AUGUST 1948

Source: *Prosperity through Competition*, London, 1958, 14

It isn't as if we had had any choice. What we had to do in this situation was to loosen the shackles. We had to be prepared to restore basic moral principles and to start with a purge of the economy of our society.

We have done more, by turning from a State-controlled economy to a market economy, than merely introduce economic measures. We have laid new foundations for our social and economic life. We had to abjure all intolerance which, from a spiritual lack of freedom, leads to tyranny and totalitarianism. We had to strive for an order which by voluntary regrouping and a sense of responsibility would lead to a sensible organic whole.

...

Following extensive discussions in Washington, the Western military governors approved the Basic Law drafted by the Parliamentary Council with some significant reservations (especially over Berlin). They prepared for the new phase in the occupation by promulgating an Occupation Statute defining their more limited continuing authority, and prepared to hand over their own functions to an Allied High Commission on the entry into force of the Basic Law.

Document 6

LETTER OF THE MILITARY GOVERNORS TO DR KONRAD
ADENAUER, PRESIDENT OF THE PARLIAMENTARY COUNCIL,
12 MAY 1949

Source: United States Department of State, *Germany, 1947–1949: the Story
in Documents,* Washington, 1950, 279–80

1. The Basic Law passed on 8 May by the Parliamentary Council has
   received our careful and interested attention. In our opinion it happily
   combines German democratic tradition with the concepts of representative government and a rule of law which the world has come to recognize
   as requisite to the life of a free people.
2. In approving this constitution for submission to the German people for
   ratification in accordance with the provisions of Article 144 (1) we believe
   that you will understand that there are several reservations which we must
   make. In the first place, the powers vested in the Federation by the Basic
   Law, as well as the powers exercised by Länder and local Governments,
   are subject to the provisions of the Occupation Statute which we have
   already transmitted to you and which is promulgated as of this date.
3. In the second place, it should be understood that the police powers contained in Article 91 (2) may not be exercised until specifically approved by
   the Occupation Authorities ...
4. A third reservation concerns the participation of Greater Berlin in the Federation. We interpret the effect of Articles 23 and 144 (2) of the Basic Law
   as constituting acceptance of our previous request that while Berlin may not
   be accorded voting membership in the Bundestag or Bundesrat nor be governed by the Federation she may, nevertheless, designate a small number of
   representatives to attend the meetings of those legislative bodies.
   ...
8. In order to eliminate the possibility of future legal controversy, we would
   like to make it clear that when we approved constitutions for the Länder
   we provided that nothing contained in those constitutions could be interpreted as restricting the provisions of the Federal constitution. Conflict
   between Länder constitutions and the provisional Federal constitution
   must, therefore, be resolved in favor of the latter.
9. We should also like it to be clearly understood that upon the convening
   of the legislative bodies provided for in the Basic Law, and upon the election of the President and the election and appointment of the Chancellor and the Federal Ministers, respectively, in the manner provided for in
   the Basic Law, the Government of the Federal Republic of Germany will
   then be established and the Occupation Statute shall thereupon enter
   into force ...

Following approval by the Military Governors, the Basic Law was
approved by the Landtage (state legislatures), not by a popular ref-

erendum. Only Bavaria withheld its consent for the time being. On 23 May 1949 the Parliamentary Council assembled for its twelfth and last sitting. The proceedings were opened by Konrad Adenauer who had presided over the Council's sessions. After his introductory remarks the members of the Council were called forward individually by the secretary, a member of the Council, to sign the completed document. Only two members refused to sign. Dr Adenauer then announced the approval by the Landtage (noting Bavarian refusal to assent), and summoned the minister-presidents of the Länder and the presidents (or speakers) of the Landtage to sign in turn on the call of the secretary. Finally, noting the Berlin City Assembly's concurrence in the 'principles and goals' of the Basic Law, Dr Adenauer invited the president of the Berlin Assembly and the governing mayor to sign. In a closing speech Dr Adenauer noted that the Basic Law would be recorded in the Federal Gazette as Law No. 1 and would take effect as from that day.

Document 7

THE SIGNING AND PROCLAMATION OF THE BASIC LAW (GRUNDGESETZ), 23 MAY 1949

Source: Parlamentarischer Rat, Stenographischer Bericht. Zwölfte Sitzung, Bonn, Monday, 23 May 1948, 270–3

President Dr Adenauer (CDU):

...

Today a new chapter is being opened in the ever-changing history of the German people. Today the Federal Republic of Germany enters the stage of history. Those who have witnessed the years since 1933 and the total breakdown in 1945 ... are with some emotion conscious of the fact that today ... a new Germany is being created. Our endeavours began with the decisions made by the Allies at the London conference in 1948. By them we were limited in regard to the latitude of the decision permitted on some points. Forces which are stronger than the will of the German people have right up to this very day made it impossible for the whole of Germany to be reconstructed into a [new] state. However, in spite of all limitations we can state: the Basic Law which we have decided on is based on the free will, on the free decision of the German people [loud cheers are recorded at this point.] Next to the representatives of the Occupying Powers the Minister Presidents and Presidents of the legislatures of the eleven Länder show by their presence today that the Länder will stand by the Federation (Bund), which also protects and guarantees their existence with affection and in good faith ...

The Roll-call Vote

Secretary **STOCK**: President Dr. Konrad **Adenauer.**—Vice-President Adolph **Schönfelder.**—Vice-President Dr. Hermann **Schäfer.**—Hans Heinz **Bauer.**—Dr. Max **Becker.**—Dr. Ludwig **Bergstraesser.**—Dr. Paul **Binder.**— Adolf **Blomeyer.**—Dr. Heinrich **von Brentano.**—Johannes **Brockmann.**— Dr. Paul de **Chapeaurouge.**—Dr. Thomas **Dehler.**—Dr. Georg **Diederichs**—Dr. Fritz **Eberhard.**—Adolf **Ehlers.**—Dr. Albert **Finck.**— Andreas **Gayk.**—Rudolf **Heiland.**—Wilhelm **Heile.**—Hubert **Hermans.**— Dr. Theodor **Heuss.**—Anton **Hilbert.**—Dr. Fritz **Hoch.**—Dr. Hermann **Höpker-Aschoff.**—Dr. Werner **Hofmeister.**—Dr. Rudolf **Katz.**—Dr. Ferdinand **Kleindienst.**—Dr. Gerhard **Kroll.**—Karl **Kuhn.**—Adolf **Kühn.**—Dr. Wilhelm **Laforet.**—Dr. Dr. Robert **Lehr.**—Lambert **Lensing.**—Dr. Fritz **Löwenthal.**—Friedrich **Maier.**—Dr. Hermann **von Mangoldt.**—Karl Siegmund **Mayr.**—Dr. Walter **Menzel.**—Dr. Willibald **Mücke.**—Friederike **Nadig.**—Erich **Ollenhauer.**—Dr. Anton **Pfeiffer.**— Heinz **Renner.**

RENNER (KPD): I will not sign the division of Germany.

Secretary **STOCK**: Max **Reimann.**

REIMANN (KPD): I will not sign.

Secretary **STOCK**: Albert **Roßhaupter.**—Hermann **Runge.**—Kaspar Gottfried **Schlör.**—Dr. Carlo **Schmid.**—Josef **Schrage.**—Carl **Schröter.**—Dr. Josef **Schwalber.**—Dr. Hans-Christoph **Seebohm.**—Dr. Kaspar **Seibold.**— Dr. Elisabeth **Selbert.**—Dr. Walter **Strauß.**—Friedrich Wilhelm **Wagner.**— Dr. Helene **Weber.**—Helene **Wessel.**—Dr. Friedrich **Wolff.**—Hans **Wunderlich.**—Gustav **Zimmermann.**—August **Zinn.**—Jean **Stock.**

PRESIDENT Dr. ADENAUER: I now invite the delegates from Greater Berlin to sign.

Secretary **STOCK**: Jakob **Kaiser.**—Paul **Löbe.**—Ernst **Reuter** (greeted with applause).—Dr. Hans **Reif.**—Dr. Otto **Suhr.**—

PRESIDENT Dr. ADENAUER: In accordance with the resolutions of the 1948 London Conference the Basic Law was transmitted to the Military Governors who, on 12 May 1949, authorized its submission to the Landtage for ratification.

The Landtag of the State of **Baden** on 18 May approved the Basic Law.
The Landtag of the State of **Bavaria** on 20 May rejected the Basic Law.
The Citizenry of the State of **Bremen** on 20 May,
The Citizenry of the State of **Hamburg** on 18 May,
The Landtag of the State of **Hesse** on 20 May,
The Landtag of the State of **Lower Saxony** on 20 May,
The Landtag of the State of **North-Rhine-Westphalia** on 20 May,
The Landtag of the State of **Rhineland-Palatinate** on 18 May,
The Landtag of the State of **Schleswig-Holstein** on 20 May,
The Landtag of the State of **Württemberg-Baden** on 18 May,
The Landtag of the State of **Württemberg-Hohenzollern** on 20 May approved the Basic Law.

I now invite the Minister-Presidents and the Presidents of the Landtage to sign.

Secretary **STOCK**:

The President of the State of **Baden**;
The Minister-President of the State of **Bavaria**;
The President of the Senate of **Hansestadt Bremen**;
The Senior Burgomaster of **Hansestadt Hamburg**;
The Minister-President of the State of **Hesse**;
The Minister-President of the State of **Lower Saxony**;
The Minister-President of the State of **North Rhine-Westphalia**;
The Minister-President of the State of **Rhineland-Palatinate**;
The Minister-President of the State of **Schleswig-Holstein**;
The Minister-President of the State of **Württemberg-Baden**;
The Minister-President of the State of **Württemberg-Hohenzollern**;
The President of the **Baden Landtag**;
The President of the **Bavarian Landtag**;
The President of the **Bremen Citizen Assembly**;
The President of the **Hamburg Citizen Assembly**;
The President of the **Hesse Landtag**;
The President of the **Lower Saxony Landtag**;
The President of the **North-Rhine-Westphalia Landtag**;
The President of the **Rhineland-Palatinate Landtag**;
The President of the **Schleswig-Holstein Landtag**;
The President of the **Württemberg-Baden Landtag**;
The President of the **Württemberg-Hohenzollern Landtag**;

PRESIDENT Dr. ADENAUER: The City Assembly of **Greater Berlin** in its 14th Extraordinary Sitting on 19 May 1949 unanimously approved the following **resolution**:

The City Assembly of Greater Berlin concurs in the principles and goals of the Basic Law for the Federal Republic of Germany approved by the Parliamentary Council on 8 May 1949.

I invite the President of the House of Assembly of Greater Berlin and the Governing Mayor of Greater Berlin to attest to this by their signature.

(The Governing Mayor, Professor Reuter, and the President of the House of Assembly, Dr Suhr, added their signatures.)

PRESIDENT Dr. ADENAUER: Ladies and Gentlemen of the Parliamentary Council! I think that I may, in the name of all Council members who have been addressed by you [the SPD Alterspräsident Paul Loebe, former President of the Reichstag] express the warmest thanks for the friendly and welcome words which you have found for us all. In our deliberations, it appears to me, we have all been givers and receivers. No one has merely contributed, everyone has received something. It seems to me that an essential gain from the work of the past nine months has been that we here in this Parliamentary Council have come to recognize and to respect the views of others. The sincerest wish of us all—I think I may express it—is that this achievement may not remain within these walls, but that it will be carried on in the struggle between the parties and that the election campaign, which must soon begin, will be conducted in a high-minded and businesslike fashion

(Applause)

and—let me again express it—in recognition of the honestly held views of others.

(Bravo!)

Ladies and Gentlemen! In accordance with Article 145, in the name and on behalf of the Parliamentary Council,

(The members rise from their seats)

and with the participation of the Members from Greater Berlin, I proclaim the Basic Law. It will take effect from today. It will be published today in Number 1 of the Federal Gazette.

Ladies and Gentlemen! We are firmly convinced that through our work we have achieved an essential step towards the reunification of the whole of the German people and also towards the return of our prisoners of war and displaced persons.

(Applause)

We wish and we hope that the day will soon come on which the whole German people will be united under this flag.

(Applause and hand-clapping)

In our work we were all guided by the idea and the goal which the preamble of the Basic Law sets forth in such a splendid manner in the following words:

conscious of its responsibility before God and men, animated by the resolve to preserve their national and political unity and to serve the peace of the world as an equal partner in a united Europe, the German people ... have ... enacted this Basic Law ...

May the spirit and the will expressed in these sentences be always present in the German people.

(Lively applause—singing of the poem *Ich hab mich ergeben*)

––––––––

Theodor Heuss was a representative of the Free Democratic Party in the Parliamentary Council who had had a political career prior to 1933. A south German liberal historian and publicist, he was a logical choice for the presidency of a state certain to be dominated by the large forces of the SPD and the CDU/CSU.

Document 8

REPLY BY PROFESSOR THEODOR HEUSS TO THE ALLIED
HIGH COMMISSIONERS ON HIS ELECTION AS PRESIDENT OF
THE FEDERAL REPUBLIC OF GERMANY, 13 SEPTEMBER 1949

Source: Beate Ruhm von Oppen, *Documents on Germany under Occupation,
1945–1954*, London, 1955, 413–4

Transl.: Tagesspiegel, 14 September 1949

I have the honour to express to you my sincere thanks for the congratulations you conveyed to me in the name of your heads of state and your Governments, as well as in your own names, on my election as President of the German Federal Republic. Simultaneously I should like to thank you for the kind words you were good enough to address to me personally.

You mentioned the great and historic importance of the election that took place yesterday. I know that the tasks before the German people and before me will make almost superhuman demands on every one of us.

But our profound faith in the common high ideals, in a democracy imbued with the spirit of Christianity, and a sense of social responsibility will give us the strength to master the difficulties which today seem almost insurmountable.

I attach great value to your remarks in which you say that it is not because of your Governments if today not all German citizens form a part of the German Federal Republic. I am thinking, at this moment, of our fellow citizens in Berlin and in all those parts of our German country who have not yet had an opportunity to profess in freedom their allegiance to the motherland.

It is the sincere desire of the German people to re-enter the great European community. For this purpose we are prepared, as provided by the Constitution, to transfer sovereign rights to international institutions and we see in the consistent realization of this plan a way to the realization of a great idea in the service of peace.

We were glad to hear you say that the Governments you represent are prepared to help us find our way back into the European community.

May I ask you to rest assured that I will do everything in my power to ensure for the Constitution—which embodies the conditions for such a policy of peace—the esteem to which the Constitution of a free people must be entitled. It is in this way that I intend to carry out the mandate which the German people has given me by yesterday's election and I should be grateful if you would convey my ideas to your respective Governments.

Dr Konrad Adenauer had been dismissed twice from his post as Lord Mayor of Cologne, first by the Nazis, and then by the British. He emerged as the dominating figure in both the CDU and the Parliamentary Council. What is particularly striking about his Petersberg statement is its emphasis on social and economic problems.

Document 9

SPEECH BY DR KONRAD ADENAUER, CHANCELLOR OF THE
FEDERAL REPUBLIC, AT THE PETERSBERG CEREMONIES, 21
SEPTEMBER 1949

Source: United States Department of State, *Germany, 1947–1949: the Story in Documents,* Washington, 1950, 321-2

I have the honour to pay you a visit in company with some of the members of my Cabinet, thereby establishing the first contact between the Government of the Federal Republic of Germany and the three High Commissioners. Now that the German Federal Assembly has convened, and the Federal president been elected, and now that I have been chosen Federal Chancellor and the members of the Federal Cabinet have been appointed, a new chapter of German history of the postwar years begins.—The disaster of the second world war had left in its wake a Germany almost totally destroyed. Our cities were in ruins. Economic life was largely smashed. All vestiges of a government had ceased. The very souls of men had suffered such injuries that it seemed doubtful whether a recovery would ever be possible. During the four years following the disaster of 1945, legislative and executive power was largely vested in the occupation powers. It was only step by step that executive and legislative functions were re-delegated to German authorities on various levels, and with a limited power to make decisions. It is fitting and proper to acknowledge gratefully that the German population was saved from starvation during these trying years by Allied help in supplying food which at the time could not be purchased with the proceeds of German exports. It was this help which made possible the start of reconstruction. Now that the governmental and legislative elements of the German Federal Republic are being built up, a large part of the responsibility and the authority to make decisions will pass into German hands. We do not, of course, possess as yet complete freedom, since there are considerable restrictions contained in the Occupation Statute. We will do our part to bring about an atmosphere in which the Allied powers will see their way clear to apply the Occupation Statute in a liberal and generous manner; only in this way will the German people be able to attain full freedom. We hope that the Allied powers will, by making a corresponding use of the revision clause in the occupation statute, hasten the further political development of our country.

It is the unshakable wish of the new Federal Government first and foremost to tackle the great social problems. The Government is convinced that a sound political entity can only develop when each individual is assured a maximum of economic opportunity to earn a livelihood. Not until we succeed in converting the flotsam millions of refugees into settled inhabitants by providing them with housing and adequate opportunities for work will we be able to enjoy inner stability in Germany. Disorder and crises in this part of Europe, however, constitute a serious threat to the security of the entire continent. For this reason, the social programme of the Federal Government should at the same time act to ensure a peaceful development in Europe. We will, of course, do everything in our power to master these problems with the forces at our command. Nevertheless, I feel I am justified in believing even now that the problem of expellees is not only a national, but an international one. To solve it, the help of the rest of the world is needed... .

If we want to establish peace in Europe we can, in the view of the Federal Government, achieve this only by working along entirely new lines. We see opportunities to do this in the efforts made for a European federation, which has just borne its first fruits [at] Strasbourg. [see also Ch.11]

Little more than a month after the capitulation, the revival of 'anti-fascist' political parties was authorized in the Soviet Zone at a time when the Red Army was still in sole occupation of Berlin.

Document 10

SOVIET MILITARY ADMINISTRATION ORDER NO.2:
ESTABLISHMENT OF ANTI-FASCIST PARTIES AND FREE
TRADE UNIONS IN THE SOVIET ZONE; 10 JUNE 1945

Source: Beate Ruhm von Oppen, *Documents on Germany under Occupation, 1945-1954,* Oxford, 1955, 37-8

... From the moment of the occupation of Berlin by the Soviet troops firm order was established in the territory of the Soviet Zone of Occupation in Germany, municipal self-government was organized, and the necessary conditions for the free social and political activity of the German population were created.

In view of all this I order:

1. The formation and activity of all anti-fascist parties having as their aim the final extirpation of all remnants of fascism and the consolidation of the foundations of democracy and civil liberties in Germany; the development of the initiative and independent activity of the broad masses of the population directed towards these ends is to be permitted in the territory of the Soviet Zone of Occupation in Germany.
2. The working population in the Soviet Zone of Occupation is to have the right to unite in free trade unions ...

G.K. Zhukov
Marshal of the Soviet Union, Supreme Chief of the Soviet Military Administration in Germany

---

Towards the end of 1945, the Communists, backed by the Soviet Military Administration, resolved on the fusion of the KPD and the SPD. Strongly assisted by Kurt Schumacher, whose oratorical skill made him the unchallenged leader of the Social Democratic masses, the anti-merger forces secured a party referendum on 29 March

1946. In the three Western sectors of Berlin the SPD won a landslide victory. However, the referendum was banned in the Soviet sector, where, as in the Soviet Zone as a whole, the pressure on East German political activity by the Soviet occupation authorities led to the KPD's absorption of the SPD (see Chapter 3).

Document 11

PRINCIPLES AND AIMS OF THE SOCIALIST UNITY PARTY OF GERMANY. 21 April 1946

Source: Beate Ruhm von Oppen, *Documents on Germany under Occupation, 1945–1954*, Oxford 1955, 121–25

... The unity of the Worker's movement and a bloc of all anti-fascist democratic parties is the most important prerequisite. ... Therefore ... the working class will unite all democratic and progressive groups of the people... .
The fusion of the Social Democratic Party of Germany and of the Communist Party of Germany is therefore the demand of the hour, whose fulfilment brooks no delay.
With these considerations in mind the Socialist Unity Party of Germany is formed... .
The Socialist Unity Party of Germany must direct ... the working class in the direction of the fight for socialism and must lead the working class and all working people towards the fulfilment of this, their historic mission... .

The People's Congress movement, pushed by the SED and strongly supported by the Soviet occupation authorities, originated in a propaganda effort to influence the negotiations over a settlement for Germany in the Council of Foreign Ministers meeting in London and to head off the formation of a West German government. Of the 2,215 delegates who came together in this haphazard and unrepresentative assembly in Berlin on 6 and 7 December, claiming to be the protagonists of German unity, three-quarters came from the Soviet Zone, half represented various 'mass organizations'.

Document 12

THE SOCIALIST UNITY PARTY APPEAL FOR A GERMAN PEOPLE'S CONGRESS FOR UNITY AND A JUST PEACE. 26 NOVEMBER 1947.

Source: Beate Ruhm von Oppen, *Documents on Germany under Occupation, 1945–1954*, Oxford 1955, 260–61

... The Socialist Unity Party of Germany ... regards it as its duty to give the German people the opportunity to make its voice heard and its will known... .

We hereby issue an invitation to a German People's Congress for Unity and a Just Peace on 6 and 7 December at the State Opera, Berlin... .
AGENDA: 1. The will of the German people to achieve a just peace, democracy, and the unity of Germany. Speeches and discussion ....
We urge all parties, organizations, and large enterprises to come to an immediate decision... .

Office of the People's Congress, Berlin N 54, Lothringer Strasse 1.
Wilhelm Pieck   Otto Grotewohl
The Party Executive of the Socialist Unity Party of Germany

With the failure of the London Council of Foreign Ministers in December 1947, the Western powers, soon joined by the Benelux powers, met in London on 23 February 1948 to discuss the fusion of their zones and the establishment of a West German Government. Shortly afterwards, the second session of the People's Congress, claiming to be the only representatives of Germany, unanimously voted to create a 'People's Council' with an executive which looked like an embryonic government. A year later the Council adopted a constitution for East Germany which, with almost diabolic subtlety, converted the Weimar blueprint into an instrument for domination by the SED which was not mentioned in the constitution.

Document 13a

UNANIMOUS RESOLUTION PASSED BY THE SECOND GERMAN PEOPLE'S CONGRESS: ESTABLISHMENT OF A GERMAN PEOPLE'S COUNCIL, 17 MARCH 1948

Source: Beate Ruhm von Oppen, Documents on Germany under Occupation, 1945–1954, Oxford 1955, 282–83

The German People's Congress hereby resolves that a German People's Council consisting of 400 members shall be elected. The German People's Council will be the debating and voting body which will remain in session between the meetings of the People's Congress.
The German People's Council will conduct the struggle for the unity of Germany and for a just peace ...

Document 13b

TEXT OF THE CONSTITUTION OF THE GERMAN DEMOCRATIC
REPUBLIC, ADOPTED BY THE GERMAN PEOPLE'S COUNCIL
ON 30 MARCH 1949 AND CONFIRMED BY THE THIRD GERMAN
PEOPLE'S CONGRESS ON 30 MAY 1949

Source: Louis L. Snyder, *Documents of German History,* New Brunswick, NJ,
195, 540–65

Preamble
The German People, imbued with the desire to safeguard human liberty and
rights, to reshape collective and economic life in accordance with the princi-
ples of social justice, to serve social progress, and to promote a secu re peace
and amity with all peoples, have adopted this constitution.
A. Fundamentals of State Authority
Article 1. Germany is an indivisible democratic republic, the foundations of
which are the German Länder... .
There is only one German nationality... .
Article 2. ... The capital of the Republic is Berlin.
Article 3. All state authority emanates from the people... .
B. Contents and Limits of State Authority
I. Rights of the Citizen
Article 6. All citizens have equal rights before the law... .
Article 10. ... Every citizen has the right to emigrate. This right may be
restricted only by law... .

As the process of constructing a government in the Western zones
proceeded, it was clear to the Communists that nothing was to be
gained by further postponing the establishment of of a separate government in East Germany whose spontaneous appearance had been
long and carefully prepared. The People's Council obliged by merely
declaring itself to be the Provisional People's Chamber *(Volkskammer)* forseen in the constitution approved earlier.

Document 14

LAW ON THE ESTABLISHMENT OF THE PROVISIONAL
PEOPLE'S CHAMBER OF THE GERMAN DEMOCRATIC
REPUBLIC. BERLIN, 7 OCTOBER 1949

Source: Beate Ruhm von Oppen, *Documents on Germany under Occupation,
1945–1954,* Oxford 1955, 282–83

Article 1

On the basis of the Constitution of the German Democratic Republic which
was adopted by the German People's Council on 19 March 1949 and confirmed by the Third German People's Congress on 30 May 1949, the Ger-

man People's Council, elected by the Third German People's Congress on 30 May 1949, hereby constitutes itself the Provisional People's Chamber of the German Democratic Republic.

Article 2

This law comes into force with its adoption. It will be engrossed and promulgated by the President of the Provisional People's Chamber.

The President of the Provisional People's Chamber of the German Democratic Republic.

Notes

1. Basic Law, Art. 146.
2. John Gimbel, *The American Occupation of Germany: Politics and the Military, 1945–1949,* Stanford, 1968, 6 Cf. Kurt Sontheimer, 'The Weimar Republic—Failure and Prospects for German Democracy,' in E.J. Feuchtwanger, ed., *Upheaval and Continuity: A Century of German History,* London, 1973, 101.
3. 'Declaration regarding the defeat of Germany and the assumption of Supreme Authority with respect to Germany …, 5 June 1945.' *Selected Documents on Germany and the Question of Berlin, 1944–1961,* London, HMSO, 1961, Cmnd. 1552, 38.
4. 'Directive of the United States Joint Chiefs of Staff to the Commander-in-Chief of the United States Forces of Occupation regarding the Military Government of Germany' (JCS 1067). US Department of State, *Germany, 1947–1949: The Story in Documents,* Washington, 1950, 23.
5. See, for example, Adolf M. Birke, 'Die aufgezwungene Demokratie? Zur Verfassungspolitik in den westlichen Besatzungszonen', in: Jürgen Heideking, Gerhard Hufnagel, Franz Knipping (Hg), *Wege in die Zeitgeschichte,* Festschrift zum 65. Geburtstag von Gerhard Schulz, Berlin, 1989, S.151–64.
6. United States Department of State: *Foreign Relations of the United States: The Conferences at Malta and Yalta, 1945,* Washington, 1956, 978.
7. Ibid., *The Conference of Berlin (Potsdam), 1945,* Washington, 1960, II, 1483, 1484.
8. Gimbel, *The American Occupation of Germany,* 16–18, 23, 52. Alfred Grosser, *Germany in Our Time: A Political History of the Postwar Years,* New York, 1971, 63.
9. *The Conferences at Malta and Yalta,* 978
10. 'Directive of the United States Joint Chiefs of Staff …' (JCS 1067), in *Germany, 1947–1949: The Story in Documents,* Washington, 1950, 21 ff. British and French instructions were similar.
11. 'Directive of the United States Joint Chiefs of Staff to the Commander-in-Chief, United States Forces of Occupation, regarding the Military Government of Germany', (JCS 1779), 11 July 1947. Ibid., 34.
12. Peter H. Merkl, *The Origin of the West German Republic,* New York, 1963, 8–15.
13. J.P. Nettl, *The Eastern Zone and Soviet Policy in Germany, 1945–50,* Oxford, 1951, 97.
14. *Akten zur Vorgeschichte der Bundesrepublik Deutschland, 1945–1949,* 1, Munich, 1979, 125.
15. For a summary of this process in the United States zone, see *Germany 1947–1949: The Story in Documents,* 169–70.
16. Merkl, *The Origin of the West German Republic,* 19; John F.Golay, *The Founding of the Federal Republic of Germany,* Chicago, 1958, 6–13; Peter Calvocoressi, *Survey of International Affairs, 1947–1948,* London, 1952, 261–3

17. Merkl, *The Origin of the West German Republic*, 58–61.
18. Merkl, ibidem, 177, cites the verdict of the distinguished (and influential) American scholar, Carl J. Friedrich, that the Basic Law was a product of a 'negative evolution'; Sontheimer, in 'The Weimar Republic,' 113, suggests that the Parliamentary Council created a 'counter-constitution' to the Weimar constitution.
19. No precise definition of the French sector of Berlin is given in this document (which reflects the text of the report submitted to the four governments on 26 July 1945). It was recorded not in the EAC, but subsequently in the Allied Control Council. See also Ch. 2.

2
Berlin

Robert Spencer

Berlin, from 1445 the seat of the Prussian rulers and from 1871 to 1945 the capital of the German Reich, and by the Unity Treaty of 31 August 1990 declared the capital of Germany, occupied a unique position in Germany and in Europe after the end of the Second World War. The old core of the city, on the banks of the Spree and the districts to the east, was from 1949 the capital of the German Democratic Republic (DDR). The larger part of the city to the west, comprising 54.4 per cent of the 883 square kilometre area included in Greater Berlin in 1922, with a population in 1980 of 1,998,000, ranked as West Germany's largest city and included extensive farmlands, lakes, and wooded areas, but was a city without a hinterland. Organized as a city-state, its status rested on the wartime agreements among the Allied powers (see also Ch.1, Doc.1) and the important restatement of its position contained in the agreements of 1971.

West Berlin's government exercised both state and municipal functions. The Social Democratic Party, revived in June 1945, dominated West Berlin's politics until 1975 and produced distinguished Governing Mayors such as Ernst Reuter (1945–53) and Willy Brandt (1957–66). In the elections of 10 May 1981, however, the CDU's Richard von Weizsäcker (later President of the Federal Republic) was elected Governing Mayor. Political change in Berlin (or in Bonn), however, did not weaken determination to preserve the position of West Berlin and its vital links with the Federal Republic (Doc. 2)

For over four decades, Berlin remained a barometer of East-West relations, and concern for its future was a reflection of the city's postwar history which was punctuated by a series of crises. The most dramatic of these was the blockade, by the Soviet Union, of the land and water access routes passing through the surrounding Soviet occupied zone in 1948/49 (see Ch.1. Doc.2). For an eleven-month period (24 June 1948 to 29 May 1949), the only link between the Western sectors and the West was the airlift, which, by bringing in food and fuel in quantities of up to 12,940 tons daily, enabled the city to survive. This operation, unparalleled in the history of aviation, depended on the earlier Four-Power agreements on the establishment of air corridors and the Berlin Air Safety Centre (Doc.3). The successful defence of Berlin was also due to the determination of the city's population to resist communist pressure, and the blockade marked a decisive stage in forging the partnership of West Berliners with what henceforth became known as the 'Protecting Powers'.

When the blockade was lifted, East and West Berlin both had separate governments, administration and utilities. In subsequent years the lines of division hardened still further, with the formation of the German Democratic Republic and the integration of the Federal Republic into the Western Alliance. The blockade had dealt a severe blow to West Berlin's economic recovery. In 1950 one in three West Berliners was unemployed. Aided by the government of the Federal Republic (Doc.4), however, West Berlin recovered from the blow and for a decade was the centre of world attention as a unique 'democratic island in a red sea', with an open frontier to the communist East. It served, as an English journalist remarked at the time, as a token of the Four-Power pledge to reunite Germany, as a refuge for the tens of thousands who after 1949 fled East Germany, and as a shop window of the West in the heart of a hostile, but still accessible East.[1]*

For the communist East, West Berlin was, as Soviet Party Secretary Nikita Khrushchev put it, 'a bone which stuck in my throat', an anachronism which prevented the consolidation of the German Democratic Republic and the source of a serious drain on its population. In 1958 he set out to solve this problem in his own way (Doc.5a). Although firm Western resistance led to abortive Four-Power talks, the stalemate was prolonged (Docs.5b and c).

In June 1961, Khrushchev challenged the West again. After a summit meeting in Vienna, the new U.S. President John F. Kennedy insisted on the basic right of the Western powers to be in Berlin and on the 'commitment to sustain—and to defend, if need be', West Berlin and its inhabitants.[2] Less than three weeks later, the government of the GDR made a desperate attempt to stop the human flood through the escape hatch of Berlin, resulting from a form of *Torschlusspanik* which had seized many of its citizens. Despite SED Party Secretary Walter Ulbricht's statement at a press conference on 15 June that 'nobody intends to build a wall',[3] the German Democratic Republic, with the full backing of its Warsaw Pact allies, proceeded to do just that. On the night of 12– 13 August 1961, in a

* *Notes for this chapter begin on p. 46.*

move which the SED leadership said was designed to put an end to 'the hostile activities of the revanchist military forces of Western Germany and West Berlin', the border between the Western and the Soviet sectors was sealed. From that date East Germans remained imprisoned by what Governing Mayor von Weizsäcker described on the twentieth anniversary of the construction of the Wall as 'a petrified rejection of humanity'(see also Ch.3).

As the 1960s wore on, West Berliners endured what Willy Brandt referred to as 'the ordeal of co-existence'.[4] Later in the decade the governments of the Western Alliance insisted on the conclusion of a satisfactory arrangement over Berlin as a precondition for moving towards a preparation of the conference on European security, for which the Soviet Union had been calling ever since the XXIII Congress of the CPSU in March 1966 (Doc.6). Negotiations between the Four Powers led to the initialling of an agreement on 3 September 1971. With the conclusion of subsequent agreements on traffic and other matters between the Federal Republic and the German Democratic Republic and the ratification by Bonn of the Moscow and Warsaw treaties, the Four-Power agreements came into effect on 3 June 1972.

With the conclusion of the agreements over Berlin, the tensions over Berlin largely disappeared and, as former Chancellor Helmut Schmidt put it, 'the existence of Berlin is secured'.[5] Nevertheless, there were many thousands of complaints over their implementation, arrests along the access routes, and reminders of the continuing element of precariousness in the situation through the reinforcing of the physical barriers by what Governing Mayor von Weizsäcker described as a 'financial wall' in the shape of major increases in the minimum currency exchange requirements. However, after 1972 trade and traffic to and from West Berlin increased, the passage across the German Democratic Republic was immeasurably eased, telephone communications between West Berlin and East Berlin and the German Democratic Republic approached 'normalcy', and several millions of West Berliners and West Germans visited the East annually. Apart from pensioners, however, until the late 1980s, Berliners and East Germans were still precluded from visiting the West.(see also Ch.3) The withdrawal of their city from the point of acute tension between East and West enabled West Berliners to concentrate on economic problems consequent on their isolated location and to tackle social problems such as those resulting from an unfavourable age structure (23 per cent of West Berlin's population were over 65) and the very large foreign community (over 10 per cent of West Berlin's population, mostly migrant workers from the Mediterranean). Bold new housing developments were constructed and attempts made to develop West Berlin into a conference centre and to add new dimensions to the city's already rich cultural and intellectual life.

West Berlin's long period of separation from the eastern part of the city came to an end with the dramatic breaching of the Wall on 9 November 1989 and the resulting human flood in both directions across the line which had divided the city since 1945. The unity of the city, its recognition as a Land of the Federal Republic, and its designation as the nation's capital, were sealed with the conclusion of the Unification Treaty of 31 August 1990 (Doc.7). When, after twenty-eight years of division by the Wall, East and West Berliners went to the polls on 2 December 1992, they gave an impressive degree of support for the CDU. Under the new government, and with the termination of Four-Power rights in the city, there began the reconstruction of unified institutions and the restoration of 'normalcy' such as the extension of conscription to Berlin, the scaling down of subsidies, and the inclusion of the city in Lufthansa's services. Six months later, on 20 June, after an impassioned debate lasting almost twelve hours, the Bundestag voted to move the seat of government to Berlin (Doc.8). When and how this agreement in principle was to be effected was left undecided. A bitter political and public debate continued in the succeeding months. Finally, on 11 December 1991, the government announced that while the Chancellery, the Federal Press Office, and ten ministries including the foreign office would move to Berlin later in the decade when facilities had been constructed for them, eight of the eighteen ministries and some parts of others would remain in Bonn.

The 1971 agreements on Berlin constituted a landmark in the city's postwar history. The protracted East-West negotiations were conducted at three levels: between the Western Powers on the one hand and the Soviet Union on the other; and, following the essential Four-Power agreement of 3 September, between the Federal Republic and the German Democratic Republic and between the Berlin Senate and the German Democratic Republic to reach supplementary agreements. In essence both sides clung to their respective legal views on the status of the divided city and on this basis agreed on general provisions for transit to West Berlin from the Federal Republic and for traffic between the two halves of the former capital. By reaffirming West Berlin's status and its links with the West, the 1971 agreements made possible Berlin's incorporation into the Federal Republic two decades later.

Document 1a

THE FOUR-POWER AGREEMENT ON BERLIN, 3 SEPTEMBER 1971, WITH APPENDICES

Source: Presse- und Informationsamt der Bundesregierung, *Documentation relating to the Federal Government's Policy of Détente*, Bonn, 1978, 87–106

The Governments of the United States of America, the French Republic, the Union of Soviet Socialist Republics, and the United Kingdom of Great Britain and Northern Ireland, represented by their Ambassadors, who held a series of meetings in the building formerly occupied by the Allied Control Council in the American Sector of Berlin,

Acting on the basis of their quadripartite rights and responsibilities, and of the corresponding wartime and postwar agreements and decisions of the Four Powers, which are not affected,

Taking into account the existing situation in the relevant area,

Guided by the desire to contribute to practical improvements of the situation,

Without prejudice to their legal positions,

Have agreed on the following:

PART I

General Provisions

1. The four Governments will strive to promote the elimination of tension and the prevention of complications in the relevant area.
2. The four Governments, taking into account their obligations under the Charter of the United Nations, agree that there shall be no use or threat of force in the area and that disputes shall be settled solely by peaceful means.
3. The four Governments will mutually respect their individual and joint rights and responsibilities, which remain unchanged.
4. The four Governments agree that, irrespective of the differences in legal views, the situation which has developed in the area, and as it is defined in this Agreement as well as in the other agreements referred to in this Agreement, shall not be changed unilaterally.

PART II

Provisions Relating to the Western Sectors of Berlin

A. The Government of the Union of Soviet Socialist Republics declares that transit traffic by road, rail and waterways through the territory of the German Democratic Republic of civilian persons and goods between the Western Sectors of Berlin and the Federal Republic of Germany will be unimpeded; that such traffic will be facilitated so as to take place in the most simple and expeditious manner; and that it will receive preferential treatment.

Detailed arrangements concerning this civilian traffic, as set forth in Annex I, will be agreed by the competent German authorities.

. . .

ANNEX I

Communication from the Government of the Union of Soviet Socialist Republics to the Governments of the French Republic, the United Kingdom and the United States of America.

The Government of the Union of Soviet Socialist Republics, with reference to Part II A of the Quadripartite Agreement of this date and after consultation and agreement with the Government of the German Democratic Republic, has the honour to inform the Governments of the French Republic, the United Kingdom and the United States of America that:

1. Transit traffic by road, rail and waterways through the territory of the German Democratic Republic of civilian persons and goods between the Western Sectors of Berlin and the Federal Republic of Germany will be facilitated and unimpeded. It will receive the most simple, expeditious and preferential treatment provided by international practice.

2. Accordingly,

    (a) Conveyances sealed before departure may be used for the transport of civilian goods by road, rail and waterways between the Western Sectors of Berlin and the Federal Republic of Germany. Inspection procedures will be limited to the inspection of seals and accompanying documents.

. . .

    (c) Through trains and buses may be used for travel between the Western Sectors of Berlin and the Federal Republic of Germany. Inspection procedures will not include any formalities other than identification of persons.

    (d) Persons identified as through travellers using individual vehicles between the Western Sectors of Berlin and the Federal Republic of Germany on routes designated for through traffic will be able to proceed to their destinations without paying individual tolls and fees for the use of the transit routes. Procedures applied for such travellers shall not involve delay.

. . .

The Four-Power agreement paved the way for negotiations between the German authorities in West and East to reach more detailed, supplementary agreements within, however, the framework of previous agreements with the Western powers.

Document 1b

LETTER OF CHANCELLOR WILLY BRANDT TO THE
AMBASSADORS OF THE UNITED STATES, THE UNITED
KINGDOM, AND FRANCE.
Source: Presse- und Informationsamt der Bundesregierung, *Documentation
relating to the Federal Government's Policy of Détente*, Bonn, 1978, 107–8

. . .

I have the honour to confirm receipt of the letter of the Ambassadors of
France, the United Kingdom and the United States of America of September 3 together with which the text of the Quadripartite Agreement signed
on September 3, 1971, in Berlin was communicated to the Government of
the Federal Republic of Germany.

I also have the honour to confirm receipt of the letter of the three
Ambassadors of the same date containing clarifications and interpretations
which reflect what their Governments understand by the declarations contained in Annex II to the Quadripartite Agreement with regard to the relationship between the Federal Republic of Germany and the Western Sectors
of Berlin.

The Government of the Federal Republic of Germany intends taking steps
immediately in order to arrive at agreements on concrete arrangements relating to civilian traffic as envisaged in Part IIA of the Quadripartite Agreement.

The Government of the Federal Republic of Germany has taken note of
the contents of Your Excellency's letter which were communicated to it in
exercising the rights and responsibilities which were retained in pursuance of
Article 2 of the Convention on Relations between the Federal Republic of
Germany and the Three Powers of May 26, 1952, as amended on October
23, 1954, and which will continue to be respected by the Government of the
Federal Republic of Germany.

The Government of the Federal Republic of Germany shares the view and
the determination that the ties between the Federal Republic of Germany
and Berlin shall be maintained and developed.

———————

In the negotiations between Bonn and East Berlin agreement was
reached, for the first time in Berlin's postwar history, on the procedures by which transit traffic between the isolated Western sectors of
the city and the territory of the Federal Republic should flow 'unimpeded' and even 'receive preferential treatment' on the access routes.

Document 1c

AGREEMENT BETWEEN THE GOVERNMENT OF THE
FEDERAL REPUBLIC OF GERMANY AND THE GOVERNMENT
OF THE GERMAN DEMOCRATIC REPUBLIC ON TRANSIT
TRAFFIC OF CIVILIAN PERSONS AND GOODS BETWEEN THE
FEDERAL REPUBLIC OF GERMANY AND BERLIN (WEST),
17 DECEMBER 1971

Source: Presse- und Informationsamt der Bundesregierung, *Documentation relating to the Federal Government's Policy of Détente*, Bonn, 1978, 115–31

The Government of the Federal Republic of Germany and the Government of the German Democratic Republic,

Desiring to render a contribution to détente in Europe, and
In accordance with the arrangements of the Agreement of 3 September 1971 between the Governments of the French Republic, the Union of Soviet Socialist Republics, the United Kingdom of Great Britain and Northern Ireland, and the United States of America,
Have agreed to conclude the following Agreement:

Article 1

The subject of this Agreement is the transit traffic by road, rail and waterways through the territory of the German Democratic Republic of civilian persons and goods between the Federal Republic of Germany and the Western Sectors of Berlin—Berlin (West)—hereinafter referred to as transit traffic.

Article 2

1. Transit traffic shall be facilitated and unimpeded. It will receive the most simple, expeditious and preferential treatment provided by international practice.

. . .

Article 21

This Agreement shall enter into force simultaneously with the Agreement of 3 September 1971 between the French Republic, the Union of Soviet Socialist Republics, the United Kingdom of Great Britain and Northern Ireland, and the United States of America, and shall remain in force together with it.

. . .

In negotiations between the West Berlin Senate and the government of the German Democratic Republic agreement was reached which permitted West Berliners to visit, for the first time since the expiry of the earlier pass agreement in 1965, East Berlin and the areas of the GDR bordering on West Berlin.

Document 1d

ARRANGEMENT BETWEEN THE SENATE AND THE
GOVERNMENT OF THE GERMAN DEMOCRATIC REPUBLIC
CONCERNING THE FACILITATION AND IMPROVEMENT OF
TRAVEL AND VISITOR TRAFFIC, 20 DECEMBER 1971

Source: Presse- und Informationsamt der Bundesregierung, *Documentation relating to the Federal Government's Policy on Détente*, Bonn, 1978, 132–3

In accordance with the arrangements of the Agreement of 3 September 1971 between the Governments of the French Republic, the Union of Soviet Socialist Republics, the United Kingdom of Great Britain and Northern Ireland and the United States of America, and desiring to render a contribution to détente, the *Senat* and the Government of the German Democratic Republic have agreed to facilitate and improve the travel and visitor traffic of permanent residents of the Western Sectors of Berlin/Berlin (West) as follows:

Article 1

(1) Permanent residents of Berlin (West) shall be granted entry one or more times into areas bordering on Berlin (West) and those areas of the German Democratic Republic which do not border on Berlin (West) for visits totalling thirty days a year.
(2) Entry under paragraph (1) above shall be approved for compassionate, family, religious and cultural reasons, and for touring.

Article 2

(1) For entry, permanent residents of Berlin (West) shall require their valid identity card and an entry permit, and for exit, an exit permit of the German Democratic Republic. The required permits are to be applied for with the competent authorities in accordance with the regulations of the German Democratic Republic.

. . .

Document 2

SPEECH BY FEDERAL PRESIDENT KARL CARSTENS ON SIGNING
THE GOLDEN BOOK, 13 JULY 1979

Source: Karl Carstens, *Reden und Interviews*, Presse-und Informationsamt der Bundesregierung, I, Bonn, 1981, 31–3

It is with the greatest of pleasure that I follow the example set by my predecessors to pay the first visit outside of Bonn after taking office to Berlin. I am grateful to you for your friendly welcome.

Every German has Berlin at heart in a special way. In the last 100 years the history of Berlin has mirrored the fate of our people. This city is a symbol of

German unity and German separation. And it is an indication of the freedom
and the desire to uphold this freedom and the basic values of our democratic state system.

. . .

This modern metropolis does not only make a large contribution to the economic strength of the Federal Republic of Germany and the European Community; it does not only shelter great memories for the whole of Germany,
but it is also the seat of important cultural institutions such as the National
Gallery, the State Library, the Philharmonic Orchestra, the German Opera,
the Foundation for Prussian Cultural Treasures (Stiftung Preußischer Kul-
turbesitz) and many others, whose effectiveness influences our whole country. Everyone who comes here feels the pulsating intellectual life. I am
confident that Berlin can make full use of its intellectual position between
East and West as a city of human, political and scientific meetings, as a city
of congresses and exhibitions. The whole of Europe will benefit therefrom.

The fact that we can make a confident prognosis for this city today is
thanks to the love of freedom and the sober political sense of the Berlin population, to the prudence and caution of Berlin's politicians and last but not
least to the determination and care of the three powers under whose protection this part of the city rests. This is an act of friendship which the three
powers perform for Germany. We are gratefully aware of this.

. . .

While no precise agreements dealing with civilian land and water
transit traffic through the Soviet-occupied Zone were concluded at
the start of the Allied occupation of Berlin, the agreement reached
on air traffic survived the blockade and subsequent crises.

Document 3

FLIGHT RULES BY ALLIED CONTROL AUTHORITY AIR
DIRECTORATE FOR AIRCRAFT FLYING IN AIR CORRIDORS
AND IN BERLIN CONTROL ZONE, 22 OCTOBER 1946
Source: Documents on Berlin, 1943–1963, Munich, 1963, 39–41

Section I

General

1. a. Object. To ensure the maximum safety in flight of all aircraft flying in
   the corridors and in the Berlin Control Zone under all conditions.

. . .

2. *Air Corridors in Germany.* The following air corridors have been
   established.

Frankfurt-Berlin
Bückeburg-Berlin
Hamburg-Berlin

Each of the above corridors is 20 English miles (32 kilometers) wide, i.e. 10 miles (16 kilometers) each side of the centre line ... .

3. *Berlin Control Zone (B.C.Z.)*

a. The Berlin Control Zone is defined as the air space between ground level and 10,000 feet (3,000 meters) within a radius of 20 miles (32 kilometers) from the Allied Control Authority Building ...

. . .

4. *Berlin Air Safety Center (B.A.S.C.)* The Berlin Air Safety Center ... regulates all flying in the Berlin Control Zone and also in the corridors extending from Berlin to the boundaries of adjacent control zones.

. . .

———

The following law, the third of its kind, laid down the validity of federal law in Berlin and specified that grants would be made annually to the Land Berlin from the federal budget.

Document 4

BERLIN AND THE FEDERAL REPUBLIC: THIRD TRANSFER LAW, 4 JANUARY 1952

Source: BGBl., I, 9 January 1952

. . .

§ 11 *Continued Validity of Existing Laws*
Laws in force before the first constituent meeting of the Bundestag which had become Federal law in the other territories within the purview of the Basic Law and which continue to be valid in the Land Berlin will be Federal law in the Land Berlin when this law is put into force in the Land Berlin according to § 19 (1) ...

. . .

§ 13 *Other Federal Laws*
Other Federal laws which are promulgated for territories within the purview of the Basic Law simultaneously with this law or after it has come into force and the validity of which is explicitly stated for the territory of the Land Berlin, shall be put into force in the Land Berlin within one month of its promulgation in the Federal Law Gazette or the Federal Gazette in accordance with Article 87, 2 of the Constitution of Berlin ...

. . .

§ 15 *General Regulations Concerning Legal Alignment*
(1) Insofar as no other stipulations arise from this law and its supplements,

the Land Berlin will adopt the Federal law with the same text with which it is in force in the other territories within the purview of the Basic Law ... .

§ 16 *Federal Grant to the Budget of the Land Berlin*
(1) The Land Berlin receives a grant to cover the deficit in the Land budget with effect from April 1, 1951. The amount of the Federal grant is determined by law on establishing the Federal budget. The Federal grant is to be transferred to the Land Berlin in monthly instalments.
(2) The Federal grant is to be assessed so that the Land Berlin can fulfil the tasks arising from its special position ... .
. . .

§ 19 *Legal Take-Over in Berlin* [6]
(1) This law shall come into force as soon as the Land Berlin decides to apply it according to Article 87, § 2.
(2) The application of this law by the Land Berlin is a prerequisite of the financial contributions to the Land Berlin to which the Federation is committed by the terms of this law.
. . .
_____

What follows is a drastically shortened version of the Soviet Note which marked the opening of the second Berlin crisis and inaugurated a prolonged war of notes and a series of conferences which failed to resolve East-West differences over Berlin.

Document 5a

NOTE FROM THE GOVERNMENT OF THE USSR TO THE GOVERNMENT OF THE UNITED STATES, 27 NOVEMBER 1958
Source: Documents on Berlin, 1945–1963, Munich, 1963, 181–95

The problem of Berlin, which is situated in the center of the German Democratic Republic but the western part of which is cut off from the GDR as a result of foreign occupation, deeply affects not only the national interests of the German people but also the interests of all nations desirous of establishing lasting peace in Europe ... . A situation of constant friction and tension has prevailed for many years in this city ... . Berlin ... has now become a dangerous center of contradiction between the Great Powers, allies in the last war ... .
    The policy of the U.S.A., Britain, and France with respect to West Germany had led to the violation of those provisions of the Potsdam Agreement designed to ensure the unity of Germany as a peace-loving and democratic state ... . The Government of the FRG, encouraged by the Western Powers, is systematically fanning the 'cold war,' and ... is nurturing plans for abolishing the GDR and strengthening at the latter's expense its own militaristic state ... .
    There is another program for uniting Germany, ... advocated by the German Democratic Republic, ... for uniting Germany as a peace-loving and

democratic state, ... that is, through agreement and contacts between the two German states and through the establishment of a German confederation ... . The Soviet Union, as well as other states interested in strengthening the peace in Europe, supports the proposals of the German Democratic Republic for the peaceful unification of Germany ... .

The Three Western Powers are ruling the roost in West Berlin, turning it into a kind of state within a state and using it as a center from which to pursue subversive activity against the GDR, the Soviet Union, and the other parties to the Warsaw Treaty. The United States, Great Britain, and France are freely communicating with West Berlin through lines of communication passing through the territory and the airspace of the German Democratic Republic, which they do not even want to recognize ... .

The Western Powers have grossly violated the Four–Power agreements, including the Potsdam Agreement, ... The Four-Power status of Berlin came into being because Berlin, as the capital of Germany, was designated as the seat of the Control Council established for Germany's administration during the initial period of occupation. This status has been scrupulously observed by the Soviet Union ... . The U.S.A., Great Britain, and France ... have chosen to abuse in a flagrant manner their occupation rights in Berlin and have exploited the Four Power status of the city for their own purposes to the detriment of the Soviet Union, the German Democratic Republic, and the other Socialist countries ... .

It is obvious that the Soviet Union, just as the other parties to the Warsaw Treaty, cannot tolerate such a situation any longer ... .

In this connection, the Government of the U.S.S.R. hereby notifies the United States Government that the Soviet Union regards as null and void the 'Protocol of the Agreement between the Governments of the Union of Soviet Socialist Republics, the United States of America, and the United Kingdom on the zones of occupation in Germany and on the administration of Greater Berlin,' of September 12, 1944, and the related supplementary agreements ... . The Soviet Government will enter into negotiations with the Government of the GDR at an appropriate time with a view to transferring to the German Democratic Republic the functions temporarily performed by the Soviet authorities by virtue of the above-mentioned Allied agreements and under the agreement between the U.S.S.R. and the GDR of September 20, 1955 ... .

Should the Government of the United States be unwilling to contribute in such a way to the implementation of the political principles of the Allied agreements on Germany, it will have no reason, either legal or moral, for insisting on the preservation of the Four-Power status of Berlin ... .

An independent solution to the Berlin problem must be found in the very near future ... . It is necessary to prevent West Berlin from being used any longer as a springboard for intensive espionage, sabotage, and other subversive activities against Socialist countries, the GDR, and the U.S.S.R. or, to quote the leaders of the United States Government, to prevent its being used for 'indirect aggression' against the countries of the Socialist camp ... .

Of course, the most correct and natural way to solve the problem would be for the western part of Berlin, now actually detached from the GDR, to be reunited with its eastern part and for Berlin to become a unified city within the state in whose territory it is situated.

However, the Soviet Government … would consider it possible to solve the West Berlin question at the present time by the conversion of West Berlin into an independent political unit—a free city, [which] could have its own government and run its own economic, administrative, and other affairs.

The Four Powers which shared in the administration of Berlin after the war could, as well as both of the German states, undertake to respect the status of West Berlin as a free city … .

For its part, the Soviet Government would have no objection to the United Nations also sharing, in one way or other, in observing the free-city status of West Berlin … . The Soviet Government is prepared to enter into negotiations with the Government of the United States of America and with those of the other states concerned on granting West Berlin the status of a demilitarized free city. In case this proposal is not acceptable to the Government of the U.S.A. then there will no longer remain any topic for negotiations between the former occupying powers on the Berlin question … . The Soviet Government proposes to make no changes in the present procedure for military traffic of the U.S.A., Great Britain, and France from West Berlin to the FRG for half a year … . If the above mentioned period is not utilized to reach an adequate agreement, the Soviet Union will then carry out the planned measures through an agreement with the GDR. It is envisaged that the German Democratic Republic, like any other independent state, must fully deal with questions concerning its space, i.e., exercise its sovereignty on land, on water, and in the air. At the same time, there will terminate all contacts still maintained between representatives of the armed forces and other officials of the Soviet Union in Germany and corresponding representatives of the armed forces and other officials of the U.S.A., Great Britain, and France on questions pertaining to Berlin … .

Caught off balance by the Krushchev ultimatum, the Western powers firmly reasserted their rights in Berlin, but wavered between toughness and conciliation as they sought a negotiated solution.

Document 5b

COMMUNIQUÉ OF THE FOREIGN MINISTERS OF THE UNITED STATES, THE UNITED KINGDOM, FRANCE, AND THE FEDERAL REPUBLIC OF GERMANY, PARIS, 14 DECEMBER 1958
Source: *Documents on Berlin*, 1943–1963, Munich, 1963, 136–7

The Foreign Ministers of France the Federal Republic of Germany, the United Kingdom and the United States [who] met on December 14, 1958, in Paris to discuss developments in the Berlin situation … had the benefit of an oral statement on the situation in Berlin by Herr Brandt, Governing Mayor of that city.

The Foreign Ministers of France, the United Kingdom and the United States once more reaffirmed the determination of their governments to maintain their position and their rights with respect to Berlin including the right of free access.

They found unacceptable a unilateral repudiation by the Soviet Government of its obligations to the Governments of France, the United Kingdom and the United States in relation to their presence in Berlin and the freedom of access to that city or the substitution of the German authorities of the Soviet Zone for the Soviet Government insofar as those rights are concerned.

. . .

The Western Powers' stand was backed by the NATO Council, whose declaration was repeatedly cited to underline the Alliance's commitment to Berlin.

Document 5c

COMMUNIQUÉ ISSUED FOLLOWING MINISTERIAL MEETING OF THE NORTH ATLANTIC COUNCIL, PARIS, WITH APPENDED DECLARATION ON BERLIN, 16–18 DECEMBER 1958

Source: NATO Final Communiqués, 1949–1974, Brussels, n.d., 121–4

. . .

2. In a comprehensive survey of the international situation, the Council gave first place to the question of Berlin. The Member countries made clear their resolution not to yield to threats. Their unanimous view on Berlin was expressed in the Council's Declaration of 16th December. The Council will continue to follow this question with close attention and will shortly discuss the replies to be sent to the Soviet notes of 27th November.

. . .

DECLARATION ON BERLIN

The North Atlantic Council examined the question of Berlin.

2. The Council declares that no State has the right to withdraw unilaterally from its international engagements. It considers that the denunciation by the Soviet Union of the inter-allied agreements on Berlin can in no way deprive the other parties of their rights or relieve the Soviet Union of its obligations. Such methods destroy the mutual confidence between nations which is one of the foundations of peace.

3. The Council fully associates itself with the views expressed on the subject by the governments of the United States, the United Kingdom, France and the Federal Republic of Germany in their statement of 14th December.

4. The demands expressed by the Soviet Government have created a serious situation which must be faced with determination.

5. The Council recalls the responsibilities which each member state has assumed in regard to the security and welfare of Berlin, and the maintenance of the position of the Three Powers in that city. The member states of NATO could not approve a solution of the Berlin question which jeopardised the right of the three Western Powers to remain in Berlin as long as their responsibilities require it, and did not assure freedom of communication between that city and the free world. The Soviet Union would be responsible for any action which had the effect of hampering this free communication or endangering this freedom. The two million inhabitants of West Berlin have just reaffirmed in a free vote their overwhelming approval and support for that position.

6. The Council considers that the Berlin question can only be settled in the framework of an agreement with the USSR on Germany as a whole. It recalls that the Western Powers have repeatedly declared themselves ready to examine this problem, as well as those of European security and disarmament. They are still ready to discuss all these problems.

. . .

In the East-West negotiations which marked the high point of détente at the end of the 1960s and the beginning of the 1970s Berlin was a key element, as the following document, dating from the early days of Willy Brandt's chancellorship, demonstrates.

Document 6

DECLARATION OF THE NORTH ATLANTIC COUNCIL, 5 DECEMBER 1969

Source: NATO Final Communiqués, 1949–1974, Brussels, n.d., 229–31

1. Meeting at Brussels on 4th and 5th December 1969, the Ministers of the North Atlantic Alliance reaffirmed the commitment of their nations to pursue effective policies directed towards a greater relaxation of tensions in their continuing search for a just and durable peace.

. . .

Germany and Berlin

8. The Ministers welcome the efforts of the governments of the United States, Great Britain and France, in the framework of their special responsibility for Berlin and Germany as a whole, to gain the co-operation of the Soviet Union in improving the situation with respect to

Berlin and free access to the city. The elimination of difficulties created in the past with respect to Berlin, especially with regard to access, would increase the prospects for serious discussions on the other concrete issues which continue to divide East and West. Furthermore, Berlin could play a constructive role in the expansion of East-West economic relations if the city's trade with the East could be facilitated.

9. A just and lasting peace settlement for Germany must be based on the free decision of the German people and on the interests of European security. The Ministers are convinced that, pending such a settlement, the proposals of the Federal Republic for a modus vivendi between the two parts of Germany and for a bilateral exchange of declarations on the non-use of force or the threat of force would, if they receive a positive response, substantially facilitate co-operation between East and West on other problems. They consider that these efforts by the Federal Republic represent constructive steps toward relaxation of tension in Europe and express the hope that the governments will therefore take them into account informing their own attitude toward the German question.

10. The Ministers would regard concrete progress in both these fields as an important contribution to peace in Europe. They are bound to attach great weight to the responses to these proposals in evaluating the prospects for negotiations looking toward improved relations and co-operation in Europe.

. . .

The future status of the city of Berlin was regulated in the Treaty, signed in East Berlin on 31 August 1990 by Wolfgang Schäuble, Federal Minister of the Interior, and GDR State Secretary Günther Krause. It entered into force on the GDR's accession to the Federal Republic on 3 October 1990 when Walter Momper, the Social Democratic Governing Mayor of Berlin, addressed the official ceremonies in Berlin's Philharmonie in his capacity as President of the Bundesrat (See also Ch 4).

Document 7

TREATY OF 31 AUGUST 1990 BETWEEN THE FEDERAL REPUBLIC OF GERMANY AND THE GERMAN DEMOCRATIC REPUBLIC ON THE ESTABLISHMENT OF GERMAN UNITY.

Source: The Unification of Germany in 1990. A Documentation. Bonn, 1991, 71-72

The Federal Republic of Germany and the German Democratic Republic Have agreed to conclude a Treaty on the Establishment of German Unity, containing the following provisions:

ARTICLE 1

LÄNDER

(1)Upon the accession of the German Democratic Republic to the Federal Republic of Germany in accordance with Article 23 of the Basic Law taking effect on 3 October 1990 the Länder of Brandenburg, Mecklenburg-Western Pomerania, Saxony, Saxony-Anhalt and Thuringia shall become Länder of the Federal Republic of Germany ... .

(2) The 23 boroughs of Berlin shall form the Land Berlin.

ARTICLE 2
CAPITAL CITY, DAY OF GERMAN UNITY

(1) The capital of Germany shall be Berlin. The seat of the parliament and government shall be decided after the establishment of German unity.

. . .

Of the five resolutions on the future seat of government debated by the Bundestag, the one sponsored by a long list of deputies headed by Willy Brandt, former Chancellor and Governing Mayor of Berlin, was passed on 21 June by a narrow majority of seventeen votes. Included in the ayes were the fifteen votes cast by the Party of Democratic Socialism (PDS), the successor of the GDR's Socialist Unity Party (SED) under the leadership of Gregor Gysi.

Document 8

MOTION ON THE COMPLETION OF GERMAN UNITY

Source: Verhandlungen des Deutschen Bundestages. 12. Wahlperiode 1990. Anlagen. Band 430. Drucksachen NV 791-920 1991, 1-7

In keeping with resolutions passed by the German Bundestag in which it has consistently made known its political desire that, on the achievement of German Unity, Parliament and Government should again be in the German capital Berlin, the Bundestag shall resolve that:

1. Berlin is the seat of the German Bundestag.
2. The Federal Government—in conjunction with the administration of the German Bundestag and the Senat of Berlin—is instructed to work out by 31 December 1991 a detailed plan for putting this resolution into effect. As a first step the facilities necessary for convening conferences of the Bundestag and of its parliamentary parties, groupings and committees, are to be created swiftly. Conditions under which work can be conducted on a normal basis are to be achieved in four years' time. Berlin is to be fully operational as the seat of Parliament and Government in 10-12 years at the latest.
3. The German Bundestag expects the Federal Government to take suitable measures to honour its responsibilities towards the Parliament in Berlin,

and accordingly to ensure its political presence there, by transferring to Berlin the core of its governmental functions.

4. Agreement is to be reached regarding a fair division of work between Berlin and Bonn, so that after Parliament has moved to Berlin, Bonn will still remain the administrative center of the Federal Republic of Germany. In particular, those ministerial departments and sections of the Government which are primarily administrative in character, are to retain their seat in Bonn. In consequence, the majority of work-places will remain in Bonn ... .

...

8. The German Bundestag assumes that Berlin is to be the principal seat of the Federal President.

9. The German Bundestag recommends the Bundesrat, in recognition of its federal traditions, to maintain its seat in Bonn.

Notes

1. Sebastian Haffner, *Encounter*, Vol.XVII, No.4, October 1961, 62–3. See also Ch.14.
2. United States Department of State Bulletin, Vol.XLV. No. 1155, 14 August 1961, 267.
3. *Dokumente zur Berlin-Frage 1944–1962*, Munich, 1962, 419.
4. Willy Brandt, *The Ordeal of Coexistence* (The Gustav Pollak Lectures, Harvard University, 1962), Cambridge, Mass., 1963.
5. Bundesministerium für innerdeutsche Beziehungen, *Zehn Jahre Deutschlandpolitik*, Bonn, 1980, 131.
6. Such a *'Berlin-Klausel'* was thereafter part of any federal laws passed by Parliament in Bonn.

3

The Two Germanies

Carl-Christoph Schweitzer

The GDR—a closed system

As the former GDR is now part of reunited Germany (see also Ch.4), a short analysis of its political system which persisted for forty years, will first be offered in this chapter. This will be followed by an overview of relations between the two postwar German states from 1949 to 1989.

The totalitarian regime in East Germany was imposed on the German people living in the Soviet Zone, without ever holding any free elections, by the victorious Soviet Forces and their unswervingly subservient tool, the Communist Party, personified at the end of the war by the so-called 'Gruppe Ulbricht' (see also Ch.1). This was a part of the old German Communist leadership which had survived fascist persecutions as well as Stalin's purges while in exile in Moscow during the 1930s and 1940s. Contemporary historians and political scientists, therefore, commonly define the first stage of development of the GDR after 1949 as 'antifascist Stalinism', comprising the entire era with Walter Ulbricht as Secretary General of the East German Communist Party (see below), and de facto Head of the Government, as well as (part of the time) Head of State from 1949 to 1971.

After the utter collapse of the regime in 1989/90 the term 'Stalinists' served as a convenient label to put the whole blame for the disastrous history of the GDR on the leaders of the Party, from Ulbricht to Honecker, who like their counterparts in the former USSR had supposedly left the path of pure doctrine and either used or contemplated the use of force right up to the end.[1]*

The early postwar years in East Germany constituted, to all intents and purposes a superimposed revolution in the Marxist-Leninist sense, since firstly the old elites in state and society were dismissed, or, at worst, physically eliminated in some of Hitler's former concentration

---

* Notes for this chapter begin on p. 72.

camps such as Bautzen or Buchenwald;[2] and secondly, since *peu à peu* all means of production in industry and agriculture, and even housing estates were, after depossession of the owners, nationalized or collectivized, with only a minority of private owners being allowed to carry on, mainly in small business or craft industries. East Germany became a totalitarian system in the acknowledged sense of the term; full state control was quickly extended to the whole spectrum of society. The educational system in schools and universities was tightly supervised with regard to the syllabus, compulsory teaching of Marxism-Leninism and the ways and means of admission, with a heavy bias in favour of ideological conformity and working-class family background. The Press, broadcasting and television stations operated exclusively on guidelines handed out by the Party. All 'Interest-groups' (see also Ch.14) with the exception of the Churches (see below)—such as Trade Unions, youth movements etc.—were 'brought into line', to use an expression of the preceding Nazi regime, in close interlinkage with the monopolistic Communist Party, which since 1946 had been called the SED (Socialist Unity Party of Germany). This new Party in German history was the outcome of an amalgamation of the two former working-class parties, the Social Democrats and the Communists, brought about by intimidation (see also Ch.1 and 8). After 1946 the Social Democratic Party of Germany was outlawed. Other 'bourgeois' parties were—in contrast to the procedures applied in the USSR—*de iure* allowed to continue or to re-instate themselves in what was euphemistically defined as the 'National Front'. However, these so-called 'Bloc Parties' *(Blockparteien)*—a new Christian Democratic Union originally, as in the West, established jointly by the Protestants and Catholics after the end of the National Socialist regime—and two liberal Parties (LDPD and NDPD, Liberal Democratic Party of Germany and National Democratic Party of Germany) were forty years later to become an especially difficult legacy of the Communist Ancien Regime. These Bloc Parties had to acknowledge in their statutes the predominant position of the SED, which in turn was firmly rooted in the official constitution of the GDR as the party representing the 'people' in this alleged 'state of the workers and peasants'. Together with its various 'offspring' or dependent organisations, such as the new Trade Union Movement (misleadingly called the Free German Trade Union Federation, FDGB) the German Women's Movement (DFB) or, the Free Communist Youth Movement (FDJ, to which practically all young Germans of both sexes had to belong) the SED held the majority in the new quasi-Parliament *(Volkskammer,* see also Ch.1). This majority was automatically assured by a fixed allocation of seats before the various sham-elections took place.

The SED State Party was, therefore, from the beginning in full control of society and government—the latter on all levels from national to regional, and local, not to mention the legal system which was subordinated to the theory of 'Socialist Justice'. (Doc.1a-d).

Finally, to point to perhaps the most important characteristic of a totalitarian system, the SED established quickly in 1950, obviously in close cooperation with the Soviet KGB—a powerful Secret Police, the 'Stasi', *(Staatssicherheit,* a new postwar German term) as the 'shield and sword of the Party' in the official language used throughout. This was and is perhaps the most damaging legacy of all bequeathed to the reunited Germany, the overall numbers of official and unofficial agents of this sprawling octopus—only gradually made known after those records were opened, which had survived last minute measures of destruction in the period immediately after the demise of the GDR in 1989—amounted to something like one hundred thousand officials and at least two hundred thousand unofficial informants (IMs).[3] This incredible figure is, seen in proportion to the total population, higher than even that for the Gestapo in the Third Reich. This can only be explained by the empirical assumption that on an average 75—85 per cent of the people in East Germany did not 'accept' their regime despite all its enforcement measures over forty years, whilst in the Third Reich the majority of Germans supported Hitler, at any rate up until Stalingrad in 1943. The agents of the Stasi over the years developed an unbelievable system of supervision and spying with electronic and other highly sophisticated devices, or with 'smell-samples' taken off bodies of temporarily arrested opponents of the regime, in order that they could be better traced later by specially trained dogs, and above all with informants planted in institutions of all kinds. There are even documented cases of some members of the same family spying on each other.

These activities apparently became ever more important from the point of view of the ruling communist class with the creation of the Wall in Berlin and along the intra-German border together with all that went with it, in August 1961, preventing the East Germans from leaving the GDR. Before that millions had fled from the East to the West of the country, a movement of people referred to as 'voting with their feet' (see Statistics 4). East Germany was from 13 August 1961 to all intents and purposes a totally 'closed society' analogous to the other Moscow controlled states. Thereafter, trying to leave the East in the direction of the West meant risking one's life. The final death-toll was about 400 people shot or otherwise killed while attempting to cross the border on foot, by boat or even balloons, with many more foiled attempts. Only the politically privileged, because absolutely politically reliable, segments of the East German population could go on visits to the West, the so-called *Reisekader,* officials and semi-officials in all walks of life. Later—as a result of the new West German policy of *Wandel durch Annäherung* (trying to achieve a change through a policy of *modus vivendi,* see also Ch.5) by the governments of Willy Brandt and his successors— pensioners over the age of 65 were allowed to leave for visits to the West while in the opposite direction basically only those who had the relatives in the East were allowed to visit. In the early years those were, of course, millions. In the last few years preceding 1989 travel restrictions were relaxed in both directions, allowing for more visits on account of 'urgent family matters.'[4] In any case this closely 'channelled' flow of travel in both directions explains why knowledge about East Germany has been very poor in West Germany during the past forty years, to the detriment of mutual understanding after reunification in 1989. There was one way in which Bonn could above all help dissidents under persecution in East Germany: more and more people could be 'bought out' since the East German government desperately needed hard currency as the years went by. In secret deals, Bonn thus bartered East Germans who wanted to regain their freedom for money—paying for example 40,000 DM for a factory worker or 120,000 DM for a medical practitioner. It is estimated that between 1963 and 1989 Bonn bought at least some 34,000 people out and paid in cash or kind 3.5 billion DM for these inhuman transactions, 'justified' by the East German Communists with the argument that the GDR had invested these sums in the training of such people.

One further means to ensure that this East German Society remained totally closed under tight party control was to conjure up an ever present 'enemy image' taught in the schools, universities and in the media: a capitalist, semi-fascist West Germany was described in the terminology of the SED throughout as *feindliches Ausland* (enemy territory or a hostile foreign country), naturally as part of the Western capitalist camp. (Doc.2) This propaganda was reinforced by the constant claim that the GDR was the only German state ever to have eradicated all roots and traces of fascism and of standing strictly for a policy of peace—two claims which never did stand the test of objective verification.[5] Logically enough in this way any repressive measure, however, severe, could be officially justified in the name of anti-fascism and the struggle for peace, the latter of course within the peace-camp of the international Communist Community. The GDR, as its geographical outpost, professed to be at all times 'on guard against the enemies of peace'. These slogans were part of the 'philosophy' behind the terrible order to 'shoot on sight' at East Germans trying to go West.[6] These contradictions between the overall domestic policy of a totalitarian system and its professed foreign policy of peace naturally became ever more difficult for the SED regime after the mechanisms of the CSCE (Conference on Security and Cooperation in Europe) seemed to bear fruit in pinning Communist governments down to a human rights policy and all that went with it. (see also Ch.5)

The chronological development of intra-German relations, i.e. of the relations between the two German states during forty years, has to be seen and evaluated within the overall international context of East-West relations.

As an analyst of postwar German history once remarked, the division of the former German Reich from 1945 onwards, resulted not so much from any specific agreement by the wartime allies to bring about such a state of affairs, but from their fundamental disagreements about the future order in Germany, in Europe and in the world at large. The Western powers and the USSR wanted a reunification of Germany only on their own terms, if at all, i.e. on the condition that such a united Germany would be part of their respective economic, political, military and ideological spheres of influence. Most of the positions adopted in the many diplomatic exchanges that occurred during the first decade after 1945, urging a reunited Germany at some future date, were almost certainly a mixture of rhetoric, lip-service and tactical manoeuvring.[7]

Neither of the German states which finally came into existence at the end of 1949 was a free agent in deciding on the future of Germany. From this perspective it seems useful to briefly consider here the various stances taken by the two German states themselves on the all-German problem and on the concept of a German nation, i.e. on German reunification. The constitutional position of the old Federal Republic of Germany remained absolutely unchanged and consistent on these questions. Basically the 'all-German' policies of all Bonn governments were guided by the goal expressed in the preamble of the Basic Law of 1949.

> The entire German people are called upon to achieve, in free self-determination, the unity and freedom of Germany.

The logical consequence of this stand was that the Federal Republic of Germany stuck rigorously to its constitutionally guaranteed 'one German citizenship'. It considered all German inhabitants of the German Democratic Republic as Germans of the same sort, i.e. as the citizens of the Federal Republic of Germany, if they wished to claim this continuing citizenship and demanded, for instance, protection and help from West German diplomatic missions in third countries. The Basic Law was and is very explicit about this in its Articles 16 and 116:

> No one may be deprived of his German citizenship ... Unless otherwise provided by law a German within the meaning of this Basic Law is a person who possesses German citizenship or who has been admitted ... to the territory of the German Reich within the frontiers of 31 December 1937 as a refugee or expellee of German stock *[Volkszugehörigkeit]* or as the spouse or descendant of such a person ...

In contrast, the German Democratic Republic has changed its policy and, therefore, also its legal code (both its constitution and various laws) in this regard several times since 1949. One could demonstrate that these changes corresponded, each time, to a changed international environment, above all to the changing 'German policy' of the Soviet Union, her relations with the other superpower and the relations between the NATO and Warsaw Pact alliances. In the first years after 1945 Moscow and East Berlin may still have entertained hopes for a united Germany on communist lines. The East German constitution of 1949, therefore, used at several points an 'all-German' language (Doc.3a). As the Cold War developed further and more and especially as the two Germanies each became part of a military, political, economic and ideological alliance which was 'antagonistic' to the other, the East felt constrained finally in 1961 to put an end to all real or feigned attempts to arrive at some kind of all-German solution, be that in the form of a confederacy or federation[8] or something else by fencing off the whole of East Germany (see also Ch.5).

The logical consequence of the new policy of the GDR after 1961 was a double one: the amendment of the constitution in 1968 to emphasize a separate *Socialist state of the German nation* (Doc.3b) and the enactment of a separate GDR citizenship law *(Staatsbürgerschaftsgesetz),* (Doc.4a,b). Both documents were an expression of an increasing desire on the part of the East German regime to get itself nationally and internationally acknowledged as a separate entity under international law.

The year 1969 marked a turning point in the internal political environment of the Federal Republic, in line with a changed international environment. For the first time ever a Social Democratic chancellor took over in Bonn—with the avowed intention of achieving a *détente,* the above mentioned *Wandel durch Annäherung* within the context of Germany in Central Europe and between the East-West camps generally. The following three years saw the breakthrough towards a new Ostpolitik, i.e. Bonn's treaties with Moscow, Warsaw, Prague, the Four-Power Treaty on Berlin and last but not least, the treaty with the German Democratic Republic.[9] As regards the latter the groundwork had been laid by Chancellor Willy Brandt in his meetings with the Prime-Minister of the German Democratic Republic, Willy Stoph, in West German Kassel and in East German Erfurth in 1970. The new West German policy guide-lines for intra-German relations *(innerdeutsche Beziehungen)*[10] were enunciated by Brandt in his so-called Kassel Points (Doc.5).

The treaty between Bonn and East Berlin of 1972 *(Grundlagen-vertrag)* with its various sub-agreements and protocol annexes (Docs.6a-d) not only made it possible for the German Democratic Republic to finally be recognized under international law by the rest of the international community, including the Western allies of the Federal Republic of Germany, but also put the relations between the two German states on a new footing of mutual recognition of each other's sovereignty. However, the West German government of Willy Brandt—as that of Helmut Schmidt or later of Helmut Kohl—made it clear that for constitutional and other reasons the Federal Republic could not and would not, in connection with these agreements, recognize the GDR under international law, that for Bonn the question of the future of an 'all-Germany' remained open and that, there-fore, an 'all-German' citizenship continued to exist. Bonn did not for that reason, establish full diplomatic relations with East Berlin. Even if a West German government or political party had wanted to bridge this continuing, decisive area of disagreement between Bonn and East Berlin, it could not have done so, unless the constitution itself were changed—with a two-thirds majority of both Houses. This legal position was reiterated authoritatively by the Federal Consti-tutional Court *(Bundesverfassungsgericht)* in an important judge-ment handed down in 1972 (Doc.7).

The consequences of Bonn's new Ostpolitik were evident above all in the so-called 'human sector' of visits (see also Ch.4) and were one of the main reasons for the second amendment of the GDR consti-tution in 1974 (Doc.3c). This time, references to an all-German nation, in being or in abeyance, were completely eliminated. The East German regime probably felt that the all-German 'germ' was getting too dangerous by virtue of increased contacts and had to be eradicated semantically as well as politically.

After the conclusion of the 1972 treaty, considerable headway in intra-German relations was made, above all with regard to the opportunities for West German journalists to work in the GDR, but also in such fields as public health or road construction between Berlin and the Federal Republic of Germany. The latter was, if any-thing, even more in the interests of the German Democratic Republic, with Bonn providing most of the necessary money. In spite of endless negotiations it was not possible to delineate the exact border-line between the two states on the river Elbe. Above all, progress was slow with regard to cultural relations, mainly due to differences over the status of West Berlin (see Ch.2) in this connection. So, all in all, one would have to say that in many of the fields singled out for more cooperation in the 1972 agreements, the actual gains achieved remained small or were not in evidence at all.

The guiding principle of the GDR's policy had remained un-changed ever since Erich Honecker raised the threshold for the intra-German process of normalisation with a speech made in the East German city of Gera in 1980 (Doc.8). Since Honecker must have known that the Federal Republic of Germany could not comply with his demands for settling the all-German question legally in line with of the GDR's wishes (in the field of citizenship, diplomatic recogni-tion etc.), it seemed clear that the Eastern side was mainly interested in a lever to exact other advantages from the West. Furthermore, the East German government created new and even stiffer barriers against meetings of West Germans with their friends and relatives in the East by increasing the amount of currency which visitors from the West were forced to exchange when entering the GDR (Doc.9).

The talks between Schmidt and Honecker in December 1981 in East Germany did not help to defuse intra-German grievances, except that they underscored once more one very important point of mutual consensus. It was made officially clear on the lines of Brandt's point 7 at Kassel (Doc.5) that both German governments, in spite of their unbridgeable ideological differences, remained determined to 'prevent another war ever taking German soil as its starting point again', to quote from the communiqué issued after the meeting.

There remained one other noticeable joint German policy approach worth mentioning: the fact that even the East German government did not want to give up the concept of a 'special rela-tionship' between the two German states in the economic sphere, i.e. regarding trade relations. Through keeping up this special relation-ship the GDR could make sure that it would continue to profit indi-rectly from the EC treaties, since the Federal Republic of Germany made certain, when signing those treaties in 1957, that its trade with the East German side would be considered as domestic trade, not subject to external tariffs and controls imposed by the EC on trade with countries outside the community (Doc.10).

While the social democratic governments of Willy Brandt and Helmut Schmidt as well as the Christian Democratic one, led since 1982 by Helmut Kohl, all officially avoided giving an appearance of democratic legitimacy to the East German regime, historians will be able to detect definite erosions in this official West-German policy line in the late 1980s. This was exemplified by the state visit of Erich Honecker to West Germany in 1987 (Doc.11) and by increasing demands from all political parties in the FRG to recognize, diplomatically at least, the East German Volkskammer—which had, after all, no democratic legitimacy—if not the Communist regime itself at any rate, its newly proclaimed GDR citizenship (Doc.5). In all political quarters of West Germany, not least amongst the intelligentsia, a tendency gained ground to play down the anti-democratic, totalitarian character of the SED regime and to upgrade at the same time mutual relations on the basis of giving up the goal of re-unification *de facto*—just paying lip-service to the idea in official pronouncements.[11] Some segments of the SPD went even further in demanding the closing of the official Institute storing records in the West on the repressive totalitarian system of East Germany, *(Erfassungsstelle Salzgitter)*. Particularly controversial in Germany was a 'Paper of Understanding' officially signed by the SPD and the SED (Doc.12). In the ensuing political debate within the SPD one side accused the other of being anti-communist and thereby endangering world peace, while the other replied with the reproach that this paper was starting off a new Munich policy of appeasement towards dictatorships. Had these trends been systematically reinforced as the 1980s went by, irreversible steps might have let to the permanent establishment of two separate German States.

Document 1a

PROGRAMME OF THE SOCIALIST UNITY PARTY OF GERMANY (SED) AS AMENDED 19 PARTY CONGRESS SED, 18–22 MAY 1976

Source: Gesamtdeutsches Institut, Bonn 1988

The SED is the conscious and organized vanguard of the working class and the working people of the socialist German Democratic Republic. It fulfils the tasks and objectives of the revolutionary Labour Movement as propounded by Marx, Engels and Lenin. Its efforts are at all times directed towards furthering the well-being of the people, the interests of the working class and of all other working people. It sees as its task the continued shaping of the socialist society already developed. Its aim is the establishment of Communist Society ...

   The SED is a branch of the International Communist Movement. It is firmly founded on proletarian internationalism. A brotherly bond links it with the Communist Party of the Soviet Union, the most tested and experienced communist party ...

Under the guidance of the SED the working class and the working peasantry of the GDR crushed for ever the rule of the German haute bourgeoisie and landed gentry, which in the course of our century unleashed two world wars. Founded on the revolutionary unity of the working class, an alliance of all democratic forces was forged. In a unified revolutionary process and in a bitter confrontation with the forces of imperialist reaction and their henchmen, the anti-fascist, democratic upheaval was achieved and the socialist revolution was carried to victory.

Under the leadership of the SED a fundamental change in the history of the German people has taken place in the GDR, the change to Socialism ...

PARTIES: Party Statutes of Bloc Parties

Source: Documents 1b-d: Katharina Behre, *Statuten und Satzungen der Blockparteien in der DDR,* Gesamtdeutsches Institut, Bonn 1984

Document 1b: LDPD
Excerpts, as amended 1982

The Liberal Democratic Party of Germany (LDP) is a democratic party active within and on behalf of socialism. It sees its historic task in shaping the developing socialist society in the GDR, under the guidance of the party of the working class and in unison with the parties and mass-organizations united within the National Front. By discharging its joint overall responsibility for our society, it makes its own distinct contribution. Within the ranks of its members and among citizens of like persuasion, in the organs of state power, in the Democratic Block, in the bodies of the National Front and in other organizations of society, it contributes through its efforts and experience, towards the all-round strengthening of the GDR as a socialist state and an inseparable constituent of the socialist community of states, and towards the securing of peace ...

Document 1c: NDP
Excerpts, as amended 1977

The National Democratic Party of Germany (NDP) is a party of the GDR linked in friendship to the Socialist Unity Party of Germany. Within its ranks it unites sections of the working population which are allied to the leading working class. Since its inception the essential values and direction of the NDP have been determined by its bond of alliance and friendship with the working class and its party, and with the Soviet Union ...

The party's main ideological task is to encourage among its members a social-ist attitude of mind towards the Socialist State; the criteria of such an attitude are thinking and acting in terms of socialist patriotism and internationalism ...

Document 1d: CDU (EAST)
Excerpts, as amended 1977

... The Christian Democratic Union of Germany (CDU) is a party of peace, democracy and socialism.... The unshakeable tenets of the political thought and action of the Christian Democrats are:
– loyalty to socialism
– trustful cooperation with the party of the working class as the guiding force of socialist society and
– friendship with the Soviet Union ...

Document 2

MEMORANDUM OF THE ACADEMY OF PEDAGOGIC SCIENCE IN THE GDR ON *PROBLEMS OF COMMUNIST EDUCATION,* 1974.

Excerpts

Source: Reinhard Günther, *Feindbild Bundesrepublik Deutschland,* Bd.II, Bonn 1976

... Above all it is the boys and girls in our republic who must be able to iden-tify the enemy clearly ... It is a dangerous and perfidious enemy ... Our con-cept of the enemy remains unchanged, even when right-wing Social Democrats are in charge of the affairs of state and military policy in the Fed-eral Republic of Germany ... We teach our pupils to hate imperialism as a system and to hate the mercenaries who, under the orders of imperialist generals and officers, raise their weapons against the might of the workers and peasants, against socialism and our friends ...

THE GERMAN NATION—AS SET OUT IN THE CONSTITUTION OF THE GERMAN DEMOCRATIC REPUBLIC

Document 3a

ART. 1 OF THE CONSTITUTION OF 1949

Source: S. Mampel, *Die Verfassung der Sowjetisch besetzten Zone,* Frankfurt, 1965, 37

Germany is an indivisible democratic republic, composed of German states [Länder].
The republic determines all matters which are essential for the existence and development of the German people as a whole, all other matters are to be determined independently by the states. The decisions of the republic are in principle to be carried out by the states.

There is only one German citizenship.

Document 3b

AMENDMENT TO THE CONSTITUTION, 1968

Source: Friedrich-Ebert-Stiftung (ed.), *Honecker's Verfassung,* Bonn, 1981, 49f.

Because of our responsibility to point the way to the entire German nation to a future of peace and socialism ... the people of the GDR ... have given themselves this socialist constitution:

The German Democratic Republic is a socialist state of the German nation. It is the political organization of the working people in the city and the country, who together bring socialism into reality under the leadership of the working class and its Marxist-Leninist Party.

Document 3c

AMENDMENT TO THE CONSTITUTION, 1974

Source: Ibid.

In continuation of the revolutionary traditions of the German working class ... the people of the German Democratic Republic have given themselves this socialist constitution:

The German Democratic Republic is a socialist state of the worker and the farmer. It is the political organization of the working people in the city and the country under the leadership of the working class and its Marxist-Leninist Party.

Document 4a

THE LAW ON CITIZENSHIP (GESETZ ÜBER DIE STAATSBÜRGERSCHAFT DER DEUTSCHEN DEMOKRATISCHEN REPUBLIK, STAATSBÜRGERSCHAFTSGESETZ), 20 FEBRUARY 1967

Source: Gesetzblatt der DDR, 1, No. 2, 23 February 1967

The citizenship of the German Democratic Republic came into existence, in accordance with international law, upon establishment of the German Democratic Republic. It is an expression of the German Democratic Republic's sovereignty and contributes to the further strengthening of all socialist countries.

The citizenship of the German Democratic Republic is membership of its residents in the first peace-loving, democratic and socialist German state, in which the working class exercises political power in alliance with the farmers' cooperative class, the socialist intelligentsia and other labouring people.

§ 1

A citizen of the German Democratic Republic is one who:
a) was a German national at the time of the establishment of the GDR, had his place of official or permanent residence in the German Democratic Republic and has not lost his German Democratic Republic citizenship since then;
b) was a German national at the time of the establishment of the GDR, had his official or permanent residence outside the German Democratic Republic, has obtained no other citizenship thereafter and, corresponding to his declaration of intent is enroled, through registration at one of the authorised German Democratic Republic's agencies, as a citizen of the German Democratic Republic;
c) obtained the citizenship of the German Democratic Republic, according to valid regulations, and has not lost it since.

§ 2

(1) The citizenship of the German Democratic Republic guarantees that the citizens of the German Democratic Republic can avail themselves of their constitutional rights and demands from them the implementation of their constitutional duties *[Pflichten]*.

. . .

§ 3

(1) According to generally accepted international law, citizens of the German Democratic Republic can claim no rights or duties of another citizenship in relation to the German Democratic Republic. (2) A citizen of the German Democratic Republic who intends to acquire citizenship from another country, requires the assent of the authorised central agencies of the German Democratic Republic ... .

. . .

§ 13

Citizens who have official or permanent residence outside the German Democratic Republic can be deprived of their citizenship for serious violation of civil duties.

[Here the point to be noted is that Germans who fled from the GDR automatically lost their GDR citizenship.]

Document 4b

ADDITIONAL LAW ON QUESTIONS OF CITIZENSHIP (ZUR REGELUNG VON FRAGEN DER STAATSBÜRGERSCHAFT), 16 OCTOBER 1972

Source: Gesetzblatt der DDR, I, No. 18, 17 October 1972

§ 1

(1) Citizens of the German Democratic Republic who, in violation of the laws of the Worker and Peasant State [Arbeiter- und Bauernstaat] left the German Democratic Republic before 1 January 1972, and who have not taken up residence in the German Democratic Republic again, lose their citizenship of the German Democratic Republic with the coming into force of this Law.

(2) Descendants of persons referred to in (1) lose their citizenship of the German Democratic Republic with the coming into force of this Law in so far as they have their residence outside the German Democratic Republic without the authorization of governmental agencies of the German Democratic Republic.

§ 2

Persons referred to in § 1 (1) will not be liable to criminal prosecution for leaving the German Democratic Republic without authorization.

Chancellor Willy Brandt and the GDR's Chairman of the Council of Ministers, Willi Stoph, met twice in 1970, first in Erfurt and then in Kassel. Brandt's visit to Erfurt in March 1970 was the first ever by a West German chancellor and led to such an enthusiastic reception for him by the East Germans that the authorities in the Eastern part of the country have never again incurred the risk of a West German chancellor meeting with the people of the German Democratic Republic. This fact was very much in evidence some eleven years later, when Chancellor Helmut Schmidt met with Erich Honecker, the leader of the GDR since 1971, in a secluded place near Berlin (December 1981). Schmidt was completely cordoned off during his visit to the town of Güstrow in the GDR. At their second meeting of 1970, in Kassel, Brandt and Stoph exchanged views and notes on the guidelines each side was putting for-

ward to normalize relations between the two states. The excerpts below
are part of a total of '20 Points' which Brandt put forward.

Document 5

KASSEL MEMORANDUM OF WILLY BRANDT

Source: Auswärtiges Amt (ed.), *Die Außenpolitik der Bundesrepublik Deutschland,* Bonn, 1972, 754

Our conception of the guidelines and treaty elements for the regulation of
an equal relationship between the Federal Republic of Germany and the
German Democratic Republic is as follows:

1. The Federal Republic of Germany and the German Democratic Republic, which are both constitutionally based on the concept of the unity of
   the nation, in the interest of peace as well as for the future and coherence
   of the nation, agree on a treaty, which regulates the relationship between
   both German states, improves the link between the people and both
   states and contributes to the elimination of existing discrimination.
5. Both sides respect the independence and self-sufficiency of each of the
   two countries in matters which concern their domestic jurisdiction.
6. Neither of the two German states can act for the other or represent the
   other.
7. The treaty-making partners declare that a war must never again begin
   from German soil.

. . .

10. The treaty must proceed from the consequences of World War II and
    from the special situation of Germany and the Germans, who live in two
    states and yet understand themselves to be citizens of *one* (my emphasis
    added) nation.

Document 6a

TREATY ON THE BASIS OF RELATIONS BETWEEN THE FEDERAL REPUBLIC OF GERMANY AND THE GERMAN DEMOCRATIC REPUBLIC (BASIC TREATY) 26 MAY 1972

Source: Presse- und Informationsamt der Bundesregierung, *Documentation
relating to the Federal Government's policy of détente,* Bonn, 1978, 178ff.

Transl.: Official

The High Contracting Parties,
In consideration of their responsibility for the preservation of peace,
Anxious to contribute to détente and security in Europe,
Conscious that the inviolability of frontiers and respect for the territorial in-
tegrity and sovereignty of all States in Europe within their present frontiers
are a fundamental condition for peace,

Recognizing that therefore the two German States are to refrain from the threat or use of force in their relations,

Proceeding from the historical facts and without prejudice to the differing views of the Federal Republic of Germany and the German Democratic Republic on questions of principle, including the national question,

Desiring to create the conditions for co-operation between the Federal Republic of Germany and the German Democratic Republic for the benefit of the people in the two German States,

Have agreed as follows:

The Federal Republic of Germany and the German Democratic Republic shall develop normal good neighbourly relations with each other on the basis of equal rights.

. . .

Article 3

In accordance with the United Nations Charter, the Federal Republic of Germany and the German Democratic Republic shall settle their disputes exclusively by peaceful means and refrain from the threat or use of force.

They reaffirm the inviolability now and in the future of the border existing between them and undertake fully to respect their territorial integrity.

Article 4

The Federal Republic of Germany and the German Democratic Republic proceed on the assumption that neither of the two States can represent the other internationally or act in its name.

. . .

Article 7

The Federal Republic of Germany and the German Democratic Republic state their readiness to regulate practical and humanitarian questions in the process of the normalization of their relations. They will conclude agreements with a view to developing and promoting cooperation in the fields of economics, science and technology, traffic, judicial relations, posts and telecommunications, health, culture, sport, environmental protection, and in other fields, on the basis of the present Treaty and for their mutual benefit. The details have been agreed in the Supplementary Protocol.

Article 8

The Federal Republic of Germany and the German Democratic Republic will exchange permanent missions. They will be established at the respective seat of government.

Practical questions relating to the establishment of the missions will be dealt with separately.

Article 9

The Federal Republic of Germany and the German Democratic Republic are agreed that the present Treaty does not affect the bilateral and multilateral international treaties and agreements previously concluded by them or concerning them.

. . .

Document 6b

LETTER FROM THE GOVERNMENT OF THE FEDERAL
REPUBLIC OF GERMANY TO THE GOVERNMENT OF
THE GERMAN DEMOCRATIC REPUBLIC ON GERMAN
UNITY, 21 DECEMBER 1972

Source: Ibid., 182

In connection with the signing today of the Treaty on the Basis of Relations
between the Federal Republic of Germany and the German Democratic
Republic, the Government of the Federal Republic of Germany has the honour to state that this Treaty does not conflict with the political aim of the
Federal Republic of Germany to work for a state of peace in Europe in which
the German nation will regain its unity through free self-determination.

Document 6c

STATEMENTS ON RECORD

Source: Ibid., 187

The Federal Republic of Germany states on record:
'Questions of nationality have not been regulated by the Treaty.'

The German Democratic Republic states on record:
'The German Democratic Republic proceeds from the assumption that
the Treaty will facilitate a regulation of questions of nationality.'

Document 6d

EXPLANATORY NOTES REGARDING THE EXCHANGE
OF LETTERS ON THE REUNITING OF FAMILIES, THE
FACILITATION OF TRAVEL AND THE IMPROVEMENT
OF NON-COMMERCIAL GOODS TRAFFIC

Source: Ibid., 191-2

With the entry into force of the Treaty on the Basis of Relations the following facilitations will take effect:

1. *Solution of problems connected with the reuniting of families*
   – Reuniting of married couples
   – Movement of parents requiring the care of their children, especially if
     only one parent is still alive. The same applies to the movement of
     grandparents to join their grandchildren.
   – In special exceptional cases, permission to marry.

2. *Improvement of border-crossing travel and visitor traffic*
  - Extension of the number of urgent family reasons for which GDR citizens may be permitted to travel to the FRG to include silver and golden wedding anniversaries.
  - Extension of the category of GDR citizens entitled to apply for travel for urgent family reasons to include half-sisters and half-brothers (same mother)... .

The government of Bavaria had applied to the Federal Constitutional Court on 28 May 1973 to declare the treaty between the Federal Republic of Germany and the German Democratic Republic of December 1972 unconstitutional, on the grounds that certain provisions of that treaty constituted a violation of the preamble and other articles of the Basic Law, all of which make it legally binding on any government in Bonn to work for a reunification of Germany. The Court rejected the Bavarian government's complaint, but emphasised the limitations placed on government action by the Basic Law. Below follow extracts from the ruling of the Court.

Document 7

BASIC PRINCIPLES UNDERLYING THE RULING OF THE FEDERAL CONSTITUTIONAL COURT ON THE VALIDITY OF THE TREATY OF DECEMBER 1972 (LEITSÄTZE, 31 JULY 1973)

Source: Bundesanstalt für Gesamtdeutsche Aufgaben, Bonn, 1974, special issue

. . .

4) It follows from the precept of reunification that no constitutional body of the Federal Republic of Germany may abandon the restoration of national unity as a political goal and that it is the duty of all constitutional bodies to work towards the attainment of this goal in their policies and to refrain from doing anything that would thwart the aim of reunification. This involves a requirement to keep alive the claim to reunification at home and to insist on it unwaveringly abroad.

5) The Constitution forbids the Federal Republic of Germany to renounce a legal title enshrined in its Basic Law, by means of which it can work towards the realization of reunification and self-determination, or to create a legal title incompatible with the Basic Law, or to be party to the establishment of a legal title which may be cited against it in its pursuit of this goal.

6) The treaty has dual character; in essence it is a treaty under international law; in substance it is specifically a treaty regulating inter-German relations.

7) Art. 23 of the Basic Law forbids the Federal Government to enter into a contractual dependence as a result of which it would no longer be able to effect the incorporation of other parts of Germany on its own, but only with the approval of the other party to the contract.

8) Art. 16 of the Basic Law assumes that the 'German citizenship', to which reference is also made in Art. 116, Para. 1 of the Basic Law, is at the same time the citizenship of the Federal Republic of Germany. It follows according to the spirit of the Basic Law that not only citizens of the Federal Republic of Germany are German citizens.

9) Any German entering the area of authority ... of the Federal Republic of Germany is entitled to the full protection of the courts of the Federal Republic of Germany and to the fundamental rights guaranteed by the Basic Law.

Document 8

SPEECH BY ERICH HONECKER, GENERAL SECRETARY OF THE SED AND CHAIRMAN OF THE COUNCIL OF STATE (STAATSRATSVORSITZENDER), ON 'TOPICAL QUESTIONS OF THE DOMESTIC AND FOREIGN POLICY OF THE GDR', AT GERA, 13 OCTOBER 1980

Source: Neues Deutschland [the official newspaper of the SED in the GDR], 14 October 1980

. . .

The GDR has made many attempts at improvements

The German Democratic Republic strives for good neighbourly relations with the Federal Republic of Germany and, just as in our policy towards other Western states, we pursue here, too, a policy of peaceful coexistence. On this basis we have done much in the past to smooth the path for progress in the relations between the German Democratic Republic and the Federal Republic of Germany. It was possible to negotiate numerous treaties and agreements which function fairly well. The results thereof were important prerequisites for a mutually advantageous cooperation based on equal rights.

Obviously it cannot be overlooked that many problems between the German Democratic Republic and the Federal Republic of Germany continue to exist and that we still have a long way to go before complete normality is attained. The main reasons for this are the Federal Republic of Germany's continued attempts, when dealing with the GDR, to disregard decisive principles of the sovereignty of our state, thereby violating the Basic Treaty *[Grundlagenvertrag]*. In this relationship, however, it is only possible to take a step forward when the existence of two sovereign states, which are independent of one another and which have different forms of society, is unconditionally accepted. Every effort to revise the European postwar arrangement must put a strain on the normalization of the relations between the two German states; indeed it puts them in doubt.

The Federal Republic of Germany prevents solutions

It is absolutely vital that the principle of non-interference is accepted without limitation by both sides in the bilateral relations as well as in the relationship to third states... . We have often pressed to have the obstructions removed, but have received no cooperation. This is true above all of the recognition of the citizenship of the German Democratic Republic. As the Federal Republic of Germany adheres to ideas which are not in accordance with international law and as they refuse to respect the citizenship of the German Democratic Republic, the jurisdiction of our state is being denied. But it is certainly a fact that there are two sovereign German states, independent of one another. There are, and this is also a fact, citizens of the socialist German Democratic Republic and citizens of the capitalist Federal Republic of Germany.

We consider it necessary for the FRG to accept reality at last, something it will not be able to avoid in the long run, in any case. This would make it easier to settle the most urgent practical questions in tourist travel, in legal aid and in various other fields. The so-called 'Registration Centre' [Zentrale Erfassungsstelle] at Salzgitter should have been dissolved long ago. An end must be put to the issuing of temporary passports for GDR citizens when staying in the Federal Republic, as well as to the issuing of FRG passports for GDR citizens by FRG embassies in third countries.

We also consider it time to exchange ambassadors as is usual in the relations between two sovereign states independent of one another, i.e. to transform the offices of the permanent representatives of the GDR and the FRG into what conforms with international law—into embassies. This would be a visible step towards a normalization of the relations between the two German states ...

Of great importance is the situation at the border of the two states, which is also the dividing line between the Warsaw Pact States and NATO. The common Border Commission of the two German states has achieved positive results and important agreements have been arrived at. It would serve the interests of peace and good neighbourly relations, if the border line along the river Elbe could be determined according to international law, an agreement which has so far failed due to the unacceptable positions adopted by the Federal Republic... .

In 1964 the GDR authorities first introduced an 'obligatory minimum exchange' for intra-German travel. The regulation of the 25 November 1964 to this effect applied to 'all visitors from West Germany, other non-socialist countries and West Berlin who enter the GDR for a private visit'. The amount of compulsory currency exchange was then fixed at 5 DM per diem per person (for West Berliners, 3 DM). This was changed to 10 DM in 1968 and to 20 DM in 1972 for all categories including West Berliners. Exempted had been women over sixty, men over sixty-five and young people under sixteen. Old people were temporarily included again in November 1973 and again in November 1974, but the amount was then reduced. Interestingly enough only five weeks later, i.e. in December 1974, pensioners were again exempted. This was the position that prevailed until 1980. The new law, quoted below, increased the amount to 25 DM and, what was even more objectionable to the Bonn government, again included pensioners. Children between the ages of six and fourteen had to pay 7.50 DM; exemption was granted only for children under the age of six. As of October 1983 children under the age of fourteen were exempted.

Document 9

REGULATION CONCERNING THE OBLIGATORY MINIMUM CURRENCY EXCHANGE [ON ENTERING THE GDR] (ANORDNUNG ÜBER DIE DURCHFÜHRUNG EINES VERBINDLICHEN MINDESTUMTAUSCHES VON ZAHLUNGSMITTELN) 10 OCTOBER 1980

Source: Gesetzblatt der DDR, Teil I, No. 29, 9 October 1980

§1

This regulation applies to persons residing temporarily in non-socialist countries and in West Berlin, who enter the German Democratic Republic for visits of limited duration.

§2

1) For each day of their stay in the German Democratic Republic including its capital city, persons referred to in §1 must exchange foreign currency equivalent in value to at least 25 marks of the German Democratic Republic at the rates of exchange currently applying in the German Democratic Republic.

2) The minimum exchange in accordance with 1) must be carried out in a convertible currency.

§3

1) Currency exchanged according to §2, 1) into marks of the German Democratic Republic cannot be reconverted.

2) Unused marks of the German Democratic Republic can be deposited or paid into an account with all bureaux of exchange and all branches of the State Bank of the German Democratic Republic. Such sums can be drawn upon in full in marks of the German Democratic Republic at any time on reentry into the German Democratic Republic.

Document 10

THE WEST GERMAN UNDERSECRETARY OF STATE FOR
FOREIGN AFFAIRS (STAATSSEKRETÄR) WALTER HALLSTEIN,
SPEAKING IN THE BUNDESTAG ON THE SPECIAL TRADE
RELATIONSHIP BETWEEN THE TWO GERMAN STATES, 21
MARCH 1957

Source: Auswärtiges Amt (ed.) *Die Aussenpolitik der Bundesrepublik Deutschland,* Bonn, 1972, 354f.

Hallstein emphasized that the federal government had, when signing the Treaties of Rome (EEC and Euratom), made clear that a reunited Germany would be free to decide on its own accession to the treaties and he went on to say in this connection: ' ... we have taken special care to safeguard the position of Berlin and the whole process of the 'intra-German trade' [Interzonenhandel] ... we are very much interested in not only preserving this instrument of intra-German trade, but in actually developing it further. For this reason the treaty on the Common Market expressis verbis contains the provision—I quote—'that the execution of the community treaty will entail neither any change in regard to the regulations for the intra-German trade as of now nor any change in the actual conduct of this same trade. It is, therefore, absolutely clear that the present state of affairs by which the intra-German trade is a purely domestic one will remain intact. The demarcation line with the Eastern zone [Zonengrenze, frontier with the German Democratic Republic] will continue not to be a customs frontier. The federal government retains its full freedom of action in regard to this intra-German trade'.

OFFICIAL VISIT OF ERICH HONECKER, THE GENERAL SEC-RETARY OF THE CENTRAL COMMITTEE OF THE SOCIALIST UNITY PARTY OF GERMANY AND HEAD OF STATE OF THE GDR, TO THE FRG ON 7TH SEPTEMBER 1987.

Document 11a

EXCERPTS FROM A SPEECH MADE BY THE FEDERAL
CHANCELLOR DR. HELMUT KOHL AT A BANQUET GIVEN
IN HONOUR OF ERICH HONECKER

Source: Bundesministerium für Innerdeutsche Beziehungen, *Texte zur Deutschlandpolitik,* Bonn, Reihe III, Band 5, 1987

'Mr General Secretary, Ladies and Gentlemen!
Herr Honecker, I bid you welcome to Bonn. It is right that we should come together for talks. The eyes of millions of Germans from Stralsund to Lake Constance, from Flensburg to Dresden—and in Berlin—are focused on your

visit to the Federal Republic and on our meeting. Many find themselves struggling with conflicting feelings: people in Germany know that two states exist here which have to resolve many practical questions with one another. But they also know that this visit has a special human and political dimension. It differs from the customary meetings between East and West.

The sense of the unity of the nation is as alive now as ever, and the determination to preserve it is unbroken. This unity finds expression in our common language, in our common cultural heritage, in a long, continuing common history. And so, many of us today have difficulty with our feelings and difficulty in deciding how this meeting fits into the continuity of German history. However, our meeting in Bonn is neither the final word nor is it a fresh start. It is a step along the road of an already long-standing development, a development marked by efforts towards achieving an acceptable modus vivendi ...

This visit can and will do nothing to alter the different outlooks of the two states on basic issues, such as the national question. On behalf of the Federal Government I repeat that the pre-amble to our Basic Law is not open to discussion, because it conforms to our convictions. It calls for a united Europe and calls upon the whole German nation to bring about the unity and freedom of Germany through free self-determination.

This is our objective. We stand by the demand placed on us by our constitution, and we have no doubt that this is the will and desire, indeed the yearning, of all the people in Germany ...

Let us in the coming days concentrate on what can realistically be achieved. Let us agree to leave issues that at present cannot be resolved in the background. Through our practical co-operation we have set an example in spite of all our differences—an example for the good of mankind and in the interests of peace. The other European nations also want the Germans in East and West to get on with each other, and to demonstrate in their mutual dealings the humanity which befits the nation of Lessing, Goethe and Schiller ...'

Document 11b

EXCERPTS FROM ERICH HONECKER'S REPLY:

Source: Ibid.

'Chancellor, Ladies and Gentlemen, dear friends and comrades!.. The development of relations between the German Democratic Republic and the Federal Republic of Germany is characterized—as we all appreciate—by the realities of the world we live in. These realities indicate that a union between socialism and capitalism is no more possible than one between fire and water ...

In accordance with our Joint Declaration of 12th March, 1985, the German Democratic Republic abides by its conviction that the inviolability of borders and respect for the territorial integrity and sovereignty of all states in Europe within their present borders, are fundamental conditions for peace. A constructive policy, which is not only of benefit to the two German states, must be based on the recognition of the existence of two separate and independent sovereign German states, each with its own social order and belonging to different alliances. On the basis of the treaties so far concluded, we will spare no effort to take steps in the relations between the German Democratic Republic and the Federal Republic of Germany, which serve the interests of peace, of détente, of mutual beneficial cooperation and thereby of mankind ...'

Document 11c

COMMUNIQUÉ ISSUED AT THE END OF THE OFFICIAL VISIT

Source: Ibid.

With due regard to given circumstances, and notwithstanding the differences in outlook on fundamental issues, including the national question, both sides declare their intention, in the spirit of the Basic Treaty, [of 1972, see above, Docs.6a-d] to develop normal neighbourly relations towards each other on the basis of equality of status, and to exploit the potential of the treaty to the full. There was agreement on preserving and building on previous achievements with regard to the principle that the two states respect each other's independence and autonomy in internal and external affairs. Co-operation between the two states which is constructive and geared towards practical results should be guided by the principles of realism and mutual understanding.

The two states acknowledge the lasting positive effects of the Four Power Agreement of 3rd September 1971 on the situation in Central Europe and on East-West relations and emphasised the need for its full implementation and strict observance.

Federal Chancellor Kohl and General Secretary Honecker dealt in detail with the issue of holiday travel and visitors, including journeys undertaken for urgent family reasons. They acknowledged the progress made so far and re-asserted the intention of working towards a further improvement and easing of the situation in the interest of the people ...

They emphasized the intention of promoting and further developing youth exchanges, in order to bring together young tourists from both sides. They welcomed the setting up of twinning arrangements between towns in the Federal Republic of Germany and in the German Democratic Republic as an important contribution towards the bringing together of citizens from both sides ....

Document 12

FROM IDEOLOGICAL CONFRONTATION AND JOINT SECURITY
Excerpts from the joint declaration: SED/SPD 1987

Source: SPD Parteivorstand, Bonn 1987

. . .

Section 3: The need for a culture based on political debate and dialogue:
We, German Communists and Social Democrats, agree that peace today
can no longer be brought about by each side preparing for war, but only
by each side coming to a mutual agreement and understanding with the
other. The consequence of this is a new community of interest in the struggle for peace.

Social Democrats and Communists both hark back to Europe's humanist
heritage. Each claims for itself the right to carry on this heritage, to represent the interests of working people and to put democracy and human rights
into practice.

Yet for seventy years, there has been a bitter conflict between Communists
and Social Democrats as to how these ends should be achieved. This conflict
is exacerbated by the fact that they often use the same terms to mean different things.

The Social Democrats see themselves as a part of Western democracy; for
them, pluralistically organized democracy with its various ways of separating
powers and exercising checks and balances, provides the framework within
which they wish to realize their conception of democratic socialism. This
frame work is binding for them and has to be defended at all costs.

For Marxist/Leninists, democracy as a system for exercising power is
characterized essentially by the ownership of the crucial means of production
and of the political power arising therefrom. For them, the transfer of the
most important means of production into public ownership and into the
political power of the working class in alliance with other working people, is
therefore the basis of comprehensive democratic rights ...

. . .

Section 5: Rules for a culture based on political debate

. . .

3. Criticism of the social conditions obtaining in the other system should be
   based on verifiable facts. It should also be accompanied by an initial
   attempt to empathize with the logic of the other side, not of course in
   order to approve of its intentions on every occasion, but to understand
   the context of its actions. Whoever undertakes such an attempt will not
   degenerate into aggressive polemicizing ...

. . .

5. Ideological disputes are to be handled in such a way as to avoid any interference in the internal affairs of other states. Criticism, even when fierce,
   must not be rejected as 'interference in the internal affairs of the other

side'. The principle of sovereign equality is also valid here, i.e. that no side may in practice claim for itself anything that it refuses to allow the other.

6. Open discussion of the competition between the systems, of their successes and failures, their advantages and disadvantages, must be possible within every system. Indeed, genuine competition requires that such a discussion be encouraged and produce practical results. Only in this fashion is it possible to compare and take stock publicly of the practice and experiences of the two systems, so that whatever is seen to have failed may be rejected, and whatever has proved itself may be retained and—if the circumstances warrant it—be adopted by the other side and elaborated on ...

Notes

1. Special concentration camps, however, in the original sense of those the British used in their wars in South Africa, were set up and kept in a state of preparedness right up to the end of 1989 with lists of people drawn up to be arrested and detained there as soon as the emergency codeword was given out.

2. According to latest estimates there were some 200,000 persons imprisoned for 'political' reasons in the former GDR. In the ill-famed Bautzen prison, Saxony, alone the Soviets had imprisoned some 26,000 people in the years between 1945 to 1950. Altogether in their zone 157,837 were taken to Soviet camps. Such figures have now become available in Russian archives. The total death-toll in both the Soviet camps and in the prisons of the GDR still can not be ascertained exactly.

3. So-called 'IMs' (unofficial informants) spied upon their fellow countrymen and women with a ratio of one such spy to eighty-five GDR inhabitants. Sometimes as many as thirty spies were put on the trail of one person under political suspicion, see now the official studies of the Federal Office for the Investigation of Stasi-activities (*Bundesbeauftragter für die Unterlagen des Staatssicherheitsdienstes in der ehemaligen DDR, Erster Tätigkeitsbericht Berlin 1993*) and ibid. *IM Statistik 1985-89, Berlin 3/1993* (Series: *BF informiert*). Altogether, some 180 km of records had to be ploughed through, a job which will still take years to accomplish. The man in charge is a former pastor, Joachim Gauck. He has at his command 3000 researchers. So far some 1.8 million applications came in—both from people who were persecuted by the communists and by heads of Civil Services who asked for the screening of their staff.

4. In 1969 some one million West Germans were able to visit relatives in the GDR, in the mid 1970s this number climbed to over 3 million. After a drastic increase of the compulsory currency exchange in 1980 (as already before in 1973), the numbers shrank once again. The figures for travel from East to West were, for obvious reasons, much more restricted. The figures for those over the age of 65 who were granted permission by the GDR authorities to visit the West show a total of approximately one million in 1969, 1.2 million in 1973 and 1.3 million annually between 1974–8. There was a significant increase in the number of exit permits given to people in East Germany to visit the West on 'urgent family grounds'(such as the marriage or death of a near relative); from 11,421 in 1973 to 48,695 in 1978. All these travellers were carefully screened and usually forced

to leave behind—a modern form of hostage taking—a spouse or child. In the mid-1980s these figures, however, increased after a new law regulating such travel was enacted in 1982. From 1983-85 they amounted to some 60,000 per annum, in 1987 and 1988 even to some 1.2 million.

See Timothy Garton Ash, *Im Namen Europas, Deutschland und der geteilte Kontinent*, München 1993, 208 ff. and Margit Roth, *Zwei Staaten in Deutschland*, Opladen 1981. For the general 'flow' of refugees and escapees see statistics, Table 4.

5. The long-time top general of the Nationale Volksarmee, Hoffmann, was the most illustrious example, cited for years in the West as having been a former Nazi. Research of SED Documents available for the first time now has revealed that in local branches of the SED, after its formation in 1946, as many as 10-15 per cent of the members had been members of the former Nazi Party, in higher echelons of the SED hierarchy the figure was as high as 30 per cent. Armin Mitter, Humboldt-University, Berlin (East) gave these figures prior to publication to the author.

6. The so-called 'order to shoot on sight' *(Schießbefehl)* was, as far as present research and the law courts ascertained given out on 6 October 1961 by the then minister for National Defence, Hoffmann. As follows '… The guards … of the frontier-forces … are under strict orders to use firearms … in order to arrest persons, who do not follow the orders of the frontier posts, i.e. their call: 'stop, here frontier post' and then do not stop after the guards have fired a warning shot, but clearly try to violate the state frontier of the German Democratic Republic… .'

In the last two years several cases have come to court where individual guards have been accused of having emptied, in some cases, a whole magazine of bullets into people who were trying to escape, and already hit, were lying on the ground wounded and then killed. See also Chs.4 and 9.

7. However, the official communiques after meetings of NATO-ministers over the years regularly referred to the 'allied' policy-goal to solve the German question on the basis of self-determination for all Germany, see C.C. Schweitzer, et al, *The Changing Western Analysis of the Soviet threat*, Pinter, London 1990. The overall policy of the USA was on historical evidence throughout the decades after 1945 in comparison to the British and French much more consistent in never giving up the goal of German re-unification. In the 1980s it was President Ronald Reagan, who appealed in public to the Soviets (in Berlin) to 'tear down that wall'. See for details on sources here: E.O. Czempiel and C.C. Schweitzer, *Weltpolitik der USA nach 1945*, (Opladen-Bonn 1989, for instance: US National Security Document No. 5727, declassified in Washington in 1982, 'On the policy of the United States towards the German question' as of December 1957: 'Germany is of vital importance to the United States: a) Germany's location in the heart of Europe and its considerable material and human resources make it a key area in the struggle between the Communist and free worlds; b) the division of Germany is a chronic source of European instability and East-West friction and a possible source of major armed conflict; the future development and orientation of the Federal Republic will significantly affect the development of Europe as a whole … West German military association with Western Europe is very important to strengthen NATO capabilities in Europe (major policy guidance): … (we must) make clear that reunification is essential to any genuine relaxation of tension between the USSR and the West, but that the US will not agree to any reunification involving a) Communist domination of a reunified Germany; b) a federated Germany which perpetuates the existing government of the German Democratic Republic; c) the withdrawal of US and other allied forces from West Germany without an effective military quid pro quo from the Soviets and the satellites …'. See also C.C.

Schweitzer, *Weltmacht USA, Kontinuität oder Wandel ihrer Aussenpolitik nach 1945,* Munich, 1983, 68ff.

8. The idea of a confederacy was first put on the overall East-West agenda by the GDR in 1956; see statement by Walter Ulbricht, the then Secretary of the East German Communist Party, of 29 December 1956, published in the official newspaper *Neues Deutschland,* 30 December 1956: 'Confederacy between the two German states as a transition stage for reunification'. The motives behind such proposals were manifold, *inter alia* to influence public opinion in West Germany against a further integration of the Federal Republic into the overall Western system (the founding of the EEC then being imminent), or to achieve international recognition for the GDR under international law etc.

9. See Ch.5 and *'Documentation Relating to the Federal Government's Policy of Détente',* published by the Presse- und Informationsamt der Bundesregierung, Bonn 1978.

10. A neat semantic change was brought about by the SPD-FDP Government under Willy Brandt 1969 in regard of the name to the ministry dealing with the relations between the Federal Republic and the GDR: From the 'All-German' *(Gesamtdeutsch)* to 'Intra-German'—Ministry *(Innerdeutsch),* the latter implying less than the former the overall goal of reunification.

11. Under the Kohl government even the CDU—in 1988—left out in its first draft of a new party programme all references to 'reunification'. However, in the end internal party pressure became so great, that the authors had to change their text and put in a passing reference to that particular goal once again.

4
Germany Reunited
1989—Her first successful revolution, and a peaceful one

Carl-Christoph Schweitzer

Before scrutinizing the dramatic events in the autumn of 1989, which with its unexpected momentum caused the whole international community to hold its breath during the crucial days when the balance was finally tipped against those who had kept the East Germans down under communist domination for forty years, one must briefly draw attention to preceding attempts made in the Soviet orbit generally to shake off detested Moscow-controlled regimes.

In this context the East Germans deserve a prize in point of time for having been the first to openly stand against a Moscow puppet government: between 15 and 17 June 1953. This dramatic event has as yet to be fully evaluated historically. It is, however, already clear that the uprising was much more widespread than officially admitted by the GDR government at the time—with some 500,000 workers and others taking part in some 400 towns and villages throughout the GDR: that it was crushed in the end only with the help of Soviet forces including tanks, even though Ulbricht and his economic policies were then already regarded with scepticism in Moscow,[1]* and that this uprising was, contrary to GDR teaching, not provoked or even inspired by Western sources of any kind.[2] Less clear is, however, still the exact mix of the underlying motives of the workers' demands which were both economic and political: on the one hand they protested against increased 'working-norms', on the other they demanded, more and more openly, as the mass demonstrations developed, freedom and democratic government.

After the brutal crushing of this uprising in 1953 by the Soviet superpower there were no further attempts to overthrow the regime in East Germany and even less, of course, to put an end to the Soviet military occupation. It was an obvious fact of international life for all to see that no one could have ejected the Soviet army from East Germany unilaterally, short of a Third World War. This, by the very nature of things, applied to all Eastern European countries in the grip of Moscow. And yet there were later dramatic uprisings in Poland and above all in Hungary 1956, in the CSSR in 1968 and again in the early 1980s in Poland—this latter being in the end successful and, therefore with a signal effect, brought about by *Solidarnosz*. Comparing the outward quietness prevailing in the GDR between 1953 and 1989 to the developments in those other bloc-countries, one must keep in mind that democratic opposition in of Eastern Europe could derive an additional strength from a historically and geographically clearly defined nation- and statehood.

In contrast, oppositional scenarios in East Germany had to cope with the fact of an artificial, but definitely most stringent division of a former (German) nation-state.

In this apparently hopeless national and international environment any opposition in the GDR was bound to develop and express itself on a highly individual basis—at least up to the early 1980s. Up to that time it was too dangerous to establish any kind of 'network' in the country with the one exception of the Churches, above all the predominant Protestant Churches (see below), which had, not least for tactical reasons, severed on their own initiative all institutionalized ties with their fellow-churches in the West in 1969. In addition—and again in marked contrast to Poland, Hungary, or the CSSR—no leading national figure personifying an opposition emerged in the course of the years in the GDR. In other words, there was no Alexander Dubzek or Václav Havel of Czechoslovakia or, above all, no Lech Walesa of Poland (with the Polish national-minded Church, in this case the Roman Catholic one, behind him).

However, as the 1960s and 1970s drew to a close, in the GDR too, more and more people seemed at least to have hoped for the possibility of achieving reforms of the communist system from within, in the direction of what used to be called in the mounting East-West conflict, a 'third way' between capitalism and communism—indeed such as Dubzek in the CSSR had stood for. That explains why today oppositional individuals in the former GDR *uni sono* point to the shattering effect the events in the CSSR of 1968 had on them. After these events, such opponents of the regime in the GDR found themselves confronted more than ever by three possibilities, apart from the almost suicidal risk of trying to escape 'illegally' (see also Ch.3 and Statistics, Table 4): to stay on in the country in spite of both petty repressions and more serious persecutions; to try and emigrate to the West on an official exit-permit, a procedure which sometimes took years and which was in any case accompanied by many punitive disadvantages in daily life; or, finally to have oneself deported *(Abschiebung, Ausweisung)*. In that latter respect a significant turning point in the official treatment of individual opponents seems to have been one of the first expatriations ever by the GDR authorities, the expatriation of the well-known poet Wolf Biermann in 1976 against his will. This led to unrest, especially in the East German world of literature which never again calmed down.[3]

And yet, as the years went by, more and more 'ordinary citizens' than was generally known at the time, or is known even today, daringly stood up for human and political rights such as freedom of expression or even free elections, at least on the local level. Highlights of such protests occurred in regard to the local elections of May 1989 (Doc.1a-c). In the early 1980s, there seems to have developed an accumulation and acceleration of such individual opposition with increasing interpersonal linkages. Otherwise there could not have been this sudden explosion which led to the mass-movement causing the unexpected collapse of an apparently tightly controlled state and society in the autumn of 1989. These dramatic events certainly caught the majority of people in the West completely by surprise, in some contrast to East Germany, where insiders had for some time seen the 'writing on the wall', i.e. particularly erosions in the economic, but also in the ideological field. All of a sudden the system collapsed totally, from the top of the government and Party to the bottom of local authorities and command-posts of the Army and even of the Secret Police, the Stasi.

This collapse was, however, not a revolution in the Marxist-Leninist sense—such as St. Petersburg in 1917 or in France in 1789. It was fortunately an entirely bloodless revolution. No one was even arrested after the formation in early 1990 of the first democratic government in East Germany under Lothar de Maizière, formerly a member of the East German CDU. The other side of this peaceful revolution was, therefore, inevitably the fact that many of the old elites in the middle and lower echelons of society, especially in the industrial sector, survived in positions of influence after reunification.

The main factors contributing to the total collapse of the GDR regime in the autumn of 1989 can now be briefly summarized as follows:

First, there had developed in the preceding years, definitely since the mid-1980s, irreversible 'contradictions' (to deliberately use Marxist-Leninist terminology) between the demands of economic policy and social policy—the rather strange synthesis of which had been proclaimed as the official goal of the Honecker regime soon after his coming into power in 1971—and, therefore, also between ideological claims and reality of life with a resulting sense of frustration and mounting discontent throughout the population. The official claim to have reached the stage of a 'socialism really existing' *(real-existierender Sozialismus)*—meant as a term of distinction—had, as the years went by, become a tool in the hand of Western, as well as domestic, critics who used that very term to unmask the government's assertion to actually be a socialist-communist state. Right to the end of the regime in 1989 there existed only very few safety-valves to this 'pressure cooker' as felt by the mass of the population, in spite of a slight relaxation (see also Ch.3) of the tight travel regulations in the direction of Western countries. It could no longer be prevented, even by threats of severe penalties, that the 'promised lands' of the West appeared night after night on the television screens of the GDR. The German revolution of 1989 was thus partly a revolution brought about by modern mass-communications successfully penetrating a closed society from the outside.

Secondly, within the preceding ten years or so the average citizen in the GDR had become less afraid of meeting with what he or she made out to be congenial minds, in all sorts of groups standing for goals which, to all outward appearances, seemed to be in line with officially proclaimed government policies, but were definitely contrary to the policies actually pursued. In this way many so-called 'citizen movements' or 'civil-rights movements' as they were and have since been named, grew up—a new democratic feature in German history. Estimates show that anything up to 150 of such citizen-initiatives developed in East Germany on a local level, prior to 1989. They stood quite openly for at least three visions or goals: peace, justice—with particular reference to the enforcement of human rights (purely on paper in the GDR constitution, cf. Ch.10)—and the preservation of the environment or, in the terminology of the most important movements, i.e. those on a religious basis, of 'God's creation' *(Bewahrung der Schöpfung)*. Calls for peace had to be condoned by the regime since the GDR officially belonged to the 'World Communist Peace Camp'. The Olaf Palme March for peace (named after the late Prime Minister of Norway) organised in 1988 between the two concentration camps Ravensbrück and Oranienburg, was in the beginning started by the Communist Youth Movement (FDJ) but then very quickly 'taken over' by protestant church groups. Such events caused confusion and consternation in the minds of local officials and served thereby to encourage and cristalize opposition groups. Points of ever more serious contention between the dissidents and the regime were the increasing demands by the former in the human rights field. They too were less liable to open persecution in comparison to earlier years after the initiation of the so-called

'Helsinki-process' (CSCE, Conference on Security and Cooperation in Europe, since 1976, cf. Ch.5 and 11). Finally, calls for an efficient environmental policy—the appalling absence of which constitutes one of the most devastating legacies of the regime right up to the present, although officially also a goal of the GDR constitution—(see below) could not be seriously penalized either.

Perhaps the most significant aspect of these pre-revolutionary developments was the fact that the majority of the dissidents gathered under the umbrella of the Protestant Churches in East Germany, which ever after the joint church-state-pronouncement in 1978 of the concept: 'a church within the socialist system' *('Kirche im Sozialismus'*—not against or for socialism, but within a socialist state) were no longer subject to direct harassment. In the previous two decades the churches had protested against indoctrination by State and Party of the children in schools, especially with regard to semi-military exercises there, against rearmament policies in the West and East (the latter clearly against the actual policy of the whole Warsaw Pact in spite of claims to the contrary) or in favour of better policies for the disabled who were indeed less well cared for in East than in West Germany. In those first decades of the GDR's existence, children of the clergy were subjected to severe discrimination in their educational careers. After the severance of all organisational ties of the Eastern protestant churches with those in West Germany in 1969, but really only after the 1978 memorandum of understanding between Honecker and the leading protestant bishop in the East, Schönherr, concerning this formula of a 'church within the socialist system,' Vicars and their families were more and more allowed a sort of 'fool's liberty'.

The Protestant, and to a lesser degree the much smaller Catholic, Church in East Germany felt at the same time that some compromises had to be made with the atheistic state in order to survive as an institution. Some clergy certainly came therefore very close to an unwarranted attitude of 'appeasement'. They were, however, very definitely in the minority. One of the most stirring acts of protest against any such appeasement on an individual basis was that of Pfarrer Brüsewitz, who in 1976, near Magdeburg, burnt himself publicly (Doc.1d).

Apart from this terrible event, the most outstanding activities on the part of the Protestant Churches laying the ground for a critical state of mind in the East German population *vis-à-vis* the regime, were the more or less regular 'prayers for peace' (Friedensgebete)[4] offered primarily in the Nikolai-Kirche in Leipzig almost every every Monday from 1982 onwards and later in churches in East Berlin.[5] Starting in 1982 the calls for the above mentioned aims: peace, justice and preservation of the environment, were echoed throughout the country especially by different church organised regional *Kirchen-tage* (mass gatherings). Pastor Schorlemmer, for instance, the 1993 winner of the annual peace award presented by the German Publishing Houses, publicly demanded as early as 1982—following a less spectacular lead from church people in Saxony—'the transformation of swords into plough shares' coupled with general demands for a reform of society (Doc.2a-c). Hence the peaceful German revolution of 1989 can with some justification be termed a 'protestant revolution', as some authors have already pointed out.

Third, and most important in triggering the revolution, was obviously the Gorbachev factor, that is the demise of the Stalinist/Breshnev regime in the Soviet Union ongoing since 1985. This had a double effect: for the first time ever pressure from Moscow was applied in favour of 'democratic' reforms, and not in the opposite direction of once more putting down, by force of arms, attempts of a hitherto satellite country within its bloc to shake off a Communist government and system—attempts for decades abused and fought against under the label of combatting 'counter-revolutionaries'. From this followed an increasing domestic pressure in the GDR on the government under Honecker, for East Germany to comply with Gorbachev's famous dictum: 'he who comes too late will be punished by life itself'.

Fourth, one must put on the list of causes the earlier revolutionary and indeed anti-Soviet 'virus' in Poland which had actually started in 1981/82. These tendencies were reinforced in the summer of 1989 by a 'Hungarian virus' which led to a mass-exodus of East Germans, especially the young, to West Germany as a result of the decision of the then, still communist government in Budapest, to let those Germans go who had sought refuge not only in the West German Embassy, but also in the country as a whole, in spite of protests by the 'semi-big brother' in East Berlin.

Fifth, however, until 1989 almost all demands from within the GDR could be interpreted as being inspired by a wish for a reform of the system, i.e., for a better socialism in reality and not for a revolution proper. That is why some observers have spoken of a 'refolution' (reformatory revolution). Calls for fundamental political changes of the whole structure of the state and government appeared on the agenda only very gradually and were really only discernible towards the end of 1989. Hence the pre-history of the revolution can be said to have been inspired by perhaps an 'apolitical' mood which only very slowly turned into a political one. The first, and perhaps most significant change in tone and form came when opposition circles tried to structure themselves into a real pressure group under the alleged freedom of association of the GDR Constitution itself, at the time a still dangerous act, and founded the so-called *Neue Forum* on 11 September 1989, supported by people like Bärbel Bohley who became one of the most well-known *Bürgerrechtler* (Civil Rights Activists) of the late GDR. (Doc.3) After the *Wende* 1989/90 the *Neue Forum* did not stand for the first free GDR elections (or the later first all-German one) as such, which in hindsight was soon considered by some to have been a fundamental mistake. Most of their founding-mothers and fathers amalgamated with the other two conspicuous groupings: *Demokratie Jetzt* and *Initiative Frieden und Menschenrechte* (founded in 1985) on 21 September 1991 into the new Federal Political Party: Bündnis 90—Die Grünen (see also Ch.8), who also declared: 'Bündnis 90 is *not* a political party but an open citizen's movement and at the same time an electable politcal association.' The bold step of actually risking the formal founding of a political party as such, was first taken by the Social Democrats. (Doc.4)

Sixth, attention must be drawn to the fact—liable, however, to be exaggerated beyond dimension today—that the East German communist regime was, especially as the 1980s went on, more and more burdened by tremendous public debts. It seems on evidence now available that the leading economic insiders in the GDR itself assumed in October 1989 that the external debt would rise by the end of that year to some 50 billion DM.[6]

Seventh and finally, all of a sudden a mass movement was sparked off which took to the streets in the crucial days of early October. These were crucial days because one can already show on available evidence, that it was 'touch and go' whether the GDR would imitate the Peking massacre of mid-summer 1989, that is launch a quasi-military attack on hundreds of thousands of people demonstrating in Leipzig, Berlin and finally in most cities and even villages of East Germany, intoning first the call 'we are the people', which slowly turned to the call 'we are one people'. The regime collapsed without resistance. The wall was first opened up on November 9th and then demolished, the headquarters of the Stasi peacefully stormed. A revolution had finally been brought about by the people themselves.

A variety of individuals and groups from different strata of society tried, at the last minute, to stem the tide: not surprisingly the Bloc Partners of the SED as mentioned in chapter 3, were still demanding at the end of November and the beginning of December *uni sono* in official pronouncements and new platforms—destined obviously to keep themselves alive politically—a reform of the old 'socialist' system, in other words, not a revolution in the strict sense. Above all, very few hints were contained in the new Programmes that these

Parties were now also aiming at reuniting the German people. (Doc.5a-d). More remarkable was the declared goal of many Citizens' Rights Movements, which even now clings to Socialism as such, and convert it into a 'democratic socialist system,' and at the same time implying that two (democratic) Germanies should continue to exist. Most remarkable of all was the attempt to collect signatures *en masse* for a public manifesto on 28 November 1989 'In favour of our Country,' *(Für Unser Land)* because it was originally signed *(Erstunterzeichner)* not only by leading dissidents, such as the above-mentioned Pastor Schorlemmer or Gerd Poppe (an MP today for the Bündnis 90-Die Grünen in the Bundestag), but also by two leading East German writers: Christa Wolf and Stefan Heym—who for many years had been collaborators of the regime, but were themselves in the end looked upon as 'unreliable' and, therefore, were also under Stasi scrutiny—and, as things went on, by Egon Krenz, the old SED hardliner who followed Honecker mid-October 1989 as the shortlived Head of the Party and Government, and who had actually applauded the Chinese for their massacre in Peking earlier in that summer. This last-minute effort also called for reforms and a continuing separate state (Doc.6). Some of the old hardliners also appeared in those weeks in public mass-gatherings to try and turn the tide also vocally—such as Markus Wolff, the long-time Chief of the GDR 'Intelligence Service', who was put on trial 1993.[7]

All such attempts proved to be in vain. The reunification of Germany, forcibly divided for over forty years was now no longer to be stopped or even slowed down. At the turn of the year 1989/90 the vast majority of the East Germans wanted reunification—whether mainly because of its obvious economic advantages or out of a longing for freedom and liberty at last, or both, can never empirically be made out. In any case, this majority was finally convinced that only the FRG could bring about a significant change in their daily lives. This state of mind in East Germany meant that in 1989/90 all official plans in West Germany, in the international community, or in the GDR itself became obsolete almost as soon as they were enunciated. This applies particularly to Chancellor Kohl's so-called Ten Points of December 1989 aiming at a transition to a German Confederation (Doc.7a,b), but also to stages of negotiation in the Two plus Four context (i.e. of the two Germanies and the four allied powers who had won the war (see also Ch.5), and other official and private proposals for a *modus vivendi* between the two Germanies after the demise of totalitarian communism. Above all, it applies to the many proposals and deliberations of the so-called Round Table *(Runder Tisch)* which was established on 7 and 8 December 1989 for the whole GDR and dissolved on 12 March 1990 prior to the first free elections in the GDR. This Round Table, with offspring in many cities under the same name, was in some ways modelled on the lines of the Polish experiment some years before, which in that country too had marked a transitional stage from communism to democracy. It consisted of representatives of the various political parties and groupings, associations etc. and was chaired mostly by leading personalities of the two Churches (Doc.8). It very quickly became apparent that even the government, led since December 1989 by a new GDR Prime Minister, Hans Modrow,[8]—who before the revolution was looked upon as a moderate reformer in the echelons of the SED, and who also attended the Round Table several times and ordered his ministers to report there on their work— could not turn the tide. This last communist government in East Germany had to concede a much earlier date for the first free elections since 1933 to a 'national' Parliament in that part of Germany, i.e. in March 1990. These Volkskammer elections led to a crushing defeat for the SED, which later transformed itself, in the united Germany, into a new entity under the name of PDS (see also Ch.8). There followed the first and last ever, in East Germany, democratically installed Prime Minister, Lothar de Maizière, with his majority of old and new Christian Democrats and other parties in a coalition government (see also Ch.8). To all intents and purposes his was purely a transitory or caretaker government whose job it was, above all, to negotiate the final financial and political agreements with the old FRG and the international community.

These contractual arrangements were carried out in three steps: first, a Monetary, Economic and Social Union was established on 1 July 1990, whereby the assets of the East Germans were converted into DM on the basis of 1:1, an exchange rate opposed from the beginning by financial experts in West Germany as economically detrimental to the future development of a united Germany (see also Ch. 14). Of course, from Chancellor Kohl's point of view this rate of exchange was also meant as an electoral gift for his East German party coalition and their supporters. But with hindsight, one would have to say that this was what the millions of East German 'revolutionaries' themselves had wanted. Such an observation applies even more to the second decisive step, that still separate, two German governments took with the overarching Agreement termed the Treaty of Unity of 1990 (Doc.9): after its ratification by both German parliaments the reunification was proclaimed on 3 October 1990, which has since become a new German national holiday (see also Ch. 10). This in turn led to the third and final step, i.e. the first all German elections in December 1990 (see also Ch.8 and 7, Statistics, Table 16).

The greatest controversy in and between the two Germanies in 1990 had devolved from the constitutional question of whether the process of reunification should be brought about on the basis of the parliamentary vote of adherence by the East German parliament, the Volkskammer, in accordance with the provisions of the Bonn Basic Law Art. 23, or by a plebiscite in the whole of Germany in accordance with Art. 146 of that constitution. (Doc.10) The final decision in favour of the method laid down in Article 23, remains important in the inner-German debate brought about by reunification even today.

Why? Because more and more East Germans have the 'feeling', that they were to all intents and purposes annexed, taken over, colonized—all these terms are now much in vogue in Germany under the new expression: *platt machen*—by the old FRG without having been asked to contribute significantly to this new 'fatherland'. On the other hand many West Germans have posed the question of whether they should not also have been involved as a whole, when such fundamental decisions had to be taken which entail heavy financial sacrifices year by year. Whether the Bundestag's Parliamentary Committee of Enquiry (corresponding more to the institution of a British Royal Commission, than to Parliamentary Committees of Enquiry in the Anglo-Saxon sense) to consider a partial revision of the Basic Law in view of the reunification of Germany, will lead to psychological and institutional improvements remains to be seen, is however, to be doubted. Under much discussion are proposals to increase the plebiscitary elements in a revised constitution. It is certain that only a minority in the now so-called old and new Länder of the re-united Germany want to change fundamental aspects of German constitutional life laid down in the Basic Law of 1949, especially those concerning the principle of a Social Market Economy, which was not ordained in the constitution of 1949 itself and could therefore theoretically be changed any time. (See also Ch.14)

The task of amalgamating the two Germanies after forty years of imposed separation, with their diametrically opposed political, economic, social, legal and ideological subsystems was, is and will continue to be a tremendous one. This is now realized, although it was not foreseen by anyone in East or West Germany during the highly emotional weeks and months of reunification in 1990. The most important goal laid down in the Treaty of Unity between West and East Germany will remain the 'adaptation of living standards' (see also Ch.14), which was, in any case already, a binding constitutional provision of the federal system in the old FRG in accordance with the

Basic Law. This applies particularly to the level of wages for equal work in the new and old Länder. The delays in this process were largely responsible for the first big strike in East Germany after reunification, in the iron and steel industry in 1993.

To list the most important problems of domestic politics in the new Germany: first and foremost, how to manage the transition—in theory and practice never before on the agenda of any government policy, now on the agenda of all formerly Moscow-controlled states including the former Soviet Union itself—from a planned, to a market economy with the inevitable result of temporarily increasing the rate of unemployment (see also Ch.14 and Statistics 8). The latter problem is, of course, the decisive one, especially when one thinks of the last years of the Weimar Republic. With figures of unemployment still mounting, especially in East Germany as this volume goes to print, people get into a mood of an increasing 'GDR-nostalgia'. They forget that while on paper there had indeed been hardly any unemployment in the old GDR, this was achieved at the cost of what later appeared as a vast system of disguised unemployment, with men and women often meaninglessly at work in an economy characterised above all by very low productivity.

Second, there is the problem of transforming the legal system away from the principle of a 'socialist party justice' to a western democratic rule of law, third, the problem of property forcibly taken away by the East German government from owners who fled to the West after 1945/49 or acquired in good faith by new East German owners. The underlying principle for a solution here is still contested: should the aim in the first place be restitution or compensation by payment? Here also the former Soviet Union came into the picture, since under their pressure in the negotiations of the contractual 'Two plus Four' agreements of 1990 the changes in property conditions carried out under military occupation between 1945-49 were exempted from any claims to restitution (see also Chs.14 and 5). Fourth, a totally new concept of social policies all round had and has to be enacted for the new Länder, with an emphasis on more individual efforts and fewer state interventions in the whole field. Here, as in the field of unemployment one must take into account the fact that in the former GDR some 91 per cent of all women were professionally employed as well as raising their families while this percentage in the old FRG amounted only to 42 per cent. Fifth, there are two of the worst legacies of forty years of socialist communism in East Germany linked together, i.e. the utterly desolate conditions of private housing (but also of historical treasures on the list of UNESCO) and, even worse, the total neglect of the environment on the part of the former GDR governments in a desolate political practise in violation of their own constitution. (Doc.11). Sixth, there is the problem of what might be called 'decommunisation' analogous to the 'denazification' which had confronted the Germans in the aftermath of the National Socialism dictatorship: how does one deal with the former senior communist functionaries, whether successfully brought to trial under German and international law (Human Rights Conventions) or not—or with the 100,000 or so officials in the former Stasi (see above) irrespective of informal agents. The latter are themselves also a problem in West Germany, where spies of the East are beginning to be brought to trial after relevant records are becoming available. Obviously, bringing former SED officials to trial on the charge of having ordered or condoned election fraud on a large scale does not make much juridical sense since this practice was implied in the system itself. Also the 2.3 million members of the former communist SED party should not as such be ostracised. However, the question arises of how to treat those who were engaged in such important professions as school or university teaching, the courts, or the media. Should teachers continue to be employed who taught—whether out of conviction or by *force majeure*—Marxism Leninism and if so in what curricular field? Obviously not all such school teachers can possibly be replaced. Under quantitative aspects the situation was somewhat easier to handle with regard to Universities. Here three criteria for continued employment where enacted in the new Länder: one, former Stasi affiliates were excluded; two, all were given the chance to show or even improve their academic standards especially with regard to publishing, which was very difficult to accomplish in the former GDR. Three, a pro forma membership in the SED state-party was in general considered irrelevant, even more so membership of the communist youth movement (FDJ) which probably some 95 per cent of all young people had to join. (See also Chap. 10)

Finally in this connection: how should society and governments at all levels cope with the phenomenon—which was also in evidence in the aftermath of National Socialist times—of 'networking' *(Seilschaften)*. Too many former SED hard-liners particularly in management positions survived successfully in their former positions of influence, now serving new masters (of capitalism), and helping each other out while many other 'ordinary' citizens had to go on the dole for lack of work.

This, by no means complete, list of problems leads to the final syndrome of problems already mentioned, i.e. to the question of the national state of mind in the new Germany sixty years after the demise of the first ever truly democratic government in German history, the Republic of Weimar. Forty years of life in different systems has led to an accumulation of mutual ignorance and even mutual prejudices. In addition to this many people in East Germany have developed, after reunification, almost a sense of collective inferiority while in the West Germany the opposite, a collective superior complex, is increasing. In the East this leads here and there to a new feeling of nostalgia with regard to the former GDR, or at least however, to the feeling that life in the former communist country did have some positive aspects which should be preserved and incorporated into the new Germany. Here, the intra-German debates in the end sometimes boil down to banalities. One such example: finally after three years, the traffic regulations which existed in East Germany, to take a right turn when straight-ahead lights are red—indicated by the so-called 'green arrow' at major road junctions—has now also been adopted in West Germany.

In both parts of Germany mutual 'complexes' are combined with a mounting sense of frustration: in the East because the process of adaptation of living standards takes such a long time, certainly much longer than was believed five years ago; in the West, because roughly a 100 billion DM which is transferred annually to the East do not yet seem to have led to significant economic growth. Certainly even more sacrifices by each individual in her or his personal income, etc. will be required in the years ahead (see Ch.14). In short, the old infamous 'wall' which had divided Germany and was eliminated in 1989/90 has here and there re-appeared in the minds of the people.

The conclusion: neither the West Germans nor the East Germans have as yet developed, in the new emerging European Union, a common national identity. The absence of such an identity must be looked upon as one of the main causes for outbursts of violence in the young generation, especially towards some of the 6.1 million foreigners living in the country. Experts agree that, in addition, the main reason for such outbursts lies in the general psychological upheaval confronting the young generation in particular after the most drastic changes brought about in all realms of life in the last decade. Of particular significance is the fact that in the former GDR many of the youth-clubs formerly run in almost every town and village by the Party, the industrial plants or other official bodies have had to shut down for lack of 'funds' (formerly cheap government money) so that the younger generation has, for the first time in their lives, to learn how to organise their leisure-time themselves. Experts equally agree that outbursts of violence have to be explained in psychological terms connected with family live, unemployment, drugs, etc. and are only marginally the result of a new radicalism of the political right or even of neo-nazis, whose leaders are few and far between and whose followers are, up to now, also relatively small in numbers as compared with other European countries. That such leaders *en miniature* will continue to try to bring about a band-waggon effect, cannot be ruled out.[9]

Document 1a

STALINISM IN THE SCHOOLS

Source: Gerhard Rein, Die protestantische Revolution, 1987-1990, Berlin, 1990 125 ff

... On 11 September 1988 four pupils from the Carl-von Ossietzky-High School in Berlin-Pankow took part in the annual rally in memory of the victims of fascism. The four pupils had brought two banners of their own with them. One bore the slogan 'Down with Fascist Tendencies', the other the slogan 'Neo-Nazis Get Out'. They were able to display their banners for about 30 seconds only, when security men came, took the banners away and made a note of the pupils' names and addresses ...

A few days later a pupil who had not been present at the rally pinned a short text written by himself to the school notice-board. In it he expressed doubts as to the point of holding military parades. He suggested that the international reputation of the German Democratic Republic and the whole peace process would benefit if the forthcoming military parade to mark the founding of the German Democratic Republic on 7th October were abandoned. The pupil handed his article round and obtained the signatures of 37 fellow pupils ...

Thereupon the headmaster, the class teachers, the Party Secretary and the officials of the Free German Youth movement began questioning the pupils. Parents were summoned, and 30 of the 37 children revoked their signatures ... The next day an extraordinary roll-call took place in the school hall. The pupils Philipp, Kai, Katja and Benjamin were called forth individually. They were told that expulsion proceedings were being instigated against them; in the meantime they were being suspended from school and had to leave the premises at once. Two other pupils were transferred to other schools; another, who had been given a reprimand, said that he felt ashamed of his school. Numerous fellow pupils wept ...

... After their eventual expulsion the pupils concerned made the following statement in which they defended themselves against the slanderous accusations levelled against them. 'We wish to live and learn in the German Democratic Republic. We wish to contribute in a creative way to the shaping of a socialist society. We wish to express our opinions openly and discuss them publicly'.

In the Carl-von-Ossietzky High School this was not possible.

Document 1b

'OUR OWN CANDIDATES'
Excerpts from a circular to Christians in the GDR and their parish representatives issued in East Berlin on 8 January 1989, e.g. by Wolfgang Ullmann and Peter Hilsberg, today MPs in the German Bundestag and its European Parliament.
Source: Ibid., 139ff.

Our suggestion that peace and environmental groups in the parishes should put forward candidates from their own membership for the local elections on 7th May 1989, is aimed at using the full framework of the law in order to help overcome internal barriers, set up by the state power structure, which prevent the people from assuming responsibility ...
  (We call for independent representatives on locally elected bodies to ...)

  – expose and prosecute cases of corruption, nepotism and the arbitrary use of power by the authorities;
  – instigate a frank and public debate on the direction and objectives of our society ...

Document 1c

A PULPIT DECLARATION BY ERFURT CLERGYMEN, 27TH MAY, 1989
Source: Ibid., 139ff.

On 11 May Erfurt clergymen wrote the following letter to the National Council of the National Front of the German Democratic Republic, in which they lodged an appeal against the official results of the local elections held on 7 May:
  'We men and women, pastors of the Protestant Church in Erfurt, protest against the officially published results of the local elections held on 7 May, according to which there were 413 valid 'no' votes in the city of Erfurt. We do this because as
  Christians we share in the responsibility for upholding the truth and maintaining confidence in the society of our country.
  Committed Christians took part in the public counting of votes in 36 polling stations in Erfurt on Sunday evening. According to the results which were announced there in public, there were 638 valid 'no' votes in the elections to the city council and 649 valid 'no' votes in the elections to the district councils. We enclose a list which we can substantiate should the need arise.
  When we take into account the total number of polling stations, it is clear that the number of 'no' votes cast in the city of Erfurt was several times higher than the figures announced for the 36 polling stations supervised.

We are addressing this protest with the same wording to the National Council of the National Front of the German Democratic Republic and to the local committee of the National Front in Erfurt. We call for an immediate investigation into the results of the elections in the city of Erfurt and, if appropriate, the holding of new elections according to § 43 of the electoral law'.

Document 1d

BRAVE PUBLIC PROTEST BY CLERGY 1975

Source: Rheinischer Merkur, Bonn, 16 August 1991

The Protestant Pastor of a little town in Thuringia, Oskar Brüsewitz, had for some years been the object of extensive Stasi observations because amongst other things he had put up on the tower of his parish church electric devices forming a cross and had time and again switched these on at night. Finally on 18th August he burnt himself on the market place carrying with him a big board with the inscription. 'Do not pervert our young people'—a protest often given expression to by him before against what he considered an evil indoctrination of the youth by the Communists.

Richard Schröder, then Pastor of a neighbouring parish, today Professor of Theology and a leading figure in the Social Democratic Party, called public attention to this deed—as desperate as it was courageous—in a sermon shortly after the event which at the time was already considered amazingly outspoken and which must be judged even more so on hindsight: In the excerpts to follow from this sermon Schröder started out by drawing attention to the brave and unfaltering witness of the Prophet Micha who stood up to King Ahab of ancient Israel. He alone had spoken up and drawn attention to the truth while all others—the story of the bible mentions 'some 400'—self-ordained experts counselled unisono in the direction of what they knew the King had wanted to hear. Schröder went on:

'... Micha does not say something just because that might have furthered his career. He displayed so much courage and independence because he knew that he was dependent on God only ... My dear parishioners: what has God in our days to do with our political stance? ... A true Christian can and will not be part of 400 people who will only say 'yes' (to those in power),. Since he participates in God's concern for all mankind he is under an obligation to look at problems very closely. When he does that, he will come up everywhere, in the East as well as in the West, against truths which are not very pleasing to eyes and ears ... he is then obliged to call attention to such truths ...

In these days a Pastor burnt himself in public nearby. This deed has taken both the Church and the State by surprise and caused them great embarrassment ... How should we ourselves judge this deed? Pfarrer Brüsewitz put up posters before burning himself meant to explain why he did what he did. When the Police appeared on the scene, the first thing they did was to con-

fiscate those posters even while Pfarrer Brüsewitz was burning. That seemed
to them the most important thing to do of all ... Since no knowledge was
spread anywhere about the contents of those posters I would like to quote
from Pastor Brüsewitz's letter of farewell to his parishioners ... *It grieves me,*
he says here, *that I cannot spare you ... what I did. It took me a long time to
come to the decision to act in this way ... my own past is certainly not worthy of
any glorification. The more so it fills me with joy that I have been called ... to
witness ... (to-day) a mighty war rages between the Light and the Dark,
(between) Truth and Lie ...'*

The heads of the Church in our Province declared in a circular letter to all
parishes that 'they could not condone this deed of our brother in Christ'.

The *Neues Deutschland*, [the official newspaper of the DDR regime, ed.]
published this circular letter, but omitted in doing so three very important
sentences; one of them having been: 'Even with this action of his Oskar
Brüsewitz wanted to point to God as being the Lord of all mankind. He was
driven on by the anxiety that our Church was not unequivocal enough in
bearing witness in our time ... On 31 August, the Neues Deutschland went
even further by publishing a long commentary on the event which is a dis-
grace in itself for this newspaper since here the deceased Pastor Brüsewitz is
being slandered by way of half-truths and outright defamation. No doubt,
we must realize what the intentions of our organs of state were when they
asked: How is it possible that in our country where everyone enjoys social
security a man can do such a thing? But we as Christians cannot condone
that Pastor Brüsewitz is now depicted as a pitiful lunatic ... For we know that
while everyone in our country probably has enough to eat, many people cannot find rest at night. We know that fear overpowers us at the thought that
we might say a wrong word in front of a wrong listener. We know that our
young people have been taught too early only to say what is expected of
them ... We know that for us too often the air to breathe in freely becomes
exhausted amidst the protection and security around us. We know that those
400 who say 'yes' only stand in higher reputation than the Prophet Micha ...
We should not say indeed: What Oskar Brüsewitz did is the way to do it. We
should also not say: that is how we must do them in. But we must ask ourselves: 'Who are we? One of those 400 or Micha? Who do we want to be
after all? Let us, therefore, ask God to grant us the courage to bear witness
to the truth out of our care for all mankind.'

Three documents from the opposition before the revolution:

Document 2a

A CALL FOR NON-ALIGNMENT IN EUROPE, EAST BERLIN, APRIL 1985
Excerpts from a published memorandum
Source: Archiv W. Ullmann, Berlin

Forty years ago the German people were freed from fascism by soldiers from America together with the other armies of the anti-Hitler alliance. We, Germans from the German Democratic Republic, remember this self-sacrificing deed today ...

(We call for negotiations to be held between East and West with the following aims:)

1. The foreign troops based in the two German states should be withdrawn to their countries of origin together with their conventional and nuclear arsenals. This withdrawal, which could also commence unilaterally, will take place in several stages. It will be paralleled by a reduction in the offensive weaponry of the two German states ...

4. All European States are to enter bilateral and multilateral negotiations with the aim of developing a pan-European treaty organization which will lay down conditions for a lasting peace and regulate economic relations, cultural cooperation and the restoration of the ecological equilibrium. In military terms this will mean the dissolution of the power-blocs and a recourse to strategies for territorial defence ...

The liberty and dignity of citizens are the key to the liberty and self-determination of peoples. That is why new initiatives towards a peace settlement in Europe are only possible given the participation of the democratic movements for peace, ecology and emancipation in East and West. The independent actions of these movements, transcending the power blocs, will lead to the attainment of full political rights for all citizens.

[40 signatories, including Bärbel Bohley, Rainer Eppelmann (now an MP, CDU), Katja Havemann, Gerd Poppe (now an MP), Wolfgang Templin and Wolfgang Ullmann (now MP-MEP]

Document 2b

TWENTY THESES FROM WITTEMBERG ON RENEWAL AND REFORM IN THE GDR, 24 JUNE, 1988 ON THE INITIATIVE OF PFARRER FRIEDRICH SCHORLEMMER
excerpts
Source: Gerhard Rein, *Die protestantische Revolution, 1987-1990,* Berlin 1990, 93ff

'The time for silence is past and the time for speaking is come', Martin Luther, 1520 ...

1. Because we—as Christians in the freedom of and commitment to our faith—feel a joint responsibility and hence a share in the blame for what becomes of our country, we consider it imperative and incumbent upon us to overcome our fear, our mistrust and our lack of expectation, to recognize and seize opportunities for making a fresh start and to attain a candour of spirit from which we may press, in critical solidarity, for the renewal of our society ...

6. Because the electoral system has so far prevented competition, we consider it necessary to provide a clear possibility of deciding between different candidates in all elections ...

9. Because the penal code and the prison system fail in many ways to live up to humanist concepts and the ideals of a new society, we consider it necessary to overhaul them as far as language, content and practice are concerned.

10. Because a world which is humane, just and capable of survival can only be created by a culture of lively debate in the search for truth and for the best way of living and working together, we consider it necessary for communists to give up their power-backed monopoly on truth and their basic claim the superiority of its social system ...

Document 2c

FROM AN ARTICLE BY BÄRBEL BOHLEY, ONE OF THE LEADING 'BÜRGERRECHTLER' IN THE FORMER GDR, NOVEMBER 1988

Source: Ibid., 120ff.

Even the authorities have been forced to recognize that threats made against a small group have not stopped people from filling the churches, and that the clamour for change in the country can no longer be suppressed. Branding individuals as 'enemies of the state' has become pointless now that there is no one left who believes that it is we who are responsible for the current situation in the German Democratic Republic.

Our opposition continues, not least in the minds of the disillusioned, who insist on the freedom to choose where they are going to live, and who want to leave for the West. Those who have not yet given this country up for good and still consider it capable of reform are also beginning to hope again, and even in the heads of those who, as party members, have until now been part of the apparatus of power, something is stirring ...

And so the authorities are having to make sacrifices ... but all such sacrifices, whether big or small, will not suffice to make the GDR gleam in its 'old colours' again. This can only be achieved by a process of democratization and the unequivocal rule of law in and for the whole of society. There are, of course, many officials in the machinery of state and party who realize this too, but resistance is great in these circles, and without hard talking no radical change will come about ...

Document 3

THE FOUNDING OF THE 'NEW FORUM'
Excerpts from first public pronouncement
Source: Archiv Heiko Lietz, Neues Forum Güstrow, Mecklenburg-Vorpommern

In our country communications between state and society have evidently broken down. Evidence of this ranges from widespread indifference to a withdrawal into the private domain or to mass emigration. Elsewhere an exodus on such a scale would be caused by poverty, famine or violence. This is not the case here... .

... We want to lead ordered lives, but we don't want to be ordered about. We want people who feel free and self-confident, but who are still mindful of the welfare of the community. We want to be protected from violence but we want to be rid of a state full of lackeys and informers ...

In order to recognize these contradictions, listen to and weigh up opinions and arguments, and distinguish general from specific interests, we need a democratic debate about the role of the constitutional state, and of our economic and cultural life. We must think and talk about these questions together, in public and throughout the land. Whether we find a way out of the current crisis in the foreseeable future, depends on our readiness and desire to do this. What matters under the present circumstances in our society is

- that a greater number of people participate in the process of social reform,
- that the multifarious individual and group activities are integrated into a concerted effort.

For this purpose we have come together to form a political platform for the WHOLE OF THE GDR. This will enable people of all vocations, social backgrounds, parties and groupings to come together to discuss and address this country's essential social problems. We have chosen to call this comprehensive movement the 'New Forum'.

The activities of the NEW FORUM are to be put on a proper legal footing, in accordance with the basic right of association, as laid down in article 29 of the constitution of the GDR, for the purpose of pursuing political interests through concerted action. We intend to register the association with the responsible bodies in accordance with the By-law of 6th November, 1975 concerning the 'Formation and Activities of Associations'.

Underlying all endeavours to which the New Forum wishes to lend its voice, is the desire for justice, democracy, peace, environmental protection and nature conservancy. These are the impulses which motivate us, and which we hope to imbue with life as we go about transforming all areas of society.

We call upon all citizens of the GDR, men and women, who wish to take part in the transformation of our society to become members of the New Forum. The time is ripe.
signed:

Die Erstunterzeichner: Michael Arnold, Student, Leipzig; Bärbel Bohley, Malerin, Berlin; Katrin Bohley, Studentin, Berlin; Dr. Martin Böttger, Physiker, Cainsdorf; Dr. Erika Drees, Ärztin, Stendal; Katrin Eigenfeld, Bibliothekarin, Halle; Dr. Frank Eigenfeld, Geologe, Halle; Hagen Erkrath, Student, Berlin; Olaf Freund, Fotolaborant, Dresden; Katja Havemann, Heimerzieherin, Grünheide; Alfred Hempel, Pfarrer, Großschönau; Rolf Henrich, Jurist, Eisenhüttenstadt; Jan Hermann, Krankenpfleger, Brandenburg; Martin Klähn, Bauingenieur, Schwerin,; Katrin Menge, Hochbauingenieurin, Berlin; Dr. Reinhard Meinel, Physiker, Potsdam; Otto Nickel, Drechsler, Dresden; Dr. Christine Pflugbeil, Ärztin, Berlin; Prof. Dr. Jens Reich, Arzt und Molekularbiologe, Berlin; Hanno Schmidt, Pfarrer, Coswig; Reinhard Schult, Betonfacharbeiter, Berlin; Jutta Seidel, Zahnärztin, Berlin; Dr. Eberhard Seidel, Arzt, Berlin; Lutz Stropahl, Musikerzieher, Berlin; Dr. Rudolf Tschärpe, Physiker, Potsdam; Hans Jochen Tschiche, Pfarrer, Samswegen; Catrin Ulbricht, Dresden

Document 4

A CALL FOR THE SETTING-UP OF AN INITIATIVE FOR THE PURPOSE OF ESTABLISHING A SOCIAL DEMOCRATIC PARTY IN THE GDR, 24 JULY, 1989
Excerpts
Source: Markus Meckel/Martin Gutzeit, *Opposition in der DDR,* Köln 1994

1. Eastern Europe is in a state of flux, and many of our people feel a strong sense of sympathy. Hopes and expectations are also beginning to grow in the GDR. Many citizens are now showing greater self-confidence. Yet it must be said that all in all the situation is still dominated by an overriding sense of impotence: people wish and hope for change, yet believe that there is nothing they can do themselves.

   Many people are consequently waiting for the ruling party to reform itself or for a man like Gorbachov to arrive on the scene. Such an attitude is passive and in the final analysis denies responsibility for the reality of the world we live in. Yet precisely when the Party (i.e. Communist) is undergoing change, there is a need for citizens who freely recognize their responsibility for the present state of affairs and are prepared to do something about it ...

2. Our society is determined by the SED's absolute claim to truth and power; all relations in state and society are ordered in accordance with this. However, the discrepancy between ideological claims and reality is becoming more and more evident. The necessary democratization of our land depends on the mounting of a fundamental challenge to these absolute claims. This includes coming to terms intellectually and openly with Stalinism, its basic assumptions and the mark it has left on past and present in the GDR.

3. The democratization of our society requires a planned, back-to-basics effort; it also requires citizens who either have or can gain the necessary competence for such an effort. This constitutes a particularly difficult problem as it was the policy of the SED over decades to obstruct intellectual and political competence outside the circle of those who were willing to swear allegiance to the Party. Faced with this situation, we consider the following step to be necessary:

a) Establishing a political alternative for our country based on political traditions of democracy and social justice. One such important tradition is socialism, but this has been largely discredited by the history of the past decades. The current situation in the socialist camp makes it simply impossible to state which economic and political structures can conform to the socialist vision ...

5. We, the undersigned, regard the formation of a social democratic party as essential for the future of our society. We know that this is at present not a legal possibility. That is why we propose to set up an initiative group, the aim of which is to work to bring about the conditions necessary for the legal establishment of such a party and to prepare for its formation ...

Programme headings

A. Concerning the organisation of state and society
  – A state founded on the rule of law with strict separation of powers.
  – Parliamentary democracy with the full range of political parties.
  – A welfare state having regard for the environment.
  – Relative autonomy for the regions (federal states), counties, urban districts and boroughs in financial, economic and cultural matters.
  – A social market economy with a strict ban on monopolies to prevent an undemocratic concentration of economic power.
  – The democratic structuring of economic life, including co-determination in the work-place.
  – The encouragement of the public sector and co-operatives (with voluntary affiliation and equal rights for private enterprise).
  – Trade union freedom and the right to strike.
  – Strict freedom of religion and matters of conscience.
  – Equality of status and opportunity for women.
  – Freedom of association and the right of assembly for all democratic organizations.
  – Freedom of the press and access to the electronic media for all democratic organizations.
  – Guarantee of asylum for political refugees.
B. Concerning foreign policy
  – Recognition of the existence of two German states as a consequence of a guilty past. This does not exclude the possibility of changes within the framework of a European peace settlement.
  – Special relations with the Federal Republic of Germany in view of our common nationhood, history and the resulting responsibilities.
  – Demilitarization of the society and territory of the GDR.

- Achievement of a European peace settlement, thus rendering Nato and the Warsaw Pact superfluous.
- Expansion of trade with the least developed countries on a fair basis and geared towards their needs.
- Solidarity with peoples and national minorities undergoing oppression and deprived of their rights.

Signed by Martin Gutzeit and Markus Meckel (the last Foreign Secretary of the first free GDR government, now an MP in the Bundestag)

Documents 5a

THE LDPD'S POSITION IN THE PROCESS OF THE DEMOCRATIC RENEWAL OF SOCIALISM IN THE GDR
(Guidelines adopted by the party leadership, 24th November 1989. Excerpts)

Source: Dokumentation zur Entwicklung der Blockparteien der DDR von Ende Sept. bis Ende Dezember 1989, Gesamtdeutsches Institut, Bonn, 1989, 46ff.

Let us face up to the truth: our fatherland, the German Democratic Republic, is in danger. It is not external enemies, however much they may want to harm us, that threaten the existence of the republic; internal tensions and contradictions, bottled up and suppressed for years, are flaring up and producing social and political conflicts. The GDR is in a deep state of crisis. Our economy paints a picture of desolation. What we referred to as democracy and the rule of law has proved to be totally inadequate. Culture, education and science have long stagnated. Young people see no future for themselves and their country. Hypocrisy, conformity and political opportunism have wreaked great moral harm. Our citizens no longer have confidence in their political leaders ...

The LDPD must take its share of the blame for the situation in which the GDR finds itself. It ought to have openly criticised and rejected the policies of the SED much sooner and much more emphatically. But we believe that, having undertaken a rigorous examination of our own past political and moral stances and having reflected self-critically on a political party's responsibility towards the people, we, the LDPD, may legitimately make our voice heard anew and intervene in social processes more stridently, more critically and more demandingly ...

What we already took to be socialism is but the shell of the edifice, the supporting walls of a new social order ...

...What results from this, for us, is a policy that can be described as follows: the existence and consolidation of the GDR as a socialist German state are of fundamental importance for the power alignments in Europe, and therefore for peace and security, as these depend on such power alignments ...

The task of Germans today consists in understanding the development of neighbourly, co-operative relations between the GDR and the FRG as an on-going process and in devising policies which will serve the people ... .

The position taken by the LDPD involves commitment to a form of socialism which

1. guarantees the political rights and liberties, and fulfils the social rights and liberties of every citizen.
2. is based on achievement and competence.
3. embraces pluralism and democracy and is unable to exist without these ... .

Document 5b

STATEMENT OF THE CDU, 28TH OCTOBER 1989
Excerpts
Source: Ibid., 86 f.

As we proceed to a new stage in the development of our society and party, we are guided by tried and tested principles:

1. The CDU is a party of Christians of differing denomination. The criteria of Christian ethics and Christian concepts of humanity are the spiritual roots of its political activities—in particular the commandment to cherish peace and love one's neighbour determines the outlook on life that we choose to promote. Peace, justice and the preservation of all things created are its foremost objectives. It represents the interests of all Christian citizens, while clinging to the fundamental distinction between party and church.
2. The CDU is a party in the GDR. It shares responsibility for formulating and putting into practice the policy of our state. Its aim, in the furtherance of which the party seeks to incorporate all the ideas and initiatives of Christian citizens, is the continued development of the state as a genuine home for all its citizens.
3. The CDU is a party of socialism. Taking as its starting point the heritage of socially progressive Christian movements, and the martyrdom of Christian anti-fascists, the CDU has made its historic decision in favour of socialism. The CDU considers that the socialist order provides a suitable foundation for a decisive and consistent policy of peace and anti-fascism, for ensuring that people feel socially secure and have a clear vision of their lives, for a just distribution of the burdens and fruits of labour and for democratic and humanist standards in public life ...

Document 5c

'WITH A REGENERATED NDPD FOR THE RENEWAL OF
SOCIALISM IN THE GDR' 4/5 November 1989
Excerpts
Source: Ibid., 117 ff.

1. The National Democratic Party of Germany affirms its full support and
   recognizes its own responsibility for the changes that are taking place in
   the development of society in the GDR. The members of our party, who
   are motivated by a deep concern for the GDR, look upon the decision
   which has brought about these changes as an act of liberation. Our friends
   within our party are caught up in the movement for change and are helping to fashion it. The National Democratic Party in Germany will do
   everything to ensure that the process of renewal is understood and implemented as a major and irreversible upheaval for preserving socialism. This
   is the avowed expectation of the majority of our members. It forms the
   basis of our actions. We must learn to overcome the constraints which
   have limited our scope for action in the past.
       Our socialism within a pluralistic party system must be rendered capable
   of meeting the needs of present and future ...
3. The National Democratic Party of Germany is a party of the German
   Democratic Republic. The essence of national and democratic politics
   remains anti-fascism and anti-imperialism, and for our party a commitment to socialism. Our identification with the GDR is based on our belief
   in socialism. If it is to be effective, socialism needs, in theory and in practice, the inseparable link with its main source of strength: the working
   class and its party. We profess this as committed socialists ... .

Document 5d

STATEMENT OF THE DEMOCRATIC PARTY OF FARMERS
AND LAND-WORKERS OF GERMANY (DBD) IN THE
PROCESS OF THE RENEWAL OF SOCIALIST SOCIETY
IN THE GDR, 4 NOVEMBER 1989
Excerpts
Source: Ibid., 156 ff.

All over our republic, in towns and villages, there is a public debate in
progress. As we go about the renewal of our society, the search is on for convincing ways of overcoming the crisis in our country and creating a better
and more attractive socialism, with the people and for the people ...
    The DBD stands by its tried and tested principles and aims. It reaffirms its
steadfast support for the constitution of the GDR. It declares its belief in

– socialism, our worker and farmworker state, and the comprehensive strengthening and protection thereof ...,
– the unswerving friendship with the Soviet Union and the other countries of the socialist community,
– the understanding between nations and solidarity with all peoples struggling for social progress,
– the constructive peace policies of socialism, peaceful coexistence between states with differing social orders, including the GDR and the FRG.

On the basis of these principles and with the aim of enhancing the DBD's standing, we are embracing new demands. The DBD wishes to shoulder greater responsibility in all aspects of the life of society, make its voice heard more loudly and make its own unmistakable contribution towards that end ...

In East Berlin a group of intellectuals and SED reformers, including the writers Stefan Heym and Christa Wolf, the Arch-Deacon Günter Krusche, Pastor Friedrich Schorlemmer, the Mayor of Dresden Wolfgang Berghofer and the film director Konrad Weiß, called on 26 of November 1989 for a socialist alternative in the GDR, with others later jumping on the same band-wagon.

Document 6

ON BEHALF OF OUR COUNTRY

Source: zitiert nach Frankfurter Rundschau, 30 Nov.1989

Our country is in a deep state of crisis. No longer can we live, nor do we want to live, as in the past. The leadership of one party had arrogated to itself total control over the people and their representative bodies; Stalinist structures had penetrated all walks of life. Through peaceful mass demonstrations the people have set in motion an irresistible process of revolutionary renewal, which is proceeding at break-neck speed. We are left with little time to bring our influence to bear on the various options which present themselves as ways out of the crisis.

Either we can insist on a separate identity of the GDR and strive—by combining our efforts and with the co-operation of such states and interest groups as are willing—to develop a supportive society in our land, in which peace and social justice, individual liberty, freedom of movement for everybody and environmental conservation are guaranteed.

Or we must accept that—owing to powerful economic constraints and the intolerable conditions attached to promises of aid for the GDR on the part of influential economic and political circles in the Federal Republic—a sell-out of our material and moral values will begin and that, sooner or later, the German Democratic Republic will be taken over by the Federal Republic. Let us go the first way ... as a socialist alternative to the FRG ...

Let us take the first option. We still have the chance of developing a socialist alternative to the Federal Republic as an equal partner amongst the states of Europe. We have not yet forgotten the anti-fascist, humanist ideals which were once our starting point. We call upon all citizens, men and women, who share our hopes and anxieties to support us by signing this appeal ... .

Document 7a

'TEN POINTS' COMMENTS BY FEDERAL CHANCELLOR DR. HELMUT KOHL IN THE GERMAN PARLIAMENTARY BUDGET DEBATE ON 28 NOVEMBER 1989 CONCERNING POLICY TOWARDS GERMANY.

Excerpts

Source: Presse- und Informationsamt der Bundesregierung, Bonn 1989

... The consistent policy with regard to the coherence of our nation is amongst the causes of the most recent changes. Since 1987, millions of fellow countrymen from the GDR have visited us, amongst them many young people. Our 'small step policy' has, in difficult times, kept awake and sharpened the consciousness for the unity of the nation, and has deepened the Germans' sense of togetherness ... .

We cannot plan the way to unity from our 'armchairs' or with our appointment calendars. Abstract models will help us no farther. We can today, however, already prepare those stages which lead to this goal. I would like to elucidate these using a Ten-Point-Programme.

. . .

Secondly: The Federal Government will, as before, continue its cooperation with the GDR in all areas where it is of direct benefit to people on both sides. This is particularly true of economic scientific and technological co-operation and of co-operation in cultural fields. It is of particular importance to intensify cooperation in the field of environmental protection. Here we will be able to shortly take decisions concerning new projects ...

Thirdly: I have offered to extensively extend our aid and cooperation should fundamental change of the political and economic system in the GDR be firmly agreed upon and put irrevocably into effect. By irrevocable, we mean that the East German leadership comes to an understanding with opposition groups concerning constitutional change and a new electoral law ...

We do not want to stabilize conditions which have become indefensible.

. . .

Fifthly: We are also prepared to take a further decisive step, namely, to develop confederative structures between the two states in Germany with the goal of creating a federation, a federal state order in Germany. A legitimate democratic government within the GDR is unrelinquishable prerequisite.

We can envisage that after free elections the following institutions be formed

– a common governmental committee for permanent consultation and political harmonization,
– common technical committees,
– a common parliamentary gremium ...

Sixthly: The development of inner-German relations remains bedded in the pan-European process and in East-West relations. The future structure of Germany must fit into the future architecture of Europe as a whole. The West has to provide pace-making aid here with its concept for a permanent and just European order of peace.

. . .

Document 7b

DECLARATION OF INTENT

Source: Bulletin, BPA (ed.) Nr. 148 20 December 1984

Helmut Kohl, the Chancellor of the Federal Republic of Germany, and Hans Modrow, the Chairman of the Council of Ministers of the German Democratic Republic, called for the comprehensive development of mutual relations and the establishment of appropriate contractual arrangements during their meeting in Dresden on 19th of December, 1989.

They agreed to conclude ... a joint treaty on co-operation and good neighbourly relations between the Federal Republic of Germany and the German Federal Republic.

Helmut Kohl and Hans Modrow announced that representatives of both governments would enter into negotiations on the text of such a treaty immediately. The projected date for the signing of the accord was to be early 1990 ...

Document 8

THE FINAL DECLARATION OF THE ROUND TABLE BEFORE ITS DISSOLUTION 12 MARCH 1990, i.e. BEFORE THE FIRST DEMOCRATIC ELECTIONS IN EAST GERMANY
Excerpts

Source: Helmut Herles/Ewald Rose, *Vom Runden Tisch zum Parlament*, Bonn 1990, 303ff

The Round Table met to hold its first session on 7 December 1989. Its initiators were responsible representatives of those new political forces and the churches which had set the peaceful revolution in motion. The participants came together out of deep concern for the crisis-ridden country and its independence. They did not want to exercise parliamentary or governmental functions, but address the public with proposals for resolving the crisis. To this end the Round Table demanded to be informed and involved by the Chamber of the People and the government before important decisions were taken on legal, economic and financial policy.

The Round Table regarded itself as an instrument of public accountability ...

(Of the Round Table's recommendations and drafts for parliamentory bills) the most important dealt with:

- legislation for the preparation and holding of elections on 18 March and 6 May 1990,
- the principles for economic reform and a social charter and for a new environmental policy,
- premises for new policies on culture, education, women's and youth issues,
- the transition to the rule of law through a new media law, judicial and administrative reform and the elaboration of principles for a new constitution ...

In their view German unification has to be brought about on the basis of observing the right of the citizens to self-determination, and on equal terms as regards both German states and Berlin. All necessary constitutional requirements were to be fulfilled by both sides acting in unison. At the same time international obligations were to be respected ...

East-Berlin, 12 March 1990

Document 9

TREATY OF UNITY—PREAMBLE

Source: Presse- und Informationsamt der Bundesregierung, 1990
(See also Ch. 5 and Ch. 10, Doc. 6)

Translation: Official

The Federal Republic of Germany and the German Democratic Republic,

Resolved to achieve in free self-determination the unity of Germany in peace and freedom as an equal partner in the community of nations,

Mindful of the desire of the people in both parts of Germany to live together in peace and freedom in a democratic and social federal state governed by the rule of law,

In grateful respect to those who peacefully helped freedom prevail and who have unswervingly adhered to the task of establishing German unity and are achieving it,

Aware of the continuity of German history and bearing in mind the special responsibility arising from our past for a democratic development in Germany committed to respect for human rights and to peace,

Seeking through German unity to contribute to the unification of Europe and to the building of a peaceful European order in which borders no longer divide and which ensures that all European nations can live together in a spirit of mutual trust,

Aware that the inviolability of frontiers and of the territorial integrity and sovereignty of all states in Europe within their frontiers constitutes a fundamental condition for peace,

Have agreed to conclude a Treaty on the Establishment of German Unity, containing the following provisions:

Document 10

ARTICLES 146 AND 23 OF THE BASIC LAW

The Basic Law shall cease to be in force on the day on which a constitution adopted by a free decision of the German people comes into force. Article 23: For the time being, this Basic Law shall apply in the territory of … (here follows a list of the original Laender in the FRG). In other parts of Germany it shall be put in force on their accession.

Document 11

ARTICLE 15 OF THE CONSTITUTION OF THE GDR AS AMENDED ON 27 SEPTEMBER 1974

Source:
1. Land is one of the German Democratic Republic's most treasured natural assets. It must be protected and used rationally. Land used for the purpose of agriculture and forestry may only be put to a different use with the approval of the state bodies responsible.
2. State and society provide for the protection of the environment in the interests of, and for the benefit of, all citizens. It is the responsibility of the relevant bodies to ensure that

   – lakes, rivers, waterways and the air are kept clean,
   – flora and fauna along with the countryside and areas of natural beauty are protected.

These matters are also the concern of the citizens.

Notes

1. According to latest research findings the death toll during the uprising amounted to some 100 people killed and about 1,000 wounded. At least 13,000 were arrested by the Soviet Military and GDR authorities after the event, a considerable number of them later executed.
2. The sources show that the United States did not, as is time and again asserted by former East German Communists, provoke the uprising behind the scene. Allan Dulles, for instance, the then Head of the CIA (brother of John Foster, the foreign

minister) declared at a—naturally secret—meeting of the US National Security Council shortly afterwards ' ... that the USA had nothing whatsoever to do with inciting these riots, and that our reaction thus far had been to confine ourselves, in broadcasts which were not attributable, to expressions of sympathy and admiration, with an admixture of references to the great traditions of 1848... (The year of European including German revolutions against absolutism), cited in C.C. Schweitzer et al, *The changing Western Analysis of the Soviet Threat*, London 1989, from: *Foreign Relations of the USA* (documents), Series 1952–54, Vol. VII, 586ff)

3. Two other famous cases must be mentioned in this connection. One, that of the scientist and philosopher Robert Havemann, who was severely persecuted under the Nazis as communist. He first held an important academic post in West Berlin after the war, then moved to the East after dismissal by the West Berlin authorities in 1950, joined the SED and held important academic posts at the East Berlin University and the East German Academy of Sciences. In 1959 he was awarded the 'Nationalpreis der DDR'. He broke with the line of the regime after Krustchevs revelation of Stalinistic terrors in 1956, provoked the East German authorities more and more and was, therefore, finally expelled from the Communist Party in 1964 and dismissed from all his positions. After that he was only able to publish (or have published) his critical works in the West, which led to complete supervision by the secret police and a *de facto* internment in his own house for years. Thus he became a focus of opposition against the regime under the flag of a 'reformed socialism'. From a similar background and personal development another academic, Rudolf Bahro, broke with the regime and 'went West' in the late 1960s to advocate too, a 'third way' between capitalism and communism.

4. The so-called 'Decades for Peace' *(Friedensdekaden)* were proclaimed first in November 1980 on the initiative of Protest Church Groups and regularly repeated year by year as a concentrated call for peace—'by way of prayers and other means such as showing the symbol: swords into ploughshares.' See e.g. Markus Meckel/Martin Gutzeit, *Opposition in der DDR—10 Jahre kirchliche Friedensarbeit,* Köln 1994.

5. Pastor Eppelmann of the East Berlin Protestant Samariter Church refused to serve in the army and then refused to pledge allegiance to the communist regime as a so-called 'Bausoldat', an alternative to military service. For this he was sentenced to 8 months imprisonment. In 1982 together with Robert Havemann he published (see footnote 3 above) a *Berliner Appell,* heavily critical of the regime. He was ever since on the black list of the secret police. After the *Wende* of 1989 he was for sometime Minister of Defence in the de Maiziere Government and after reunification joined the Bundestag as an MP for the Christian Democrats in 1990.

6. See Timothy Garton Ash, *Im Namen Europas,* 237 and 648

7. After reunification some of the former GDR big shots were put on trial: Erich Honecker in the first place on charges mainly connected with the 'order to shoot on sight'. Before court proceedings could get anywhere he had to be released on account of his health and was then allowed to go into exile in Chile, where he died in May 1994. The long time head of the Secret Police, Mielke, was also soon imprisoned. In order to secure a court sentence the attorney-general first brought up charges connected with Mielke's involvement, as a young Communist before 1933, in the murder of policemen in Berlin. This and other trials showed that the problem could so far not be solved as to how to charge people *ex post* with having violated German (West and pre-1933 law). The only line that could and can be taken with any prospect of success is to base charges on violation even of East German Law in force at the time of the offences committed, as agreed in the Treaty of Unity 1990. In addition, charges were based on the violation of the UN-Pact for

Civic and Political Rights of 1976. Germany's Supreme Court of Appeal *(Bundes-gerichtshof)* finally in July 1994 confirmed a sentence passed by the lower courts which, therefore, now comes into force against leading members of the former GDR 'National Defence Council' (between four and a half and seven and a half years imprisonment) on the grounds of having violated both GDR law in its regulations on 'wilful murder', (obviously not meant to be taken literally under former conditions pertaining to the *Schießbefehl*, see above) *and* the above mentioned International Pact of the United Nations.

8. Records, particularly those of the SED-Party headquarters now open for research, seem to reveal step by step that Hans Modrow, since 1990 MP for the new Communist Party PDS, (see also Ch.8) was also part of a regime intent on crushing any opposition from within, if necessary by means of force. Modrow and others were, however, sentenced on probation for having been privy to manipulations of the election results in the former GDR especially in May 1989 (see Doc. 1c above).

9. Interesting details are given in the report by the Special Advisor to the Government on problems of foreigners living in Germany (a high-ranking government post within the Federal Ministry of Labour and Social Policy):
Bericht der Beauftragten der Bundesregierung für die Belange der Ausländer über die Lage der Ausländer in der Bundesrepublik Deutschland 1993, Bonn 1994.

5
Foreign Policy
Robert Spencer

In many respects, for its first forty years, until the tumultuous events of 1989–90, the foreign policy of the Federal Republic of Germany has been unique. More dependent than most other states on the international system which gave birth to it, the Republic in its earlier years had to endure a long period of apprenticeship.[1]* It had no foreign ministry until 1951, no foreign minister separate from the chancellor until 1955, the year in which sovereignty was regained in most essentials. Even after that date, however, the Federal Republic remained, as Willy Brandt described it in the 1964 election campaign, 'an economic giant, but a political dwarf'.[2] Just why this pattern should have prevailed after 1949 is explained in part by the Republic's origins. The government established in 1949 was endowed with only a limited and revocable degree of sovereignty, and only gradually were the reins of the occupying powers relaxed (Docs. 1 and 2). From the very start, the goal of political recovery by the Federal Republic meant, as it could only mean, the right to have a foreign policy and to bring about conditions in which it could be exercised.[3]

Other factors also circumscribed Bonn's foreign policy from the start. In the first place, the Federal Republic comprised not all, but only a part of the territory of the former German Reich. The importance of this consideration is suggested by the fact that the central goal of foreign policy was laid down in the preamble to the Basic Law: 'The entire German people are called upon to achieve in free self-determination the unity and freedom of Germany.' The Basic Law also committed the Federal Republic to 'serve the peace of the world as an equal partner in a united Europe'. Not only, that is, was the Republic committed to the causes of unification and of peace but, as was the case in a number of other countries such as Italy, the goal of European unity was enshrined in its constitution. The regaining of sovereignty was also coupled with the constitutional authority to 'transfer sovereign powers to inter-governmental institutions' and to enter 'a system of mutual collective security' (Art. 24). Active par-

* Notes for this chapter begin on p. 146.

ticipation in a highly multilateralized international security system has been a hallmark of the Federal Republic's foreign policy.

In line with these provisions the Bonn government's early steps towards regaining sovereignty were paralleled by an active policy of *Westpolitik,* i.e. participation in the progress towards European integration, which was to lead in 1993 to the formation of the European Union with the Maastricht Treaty. In 1950 it overcame its hesitations over the dispute with France over the Saar and entered the newly established Council of Europe in the hope of securing 'appreciable alleviations' in the occupation regime.[4] In the same year it also eagerly embraced the proposal of French Foreign Minister Robert Schuman to pool the resources of heavy industry in Germany, France, Italy and the Benelux countries to form the European Coal and Steel Community on the basis of full equality for the Federal Republic (Doc.3).

In the realm of security policy, with the failure in 1954 of the French proposal for an integrated European army which would have enabled the Germans to make a contribution to the defence of the West, without the political risks attendant on the revival of a national German army, the Federal Republic joined in steps which led, a year later on 9 May 1955, to its admission to the North Atlantic Treaty Organization (NATO) as the Alliance's fifteenth member (Doc.4). After 1955 the West German partnership in the Atlantic Alliance, was the cornerstone of the country's security policy and the basis of the relationship with the former occupying powers, who until the conclusion of a peace treaty were to retain special responsibility 'relating to Berlin and to Germany as a whole,'[5] and especially with the United States which provided the vital nuclear shield. A bilateral relationship which was of great importance both within the European community and, more broadly, in the Western Alliance was the Franco-German reconciliation. This, as Adenauer recorded later on, was a special attraction of the Schuman Plan.[6] It was sealed by the Franco-German Treaty of 1963 (Doc.5), a development of historic proportions.

While it took until the 1970s for a line to be drawn under the legacy of the Second World War in the East, the process of meeting moral obligations elsewhere began two decades earlier. The principal thrust in this direction was the attempt to provide compensation for the special victims of the National Socialist system, the Jews. As early as 1951 Chancellor Adenauer, supported by a broad coalition in the Bundestag which included his own party and the Social Democrats, then in opposition, initiated and executed a policy of substantial restitution payments to Israel which by 1975 had

amounted to DM 3.5 billion (Doc.6). Restitution also involved payments to countries such as Norway which had been occupied and
despoiled by the Nazis (Doc.7).[7]

From the start, the Federal Republic's relations with eastern
Europe were governed by the inescapable fact that the Soviet Union
and its system of satellites stood in the way of German reunification
(Doc.8). The other German state, formed in the Soviet Zone of
Occupation with its self-proclaimed capital in the Soviet sector of
Berlin, was linked with the other central European satellites in the
Soviet-led Warsaw Treaty of 1955, and, behind its barbed wire and
chain of watch towers, pursued a campaign of vilification against the
Federal Republic.(see also Ch.3).

Moreover, it was perceived in Bonn that any threat to the Federal
Republic's security could only come from Moscow. While seeking
integration with the West and preparing to contribute to Western
defence, the Republic's first chancellor, Konrad Adenauer, did not
neglect the need to tackle the problems involved in normalizing relations with the East. His historic visit to Moscow in September 1955,
four months after Bonn had joined the North Atlantic Treaty Organization, opened the way to the establishment of diplomatic relations
between Bonn and Moscow (Doc.9); it also recalls the comment by
Gustav Stresemann in 1927 on his Locarno policies: 'I never thought
more about the East than during the time I was looking for an
understanding in the West.'[8] Bonn's hopes to use the link with
Moscow to solve the problem of reunification were stillborn, however, and the Federal Republic turned to the more promising
prospects in the West (Doc.10). At the same time, it enunciated the
'Hallstein Doctrine', which promised diplomatic retaliation against
third-party states which granted diplomatic recognition to East
Berlin (Doc.11).

West German-Soviet relations deteriorated sharply as the crises
over Berlin in 1958 and 1961 demonstrated (see also Ch.2). But in
the early 1960s Foreign Minister Gerhard Schroeder, who after Adenauer's retirement in 1963 was able to exercise greater freedom of
action, made significant efforts towards reconciliation with the East,
and in its last days the government of Ludwig Erhard, who had succeeded Adenauer as chancellor, launched a broad assault on the
problem with the Peace Note *(Friedensnote)* of March 1966
(Doc.12). However, this initiative, too, was stillborn. The 'Great
Coalition' government of Kurt-Georg Kiesinger, in which the SPD
leader Willy Brandt was Foreign Minister, enunciated policies looking to reconciliation with the East which took account of the criticisms levelled at the rigidities of CDU policies (Doc.13). In large

measure pursuing the ideas advanced earlier by the SPD, it succeeded in establishing diplomatic relations with Romania and, in a breach of the Hallstein Doctrine, in re-establishing diplomatic relations with Yugoslavia which had been broken off a decade earlier. Repeatedly expressed desires on the part of the Kiesinger government to improve relations were rejected by the USSR. And from East Berlin Walter Ulbricht succeeded in rallying Poland and Czechoslovakia into an 'iron triangle'[9] to resist German advances.

In the end, it was the new Eastern Policy *(Ostpolitik)* initiated by Chancellor Willy Brandt, following the success of the Social Democratic Party in the elections of September 1969 and the formation of the Socialist-Liberal coalition, which broke the log jam (Doc.14)(see also Ch.8 and 9). This opened the way to the abandoning of the outdated and unrealistic concepts of the Hallstein Doctrine and the *Alleinvertretungsanspruch* (the right of Bonn to speak for all Germans). It led to the conclusion of treaties with Moscow and with Poland in 1970 (Docs.15 and 16) and, two years later, of the treaty governing relations between Bonn and East Berlin, 'the two states within the German nation' according to the view enunciated by Chancellor Brandt in 1969 (see also Ch.3). The reconciliation with Czechoslovakia was delayed until December 1973 (Doc.17).

While pursuing its *Ostpolitik*, the Brandt government also launched a bold initiative towards European integration (Doc.18).

Although the Federal Republic had long been represented at the United Nations by an observer, membership in the organization had to await this settlement in the East. It was thus not until 1973, as a byproduct of the Eastern treaties, that the governments of the four occupying powers could support the admission of both the Federal Republic of Germany and the German Democratic Republic to the UN and so enable Bonn to play its full role in the world body (Doc.19). Well before this, however, the Federal Republic had assumed its share of the obligations of other western industrialized nations in providing assistance to less developed countries. The conditions governing development assistance have been made more specific (Doc.20).

While many aspects of Bonn's policies enjoyed a broad measure of domestic support, others from time to time provoked sharp controversy. The Adenauer policy of European integration and of adherence to the Atlantic Alliance was at first opposed by the Social Democrats, mainly because they feared this would make difficult, if not impossible, German reunification. However, since about 1960 the Social Democrats have embraced, and indeed enthusiastically endorsed, these aspects of Adenauer's foreign policy. In the late

1960s and the early 1970s, the Christian Democratic opposition violently attacked the *Ostpolitik* of the Brandt-Scheel government, arguing that Bonn was 'giving' too much through acceptance of the territorial status quo and the 'recognition' of the GDR and not 'receiving' sufficient in return from Moscow and its Warsaw Pact allies. By the late 1970s, however, with the high point of détente following the conclusion of the Final Act of Helsinki by the Conference on Security and Co-operation in Europe (CSCE), the Christian Democratic opposition had largely accepted the government's position, and the main features of the Federal Republic's foreign and defence policies enjoyed bipartisan support.

Helmut Schmidt (see also Ch.9), who had succeeded Willy Brandt as chancellor in 1974, continued the *Ostpolitik* established by his predecessor. Together with his foreign minister, Hans Dietrich Genscher (who was to occupy the post for a further eighteen years) he attempted to reconcile harmony in the Atlantic Alliance and the need for military strength with a continuing policy of détente with the East. In the early 1980s, as détente broke down when Soviet forces shocked the world by the invasion of Afghanistan, and Moscow appeared to threaten military action against the reformist movement in Poland, domestic consensus was destroyed. Chancellor Schmidt advanced proposals for theatre nuclear modernization, if negotiations with Moscow failed to remove the threat to its new intermediate range missiles. This stand encouraged the development of a strong peace movement, in which the new Green Party played a prominent role (see also Ch.8). At the same time leading elements in the SPD moved leftward towards less Atlanticist emphasis on peace and isolated the chancellor. When the FDP deserted the coalition, Schmidt's government fell in October 1982.(see also Ch.7)

The new coalition, headed by Helmut Kohl, had to maintain a balance between the CSU, led by Franz-Josef Strauss, which emphasized the failure of détente, and the FDP under Foreign Minister Genscher which adhered to the Eastern policy of the previous SPD-led government (Doc.21). The issue of theatre nuclear modernization continued to provoke an outspoken response from the peace movement and to provide a subject of controversy in the 1983 election campaign. Chancellor Kohl (see also Chs.3 and 6) interpreted his success at the polls on 6 March as a mandate to pursue the strengthening of the Alliance and closer co-operation with the United States. While in early 1983 he spoke of the 'expansionist policy' of the USSR, his concern for relations with Germany's eastern neighbour also suggested continuity with the policies pursued by his two predecessors (Doc.22). As the 1980s progressed, Foreign Minister Genscher increasingly sought to portray himself as the champion of détente and arms control. However, the advent of Mikhail Gorbachov at the helm of the Soviet Union in March 1985 was greeted with a scepticism which persisted through to 1988 when the first signs of change in the Soviet Union were becoming apparent (Doc.23). When Gorbachov visited Bonn in June 1989, in an atmosphere charged with 'Gorbymania', the two leaders issued a joint declaration which was long on rhetoric but short on specifics, especially as regards the key question of unification. On the eve of the dramatic events of 1989–90, however, on the occasion of the fortieth anniversary of the signing of the Washington Treaty, Chancellor Kohl underlined the importance of the NATO for German security and for the search for the development of a stable relationship with its eastern neighbours (Doc.24).

The unforeseen events which led to unification in 1990 (described in detail in Ch.4) had an immediate impact on German foreign policy. Foreign Minister Genscher used his address to the United Nations General Assembly to issue the first of a series of statements intended to reassure Germany's Eastern neighbours of Bonn's intention to adhere to its treaties and to its obligations to the EC and the CSCE. On the morrow of the breaching of the Berlin Wall he telephoned similar assurances to Soviet Foreign Minister Shevardnadze in Moscow (Doc.28). A month later, together with the new GDR Minister-President Hans Modrow, Chancellor Kohl pledged to work for a peaceful evolution of Europe within the framework of the CSCE (Doc.26).

The prospect of early political unification (see also Ch.4) brought to the fore the question of the future orientation of the united Germany. While Bonn repeatedly insisted on its continued adherence to NATO, Moscow insisted that 'it is necessary to proceed on the basis of post war realities—namely, the existence of two sovereign states', and continued to argue for neutrality or joint membership for united Germany in NATO and the Warsaw Pact. Not until mid-July 1990, and only after the Atlantic Alliance had turned in a revolutionary fashion from a posture of confrontation to co-operation with the states of Eastern Europe, did the USSR guarantee the newly united Germany the option to chose its alliance allegiance (Doc.27).

The external aspects of German unity were settled in the 'Two-plus-Four' talks (the two German states plus the four war-time allies), (Doc.28). With the suspension of the rights which the occupation powers had assumed in 1945, the new, fully sovereign State of 'Germany' took its place in the United Nations. On 4 October, the day following the ceremonies marking the emergence of the new state, Chancellor Kohl outlined to the Bundestag, meeting in the old Reichstag Building in Berlin, the government's post-unification foreign policies. Recognizing that unification had bred fresh anxieties abroad, he stressed continuity with the Federal Republic's policies in the past: commitment to the Atlantic Alliance, progress towards European unification, support for the CSCE, good neighbourliness with the Warsaw Pact countries, and support for arms control measures. The new Germany, it seemed, would be 'bigger and better'.[10]

In the months which followed, the rapidly unfolding international situation confronted the new Germany with unforseen challenges. German hopes for 'normalization' after the hectic year of unification and the termination of the constraints which had governed foreign and security policies for four decades were disappointed.[11] After 1990, Germany was bound to be powerful; it was not yet clear how it would employ its power. Within a year Germany's international situation was further complicated by the dissolution of the Warsaw Treaty Organization (May 1991) and of the USSR (December 1991), followed swiftly by the resignation of Mikhail Gorbachov on whom the Bonn government had placed such reliance. Confronted at home with the huge and underestimated costs of integrating the new eastern Länder into its fabric (see also Ch.4), and abroad with the new and dramatically changed international situation, the hesitant actions of the Bonn government were in sharp contrast to the sure-footed way in which the Chancellor and Foreign Minister had seized and exploited the window of opportunity which had led to the lightning process of unification.

The collapse of communism in Central and Eastern Europe called for a restatement of Germany's relations with its eastern neighbours. The comprehensive Treaty of Good Neighbourliness, Partnership, and Cooperation with the Soviet Union drew a line under the Second World War and its consequences, and provided the model for the treaties between Germany and Poland, Czechoslovakia, and Romania[12] (Doc.29). Convinced, as Chancellor Kohl put it, of the need 'to stabilize the political, economic, and social conditions in Central and southeastern Europe as well as in the successor states of the Soviet Union,' Bonn led in providing economic support, including financial support directed towards achieving the withdrawal of Soviet troops from the former GDR, first for the USSR and then for Russia. The North Atlantic Co-operation Council (NACC), formed in December 1991 on a German-American initiative on the eve of the dissolution of the Soviet Union, appeared a more promising instrument than the CSCE on which Foreign Minister Genscher had placed such reliance.

Washington's strong response to Iraq's invasion of Kuwait on 2 August 1990 caught the Bonn government by surprise. Massive demonstrations against the war revealed an underlying animosity towards the United States, while Washington experienced a strong sense of disappointment in the light of President Bush's May 1989 'partners in leadership' appeal and its unwavering support for German unification. When military action by the United States-led coalition began in February 1991, Germany's international reputation suffered when it failed to demonstrate solidarity with its partners in support of UN resolutions until jolted by a barrage of criticism into a somewhat frantic response which could not reverse the severe loss of credibility. Further criticism was averted by massive financial support for the operation. The reluctant despatch of forces to defend a NATO ally, Turkey, contrasted with the West's resolute defence of the Federal Republic during the Cold War. And there was also shock at the revelation that the Iraqi Skud missiles directed towards Israel owed much to the contribution of German technicians (see also Ch.6).

The outbreak of full-scale civil war in the former Yugoslavia also pushed German policy into new directions. Foreign Minister Genscher had at first backed the country's territorial integrity and then, realizing that Serbian policy made inevitable the demise of Yugoslavia, gave in too lightly to domestic pressure by goading his EC partners into a precipitate recognition of the independence of Croatia and Slovenia. Three quarters of the refugees fleeing the former Yugoslavia and seeking sanctuary in Europe were able to enter the Federal Republic thanks to its liberal asylum law. The conflict produced a bitter debate on the role for German armed forces permitted by the somewhat ambiguous terms of the constitution *(Grundgesetz)*. In April 1993 the Constitutional Court in Karlsruhe narrowly approved German participation in surveillance flights by multination manned AWACs aircraft on the *political* grounds that a German refusal to do so would endanger the trust of Germany with the (NATO) alliance. The constitutional issue was finally decided by the *Bundesverfassungsgericht* in 1994 (see Ch.6, Doc.10). In an historic judgement with profound implications for Germany's foreign policy, the Court ended a long-standing controversy and marked a decisive stage in the country's march to normalcy by ruling that the sending of German troops to fight abroad under the aegis of the United Nations or NATO did not violate the provisions of the Basic Law (Grundgesetzt). In its 48-page judgement the Constitutional Court rejected the objections of the Social Democratic and Free Democratic Parties and ruled that German troops could be despatched abroad on approval on each occasion by a simple majority of the Bundestag.

Ironically, the judgement came the same day as President Bill Clinton strode through Berlin's Brandenburg Gate and appeared to single out Germany as the United States's leading European partner. In welcoming the judgement Chancellor Kohl underlined that if Germans were to benefit from membership in the United Nations they have also to fulfil the resultant obligations, while Foreign Minister Kinkel assured the international community of German restraint in any future military assignments.

European integration and loyalty to the Atlantic Alliance have remained hallmarks of Bonn's foreign policy. In the years since unification German leaders have resolutely stressed the 'irreversible' process of European union, proclaiming without hesitation or equivocation their commitment to a 'European Germany' (Doc.30), and have urged the development of representative and democratic institutions to which they would be prepared to cede sovereign powers. Bonn's willingness to see the DM replaced by a single European currency provided the European parliament was given more authority, led to the single supranational item in the Maastricht Treaty of December 1991, the formation of a European central bank modelled on the politically independent Bundesbank to be located in Frankfurt.

Having won the right in the Two-plus-Four talks to choose its alliance orientation, Bonn has continued its commitment to collective defence in the framework of NATO as the single functioning security structure in Europe and a hedge against United States neo-isolationism, 'the irreplaceable instrument providing reassurance against crises'.[13] This has required a delicate balancing act in view of French ambitions (Doc.31). The belated French realization that the Americans will not remain in Germany as mercenaries and that a continued American voice in Europe will require acceptance of NATO's pre-eminent role eased Bonn's efforts to reinforce its shaky alliance with Paris.

The sudden and unexpected resignation of Hans-Dietrich Genscher on 17 May 1992 after eighteen years at the Foreign Office caught the country and the world by surprise. His dominating role had made the Foreign Ministry into what was known as 'Genscher's Reserve', and he was at the height of his international reputation as a consequence of his role in unification. The hasty appointment as his successor of the relatively unknown forty-five-year old Klaus Kinkel was influenced by the FDP desire to hold on to the foreign affairs portfolio. The challenge to redefine military policies has been seen by the new Foreign Minister and his colleague in defence, Volker Rühe, as a welcome relief from domestic politics. Both have strongly advocated German peacekeeping missions abroad and a determination to end the constitutional hurdles which have limited them, and at their urging Germany has assumed a more active role in the former Yugoslavia, in Cambodia, and in Somalia. While abstaining from any initiative, the Foreign Minister has also made it clear that if a change in the composition of the Security Council is actually considered, Germany will also seek a permanent seat.

A little over a year after giving their approval of the Basic Law for the new Federal Republic of Germany, the Western occupying powers, while retaining their occupation role, projected further steps towards the recovery of sovereignty by the West German state.

Document 1

DECLARATION BY THE FOREIGN MINISTERS OF GREAT BRITAIN, THE UNITED STATES AND FRANCE, LONDON, 13 MAY 1950

Source: London Conferences. Tripartite Talks between the Foreign Ministers of the United States, United Kingdom and France, May 11–13 1950, London, 1950, Cmd. 7977, 5–6

Following the London Agreements of June, 1948, and the Washington Agreements of April, 1949, the United States, France and the United Kingdom replaced the military authority and the direct administration of the occupied territories in force since 1945 by a civilian regime simply of supervision ... .

In the domain of foreign relations the Petersberg Protocol made provisions for the appointment of German consular and commercial representatives abroad. During the last few months steps have been taken by the Western Powers to secure the accession of the Federal Republic to a number of international organizations, including the Organization for European Economic Co-operation. Finally, she has been invited to join the Council of Europe ... .

...

2. The Allies are resolved to pursue their aim laid down in the Washington Agreement of April 1949 and reaffirmed at the Petersberg that Germany shall re-enter progressively the community of free peoples of Europe. When that situation has been fully reached she will be liberated from controls to which she is still subject and accorded her sovereignty to the maximum extent compatible with the basis of the Occupation regime. This regime is imposed on the Germans and on the Allies by the consequences of the division of Germany and of the international position; until this situation is modified it must be retained in accordance with the common interests of Germany and of Europe.

The Western Powers desire to see the pace of progress towards this end as rapid as possible ... . The Ministers accordingly agreed to set up a study

group in London to undertake the necessary preparatory work to enable the
Occupation Statute to be reviewed at the appointed time and to make recommendations for eliminating the major practical inconveniences arising in
the countries concerned from the state of war, on the understanding that in
the present situation of Europe supreme authority must remain in the hands
of the Allied Powers.

. . .

4. While retaining the framework outlined above, the Allies intend to give
   Germany the possibility of developing freely, while at the same time safeguarding the possibility of peaceful reunification of Germany, which
   remains the ultimate object of their policy … .

The Federal Republic's participation in the evolving European institutions—at this early stage the Council of Europe and the Coal and
Steel Community—involved further steps towards limiting the
restrictions of the occupation regime and a consequent regaining of
sovereignty.

Document 2

STATEMENT ON WEST GERMAN SOVEREIGNTY BY THE
THREE WESTERN FOREIGN MINISTERS AND THE FEDERAL
CHANCELLOR, PARIS, 22 NOVEMBER 1951
Source: United States Department of State Bulletin, Vol. XXV, 649, 3 Decem-
ber 1951, 891–2

The Foreign Ministers of France, the United Kingdom, and the United
States met today with Dr. Adenauer.

This meeting, the first occasion on which the Chancellor and Foreign
Minister of the German Federal Republic had jointly conferred with the foreign ministers of the three Western Powers, marked in itself a notable
advance in the progressive association of the German Federal Republic with
the West on the basis of equal partnership.

. . .

The general agreement will be a decisive step toward the realization of the
common aim of the three Western Powers and the Federal Government to
integrate the Federal Republic on a basis of equality in a European community itself included in a developing Atlantic community.

With the coming into force of the general agreement and the related convention, the Occupation Statute with its powers of intervention in the
domestic affairs of the Federal Republic will be revoked, and the Allied High
Commission and the Offices of the Land Commissioners will be abolished.
The three powers will retain only such special rights as cannot now be
renounced because of the special international situation of Germany, and

which it is in the common interest of the four states to retain. These rights relate to the stationing and the security of the forces in Germany, to Berlin and to questions concerning Germany as a whole ... .

The Federal Republic will undertake to conduct its policy in accordance with the principles set forth in the Charter of the United Nations and with the aims defined in the Statute of the Council of Europe.

The four ministers are agreed that an essential aim of the common policy of their Governments is a peace settlement for the whole of Germany freely negotiated between Germany and her former enemies, which should lay the foundation for a lasting peace. They further agreed that the final settlement of the boundaries of Germany await such settlement ... .

As this document underlines, West German interest in European integration was inspired by more than short-term economic aspirations and looked to political union on a supranational basis.

Document 3

KONRAD ADENAUER IN THE BUNDESTAG ON THE
EUROPEAN COAL AND STEEL COMMUNITY, 12 JULY 1952

Source: Auswärtiges Amt (ed.), *Die Auswärtige Politik der Bundesrepublik Deutschland*, Cologne, 1972, 1 76–9

. . .

As with every agreement, this agreement by six members is a compromise. None of the participants in the negotiations would or could claim that the outcome of the negotiations was a hundred per cent correct or satisfied him a hundred per cent. One should not focus too narrowly on the details of such a set of agreements, but rather consider the basic idea, the purpose of the agreement as a whole ...

The idea was that when these six European countries had learnt to cooperate in such an extremely important economic field, then the incentive ensuing from this mutual work would suffice in order to achieve cooperation in further economic fields ... .

It is my opinion and belief that the parliaments of the six European countries which will have to deal with this European Coal and Steel Community realize ... that the political goal, the political meaning of the European Coal and Steel Community, is infinitely larger than its economic purpose ... .

For the first time in history, certainly in the history of the last centuries, countries want to renounce part of their sovereignty, voluntarily and without compulsion, in order to transfer the sovereignty to a supranational structure ... . A beginning has finally been made . . . and in this way nationalism, the inveterate evil of Europe, will be dealt a death blow ... .

The Federal Republic's entry into the North Atlantic Treaty Organization within a decade of the defeat of the Third Reich was a dramatic shift from foe to ally and took place within carefully circumscribed limits.

Document 4

FINAL ACT OF THE NINE-POWER CONFERENCE, LONDON, 28 SEPTEMBER-3 OCTOBER 1954

Source: Nine-power Conference. Final Act of the Nine-Power Conference held in London, Sept. 28 to Oct. 3, 1954, London, 1954, Cmd. 9289, 10–11

DECLARATION BY THE GOVERNMENTS OF FRANCE, THE UNITED KINGDOM AND UNITED STATES OF AMERICA

The following declarations were recorded at the Conference by the German Federal Chancellor and by the Foreign Ministers of France, United Kingdom and United States of America:

Declaration by Federal Republic of Germany

The Federal Republic of Germany has agreed to conduct its policy in accordance with the principles of the Charter of the United Nations and accepts the obligations set forth in Article 2 of the Charter.

Upon her accession to the North Atlantic Treaty and the Brussels Treaty, the Federal Republic of Germany declares that she will refrain from any action inconsistent with the strictly defensive character of the two treaties. In particular the Federal Republic of Germany undertakes never to have recourse to force to achieve the reunification of Germany or the modification of the present boundaries of the Federal Republic of Germany, and to resolve by peaceful means any disputes which may arise between the Federal Republic and other States.

Declaration by the Governments of the United States of America, United Kingdom and France

The Governments of the United States of America, the United Kingdom of Great Britain and Northern Ireland and the French Republic ... .

Take note that the Federal Republic of Germany has by a Declaration dated the Third of October, Nineteen hundred and Fifty Four accepted the obligations set forth in Article 2 of the Charter of the United Nations and has undertaken never to have recourse to force to achieve the reunification of Germany or the modification of the present boundaries of the Federal Republic of Germany, and to resolve by peaceful means any disputes which may arise between the Federal Republic and other States:

DECLARE THAT:

1. They consider the Government of the Federal Republic as the only German Government freely and legitimately constituted and therefore entitled to speak for Germany as the representative of the German people in international affairs.
2. In their relations with the Federal Republic they will follow the principles set out in Article 2 of the United Nations Charter.
3. A peace settlement for the whole of Germany, freely negotiated between Germany and her former enemies, which should lay the foundation of a lasting peace, remains an essential aim of their policy. The final determination of the boundaries of Germany must await such a settlement.
4. The achievement through peaceful means of a fully free and unified Germany remains a fundamental goal of their policy.
5. The security and welfare of Berlin and the maintenance of the position of the Three Powers there are regarded by the Three Powers as essential elements of the peace of the free world in the present international situation. Accordingly they will maintain armed forces within the territory of Berlin as long as their responsibilities require it. They therefore reaffirm that they will treat any attack against Berlin from any quarter as an attack upon their forces and themselves.

The Franco-German reconciliation—perhaps the most far-reaching and certainly one of the unpredictable developments of the postwar era—culminated in a formal treaty. It was concluded in the last months of Adenauer's tenure as chancellor and had perhaps a symbolic rather than a practical importance.

Document 5

JOINT DECLARATION BY CHANCELLOR ADENAUER AND PRESIDENT DE GAULLE, 22 JANUARY 1963

Source: Auswärtiges Amt (ed.), *Die Auswärtige Politik der Bundesrepublik Deutschland*, Cologne, 1972, 490

The Federal Chancellor of the Federal Republic of Germany, Dr. Konrad Adenauer, and the President of the French Republic, General de Gaulle,
- at the close of the conference from 21–22 January 1963 in Paris, with the participants from the German side being the Federal Foreign Minister, the Federal Minister of Defence and the Federal Minister for Family and Youth Affairs, and from the French side being the Prime Minister, the Foreign Minister, the Minister of the Army and the Education Minister,
- in the conviction that the reconciliation between the German and French people, which has ended a rivalry of centuries, presents an historical occurrence which shapes afresh the relationship between the two peoples from the ground up,

- in view of the fact that the youth in particular have become conscious of this solidarity and that they have been allotted a critical role in the strengthening of the German-French friendship,
- in recognising that the strengthening of the cooperation between both countries means an essential step on the path toward a united Europe, which is the goal of both peoples,

have agreed to the organization and the principles of cooperation between the two states, as they have been laid down in the treaty signed to-day.

The persecution of Europe's Jews culminating in the extermination camps presented the new Republic with a continuing problem. A notable feature of its foreign policy, very early in its history, was its provision of some form of restitution for Nazi crimes against the Jews.

Document 6

STATEMENT BY CHANCELLOR ADENAUER TO THE BUNDESTAG CONCERNING THE ATTITUDE OF THE FEDERAL REPUBLIC TOWARDS THE JEWS, 27 SEPTEMBER 1951
Source: Ibid., 179–81

Of late, the world public opinion has repeatedly been concerned with the attitude of the Federal Republic of Germany towards the Jews. Here and there doubts have arisen as to whether our new policy is guided, in regard to this important question, by principles which take into account the terrible crimes of the past epoch and which place the relationship between the Jews and the German people on a new and healthy footing.

The attitude of the Federal Republic of Germany to its Jewish citizens is clearly defined through the Basic Law ... . These legal norms are the law of the land and oblige every German citizen, and especially every state official, to reject any form of racial discrimination. In the same spirit, the German government has also signed the Human Rights Convention adopted by the Council of Europe and has pledged itself to the realization of the legal concepts laid down in this Convention.

... The German government, and with it the majority of the German people, are conscious of the immeasurable sorrow that was brought upon the Jewish people in Germany and in the occupied territories during the period of National Socialism. There was a predominant majority of German people who abhorred the crimes committed against the Jews and did not take part in them. There were many Germans during the time of National Socialism who, at their own risk, showed their willingness to help their Jewish compatriots for religious reasons, in a conflict of conscience, and out of shame because the

German name had been disgraced. The unmentionable crimes committed in the name of the German people demand a moral and material restitution. This includes both the damages inflicted on individual Jewish people and on Jewish property for which the individuals entitled to restitution no longer exist. The first steps have been taken in this area. Much more, however, remains to be done. The German government will see to a quick settlement concerning the restitution legislation and its fair implementation. A part of the identifiable Jewish property has been returned; additional restorations will follow ... .

The Federal Government is ready, together with representatives of Jewish interests and the State of Israel, which received so many homeless Jewish refugees to bring about a solution of the material restitution problems and thereby to prepare the way to a moral adjustment of this infinite sorrow. The German government is deeply convinced that the spirit of true humanity must be revived and made fruitful again ... .

In its foreign policy the Federal Republic also assumed responsibility for the crimes committed as a result of the wartime conquests and occupation by the Third Reich.

Document 7

TREATY BETWEEN THE FEDERAL REPUBLIC OF GERMANY AND THE KINGDOM OF NORWAY, 7 AUGUST 1959.

Source: Ibid., 410

The Federal Republic of Germany and the Kingdom of Norway have agreed as follows:

Art. I

(1) The Federal Republic of Germany will pay 60 million German marks to the Kingdom of Norway for the benefit of the Norwegian citizens concerned who have been persecuted by the National Socialists because of their race, belief or Weltanschauung, who have thereby endured injury to their freedom or health, as well as for the benefit of the bereaved of those who died as a result of this persecution

(2) The distribution of the amount is left to the discretion of the Kingdom of Norway ... .

Paul Loebe, a member of the SPD and a former speaker of the old Weimar Reichstag, was delegated, as the Bundestag's oldest member, to make this declaration on behalf of all the parties represented in it.

Document 8

DECLARATION ON THE ODER-NEISSE LINE BY PAUL LOEBE,
SPD, THE SENIOR MEMBER OF THE BUNDESTAG, 13 JUNE 1950
Source: H. Siegler, *The Reunification and Security of Germany*, Bonn, 1957,
123–4

In the name of all the Fractions and groups in the Bundestag, with the exception of the Communist Fraction, and with the assent of the Federal Government and the Bundesrat, I make the following declaration:

In the Agreement signed on 6th June 1950 by a delegation of the so-
called provisional Government of the German Democratic Republic and by
the Government of the Polish Republic, the assertion, untenable in international and constitutional law, is made that a so-called peace frontier has been
established between the Soviet Occupied Zone of Germany and Poland.
Under the Potsdam Agreement, the German territory east of the Oder and
Neisse was handed over as part of the Soviet Occupied Zone of Germany to
the Polish Republic only for temporary administration purposes. That territory remains part of Germany ... .

The settlement of this question, as of all other questions affecting the German frontiers, both eastern and western, can be effected only by a peace
treaty, and such a treaty must be concluded a soon as possible by a democratically elected German Government as a pact of friendship and good neighbourliness with all nations ... . The Bundestag knows that it is speaking in
the name of the Germans in the Soviet Occupied Zone, too.

. . .

———

Within a few months of the Federal Republic's joining NATO,
Chancellor Adenauer journeyed to Moscow in the interests of
normalizing diplomatic relations with the USSR. Here, on his
return, he defends his *Ostpolitik*.

Document 9

CHANCELLOR ADENAUER IN THE BUNDESTAG ON THE
AGREEMENT WITH THE USSR, 22 SEPTEMBER 1955
Source: Die Auswärtige Politik der Bundesrepublik, Cologne, 1972, 308–13

. . .

In the course of the talks with representatives of the Soviet government, the
delegation of the Federal Republic of Germany has very clearly pointed out
that a normalization of relations can, under no circumstances, consist of
legalizing the anomalous condition of Germany's division. It was also
pointed out that the existence of diplomatic relations between two states was
not to be put on a par with a friendly pact relationship; our Soviet discussion

partners themselves have stated that they also maintain diplomatic relations with states with which they otherwise have considerable political and ideological differences of opinion ... .

The establishment of diplomatic relations means that the Federal Republic of Germany, whose effective sovereign power includes three-quarters of our nation and 80 per cent of its productive force and behind whose policy—we are convinced—at least 90 per cent of the population of the Soviet Occupied Zone stands as well, is now also recognized by the Soviet Union ... .

In due form I wish to declare for myself, for the Federal Government, for the whole German nation in the West and in the East: Germany is a part of the West, in conformity with its spiritual and social structure, its historical tradition and the will of its population ... .

The establishment of diplomatic relations between the Federal Republic and the Soviet Union does not therefore conflict with Western interests. I even believe I can go further: it serves Western interests. As the Federal Republic, in the role of a clearly Western power which is orientated towards Europe, will now also have a representative in Moscow, it will further strengthen the voice of the West there.

The establishment of relations has yet a further meaning. It contributes to the difficult task of easing the international situation and thereby contributes to world peace ... . We have made the reservations under international law necessary to maintain our juridical standpoint of which the Soviet Union has taken notice. In extremely difficult negotiations, we have extracted as much as was possible out of the given situation for the human and political spheres ... .

The disappointing results of the establishment of diplomatic relations with Moscow and the gloomy outlook for the reunification of Germany in view of the hardening of the lines of division following the entry of the Federal Republic into NATO, suggested to Adenauer the critical importance of moving forward along the road towards European economic and political integration.

Document 10

MEMORANDUM OF CHANCELLOR ADENAUER TO THE FEDERAL MINISTERS, 19 JANUARY 1956

Source: Auswärtiges Amt (ed.), *Die Auswärtige Politik der Bundesrepublik,* Cologne, 1972, 317–8

The present situation in foreign affairs confronts us with extraordinary dangers. Decisive measures are required to avoid these dangers and to initiate favourable developments. Above all, a clear, positive German attitude to European integration is necessary ... .

The resulting guideline for our policy is that we must carry out the Messina Resolution in a decisive and honest manner. The political character of this decision must be taken into consideration more strongly than before. It is a decision intended not only to lead to a technical cooperation based on specialized considerations, but to a community which ensures coordination of political purpose and action and is also in the interests of reunification ... .

In particular the following must apply for the realization of the Messina programme:

(1) Integration of the six members at first is to be furthered by *all* possible methods, i.e. in the field of general (horizontal) integration as well as suitable partial (vertical) integration.

(2) Right from the beginning and as far as possible, the establishing of suitable common institutions is to be aimed at in order to achieve a firm tie between the six members based on the main political goals.

(3) The fairly successful talks on establishing a common European market—i.e. a market which is similar to an inland market—must be vigorously brought to an end. At the same time, European institutions with decision-making rights must be established in order to secure the functioning of the market and simultaneously advance political development.

(4) Based on the idea of the Common Market, a genuine integration of the six with regard to traffic must be strived for. This applies especially to air-traffic; a fundamental refusal or delay in plans for the integrated production, supply and management in this field is politically irresponsible.

(5) The same applies to energy, especially to nuclear energy. It is an absolute political necessity to remove every doubt that we continue to stand by our Messina statements according to which a European Atomic Community with decision-making rights, common institutions and common financial and other operational means should be established ... .

I request that the above be regarded as guidelines of federal government policy and be followed as such.

The Federal Republic's concern to keep open the door for reunification prompted it, in a formal statement, to threaten diplomatic counter-measures against states which recognized what at the time was referred to as the 'so-called German Democratic Republic' or the 'Soviet Occupied Zone'. The resulting 'doctrine' came to be known by the name of the then Under-Secretary in the Foreign Office, Walter Hallstein.

Document 11

GOVERNMENT DECLARATION, 28 JUNE 1956: THE
HALLSTEIN DOCTRINE

Source: H. Siegler, *The Reunification and Security of Germany*, Bonn, 1957,
141–2

. . .

... The recognition of the German Democratic Republic would mean
international recognition of the partition of Germany in two States. Reunification would then no longer present itself as the elimination of a temporary disturbance in the organism of our all-German State: it would change
into the infinitely more difficult task of uniting two separate States. The
history of the unification of Germany in the 19th century illustrates what
that can mean. Were the Federal Republic to take the lead in recognition,
she would herself contribute to a state of affairs in which Europe and the
world would lose consciousness of the anomaly of the present situation and
become resigned to it. She would relieve the Four Powers of their responsibility for the re-establishment of the national unity of Germany, a responsibility which they—including the Soviet Union—have so far always
recognized. Instead, she would accord to Pieck, Grotewohl and Ulbricht
the right of vetoing any reunification. Furthermore, the recognition of the
'German Democratic Republic' would mean that the Federal Republic
would relinquish its claim to be the spokesman of the entire German people, a claim established in our constitution and which no Federal Government can ignore.

The Federal Government cannot refrain from making it clear once again
that it will feel compelled in future to regard the establishing of diplomatic
relations with the so-called German Democratic Republic by third States
with which the Federal Republic maintains diplomatic relations, as an
unfriendly act calculated to intensify and aggravate the partition of Germany. The Federal Government would in such a case have to re-consider its
relations to the State in question.

The question has been variously discussed in recent times as to whether or
not it is useful and possible to establish relations with Germany's eastern
neighbours. The Federal Government has examined this problem in all its
detail and has come to the conclusion that, under present circumstances,
diplomatic relations cannot be established with those countries. That does
not mean that the Federal Government is not interested in the establishment
of normal relations with the countries in question.

The attempt to unfreeze the situation in central Europe through the
Peace Note of March 1966 suggests the concern over the dead end
into which Adenauer's policies had led the Republic.

Document 12

PEACE NOTE *(FRIEDENSNOTE)* OF THE FEDERAL REPUBLIC OF GERMANY, 29 MARCH 1966

Source: The Bulletin, 29 March 1966

Transl.: Official

I

The German people wish to live in peace and freedom. They consider it their greatest national task to remove the partition of Germany under which they have suffered for many years. The Government of the Federal Republic of Germany has repeatedly stated that the German people would be prepared also to make sacrifices for the sake of their reunification. They are determined to solve this problem by peaceful means only ... .

As in the past, the Government of the Federal Republic of Germany still holds the view that a world-wide, general and controlled disarmament must be the objective. Nor will this objective be changed by monotonous propaganda which seeks to question and misrepresent the standpoint of the Federal Government on problems of disarmament and security ... .

II

The Federal Government considers that given good will and honest intentions on all sides, even the most difficult problems between nations can be resolved in a peaceful and equitable manner. Thus, on this basis it has reached agreement with Germany's neighbours in the West on all problems that were still open after the war.

The German people desire to live on good terms with all, including their east European neighbours. Hence the Federal Government has been trying in various ways to improve relations with the States and peoples of eastern Europe ... .

Despite the fact that the Federal Government has made particular efforts to cultivate relations with Poland, the country which suffered most of all among the east European nations in the Second World War, it has made but little progress in this direction. Although the Polish Government is obviously interested in more lively trade between Germany and Poland, it has hitherto not given any indication that it is interested in achieving a conciliation between the two nations. Rather does it hamper the cultural contacts we seek, stand for the continued division of Germany and at the same time calls upon the Federal Government to recognize the Oder-Neisse line, though it is generally known that, under the allied agreements of 1945, the settlement of frontier questions has been postponed until the conclusion of a peace treaty with the whole of Germany and that, according to international law, Germany continues to exist within its frontiers of 31 December 1937 until such time as a freely elected all-German Government recognizes other frontiers.

If, when the occasion arises, the Poles and the Germans enter into negotiations on frontier questions in the same spirit that led to the conciliation between Germany and her western neighbours, then Poles and Germans will also find their way to agreement. For in this question neither emotions nor alone the power of the victor, but rather reason, must prevail.

. . .

The policy pursued by the Federal Government is neither revanchist nor restorative. It is looking forward, not backwards, and its aim is an equitable European order on the basis of peaceful agreements, an order in which all nations can live together freely and as good neighbours.

. . .

V

4. The Federal Republic of Germany and its Western allies have already exchanged declarations renouncing the use of force. As the Governments of the Soviet Union and some other east European countries have repeatedly expressed their anxiety, unfounded as it is, over a possible German attack, the Federal Government proposed that formal declarations be exchanged also with the Governments of the Soviet Union, Poland, Czechoslovakia and any other east European State, in which either side gives an undertaking to the other people not to use force to settle international disputes.

. . .

6. Finally, the Federal Government is prepared to participate and to co-operate in a constructive spirit in a world disarmament conference or in any other disarmament conference promising success ... .

. . .

While reiterating themes familiar in the Adenauer era, Chancellor Kurt Georg Kiesinger's government reflected Social Democratic policies by striking out for improved relations with the countries of Eastern Europe.

Document 13

THE DECLARATION BY THE GREAT COALITION GOVERNMENT, 13 DECEMBER 1966.

Source: The Bulletin (English edition), 20 December 1966

The German Government advocates a consistent and effective peace policy apt to remove political tension and to check the arms race ... . The Federal Republic has given an undertaking to its partners in the alliance to renounce the production of atomic weapons, and has in that respect submitted to international controls. We seek neither national control nor national ownership of atomic weapons ... .

The previous Federal Government in its peace note of last March offered an exchange of declarations renouncing the use of force also to the Soviet Union, in order to make it clear once again that it did not seek to attain our aims by other than peaceful means. The Federal Government today repeats this offer ... . Large sectors of the German people very much want reconciliation with Poland whose sorrowful history we have not forgotten and whose desire ultimately to live in a territory with secure boundaries we now, in view of the present lot of our own divided people, understand better than in former times ... . The German people also wish to come to an understanding with Czechoslovakia. The Federal Government condemns Hitler's policy which was aimed at destroying the Czechoslovakian state. It shares the view that the Munich Agreement, which came into being as the result of the threat to use force, is no longer valid ... .

Willy Brandt's policy statement, the first by a Social Democratic Chancellor in the Federal Republic's history, while including in its introductory paragraphs the pregnant phrase 'We want to venture more democracy', spelled out bold initiatives in foreign (and German) policy.

Document 14

GOVERNMENT DECLARATION, 28 OCTOBER 1969
Source: The Bulletin (English edition), 4 November 1969

. . .

We must prevent any further alienation of the two parts of the German nation, that is, arrive at a regular *modus vivendi* and from there proceed to co-operation ... The Federal Government will continue the policy initiated in December 1966 and again offers the Council of Ministers of the GDR negotiations at Government level without discrimination on either side, which should lead to contractually agreed co-operation. International recognition of the GDR by the Federal Republic is out of the question. Even if there exist two states in Germany, they are not foreign countries to each other; their relations with each other can only be of a special nature ... . The Federal Government will advise the USA, Britain, and France to continue energetically the talks begun with the Soviet Union on easing and improving the situation of Berlin. The status of the city of Berlin under the special responsibility of the Four Powers must remain untouched. This must not be a hindrance to seeking facilities for traffic within and to Berlin ... . The foreign policy of this Federal Government follows up on the Peace Note of March 1966 and on the Policy Statement of December 1966 ... . The German people needs peace in the full sense of that word also with the peoples of the Soviet Union and all peoples of the European East. We are prepared to make an honest attempt at understanding, in order to help overcome the aftermath of the disaster brought on Europe by a criminal clique ... .

In continuation of its predecessor's policy the Federal Government aims at equally binding agreements on the mutual renunciation of the use of threat of the use of force. Let me repeat: This readiness also applies as far as the GDR is concerned. And I wish to make as unmistakably clear that we are prepared to arrive with Czechoslovakia—our immediate neighbour—at arrangements which bridge the gulf of the past.

Within a year of taking office as chancellor, Willy Brandt and his associates had concluded a treaty with the Soviet Union in which the Federal Republic accepted 'current realities'. But as the accompanying letter shows, the ultimate right to 'unity in free self-determination' was preserved.

Document 15a

TREATY BETWEEN THE FEDERAL REPUBLIC OF GERMANY AND THE UNION OF SOVIET SOCIALIST REPUBLICS, 12 AUGUST 1970

Source: Presse- und Informationsamt der Bundesregierung (ed.), *Documentation Relating to the Federal Government's Policy of Détente*, Bonn, 1978, 17–19

Art.1

The Federal Republic of Germany and the Union of Soviet Socialist Republics consider it an important objective of their policies to maintain international peace and achieve detente.

They affirm their endeavour to further the normalization of the situation in Europe and the development of peaceful relations among all European States, and in so doing proceed from the actual situation existing in this region.

. . .

Art.3

In accordance with the foregoing purposes and principles the Federal Republic of Germany and the Union of Soviet Socialist Republics share the realization that peace can only be maintained in Europe if nobody disturbs the present frontiers.

- They undertake to respect without restriction the territorial integrity of all States in Europe within their present frontiers;
- they declare that they have no territorial claims against anybody nor will assert such claims in the future;

– they regard today and shall in future regard the frontiers of all States of Europe as inviolable such as they were on the date of signature of the present Treaty, including the Oder-Neisse line which forms the western frontier of the People's Republic of Poland and the frontier between the Federal Republic of Germany and the German Democratic Republic.

Document 15b

LETTER ON GERMAN UNITY, 12 AUGUST 1970

Source: Presse- und Informationsamt der Bundesregierung (ed.), *Documentation Relating to the Federal Government's Policy of Détente*, Bonn, 1978, 20

On the occasion of the signing of the Treaty, the Federal Government handed over in the Soviet Foreign Ministry the following letter:

Dear Mr. Minister,

In connection with today's signature of the Treaty between the Federal Republic of Germany and the Union of Soviet Socialist Republics the Government of the Federal Republic of Germany has the honour to state that this Treaty does not conflict with the political objective of the Federal Republic of Germany to work for a state of peace in Europe in which the German nation will recover its unity in free self-determination.

I assure you, Mr. Minister, of my highest esteem.

Walter Scheel

In view of the long history of German/Polish hostility and of the suffering inflicted on the Poles by the Third Reich (and of the fact that Poland was the chief beneficiary of the partition of Germany) the reconciliation between Bonn and Warsaw was of special importance. A very sensitive issue was the repatriation of many Germans who still lived in these former East German territories. The Polish side was at the time only willing to admit that 'some 65,000' Germans were still willing—and anxious—to leave the 'new' Poland for the 'new' (without its former Eastern territories) Germany. The West German side unofficially claimed—on evidence of the Red Cross—at least one million, the refugee organisations anything up to two million. For the actual numbers who left between 1970 and 1990, see Statistics, Table 2. (Doc. 16c).

Document 16a

TREATY BETWEEN THE FEDERAL REPUBLIC OF GERMANY AND THE PEOPLE'S REPUBLIC OF POLAND, 7 DECEMBER 1970, CONCERNING THE BASIS FOR NORMALIZING THEIR MUTUAL RELATIONS, AND RELATED STATEMENTS

Source: Ibid., 8ff.

THE FEDERAL REPUBLIC OF GERMANY AND THE PEOPLE'S REPUBLIC OF POLAND

Considering that more than 25 years have passed since the end of the Second World War of which Poland became the first victim and which inflicted great suffering on the nations of Europe,

Conscious that in both countries a new generation has meanwhile grown up to whom a peaceful future should be secured,

Desiring to establish durable foundations for peaceful coexistence and the development of normal and good relations between them,

Anxious to strengthen peace and security in Europe,

Aware that the inviolability of frontiers and respect for the territorial integrity and sovereignty of all States in Europe within their present frontiers are a basic condition for peace,

Have agreed as follows:

Article I

(1) The Federal Republic of Germany and the People's Republic of Poland state in mutual agreement that the existing boundary line the course of which is laid down in Chapter XI of the Decisions of the Potsdam Conference of 2 August 1945 ... shall constitute the western State frontier of the People's Republic of Poland.

(2) They reaffirm the inviolability of their existing frontiers now and in the future and undertake to respect each other's territorial integrity without restriction

(3) They declare that they have no territorial claims whatsoever against each other and that they will not assert such claims in the future

Article II

(1) The Federal Republic of Germany and the People's Republic of Poland shall in their mutual relations as well as in matters of ensuring European and international security be guided by the purposes and principles embodied in the Charter of the United Nations.

(2) Accordingly they shall, pursuant to Articles 1 and 2 of the Charter of the United Nations, settle all their disputes exclusively by peaceful means and refrain from any threat or use of force in matters affecting European and international security and in their mutual relations.

Article III

(1) The Federal Republic of Germany and the People's Republic of Poland shall take further steps towards full normalization and a comprehen-

sive development of their mutual relations of which the present Treaty shall form the solid foundation.

(2) They agree that a broadening of their co-operation in the sphere of economic, scientific, technological, cultural and other relations is in their mutual interest.

Article IV

The present Treaty shall not affect any bilateral or multilateral international arrangements previously concluded by either Contracting Party or concerning them.

. . .

Document 16b

NOTE FROM THE FEDERAL GOVERNMENT TO THE THREE WESTERN POWERS, 19 NOVEMBER 1970

Source: Ibid.

. . .

In the course of the negotiations which took place between the Government of the Federal Republic of Germany and the Government of the People's Republic of Poland concerning this Treaty, it was made clear by the Federal Republic that the Treaty between the Federal Republic of Germany and the People's Republic of Poland does not and cannot affect the rights and responsibilities of the French Republic, the United Kingdom of Great Britain and Northern Ireland, the Union of Soviet Socialist Republics, and the United States of America as reflected in the known treaties and agreements. The Federal Government further pointed out that it can only act in the name of the Federal Republic of Germany.[14]

The Government of the French Republic and the Government of the United States of America have received identical notes.

. . .

Document 16c

INFORMATION FROM THE GOVERNMENT OF THE PEOPLE'S REPUBLIC OF POLAND (UNDATED)

Source: Presse- und Informationsamt der Bundesregierung (ed.), *Documentation Relating to the Federal Government's Policy of Détente*, Bonn, 1978, 28ff.

. . .

(1) In 1955 the Polish Government recommended the Polish Red Cross to conclude an agreement with the Red Cross of the Federal Republic of Germany on the reunion of families; under that agreement, roughly one-quarter million people left Poland up to 1959. Between 1960 and 1969, an

additional 150,000 people have departed from Poland under normal procedures. In carrying out measures to reunite families, the Polish Government has been guided above all by humanitarian motives. However, it could not, and still cannot, agree that its favourable attitude regarding such reunions be exploited for the emigration of Polish nationals for employment purposes.

(2) To this day, there have remained in Poland for various reasons (e.g. close ties with their place of birth) a certain number of persons of indisputable ethnic German origin and persons from mixed families whose predominant feeling over the past years has been that they belong to that ethnic group. The Polish Government still holds the view that any persons who owing to their indisputable ethnic German origin wish to leave for either of the two German States may do so subject to the laws and regulations applicable in Poland.

Furthermore, consideration will be given to the situation of mixed and separated families as well as to such cases of Polish nationals who, either because of their changed family situation or because they have changed their earlier decision, express the wish to be reunited with near relatives in the Federal Republic of Germany or in the German Democratic Republic ... .

. . .

(4) Co-operation between the Polish Red Cross and the Red Cross of the FRG will be facilitated in any way necessary ... .

(5) As regards the traffic of persons in connection with visits to relatives, the appropriate Polish authorities will, after the entry into force of the Treaty concerning the basis for normalizing relations between the two States, apply the same principles as are customary with regard to other States of Western Europe.

While there were many former Sudeten Germans living in the Federal Republic after having been expelled by the Czechs, it was less the pressure from expellees than the more complicated legal questions resulting from the Czechoslovak demand that the Munich Treaty of 1938 (to which Britain, France and Italy were also parties) be declared invalid *ab initio* which delayed the settlement with Czechoslovakia until 1973. As with the Polish treaty three years earlier, by an exchange of notes the validity of Article II was extended to include Berlin (West).

Document 17

TREATY BETWEEN THE FEDERAL REPUBLIC OF GERMANY
AND THE CZECHOSLOVAK SOCIALIST REPUBLIC, 11
DECEMBER 1973

*Source: Documentation Relating to the Federal Government's Policy of
Detente*, Cologne, 1972, 68–71
Transl.: Official

. . .

Article II

(1) The present Treaty shall not affect the legal effects on natural or legal
persons of the law as applied in the period between 30 September 1938 and
9 May 1945.
This provision shall exclude the effects of measures which both Contracting
Parties deem to be void owing to their incompatibility with the fundamental principles of justice.
(2) The present Treaty shall not affect the nationality of living or deceased persons ensuing from the legal system of either of the two Contracting Parties.
(3) The present Treaty, together with its declarations on the Munich Agreement, shall not constitute any legal basis for material claims by the
Czechoslovak Socialist Republic and its natural and legal persons.

Article III

(1) The Federal Republic of Germany and the Czechoslovak Socialist
Republic shall in their mutual relations as well as in matters of ensuring
European and international security be guided by the purposes and principles embodied in the United Nations Charter.
(2) Accordingly they shall, pursuant to Articles 1 and 2 of the United
Nations Charter, settle all their disputes exclusively by peaceful means and
shall refrain from any threat or use of force in matters affecting European
and international security, and in their mutual relations.

Article IV

(1) In conformity with the said purposes and principles, the Federal Republic of Germany and the Czechoslovak Socialist Republic reaffirm the inviolability of their common frontier now and in the future and undertake to
respect each other's territorial integrity without restriction.
(2) They declare that they have no territorial claims whatsoever against each
other and that they will not assert any such claims in the future.

Especially striking—in view of earlier SPD scepticism and indeed
outright opposition to European integration—were SPD Chancellor
Brandt's early attempts to 'get Europe moving'. This speech was

delivered within a few weeks of his enunciation in his first government declaration of his new *Ostpolitik.*

Document 18

SPEECH OF CHANCELLOR WILLY BRANDT AT THE
EUROPEAN COMMUNITY'S SUMMIT CONFERENCE, THE
HAGUE, 1 DECEMBER 1969

Source: Auswärtiges Amt (ed.), *Die Auswärtige Politik der Bundesrepublik Deutschland*, Cologne, 1972, 716–17

. . .

If things were going well in Europe, we would not have met here today. If our community had been ready to speak out with a united voice, then our main theme would have been foreign policy: the question of a European order of peace, negotiations with the states of Eastern Europe and our interests in view of the conflict in the Middle East.

Therefore, I say in complete frankness: the German parliament and public opinion expect me not to return from this conference without a concrete agreement concerning the question of the broadening of the Community ... .

Firstly, experience has shown that postponing the expansion of the Community threatens to cripple it.

Secondly, it serves our mutual interests if the Community expands at a time in which we are making efforts to get West and East closer together.

Thirdly, the Community must outgrow the Six if it wants to maintain an economic and technological equivalence with the giants and fulfil its world-wide political responsibility.

I do not hesitate to add a fourth argument: he who fears that the economic weight of the Federal Republic of Germany could prove detrimental to the balance within the Community, should, for this reason, favour expansion.

In any case, I say that without England and the other nations, which are willing to join, Europe cannot be what it should be and what it can be ... .

The people of Europe wait and urge that state officials must add to the logic of history the will for success. Europe needs our success.

. . .

———

Not until the two German states had come to an understanding in the Basic Treaty of 1972 (see Ch.3. Docs.6a-c) was it possible for the Federal Republic, along with the GDR, to seek full membership in the United Nations.

Document 19

DECLARATION OF THE GOVERNMENTS OF THE UNITED
STATES, FRANCE, THE USSR AND GREAT BRITAIN, 18 JUNE
1973
Source: *The Federal Republic of Germany, Member of the United Nations*, 3rd
ed., Bonn, 1977, 170

The Governments of the United States of America, the French Republic, the
Union of Soviet Socialist Republics and the United Kingdom of Great
Britain and Northern Ireland, having been represented by their Ambassadors, who held a series of meetings in the building formerly occupied by
the Allied Control Council, are in agreement that they will support the
applications for membership in the United Nations when submitted by the
Federal Republic of Germany and the German Democratic Republic, and
affirm in this connection that this membership shall in no way affect the
rights and responsibilities of the Four Powers and the corresponding related
quadripartite agreements, decisions, and practices.

From the 1960s onwards, German government statements (and policy)
reflect an increasing preoccupation with the question of developmental
assistance. As a result of controversy over which countries were to be eligible for developmental assistance, specific criteria have been developed.

Document 20

NEW POLICY CRITERIA OF THE FEDERAL MINISTRY FOR
ECONOMIC COOPERATION
Source: Statement by Carl-Dieter Spranger, Federal Minister for Econommic
Co-operation, to the 'Bundespressekonferenz', Bonn, 10 October 1991
Transl.: Official

. . .

In the future five criteria will be of central importance for the granting of
development assistance.
These criteria are:

1. respect for human rights
2. popular participation in political decision-making processes
3. certainty of the law
4. the creation of a 'market-friendly' economic system
5. the development-orientation of government activities.

Respect for human rights is not only a moral imperative, it is also indispensable if a strategy which 'focuses on people' is to be credible. Freedom from torture, the granting of basic rights in connection with arrests and legal proceedings, the application of the principle 'no punishment without law', religious freedom and the effective protection of minorities are yardsticks against which the human rights situation in a given country will be measured.

Popular participation in political decision-making processes is a further criterion for the granting of development assistance. It should not mean measuring individual developing countries using the criteria for historical constitutional models, with out giving any consideration to socio-cultural differences. It is important, however, for the basic elements of a democratic system to be realised. These include a democratic election system, freedom of association, freedom of speech, freedom of the press and freedom of information—in other words the basic civil rights as laid down in the human rights convention, which have been ratified by the developing countries.

Certainty of the law and the rule of law constitute the third criterion. The independence of the judiciary and the application of the principle of 'equality before the law' are fundamental elements of a system based on the rule of law. There is more to certainty of the law than just safeguarding of individual rights, however. It also requires that government activity be transparent and predictable. Only on this basis can economic planning and activities be carried out on a rational basis and in accordance with the rules of a social market economy.

A further criterion for the granting of development assistance is the existence of what the World Bank, in its most recent World Development Report, called a 'market-friendly economic order'... .

Economic and social progress, particularly in the developing countries, depends in the end largely on the extent to which the state accepts responsibility for its central tasks and the degree of efficiency with which it fulfils them. Hence 'development-oriented government action' is the fifth criterion. This means in particular, that priority must be given within government policy to improving the economic and social situation of the poorer sections of the population, to preserving natural life-sustaining resources and, not least, to taking appropriate action to limit population growth.

In order that priority may be given to the pursuit of these objectives within the framework of government activities, these objectives must also take priority with regard to the distribution of a developing country's own funds. In many countries it will not be possible to achieve this without reducing excessive military spending ... .

A notable feature of the Federal Republic's foreign policy has been the assumption of responsibility for the crimes committed during wartime by the Third Reich. Doc.17 illustrates the pattern in which this obligation was discharged in Europe. The much more far-reaching attempt, very early in the history of the Federal Republic, to provide some form of restitution for Nazi crimes against the Jews is suggested by Doc.18.

The balancing act of the new CDU-FDP coalition government formed following the non-confidence vote of October 1982 which ended thirteen years of SPD-FDP rule was illustrated by the policy statement of the new chancellor.

Document 21

CHANCELLOR HELMUT KOHL'S POLICY STATEMENT, 13 OCTOBER 1982

Source: Survival, January/February 1983, 35-36

This country's foreign and security policy is founded on the North Atlantic Alliance and our friendship with the United States of America. It is an alliance that threatens no-one and does not aspire to superiority, but cannot, for the sake of preserving peace, accept permanent inferiority ...

First, we shall dispel the doubts that have fallen on German-American relations by reaffirming and stabilising our friendship ...

Second, the Federal Government reaffirms its commitment to the Atlantic Alliance ... We support without reservation the overall alliance strategy for our relations with the East as laid down in the Harmel Report and reaffirmed at the Bonn NATO Summit ...

Third, our prime objective is to establish and stabilize the necessary military equilibrium at the lowest possible level of armaments by means of concrete, balanced and verifiable negotiated results.

To create peace without weapons: this is an understandable aspiration but a dangerous illusion. To create peace with weapons alone: this would be a fatal delusion. To create peace with ever fewer weapons: this is the challenge of our time.

. . .

We therefore support the initiatives agreed on in the alliance which, in their entirety, represent the most comprehensive offer on arms control yet made to the Soviet Union.

The Federal Government is wholly committed to the NATO dual-track decision of 1979 which proposes negotiations on the reduction and limitation of Soviet and American intermediate-range nuclear systems. It will stand up for the two parts of the decision and put them into effect, the part relating to negotiations and, if necessary, the part on arms modernization, and it will call to mind that the credit for demanding the decision and asserting it in the alliance goes to a Social Democratic Chancellor.

In his emphasis on the role of the Federal Republic in Central Europe Chancellor Kohl's government statement following his electoral victory on 6 March 1983 was hardly distinguishable from the pronouncements of his Social Democratic predecessor.

Document 22

GOVERNMENT DECLARATION BY CHANCELLOR HELMUT KOHL BEFORE THE BUNDESTAG, 4 MAY 1983

Source: Europa Archiv, 38. Jahr, Folge 12, 25 June 1983, 307-14 [Verhandlungen des Deutschen Bundestages. 10 Wahlperiode 1983 Bd.124. Stenographische Berichte 1-17 Sitzungen 1983. 4. Sitzungen 4 May 1983, S.307-15]

. . .

German Foreign Policy ... means above all the preservation of freedom and the consolidation of peace in Europe and the World. For us an active peace policy is a political necessity and a moral duty. As a country we are open to the world and wish to remain so. We want to live in harmony with our European neighbours. We need partners and friends in the world. We have them. We want to keep their friendship. And we can do this because our policies are dependable and predictable and because we honour our commitments. Our friends can rely on us. Our policies are determined by the United Nations Declaration on Human Rights and the European Convention on Human Rights. As the free part of a divided people we remain pledged to speaking on behalf of the human rights of all Germans. The Final Act of Helsinki imposes an obligation on all who have signed it. The renunciation of violence lies and will continue to lie at the heart of our peace policy. The rejection of violence embodied in the Charter of the United Nations applies to everyone everywhere.

We live on the line that divides East from West. This places a special burden on us for our security; to an exceptional degree it forces us to come to terms—intellectually and politically—with the Communist social system. It also obliges us to strive for greater mutual understanding. In our situation it is important that the picture of our country, of our people and of our history that the rest of the world has of us, is a living, accurate one. We need the friendship and goodwill of other peoples ...

Because of our geographic situation and our history we Germans are committed to fostering good relations with both West and East. For us Germans there are numerous historical ties with the East. We have a profound understanding of the cultural unity of Europe in all its variety and diversity. We regard our neighbours in Central and Eastern Europe as being a part of Europe, not only in this cultural sense.

We understand the need of all states for security. We appreciate the historically-rooted need of the Soviet Union for security. Nothing, however, justifies the Soviet Union's over-armament, which threatens the security of its neighbours and serves the end of political coercion. And nothing justifies Moscow's policy of expansion, which has led to the invasion of Afghanistan and is also placing constraints on the Polish people's freedom of determination ...

Even after the first signs of change appeared in the Soviet Union following the succession to the leadership of Mikhail Gorbachev in

March 1985, memories of the fate of earlier reform attempts caused official opinion in the Federal Republic (as elsewhere in the West) to exhibit a mixture of hopefulness and scepticism.

Document 23

STATEMENT OF CHANCELLOR HELMUT KOHL TO THE BUNDESTAG, ON HIS RETURN FROM MEETING MIKHAIL GORBACHOV IN MOSCOW, 10 November 1988

*Source: Verhandlungen des Deutschen Bundestages, 11.*Wahlperiode 1988, Stenographische Berichte, 106. Sitzung, 7280-84

. . .

What again impressed me in these talks was the soberness of analysis, the frankness with which problems were discussed but at the same time the determination, having chosen a course, to pursue it, however difficult ...

We discussed the historical basis of our relations. We re-affirmed our resolve to take the positive and constructive traditions of our common history as a starting point and build on them. We were in agreement on the evaluation of our talks and in our belief that there was now an opportunity to open a new chapter in our relations, one that offered a positive outlook ...

We spoke above all about developments in Europe and about the cultural and human dimension that these developments are assuming. General Secretary Gorbachov outlined his idea of a 'Common European House' and emphasized repeatedly that the USA and Canada were naturally an integral part of this. He also stressed that the systems of alliances should remain unaffected and the differing social orders should be mutually respected ... .

In all these talks I told General Secretary Gorbachov that, given the perspective of a Europe that is healing its old wounds, recalling its historical and cultural unity and seeking joint approaches to the future, we too, as Germans, wish to overcome the division of our fatherland ...

I also had very intensive and serious discussions with General Secretary Gorbachov on the situation in and around Berlin ...

. . .

... in his final appraisal of our meeting, General Secretary Gorbachov stated that we had experienced and helped to shape a 'major turning point' in German Soviet relations on the occasion of this visit to Moscow. I should like to make this phrase my own, adding that we wish to take maximum advantage of the favourable objective circumstances in the light of geo-political developments, which I outlined earlier, in order to raise our relations to a new, higher plane. We want to concentrate our political will and all our energy on setting in motion what can realistically be achieved at present, while not losing sight of our wider objectives as a result of the inevitable difficulties lurking in the details. We want to contribute to an overall improvement in the spirit of our relations in the interests of East-West ties and to the lasting establishment of good neighbourly relations for the benefit of all our European neighbours ...

With the ending of Cold War confrontation and after the setbacks of the so-called period of stagnation, we pin our hopes, henceforth, on the way being open for increased dialogue and cooperation in our continent. This will enable both West and East to concentrate on common future goals. It will also enable West and East to discharge their responsibilities towards the peoples of the Third World and to help building a peaceful future for all lands and peoples.

On the eve of the revolutionary events which were dramatically to alter the European landscape Helmut Kohl reaffirmed the Federal Republic's adherence to and reliance on the North Atlantic Alliance which had provided security for the Federal Republic through its own forty year history.

Document 24

'FORTY YEARS OF FREEDOM AND SECURITY UNDER THE NORTH ATLANTIC TREATY'; STATEMENT BY CHANCELLOR HELMUT KOHL, 4 April 1989

Source: 40 Jahre Außenpolitik der Bundesrepublik Deutschland. Eine Dokumentation. Herausgegeben vom Auswärtigen Amt, Bonn 1989, 556-58

... NATO is only a few weeks older than the Federal Republic of Germany. That our country can celebrate the 40th anniversary of its existence in peace—as it has been able to celebrate each day since its founding—is essentially thanks to NATO, and by no means self-evident ...

The incorporation of the Federal Republic of Germany into this alliance in 1955 was a visible indication to the whole world that the second German Republic had been admitted into the circle of Western democracies. In this way our new partners showed their acknowledgement of a policy for which one name stands above all: that of Konrad Adenauer. Under Adenauer our country opted for unequivocal ties with the West and clearly repudiated any idea of a 'special German way'. We have decided irrevocably in favour of the community of Western democracies, a free Europe and the transatlantic partnership.

This fundamental decision on the part of our people has been upheld by all succeeding federal governments. It is still shared by the overwhelming majority of our citizens today ...

40 years of NATO are 40 years of success. This is borne out by the peace in which our peoples live, free and under the rule of law. This is also borne out by the political conception, set out by the alliance in the Harmel Report of 1967, which is today still as relevant for the present and the future as it was then:

- maintenance of sufficient military strength and political solidarity in order to
- achieve, on this basis, more stable relations between West and East through dialogue and cooperation.

Our aim is the creation of a just and lasting order of peace in a Europe without divisions... .
NATO needs the Federal Republic of Germany and vice versa. This will remain so in the future ...
NATO is much more than a conventional military alliance. It is a community standing for peace and recognized values.

As the dramatic scenes which accompanied the breaching of the Berlin Wall on 9 November heralded the final crisis of the German Democratic Republic, hitherto the strong bastion of Moscow's East European empire, Foreign Minister Genscher moved to reassure the Federal Republic's eastern neighbours, and especially the Soviet Union.

Document 25

TELEPHONE CONVERSATION BETWEEN FOREIGN MINISTER GENSCHER AND SOVIET FOREIGN MINISTER EDUARD SCHEVARDNADSE, 11 November 1989.
Source: Umbruch in Europa. Die Ereignisse im 2. Halbjahr 1989. Eine Dokumentation. Herausgegeben vom Auswärtigen Amt, Bonn, 1990, 85

Today, 11th of November 1989, Foreign Minister Hans Dietrich Genscher had a telephone conversation with the soviet Foreign Minister Eduard Shevardnadse. He welcomed the recent decision of the GDR leaders to lift restrictions on travel. He thanked the Soviet Union for its understanding standpoint in this matter.

In their conversation Foreign Minister Genscher reaffirmed that the Federal Republic of Germany stood by all treaties that it has signed and by all commitments that it has undertaken. That included the Moscow Treaty, the Warsaw Treaty, the Treaty with the Republic of Czechoslovakia, the Basic Treaty with the GDR and the CSCE process. He told Shevardnadse that he had also assured the Polish Foreign Minister Skubiszevski of this in Warsaw on Friday.

Foreign Minister Genscher stressed the importance of advancing the CSCE process along constructive lines and pursuing energetically efforts towards disarmament. He said that the Federal Government attached great significance to the joint German Soviet Declaration of 13 June 1989. This, he said, had created the possibility of further strengthening ties between the Federal Republic of Germany and the Soviet Union on the basis of the Moscow Treaty. Foreign Minister Genscher made appreciative mention of the part played by General Secretary Gorbachev and Foreign Minister Shevardnadse in the important developments of the last few months and years.

Foreign Minister Genscher assured his opposite number that the Federal Government wished to see the reform movements in central and Eastern

Europe proceed without hindrance or upset. On the part of the Federal Republic of Germany nothing would be done to take advantage of difficulties arising from the reform movements. He stressed that we were interested in preserving a stable framework of relations.

Foreign Minister Shevardnadse thanked Foreign Minister Genscher for his initiative in choosing to make contact in this personal way. There was agreement between both ministers on the need for all states to exercise responsibility in the interest of stability in Europe.

Following the resignation of Erich Honecker after eighteen years as state and party chief, and the end of the short-lived regime of his successor, Egon Krenz, the Dresden SED chief Hans Modrow was elected to head the DDR Ministerial Council. On 20 December he and Chancellor Helmut Kohl met in Dresden.

Document 26

JOINT STATEMENT ISSUED FOLLOWING THE MEETING OF FEDERAL CHANCELLOR KOHL AND PRIME MINISTER MODROW IN DRESDEN, 19-20 December 1989.

Source: Umbruch in Europa, *154-58*

. . .

Federal Chancellor Kohl and Prime Minister Modrow agreed that a good-neighbourly relationship between the two German States was of great importance for stability in Europe and constituted a contribution to a new European architecture. Such a relationship is to be based on a shared responsibility for peace and on a community whose relations are subject to binding accords.

In their opinion the changes which have taken place so far justify the hope that the division of Europe can be overcome and that a new order of peace for Europe in line with the goals of the Final Act of Helsinki and other CSCE documents can be brought about. Such an order must be founded on unconditional respect for the principles and norms of international law, with particular regard to human rights and the right of peoples to self determination ... .

As unification loomed closer on the horizon, the Bonn government repeatedly rejected neutralism, insisted on its continued membership in NATO, and stressed the continuing importance of the transatlantic link with the North American democracies. After a visit to the Soviet Union 14-16 July, Chancellor Kohl was able to report that he and President Gorbachov had reached agreement which allowed for continued German membership in NATO.

Document 27

STATEMENT TO THE PRESS BY CHANCELLOR KOHL CON-
CERNING POLICY ON GERMANY AND HIS VISIT TO THE
SOVIET UNION, BONN, 17 July 1990

Source: Presse- und Informationsamt der Bundesregierung (ed.), *The Unification of Germany in 1990. A Documentation.* Bonn 1991, 65-67

An Agreement has now been reached on all external aspects between ourselves and the Soviet Union ...
FIRST,
The unification of Germany will involve the Federal Republic of Germany,
the GDR and all of Berlin.
SECOND,
With the establishment of the unity of Germany, Four Power rights and
responsibilities with regard to Germany as a whole and Berlin will be terminated. United Germany will acquire its full and unrestricted sovereignty at
the time of unification.
THIRD,
United Germany can decide freely and independently in exercise of its full
and unrestricted sovereignty whether it wants to belong to an alliance and,
if so, what alliance. This is in keeping with the CSCE Final Act.
I indicated that it was the view of the Government of the Federal Republic
of Germany that a united Germany would like to be a member of the
Atlantic Alliance and I know that this corresponds to the wishes of the GDR.
Prime Minister de Maizière made this clear yesterday and we confirmed this
in our discussion this morning ... .

Six months of negotiations between the foreign ministers of the four
occupation powers and the two German states resulted in the agreement of 12 September 1990

Document 28

TREATY ON THE FINAL CONDITIONS WITH RESPECT TO
GERMANY, MOSCOW, 12 September 1990
Source: Ibid., 99-102

ARTICLE 1

(1) The united Germany shall comprise the territory of the Federal Republic of Germany, the German Democratic Republic and the whole of Berlin.
Its external borders shall be the borders of the Federal Republic of Germany
and the German Democratic Republic and shall be definitive from the date

on which the present Treaty comes into force. The confirmation of the definitive nature of the borders of the unified Germany is an essential element of the peaceful order in Europe.

(2) The united Germany and the Republic of Poland shall confirm the existing border between them in a treaty that is binding under international law.

(3) The united Germany has no territorial claims whatsoever against other states and shall not assert any in the future ... .

. . .

ARTICLE 4

(1) The Governments of the Federal Republic of Germany, the German Democratic Republic and the Union of Soviet Socialist Republics will settle by treaty the conditions for and the duration of the presence of Soviet armed forces on the territory of the present German Democratic Republic and of Berlin, as well as the conduct of the withdrawal of these armed forces which will be completed by the end of 1994, in connection with the implementation of the undertaking of the Federal Republic of Germany and the German Democratic Republic referred to in paragraph 2 of Article 3 of the present Treaty ...

. . .

ARTICLE 6

The right of the united Germany to belong to alliances, with all the rights and responsibilities arising therefrom, shall not be affected by the present Treaty.

ARTICLE 7

(1) The French Republic, the Union of Soviet Socialist Republics, the United Kingdom of Great Britain and Northern Ireland and the United States of America hereby terminate their rights and responsibilities relating to Berlin and to Germany as a whole. As a result, the corresponding, related quadripartite agreements, decisions and practices are terminated and all related Four Power Institutions are dissolved.

(2) The united Germany shall have accordingly full sovereignty over its internal and external affairs ...

The treaty, signed in Moscow on 13 September 1990, came into force on 15 March 1991 on being ratified by the Soviet Union. Building on and extending the provisions of the Moscow Treaty of 12 August 1970, it established the framework for relations between the new German state and its former adversary. No mention is made in the Treaty of the economic assistance which the Federal Republic provided during the succeeding months.

Document 29

TREATY BETWEEN THE FEDERAL REPUBLIC OF GERMANY AND THE UNION OF SOVIET SOCIALIST REPUBLICS ON GOOD-NEIGHBOURLINESS, PARTNERSHIP AND COOPERATION:
Source: International Legal Materials, Vol XXX, No 2, March 1991, 505-14.

Article 1

The Federal Republic of Germany and the Union of Soviet Socialist Republics will, in developing their relations, be guided by the following principles: They will respect each other's sovereign equality, territorial integrity and political independence ... .

Article 2

[They] undertake to respect without qualification the territorial integrity of all States in Europe within their present frontiers.
They declare that they have no territorial claims whatsoever against any State and will not raise any in the future ... .

Article 3

[They] reaffirm that they will refrain from any threat or use of force which is directed against the territorial integrity or political independence of the other side or is in any way incompatible with the aims and principles of the United Nations Charter or with the CSCE Final Act ... .

Article 4

[They] will seek to ensure that armed forces and armaments are substantially reduced by means of binding effectively verifiable agreements in order to achieve ... a stable balance at a lower level ... which will suffice for defence but not for attack ... .

In view of its size and power-potential, and of the new importance acquired by the United Nations as a result of the Gulf crisis, the possibility of Germany's securing of a permanent seat on the Security Council appeared logical. Such a step could not be contemplated, however, until the constitutional crisis concerning the deployment of armed forces abroad was resolved. Here Foreign Minister Kinkel sets out briefly the German position.

Document 30

FOREIGN MINISTER KINKEL TO THE UNITED NATIONS
GENERAL ASSEMBLY, 23 September 1993
Source: *UN Document A/47/PV8*, 30 September 1992

... The system of collective security of the United Nations, and of regional arrangements like the CSCE, must be made a powerful instrument ... The Security Council is the guardian of international peace. Its effectiveness and credibility are of equal importance. A debate on reforming the Council is under way. We Germans will not take the initiative in this respect, but if change in the Council's composition is actually considered we too shall make known our intention to seek a permanent seat.

Notes

1. Alfred Grosser, *Germany in Our Time: A Political History of the Postwar Years*, New York, 1971, 291
2. Cited in Philip Windsor, 'West Germany in Divided Europe,' in F.S. Northedge, ed., *The Foreign Policies of the Powers*, London, 1968, 237
3. Wolfram F. Hanrieder, *The Stable Crisis. Two Decades of German Foreign Policy*, New York, 1970, 45; Grosser, *Germany in Our Time*, 291
4. Konrad Adenauer, *Memoirs 1945–1953*, transl. Beate Ruhm von Oppen, London, 1965, 259
5. Protocol on the Termination of the Occupation Regime in the Federal Republic of Germany, 23 October 1954, Selected Documents on Germany and the Question of Berlin, 1944–1961, London, HMSO, Cmnd. 1552, 209. See also Ch.2.
6. Konrad Adenauer, *Memoirs 1945–1953*, 260
7. Total restitution payments by the 1990s amounted to some DM 52 billion. See *Die Auswärtige Politik der Bundesrepublik Deutschland*, Cologne, 1972, 954
8. Cited in Gerald Freund, *Unholy Alliance: Russo-German Relations from the Treaty of Brest-Litovsk to the Treaty of Berlin*, London, 1957, 245
9. Karl Kaiser, *German Foreign Policy in Transition. Bonn Between East and West*, London, 1969, 90 f. See also Ch 3
10. Robert Gerald Livingston, 'United Germany: Bigger and Better', *Foreign Policy*, No 87, Summer 1992, 157-74
11. Ronald D. Asmus, 'Germany and America: Partners in Leadership?', *Survival*, XXXIII, No 6, November/December 1991, 546-66
12. Stuart Drummond, 'Germany: moving towards a new Ostpolitik', *The World Today*, Vol 49, No 7, July 1993, 132-35
13. Klaus Kinkel, 'Responsibility, Realism: Providing for the future German Foreign Policy in a World undergoing process of restructuring', *Frankfurter Allgemeine Zeitung* 19 March 1993, and 'NATO's enduring role in European security', *NATO Review*, Vol 40, No 5, October 1992, 3.
14. This reservation has been strongly re-emphasised by a part of the CDU/CSU, after they came into power in 1982.

6
Defence policy and the Armed Forces
Carl-Christoph Schweitzer

The Basic Law stipulates very clearly 1) the exclusively defensive aim of Germany's foreign and defence policies; 2) the exclusive power of the Federation to set up federal armed forces (Bundeswehr) and to subject them to rigorous political control and 3) the principle both of compulsory military service, if need be, and of the right of 'conscientious objection', the latter being linked to the obligation to serve the country in a 'civilian alternative service' *(Ziviler Ersatzdienst)*.

The constitutionally binding preamble of the Basic Law made it absolutely clear that the foreign and defence policies of the 'old' Federal Republic were committed to three basic goals: '... to preserve its national and political unity and to serve the peace of the world as an equal partner in a United Europe'.

Art. 26 (1) elaborates on the problem of war and peace in the context of these goals and states that 'acts tending to and undertaken with the intent to disturb the peaceful relations between nations, especially to prepare for aggressive war, shall be unconstitutional. They shall be made a punishable offence'.

Hence even to draw up offensive plans for military action would for the first time in German history constitute a violation of the constitution. Another significant break with the German past was the fact that a General Staff (Generalstab) was not established again when the Federal Republic was finally permitted to set up a new military force in 1955.

The rearming of West Germany after 1949 was debated for some five years and possibly would not have materialised at all, certainly not so relatively early after 1945/49, had it not been for the outbreak of the Korean War in 1950.[1]* Chancellor Adenauer, when 'offering' German rearmament to the Western Powers in 1950, was obviously motivated by German security interests (Doc.1). The actual setting up of the new armed forces was, in the end, part of a package which included West Germany's entry into the NATO alliance, her regaining of national sovereignty (with the continuing

* *Notes for this chapter begin on p. 171.*

exception of reservations previously imposed by agreements made at Potsdam in 1945 and Paris in 1954, see also Ch.5) and the renunciation of any further attempt to produce ABC weapons.[2] In addition the founding fathers themselves had made provision for giving up national sovereignty rights in favour not only of a 'supra-national' European organization but also of 'collective security arrangements' expressly referred to in Art. 24 of the Basic Law. In this connection it is important to point out that from the beginning practically all the German armed forces have been assigned to NATO's supreme command even in peace-time—quite in contrast to other NATO countries, above all to France, which in 1966 withdrew from the integrated military command of NATO altogether. The Federal Republic provided at times some 50 per cent of the NATO's land forces in Central Europe (excluding France), 50 per cent of the groundbased air-defence, 30 per cent of the combat aircraft, 100 per cent of the naval air forces in the Baltic and nearly 100 per cent of the naval forces in the Baltic. In absolute figures West Germany made the second biggest financial contribution to NATO, which adds up to a considerable portion of the overall federal budget.[3]

Apart from the articles that were in the Basic Law from the beginning, amendments were enacted in the field of defence after the allied decision of 1955 to rearm the Federal Republic. A first set of these amendments concerned the organizational structure of the armed forces. Art. 87a, enacted in 1956, stating that the 'numerical strength and general organizational structure shall be shown in the annual budget', was intended to ensure that parliament would not only provide the necessary money, but would also exercise a general oversight. Furthermore, Arts. 65a and 115 (as amended) of the Basic Law made certain that the supreme political control over the armed forces could not be called into question again. Here the law-makers were mindful of the Kaiserreich (1871–1918) and the Weimar Republic (1919–1933), not to speak of the Nazi regime.[4] In peacetime the supreme authority over the armed forces lies in the hands of a civilian minister of defence; in wartime it would be in the hands of the chancellor. Chancellor and minister of defence are, of course, politically responsible to Parliament.

The Bundestag has a special instrument of control through its Defence Commissioner (Wehrbeauftragter), a sort of Ombudsman for the armed forces. A continuous legal overview is guaranteed by its Committee on Defence. Finally, only the Bundestag as a whole, or its emergency subparliament (Gemeinsamer Ausschuß)[5] can determine constitutionally that the Federal Republic of Germany is at war, which would then be legally proclaimed by the head of state.

Euphemistically, the Basic Law does not envisage a 'state of war', but a 'state of defence'. In possible 'internal upheavals', the powers of the federal government to use troops would be very narrow indeed. Art. 87a (4) states: '... should ... the police forces and the Federal Border Guard [Bundesgrenzschutz] be inadequate, the Federal Government may use the armed forces to support the police and the Federal Border Guard in the protection of civilian property and in combating organized and military armed insurgents ...'.

In accordance with Art. 12a the Bundestag, in 1956, passed the Law of Compulsory Military Service (*Wehrpflichtgesetz*, Doc.2a) as well as that for Civilian Alternative Service (*Ziviler Ersatzdienst*, Doc.2b). Today a very heated and still 'open' public debate revolves around the problem of how to improve the process of recognition of a conscientious objector. The difficulty lies in defining and proving a point of conscience.[6] An additional factor in this problem is that in the future the Federal Republic seems likely to have a serious shortage of professional soldiers. Additional constitutional provisions have been introduced for the calling-up of men and women in times of a national emergency, with women serving in non-military activities. In an age of equality between men and women and, above all, in view of the shortages in the nursing profession, another as yet undecided public debate has turned on the possibility of once more revising the Basic Law in order to make a call-up of women possible even in peace-time. So far the political odds are against such an innovation.

One of the main features of the new German armed forces has been the extreme care devoted to, and emphasis put on, the safeguarding of democratic standards in the day-to-day life of conscripts and professional soldiers. The Germans have given this phenomenon the overall term (as peculiar as it is untranslatable) of Innere Führung (Leadership) (Doc.3), meaning certain principles of conduct within the armed forces. A very extensive Central Service Regulation (Zentrale Dienstvorschrift) of 1972 was devoted to this problem which has since been the subject of further official pronouncements. The principle of Innere Führung was given legal force by Parliament through the Soldiers' Act (Soldatengesetz, Doc.4) and the Military Appeal (Complaint) Act (Wehrbeschwerdeordnung) for the armed forces (Doc.5). Innere Führung is based on the central hypothesis that it is necessary in a democratic society with a viable military establishment to strike a balance between obligations and rights of the individual in the armed forces. Its members have obligations, above all, to defend their country. While on this duty, they have to forego some basic civil rights 'for the time being', such as the right to assemble at any time or to associate themselves with others. They retain, however—and this is the main point—other important rights, since they remain citizens, or citizens in uniform, as another German concept puts it. This was very clearly embodied in the Central Service Regulation (Doc.3). Above all, the members of the armed services can claim to be treated in accordance with their basic constitutional right to the 'inviolability of their human dignity' (Art. 1, Basic Law); they have the right to make complaints against superiors (Doc.5), and they are part of a community in which other principles are supposed to be cherished, such as comradeship, loyalty, determination of purpose, tradition (Doc.6) or the claim to a continuing general and professional education within the forces. The latter applies especially to the field of civic studies, which is on the weekly curriculum for all units. All these rights are committed—over and above the normal enforcement of laws—to the special care and supervision of the Defence Commissioner. He receives complaints directly from any member of the armed services, investigates them and issues a yearly report on his findings to the Bundestag (Doc.7).

Throughout its relatively short history, the Bundeswehr has been confronted by problems not of its own making, i.e. by problems emerging from the overall domestic and international environment. In the first years of its existence the Bundeswehr had to grapple with the legacies of the Third Reich. In the 1950s most Germans did not, really, want an army again. In those years, especially after the stationing of the first atomic weapons on German soil, the country resounded with slogans such as the famous 'count me out' ('Ohne mich') in regard to the rearming of West Germany. These views were by no means confined to the young. All this explains the decrees and laws mentioned above, to provide a maximum of democratic guarantees for the members of the armed forces—to be used as guidelines, also, for the formation of a new corps of officers.

In the 1980s, new developments took place in the national and international situation. A second peace movement arose some of whose aims were reflected in the slogan of young demonstrators at the National Conference of the German Protestant Churches (Kirchentag) in Hamburg in 1981: 'What will the governments do when they start their war and we just won't show up?'(see also Ch.13, Doc.9). The West German peace movement had not only been part of a larger Western European peace movement,[7] but it is was actually at the forefront of that effort. Hundreds of thousands marched for peace in West Germany in 1981 and 1982. There were, in the West German Federal Republic, a great number of calls for peace (Friedensappelle) from all walks of life.[8] The most radical one was the Krefelder Appell of 1981, directed against the NATO dual-track decision of 1979 (Doc.8). The people behind such appeals could by no means be dismissed as communist stooges, as was also made clear by the last Social-Democratic defence minister Hans Apel in a key address in October 1982 (Doc.9).

Chancellor Schmidt had to leave office in 1982 because he was unable to carry his party with him on the road towards ratifying the NATO Dual Track decision (see Ch.5). These arrangements were finally passed by the Bundestag at the beginning of Helmut Kohl's chancellorship and his coalition with the Free Democrats, who had changed sides non the least because of that overall issue in 1982-83 (see also Ch.8).

Thereafter problems of German defence policy were part of the wider discussion within NATO, the European Union, the WEU, and formed part of the CSCE and the European-US dialogue because Washington announced a reduction of US forces in the European theatre. A side-line was the setting up of an integrated Franco-German Corps which caused irritation in Washington and other NATO capitals during its early stages; however, these problems have been overcome after other such integrated corps have been set up.

With the final Two-plus-Four Agreements on the reunification of Germany (see also Ch.5) the former GDR Army, (Nationale Volks-sarmee, NVA) became part of the Bundeswehr, with many high ranking officers having to be retired early because of their involvement in former SED party activities (see also Ch.4). In addition, the difficult process of the withdrawal of some 500,000 Soviet troops from East Germany when reunification came, had to be carried out by the middle of 1994. The new Germany has restricted itself since to a total number of armed forces in the order of 370,000, probably to be diminished even further, due to both lack of funds and the absence of meaningful military threats from the former East.

The German domestic political scene was, in 1993, dominated by the controversy between the Government and the opposition parties over the question of German military participation in both NATO out of area conflicts (lack of German participation in the Iraq/ Kuwait war was as an important issue, as were the ongoing problems in the former Yugoslavia), and in UN missions generally whether peace-keeping, humanitarian, or fighting operations. Both pacifists and legal experts interpreted the Basic Law as prohibiting such missions, in view of Article 87 of the Basic Law, and were in conflict with other experts who stressed that Article 24 of the Basic Law authorizes any German government to participate in arrangements of collective security and that this can be applied automatically to the new national and international exigencies in the 1990s and who further argue that the reunited Germany must, fifty years after the end of the Second World War, finally shoulder its full responsibility in world affairs, with or without becoming a permanent member of the United Nations Security Council. The issue was finally decided by the Bundesverfassungsericht in 1994.

Document 1

MEMORANDUM OF CHANCELLOR KONRAD ADENAUER
TO THE ALLIED HIGH COMMISSION ON THE SECURITY OF
THE FEDERAL REPUBLIC, 29 AUGUST 1950

Source: K. von Schubert (ed.), *Sicherheitspolitik der Bundesrepublik Deutschland, Dokumentation*, Teil I, 79ff.

I.

The development in the Far East has aroused alarm and uncertainty within the German population. Confidence that the western world would be prepared swiftly and effectively to react to aggression against Western Europe is in the process of dwindling to such an extent as to cause fear, and has led to a dangerous lethargy in the German population ... .

II.

According to confirmed reports, two corps of mobile troops with nine motorized divisions and four tank corps with thirteen divisions, that is to say, a total of twenty-two motorized and tank divisions of Soviet troops are presently located in the East Zone ... . Their deployment displays the motorized mobile troops on the front line, the heavy tank units behind them, with special artillery and anti aircraft units in between. This picture must be designated as a marked offensive deployment.

The number of tanks ready for action must be assumed to be 5000 to 6000 ...

In addition to these extraordinarily strong Soviet Russian forces, the building up of the Volkspolizei [People's Police] has made considerable progress in the last few months. Their development from police force to police army demands attention. In the last few months, around 70,000 men have been taken out of the General Police of the East Zone and organized into military-like formations and have been militarily trained ... .

It can be assumed that the Volkspolizei will have some 150,000 men in the near future who, according to the overall plan, should be brought up to around 300,000 men.

All information regarding the setting of the objective, which is being given to these troops by the Soviet and East Zone governments indicates that it would be their task in the near future to free West Germany from its allied tyrants, to eliminate the 'collaborating government' of the Federal Republic, and to unify West Germany with the East Zone in a satellite-like state. Along with the public declarations of the East German politicians Pieck and Ulbricht, one must assume that preparations are being made in the East Zone for an operation which, from many viewpoints, brings to mind the development of the action in Korea ... .

III.

As a counteracting force to this adversary there are two American and British divisions apiece, and one French unit in West Germany. Apart from the weak forces comprising the customs guards, the Federal Government has no power at its disposal. In the British Zone there is a police force which is organized on a local level ... .

IV.

The problem of the security of the Federal Republic, to begin with, is a problem of foreign affairs. The defence of the Federation against outside attacks lies primarily in the hands of the occupation troops. The Chancellor has repeatedly requested a strengthening of the occupation troops and, herewith, renews this request in a most urgent form. For the strengthening of the allied occupation troops alone can make visibly known to the people the determination of the Western powers that West Germany will actually be defended under emergency conditions ... .

The Chancellor has furthermore repeatedly made clear that he is prepared, if an international West European army is to be set up, to provide a contribution in the form of a German contingent. It has since been clearly stated that the Chancellor rejects a remilitarization of Germany through setting up independent national military forces.

V.

The security problems of the Federal Territory present themselves moreover under a domestic perspective ... .

The Federal government, therefore, proposes to set up immediately, on a federal basis, a police force which must be strong enough to guarantee its internal security

. . .

Because preparations must be immediately begun, it is necessary that the Allied High Commission furnish the Federal government with the directive for the necessary steps to initiate the creation of this police force.

The democratic control of this police force shall be guaranteed through a committee set up by the Bundestag which would be given the power to inspect the build-up and the personnel arrangements of this police force.

International control of this force could be exercised by the Allied Office for Military Security ... .

From 1956 right through to the present the Federal Ministry of Defence has relied on calling up males above the age of eighteen— roughly 51,500 every three months to make up between 45 and 50 per cent (i.e. some 220,000 men) of the total strength of the three services. There is now a serious shortage of senior NCOs whose duties are, therefore, often assigned to corporals or junior sergeants.[9]

Document 2a

COMPULSORY MILITARY SERVICE ACT *(WEHRPFLICHTGE-SETZ)* 21 JULY 1956

Source: BGBl., I, 1956, 651ff.
[Subsequently ammended several times, ed.]

1. Extent of Compulsory Military Service …

§ 1 *General Compulsory Military Service*
(1) From the age of 18 onwards all men who are German citizens according to the Basic Law are obliged to perform military service, if the following conditions are fulfilled:

1. If they have a permanent residence within the domain of this law or
2. If they have their residence outside the territory of the German Reich as it stood on December 31, 1937 and either
   a) had their last German permanent residence within the domain of this law or
   b) possess a passport or certificate of nationality of the Federal Republic of Germany or have put themselves under its protection in some other way.

(2) Compulsory military service is suspended for Germans who have their permanent residence and means of subsistence outside the Federal Republic of Germany if the facts support the belief that they intend to keep their permanent residence abroad. This applies particularly to German citizens with a dual nationality.

. . .

§ 5 *Basic Military Service*[10]
(1) Conscripts up to the age of twenty-eight perform a basic military service. Those conscripts who are used mainly for special military duties because of their professional qualifications or those who were not conscripted before the age of twenty-eight because of a military service exemption … have to perform military service up to the age of thirty-two. Basic military service lasts for fifteen months and begins as a rule in the calendar year when the conscript reaches his nineteenth birthday. Applications from the conscript to perform basic military service before the call-up of conscripts of his age should be met but not before the conscript's eighteenth birthday.

. . .

§ 12 *Temporary Exemption from Military Service*
(1) Those who are temporarily exempt from military service are:

1. those who are temporarily unable to perform military service

2. those who ... are serving a prison sentence or ... are being cared for in a psychiatric hospital or ... are in a social-therapeutic institution or in an institution where withdrawal treatment for addicts is administered.

3. Anyone who is currently placed in the care of a guardian.

(2) Conscripts who are preparing themselves for holy orders ... are exempted on application.

(3) If a conscript has agreed to stand for an election to the Bundestag or to one of the Länder parliaments he will be exempted until that election. If he has taken his seat, he may only be called up for service during parliamentary recesses for the duration of his term of office unless he requests otherwise.

(4) A conscript should be exempted from military service,

1. if being called up for military service would mean for him a special personal, in particular, a domestic; economic or professional hardship. Such would be the case, as a rule, if the calling up of a conscript put at risk either a) his provision for his family or needy relatives or other needy people for whom he must supply a livelihood on either legal or moral grounds or b) if particular distress were to result for his nearest kin.

2 . If the conscript is indispensable for the upkeep and maintenance of his own or his family's farm or firm.

3. If the calling up of the conscript would interfere with
a) a period of training which was already greatly advanced
b) his secondary education leading to a university degree or a diploma of higher education
c) primary professional training or the first part thereof

and in the case of c) when neither a university degree nor a diploma of an institution of higher education has been obtained, nor when the normal length of the training or part of the training exceeds four years.

. . .

§ 25 *Effects of Conscientious Objection*

Anyone who objects to taking part in an armed conflict between states for reasons of conscience and therefore refuses to perform armed service in war must render civilian service outside the armed forces. He can be recruited to unarmed service within the armed forces if he applies for this.

The alternative civilian service (in hospitals, nursing homes for the aged and disabled, in forestry work etc.) lasted one month longer for conscripts recognized as conscientious objectors than the term for those serving in the armed forces. Hitherto special tribunals have had to take the decision to recognize conscientious objectors. It has now been decided to abolish these tribunals and to extend the term for those serving in the 'civilian alternative' to twenty months, as against fifteen months in the armed forces.

Document 2b

CIVILIAN ALTERNATIVE SERVICE ACT *(ZIVILDIENSTGE-SETZ),* 3 JANUARY 1960, HERE AS AMENDED 26 JUNE 1981
Source: BGBl., I, 1981, 553ff.

1. *Duties of Civilian Alternative Service*
In civilian alternative service, recognized conscientious objectors fulfil duties which serve the public welfare with priority in the social services area.

2. *Organization of Civilian Alternative Service*
(1) This law will be executed by the federal administration, in so far as not otherwise determined herein.

. . .

7. *Fitness*
Fitness for civilian alternative service is determined by the fitness standard applied to the military service. Those qualified for military service can be drafted into civilian alternative service; those momentarily not fit for military service are momentarily not fit for civilian alternative service, and those not fit for military service are not fit for civilian alternative service. In compliance with Art.8, Para. 2 of the law of compulsory military service, types of employment established on the basis of the physician's examination must be taken into consideration in the assignment of activities for the men who are liable to serve.

8. *Unfit for Civilian Alternative Service*
Not to be called upon for civilian alternative service are:
(1) those not capable of civilian alternative service,
(2) those under guardianship.

. . .

19. *Conscription*
(1) Those liable to serve will be called up for civilian alternative service according to the conscription regulations of the Minister for Labour and Social Affairs [now Minister of Youth, Family and Health Affairs], as long as they are not transferred according to section (2) below to a term of employment according to this law. Those who are discharged from the basic military service after having been recognized as conscientious objectors should be called up immediately for civilian alternative service.
(2) Service in the armed forces already begun can be commuted through an agreement in the form of a written reply from one of the administrative offices set up by the Federal Minister of Defence to a term of employment according to this law, if the soldier is recognized as a conscientious objector.

. . .

24. *Length of Civilian Alternative Service*
(1) Men liable to serve who have not yet completed their twenty-eighth year render civilian alternative service. Those liable to serve who, with their consent, intend to fulfil particular duties in the civilian alternative service remain liable, after completion of their professional training, to render civilian alter-

native service until the completion of their thirty-second year. Civilian alternative service lasts sixteen months ... .

Document 3

REGULATION 10/1 OF 1972 (ZDV), ISSUED BY THE MINISTRY OF DEFENCE, ON PRINCIPLES OF LEADERSHIP *(INNERE FÜHRUNG)* IN THE ARMED FORCES

Source: Ministry of Defence

Chapter 2: Leadership

I. Aims

. . .

202. It is the aim of *Innere Führung* (Leadership) to enforce the performance of the soldier's duties, and at the same time to guarantee his rights. The principles of Leadership, on which the order of the federal armed forces depends, balance out the tension between the rights and the duties of the soldier ...

. . .

205. The principles and practices of Leadership are adaptable to the intellectual, political, and technical development within society ...

II. Principles

206. (1) *Innere Führung* (Leadership) serves the federal armed forces' state of preparedness within the framework of our legal order. The principles of Leadership are therefore firmly established in the Basic Law, in military laws, decrees, ordinances, and service regulations.

(2) The senior officer should utilize the latitude which these regulations allow, in exercising Leadership ...

. . .

210. The legally determined duties of the soldier are derived from the requisites of military service.

. . .

212. Senior officers and subordinates alike are responsible for cohesion within the federal armed forces. This presupposes trust, which must be valued and which demands mutual respect.

(1) The representatives of the other ranks *(Vertrauensmänner)*, of the non commissioned officers and the officers should contribute to, and thereby strengthen, in the areas for which they have been elected, the inner order of the federal armed forces towards responsible cooperation between superiors and subordinates, as well as the maintenance of trust between comrades ... [the election of the Vertrauensmänner is prescribed by law].

. . .

IV. Self-Image of the Soldier

222. The federal armed forces have many relationships with society at large. The federal armed forces, in so far as their tasks permit, take part in the intellectual, political and technical development of society.

223. Today's soldier is not only a soldier. He may also be, for example, a member of a church, a party, a professional organization, association or other organizations. From this, many links have been forged between the federal armed forces and society.

224. Our liberal society is characterized by a plurality of interests, opinions, conceptions of values and aims (Pluralism). Willingness for objectivity, compromise, and democratic decisions guarantee that conflicting interests and opinions can be resolved without use of force. This willingness also applies to the federal armed forces if, during the fulfilment of duties, they come into conflict with other groups ...

. . .

232. Soldiers can be proud of their profession. Like members of other professions, this pride in the soldier's profession depends on his own performance but, above all, on the performance of the group, the unit, or the task force.

. . .

234. The tasks of the federal armed forces in the midst of a modern industrial society demand from each superior
  – Education and specialized knowledge,
  – Powers of judgement and decision,
  – Commitment and ability to differentiate,
  – Loyalty and comradeship.

. . .

Document 1

FEDERAL LAW GOVERNING THE LEGAL STATUS OF SOLDIERS (SOLDIERS' ACT, *SOLDATENGESETZ*), 19 MARCH 1956, AS AMENDED IN 1975

Source: BGBl., I, 1975, 2275ff.

. . .

§ 6 *A Soldier's Rights as a Citizen*
A soldier enjoys the same rights as any other citizen. His rights are limited within the framework of the requirements of military service through the obligations placed on him by law.

§ 7 *The Basic Duty of a Soldier*
A soldier has the duty to serve the Federal Republic of Germany loyally and to defend valiantly the rights and liberties of the German people.

§ 8 *Commitment to the Democratic Basic Order*
A soldier must recognize the free democratic basic order as defined by the Basic Law and show himself committed to its preservation by his whole behaviour.

§ 9 *The Oath and Solemn Pledge*

(1) Professional soldiers and short-service soldiers must take the following oath of office:

'I swear to serve the Federal Republic of Germany loyally and to defend valiantly the rights and liberties of the German people, so help me God.'

The oath can also be taken without the words 'so help me God'. If a Federal law allows members of a religious body to use another term of affirmation instead of the words 'I swear' the member of the religious body may use this form of affirmation.

(2) Soldiers performing military duty because they are required to by compulsory military service pledge themselves to their duties by the following solemn promise 'I promise to serve the Federal Republic of Germany loyally and to defend valiantly the rights and liberties of the German people'.

§ 10 *Duties of a Superior Officer*

(1) A superior officer must set an example by his behaviour and devotion to duty.

(2) He has the duty to supervise and is responsible for the discipline of those under his command.

(3) He must take care of those under his command.

(4) He may only give orders in the exercise of duty and in compliance with international law, the national law and service regulations.

(5) He must bear the responsibility for his orders. He must see that orders are carried out in a way that is appropriate to the circumstances.

(6) Officers and non-commissioned officers must, both on and off duty, preserve that restraint in their language which is necessary to uphold the confidence and trust placed in them as superior officers.

§ 11 *Obedience*

(1) A soldier must obey his superiors. He must carry out their orders to the best of his ability, to the letter, conscientiously and promptly. A soldier is not guilty of disobedience if he refuses to carry out an order which violates human dignity or which has not been given in the line of command. The false supposition that such an order had been given only absolves the soldier from responsibility if the mistake was unavoidable and if he could not, in the circumstances known to him, be expected to oppose the order by lawful means.

(2) An order may not be followed when a punishable offence would thereby be committed. If the soldier carries out the order notwithstanding he can be blamed only if he recognizes or if it is apparent from the circumstances known to him that a punishable offence is thereby being committed.

§ 12 *Comradeship*

The cohesion of the armed forces rests essentially on comradeship. This obliges every soldier to respect the dignity, honour and rights of his comrades and to stand by them in distress and danger. This includes the mutual recognition of, consideration for, and respect for, different outlooks and ideas.

. . .

§ 15 *Political Activity*
(1) A soldier may not while on active service promote or discredit a particular political view. The right of the soldier to express his own opinion among his comrades remains intact.
(2) Within military quarters and installations and off duty the right of free expression is restricted by the basic rules of comradeship. A soldier must behave in a way that does not seriously disturb the cooperative spirit of the service. Above all a soldier may not actively canvas support for a political group by holding meetings, disseminating literature or working as a representative of a political organisation. Mutual respect must not be put at risk.
(3) A soldier may not wear uniform at a political meeting.
(4) A soldier may not as a superior officer influence his subordinates for or against a political opinion.

§ 16 *Behaviour in Other Countries*
Outside the domain of the Basic Law a soldier is forbidden to involve himself in the affairs of the country where he is residing.

§ 17 *Behaviour On and Off Duty*
(1) A soldier must maintain discipline and respect the rank of a superior officer also off duty.
(2) His behaviour must be fitting to the high standing of the armed forces as well as to the respect and trust which his duties as a soldier command. When off duty and not present in his military quarters or on military installations he must behave in such a way that he does not seriously impair the high standing of the armed forces or the respect and trust which his official position demands.

. . .

Document 5

MILITARY APPEAL (COMPLAINT) ACT *(WEHRBESCHWERDE-ORDNUNG),* 23 DECEMBER 1956

Source: BGBl., I, 1956

The Bundestag has passed the following law:

§ 1 *The Right of Complaint*
(1) A soldier may complain, if he considers himself to have been improperly treated by a superior or a section of the armed forces or if he feels himself to have been hurt by the unsoldierly behaviour of his comrades.
(2) A complaint can also be based upon the fact that no response to a petition of his has been forthcoming after two weeks have elapsed without adequate reasons being given.
(3) A complaint against an official judgement of personal performance cannot be entertained.
(4) Collective complaints are not permitted. The Right of Petition according to Art. 17 of the Basic Law is thus restricted.

. . .

§ 4 *Mediation and Expression of Views*

(1) The complainant may, before registering a complaint, call upon a mediator, if he feels personally offended and a favourable settlement seems possible to him.

(2) The mediator may be called upon at the earliest after one night has elapsed and must be called upon within a week of the complainant's becoming aware of the cause for complaint.

(3) A complainant must choose as a mediator a soldier who enjoys his personal confidence and who has no part in the matter. A soldier who has been called upon as a mediator may only refuse with good reason to carry out the mediation. Direct superiors of the complainant or the one about whom the complaint is being made ... and the 'man of confidence' (Vertrauensmann) may not take on the role of mediator.

(4) The mediator should personally familiarise himself with the subject matter of the complaint and make an effort to ensure a settlement.

(5) If a complainant asks the person he has complained about to have a discussion either before the mediation or instead of it then the latter must give him the opportunity to put forward his point of view.

. . .

§ 7 *Failure to Meet the Deadline*

If the complainant is prevented from adhering to a deadline either by military duty, act of God or other unavoidable occurrence, the deadline will not expire until three days after the ending of the obstruction.

. . .

§10 *Preparation of the Decision Regarding the Complaint*

(1) The superior who takes the final decision in the matter has to clarify the issue by way of oral or written proceedings. He may commission an officer to clarify the issue. A short concluding report must be made on all oral proceedings, in writing ... .

. . .

§ 12 *Notification of the Final Decision*

(1) The decision must be made in writing. The reasons for the decision must be given ... .

(2) In so far as the substance of the complaint concerns an action which is subject to prosecution under the legal code involved, the matter must be handed over immediately to the relevant office of the public prosecutor ... .

. . .

§ 13 *Contents of the Decision*

(1)In so far as the complaint proves to be justified, the decision must be complied with ... . In this connection orders or measures which are proved to have been out of order or irrelevant [unzulässig oder unsachgemäß] must be revoked or changed. If the relevant order has been already executed, or become irrelevant, it must be made clear [in the decision] that the order should not have been given. Measures called for but not taken must be executed, as far as this is still possible.

———

The directive below is the second of its kind, the first having been issued in 1965 by the then CDU-governed Cabinet. In its introduction to the directive of 1982 the then Social Democratic-led Ministry of Defence said, interestingly enough, that 'for instance' para. 17 of the old directive was 'historically not tenable'; this paragraph had asserted that it was 'a part of the good tradition of the German military, that ever since the time of the Prussian reforms [during and after the Napoleonic Wars] the German army has participated in political thinking and been ready to take on political responsibilities.'

Document 6

NEW DIRECTIVE ON THE PROBLEM OF TRADITIONS IN THE ARMED FORCES *(NEUE TRADITIONSRICHTLINIEN DER BUNDESWEHR)*, ISSUED BY THE MINISTRY OF DEFENCE 20 SEPTEMBER 1982

Source: Ministry of Defence press release, 20 September 1982

I. *Basic Principles*

1. Tradition is the passing on of values and norms. They are formed through a value-orientated analysis of the past. Tradition binds generations, safeguards an identity, and builds a bridge between the past and the future. Tradition is an essential foundation of man's culture. It presupposes an understanding of the historical, political and social context.
2. The yardsticks for an understanding and preservation of traditions in the German Federal armed forces are the Basic Law and the delegated assignments and duties of the army. The Basic Law is the response to history. It allows much latitude yet entails definite limits.

    The portrayal of common, united values and a democratic awareness of the armed forces is the foundation of the preservation of their tradition.
. . .
5. Political-historical education contributes decisively to the development of a common understanding of tradition in conformity with the Basic Law and an up-to-date preservation of that tradition. This demands an approach that incorporates the whole of German history and omits nothing.
6. The history of the German armed forces has not been without abrupt changes of a serious nature. The armed forces were both instruments and victims of political abuse during the period of National Socialism. An unjust regime, such as the Third Reich, cannot found a tradition.
. . .

15. In the preservation of tradition in the German Federal armed forces, such records of conduct and experiences from history should be preserved which, as ethical and constitutional, free and democratic traditions, can serve as examples and are worthy of remembrance today.

16. In the preservation of tradition in the German Federal armed forces, events should be remembered such as those in which soldiers, beyond their military performance, took part in progressive political activities which contributed to the emergence of a mature citizenry and led the way to a free, republican and democratic Germany.

17. In maintaining the tradition of the German Federal armed forces special emphasis should be placed on the following political stances and modes of behaviour:

1) Critical acceptance of German history, love of the homeland and mother country, orientation not only towards success and the successful, but also towards the suffering of the persecuted and the humiliated.

2) Political participation and common responsibility, awareness of democratic values, judgment without prejudice, tolerance, readiness and ability to discuss the ethical aspects of military service, the will for peace.

3) Conscientious obedience and loyal fulfilment of duties in everyday life, comradeship, determination and will to fight when defence is required.

. . .

20. The German Federal armed forces preserve their own established traditions, which should be further developed. Those included above all are:

1) The mission to preserve peace in freedom as the foundation of a soldier's commitment.

2) Abstention from creating ideologically-motivated images of an enemy or from cultivating feelings of hatred.

3) Participation in the Atlantic Alliance and comradely cooperation with Allied troops on the basis of common values.

4) The model of 'Citizen in Uniform' and the principles of Innere Führung.

5) The active contribution to the shaping of democracy through the role of the soldier as a citizen.

6) An open-minded attitude to social change and the readiness for contact with the civilian citizen.

7) Assistance to the civilian population in emergency and catastrophe at home and abroad.

These are unchangeable characteristics of the German Federal armed forces.

These annual reports, regularly debated in Parliament, often touch on points of principle relating to the overall situation of the armed forces within state and society today. Their main purpose is, however, to list, evaluate and act upon complaints lodged by the members of the forces. In 1980 (dealt with in 1981, see Deutscher Bundestag, 9th leg. per., Drucksache 9/1406) for instance, 400 complaints were brought forward. Of those, sixty-nine concerned problems of conscientious objectors, sixty-eight questions of human dignity, sixty-six the principle of equality, fifty-three general principles of the Basic Law, forty-nine violations of the inviolability of the individual, forty-five problems of freedom of expression and so on. The incident listed below may be seen as typical of the work of the Defence Commissioner. One of the most serious incidents investigated by the Commissioner (and brought to court) occurred in 1962 in Nagold during a river-crossing as part of a military exercise which led to loss of life.

Document 7

REPORT OF THE DEFENCE COMMISSIONER TO THE BUNDESTAG FOR THE YEAR 1963, ISSUED 1965

Source: Deutscher Bundestag, 4th legislative period, Drucksache 4/2305, 13

. . .

4. *Maltreatment of a Subordinate*
A company 1st sergeant kicked a soldier who was lying on his bed and sleeping during barracks' detail, in order to wake him. The company 1st sergeant was sentenced to detention.

. . .

Private 1st class A., member of a signal company, filed a complaint with the Defence Commissioner regarding the following incident:

After reveille, he and a few other soldiers from his unit were ordered to stay in quarters until 8 a.m. There they lay down fully dressed upon the beds and he, the complainant, fell asleep. At around 7.40 a.m. the company 1st sergeant woke him with a 'kick in the loins'. He requested verification of his grievances.

The regimental commander, whom the Defence Commissioner had requested to investigate the matter, established that the statements of private 1st class A. did not prove true on all counts. According to his findings, the incident occurred in the following manner:

Following the end of reveille, private 1st class A. and some other soldiers who were not taking part in the company's general detail, were sent to the quarters for barracks' detail.

As the company 1st sergeant went through the mens' quarters during this detail, he established that the private 1st class, and soldiers B. and C., were lying on their beds sleeping. Upon his loud shout, B. and C. got up, while A. remained lying. In order to motivate him to get up, the company 1st sergeant kicked him in the hip region.

The assertion of private 1st class A. that he received a kick 'in the loins' was not confirmed by the medical officer who had examined him; signs of use of violence were not established. And furthermore, because witnesses agreed that they had not had the impression that the company 1st sergeant had intended to abuse private 1st class A., the incident was not reported to the public prosecutor's office. The company 1st sergeant was sentenced to three days detention. In light of the company 1st sergeant's irreproachable conduct up to the time of the incident, the sentence was suspended in favour of a five months probation period.

The Defence Commissioner considered the settlement of the matter appropriate ... .

This appeal, one of many at the time in the Federal Republic, but the most widely publicized, was issued jointly by individuals and groups from the churches, the trade unions, the ecological movements, youth organizations (in particular from the socialist and liberal parties), some members of the Bundestag (of the Social Democratic Party only), teachers, doctors, university professors, novelists, former officers of the Bundeswehr and, last but not least, sections of the Communist Party of Germany (DKP). By the end of 1981, it was claimed that some one million signatures had been collected.

Document 8

APPEAL OF KREFELD *(KREFELDER APPELL)* AGAINST NATO'S DUAL TRACK DECISION OF 1979, ISSUED IN NOVEMBER 1980
Source: *Unsere Zeit*, 8 November 1980

NATO resolution a fateful mistake
European nations should not be exposed to unbearable risks

More and more obviously the NATO rearmament resolution of 12 December 1979 is proving to be a fateful mistake. The hope for agreements between the USA and the Soviet Union over a restriction of Euro-strategic arms systems before a new generation of American middle-range nuclear weapons is stationed in Western Europe will apparently not be fulfilled.

A year after Brussels, [the taking of the decision, ed.] not even the commencement of such talks is in sight. On the contrary: the newly elected president of the USA frankly declares that he does not even want to accept the Salt II treaty on the restriction of Soviet and American strategic nuclear weapons and therefore does not want to pass it on to the Senate for ratification.

However, the American refusal to ratify the treaty would unavoidably push the chance of talks on restricting Euro-strategic nuclear arms into the distant future. A suicidal arms race would not be stopped at the last moment; its increasing acceleration together with increasingly specific speculations about the possibility of limiting a nuclear war necessarily exposes the European nations, above all, to unbearable risks.

The participants in the Krefeld Talks of 15 and 16 November 1980 therefore jointly appeal to the Federal government:

> To withdraw their consent to stationing Pershing II rockets and cruise missiles in Central Europe; to take an attitude within the alliance which no longer leaves room to suspect our country of wanting to be the forerunner of a new nuclear arms race which would endanger the Europeans above all.

Worry about recent developments is growing among the general public. The possibilities of an alternative security policy are being discussed with more and more determination. Such deliberations are of great importance for the democratic process of opinion-forming and can contribute to preventing our nation from suddenly being confronted with a *fait accompli*.

The whole population is therefore asked to support this appeal in order to enforce by unceasing and increasing pressure of public opinion a security policy:

> which does not permit Central Europe to be equipped as a nuclear arms platform for the USA; disarmament is considered more important than deterrent; the development of the armed forces is to be orientated to achieve these goals.

Krefeld, 16 November 1980

Document 9

SPEECH BY THE LONG-SERVING SOCIAL DEMOCRATIC MINISTER OF DEFENCE, HANS APEL, DELIVERED ON 27 OCTOBER 1982 TO THE COMMANDING OFFICERS OF ALL THREE SERVICES AT THEIR REGULAR (25th) MEETING IN INGOLSTADT

Source: Ministry of Defence press release, 27 October 1982

, , ,

20. The Bonn peace demonstration and its non-violent course made it clear to everyone that it expresses the motives and anxieties of parts of our population. Before and after the event this somehow seemed to some people to be a centrally steered, remote-controlled Communist campaign. In actual fact it was nothing of the sort, but was rather the result of innumerable individual initiatives in our country's towns and villages. Certainly, part of the organization lay in the hands of Communist groups which are trained in organizing such meetings. According to my information there were 23,000 Communists amongst the 250,000 to 300,000 demonstrators. That is a lot, if you remember that there are only 40,000 Communist Party members in the Federal Republic of Germany. But they were lost amongst the masses of people who made up this demonstration: ecologists, neutralists, pacifists, supporters of unilateral disarmament, entire school classes, unionists, feminists and above all

Protestant and Catholic youth groups. The two Protestant Church orga-
nizers, the Aktion Sühnezeichen and the Aktionsgemeinschaft Dienst für
den Frieden, were themselves surprised by the number of demonstrators
who travelled to Bonn and the high participation rate of Christians.

Nevertheless, we should not let ourselves be impressed by the number of participants at demonstrations. This becomes clear, if you compare the percentage of demonstrators to the electorate. Not only the size
of a demonstration counts, but rather the goals it seeks to advance.

21. It is the fight against so-called rearmament which unites all groups.
    Apart from this, the peace movement has hardly one common platform.
    So far, no consensus of the various groups on a constructive alternative
    to the existing security policy is in sight.

22. Certain anti-American tones are not representative of our population's
    opinion. Today 56 per cent are in favour of closer cooperation with the
    United States; in May 1973 it was only 36 per cent. Especially in diffi-
    cult political times, the Germans know that they cannot have security
    without American protection. Likewise it is certain that the majority of
    the public supports NATO's dual-track decision. This summer, two sur-
    veys showed that 58 per cent of the population agree with the dual-track
    decision as a means of making the Soviet Union negotiate. About 30 per
    cent are against any form of rearmament. Only 10 per cent are correctly
    informed about the contents of the dual-track decision, i.e. to station all
    planned American medium-range systems, if concrete arms limitation
    measures have not been agreed by the end of 1983. About 30 per cent
    think the decision only concerns rearmament. This is also a result of
    poor information.

23. References to and evidence for the fact that deterrence has functioned
    for thirty-six years do not suffice in a debate with young people. This
    deterrence system is certainly not a guarantee of eternal peace; it has its
    own built-in dynamics which stem from technical progress and the
    necessity of maintaining a balance of power. This is, however, the pre-
    requisite, if deterrence is to remain plausible. In the long run, this deter-
    rence system is only bearable, if it is supplemented by arms control and
    if thereby the balance of power is kept on the lowest level possible. We
    must say and explain this to our public which has become more critical
    on questions of security policy. And we must tell them that we cannot
    have unilateral arms limitation and arms control. The Soviet Union has
    to put a stop to its rearmament spiral. Unilateral Western concessions
    made in advance increase the danger of martial conflicts. Our country
    can only secure its future in a Western alliance and on that basis pursue
    its détente policy with a chance of success.

24. The main accusation levelled by critics of our security policy amounts to
    the statement that defence is no longer possible today. It is true that
    defence, in the sense of effective protection of our country and its inhab-
    itants in a nuclear war, is out of the question. But that is not the issue.
    The issue is deterrence. We must have armed forces as a protection
    against war and military threat so that we are not faced with foreign

demands or ideological situations we do not want. It is a matter of preventing war ... .

25.

...

Questions concerning our security policy are posed more critically and probably more intelligently today. 'Critical peace research' which did not exist originally [as a discipline] has effectively prepared the ground for the present peace movement. We, too, should seek to talk with serious peace researchers. Discussions with critics of this security policy have become more difficult ... . Each generation has to think over the basic questions of peace anew, and the political and ethical legitimation of our security policy and armed forces as a part of this policy has to be transmitted to each generation. This inner credibility can only be created by open debate.

The armed forces cannot avoid taking an active part in this debate. Explaining the rationale of security policy is certainly a task for politicians as well as for the whole of society, especially for parents and schools. When questions of the legitimacy of their mission are involved, however, the federal armed forces also must become responsive to the intellectual challenge. In the eyes of young people in particular, the task of the federal armed forces cannot be separated from our democracy and the duty of every one of us to support it daily.

26. I ask you to take every opportunity to discuss and publish information on the basic questions of our security policy. You should be guided therein by three principles:

Firstly: The soldier's contribution to securing peace in freedom is his actual and most important task. However, this contribution is only credible if the armed forces possess combat effectiveness. At this point, the critics of deterrence have to be told that it is necessary to be *able* to fight in order not to have to fight.

Secondly: We all long for and want peace. However, that does not suffice for a credible security policy. Allow me to put it differently: a highly admirable, individually ethical pacifism or neutralism is not a security policy which the Federal Republic of Germany can afford.

Thirdly: I emphatically reject those who see a cause for tension and dangers of war in the armed forces and claim that they alone know the right way to keep peace. On several public occasions I have stressed the fact that the Federal Government and the armed forces let no one surpass them in their desire and determination to preserve peace in freedom.

Document 10

PRINCIPLES *(LEITSÄTZE)* OF THE RULING OF THE FEDERAL CONSTITUTIONAL COURT; DECISION OF JULY 1994, CONCERNING DEPLOYMENT OF GERMAN ARMED FORCES ABROAD

Source: Frankfurter Allgemeine Zeitung, 13 July 1994

Approval by the Bundestag needed

1. The powers invested in Art. 24 Para. 2 of the Basic Law authorize the Federal Government not only to enter into a system of mutual collective security and to agree to restrictions thereby being placed on its sovereignty. They also provide the constitutional basis for undertaking tasks which are typically associated with membership of such a system, and consequently also for deploying the Bundeswehr in missions that take place within the framework and according to the rules of this system.

2. Art. 87a of the Basic Law does not conflict with the application of Art. 24 Para.2 of the Basic Law as the constitutional basis for deploying armed forces within the framework of a system of mutual collective security.

3a. The Basic Law obliges the Federal Government to obtain the constitutional consent of the German Bundestag—in principle prior to any deployment of the armed forces.

3b. It is a matter for the legislator—beyond the minimum requirements and limitations on Parliament's reservations regarding the deployment of armed forces, as put forward in this ruling—to determine the form and extent of Parliament's assent more closely.

4. For the preservation of peace the Federal Republic of Germany may—in accordance with Art. 24 Para. 2 of the Basic Law—consent to 'restrictions' being placed on its sovereignty by committing itself to decisions taken by an international organization without thereby transferring to this organization sovereignty in the sense of Art. 24 Para. 1 of the Basic Law.

5a. The distinguishing feature of a system of mutual collective security in the sense of Art. 24 Para.2 of the Basic Law is that—by a set of rules for ensuring peace and by setting up a specific organization—it lays the foundation for a status that is binding on each member under international law. This status imposes a mutual committment to preserving peace and providing security. Whether the system in this respect is meant —exclusively or primarily—to guarantee peace among member states or to commit them to collective mutual assistance in the case of an external attack, is immaterial.

5b. Alliances for the purpose of collective self-defence can also be systems of mutual collective security in the sense of Art. 24 Para. 2 of the Basic Law if and insofar as they are strictly committed to the preservation of peace.

6. Having consented to incorporation into a system of mutual collective security, the legislator's consent also extends to the involvement of armed forces within integrated units of the system or to the participation of soldiers in military actions carried out by the system under its military com-

mand, insofar as such involvement or participation have already been provided for in the articles of association or statutes which underlay the consent. The acceptance of limitations on sovereignty implicit therein also applies to the participation of German soldiers in military ventures undertaken on the basis of cooperation between security systems within their respective framework, if Germany's incorporation into these systems has received Parliamentary approval.

7a. Measures within the domain of foreign and defence policy not covered by the circumstances of Art. 59 Para. 2 Sentence 1 of the Basic Law fall as a matter of principle within the competence of the government. Art. 59 Para. 2 Sentence 1 of the Basic Law cannot be taken to imply that whenever an action of the Federal Government under international law regulates the political relations of the Federal Republic or relates to matters of federal legislation the form that must be chosen is a treaty requiring legislative approval ...

Following are the excerpts from articles 24 and 87a of the Basic Law referred to in the above decision:

Article 24 (Entry into a collective security system)

(1) The Federation may by legislation transfer sovereign powers to intergovernmental institutions.

(2) For the maintenance of peace, the Federation may enter a system of mutual collective security; in doing so it will consent to such limitations upon its rights of sovereignty as will bring about and secure a peaceful and lasting order in Europe and among the nations of the world ... .

Article 87a (Build-up, strength, use and function of the Armed Forces)

(1) The Federation shall build up Armed Forces for defence purposes. Their numerical strength and general organizational structure shall be shown in the budget.

(2) Apart from defence, the Armed Forces may only be used to the extent explicitly permitted by this Basic Law ... .

Notes

1. The relevant volume of the series Foreign Relations of the United States for the year 1950 shows that not only were the Joint Chiefs of Staff already considering West German rearmament before the outbreak of the Korean War, but so was the British government. Here, no doubt, the prime motive was to reduce the financial liabilities in regard to the British Army of the Rhine. The impression which the then US High Commissioner in Bonn, John McCloy, cabled home to his government was that Adenauer pressed for rearmament both for security reasons and to pressure the Western allies into hastening the process of the Federal Republic regaining sovereignty.

2. See also Ch.5 on foreign policy. The whole issue came to the fore again in 1982 as new reports spread about the stationing of US army chemical weapons on German soil. Very strong protests, especially from the trade unions in the Palatinate, followed. The Federal Constitutional Court was appealed to.

3. See as an example: White Paper 1979, The Security of the Federal Republic of Germany and the developments of the Federal armed forces, published in English by the Ministry of Defence in Bonn 1979, as in the following years, the latest 1993/94. See also Statistics, 14.

4. In the Weimar Republic the German army had become what was then called a 'state within the state'—one of the reasons for the collapse of the Republic in the early 1930s.

5. See Ch.7 for the Law on the Defence Commissioner, the Bundestag Committee on Defence and the 'emergency parliament'.

6. The Social Democratic government and its majority in the Bundestag had wanted to make it possible for potential conscientious objectors to claim their status 'by postcard' as it were, i.e. doing away with special boards. The new Christian-Democratic government of Chancellor Kohl introduced a new bill in parliament because the Federal Constitutional Court had stepped in.

7. In the German Democratic Republic the Protestant Church hosted some very courageous efforts especially by the younger generation to call for disarmament in East and West under the slogan: 'Swords into plough shares'. Otherwise 'calls for peace' in all Communist countries have, ever since the 1950s, been officially sponsored as part of an overall Moscow diplomatic strategy and, therefore, been restricted to demands for disarmament by NATO. (See also Chs.3 and 4)

8. Other calls for peace, more in line with the policies of the then government and of NATO were issued primarily by the trade unions.

9. See White Paper, 1979, above (n.3), 229ff., 261ff. and Statistics, 14.

10. As of 1994 the term of service is 12 months in the armed forces and 15 in the civilian alternative service. *(Ziviler Ersatzdienst)*. These terms are likely to be lowered even further by the Bundestag in the near future.

7
Parliamentary Democracy: the Bundestag

Carl-Christoph Schweitzer

According to democratic theory and the German Basic Law, the Bundestag, directly elected by the sovereign people, has precedence over the other two 'powers', i.e. the executive and the judiciary. The fathers of the Basic Law wanted to establish the Federal Republic of Germany very clearly as a parliamentary democracy. Remembering their experiences with the Weimar Republic, whose head of government was responsible to both parliament and the president as Head of State, they made sure that the executive branch of government, the chancellor *(Bundeskanzler)* with his cabinet *(Bundesregierung)*, is politically responsible to the Bundestag and is elected by its members by secret ballot. (see also Ch.9)

The president of the Bundestag *(Bundestagspräsident,* 'speaker'), automatically elected at the beginning of each legislative period *(Wahlperiode)* on the nomination of the majority party in the Bundestag, conducts the business of the House within a set of very specific Standing Orders *(Geschäftsordnung des Bundestages,* Doc.1). He is assisted by Vice-presidents, representing the other parties in the Bundestag, and by the Council of Elders *(Ältestenrat)* made up of 'government' and 'opposition' Members of the Bundestag (MdBs, referred to below as 'members'). This body draws up, by mutual agreement, the weekly timetable of the House and in this way exercises control over its own business in a formal way not followed in Great Britain or Canada.

The members are not only governed by these Standing Orders of the Bundestag, but also by Standing Orders of their party caucuses *(Fraktionsgeschäftsordnungen,* Doc.2). The party caucuses constitute themselves formally and automatically after each general election. They are, however, recognised only when and if the elected members of a given political party make up at least 5 percent of the overall Bundestag membership of 656 (see also Chs.2 and 8 for post-reunification). There have been so far no cases of members being elected to the Bundestag as independent representatives. Some left their party and, therefore, also their caucus in parliament during a four-year-legislative period of the Bundestag and then remained members for the rest of that period as independents. In this capacity they lost, for example, the important right to sit on Bundestag committees, because members can only be chosen for or withdrawn from those committees by party caucuses. These caucuses *(Fraktionen)* are highly organized bodies with working groups *(Arbeitsgruppen)* and coordinating committees *(Arbeitskreise)*, comprising several working groups, which consider the various areas of policy covered by the Standing Committees of the Bundestag *(Bundestagsausschüsse,* Doc.3), such as, for instance, the Budget Committee, or the Judicial Committee. These committees in turn correspond more or less to the Federal Ministries they are supposed to supervise (Docs.3 and 4). One whole day of each weekly parliamentary timetable is devoted to meetings of the caucuses and their working-groups, another one to the meetings of the Standing Committees of the Bundestag itself.

So much for the structure of the Bundestag. Two important questions then arise: firstly, what are the functions of the Bundestag, its 'effective parts'—to use W. Bagehot's famous terminology[1]*—as they are spelt out in the various Standing Orders as well as in the Basic Law itself? Secondly, what powers do the 656 supreme representatives of the people have in actual political practice—the individual members, the caucuses or the Bundestag as a whole? To begin with, the Bundestag has *elective functions.* With a so-called 'chancellor majority' (of at least 329 members, one more than half the total membership) the Bundestag chooses at the beginning of each legislative period the chancellor, who then can only be voted out of office by a so-called *constructive vote of no-confidence.* This requires that the Bundestag must elect a successor to the chancellor if it wishes to remove him. The chancellor himself can also at any time ask for a *vote of confidence.* Only if he loses it can the Bundestag be dissolved within a legislative period. There is no other way than that of calling general federal elections within the constitutionally prescribed period of four years. The Basic Law says in regard to the election of a chancellor in Art. 63:

(1) The Federal Chancellor shall be elected, without debate, by the Bundestag upon the proposal of the Federal President
(2) The person obtaining the votes of the majority of the members of the Bundestag shall be elected. The person elected must be appointed by the Federal President.
(3) If the person proposed is not elected, the Bundestag may elect within fourteen days of the ballot a Federal Chancellor by more than one-half of its members.

* *Notes for this chapter begin on p. 197.*

(4) If no candidate has been elected within this period, a new ballot shall take place without delay, in which the person obtaining the largest number of votes shall be elected. If the person elected has obtained the votes of the majority of the members of the Bundestag, the Federal President must appoint him within seven days of the election. If the person elected did not obtain such a majority, the Federal President must within seven days either appoint him or dissolve the Bundestag.

The provisions for a vote of no-confidence are stated in Art. 67:

(1) The Bundestag can express its lack of confidence in the Federal Chancellor only by electing a successor with the majority of its members and by requesting the Federal President to dismiss the Federal Chancellor. The Federal President must comply with the request and appoint the person elected ... .

and the provisions for a vote of confidence, possibly leading to new elections, are spelt out in Art. 68:

(1) If a motion of the Federal Chancellor for a vote of confidence is not assented to by the majority of the members of the Bundestag, the Federal President may, upon the proposal of the Federal Chancellor, dissolve the Bundestag within 21 days. The right to dissolve shall lapse as soon as the Bundestag with the majority of its members elects another Federal Chancellor ... .

Since 1949 a vote of no-confidence has been attempted only twice. In 1972 it failed against Chancellor Willy Brandt; in 1982 it succeeded against Chancellor Helmut Schmidt (Doc.5). Three votes of confidence were asked for: the first by Willy Brandt in 1972 in order to make new elections possible, i.e. with the members of parliament from the government bench deliberately abstaining so as to lose the vote; the second asked for and won by Helmut Schmidt in 1982; the third asked for by Helmut Kohl and again deliberately lost, in December 1982, in order again to arrive at new elections. Procedures then adopted by the majority in parliament gave rise to most heated constitutional and political debates in the Federal Republic at the turn of the year and led to a pronouncement of the Federal Constitutional Court on the subject in February 1983 (see also Ch.9). So far no amendments of the Basic Law have been made to enable a Parliament to dissolve itself.

The chancellor alone is responsible to the Bundestag as Head of the Cabinet. He alone can be dismissed on a vote of no-confidence, individual ministers cannot. In other words, there is collective, but no individual cabinet responsibility to parliament. In the Federal Republic of Germany there is, just as in other parliamentary democracies, no 'incompatibility' in being both a member of the Bundestag and a member of the cabinet. Consequently, with two or three exceptions, all cabinet members have been at the same time sitting members. In the first cabinet of Willy Brandt, for instance, the Minister for Science and Education, Hans Leussink, was a member of the cabinet, but not of the Bundestag, where he had no seat, no functions or privileges, but where he could speak or had to speak and answer questions for the Government.

Secondly, the Bundestag has the *function of law-making*, i.e. it is the supreme federal law-making body. However, it is important to point out that the second chamber, the Bundesrat, representing the governments of the eleven Länder (sixteen since 1990) of the Federal Republic, has a veto on bills—a suspensive one on all, an absolute one on some, depending on the substantive matter concerned (see also Ch.12). For this reason the Mediation Committee of both Houses (the *Vermittlungsausschuß*, Doc.6) is a very important instrument of law-making. Here compromises are thrashed out which the two houses have then to vote on again, but which are usually carried unless the absolute veto of the Bundesrat can apply. Two points have to be taken into account: firstly, that some 80 per cent of all federal bills later enacted are *introduced* into the Bundestag by the government (and not by the Bundestag itself, by a caucus or by the Bundesrat—all of which are constitutionally possible); such a percentage is considered fairly normal in Great Britain or Canada, where practically all business is introduced into parliament by the government.[2] However, this is not accepted as normal by German political theorists. Secondly, government bills are seldom changed in important points during their parliamentary passage. The reason for the first phenomenon is mainly that the government, with its ministries, has far more expertise at its disposal, even though the members have for some years now been given an assistant each, as well as access to a sophisticated Legislative Reference Service *(Wissenschaftlicher Dienst)* with many specialists for all fields. The reason for the second phenomenon will be referred to again below: the government can, in the law-making process as in other matters, generally rely on its majority in the Bundestag.

Thirdly, the Bundestag has (again at least on paper) a number of opportunities to exercise the function considered to be most important by theorists of parliamentary democracy, i.e. that of *controlling* the policies of the government in power. In Germany theoreticians distinguish here between control of the overall direction of policies *(Richtungskontrolle)* and of control of the performance of the government *(Leistungskontrolle)*. The former means that the Bundestag can try to ascertain government policy or, having ascertained it, to criticise that policy. It can do so by means of the Question Time *(Fragestunde)* twice a week for ninety minutes during twenty-six weeks a year, when the Bundestag is in session. It can do so by means of an *ad hoc* debate (the so-called *Aktuelle Stunde)*, which is a debate confined to sixty minutes with speeches limited to five minutes each. It can do so by means of a formal written question or set of questions introduced by a group of members collectively (the so-called *Kleine* or *Große Anfrage)*. Finally—and most extensively in point of time— the Bundestag can control the overall direction of policies by means of a full-scale debate which any member of the cabinet or the chancellor himself can be 'compelled' to attend, in order to answer questions. That is constitutionally possible because Art. 43 of the Basic Law says in its first paragraph: 'The Bundestag and its committees may demand the presence of any member of the Federal Government'. A famous case occurred in 1974 when—on the motion of the then opposition (CDU/CSU), supported by members of the governing party—SPD Chancellor Helmut Schmidt was compelled by a vote of the House not to proceed with an intended schedule outside Bonn, but instead to attend a debate on a problem of foreign policy. The Bundestag adjourned for thirty minutes in order to give the chancellor a chance to change his schedule.

Full-scale debates take place on an average of one-and-a-half days a week when parliament is in session. Here the Bundestag exercises an important educative function, i.e. acts in the full limelight of the public as the central forum for political controversies in the nation.

The main instrument for controlling the performance of the government is provided by the Standing Committees, already mentioned. As in other Western democracies perhaps the most powerful Committee is that for the Federal Budget *(Haushaltsausschuß)*. All committees meet, as a rule, in executive session and are closed to the public and press. Public hearings are possible, but have been extremely rare, though of late the number has increased. It is not least in such hearings that influence can be brought to bear on the political process by interest groups, whose role in politics must also be seen in the light of historic 'affiliations' between some of these groups and certain political parties.[3]

The Bundestag provided itself in 1957 with an unique instrument for controlling the German military establishment by creating—in addition to the Defence Committee—a Defence Commissioner, or Parliamentary Ombudsman for the Armed Services *(Wehrbeauftragter des Bundestages,* Doc.7). Similarly, the Bundestag has insisted on its prerogative of controlling government activities in the field of the secret services. They are supervised by a special Committee of three members *(Vertrauensmännergremium,* or Confidential Group), one from each caucus. So far this has not led to any security leakages.[4] It sits in secret sessions only, with no other members being able to 'listen in', as they can in most other committees. In this connection mention must also be made of the Joint Committee of thirty-two members of the Bundestag and sixteen from each of the Länder *(Gemeinsamer Ausschuß,* in accordance with Art. 53a Basic Law), to control the government in times of national emergencies. This 'parliament in miniature' would only go into action when and if the Bundestag and Bundesrat as a whole were not in a position to assemble. Its members could be flown within minutes to the big atomic shelter and command centre near Bonn, there to 'govern' the country constitutionally from underground—a perfectionist German device to make sure that Germany remains 'safe for democracy'. Finally, there is the possibility of setting up any time, as instruments of control in addition to the Standing Committees, *ad hoc* Committees of Investigation *(Untersuchungsausschüsse,* Doc.8). These Committees constitute (again on paper) a very important 'minority right', since the opposition can have them set up even if the government parties are not in favour. Art. 44 of the Basic Law states that they must be set up if one quarter of the Bundestag membership demands it. However, since *all* committees (standing or *ad hoc)* are established on the basis of proportional representation which governs the composition of the Bundestag itself, the committees 'mirror' the majority and minority in parliament at any given time. Hence, when it comes to a committee vote on resolutions, bills, treaties or reports, the opposition will, as a rule, be in a minority. The chairmanships in all committees are also distributed to the various party caucuses on a proportional basis.

At this point the overall question again poses itself as to whether in actual fact the Bundestag can *effectively* control the government in power. The answer is the same—as it would be for all parliamentary democracies of the same type: there is, firstly, no system of checks and balances between the government and the Bundestag as a whole, because the majority in parliament will generally support 'its' government through thick and thin. Since, secondly, the opposition in parliament will always be in a minority, the only effective controlling bodies of parliament are, hence, the caucuses of the government parties (or of the government party). So far it is only possible to speculate on the effectiveness of actions taken by majority caucuses of the Bundestag in controlling 'their' government, since the regular minutes of caucus meetings are only gradually becoming available for research. Regular votes are taken at those meetings which cabinet ministers—including the chancellor—attending their respective party caucus would be obliged to follow politically because, after all, the government depends on the support of its basis. Votes are also taken in the opposition caucus (or caucuses as the case may be) to determine the line to be taken by the opposition in plenary sessions.[5]

The final problem is, then, basically the same in all party caucuses of the Bundestag, i.e. the question of the relationship between what is called in German terminology *Fraktionszwang* (caucus-pressure), applied by the leadership towards rank and file members with the aim of forcing them into a certain voting behaviour (or other forms of conformity) on the one hand, and *Fraktionsdisziplin* (a self-ordained party-discipline) on the other. To apply *Fraktionszwang* openly would, in a very German way, be against 'the law', i.e. the Basic Law itself, whose Art. 38 clearly stipulates:

> (1) The members of the German Bundestag ... shall be representatives of the whole people, not bound by orders and instructions, and shall be subject only to their conscience ...

Nevertheless, in this connection, too, one must speak of indirect deviations from the prescribed norm in so far as the party-leadership has many subtle means at its disposal to dissuade potential or actual rebels from voting against their party in the House. There have, however, been a number of recorded cases since 1949, where individual members did vote against their own party on a 'point of conscience' concerning important matters of substance.[6] What is 'conscience' and what personal political calculation is, of course, difficult to prove (Doc.9). But the rule in the Bundestag has been—and still is—for caucus members to observe a maximum of '*Fraktionsdisziplin*'. The philosophy behind this tendency is obvious: caucuses must try to exert a maximum of influence on the political process in parliament in order to achieve their overall policy objectives. This presupposes a maximum of internal cohesion.[7]

Political scientists and constitutional lawyers have written a good deal on the conflict built into the Basic Law itself through its combined articles 38 and 21: Members of Parliament are supposed to be entirely free agents under Art. 38 Basic Law, but they are, in fact, elected to parliament through their affiliations to political parties, which constitute to all intents and purposes 'organs of the state' by virtue of Art. 21 Basic Law. German parliamentary democracy has been based on the principle of *party-government* (see also Ch.8), which was, for the first time called into question by new movements towards 'direct democracy'—by way of citizens' action groups or by 'green' and other alternative groups of all sorts. (see also Ch.13)

To sum up this introduction: according to the constitutional theory of the Federal Republic of Germany the Bundestag is the supreme body in the country and constitutes the 'sovereign parliament', as in Great Britain or Canada. In Germany many aspects of parliamentary life have been laid down in very precise and detailed Standing Orders of the Bundestag as a whole and of the party caucuses. Even so, however, the political practice often does not, for the reasons mentioned above, conform to the prescribed norms—a problem for all parliamentary democracies of our time. New developments arose in the 1980s and early 1990s on four accounts: one, that a new party in opposition to the Federal Government, the Greens *(Die Grünen)* overcame the 5 per cent hurdle of the Federal Election Law successfully in 1983, failing however in 1990 as far as West Germany was concerned.[8] They were then superseded by a similar party in the New Länder, *Bündnis 90.* Both parties have now been fused into one. Secondly, that with the reunification of Germany in 1990 for the first time since 1949–53 there are again members representing the extreme left sitting in the Bundestag under the name of PDS, emanating from East Germany as remnants of the former communist SED (see also Ch.8) with a few others from the old Länder. Thirdly, due to reunification, and the additional 16 million German citizens, the overall number of seats in the Bundestag had to be increased to 656.[9] And fourth, that the German Bundestag has lost and is losing more competences in favour of European supra-nationality, unfortunately, however, still not to a European Parliament with full powers of democratic control.

Document 1

STANDING ORDERS OF THE BUNDESTAG *(GESCHÄFTSORDNUNG)*

Source: Text as amended by the Bundestag in June 1980 (Deutscher Bundestag, 8th legislative period, Drucksache 8/3460; cf. BGBl.I, 1237) and 12 November 1990 (BGBl.I, 2555)

. . .

§5: The president and his deputies (vice-presidents) form the presidency.

§6: *The Council of Elders*

(1) consists of the president, his deputies and twenty-three additional members to be chosen from the caucuses according to § 12 below. It is the president's duty to summon and chair its meetings. He must summon the council, if a caucus requests it.

(2) The council of elders aids the president in conducting parliamentary business. Through it, agreements are brought about between caucuses regarding nominations to the positions of committee chairmen, as well as the weekly agenda of the Bundestag ...

. . .

§8: *The Chair*

In meetings of the Bundestag (plenary sessions) the president *pro tempore* and two secretaries (MdBs as Schriftführer) constitute the chair ... .

. . .

§10: *Formation of Caucuses*

(1) The caucuses are associations of at least five per cent of the Bundestag membership, who belong to the same party or parties that are not in competition with each other in any Land on the grounds that they pursue similar political goals ... .

(2) The forming and naming of a caucus, the names of its chairmen, members and guests are to be communicated to the president in writing ... .

(4) Members of the Bundestag who wish to associate without having achieved the minimum percentage required to form a caucus can be recognised as a 'group' ... .

. . .

§12: *Positions Apportioned to the Caucuses*

(1) The composition of the council of elders and of the Bundestag committees as well as the apportioning of the chairmanships in those committees is determined by the proportionate strength of the different caucuses.[8] The same principle applies to the election of members to other bodies by the Bundestag ... .

§13: *Duties of the Members of the Bundestag*

(1)Bundestag members are obliged to take part in the business of the Bundestag.

(2) On every session-day an attendance sheet will be laid out; members are to register themselves. The consequences of non-registration and non-participation follow from the law on remuneration for members.

. . .

[Non-registration is penalised by a fine for each day, ed.]

. . .

§19: *Plenary Sessions (Meetings)*

(1) The meetings of the Bundestag shall be public. The public can be excluded in accordance with Art. 42, 1, Basic Law: '... on a motion of one-tenth of its members, or upon a motion of the federal government, the public may be excluded by a two-thirds majority. The decision on the motion shall be taken at a meeting not open to the public'.

. . .

§27: *Recognition of Speakers and the Way to Ask for Recognition*

(1) ... Members of the Bundestag who wish to speak on a point on the agenda have, as a rule, to indicate their wish to do so to that secretary who is listing members desiring to be called ...

. . .

§43: *Right to be Heard at all Times*
The members of the government (federal) and of the Bundesrat, as well as persons commissioned by them, must, upon their request, be heard any time. (Cf. Art. 43, 2, Basic Law.)

. . .

§54: *Standing Committees and ad hoc Committees*
(1) The Bundestag sets up standing committees which prepare the business of the day. For specific matters special committees can be set up ...

. . .

§69: *Closed Committee Meetings*
Committee deliberations are on principle carried out in closed meetings. The committee can decide for a specific subject under debate, or parts thereof, to admit the general public. The meeting is considered to be an open one if members of the press and/or any other listeners are allowed to be present ...

§70: *Public Hearings*
(1) Public hearings of experts, representatives of interest groups and other persons supplying information can be undertaken by a committee in order to become informed about a subject under deliberation ...

[In the legislative period of the Bundestag 1976 to 1980 only four out of some 2,000 committee meetings (see §69 above) were open to the public. In the same period some 170 hearings with experts were conducted (see §70 above), of those only some seventy were open to the public. Meetings of the Committee on Foreign Affairs or the Defense Committee have never been, inter alia, open to the public.

. . .

§76: *Papers Submitted by Members*
(1) Any business can be brought to the attention of the Bundestag by members if a request to do so has been signed by a caucus or by five per cent of the members of the Bundestag ...

. . .

§78: *Reading of Bills*
(1) Drafts of a bill are dealt with in three readings. Treaties with foreign states and similar treaties or agreements which regulate the political relations of the federation or relate to matters of federal legislation are in general deliberated upon in two readings only, by decision of the Bundestag in three. All other business is deliberated upon only in one reading.

. . .

§105: *Questions by Individual Members of the Bundestag*
Any member of the Bundestag is entitled to put questions to the federal government during question-time or in writing. For details see the special rules of procedure in the annex hereof No. 4. (Cf. ibid. section II: Handing in of questions: ... 'Questions have to be handed in to the president [his bureau for parliamentary affairs] with two copies thereof ...'.)

Standing orders of the SPD caucus have, basically, been in force with only insignificant changes since 1949. Their main features are the same as those of the standing orders of the other caucuses; for example, those of the CDU which, together with its Bavarian Counterpart, the CSU (see Ch.8), has since the days of Chancellor Adenauer established a joint caucus at the beginning of each new legislative period, and those of the liberal FDP. The excerpts below demonstrate once again that in practical politics there are always deviations from the prescribed norm since, for instance, §3 stipulates that members wishing to speak in the house must channel their request through their whips, while the standing orders of the higher-ranking Bundestag stipulate in §27 that members wishing to speak need only indicate their wish to the chair. Even more questionable is the stipulation of §5, 3 below.

Document 2

STANDING ORDERS OF THE SPD-CAUCUS (FRAKTION)
Source: Standing Orders of the SPD-Fraktion, as amended, 1970

. . .

§2: *Speakers for the Caucus in Plenary Sessions*
The caucus determines the speakers who are to represent its views in plenary sessions of the Bundestag.

§3: *Participation in Plenary Debates*
If a caucus member wishes to participate as a speaker in a plenary debate he will come to an understanding with the caucus officer in charge of the appropriate Bundestag committee (Obmann) as well as with the caucus whip (Parlamentarischer Geschäftsführer, see below 8).

§4: *Nominations to Committees of the Bundestag, other Bodies and Delegations*
Nominations to such committees, other bodies and delegations are decided upon by the caucus. Candidates for offices and functions of the Bundestag who have to be put forward by the caucus are elected by the same on the proposal of the caucus's executive committee (see below 8). If in addition nominations are put forward from the midst of the caucus, a list of all candidates proposed will be put to the vote of the caucus in alphabetical order ...

§5: *Introduction of Interpellations, Resolutions and Drafts for Bills*
   (1) The caucus decides on the introduction of bills and other motions as well as any other interpellations (Große und Kleine Anfragen).
   (2) Any initiatives taken by individual members in this respect which are not be introduced by the caucus as such, have first to be put before the caucus's executive committee via the relevant working group of the caucus ... .

(3) Questions for question time have to be submitted to the parliamentary whip first.

. . .

§7: *General Duties of the Caucus Members*

The caucus members are obliged to participate in the meetings and the general work of the caucus as well as of the Bundestag and its committees. The caucus adopts more specific regulations to guarantee that participation and to grant leave of absence.

§8: *Caucus Executive Committee, its Composition*

(1) The caucus executive committee consists of its chairman, his deputies, the other members elected by the whole caucus and the parliamentary whips.

. . .

(3) ... Social Democratic members of the government and ministers of state participate in the meetings of the executive committee ...

§9:

The caucus elects by secret ballot, separately, the chairman of the caucus, his deputies, the parliamentary whips and the other members ...

. . .

§18: *Working Groups*

The members of a Bundestag committee form a working group of the caucus. The caucus elects for each of these a chairman (Obmann) ...

. . .

§23: *Formation of Working Committees (Arbeitskreise) and Working Groups (Arbeitsgruppen) to Deal with Specific Problems*

(1) The caucus sets up working committees for different subject matters in order to facilitate its work in the Bundestag. In addition to the working groups in accordance with §18 above further such groups can be set up to deal with specific problems. All working groups submit their findings to the working committees for a decision to be taken.

(2) The chairmen of the working committees and their deputies as well as the chairmen of working groups for specific problems are elected by the caucus on the proposal of the executive committee ...

§24: *Meetings of Working Committees and Working Groups*

All members of the caucus are entitled to take part in meetings of any such working committee or working group ...

At the beginning of each legislative period the chairmanships of the standing committees, whose overall number has been more or less constant since 1949, are apportioned almost equally between government and opposition caucuses. The committees themselves appoint by vote, on the proposal of the senior caucus members from all parties, 'rapporteurs' *(Berichterstatter)* for most matters on the agenda, such as the consideration of bills, treaties, resolutions, reports etc. There are always two, one from the government, one from the opposition parties. Ever since the days of the old German Reichstag in the last century the chairman of the important Budget Committee has been a member of the opposition.

Document 3

STANDING COMMITTEES OF THE BUNDESTAG AND AD HOC COMMISSIONS

Source: Handbuch des Deutschen Bundestages, 1983–91, Bonn, 1994

A. Standing Committees

Number		Number of members
1	Committee for the Scrutiny of Elections, Immunity and the Rules of Procedure	19
2	Petitions Committee	33
3	Committee on Foreign Affairs	41
4	Committee on Internal Affairs	41
5	Sports Committee	19
6	Legal (Judicial) Committee	29
7	Finance Committee	41
8	Budget Committee	39
9	Committee on Economic Affairs	41
10	Committee on Food, Agriculture and Forestry	35
11	Committee on Labour and Social Affairs	37
12	Defence Committee	37
13	Committee on Family Affairs and Senior Citizens	29
14	Committee on Women and Youth	29
15	Committee on Health	29
16	Committee on Transport	41
17	Committee on Environment, Natural Resources and Safety of Atomic Plants	41
18	Committee on Posts and Telecommunications	19
19	Committee on Regional Planning, Building and Urban Development	31
20	Committee on Research, Technology and Technology Assess.	35
21	Committee on Education and Science	31
22	Committee on Economic Co-operation	35
23	Committee on Tourism	19
24	EC-Committee	33
25	Treuhand-Committee [See Ch.14]	24
B.	Special Committees:	
	a) Protection of the Unborn	42
	b) Joint Committee of Bundestag and Bundesrat for the Revision of the Constitution	64

C.   Enquete Commissions as of 1994 (the equivalent of Royal Commissions in Great Britain to promote new legislation) since 1980:

These Enquete Commissions have operated since 1969 when the Rules of Procedures for the Bundestag were amended to include a new Art. 74a.

1. On new technics of information and communication
2. On the protest of the young generation in a democratic society
3. On the future of atomic energy policies
4. On chances and risks of genetic engineering
5. On technology assessment
6. On the dangers of Aids and effective means of combatting them
7. On the Reform of the Public Health Insurance System
8. On preventive measures to protect the atmosphere of the earth
9. On future educational policies, 'Bildung 2000'
10. On the protection of the human race and its environment ...
11. On researching into the history of the dictatorship of the SED and the consequences therof
12. On demographic changes

Documents 4a–d

SOME AGENDAS OF STANDING COMMITTEES OF THE BUNDESTAG

Source: Committee Publications, Deutscher Bundestag 1976 and 1980

Here we have 'typical' orders of the day for meetings of two important Bundestag committees, both restricted to committee members only: the Committee on Foreign Affairs and the Defence Committee. The case of Doc.4a below may be taken as typical of a treaty to be ratified by parliament in accordance with Art. 59, 2, of the Basic Law:

...

(2) Treaties which regulate the political relations of the federation or relate to matters of federal legislation shall require the consent or participation, in the form of a federal law, of the bodies competent in any specific case for such federal legislation ...

On the agenda given in Doc.4a was the treaty between the Federal Republic and Poland signed in 1975, as a further and final breakthrough in German-Polish relations after the Treaty of Warsaw of 1970 (see Ch.5). The then Minister for Foreign Affairs (Genscher) was himself in attendance to answer questions and criticisms of the members. Document 4d demonstrates the ability of the Defence Committee to transform itself (the only one which can do so) into a special 'committee of investigation' (see also below Doc. 8), the idea being that the Bundestag wished to have special emergency powers to control the new armed forces. (see Ch.6)

Document 4a

German Federal Parliament   Bonn, 6 January 1976
7th Term [legislative period]
Third Committee
-712-2401-

Anouncement
The 68th session of the Committee on Foreign Affairs
takes place on Wednesday,
14 January 1976, 10.00 a.m ... .

Agenda

1. Deliberation
a) on a bill regarding the agreement of 9.10.1975 between the Federal
   Republic of Germany and the People's Republic of Poland on pension
   and accident insurance together with the agreements on this matter of
   9.10.1975
b) on government information about the agreements with the People's
   Republic of Poland which were signed in Warsaw on 9.10.1975

Rapporteurs for a) and b): Schlaga MdB
                           Dr. Wallmann MdB

2. Naming a rapporteur for the bill ... regarding the agreement on establishing an association between the European Economic Community and
   Greece ... (1975)
3. Miscellaneous

                                                                Mattick
                                                         Deputy Chairman

Document 4b

German Federal Parliament   Bonn, 20 June 1980
8th Term
Defence Committee
-715-2401-

Announcement
The 103rd session ofthe Defence Committee takes place on Wednesday, 2
July
1980, 9.00 a.m ... .

Agenda

1. Decision on the FDP caucus motion of 18.6.1980 concerning infrastructure
2. Report from the Federal Ministry for Defence on a concept for an army
   tank in the 'nineties
3. Report from the Federal Ministry for Defence on armament planning
4. Annual report 1979 from the Defence Commissioner of the German Federal Parliament
Rapporteurs: Ernesti MdB
             Horn MdB

5. Report of the Commission of the Federal Ministry for Defence on strengthening leadership ability and responsibility for decisions in the armed forces (de Maizière report)

. . .

Dr. Wörner
Chairman

Document 4c

German Federal Parliament   Bonn, 26 May 1976
7th Term
Third Committee
-712-2401-

Announcement

The 78th session of the Committee on Foreign Affairs takes place on Wednesday,
2 June 1976, 3.30 p.m.
Bonn, Bundeshaus, Chamber 2704 NH

Agenda

1. Government report on the spring conference of the NATO Council Ministers in Oslo
2. Government report on the situation in Israel
3. Government report on the Trade and Development Conference of the United Nations (UNCTAD IV) in Nairobi
4. Government report on the consular agreement between the United Kingdom and the GDR
5. Deliberation on the draft of the Ministry for Foreign Affairs concerning defence aid for Turkey (9th Tranche) ...
6. Deliberation on the resolution of the European Parliament concerning the UN General Assembly's resolution on Zionism ...
7. Deliberation on the resolution of the European Parliament concerning the present state of the Euro-Arabian dialogue ...
8. Discussion of the CDU/CSU parliamentary caucus's motion concerning aid for the victims of the earthquake catastrophe in Northern Italy ...
9. Miscellaneous

Dr. Schröder
Chairman

Document 4d

German Federal Parliament   Bonn, 31 July 1980
8th Term
Defence Committee as the
2nd Committee of Investigation
-715-2401-

Announcement
The 110th session of the Defence Committee—
8th session as the 2nd Committee
of Investigation in accordance with Art. 45a, para. 2 Basic Law—
takes place on
Tuesday, 5 August 1980, 9.00 a.m ... .

Agenda

Questioning of the expert witness Federal Minister Gerhart Baum, MdB	on 1. 2, 3, 4, 5, 6 in open session
Hearing Representatives of the 'Land Office for the Protection of the Constitution', Hamburg	in closed session
Police counsellor (Polizeirat) Elbrecht, Bremen	in open session
Under Secretary of State, Baier, Niedersachsen	in open session
Questioning of the expert witness Dieter Mützelburg	on 1.6 in open session

. . .

The constructive vote of no-confidence, provided for in Art. 67 of the Basic Law, prevents the Bundestag from dismissing the chancellor without at the same time electing his successor by a majority of its members. Helmut Kohl's election as the new chancellor following the no-confidence vote was the first time in the Federal Republic's history that a government had been replaced without a general election (see Ch.9). The following extract is from the parliamentary debate over the 1972 motion for a no-confidence vote against Chancellor Brandt.

Document 5

CONSTRUCTIVE VOTE OF NO-CONFIDENCE

Source: Deutscher Bundestag, *183rd Parliamentary sitting*, Sten. Berichte, 27 April 1972

President von Hassel: The proceedings are opened. I call for point 3 of the agenda: discussion of the motion of the CDU/CSU caucus according to Art. 67 of the Basic Law-Order Paper VI/3380-
I call on Member Dr. Kiesinger (for the motion).

Dr. h.c. Kiesinger (CDU/CSU):

. . .

We have chosen the possibility of moving a motion in accord with Art. 67 of the Basic Law for a 'Constructive Vote of No Confidence' not in order—as a speaker from the government coalition claimed yesterday—'to sneak into power', but in order to relieve a government and a policy which we are convinced has failed and has damaged the interests of our people.

(Applause from the CDU/CSU)

We have not chosen this path because we are afraid of a new election. On the contrary! But according to the Basic Law the opposition does not have the power to bring about such elections. Neither have we chosen this path out of a narrow-minded party interest with short-lived tactical considerations. Many of our friends have advised us to let this coalition, this government, this chancellor carry on even deeper into the dead-end of its failed policy in order to win better chances for ourselves in the next election. If it were only a matter of the fate of this government we would have followed this advice. But it is a matter of the interests of our people. And it was in order to avert their being further endangered that we determined on this course.

. . .

The fathers of the Basic Law, remembering the Weimar Republic, rejected with good reason a simple 'Vote of No Confidence'. For by this a heterogeneous majority could bring down a government without being in a position or wanting to form a new government itself.

The Social Democrat Member Dr. Menzel argued at the time in the Parliamentary Council that one ought to transform the 'Vote of No Confidence' as it was put to previous ill use [in the Weimar Republic, ed.] as a politically destructive mechanism into a weapon of a positively oriented parliamentary democracy.

. . .

Chancellor Brandt:

. . .

The decision of the CDU/CSU to try to bring down the government accords with the opportunities offered by the Constitution and is not difficult to understand either as power politics or psychologically. If you will allow me a judgement on the latter: This is an attempt at a 'forward escape', out of the irresponsibility of a sterile 'No' to matters of the fate of our people, but with the risk of going into a responsibility whose bitterness you would soon feel. For Dr. Barzel and his friends would only obtain this responsibility if they were to receive a 'Yes' from a few members of this respected house of whom one would be able to say that they had strained their conscience beyond the point of recognition.

(Cheers from the government side. Shouts
from the CDU/CSU: 'Rubbish, outrageous')

. . .

President von Hassel:

Ladies and Gentlemen, there are no more speakers. I hereby conclude the proceedings.

We come to the vote. The CDU/CSU proposed the motion, which is on the order paper No VI/3380 before you, that Member Dr. Barzel be elected as successor to Chancellor Willy Brandt.

According to § 98 of our rules of procedure a successor has to be elected by secret ballot. He is only elected when the votes of the majority of the members of the house—this means at least 249 votes—fall to him.

(The vote is taken. After that thesitting is interrupted from
12.59 hrs-13.22 hrs to count the vote)

. . .

Ladies and gentlemen, the sitting is resumed.
I will give the results of the vote. Of the members entitled to vote 260 votes were cast, from the Berlin members eleven votes. From the 260 entitled members 247 have voted yes for the motion, ten voted no, three abstained. From the Berlin members ten voted yes and one no, with no abstentions … .
[With few exceptions the SPD/FDP members did not take part in the vote, two from the CDU/CSU must have been 'defectors'.] This has been a matter for controversial debate ever since.
I hereby declare that the Member Dr. Barzel proposed by the CDU/CSU caucus has not obtained the votes of the majority of members of the German Bundestag.

(Stormy applause from the government parties. The SPD and numerous
FDP members rise to their feet. Dr. Barzel congratulates Chancellor
Brandt and Minister Scheel.)

The motion of the CDU/CSU on the order paper VI/3380 is thus defeated

…

As can be seen from the statistics, the Conference Committee of the two houses has a high record of achieving compromise solutions. The legislative history of the law on universities, for instance (see Ch.12), which could have been subject to a final veto by the Bundesrat, provides a good example of the way in which the original bill passed by the Bundestag finally got on the statute book in a very diluted fashion, after prolonged deliberations and votes taken in the *Vermittlungsausschuß*. Criticism is mounting in Germany against this Conference Committee acting as a sort of 'second track' lawmaking body, very often circumventing the will of the majority of the elected Bundestag.

Document 6

JOINT RULES OF PROCEDURE OF THE BUNDESTAG AND BUNDESRAT FOR THE COMMITTEE ACCORDING TO ARTICLE 77 OF THE BASIC LAW: MEDIATION (OR CONFERENCE) COMMITTEE *(VERMITTLUNGSAUSSCHUSS)*

Source: BGBl.; II, 1951, 104

1 *Permanent Members*
Bundestag and Bundesrat each delegate 12 of their members, who form the mediation committee.

2 *Chairmanship*
The committee elects one member of both the Bundestag and Bundesrat, who act in turn as chairman every three months ...

. . .

8 *Majority*
The committee takes its decisions with the majority vote of its members present.

9 *Sub-committees*
The committee can appoint sub-committees.

. . .

12 *Conclusion of the Mediation Procedures:*
1) Should a unified motion not be decided upon in a second meeting called for consideration of the same subject matter, then any member of the committee can move that the procedures be concluded.
2) Procedures are to be considered as concluded if a unified motion fails to get a majority at the meeting thereafter.
3) Procedures can otherwise not be concluded without a unified motion.
4) The chairman has to certify the conclusion of mediation procedures and give notice to this effect on the same day to the presidents of the Bundestag and of the Bundesrat ...

The 'Ombudsman' of the Bundestag for the members of the armed forces has, on the whole, done good work since 1957, by drawing attention to failings which are inevitable in any system. The German Basic Law of 1949 guarantees that there can be no repetition of dangerous tendencies in past Prussian-German history which were caused in part by a lack of political control over the armed forces.

Document 7

DEFENCE COMMISSIONER *(WEHRBEAUFTRAGTER DES DEUTSCHEN BUNDESTAGES)* LAW OF 26 JUNE 1957, AS AMENDED BY THE LAW OF 2 MARCH 1974

Source: BGBl., I, 1974, 469f.

§1 *The Defence Commissioner of the Bundestag is to observe the requirements of Article 45b of the Basic Law.*

§2

1. The Defence Commissioner will examine particular matters at the directive of the Bundestag or of the Standing Defence Committee. The latter can only issue the directives if it is not making the matter the subject of its own investigation. The Defence Commissioner must submit, if requested, a specific report on the result of his examination.
2. The Commissioner will, after due consideration intervene when, in exercising his rights under §3 (4), he learns of complaints from soldiers, passed on by members of the Bundestag, or if he learns in other ways of circumstances which lead to the conclusion that the basic rights of soldiers or the basic codes of internal conduct have been infringed. He reports to the Bundestag on the result of his examination in a report about the particular case or as a part of his annual report.
3. The Commissioner prepares a written complete report at the end of the calendar year.

§3

In exercising his duties the Defence Commissioner has the following powers:

1. He can demand information and access to files from the Minister of Defence and all subordinate offices and persons. This right can only be refused him where the subject in question is strictly classified. The decision about this refusal is taken by the Minister of Defence himself, or his permanent deputy in office, who is accountable for his decision to the Defence Committee ...

...

3. He can pass on any complaint to the authorities responsible for initiating disciplinary actions or court procedures.
4. He can visit without previous notice any barracks, headquarters or other premises of the armed forces ... at any time.
5. He has the right to demand from the Minister of Defence overall reports on the discharge of disciplinary powers in the armed forces and statistical reports from the Federal Minister of Justice or the ministers of justices of the Länder concerning procedures under the penal code as far as members of the armed forces and their dependants are affected thereby.
6. He can ... sit in on proceedings of the courts, also in as far as these deliberate in closed sessions. He has the right of access to material under consideration by the courts in the same way as the public prosecutor.

...

§6
The Bundestag and its Defence Committee can demand at any time that the Commissioner be present.

§7
Every member of the armed forces has the right to approach the Commissioner individually or collectively without going through normally prescribed channels. He may not be ... discriminated against by his superiors for having appealed to the Commissioner.

. . .

The Bundestag Defence Committee constituted itself in 1980 as a special Committee of Investigation (there have been twenty such *ad hoc* committees since 1949) to probe into possible failures on the part of Bund and Länder institutions to foresee and handle violent demonstrations of the extreme left against the celebrations of the 25th anniversary of the new German armed forces within NATO, in Bremen in May 1980. The Committee heard, partly in secret sessions (see above, Doc.4d), federal ministers, chiefs of staff, heads of military intelligence and of the Offices for the Protection of the Constitution *(Ämter für Verfassungsschutz)*. All investigating committees *(Untersuchungsausschüsse)* can apply the German code of court procedure, i.e. subpoena witnesses etc. In contrast to the British practice of parliamentary committees of investigation and inquiry and more analogous to the US one, there are no 'neutral' judges involved, only parliamentarians. In the case in question the end result of long investigation was both a majority and a minority report, trying to blame and exonerate the Bonn government. The excerpts below, however, show a minimum of consensus in regard to consequences to be drawn for the future.

Document 8

THE DEFENCE COMMITTEE AS A COMMITTEE OF INVESTIGATION *(UNTERSUCHUNGSAUSSCHUSS):* FINAL REPORT
Source: Deutscher Bundestag, 8th legislative period, Drucksache 8/4472

Section H: *Dangers and Consequences*
1. Personal injuries and damage to property
. . .

Approximately 300 Bremen police officers were injured; five police officers required hospital treatment. Nearly fifty of the assisting police officers from Lower Saxony were injured. In addition there were five injured soldiers.

The number of injured demonstrators is unknown; a much lower figure is estimated.
Material damages include eight demolished and damaged army vehicles (total damages approx. DM 112 400) as well as damage to equipment in front of the Weser stadium, to streets in the area and to police clothes and equipment.

Judicial Proceedings
Seventy-four suspected persons are under investigation. The first charges have been preferred. 30 per cent of the suspects come from the area around Bremen. Some offenders from Hamburg are thought to belong to the terrorist scene in the broadest sense. Probable offenders also come from so-called undogmatic groups. Offenders from democratic organizations or from orthodox Communist groups have not been identified ... .

Fundamental Conclusions Drawn from the Events
However much the Defence Committee supports the standpoint of the Federal Minister for Defence that the army will not allow itself to be chased from one city to another whenever organizing its official events by violent demonstrators or shut itself up in its barracks, the matter cannot be left there.

First of all, the Bremen incident throws a light on the potential of radical opponents of the Federal Republic's armed forces and its political attachment to the alliance, a potential whose size should not be exaggerated but which should be taken seriously. Various activities can be expected from this potential in the future, too ...

[Compare *inter alia* the violent demonstrations by a similarly violent minority during the visit of the American Vice President to Krefeld in 1983. ed.]

The protests and actions directed against the official event were based on a number of partly overlapping motives:

Especially widespread was the opinion that the public ceremony of the taking of the military oath, seen in a foreign policy context with the crises in Afghanistan and Iran, was considered as being adverse to détente, even conducive to promoting war. Such ideas were related to the notion of the public oath and the military tattoo being pre-democratic military rituals which were considered old-fashioned and unnecessary. Besides these voices which did not throw any basic doubt on the task of the state to provide the country with a military defence system were others which made the Bremen riots against the army, in its role as an institution upholding the state, into a symbol of the fight against this state. This opposition apparently avails itself of political-intellectual trends of a deeper dimension which can be especially observed in sections of the younger generation. This view is not only supported by the unusually large number and variety of the organizations and persons who have taken part in protests and counter-demonstrations in Bremen, but also by the number of 10,000 to 15,000 chiefly young citizens who let themselves be sent onto the streets by this topic. The main factor here is not only the defence policy opposition in the narrow sense but a basic mood which opposes the outward manifestations of the state ...

The task of politics is to define the necessity of an efficient defence system, arising from the external and security policy conditions, but only credible and effective if it can meet the possible outside threat. State and social institutions must digest and hand on this knowledge. Left alone, the army is not capable of sufficiently promoting acceptance of the need to defend a country. Rather more, this is the task of all forces which carry responsibility in the state and in society. The committee therefore suggests examining what further and increased efforts in this basic intellectual discussion are necessary. Furthermore, the following possibilities should be considered:

Political parties, associations and Churches should stress the need for the country's defence more strongly and take part accordingly in official events. They should encourage relevant information and discussion in their field of responsibility. On the one hand, special importance is to be attached to the dialogue with critical sections of the population, above all with the younger generation. On the other, it is necessary to keep the appropriate distance from forces guided by undemocratic intentions in order to counter-balance the danger of any misleading actions by such groups; this also applies when demonstrations take place.

In the field of schooling and education, increased efforts have to be made to acquaint the younger generation more intensively with questions concerning the country's defence and compulsory military service. Here reference is made to Corresponding suggestions of the Defence Committee made in June 1980 ... .

The possible, because inherent, conflict mentioned above between Art. 38 and Art. 21 of the Basic Law explodes when 'rebels' speak and vote against their own caucus in the Bundestag. They risk being expelled from their party and caucus (the latter has never been done without the former) for their stand, as happened again in two cases in 1981/82 in regard to the then governing SPD. The excerpts to follow are part of a speech made by Dieter Lattmann, a writer who belonged to the left wing of his party and caucus and who decided not to return to parliament in the following legislative period. At the time terrorism was much in evidence in West Germany and numerous laws were enacted or amended to cope with the situation, *inter alia* to prevent abuse of contacts between an accused and his lawyer (taking messages from the imprisoned on trial to outside sympathizers and followers etc.).

Document 9

SPEECH BY A DISSENTING MEMBER OF THE SPD CAUCUS IN 1978

Source: Deutscher Bundestag, 72nd Parliamentary sitting,8th legislative period, Sten. Berichte, 16 February 1978

. . .

Lattmann (SPD)
The members of the German Federal Parliament are representatives of the whole nation, not tied to orders and instructions and only bound to their conscience. With this reference to the contents of Art. 38 of the Constitution I explain why my convictions differ from those of the majority of my own caucus.

. . .

We are all faced with the question whether we submit to the terrorists' plan by letting ourselves be provoked by their murderous actions into restricting basic rights and increasingly arming the state with weapons or whether we want to defend our free basic rights even more decisively because of terrorism. Of course everybody talks about freedom. No cliché rolls off the tongue of right-wing politicians of order more often than the one about the free democratic system. People should stop making boasting noises about freedom; they should put freedom into practice!

(Applause from parts of the SPD and the FDP
-Shouts from the CDU/CSU)

This also means fearlessly describing what is happening in Parliament at a moment like this.

. . .

All of a sudden it is apparently not a matter of a bill whose meaning and usefulness are to be objectively examined but a matter of the ritual of power.

. . .

Accordingly I shall vote together with my caucus colleagues Manfred Coppik, Karl-Heinz Hansen and Erich Meinike against the bill. Our proximity to the CDU/CSU in the minutes will be only a typographical one ... .

Notes

1. See W. Bagehot, *The English Constitution*, Oxford 1958, 118ff.
2. For the total number of laws between 1949 and 1990 which failed to get on the statutes because of an absolute veto of the Bundesrat and for the origin of bills introduced, see Statistics, 17.
3. For instance, between the Trade Unions and the SPD or the Catholic Church and the CDU/CSU, see Ch.8.
4. On the military side there is the MAD (Militärischer Abschirmdienst, counter espionage) and the BND (Bundesnachrichtendienst, espionage), on the civilian side the

Bundesamt für Verfassungsschutz (Federal Office for the Protection of the Constitution). The latter—strictly regulated by law—gathers material on any revolutionary activities directed against the democratic order as such, not against the government in power. It has no powers to arrest etc. In 1978 Parliament established by law a special supervising body of the Bundestag for the three secret services. See also Doc.4d and Ch.12.

5. It has been shown that, for instance, between 1972 to 1976 there were three or four instances of political importance, when measures already announced or announced as pending by the government, had to be cancelled because opposition within the then SPD government caucus was too strong, see: C.C. Schweitzer, *Der Abgeordnete im parlamentarischen System der Bundesrepublik,* Opladen 1979.

6. Subtle means of exerting pressure on individual MdBs could consist of offering or withdrawing nominations to certain positions in the caucus or on parliamentary committees, or to send or not to send MdBs on official trips abroad which are generally very 'popular'. Famous dissenting votes in the Bundestag were recorded in connection with the introduction of compulsory military service, the reform of the law on abortion and the law on emergency-regulations. See Schweitzer, *Der Abgeordnete im parlamentarischen System der Bundesrepublik,* op. cit.

7. G. Leibholz has highlighted this in his book: *Strukturprobleme der modernen Demokratie,* Karlsruhe 1967 (3rd edition).

8. On the mathematical basis of proportional representation and formulae adopted see Ch.8.

9. As of 1994, the total number of seats is 'normally' 656. However, the intricate German electoral law still provides for the possibility of so called *Überhangmandate,* i.e additional seats gained in those Länder where more members of the Bundestag have been directly elected for a particular party than this party is entitled to in each Land on the decisive basis of proportionate representation. The Bundestag elected on 16 October 1994 has, therefore, a total of 672 members, i.e. 16 holding *Überhangmandate.* See also Ch.8 and Statistics 16.

8
Political Parties

Anthony Nicholls

Political parties in Germany are not only recognized in law and regulated by it, they are even referred to in the Federal German Constitution (Basic Law). Art. 21 of the Basic Law is clearly designed to ensure that political parties respect the principles of democracy. It reads as follows:

> (1) Political parties shall participate in the forming of the political will of the people. They may be freely established. Their internal organisation must conform to democratic principles. They must publicly account for the sources of their funds.

> (2) Parties which, by reason of their aims or the behaviour of their adherents, seek to impair or abolish the free democratic basic order or to endanger the existence of the Federal Republic of Germany shall be unconstitutional. The Federal Constitutional Court shall decide on the question of unconstitutionality.

> (3) Details shall be regulated by federal laws.[1]*

This provision in the Basic Law was designed to prevent a recurrence of the situation which had developed in the Weimar Republic, when parties like the Nazis and Communists had abused the freedom given to them under the constitution to attack democracy itself. In the early years of the Republic the restrictions in the Basic Law were indeed implemented against threats from the right and left. The neo-Nazi Socialist Reich Party (SRP) was banned in 1952, and in 1956 the German Communist Party (KPD) suffered the same fate (see also Ch.11).

Nevertheless, it took some time before the Federal legislation referred to in the last paragraph of Art.21 passed through parliament. It was not until July 1967 that the Law on Political Parties was finally approved by the Bundesrat (Doc.1). The law defines political parties and lays down rules about their statutes and organization. The rights of members, election of officers, and the regulation of finances are established in this law.

The question of party finances has been the subject of both legislation and judicial proceedings. In general, strict rules are established

Notes for this chapter begin on p. 236.

about the public declaration of financial contributions. On the other hand parties are generously treated by comparison with Anglo-Saxon counterparts, in that they receive direct financial assistance from the state in direct proportion to their performance at the polls. Contributions to party funds are also, if only to a limited extent, exempt from personal taxation. The way in which these matters are regulated in the Party Law is set out in Doc.2.

The electoral process in the Federal Republic is also carefully circumscribed by statute. Art. 38 of the Basic Law stipulates that the members of the Bundestag shall be elected in 'general, free, equal and secret elections'.

The Bundestag and Land parliaments are elected according to a system which combines direct election with proportional representation (Doc.3). The aim is to combine fairness of representation with political stability; it is assumed that 'pure' proportional representation would lead to a multiplicity of small parties and weak coalition governments.

Since 1990 the Bundestag has had a normal total of 656 members (see also Ch.7). Half are directly elected in constituencies—the other half from party lists drawn up in each Land. This illustrates the importance of legally defining political parties in Germany, since the electoral process would not work if the fiction were maintained that such parties did not exist.

Electors have two votes, the first of which is given to a candidate and the second to a party list. In each of the 328 constituencies one candidate is directly elected by simple majority. Then electors' second votes are put together with those from other constituencies and a total figure for each party in the Federal Republic is obtained (Electoral Law, section 6, paras. 1 and 2). Once each party's total entitlement has been defined, its seats are divided among the Land lists according to the second votes cast in the various Länder, although the number of directly elected members is subtracted from the total entitlement in each case. If a party has more directly elected members than its total of second votes in any one Land would warrant, it is allowed to keep the extra members and the number of seats in the Bundestag from that Land is increased accordingly. This was important for the CDU/CSU in the 1994 Bundestag elections. Voters may choose different parties with their first and second votes and such 'tactical' voting is not uncommon. The decisive vote for determining the strength of the parties is the second vote. In order to gain seats from the Land lists at all, parties must obtain at least 5 per cent of the valid votes cast or be successful in direct elections in three constituencies (section 6, para. 11). This so-called '5 per cent hurdle' has been a serious obstacle to the emergence of small parties in the Bundestag and is a constant threat to the FDP. The law also sets out rules for the presentation and selection of party candidates. All such candidates must be elected by constituency parties according to defined procedures (sections 20 and 21).

In comparison with some Anglo-Saxon countries, membership of political parties is high in the Federal Republic. Electoral participation is also very impressive, even if the turnout at the 'unification' Bundestag election, in December 1990, was 77.8 per cent, the lowest recorded in the history of the Federal Republic. This could partly be accounted for by relatively low turnouts in the new federal states of the former GDR, but it was noteworthy that most of the old federal states produced lower electoral participation than in any Bundestag election since 1949. Nevertheless, by Anglo-American standards, the turnout remains high. One reason for this may be the attention paid to political education in German schools. More important is possibly the fact that elections in Germany are held on a Sunday, so that working people are given a fair chance to go to the polling booths. It is also relatively easy to obtain a postal vote. However, it should be remembered that proportional representation itself encourages a high turnout because no elector needs to feel that he is wasting his vote.

In accordance with the laws established for political parties, their statutes set out in detail their aims, membership, organization and financing arrangements. The laws require that the parties should be organized on strictly democratic lines.

Examples from contrasting political groups illustrate the extent to which party life is based on firm legal foundations.

The first example is the statute of the Christian Democratic Union, Germany's most important conservative party and a ruling party in Bonn coalitions, 1949–1969 and 1982 to the present (Doc.4).

The second example is that of the Social Democratic Party, the main opposition group, 1949–1965, and the foundation of coalition governments, 1969–82 (Doc.5).

So far as the Christian Democrats and Social Democrats are concerned, their statutes do not reveal striking differences, except that the SPD is rather more centralized in its organization than the CDU. This reflects different attitudes to the issue of Federalism; the Christian Democrats have always stressed the importance of the Land divisions within the Federal Republic.

In all parties, policy is defined by the party conference. Party leaders, even when they are in government, cannot dispense with the confidence of the party conference. An example of this was Chancellor Schmidt's difficulty in carrying his party with him on defence and economic matters in 1982.

Party Finances

The financial affairs of political parties are carefully regulated in their statutes. Party subscriptions are often levied in relation to a member's income, as in the case of the SPD (Doc.6).

Party Programmes

In the early years of the Federal Republic there were clear programmatic differences between the parties. The Christian Democrats stood for a decentralized Germany, integrated into Western Europe and NATO. They were in favour of Church influence on German cultural life, believed in private property and, by 1949, they were committed to free enterprise in the economy. However, this was tempered by a commitment to social welfare—the so-called 'Social Market Economy'(see also Ch.14). The Social Democrats wanted a centralized Germany with a strong emphasis on social equality. They favoured an economic policy involving state planning and the socialization of major industries. The Free Democrats also wanted a strong central government and were specially concerned to see Germany reunified. They, like the Social Democrats, were opposed to clerical influence in education. However, they were completely against state interference in the economy or state control of industry. If anything, the Free Democrats, despite their liberal-sounding name, were socially more conservative, more nationalist and more committed to laissez-faire economics than the CDU.

After the first decade of Federal German politics, differences between the parties began to blur. The SPD, for example, discouraged by poor Federal election results and headed by a new generation of leaders, changed its programme so that it accepted the free market, at least in modified form, and committed itself to national defence. This was enshrined in the Godesberg Programme of November 1959 (Doc.7).

In the 1960s the Free Democrats also faced divisions of loyalty and began to move towards a form of liberalism which stressed individual freedom rather than nationalism or business interests. In October 1971 at their Congress in Freiburg, they enshrined this humane liberalism into the 'Freiburg theses' which formed the basis of their programme and the theoretical justification for political collaboration with the Social Democrats (Doc.8). In 1982 the FDP moved back into coalition with the CDU and since then has tended to put more emphasis on the importance of private property, private enterprise and low taxation. As a junior partner of the CDU/CSU since 1982, the FDP seems to have become narrower in its appeal. Younger people, left-liberals and even self-employed business people no longer support it as firmly as before. This has been particularly damaging in Land elections, eight of which in 1994 saw the FDP failing to obtain representation in the respective Land parliaments. In the 1994 Bundestag election it only just got over the five per cent hurdle, probably as the result of CDU supporters using their second votes to help the Christian/liberal coalition. Nevertheless, the fact that the FDP stayed in the Bundestag meant that Chancellor Kohl received a mandate for a further term of office.[2]

The Christian Democrats have found it possible to retain most of their basic principles, though they have felt the need to put a new gloss on some aspects of their policies, such as those dealing with the protection of the environment or women's rights. The general principles of Christian Democracy are well set out in the statement by the CDU Federal Executive issued in October 1993 (Doc.9).

It will be seen that at least by the early 1970s the area of common ground between the parties represented in the Bundestag had become very large. Today, differences in electoral programmes rarely concern fundamental matters of principle, but are about the priority to be given to different objectives. In many ways this is a source of stability in the system. The events of 1989/90, however, created difficulties for all the traditional parties. At first the CDU/CSU and FDP coalition seemed to carry all before it, rapid unification being a triumph for the foreign policy of Hans-Dietrich Genscher (FDP) and the leadership of the Federal Chancellor, Helmut Kohl.

The SPD, on the other hand, was less happy with the rush for unification, and its Chancellor-candidate, Oskar Lafontaine, who did not seem very enthusiastic about unification, warned that the price to be paid by German tax-payers would be very heavy. The Bundestag elections were a resounding victory for the CDU/CSU/FDP coalition. Soon, however, the euphoria began to wear off and serious problems appeared. It was clear that the 'old' federal states of West Germany would have to make sacrifices for the rehabilitation of the East (see Ch.14, Doc.10), and the SPD differed strongly from the CDU—and even more from the business-orientated FDP—about where to place the burdens. Social Democrats were strongly opposed to cuts in social spending or attacks on public subsidies which might exacerbate unemployment. Another burning issue was that of asylum-seekers and immigrants of German descent from Eastern Europe and the Soviet Union who were entering the Federal Republic in very large numbers (See also Ch.14, Doc.6, and Statistics, Tables 2–4). This matter aroused great popular discontent, since asylum-seekers were spread throughout the country and were supported and housed without being obliged—or even allowed—to work. The CDU, and especially the CSU, were eager to change the Basic Law to inhibit such immigration—the FDP and SPD were far more reluctant. Similarly, Social Democrats resisted the view, which developed strongly as a result of the Gulf War, 1991-2, that a united Germany should be ready to shoulder international responsibilities and deploy troops outside the NATO area. The most they were prepared to contemplate was that German soldiers could serve in UN peace-keeping forces (see also Ch.6, Doc.10), and even that was a source of disagreement within the party.

Apart from new tensions between the established parties, there had already been indications that these parties were not satisfying the aspirations of those who felt themselves unrepresented by the social/liberal consensus in West Germany. In the early 1980s, for example, a new party, the Greens, emerged to challenge the traditional ones. The Greens were founded on 17 March 1979 in Frankfurt/Sindligen, also calling themselves the 'Other Political Association' *(Die Sonstige Politische Vereinigung)*. They were formed out of an amalgam of ecological and citizens' action groups from various parts of Germany. On 13 January 1980 they established themselves as a Federal Party. The Greens opposed nuclear power, nuclear armaments and Cold War alliances. Their programme involved a fundamental rejection of the premises upon which West Germany's post-war prosperity was based—especially the concept of economic growth. In March 1983 they polled 5.6 per cent or over two million, of the second votes cast in the Bundestag elections and gained twenty-seven seats. The Greens did even better in the 1987 Bundestag elections, their vote rising to 8.3 per cent. Since then, however, the collapse of the Cold War has removed one of their strongest concerns, the threat of global nuclear war. Splits developed between fundamentalists who refused to work within the system *(Fundis)* and more pragmatic leaders *(Realos)* who wanted to make coalitions with the SPD—coalitions which have appeared in a number of Land governments. These splits, and a confused reaction to the prospect of German unification under the leadership of Helmut Kohl, caused a severe loss of support for the Greens in 1990, and their only link with the Bundestag was through their relationship with former oppositionist groups in the GDR, the 'Alliance 90' *(Bündnis 90)* (see below and Doc.13). Thereafter the *Realos* gained the upper hand and the party did better in Landtag elections.

There have also been threats from the extreme Right and Left. In the middle years of the 1960s, when a minor economic set-back occurred, the political system in the Federal Republic was challenged by a radical nationalist party, the National Democrats or NPD. It obtained some impressive results in Land elections, but was never able to overcome the 5 per cent hurdle in a Bundestag election. On the Left, Radical Marxist parties also exist, despite the banning of the Communist Party (KPD) in 1956 (see also Ch.11). The party which claims to be the successor to the KPD, although carefully defining itself as compatible with the Basic Law, is the German Communist Party (DKP), which was set up in 1968. As in other European countries, there occurred in the 1980s a revival of right-wing nationalism on the fringes of West German political life. Firstly, this might be explained by the sluggishness of the economy. Despite some improvement after the change of government to a Christian/FDP coalition in 1982, the level of unemployment remained relatively high, and the buoyant optimism of earlier decades had faded. Secondly, the presence of many foreigners in Germany aroused hostility. Although many foreign workers had been sent home after the oil crisis of 1973, large numbers of Turkish or Southern European origin remained, with their families. Some parts of major cities, such as the district of Kreuzberg in West Berlin, were regarded as having become Turkish in Character, and this led to social tensions with non-Turkish residents.

There were also changes in working-class culture which created resentments amongst the less fortunate. The unskilled and the poorly educated were likely to find themselves missing out on the good things of life, and blamed this on the state authorities or on alien immigrants. Such resentments were combined with contempt for apparently permissive trends in education and culture, and the belief that Germany was being betrayed by those who had sold out to her former enemies or to some supra-national European movement.

Two parties on the right fringe of politics came to express this viewpoint, the German People's Union *(Deutsche Volksunion* or *DVU)*, led by Gerhard Frey, and the Republican Party *(Republikaner* or *Reps)*, led by Franz Schönhuber. The DVU was xenophobic but rather old-fashioned in its approach, and did not seem to pose much of a threat to established parties.

The Republicans had their roots in Bavaria, where, of course, the NSDAP had begun its operations in the early years of the Weimar Republic. They were founded on 27 November 1983 by two former CSU members of parliament who had been outraged by Strauss's willingness to grant credits to the GDR and by his generally high-handed methods of leadership. The most effective spokesman for the Reps, however, was Franz Schönhuber, a successful TV presenter whose unashamed references to his past in the *Waffen SS* had been a factor in his break with Bavarian Television.

Both the DVU and the Reps were careful to avoid activities or policy statements which could lead to action to ban them under Article 21 of the Basic Law. The Republicans stressed national unity, urged changes to the constitution which would weaken parliamentary parties by introducing plebiscites and a popularly elected president, and stressed the need to protect the traditional middle class of Germany, or *Mittelstand* (Doc.10).

In January 1989, the Reps caused something of a sensation in West Berlin, where they gained 7.5 per cent of the vote and thereby entered a Land parliament for the first time, and in June 1989 they also did well in European elections.[3] Although it was clear that many of these were protest votes, and although the turnout for European elections was low, the result was a boost for the Reps, who now seemed to be challenging the established parties from the right.

From November 1989 until December 1990 the achievement of German unification, and particularly the leading role in it played by the Christian Democrats under Helmut Kohl, weakened the appeal of the far-right parties, and the Republicans seemed to go into decline. In the unification Bundestag election of 2 December 1990 the Reps only won 2.1 per cent of the vote, falling well below the 5 per cent hurdle they needed to clear to obtain representation in Bonn.

Once the difficulties involved in unification became apparent, however, and with increasing pressure on the Federal Republic as the result of asylum-seekers and other immigrants, the Reps bounced back. The tensions created by economic difficulties and professional purges in the former GDR were also grist to their mill. The Reps argued that the treatment of former SED members was similar to the denazification procedure in West Germany after the war, and that it was just as unfair.

The difficulties of the European Community have also helped the Reps. The Maastricht Treaty of December 1991, with its commitment to monetary and economic union, seemed to threaten Germany's monetary sovereignty, and especially the status of the D Mark. Since monetary union with East Germany had already created grave economic difficulties and increased inflation, a threat to the stability of the currency was particularly worrying. The Reps have exploited the European issue, since the established parties rarely criticise the EU, and some Germans see this as an example of their lack of concern for the 'little man' whose interests are damaged by EU directives (Doc.11).

Despite their raucous campaigning however, the Reps have so far never been able to gain the necessary five per cent of the votes needed to enter the Bundestag—and thereby becoming the first party of the extreme right to do so. One of their problems remained the rivalry with the DVU—in the Hamburg Land elections of September 1993 the two extreme right parties obtained 7.6 per cent of the votes cast, but since only 4.0 per cent went to the Reps, they were kept out of the Land parliament. In the Bundestag election of 16 October 1994 they fared even worse, gaining only 1.9 per cent of the vote and failing to obtain representation in the Bundestag.

If unification affected the right-wing of the political spectrum, it also had an impact on the left (see also Ch.4). With the collapse of the communist regime in the GDR, in November/December 1989, the SED was totally discredited and many of its members resigned. It renamed itself the 'Party of Democratic Socialism' or PDS. The PDS admits 'the mistakes and the crimes committed in the name of socialism' but still seeks to develop an alternative to capitalist society. Like the Reps, it publicly supports the Federal Republic's constitution. The PDS makes a particular appeal to those who feel they have lost out in the former GDR as the result of unification, and is supported by the old *Nomenklatura* of the former GDR, whose commitment to Western-style pluralistic democracy must be doubted. (See Doc.12 and also Ch.4).

In the first Bundestag elections held in united Germany on 2 December 1990, it was ruled, exceptionally, that for parties competing for votes in the former GDR the five per cent hurdle would be relaxed so that it only applied to the area of the 'new' federal states. As a result the PDS obtained representation in the Bundestag, even though it only obtained 2.4 per cent of the Federal vote. Since then support for the PDS has hardened in some of the 'new' federal states, and especially East Berlin. In the Bundestag elections of October 1994, it was able to circumvent the five per cent hurdle by winning four direct mandates in constituencies in East Berlin. It was therefore entitled to thirty seats in the Bundestag, despite the fact that it only achieved 4.4 per cent of the vote.

The relaxation of the five per cent clause in the former GDR in December 1990 also helped another group whose claim to represent a true alternative to the established system was perhaps somewhat more credible. During 1989, in what proved to be the last year of the SED dictatorship, opposition groups had sprung up in the GDR demanding more freedom and democracy. (see also Ch.4) The most important of these groups were the 'New Forum' and 'Democracy Now'. They wanted a genuine democracy, but were concerned to preserve a separate identity for the former GDR, and to protect the right to work and the rights of women.

In the early months of 1990 the New Forum and its allies were swept aside by the more professionally organized parties associated with counterparts in West Germany, and by the irresistible pressure for rapid unification, which meant that there would not be a new constitution for a united Germany, but that the GDR would simply join up with the Federal Republic. New Forum and Democracy Now joined with another group, the Initiative for Human Rights, to form an electoral pact 'Alliance 90', which was associated with the East German Greens. It only obtained 1.2 per cent of the federal vote in the December 1990 Bundestag elections, but—as with the PDS—it was able to gain a small number of seats in the Bundestag. Ironically, this was the only Green representation in Bonn, since the West German Party fell below the five per cent hurdle.(see also Ch.4)

There followed negotiations between Alliance 90 and the Greens in West Germany, and in November 1992 a contract of association was drawn up between the two organizations. This included commitment to basic values and human rights, ecology, democracy, social justice, social equality of men and women, and freedom from force *(Gewaltfreiheit)*. The new alliance also urged a new type of political culture and a new form of political organization (Doc.13).

In September 1993 the Land elections in Hamburg, where a green 'alternative' list gained over 13 per cent of the poll, encouraged the Greens to believe that the prospects for the new alliance would be quite good in the election year of 1994. In fact, they did manage to overcome the five per cent hurdle in the Bundestag election of 16 October 1994, and received 49 seats in the Bonn parliament.

Document 1

THE LAW ON POLITICAL PARTIES *(PARTEIENGESETZ)*
Amended version: 31 January 1994
Source: Documents on Politics and Society in the Federal Republic of Germany (Inter Nationes, Bonn, 1994).
Transl.: Official

I: General Provisions

Art.1. Constitutional Status and Functions of the Parties

(1) Political parties form a constitutionally integral part of a free democratic system of government. Their free and continuous participation in the formation of political opinions amongst the population enables them to discharge the public tasks which are incumbent upon them pursuant to the

Basic Constitutional Law (Grundgesetz) and which they undertake to fulfil to the best of their ability.

(2) The parties participate in the formation of the political will of the people in all fields of national life, in particular by:

bringing their influence to bear on the shaping of public opinion; inspiring and furthering political education;
promoting an active participation by individual citizens in political life;
training talented people to assume public responsibilities;
participating in Federal, Land and Local Government elections by nominating candidates;
exercising an influence on political trends in parliament and the government;
initiating their defined political aims in the national decision-making processes; and
ensuring continuous, vital links between the people and the public authorities.

(3) The parties shall define their aims in the form of political programs.

Art.2. Definition of the Term 'Political Party'

(1) Parties are associations of citizens who set out to influence either permanently or for a long period of time the formation of political opinions at Federal or Land level and to participate in the representation of the people in the ... Bundestag or regional parliaments.

. . .

Art.4. Designation

(1) The name of a party must be clearly distinguishable from that of any existing party ... .

. . .

Art.5. Equality of Treatment

(1) Where a public authority provides facilities or other public services for use by a party, it must accord equal treatment to all other parties ... .

II: Internal Organization

Art.6. Statutes and Program

(1) A party must have written statutes (articles of association) and a written program.

. . .

(2) The statutes must contain provisions on:

1. the name and acronym (if used), the registered seat and the activities of the party;
2. the admission and designation of members;
3. the rights and duties of members;
4. admissible disciplinary measures against members and their exclusion from the party (Art.10, paras. 3 to 5);
5. admissible disciplinary measures against regional associations;
6. the general organisation of the party;

7. composition and powers of the executive committee (Vorstand) and other bodies (Organe);
8. matters which may only be decided upon by a meeting of members and representatives pursuant to Art.9;
9. the preconditions, form and time limit for convening meetings of members and representatives and the official recording of the resolutions;
10. regional organizations and organs which are authorised to submit or sign election proposals for elections to parliaments inasmuch as there are no legal provisions on this matter;
11. an overall vote by members and the procedure to be adopted when the party convention has passed a resolution to dissolve the party or a regional association or to merge with another party;

. . .

Art.7. Organisation

(1) Parties are subdivided into regional organizations. The size and scope of these units are determined in the statutes. The regional structure of the party must be developed to a sufficient degree to enable individual members to participate on an appropriate scale in the formation of political opinions within the party ... .

Art.8. Organs

(1) The members' meeting and executive committee constitute the essential organs of the party and the regional organizations ... .

. . .

Art.9. Members and Delegates' Assemblies (Convention, General Assembly)

(1) The assemblies of members' delegates (convention, General Assembly) constitute the supreme organ in the given regional organization. It is designated as a party convention *(Parteitag)* in higher level regional organizations and general assembly *(Hauptversammlung)* at the lower levels ... Party conventions are convened in at least every second calendar year.

(2) Pursuant to the statutes, members of the executive committee and members of other bodies in a regional organization ... may participate in a representatives' meeting. However, in this case they may only be given voting rights on a scale corresponding to one-fifth of the total number of members at the assembly who are entitled to vote.

(3) ... the party convention decides on programmes, statutes, subscriptions, arbitration procedure, dissolution of the party and merging with other parties.

(4) The party convention elects the chairman *(Vorsitzender)* of the regional organization, his representatives and the other members of the executive committee ... .

Art.10. Members' Rights

(1) ... No justification need be given for refusing an application for membership. Neither general nor temporary embargoes on new members are permissible ... .

(2) Members of the party and representatives in the party bodies have equal voting rights ...

(3) The statutes contain provisions governing:

1. admissible disciplinary measures against members;
2. reasons for such measures;
3. those bodies within the party which may initiate disciplinary measures.

If a member is deprived of his party offices or his qualification to hold them, the justification for such a decision must be stated.

(4) A member may only be expelled from the party if he deliberately infringes the statutes or acts in a manner quite contrary to the principles or discipline of the party and thus seriously impairs its standing.

(5) The arbitration court competent in accordance with the arbitration procedure code decides upon expulsion from the party. The right to appeal to a higher court is guaranteed ... .

Art.11. Executive Committee (Vorstand)

(1) The executive committee must be elected at least every second calendar year. It must comprise at least three members.

(2) ... the executive committee may include members of parliament and other high-ranking persons in the party if they hold office or mandate as the result of an election. The proportion of members not elected under the provisions of Art.9, para.4, may not exceed one-fifth of the total number of executive committee members ... .

. . .

Art.13. Composition of Delegates' Assemblies

The composition of a delegates' assembly or that of any other body wholly or partly comprising representatives from regional organizations is laid down in the statutes. The number of representatives from a regional organization is primarily calculated on the basis of the number of represented members. The statutes may provide that the composition of the rest of the representatives from the regional organization, at most one-half of the total, shall be determined in accordance with the proportion of votes polled at regional organization level in previous parliamentary elections ... .

Art.14. Party Arbitration

(1) The party and the highest-level regional organizations set up courts of arbitration to settle and decide disputes between the party or a regional organization and individual members as well as differences of opinion about the interpretation and implementation of the statutes ... .

Art.15. Decision-Making Party Organs

(1) The party organs adopt their resolutions on the basis of a simple majority vote inasmuch as an increased majority vote is not stipulated by law or by the statutes.

(2) The ballots for members of the executive committee and representatives for representatives' meetings as well as for the bodies of higher-level regional associations are secret ... .

(3) The statutory provisions governing the submission of motions must be such as to ensure a democratic formation of opinions and in particular adequate discussion of the proposals put forward by minorities ... .

Art.16. Measures against Regional Organizations

(1) The dissolution and exclusion of subordinate regional associations ... are only permissible in cases of serious infringement of party principles or discipline. The statutes stipulate:

1. the reasons justifying the measures;
2. which higher-level regional organization and which regional organization body may adopt such measures ... .

III: Nomination of Candidates for Election

Art.17. Nomination of Candidates

Candidates for election to parliament must be chosen by secret ballot. The nomination procedure is governed by the election laws and the party statutes ... .

The Law regulates the manner in which political parties may be assisted from public funds when meeting election expenses. The accounting procedures of the parties are also strictly defined.

Document 2

THE LAW ON POLITICAL PARTIES: FINANCES

IV: Public Financing

Art.18. Principles and Extent of Public Financing

(1) The State shall grant the parties funds to partly finance their general activities pursuant to the Basic Law. The criteria for the distribution of public funds shall be the parties' performance in European Bundestag and Landtag (state parliament) elections, the sum of its membership contributions and the amount of donations received.

The maximum annual amount of public funds which may be granted to all parties together shall be DM 230 million (absolute limit) at the time of entry into force of this provision.

(3) The parties shall receive each year

1. DM 1.00 for each valid vote cast for the party list or
2. DM 1.00 for each vote cast for the party in a constituency where in the state concerned a list for that party was not permissible, and
3. DM 0.50 for each DM received from other sources (members' subscriptions or lawful donations); only amounts up to DM 6,000 per person are taken into account.

In derogation of numbers 1 and 2 above, the parties shall receive DM 1.30 per vote up to five million valid votes.

(4) Parties who according to the final result of the most recent European or Bundestag election have polled at least 0.5% or, in a state election, 1% of the valid votes coast for the party lists shall be entitled to public funds in accordance with Para. 3 nos. 1 and 3; in order to qualify for payments under Para. 3, Sentence 1 No. 1 and Sentence 2, a party must meet these requirements in the election concerned. Parties who according to the final election result have obtained 10% of the valid votes cast in a constituency have a right to public funds under Para. 3, No. 2. The first and second sentences do not apply to parties of national minorities.

(4) Parties who according to the final result of the most recent European or Bundestag election have polled at least 0.5% or, in a state election, 1% of the valid votes cast for the party lists shall be entitled to public funds in accordance with Para. 3, Nos. 1 and 3; in order to qualify for payments under Para. 3, Sentence 1, No. 1 and Sentence 2, a party must meet these requirements in the election concerned. Parties who according to the final election result have obtained 10% of the valid votes cast in a constituency have a right to public funds under Para. 3, No. 2. The first and second sentences do not apply to parties of national minorities.

(5) The amount of public funds may not exceed the party's own annual income (relative limit, Article 24, Para. 2, Nos. 1 to 5 and 7). The amount of funds made available to all parties together may not exceed the absolute limit

(6) Upon the entry into force of this Law the Federal President shall appoint a committee of independent experts. This committee shall initially draw up a basket of goods and services that represent typical party expenditure. Using this as a basis the committee shall each year, beginning in 1995 and relating to 1991, determine the increase in the prices of party-relevant items. The committee shall submit the results to the President of the German Bundestag. The committee shall be appointed for the duration of the term of office of the Federal President.

(7) Before making any changes in the structure and amount of public financing in excess of the price increases established in accordance with Para. 6, the committee referred to in Para. 6 shall submit recommendations to the German Bundestag. This applies especially to the assessment whether conditions have changed considerably and whether, therefore, an adjustment of the total volume or a change in the structure of public financing is called for.

(8) If a party is dissolved or banned it shall from then on receive no public funds.

Art.25. Donations

(1) Political parties are entitled to accept donations. The following are excluded:

1. Donations from political foundations and parliamentary groups.
2. Donations from corporate bodies, associations of persons and estate which, under statutes, foundation rules or other consitutions and, by virtue of actual business procedure, are exclusively and directly intended

for non-profit, charitable or church purposes (Paras. 51 to 68 of the Taxation Code).

3. Donations from outside the sphere of validity of this Law unless:

    a) they flow directly to a party from the assets of a German as defined by the Basic Law, citizen of the European Union, or of a business enterprise whose shares are more than 50 percent owned by Germans as defined by the Basic Law;

    b) they are donations to parties of national minorities, transferred from countries which are adjacent to the Federal Republic of Germany and where members of their ethnic group live, by that political party's parliamentary group in the European Parliament or by a foreign member of the European Parliament, or

    c) It is a donation by a foreigner not exceeding DM 1,000.

4. Donations from professional organizations which are made with the proviso that they be passed on to a political party.

5. Donations which, in each individual case, exceed DM 1,000 and whose donors cannot be determined or who are obviously merely passing on the donations of third parties not named.

6. Donations which are clearly made in the expectation of some specific economic or political advantage.

Document 3

THE ELECTORAL LAW OF THE FEDERAL REPUBLIC OF GERMANY (BUNDESWAHLGESETZ), 7 MAY 1956

Source: Documents on Politics and Society in the Federal Republic of Germany,
Inter Nationes, Bonn, 1980, citing BGBl., I, 1975, 2325
Transl.: Official
Modified to take account of alterations in the *Neufassung des Bundeswahlgesetzes* 21 July 1993, BGBl.I, 1993, 1217, and 29 July 1993, BGBl.I, 1290

Electoral System

§1: *Composition of the German Bundestag and Suffrage Principles*
(1) Subject to variations resulting from this law, the German Bundestag shall consist of 656 members. They shall be elected in a universal direct, free, equal and secret ballot by the Germans entitled to vote, in accordance with the principles of proportional representation combined with the personal election of candidates.
(2) Of the members, 328 shall be elected from constituency nominations in the constituencies and the rest from Land nominations (Land Lists) ...
. . .

§4: *Votes*
Each voter shall have two votes, a first vote to be cast for a Member of Parliament representing a constituency and a second vote be cast for a Land list.

§5: *Polling in the Constituencies*

In each constituency one member shall be returned to Parliament. The candidate obtaining the majority of the votes cast shall be deemed elected … .

§6: *Election by Land List*

(1) For the distribution of the seats to be occupied on the basis of Land lists, the second votes cast for each Land list shall be added up. In cases where a successful candidate in a constituency is one who has been nominated in accordance with §20, subsection (3), or by a party not entitled to submit a Land list in the Land in question, the second votes of those voters whose first votes were cast for him shall be disregarded. There shall be deducted from the total number of Members of Parliament (§1, sub-section (1) the number of successful constituency members referred to in the second sentence above or nominated by parties which, in accordance with sub-section (4) of the present section, are not to be taken into consideration.

(2) The remaining seats referred to in the last sentence of sub-section (1) above shall be distributed among the Land lists in proportion to the totals of their second votes to be taken into account according to the first and second sentence in the same sub-section. The total number of seats left over [after the direct election of the constituency members] is multiplied by the number of votes received by a Land [i.e. Party's] List throughout the Federal Republic and then divided by the total number of second votes on all Land lists which are to be taken into account. Each Land list receives in the first instance as many seats as it is entitled to on the basis of whole numbers. After that the seats are to be distributed among the Land lists in order according to the largest fractions of whole numbers required to elect a member of the list, according to the method given above.[4] If there are equal fractions of votes the Federal Returning Officer shall decide the assignment of the seat by drawing lots.

(3) If a party's Land list receives more than half the votes cast for all eligible Land lists but does not receive more than half of the seats to be distributed, then, disregarding the provisions of the previous sub-section, it shall receive an extra seat from those being distributed on the basis of fractional proportions of the second votes. Thereafter, the seats shall be distributed as in the last two sentences of sub-section 2, above.

(4) From the number of members thus arrived at for each Land list, the number of seats won by the party in question in the constituencies of the respective Land shall be deducted. The remaining seats shall be filled from the Land list concerned in the order laid down therein. Candidates who have been elected in a constituency shall be disregarded in the Land list … .

(5) Any party shall retain all the seats it has gained in the constituencies even if they exceed the number arrived at in accordance with sub-sections (2) and (3). In this event the total number of seats (Para 1, sub-section (1)) shall be increased to take account of the extra numbers: renewed calculation as under sub-sections (2) and (3) shall not take place.

(6) In distributing the seats among the Land lists, only such parties shall be taken into consideration as have obtained at least 5 per cent of the validly cast second votes in the Federal Republic or have won a seat [by direct election through first votes-AJN] in at least three constituencies … .

. . .

Franchise and Eligibility

§12: *Franchise*
(1) All Germans within the meaning of Art.116 Para.(1) of the Basic Law
shall be entitled to vote, provided that on the day of election they:
1. have reached the age of 18 years;
2. have had a domicile or have otherwise been permanently resident for at
   least three months within the Federal Republic of Germany;
and
3. are not disqualified from voting under §13 ... .

[§13 refers to those incapacitated by mental illness or disqualified by judicial
decision.]

. . .

§15: *Eligibility to Stand for Parliament*
(1) There shall be eligible to stand for parliament such persons as, on
election day:

1. have been Germans within the meaning of Art. 116 para. (1) of the Basic
   Law for at least one year;
and
2. have reached the age of 18 years ... .

[§13 also applies to deny eligibility for election to those incapacitated by
mental illness or disqualified by the courts.]

Preparations for the Election

§16: *Election Day*
The Federal President shall decide the day on which the general election is
to take place (election day). The election day must fall on a Sunday or on a
statutory public holiday ... .

. . .

§18: *Right to Nominate Candidates for Election*
(1) Nominations of candidates may be submitted by parties and, in accordance with §20, by persons entitled to vote ... .

. . .

§20: *Content and Form of Constituency Nominations*
(1) A constituency nomination may only contain the name of one candidate. Each candidate may only be named in one constituency and there only
in one nomination. A person may only be nominated if he or she has given
his or her consent in writing; such consent shall be irrevocable.
(2) Constituency nominations by parties must bear the personal and handwritten signatures of the executive committee of the Land party organisation ... .
(3) Other constituency nominations must bear the personal and handwritten signatures of at least 200 persons entitled to vote from the constituency concerned ... .

§21: *Selection of Party Candidates*

(1) A person may only be named as candidate of a party in a constituency if he or she has been selected for this purpose in an assembly of party members for the selection of a constituency candidate or in a special or general assembly of party representatives ... .

. . .

(3) The candidates and the representatives for the assemblies of representatives shall be selected by secret ballot. Elections may take place at the earliest thirty two months, in the case of the representatives' assembly at the earliest twenty three months, after the beginning of the legislative term of the German Bundestag; this shall not apply if the period of legislature ends prematurely ... .

. . .

§27: *Land Lists*

(1) Land lists may only be submitted by political parties. They must bear the personal and handwritten signatures of the executive committee of the Land party organisation or, where Land organisations do not exist, those of the executive committees of the next lower regional organisations ... existing within the territory of the Land; moreover, in the case of the political parties mentioned in §18, subsection (2), they must be so signed by one per 1,000 of the persons entitled to vote in the Land at the last elections to the Bundestag, but by not more than 2,000 persons entitled to vote ... .

(2) Land lists must show the name of the party submitting them as well as any shortened form of its name if such form is used by it.

(3) The names of the candidates must be listed in recognizable sequence ... .

(4) A candidate may only be nominated in one Land, and there only in one Land list. Only such persons as have given their consent in writing may be named in a Land list; such consent shall be irrevocable.

. . .

§30: *Ballot Papers*

. . .

(2) The ballot paper shall contain:

1.for the constituency elections, the names of the candidates of the accepted constituency nominations; additionally, in the case of constituency nominations by parties, it shall show the names of these parties ... ;

2.for elections by Land lists, the names of the parties ... as well as the names of the first five candidates on the Land lists accepted.

3)The order of the Land lists of parties which were represented in the last Bundestag shall be determined by the number of second votes which each obtained in the last Bundestag election in the Land concerned ... .

. . .

Special Regulations for By-elections and Repeat Elections

§43: *By-elections*

(1) A by-election shall take place:

1. if an election has not been held in a constituency or a polling district;

2. if a constituency candidate dies after the acceptance of his or her nomination, but before the election ... .

§48: *Appointment of Successors from the Lists, and Replacement Elections*

(1) If an elected candidate dies or refuses to accept election, or if a member dies or subsequently withdraws from the Bundestag for any other reason, the vacant seat shall be filled by an appointment from the Land list of that party for which the departed member stood at the election. In the selection of the successor those candidates on the list who have—subsequently to the drawing up of the Land list—resigned from the party concerned shall not be taken into consideration. If the list is exhausted, the seat shall remain vacant ... .

Document 4

STATUTES OF THE CHRISTIAN DEMOCRATIC UNION (CDU), 1 April 1993

Source: *CDU Bonn*, n.d.

A. Function, Name, Headquarters

§1. *Function*

The aim of the Christian Democratic Union of Germany (CDU) is the democratic structuring of public life in the service of the German people and the German fatherland, in accordance with a Christian sense of responsibility and the Christian moral code, and on the basis of personal liberty.

§2: *Name*

The name of the party is the Christian Democratic Union of Germany (CDU) ...

B. Membership

§4: *Conditions of membership*

(1) Anyone can become a member of the Christian Democratic Union of Germany if he is willing to further its objectives, if he is at least sixteen years old and has not been deprived of his active or passive electoral rights by judicial decision ...

(2) A person who does not have German nationality may work with the party as a guest. He can be accepted into the party when he can prove uninterrupted residence for at least three years in the territory covered by the Basic Law [i.e., the FRG].

. . .

§11: *Expulsion from the party*

(1) A member can only be expelled from the party if he has wilfully violated the party's constitution or gravely flouted its principles or regulations, thereby causing it serious harm.

(2) Motions calling for the expulsion of a member are put by the locally responsible constituency or regional executive or by the party's federal executive and are decided on by the responsible Party Tribunal which is established according to the party statute governing tribunals.

. . .

(5) Decisions taken by the Party Tribunals in expulsion proceedings must be explained in writing.

. . .

§12: *Damaging Behaviour*
Behaviour that is damaging to the party is displayed by anyone who
1. belongs to another political party at the same time.
2. makes statements contrary to the official policy of the CDU at meetings of political opponents, in their radio and television broadcasts or their party newspapers.
3. is elected to a representative body as a candidate of the CDU, but withdraws from or refuses to join the CDU as a caucus.
4. publishes or leaks to political opponents information on confidential party matters.
5. misappropriates property belonging to, or at the disposal of, the party.

. . .

C. Organizational Structure

§15: *Levels of Organisation*
(1) The CDU is organized at the following levels:

1. The Federal party.
2. The regional *(Land)* associations.
3. The District *(Kreis)* associations.
4. The local or urban district associations ...

§16: *Regional Associations [Landesverbände]*
(1) The regional associations are the organisations of the CDU in the *Länder* of the Federal Republic of Germany. The CDU in Lower Saxony consists of the regional associations of Brunswick, Hanover and Oldenburg. The regional association is responsible for all political and organisational questions in its area, in so far as they do not touch upon the interests of several regional associations and therefore have to be decided in consultation with the party authorities at federal level ... .

. . .

§28: *Composition of the Federal Party Conference*
(1) The Federal Party Conference is composed of 1,000 delegates from the regional associations, who are elected by the district, area or district or regional party conferences, together with the honourary chairmen. Of the thousand delegates from the regional associations, 200 are allocated in proportion to the number of 'second'votes cast for each of the CDU's Land lists in the last election to the German Bundestag, and 800 are chosen in proportion to the number of party members in each regional association ...

. . .

(4) The Federal Party Conference meets at least once every two years and is convened by the party executive. It must be convened on the motion of the Federal Committee or at least one third of the regional associations ...

. . .

§29: *Powers of the Federal Party Conference*
Functions of the Federal Party Conference:

(1) It lays down the principles of the Christian Democratic Union and its party programme; these form the basis of the work of the CDU caucuses and CDU-led governments in the Federation and the Länder and are binding on them.

(2) It elects in separate ballots the following members to the Federal Executive:

1. The Chairman
2. On the proposal of the Chairman, the General Secretary.
3. Four Vice-chairmen
4. The Federal Treasurer
5. A further seven members to the Präsidium.
6. A further 26 members of the Federal Executive.

. . .

Document 5

ORGANIZATION STATUTE OF THE SOCIAL DEMOCRATIC PARTY OF GERMANY. As of 29 May 1991
Source: SPD Bonn, n.d.

Name, Headquarters, Area of Activity

§1:
(1) The name of the party is the Social Democratic Party of Germany (SPD).
(2) The area of activity is that of the Federation and the Länder [of Germany]
(3) The headquarters of the party is in Bonn and Berlin.

Structure

§8:
(1) The SPD comprises local branches, sub-districts and district associations. Within this framework the will of the party expresses itself from the bottom upwards ... .
(2) The basis of the organization is the district, the boundaries of which are determined by the party executive on the grounds of political and economic expediency. The boundaries of the sub-districts are determined on the same lines by the district executives, those of the local branches by the sub-district executives.
(3) In Länder containing more than one district, Land associations can be formed as further organisational bodies if it is felt to be politically expedient

to do so, provided that all districts in the Land approve. The status of the districts as the basis of the organization is not affected by the formation of a Land association.

. . .

Commissions of Arbitration

§34:
(1) Commissions of Arbitration are formed at sub-district, district and Party Executive Committee levels ... .
(2) Commissions of Arbitration are responsible for making decisions regarding:

1. disciplinary proceedings within the party;
2. disputes concerning the application and interpretation of the Statutes of Organization, the Constitutions, the basic precepts ... and the operational guidelines of the study-groups;
3. procedures for contesting elections or declaring elections null and void ...

. . .

(5) The members of the commissions of arbitration are elected at Party Conferences by secret ballot for a period of two years ... .

. . .

(7) The procedures of the commissions of arbitration are governed by a set of rules to be laid down by the Party Conference as an integral part of these statutes.

Disciplinary Proceedings

§35:
(1) Disciplinary proceedings are to be taken against a member who damages the interests of the party by persistently flouting decisions of the Party Conference or party organization, or who commits a dishonourable deed or a gross violation of the precepts of the party.
(2) The following sanctions can be imposed as a result of disciplinary proceedings:

1. the censure of a member,
2. the loss for a period of up to three years of the right to hold a specific office or all offices ...
3. the temporary suspension of a specific right or all rights arising from membership for a period of up to three years,
4. expulsion from the party.

(3) A decision to expel a member can only be taken when he or she has wilfully violated the Statutes or gravely contravened the precepts or rules of the party, thereby causing the party serious harm.
(4) A motion calling for disciplinary proceedings to be taken can be submitted by any of the party's structural organizations (§8) to the commission of arbitration of the sub-district of which the individual concerned is a member ... .

Ballot of Party Members

§36:
In the event of the Party Conference voting to disband the party or to amal-

gamate it with another party or parties, a ballot of members shall take place. The resolution of the Party Conference is either confirmed or invalidated by the result of the ballot; it may not be put into effect until it has been confirmed by the ballot.

. . .

Amendments to the Statutes

§40:

(1) The Party Statutes can only be amended by a Party Conference with a two-thirds majority.

(2) Motions calling for amendments to the Statutes can only be debated if they have been tabled within the time-limits prescribed by §18. Failure to comply with the time-limits can be overcome if the Party Conference votes by a three quarters majority to debate the motion.

. . .

Document 6

SPD SUBSCRIPTIONS

Source: *Organisationsstatut, Wahlordnung, Schiedsordnung, Finanzordnung der Sozialdemokratischen Partei Deutschlands as at 29 Mai 1991* (Bonn n.d.), 73–75.

Membership Subscriptions (SPD)

§1

(1) Membership subscriptions are based on net monthly earnings according to the following table:

Net Monthly income (DM)						
600 to 1200	1200 to 1500	1500 to 2000	2000 to 3000	3000 to 4000	4000 to 7000	over 7000
Monthly subscriptions (DM)						
5.00	6.00	8.00	12.00	50.00	120.00	400.00
7.00	9.00	15.00	60.00	150.00		
	10.00	20.00	70.00	200.00		
	11.00	25.00	80.00	250.00		
			30.00	100.00		
			35.00			
			45.00			

Explanatory note: Each member selects his own position within the various payment bands. The first number given is the expected *minimum* payment.

(2) For members with no income or with very little income the monthly subscription is 3 DM.

(2a) For the creation and development of the party in the area of the former GDR all members will pay a special designated contribution to a fund set up for this purpose by the party executive. This contribution will be levied during the period 1 January 1991 until 31 December 1994 ... The special contribution is fixed at 10 per cent of the membership subscription—with a minimum, however, of 2 DM. For members covered by section (2) above, the special contribution will be 1 DM ... .

(4) It is the Party Conference which, as a matter of principle, fixes the level of subscriptions ... .

Contributions from Office holders

§2

(1) Members of parliamentary delegations will pay special contributions in addition to those set out in the statutes above.

(2) Members of the SPD who receive fees or similar gratuities as a result of discharging public offices or holding mandates as members of supervisory boards, must pay 30 per cent of their gross remuneration to the party at the appropriate organisational level ... .

PARTY PROGRAMMES: THE FUNDAMENTAL PRINCIPLES
Document 7

THE GODESBERG PROGRAMME OF THE GERMAN SOCIAL DEMOCRATIC PARTY, NOVEMBER 1959

Source: Basic Programme of the Social Democratic Party of Germany, Bonn, n.d.

Fundamental Values of Socialism

Socialists aim to establish a society in which every individual can develop his personality and as a responsible member of the community, take part in the political, economic and cultural life of mankind ... .

Democratic Socialism, ... in Europe is rooted in Christian ethics, humanism and classical philosophy ... .

The Social Democratic Party is the party of freedom of thought ... .

We are fighting for democracy. Democracy must become the universal form of state organisation and way of life ... .

We resist every dictatorship, every form of totalitarian or authoritarian rule.

. . .

The Order of the State

The Social Democratic Party of Germany lives and works in the whole of Germany. It stands by the Basic Law of the German Federal Republic. In accordance with the Basic Law it strives for German unity in freedom.

The division of Germany is a threat to peace. To end this division is a vital interest of the German people ... .

National Defence

The Social Democratic Party affirms the need to defend the free democratic society. It is in favour of national defence ... .

The Federal Republic of Germany must neither produce nor use atomic or other means of mass destruction ... .

The armed forces must only be used for national defence ... .

The Economy

The goal of Social Democratic economic policy is the constant growth of prosperity and a just share for all in the national product ... .

Economic policy must secure full employment whilst maintaining a stable currency, increase productivity and raise general prosperity ... .

More than a third of the national income passes through the hands of the government. The question is therefore not whether measures of economic planning and control serve a purpose, but rather who should apply these measures and for whose benefit ... .

Free choice of consumer goods and services, free choice of working place, freedom for employers to exercise their initiative as well as free competition are essential conditions of a Social Democratic economic policy. The autonomy of trade unions and employers' associations in collective bargaining is an important feature of a free society. Totalitarian control of the economy destroys freedom. The Social Democratic Party therefore favours a free market wherever free competition really exists. Where a market is dominated by individuals or groups, however, all manner of steps must be taken to protect freedom in the economic sphere. As much competition as possible—as much planning as necessary.

Ownership and Power

A significant feature of the modern economy is the constantly increasing tendency toward concentration ... .

Wherever large-scale enterprises predominate, free competition is eliminated. Those who have less power have fewer opportunities for development, and remain more or less fettered. The consumer occupies the most vulnerable position of all in the economy ... .

The key task of an economic policy concerned with freedom is therefore to contain the power of big business. State and society must not be allowed to become the prey of powerful sectional groups.

Private ownership of the means of production can claim protection by society as long as it does not hinder the establishment of social justice ... .

Effective public control must prevent the abuse of economic power. The most important means to this end are investment control and control over the forces dominating the market.

Public ownership is a legitimate form of public control which no modern state can do without. It serves to protect freedom against domination by large economic concerns ... .

Wage and salary earners whose contribution to production is decisive have so far been deprived of an effective say in economic life. Democracy, however, demands that workers should be given a voice and that co-determination be extended to all branches of the economy. From being a servant the worker must become a citizen of the economy ... .

Social Responsibility

. . .

Every citizen has the right to a minimum state pension in case of old age or inability to earn a living, or at the death of the family's provider ... .
The Social Democratic Party ... demands comprehensive health protection.
. . .

All labour and social legislation should be ordered and compiled in a surveyable code on labour legislation and a code on social legislation.
Everyone has a right to a decent place in which to live. It is the home of the family. It must therefore continue to receive social protection and must not be the mere object of private gain ... .

Woman-Family-Youth
Equality of rights for women should be realised in the legal, economic and social spheres.
. . .

Cultural Life

. . .

Religion and Church
. . .

Socialism is no substitute for religion. The Social Democratic Party respects churches and religious societies. It affirms their public and legal status, their special mission and their autonomy ... .

Education
Education must give an opportunity to all freely to develop their abilities and capacities. It must strengthen the will to resist the conformist tendencies of our time. Knowledge and the acquisition of traditional cultural values, and a thorough understanding of the formative forces in society, are essential to the development of independent thinking and free judgment ... .
School systems and curricula must give full scope to the development of talent and ability at all stages. Every gifted pupil should have access to advanced education and training ... .

The International Community

The greatest and most urgent task is to preserve peace and protect freedom. Democratic Socialism has always stood for international co-operation and solidarity ... .
Normal diplomatic and trade relations with all nations are indispensable in spite of differences in system of government and social structure ... .

[The programme continues with support for International Courts and the U.N.]

Document 8

THE 'FREIBURG THESES' OF THE FREE DEMOCRATIC PARTY, OCTOBER 1971

Source: Freiburger Thesen der F.D.P. zur Gesellschaftspolitik, Bonn, n.d.

Introduction

Liberalism is ... both heir to and champion of the tradition of human liberty and dignity which informed the democratic revolutions in America and France at the end of the eighteenth century.

The liberal tradition grew out of these middle-class revolutions and was later assimilated by reform movements within the state ... .

. . .

In our country a free democratic liberal party has the ... responsibility of guarding and upholding this tradition of classical liberalism in the face of state measures and social developments which threaten liberty and right.

Today we stand at the beginning of the second phase of a reform movement which stems from the middle-class revolution ... .

This new phase of democratisation and liberalisation ... springs from a changed understanding of liberty. It opens up the new political dimension of a liberalism which is no longer just democratic, but also social.

. . .

For this social liberalism rights and liberties should not be mere formal pledges given by the state to its citizens, but real opportunities presented to them in their day-to-day life.

. . .

In our party this new spirit of democratisation in society has above all forged ahead in the field of educational policy, in the struggle for equal educational and vocational opportunities, in short for the citizens' right to education. The following theses on liberal social policy outline ways of putting these ideas into political practice ... .

. . .

Thesis 1: Liberalism stands for human dignity through self-determination ... .
Thesis 2: Liberalism stands for progress through reason ... .
Thesis 3: Liberalism calls for the democratisation of society ... .
Thesis 4: Liberalism calls for the reform of capitalism ... .

Supported by competition and the individual's will to work, capitalism has led to great economic successes, but also to social injustice. The liberal reform of capitalism aims at halting the imbalance of opportunity and the massing of economic power, which result from the accumulation of money and property and from the concentration of ownership of the means of production in the hands of a few ... .

Property

Thesis 1: Liberty needs ownership of property. Ownership of property creates liberty. It is a means to the end of preserving and increasing human liberty, not an end in itself ... .

. . .

Thesis 4: The right of the individual to exploit his property and to use it privately and professionally, must ... end at the point where this imposes improper and unreasonable restrictions on the freedom of others or interferes with public welfare.

Landed Property

. . .

Thesis 1: The main aims of land policy must be to provide all population groups with sufficient living space and to guarantee humane town-planning ... .
Thesis 2: The local authorities must be enabled to pursue appropriate land supply policies ... .

The Formation of Private Wealth
Worker Participation in Industrial Assets

Preliminary Note:
Today the increment of productive capital arising from profits is concentrated in the hands of a small number of holders of capital. This is politically dangerous, socially unjust and incompatible with liberal demands for equality of opportunity and for the best possible conditions for the development of individual personality. Liberal policy on the formation of wealth, therefore, aims at a more even distribution of wealth. This is not to be brought about by a once-and-for-all adjustment of the status quo, but rather by the permanent participation of a broader cross-section of the community, particularly in the increment of productive capital ... .
Thesis 1: Above a stipulated figure of capital appreciation, private and public companies will be obliged to grant to the public the right to participate in the companies' capital gains.

. . .

Estate Levy

Preliminary Note:
Death duties, as they have hitherto been in force, perpetuate an outmoded system that has an adverse effect on our economic and social order and its free development.

. . .

These shortcomings and disadvantages are to be overcome by replacing the present death duties by a levy on a dead person's estate and by reorganizing gift taxes correspondingly. Once divested of its tax character, the levy on large fortunes is to be incorporated into the system of participation in industrial

assets. By focusing more closely on very great fortunes, proper account is being taken of the fact that very great fortunes cannot normally be acquired without the vital contribution rendered by third parties and society ... .
[The programme goes on to detail the various conditions of the levy system.]

Co-determination on the Shop Floor

As an employee, the mature and enlightened citizen still wants to be an active individual and not feel himself to be the passive victim of decisions and processes he doesn't understand ... .
[The Free Democrats were concerned that worker participation should not undermine business efficiency, and that managerial staff should play an important role in decision-making.]
As a matter of principle the senior salaried staff have the same social rights as all other employees in the firm. Appropriate account must be taken of their special status as belonging both to the management and to the workforce ... .
The protection of minorities in a firm is to be intensified. In its composition the workers' council should reflect the social strata of the whole firm and the ratio of men to women ... .

Co-determination at the Board Level

Preliminary Note
Liberal social policy cannot be satisfied with a form of co-determination that only allows employees to participate in the running of the workshop and in the determining of working conditions on the shop floor.
. . .

... the hereafter outlined liberal model for co-determination at the board level on the part of employees in their own company adopts a new approach, both regarding the commensurate participation of the three factors of production—capital, management and labour—and their relative numerical strengths and joint operational procedures. The essence of this approach is codetermination at the board level, organised internally and based on parity.
Thesis 1: Co-determination is to be introduced into the controlling bodies of large-scale industrial enterprises run as joint-stock companies. Such co-determination assumes joint responsibility on the part of the factors capital, management and labour.
. . .

Thesis 4: To ensure the overriding interests of the company, it is vital that on the one hand the share-holders ('capital' factor) should not be absolved from their responsibility; on the other hand, the company employees ('management' and 'labour' factors) must be able to assert their interests without being outvoted.
. . .

Thesis 5: In accordance with the above-mentioned principles, ... the 'capital', 'labour' and 'management' factors are to participate in the supervision of large scale industrial enterprises in the ratio 6:4:2 ... .
Thesis 6: The 'management' factor on company boards of supervision is composed of senior salaried staff of the company. Elections are by the majority decision of the senior salaried staff.

. . .

Environmental Policy ...

Environmental policy is a response to one of the challenges of industrial society. Population increase, urbanisation, urban sprawl, uninhibited technical advances and growing prosperity lead to the overutilisation and destruction of the natural elements—the soil, raw materials, the atmosphere and water. Noise levels, particularly in conurbations, are becoming unbearable; chemicals in the environment are threatening to poison our food. The environmental crisis is world-wide.

Thesis 1: The protection of the environment has priority over the pursuit of profit and over personal gain. Harming the environment is a criminal offence.

. . .

Document 9

FREEDOM AND RESPONSIBILITY: DRAFT PROPOSALS OF THE CDU FEDERAL EXECUTIVE October 1993
Source: Freiheit und Verantwortung: Leitantrag des CDU-Bundesvorstandes October 1993 (n.p.).
Transl.: Author

1. Who we are:

   1. The Christian Democratic Union is a People's Party. It appeals to all persons in all classes and groups of our society. Our policy is based on the Christian understanding of the human being and his responsibility before God.
   2. We are aware that no particular political programme can be deduced from the Christian faith. We do not claim that, on the basis of our commitment to Christian beliefs, political action of a responsible Christian kind is only possible within the Christian Democratic Union. The CDU is open to anybody who supports the worth and freedom of all human beings and the fundamental principles which spring from that and which underpin our policies. This is the basis for the common action of christians and non-Christians within the CDU.

   . . .

   4. On the basis of a belief in common values, the members of the CDU demonstrated their responsibility and carried through the fundamental decisions which had to be taken in the free part of Germany—for free democracy with a rule of law, for the social market economy and the integration of the Federal Republic of Germany into community of Western values and the Western defence community; and for the unity of the nation and the unification of Europe.

   . . .

6. The Christian assessment of human beings is our spiritual foundation and the historic starting point of our party. Our values include conservative as well as Christian-social and liberal convictions. We want to continue with this tradition, thereby retaining that which has proved itself whilst developing new ideas.

Our understanding of human beings:

7. We declare our faith in the value of human beings. Human life and human dignity—including that of the unborn child—are inviolable. We respect every human being as a unique and independent person. The value of all [human beings] is equal—independent of sex, race, nationality, age, handicap, religious or political belief, health and strength, success or failure and of the judgement of others.

. . .

Freedom

. . .

16. The realisation of freedom requires a life-style based on personal responsibility exercised according to the principle of subsidiarity. For this reason the state must refrain from taking over tasks which the individual or appropriate smaller communities are capable of tackling. That which can just as well be done by the citizen alone, within the family and in voluntary collaboration with others, should be left to him. The principle of subsidiarity should also operate between smaller and larger public institutions and between independent associations and state authorities ...

. . .

Solidarity

. . .

23. Social security is based on the principles of solidarity and subsidiarity. Social security protects people by community action against risks which the individual cannot overcome by himself. Social security has a liberating and life-enhancing effect. Solidarity is not possible without sacrifice. He who expects help and solidarity from others must himself be prepared to help others ...

. . .

Justice

. . .

29. Justice includes the assumption of duties which relate the competence of the individual to the common good. Social justice demands above all that those people should be helped who are not sufficiently capable of looking after themselves and who cannot adequately represent or attain their own interests. For us it is a matter of principle not to allow anyone to fall by the wayside and to secure humane conditions for all in our society.

[The programme goes on to urge that the opportunities of German unification should be seized upon to create a really free society.]

For an Ecological and Social Market Economy

66. The ecological and social market economy is an economic and social programme for all. It has its spiritual foundation in the Christian concept of that responsible freedom which belongs to all human beings, and which is in contrast both to the socialist planned economy and to uncontrolled laissez-faire liberalism [*Wirtschaftsformen liberalistischer Prägung*] ...

67. The [free] Market and Competition are central elements in our economic system and help the realization of freedom by decentralizing power ...

. . .

68. The economic and the social order are inextricably bound together. They complement and delimit each other. An economic policy without social justice fails to create social peace and would lead to economic losses ... .

69. We Christian Democrats extend the Social Market Economy into an ecological dimension. We want to deploy the powers and steering mechanisms of the market more strongly than before in order to achieve a harmonious relationship with nature and the environment ... .

. . .

Co-determination

95. Co-determination and participation by employees in factories and businesses are for us an essential element of our economic and social system and the expression of Christian-social principles ... .

. . .

Federalism and communal self-administration are the hallmarks of our federal state.

. . .

114. German unity has put new life into federalism. Federalism and communal self-administration divide state power and create additional possibilities for democratic participation. The diversity thus created facilitates competition and respect for regional peculiarities. We want also to implement the principle of subsidiarity in the formation of the European Union. We only want to transfer those powers and responsibilities to the European Union which it alone can implement effectively ... .

Document 10

THE REPUBLICANS PARTY PROGRAMME
Promulgated at the federal party congress in Rosenheim, 13/14 January 1990.

Source: Die Republikaner: Parteiprogramm, Bundesgeschäftsstelle der Republikaner (Bonn 1990).

We dedicate ourselves to Germany ...

... we reject the willingness of the old parties to accept a policy of continuing enemy war propaganda, using the methods of re-education and education, infiltration and [control of] the media. We reject a policy of unceasing redemption of guilt which the Germans have been forced to swallow for decades, from generation to generation ...

[The programme goes on to demand the recreation of united Germany]
...

The Republicans commit themselves to the fundamental principles of a free and democratic order ... .

The Republicans support a pluralistic state based on the rule of law. The freedom of the individual meets its limits at the point where it threatens the freedom of others.

To strengthen democracy the Republicans demand:

The introduction of plebiscites such as those in use in Austria and Switzerland.

The direct election of the President by the people.

Observance of the principle of the division of powers and a ban on directorships for members of parliament.

Resistance to the abuse of state institutions by political parties and groups.

[After demanding the restoration of a unified German state ...]

... The recreation of Germany as a nation has priority over European unification ...

The Political aim of the Republicans is not the 'united states of Europe', but 'Europe of the Fatherlands' ...

Domestic Security and the Rights of Foreigners

We Republicans are the party of law and order ... Security 'on the street' should be restored. New forms of that criminal behaviour which threatens us all must be combated effectively. We will therefore strengthen the authorities charged with protecting us and give them back their capacity to act *(Handlungsfähigkeit)* ...

The Rights of Foreigners: Our principles:

Our country is not a country of immigration.

We say NO to 'multi-cultural' society, and therefore to a state with a multiplicity of peoples.

We say NO to foreigners having the right to vote, even if they are EC members ... .

There should be no right to claim citizenship ... [The programme goes on to demand more stringent and more rapid treatment for asylum-seekers] ...

... Agriculture, Forestry ...

The Republicans Demand:

An end to the destruction of any more independent *[mittelständisch]* family farms ...

We urge the renationalisation of agricultural policy so that the family farm can survive and can consolidate itself by integration into the social market economy. The national agricultural policy of the Swiss should be a model for us.

... **The agricultural policy of the EC has collapsed** ...

Middle Class (Mittelstand) *and craft industry.*

The Republicans are the party of the workers, farmers, free professions and the traditional middle class. Christian Democrats and Liberals are orientated towards big business and the Socialists are dominated by the trade unions. The *Mittelstand* has for that reason only heard flattering words, but has seen no political deeds. In practice the marginal groups and the parties which support them overload the *Mittelstand* with taxes and with social welfare contributions, and hold them back in their work by ever more intolerable bureaucratic requirements.

The *Mittelstand* is the bearer and guarantor of welfare, employment and public finances, and therefore of the entire economy ... .

Document 11

Leaflet put out in Munich by the leader of the Reps Land working group for finance economics and transport. (c.1992)

Transl.: Author

Save the German Mark. The DM may not die!
No European soft currency—ECU. No European central bank. What are the old parties planning? They are planning to throw the hard DM and other softer currencies as well as strong and weak economies into a common Euro stew [*Suppentopf*]!
The result will be an insipid, homogenized brew.
Who is giving away security and sacrificing stability? We Germans. Who is profiting thereby? Not us ...

. . .

We Republicans demand: No right to vote for foreigners, not even for EC members. A stop to the Euro-Juggernaut. The proliferating Euro-bureaucracy with its appallingly high salaries must be drastically cut back. There should be no EC at the expense of German taxpayers—we are not the golden donkey [*Dukatenesel*] of Europe.
We are now paying 16.6 billion DM net per annum to the EC and what do we get for it: more rapid deprecation of the value of our money. More state debts and higher unemployment.
We Republicans represent GERMAN interests.

Document 12

PROGRAMME OF THE PARTY OF DEMOCRATIC SOCIALISM (PDS) 1993

Source: Published and translated by Bundesgeschäftsführer der PDS (Berlin n.d.)

Programme of the Party of Democratic Socialism

The Party of Democratic Socialism is issuing this programme at a time characterized by historically unprecedented upheavals in the conditions of global development and a crisis of existence affecting the whole of humankind as well as by the collapse of the socialist experiment in Eastern Europe. The economic and social decline and wholesale political discrimination in east Germany, the undermining of democratic, social and legal rights, the chauvinist, nationalist and right-extremist trends across Germany, are all assuming threatening proportions ... .

. . .

Federal Republic of Germany

The attachment of the GDR to the FRG has not eradicated the contrast between east and west Germany. Through the policy of the ruling circles extensive regions in the eastern federal states have been deindustrialised, agriculture to a large extent ruined. Social and individual impoverishment have assumed an alarming scale. The scientific, economic and cultural potential associated with the name 'GDR' has been 'liquidated'. Highly discriminatory questionnaires imposed on employees have ousted any well-considered reassessment of the GDR's past. The chosen practice has been court proceedings instead of the discussion of history. Through the policy of the established parties the former citizens of the GDR have been written off as people with limited rights for years to come, if not decades ... .

Socialist renewal

For us socialism is an indispensable goal—a society in which the free development of each is the condition for the free development of all. For us socialism is a movement against the exploitation of people by other people, against patriarchal oppression, against the plundering of nature, for the preservation and development of human culture, for the implementation of human rights, for a society where people run their affairs democratically and rationally. For us socialism is a system of values in which liberty, equality and solidarity, human emancipation, social justice, conservation of nature and peace are inseparably united ...

. . .

Ending the cold war in Germany

Owing to the destructive strategy of the Federal Government and its consequent costs, as well as intensifying global conflicts, the rapid levelling out of living standards in East and West as promised by the leading politicians is not going to take place.

Unlike the established parties we want no 'Westification' of the East, because we want no 'two-thirds society', no mass unemployment, no wealth at the cost of underdeveloped countries, and no destruction of nature. We are fighting for a way of development in the Federal Republic which incorporates what was positive in the former FRG as in the GDR, and which faces up to the global challenges. Improving the difficult situation of very many people in east Germany strikes us as an outstanding task of internal policy in the coming decade.

Priority should be given to satisfying the following demands:

—We firmly object to the rewriting of post-war history in order to deprive former GDR citizens of their identity and with that the pre-condition for a confident advocacy of their interests.

. . .

The principle, 'restitution before compensation' must be quashed. Land and soil, buildings and enterprises, should not be returned to dispossessed owners of huge estates, war criminals or convicted Nazis or to their heirs, nor should compensation be paid to them. Restitution of such property already made must be declared illegal. Former GDR state property should as far as possible be turned into communal and cooperative property ... .

Document 13

Statute of the Federal Association of Alliance 90 and the Greens. June 1993

Source: Extracts from *Bündnis 90 Die Grünen: Satzung des Bundesverbandes* Stand: Juni 1993. Cologne n.d.

Preamble
(1) We, THE GREENS and the ALLIANCE 90, rooted in the opposition culture of the two German states, united together to form 'Alliance 90/the Greens' in order to fight for our democratic reform objectives as a joint political force, responding to the new national and global challenges and seeking to assume political responsibility.

. . .

(3) We know that the missed chances in the German unification process and the heavy burden of the false beginning [to unification] can only be cleared away if we break down the barriers in our hearts and minds and accept each other with honour and respect.

Basic Values: Human rights ...

. . .

(5) Respect for human rights can be regarded as a precise way of measuring the free and humane character of a political system ... .

. . .

(7) These human rights, including the right to asylum, must be established beyond the UNO-conventions by being written into the [German] constitution and into law as legally defensible basic rights of every person. Elementary rights ... must not be any longer restricted in our constitution exclusively to Germans, but must apply without limitation to all persons. In order to achieve a complete realisation of human rights we require the full participation of foreign citizens in political life, the complete equality of the sexes, the rejection of every sort of discrimination and the consistent pro-

tection of the rights of minorities, since in a democracy human rights have the important political function of protecting the identity of minorities.
. . .

Democracy
(18) Democracy shall ensure the equal right for all persons to participate in the formation of society ... we demand democracy in all areas of life ... .
. . .

(20) However, the desire for self-determination and participation is far from being met by the actual possibilities available to people. The apparent omnipotence of the parties and the powers which stand behind them in the state and in the economy confront a constantly growing impotence on the part of the citizenry. This impotence and the lack of real possibilities for participation are an important reason for the growing 'indifference to politics' *[Politikverdrossenheit]*. At the same time governments are taking more and more decisions out of the hands of the people and even out of the hands of parliaments, claiming the need for 'centralization', 'harmonization', 'speeding up' or 'simplification'.
(21) This is particularly true of the European Community, the executive organs of which are taking more and more authority upon themselves. The dismantling of democratic rights in the member states is thus further intensified by the luxuriant growth of a centralized bureaucracy which is not subject to democratic control.
. . .

Social equality of men and women
(34) Alliance 90/The Greens commits itself to the realization of human rights for women as a precondition for a peaceful, democratic and ecological society. The patriarchal structures of our culture and society attest to the continuation of discrimination, repression, and disadvantagement ... .

Notes

1. For the English translation, see *The Law on Political Parties* (Inter Nationes, Bonn, 1978), 5–6
2. The SPD again became the principle party in opposition to the government, this time under Rudolf Scharing, their candidate for the chancellorship in the 1994 election.
3. N. Lepszy, *Die Republikaner: Ideologie—Programm—Organisation und Wahlergebnisse*, (St. Augustin/Forschungsinstitut der Konrad-Adenauer-Stiftung, 1989), 19–22
4. The votes in all Länder are added together to arrive at a total for the whole Federal Republic. To take a hypothetical example of the way in which the seats are then distributed, let us suppose that there are thirty million valid second votes and that Party A receives three million votes in the entire FRG. These would be multiplied by the 328 seats left for distribution and divided by the total number of valid second votes cast (in this purely hypothetical example, 30 Million). This would yield 32 seats on 'whole numbers' and probably one extra seat on 0.8 as a fraction left over.

9
Chancellor, Cabinet, and President
Donald P. Kommers

Executive authority in the Federal Republic is vested in the federal chancellor *(Bundeskanzler)* and his cabinet, collectively known as the federal government *(Bundesregierung)*. The federal president *(Bundespräsident)* is the Federal Republic's highest ranking public official, but he functions mainly as a ceremonial head of state, a vestigial reminder of the once-thriving presidency in the Weimar Republic. The Basic Law concentrates effective political power—and leadership—in the hands of the chancellor. He is responsible for determining the general policies of the government, he decides on the number of ministries to be established within the cabinet, and he appoints all cabinet ministers who in turn are directly responsible to him. The cabinet's standing orders *(Geschäftsordnung der Bundesregierung)*, which require the approval of the federal president (Docs.1 and 4), govern the process of decision-making in the cabinet. These procedures bind the chancellor as well as all cabinet members.

Constitutionally responsible for setting forth the general guidelines of national policy (Art. 65), the chancellor could theoretically maintain his position even against the wishes of a parliamentary majority, a power that flows from the so-called constructive vote of no confidence. Under Article 67 of the Basic Law, the Bundestag may dismiss the chancellor only when a majority of its members simultaneously elects his successor. The constructive vote of no-confidence has succeeded only once, in 1982, when the Bundestag voted Helmut Schmidt out of office after the FDP's withdrawal from the coalition cabinet (see also Ch.7). The stabilizing effect of Article 67, together with the fourteen-year tenure and the legacy of strong leadership provided by West Germany's first chancellor, Konrad Adenauer, has led many observers to characterize the Federal Republic a 'chancellor democracy'.

One of the most powerful instruments of executive leadership today is the Office of the Federal Chancellor *(Bundeskanzleramt)*, which is analogous to the White House Office of the United States President and to some extent also to the Offices of the British and

Canadian Prime Ministers. Originally a small secretariat serving the chancellor's personal needs, the federal chancellery has developed into an agency of major political importance. It contains departments corresponding to the various federal ministries, as well as a planning bureau, created in 1969, to engage in long-range social and economic planning, in the coordination of policies relating to the European Union, and in overseeing the secret services. Its staff of over 500 persons keeps the chancellor informed on domestic and foreign affairs, coordinates policy among the federal ministries, and monitors the implementation of cabinet decisions. The office is headed by a chief of staff, usually a personal confidant of the chancellor. Finally, the chancellor is served by a Federal Press Secretary *(Bundespressechef)*, who in turn heads the Federal Press and Information Office *(Presse- und Informationsamt der Bundesregierung)*, with its staff of some 700 employees. It, too, is under the chancellor's direct control.

There have been six chancellors since 1949: Konrad Adenauer (1949–63); Ludwig Erhard (1963–66); Kurt-Georg Kiesinger (1966–69); Willy Brandt (1969–74); Helmut Schmidt (1974–82); and Helmut Kohl (1982–94) (Doc.2). All save Brandt and Schmidt have been Christian Democrats. The chancellor is elected by a majority (see also Chs.7 and 8) of the Bundestag in a secret ballot. Given the nature of the German party system, he is normally the leader of his party outside parliament. Since all the chancellors have been party leaders, they have been politically experienced persons who have spent most of their lives in public office. The age at which they assumed the chancellorship has been declining. Adenauer was seventy-three, Erhard and Kiesinger were in their sixties; Brandt and Schmidt were fifty-six; Kohl was fifty-two.

As Art. 65 of the Basic Law indicates, the chancellor's power can be offset when the cabinet acts a collegial organ. When votes are taken the chancellor is reduced to the status of first among equals. The collapse of Schmidt's government in 1982 stemmed largely from the problems the chancellor faced with his coalition partner, the FDP, and its powerful leader and foreign minister, Hans-Dieter Genscher. In short, whether a strong chancellor prevails, or whether the focus of ultimate decision-making lies with the cabinet as a whole, depends on whether the government consists of a coalition in which the chancellor, together with his political friends inside and outside the cabinet, has to take into consideration the views expressed by the partner in the coalition. In addition, as the Adenauer years showed, it also depends on whether the office of the chancellor is held by a dominating or by a more accommodating personality.

Germany's multi-party system (see also Ch.8) usually results in coalition governments. (Only Adenauer, following the 1957 election, had the luxury of ruling with a parliamentary majority of his own party.) The formation of a coalition government is usually preceded by negotiations between potential partners in the governing coalition. These negotiations lead to a formal coalition agreement (Doc.3) spelling out the areas of policy consensus between the partners. Tensions between coalition partners may nevertheless persist. In 1966 the CDU/CSU coalition with the FDP collapsed, making way for the 'great coalition' between the CDU/CSU and the SPD. But after the 1969 election, when Social Democrats reached a new high of 42.7 per cent of the popular vote, the SPD formed a government with the FDP as junior partner. This coalition survived three national elections. Fundamental differences over economic and social policy, however, prompted the FDP in September 1982 to drop out of the governing coalition with the SPD and join hands once again, after sixteen years, with the CDU/CSU. Schmidt fought hard to retain the chancellorship and even declared his intention to continue at the helm of a minority government, should the no-confidence vote fail to designate his successor. This hope was dashed when the new CDU/CSU-FDP alliance elected Helmut Kohl as chancellor on 1 October 1982 by a vote of 256 to 235 members of the Bundestag.

As noted above, the chancellor is constitutionally empowered to appoint and dismiss cabinet members (Doc.5). Yet political considerations limit his leverage over the formation of his cabinet. There is a practical need to distribute cabinet seats among various 'wings' of the major coalition party, and leaders of the minor party in the coalition are in a position to 'demand' the control of certain ministries. At times feuding breaks out among cabinet members and occasionally between a minister and the chancellor himself. A notable example of the latter was the joust in 1982 between Chancellor Schmidt and Economics Minister Otto Graf Lambsdorff. Schmidt actually rebuked Lambsdorff publicly, describing his proposals to limit welfare spending as 'one-sided and disappointing' and 'in flagrant contradiction to official policy'. In addition there are two principal constitutional limitations upon the chancellor in his dealing with his ministers. Under Article 65a of the Basic Law, the minister of defense is to serve as commander-in-chief of the armed forces while Article 112 requires the consent of the minister of finance before expenditures in excess of budgetary appropriations can be approved (Docs.1 and 4).

The office of the parliamentary state secretary (see also Ch.7) (or minister of state), to be distinguished from the permanent under secretaries of the various ministerial bureaucracies, was introduced in 1967 (Doc.6). Parliamentary state secretaries are selected from among the more junior members of the Bundestag to help the ministers run their departments, defend their records in parliament, and to maintain contact with the public. A feature of recent cabinets under Schmidt and Kohl are the high number of former parliamentary state secretaries who have been elevated to cabinet posts. The office is now widely recognized as a stepping stone to a cabinet post.

The federal president is actually Germany's highest ranking public official. As the formal head of state, he accredits and receives envoys and represents the nation in international relations. He also plays an important role as a non-partisan spokesman for the nation (Doc.8). In the Weimar Republic, the president was directly elected and able to wield decisive executive power at critical junctures. In the Federal Republic, by contrast, he is elected indirectly for a term of five years by a federal convention consisting of all members of the Bundestag and an equal number of representatives elected by the various Land parliaments and has no executive powers whatsoever. He may be reelected to a second term only. Many Germans perceive the president as a *pouvoir neutre* (Docs. 7a and b). So far, however, all seven presidents had been noted party leaders or widely known and respected public officials at the center of national government power before they took office.

On 23 May 1994, Roman Herzog, President of the Federal Constitutional Court and a Christian Democrat, became the FRG's seventh president. He was preceded by Theodor Heuss (FDP; 1949–1959), Heinrich Lübke (CDU; 1959–1969), Gustav Heineman (SPD; 1969–1974), Walter Scheel (FDP; 1974–1979), Karl Carstens (CDU; 1979–1984), and Richard von Weizsäcker (CDU; 1984–1994). Until 1974, an incumbent president otherwise competent and prudent in the exercise of his office could expect, if he wished, to be reelected to a second term. The 1979 election, however, was largely an exercise in partisan politics. Scheel withdrew as the SPD-FDP candidate when the CDU-CSU entered the federal convention resolved, with a slim majority of 26 votes, to elect its own candidate, Karl Carstens.

By contrast, the 1984 election was unusual for its lack of partisan maneuvering. Supported by both the governing centre-right coalition and a considerable part of the opposition SPD, the federal convention chose Richard von Weizsäcker, the once popular Christian Democratic mayor of West Berlin and scion of a patrician line of statesmen and theologians with a considerable majority. He eventually emerged as a strong president determined to speak his mind on controversial issues. Many Germans and non-Germans alike regarded him as the conscience of his country as he reminded Germans again and again of their past and also of their present responsibilities.

In 1994, the presidency once again became the focal point of a hard fought political battle in which chancellor Kohl played a major role. Kohl's first candidate for president was Steffen Heitman, the relatively unknown minister of justice in the eastern Land of Saxony. After considerable intra-party wrangling and Heitman's renunciation of the candidacy, the CDU-CSU chose Roman Herzog as its presidental candidate. Widely seen as Chancellor's Kohl's man, Herzog won the presidency on the third ballot when the FDP joined hands with the CDU-CSU to defeat Johannes Rau, the candidate of the SPD.

In early 1983, for the first time since 1949, the president faced a court challenge over the exercise of his constitutional functions and thereby the prospect of having an important presidential decision overturned. A number of SPD and FDP members of parliament challenged President Carstens' January 1983 decision to dissolve the Bundestag on the advice of Chancellor Kohl after a contrived loss of a vote of confidence initiated by the chancellor himself. In a decision widely regarded as the most important in its history, the Constitutional Court, by a majority vote, ruled that the president's action in dissolving the Bundestag was in conformity with the Basic Law (Doc.9).

The following articles of the constitution relate to the powers and duties of the federal chancellor, federal president and federal ministers. Certain features of the 'executive branch' under the Bonn Constitution differ from the practice under the Constitution of the Weimar Republic. For example, prior to 1933 the president was popularly elected for a seven-year term. He had the power to appoint the chancellor and, on the latter's recommendation, the national ministers. Both chancellor and ministers were individually responsible to the national assembly. They could be removed by parliament, unshielded by the modern constructive vote of no-confidence, the net result of which was a succession of weak governments during the Weimar period.

Document 1

ARTICLES OF THE BASIC LAW
Source: Presse- und Informationsamt der Bundesregierung

Art. 55. No Secondary Occupation

(1) The Federal President may not be a member of the government nor of a legislative body of the Federation or of a Land.

(2) The Federal President may not hold any other salaried office, nor engage in a trade or occupation, nor practice a profession, nor belong to the management or the board of directors of an enterprise carried on for profit.

Art. 57. Representation

If the Federal President is prevented from acting, or if his office falls prematurely vacant, his powers shall be exercised by the President of the Bundesrat.

Art. 58. Countersignature

Orders and decrees of the Federal President shall require for their validity the countersignature of the Federal Chancellor or the appropriate Federal Minister. This shall not apply to the appointment and dismissal of the Federal Chancellor, the dissolution of the Bundestag under Article 63 and the request under paragraph (3) of Article 69.

Art. 65. Distribution of Responsibility

The Federal Chancellor shall determine, and be responsible for, the general policy guidelines. Within the limits set by these guidelines, each Federal Minister shall conduct the affairs of his department autonomously and on his own responsibility. The Federal Government shall decide on differences of opinion between the Federal Ministers. The Federal Chancellor shall conduct the affairs of the Federal Government in accordance with rules of procedure adopted by it and approved by the Federal President.

Art. 65a. Power of Command over Armed Forces

Power of command in respect of the Armed Forces shall be vested in the Federal Minister of Defence.

Art. 75. Bills

(1) Bills shall be introduced in the Bundestag by the Federal Government or by members of the Bundestag or by the Bundesrat.

(2) Bills of the Federal Government shall be submitted first to the Bundesrat. The Bundesrat shall be entitled to state its position on such bills within six weeks. A bill exceptionally submitted to the Bundesrat as being particularly urgent by the Federal Government may be submitted by the latter to the Bundestag three weeks later, even though the Federal Government may not yet have received the statement of the Bundesrat's position; such statement shall be transmitted to the Bundestag by the Federal Government without delay upon its receipt.

Art. 112. Expenditures in Excess of Budgetary Estimates

Expenditures in excess of budgetary appropriations and extra-budgetary expenditures shall require the consent of the Federal Minister of Finance. Such consent may be given only in the case of an unforeseen and compelling necessity. Details may be regulated by federal legislation.

CHANCELLORS FROM 1949 TO PRESENT
REPRESENTATIVE SPEECHES

All German governments have reflected to a greater or lesser degree the personality of the chancellor, just as the chancellor has given expression to the dominant views of the political party or coalition that elected him. Presented below are brief notes on each of the six chancellors who have held power since 1949, together with excerpts from major policy statements which suggest aspects of their leadership.

KONRAD ADENAUER (1949–63)

The Federal Republic's first (and to date the longest serving) chancellor was an unlikely candidate for the post. Seventy-two years of age in 1949, he had reached the stage when most men have sought retirement. While he had had a long and distinguished career under the Weimar Republic as Lord Mayor of his native Cologne, had become a member of the Prussian State Council, and in the mid 1920s had been considered for the post of chancellor, in 1945 he hardly ranked as a major national figure. However, twice dismissed from his post as mayor—first in 1933 by the Nazis and again in 1945 by the British (after having been reinstated in office by the Americans following the capture of Cologne, six months earlier), this elderly Catholic Rhinelander skillfully exploited his new freedom to embark on a political role in a wider sphere. Manoeuvering his way to the chairmanship of the newly-emerged Christian Democratic Union (which replaced the old pre-1933 Centre Party) in the British Zone, he became chairman of the Parliamentary Council *(Parlamentarischer Rat)*, established in 1948 to draft a constitution for the provisional government of the three Western occupation zones. Supported by the liberal economic policies of the former Bavarian Economics Minister, Ludwig Erhard, Adenauer emerged as the dominant political figure in West Germany and in 1949 was elected as the Federal Republic's first chancellor. A conservative and rather authoritarian figure, he dominated the political scene for the next fourteen years and gave his name to an era. His chancellorship embodied a major period of post-war German history: a period of domestic institutional reconstruction, of economic recovery, and of the re-entry of Western Germany into the Western family of nations. He was also a leading advocate of and partner in the integration of Western Europe, and especially of the critical and hardly foreseeable reconciliation with France which culminated in the 1963 treaty.

Document 2a

MAJOR POLICY SPEECH BY ADENAUER IN AUGUST 1957, BEFORE THE GENERAL ELECTIONS

Source: The Bulletin, 10 September 1957
Transl: Official

Faithful cooperation with the partners of the Atlantic Community and the peoples of the free world is and remains the cornerstone of our foreign policy. This includes friendly relations with the United States, which in our view is the nucleus of the defence alliance and the backbone of Europe's freedom. The danger of Communist infiltration and subversive attempts in many parts of the world remain unchanged. As long as we have to face this menace, the defence alliance of the free world must not be weakened.

Three Major Objectives

In the coming years we will strive for the realization of three major objectives: cementing of peace, restoration of German unity, and continuation of European integration.

It is self-evident that German reunification is our great national concern, and all our hopes are directed towards its realization. German reunification is a true test for the sincerity of the Soviet Union and its future intentions. As long as the Soviet Union refuses to agree to Germany's reunification in peace and freedom, it is not willing to contribute toward relaxation of world tensions and to give real guarantee of world peace.

Supporting Disarmament

To promote relaxation, Germany's foreign policy will support the efforts of the London Disarmament Committee. We welcome any disarmament and control efforts that are aimed at creating security against surprise attacks and that help to prepare a world-wide relaxation for the cementing of peace.

The present border of the Soviet zone of occupation running through Germany, however, must under no circumstances become the 'central line' of an inspection area. Creation of a demilitarized zone on German or Central European soil that could be a temptation for an aggressor must also be avoided.

The attempt to reach relaxation through controlled general disarmament is more comprehensive than the Socialist proposed European agreement with the Soviet Union … . I therefore consider such proposals not only untimely but a hopeless diversion from the more important task, already begun, of creating a feeling of security and an atmosphere which allows the tackling of hitherto unsolved problems through arms reductions and controls …

LUDWIG ERHARD (1963–66)

The Federal Republic's second chancellor Ludwig Erhard, widely regarded as the 'father' of West Germany's postwar economic revival, was born in Bavaria on 4 February 1897. After service in the first World War he studied economics, and from 1928 to 1942 he was special assistant and later deputy director of the Nürnberg Institute of Economic Observation. After the collapse of the Third Reich he taught economics briefly at the University of Munich. More importantly, he played a key role as Bavarian Minister of Economics (1945–47) and later as Director of the Economic Administration of the Western zones of occupation. A member of the CDU, he was chosen by Chancellor Adenauer in 1949 to head the Federal Ministry of Economics, a position he held until Adenauer's retirement. Adenauer had not wanted him as his successor, but in the end could not prevent it. His rather unhappy three-year chancellorship came to an end with the economic and political crisis of 1966. The extracts below underscore one of the main characteristics of his approach to politics and government.

Document 2b

ERHARD'S STATEMENT OF 16 OCTOBER 1963 ON GOVERNMENT POLICY AFTER HAVING BEEN SWORN IN AS THE NEW CHANCELLOR IN THE BUNDESTAG

Source: The Bulletin, 22 October 1963

… I feel sure that I am expressing the concern and, at the same time, a demand of the German people when I call upon the Government and Parliament to look beyond the wishes and interests of individual groups and to devote themselves with more determination to the essentials of our political life.

Above all, young people want to measure their actions by superordinate values and standards, and they expect the Government to adhere to these maxims as well. The youth of our country wish to be given tasks to fulfil and problems to solve. The more conscious we are of this fact and the more genuine our appeals to youth, the better we will succeed in diverting them from the wrong path of simply wanting to earn money and to enjoy being provided for.

Let us also endeavour not to hasten to stamp every demand made on the German Government with the word 'social' or ' just' when in fact they are only too often merely wishes of this or that particular group. Nor should we close our eyes to the fact that whereas distinct emphasis is placed on private and group interests the sense of civic responsibility is more and more lacking. This is all the more grave since the federal Republic concedes to its citizens an unusual measure of freedom in their private activities and manifests its great respect for the value of individual development.

We must strive incessantly to make all our citizens aware of the values set by our Constitution, and to make clear again and again that freedom must go hand in hand with responsibility if it is not to degenerate into chaos. Thus we must repeatedly ask ourselves what in each individual case the need for a

continued development of our liberal order and the need for true social justice call for. Confidence in our constitutional State will only be assured for
as long as the people bearing political responsibility set a good example by
their own behaviour.

If it is therefore indispensable to make clear to the pressure groups the
limits to their claims, this would appear credible only if the State, too, knows
how to set the right standards. The State is not an abstract entity, detached
from the community of a nation, though it is certainly more than just the
sum of its citizens.

KURT-GEORG KIESINGER (1966–69)

Ludwig Erhard's successor, Kurt-Georg Kiesinger, practiced law in
Tübingen after the war and in 1949 was elected as a CDU member of
the first Bundestag. He was a member of the CDU/CSU national
executive under Adenauer, and served as Vice-President of the Con-
sultative Assembly of the Council of Europe from 1955 to 1958.
Elected Prime Minister of the state of Baden-Württemberg in 1958,
he served in Stuttgart with distinction for the next eight years. In the
wake of the crisis which followed the collapse of Erhard's government—West Germans in the fall of 1966 were fearful of an economic
collapse and concerned about the local successes of the neo-Nazi
National Democratic Party *(Nationaldemokratische Partei,* or *NPD)*—
it was mutually advantageous for the leaders of both parties to form a
'Grand Coalition' of CDU/CSU and SPD. This was a critical step in
the SPD's achievement of political dominance in the period 1969–82.
Kiesinger was thus the first—and until now the last—chancellor who
has had to work with a coalition government of partners equal in
number and political importance—a task for which his southwest
German temperament eminently fitted him.

Document 2c

KIESINGER'S STATEMENT OF 16 DECEMBER 1966 ON GOVERNMENT POLICY IN THE BUNDESTAG AFTER TAKING OFFICE

Source: *The Bulletin,* 20 December 1966

Mr President,
Ladies and Gentlemen, ...

The formation of the present Federal Government, in whose name I have
the honour to speak to you, was preceded by a long smouldering crisis, the
causes of which can be traced back over a good number of years. That crisis
came to a head barely a year after the elections to the fifth German Bun-

destag, which had proved to be an impressive vote of confidence for my predecessor, Professor Ludwig Erhard, and had enabled the ruling parties to continue their coalition. Subsequently, domestic difficulties, internal party strife, and problems of foreign policy burdened the work of the Government, until the disagreement on the balancing of the Federal budget for 1967 and on the required long-term measures of financial policy ultimately led to a split in the coalition and hence to a minority cabinet. From the following negotiations for a coalition which were an inevitable consequence of that breach the present grand coalition government emerged. In their negotiations the parties have surely carried out the most thorough stocktaking up to now of the possible courses and necessary steps open to German policy before the making of a government.

The Christian Democratic Union and the Christian Social Union and the Social Democratic Party have for the first time resolved to form a joint government at the federal level. This is without doubt a landmark in the history of the Federal Republic, an event with which many of the hopes and anxieties of our people are linked. It is hoped that the grand coalition which has such a great majority in the Bundestag exceeding by far two-thirds of its members will succeed in solving the difficult tasks ahead of it, especially of putting the public finances in order, running an economic, thrifty administration and of ensuring the growth of our economy and the stability of our currency. All these are prerequisites to the private and public weal, as much in our country as in any other country. They are the source of the strength which Government and Parliament need to enable them to act in all domains of domestic and foreign policy. Many people are worried about the possible dangers inherent in a grand coalition faced by only a comparatively small opposition.

We are resolved to do our utmost to fulfil the hopes which have been placed in us and to ward off the dangers people are afraid of. In this coalition there will be no sharing of power and sinecures between the partners, there will be no glossing over of mismanagement, and the forces of parliamentary life will not be paralyzed by arrangements behind the scenes, as has been alleged by the slogan 'proportional democracy'. The opposition will be given all parliamentary opportunities to present and bring to bear its views.

The strongest safeguard against any possible abuse of power is the firm determination of the partners in the grand coalition to maintain the coalition only for a limited period, in other words, until the end of the present term ... .

WILLY BRANDT (1969–74)

The chief beneficiaries of the Grand Coalition experiment of 1966 were the SPD and Willy Brandt, who had served alongside Chancellor Kiesinger as vice-chancellor and foreign minister. Born in Lübeck in 1913, Brandt had been active in the socialist youth movement. Following the Nazi seizure of power in 1933 he managed to escape at the very last moment to Norway, where as a Norwegian citizen he continued his political activities and took up journalism. When the Germans invaded that country in 1940, he was successfully hidden by Norwegian friends and eventually escaped to Sweden. After the end of the war he returned to Germany as a Norwegian press attaché and then resumed a journalistic career as editor of the *Berliner Stadtblatt*. Resuming German citizenship, he was elected to the Berlin House of Representatives in 1955 and, two years later, on the eve of the prolonged Berlin crisis of 1958–61, he was chosen Governing Mayor of the former capital. In the meantime, as a leading exponent of the 'Berlin Course' of modernizing and reshaping the SPD to broaden its electoral appeal, Brandt had risen to prominence within it. Chosen to lead his party in the federal elections of 1961 and 1965 he substantially increased its share of the vote from 36.2 per cent to 39.3 per cent in 1965 (against Erhard). Political power at the national level eluded him, however, until the formation of the Grand Coalition in 1966, in which his party shared power with the CDU/CSU and he became vice-chancellor and foreign minister. His success as foreign minister, and especially the initial phases of his *Ostpolitik*, helped to produce a further electoral gain in 1969 (42.7 per cent) and secured enough seats in the Bundestag to enable the SPD to assume a leadership role, in coalition with the smaller Free Democratic Party, which endured to 1982. Brandt, however, chose to resign in 1974 following the unmasking of a spy in his office. In the course of his chancellorship Brandt tried to usher in a series of social and economic reforms and to breathe new life into the German political system; Germany was to 'venture more democracy', as he put it. In foreign policy he was influential in pressing for further steps in European integration and through his *Ostpolitik* he achieved a breakthrough in West Germany's relations with the East, above all with Poland, while securing a restatement of the guarantees for West Berlin.

Document 2d

BRANDT'S STATEMENT OF 28 OCTOBER 1969 ON
GOVERNMENT POLICY IN THE BUNDESTAG
Source: *The Bulletin*, 28 October 1969
Transl.: *Official*

. . .

We are resolved to uphold the security of the Federal Republic of Germany and the coherence of the German nation, to preserve peace and to co-operate in a European peace arrangement to extend the freedoms and prosperity of our people and to develop our country in such a way that its standing will be recognized and assured in the world of tomorrow. The policy of this Government will be one of continuity and of renewal.

Our respect is due to what has been achieved in the past years—in the Federation, in the Länder and in the municipalities—by all strata of our people. I name Konrad Adenauer, Theodor Heuss and Kurt Schumacher in lieu of many others with whom the Federal Republic of Germany has lived through a period of which it can be proud. No one will deny, doubt or look down on the achievements of the past two decades. They have become history.

The stability of our democratic way of life has been reaffirmed on 28 September. I thank the voters for their unequivocal rejection of any extremism which we will have to fight also in future.

Twenty years after its constitution, our parliamentary democracy has proved its capacity for change and thus stood the test. This has been noted also outside our frontiers and has helped our State to new confidence in the world.

The strict observance of the forms of parliamentary democracy is but natural for political groups which have fought for German democracy for a good hundred years, made heavy sacrifices in its defence and taken great pains to rebuild it. Divided on material issues but united in the service of the nation, Government and Opposition have the common responsibility and duty to secure a good future for this Federal Republic.

The Federal Government knows that to cope with that task it needs loyal cooperation with the legislative bodies. For that co-operation it offers its good will to the German Bundestag and, of course, to the Bundesrat.

Our nation must have its internal order just as any other nation. In the seventies, however, we shall have order in this country only to the extent that we encourage our citizens to share responsibility. Such democratic order demands extraordinary patience in listening to others and extraordinary endeavour to understand one another.

We want to venture more democracy. We shall expose our method of working to view and satisfy the critical mind's need for information. We shall try to ensure—through hearings in the Bundestag, through constant contact with the representative groups of our people and through comprehensive information on the Government's policy—that every citizen is placed in a position to participate in the reform of state and society.

We address ourselves to the younger generation that has grown up in peaceful times, that is not and must not be encumbered with the mortgages of the older; those young people who want to—and should—take us at our word. These young people must understand, however, that they, too, have obligations towards state and society.

We shall present to this Assembly a bill to lower the franchise age from twenty-one to eighteen and the eligibility age from twenty-five to twenty-one. We shall also review the age of adulthood.

Joint management, joint responsibility in the various sectors of our society will be a motive force in the years to come. We cannot create perfect democracy. But we want a society offering more freedom and demanding greater participation in responsibility. This Government wants discussion; it seeks the critical partnership of all those bearing responsibility, be it in the churches, in the spheres of art and science, in economic life, or in other sectors of society.

This goes not least for the trade unions whose trustful cooperation we are seeking. There is no need to specifically certify their eminent importance to this State and to its further development into a social state under the rule of law.

If we want to achieve what must be achieved we need to muster all the active forces in our society. A society that wants to give room to all ideological and religious convictions, lives on the ethical impulses which manifest themselves in serving one's neighbour in the spirit of solidarity. We should not only have the churches care for the families, youth, or education. We visualize our common tasks especially where old and sick people, physically or mentally handicapped in their distress, are in need of not only material support but of human solidarity. In serving man—not only in our own country but also in the developing countries—the work of religious and social groups and political action converge.

We shall endeavour to bring the justified wishes of the various forces of society and the political will of the government into harmony.

HELMUT SCHMIDT (1974–82)

Brandt's successor in 1974, the perennially youthful looking Helmut Schmidt, came to the chancellery with a reputation for expertise in the areas of economics and finance as well as in defence. Born in Hamburg in 1918, he was of the age group involved in military service during the Second World War. After 1945 he returned to Hamburg, joined the SPD, and embarked on the study of economics. In 1953, after working for the Hamburg city government, he was elected to the Bundestag and assumed an increasingly prominent role in the leadership cadres of the SPD. In 1961 he returned to Hamburg as that state's Minister of the Interior. When flood waters devastated large parts of the city the next year, Schmidt's energetic handling of emergency measures earned him a reputation as a forceful organizer. In 1969, when the Brandt-led government was formed, he became Minister of Defence. He later headed both the Ministries of Economics and Finance. When Brandt resigned in 1974 following the discovery of an East German spy on his personal staff Schmidt, as the SPD's deputy party chairman, succeeded to the chancellor's office. In his eight years in office he dominated not only German domestic politics, but also the international arena, especially as an expert in international economic affairs.

Document 2e

SCHMIDT'S STATEMENT ON GOVERNMENT POLICY IN THE BUNDESTAG OF 24 NOVEMBER 1980 AFTER THE FORMATION OF HIS SECOND GOVERNMENT

Source: Statements and speeches (prepared by Press Office of the Embassy of the Federal Republic of Germany in Washington, D.C.), 28 November 1980

. . .

The basic lines of our foreign policy are:

First: Without equilibrium there is no dependable peace in the world. We can feel secure because the Atlantic Alliance maintains the equilibrium to which we have contributed by placing our whole political and military weight on the western side of the scales.

Second: Equilibrium is a necessary if insufficient condition for peace. Peace therefore has to be safeguarded by a policy of arms limitation and cooperation as well. 'Military security and a policy of détente' (Harmel Report, December 1967) have been the two main elements of the Alliance's security policy concept for over ten years. We shall continue the policy of cooperation with our eastern neighbours in the interest of peaceful development in Europe and of the future of the whole German nation.

Third: The European Community remains the indispensable basis for peace and freedom and for social and economic progress. It also helps preserve the equilibrium.

. . .

Together with our partners in the Alliance we are making efforts in the arms control negotiations with the East to achieve a stable military balance at the lowest possible level in order to halt the arms race and reduce the burden of military expenditure. Mankind could arm itself to death if the arms race were not stopped. That is why the negotiations between the superpowers on the limitation of strategic arms are of central importance. We strongly advocate the continuation of the SALT process. After my discussion with President-elect Reagan, I am pleased to be able to report to the Bundestag that he is thinking along the same lines.

. . .

Our long-term efforts to improve the situation of the Germans who are suffering from the division of Germany has put many things in motion: millions of people have made journeys, relatives make telephone calls to each other, families have been reunited. Roads to Berlin are being built. Trade has shown a vigorous development—to name a few examples. All in all, we have been able to keep the Germans from drifting apart from each other.

This policy is and remains an integral part of the general policy of reconciliation between West and East.

. . .

Our relationship with the Soviet Union is marked by the willingness for long-term cooperation. I recall the statements on the occasion of my meetings with General-Secretary Brezhnev here in Bonn two years ago and in Moscow last summer. These also express the Soviet Union's interest in cooperation between the two German states. Precisely in difficult times, the Federal Government does not want to allow the dialogue with the Soviet Union to be interrupted.

HELMUT KOHL (1982 to the present)

Helmut Kohl, who succeeded to the chancellorship in October 1982 following the disintegration of Helmut Schmidt's socialist-liberal coalition, was at fifty-two years of age, the youngest head of government in the Federal Republic's history. A tall and warm-hearted south German from Ludwigshafen, he had earned a doctorate in political science at Heidelberg University and worked in a chemical company before achieving prominence in politics. Joining the CDU as early as 1947, he became a member of the party's executive in the Rhineland-Palatinate in 1955 and four years later was elected to the state parliament in Mainz. From a strong local political base he rose steadily in the CDU national ranks to become deputy chairman in 1969 and chairman four years later. In 1976 he took on the unenviable task of leading the CDU in the electoral battle against the popular Helmut Schmidt. In the next election he was forced to step aside when the party chose to back the CSU leader, Franz-Josef Strauss, as its candidate for the chancellorship. Strauss was less successful against Schmidt than Kohl had been in 1976, however, and when Schmidt's government collapsed in 1982 Kohl was the logical choice of his party to lead a coalition of CDU/CSU and FDP. Pledged to secure ratification of the mid-term change of coalition at the polls, Kohl secured a controversial dissolution of the Bundestag and led his party to a stunning victory on 6 March 1983.

Since then, Kohl has grown in the office, surprising Germans and foreigners alike with his self-confidence and leadership ability. As the youngest chancellor in the FRG's history and an unpretentious representative of the new, more progressive generation of CDU party leaders, Kohl surprised everyone again in the January 1987 federal election, a victory that set the stage for his response to the extraordinary events of 1989. Despite misgivings in many quarters, he seized upon a virtual blank cheque from Washington to negotiate the quick and complete reunification of Germany, setting the stage yet again for his election in 1990 as the first freely chosen chancellor of *all* the German people since 1932 (see also Chs.5 and 4). On 15 November 1994, he was reelected by a majority of 338 votes, one more than constitutionally required.

Document 2f

KOHL'S ADDRESS ON THE EVE OF GERMAN UNITY, 2 OCTOBER 1990

Source: Presse- und Informationsamt der Bundesregierung (ed.), *The Unification of Germany: A Documentation,* Bonn 1991, p. 137
Transl.: Official

My fellow countrymen.

In a few hours a dream will become reality. After over forty bitter years of division Germany, our fatherland, will be reunited. This is one of the happiest moments of my life. From the many letters and conversations I have had, I know the great joy also felt by the vast majority of you.

On such a day we naturally look ahead. Yet despite our great joy, we must first think of those who particularly suffered from the division of Germany. Families were cruelly torn apart. Political prisoners were incarcerated. People died at the Wall.

Fortunately, this is now a thing of the past. It must never be forgotten. We owe it to the victims to recall this. We owe it to our children and grandchildren. They must be spared such experiences for ever. For the same reason we have not forgotten those to whom we owe the unity of our country. We would never have achieved it on our own. Many played a part in this process.

When has a nation ever had the opportunity of overcoming decades of painful separation in such a peaceful manner? We are reestablishing German unity in freedom in full agreement with our neighbors.

. . .

Particularly at this moment, we Germans must show solidarity towards one another. A difficult path lies before us. We want to proceed along it together. If we stick together and are prepared to make sacrifices, we will have a very [good] chance of joint success.

. . .

We call upon all Germans to show that we are worthy of our shared freedom. The third of October is a day of joy, gratitude and hope. The young generation of Germans, more than any other previous generation, have every chance of spending their whole lives in peace and freedom. We know that our joy is shared by many people throughout the world. With them we share our feelings at this moment; Germany is our fatherland, the united Europe is our future!

With the exception of Adenauer's third cabinet formed in 1957—and that only for three out of four years—all German governments have been formed by party coalitions. The formation of a coalition is preceded by negotiations leading to a coalition agreement such as the following between the SPD and the FDP subsequent to the 1980 election.

Document 3

THE COALITION AGREEMENT BETWEEN SPD AND FDP, 1980
(see also Ch.8)

Source: Supplied in typescript, n.d.

On 7 October 1980 the SPD and the FDP issued a joint statement on their wish to continue the social-liberal coalition. They expressed their desire to continue their successful foreign and security policies as well as their German and Berlin policies.

In a further joint statement on co-determination, dated November 4, the SPD and FDP agreed to continue serious discussions with the aim of arriving at a mutual solution.

In addition, both coalition parties agreed to the following items:

Financial Policy

The 1981 Federal budget has to set the course for financial policy in the new legislative period: Growth rates of the 1981 Federal budget about 4 percent; net borrowing in 1981 about 27 billion DM. This will result in the following tax and subsidy policies:

a) From 1 April 1981 tax on mineral-oil will be raised by 7 pfennigs per litre for petrol, 3 pfennigs per litre for diesel oil. The possibility of giving community traffic a part sum (0.51 pfennig) out of the mineral-oil tax raise is being examined. Tax on liquors will be raised by 300 DM per 100 litres on 1 April 1981.

The Federal Government will introduce a bill to apportion automobile tax onto mineral-oil tax; it hopes to reach an agreement with the Länder by legislative procedures.

It is not intended to increase the general tax burden during the coming legislative period. In the case of a tax reduction, the basic allowance and tax regulations for health insurance payments of the self-employed are to be improved. The Federal government is still trying to get the tax offices to disburse family allowances.

Housing and Urban Policy

Improvement of skeleton conditions for privately financed housing construction: Obligatory rent comparison, simplification of rent-raising procedure and progressive rents for first lets or lets of living-space rendered habitable after 1 January 1981. Greater consideration of market economy elements in council housing construction: continuation of yearly interest increases for construction loans. An attempt to alter present competence spheres. People living in council housing and whose income is actually too high for them to have the right to benefit from the subsidized rents should pay compensation to the community.

Better protection of the tenants against commutation, alienation, and overmodernization as well as in regard to rent deposits. Encouragement of modernizing housing by the tenant.

Policy on Women's Rights

Progress in putting women's equal rights into practice in every respect. Examine whether the non-discrimination law can confirm actual existing disadvantages for women compared to men. Further practical report on § 218 StGB, [the abortion law].

The standing orders of the federal cabinet define the status of the ministers and their general relationship to the chancellor. They also set forth the cabinet's functions and decision-making procedures, including the method of resolving differences of opinion among cabinet members.

Document 4

STANDING ORDERS OF THE FEDERAL CABINET
(GESCHÄFTSORDNUNG DER BUNDESREGIERUNG)
Source: GMBl., 11 May 1951, 131ff., as amended up to and including 1 January 1970

I. The Federal Chancellor

Art. 1

(1) The Federal Chancellor shall determine general policy in domestic and foreign affairs. These policies shall be binding upon the Federal Ministers and be carried into effect by them within their sphere of competence and on their own responsibility. In cases of doubt a decision of the Federal Chancellor shall be obtained.

(2) The Federal Chancellor shall have the right and the duty to see to the adherence of the general policy [guidelines].

Art. 2

In addition to determining general policy the Federal Chancellor shall also make efforts toward the harmonizing of the operation of the Federal Cabinet.

Art. 3

The Federal Chancellor shall receive from the departments of the various Federal Ministers information on measures and plans which are of significance for the determination of general policy and for the conduct of operations of the Federal Cabinet.

Art. 4

Whenever a Federal Minister deems an extension or change of general policy necessary he shall inform the Federal Chancellor, giving his reasons and requesting the Chancellor's decision.

Art. 5

The Federal Chancellor shall keep the Federal President informed on his policies and the work of the various Federal Ministers by transmitting to him essential records or written reports on matters of particular significance, or, if necessary, by reporting in person.

Art. 6

The Federal Chancellor shall guide the operations of the Federal Cabinet in accordance with Section IV.

Art. 7

(1) The Under Secretary of the Federal Chancellery shall also act as a Secretary of State of the Federal Cabinet.

(2) He may forward directly to the appropriate Federal Minister correspondence addressed to the Federal Chancellor or transmitted to the Federal Chancellor by the Federal President. If the appropriate Federal Minister recommends a reply by the Federal Chancellor, the Under Secretary shall submit an appropriate draft reply to the Federal Chancellor.

. . .

III. The Federal Ministers

Art. 9

The spheres of competence of the various Federal Ministers shall be determined in their general outlines by the Federal Chancellor. In cases of overlapping and differences of opinion resulting therefrom among several Federal Ministers the Federal Cabinet shall decide by a resolution [vote].

Art. 10

(1) Deputations shall, as a rule, be received only by the appropriate Minister in charge, or by his deputy. Deputations shall be asked beforehand for a statement of the subject of negotiation. If a joint reception appears to be appropriate the Federal Minister appealed to shall inform the other Federal Ministers concerned.

. . .

Art. 12

Statements by a Federal Minister made in, or intended for, the public must be in accord with the general policies laid down by the Federal Chancellor.

Art. 13

(1) Each Federal Minister shall notify the Federal Chancellor whenever he shall leave the seat of the Federal Cabinet for longer than one day. Agreement shall be reached with the Federal Chancellor regarding any absence of longer than three days.

(2) The consent of the Federal Chancellor shall be necessary for the acceptance of invitations for visits abroad.

(3) Before leaving the seat of the Federal Cabinet a Federal Minister shall leave with the Federal Chancellor the address at which he can be reached during his absence.

. . .

IV. The Federal Cabinet (Federal Government)

. . .

Art. 15

(1) The Federal Cabinet shall be furnished, for its considerations and decisions, with all matters of general importance in domestic, foreign, economic, social, financial or cultural policy, particularly

(a) all legislative bills;
(b) all drafts of ordinances of Federal Cabinet *[Verordnungen]*;
(c) drafts of other orders, if they are of particular political importance;
(d) statements by the Bundesrat of its position on Bills submitted by the Federal Cabinet;
(e) all matters in which the Basic Law or these Standing Orders so require;
(f) differences of opinion among various Federal Ministries; ...

. . .

Art. 17

(1) Differences of opinion among Federal Ministers shall be submitted to the Federal Cabinet only after the Federal Ministers involved, or, in the event of their disability, their deputies, have personally made an unsuccessful attempt at reaching agreement.

(2) Before discussion in Cabinet session the Federal Chancellor may first discuss the differences of opinion with the Federal Ministers involved in a ministerial conference under his chairmanship

Art. 24

(1) The Federal Cabinet shall have a quorum when one half of the Federal Ministers, including the chairman, are present.

(2) The Federal Cabinet shall render its decisions by majority vote. In cases of tie votes the chairman shall cast the deciding vote.

Art. 25

The text of decisions of the Federal Cabinet shall be determined by the chairman at the conclusion of the oral deliberation of each subject.

Art. 26

(1) In the event that the Federal Cabinet, in cases other than those under Articles 20 and 21 of the Budget Statute *(Haushaltsordnung)*, act in opposition to or without the vote of the Federal Minister of Finance in questions of financial importance, he may explicitly lodge a protest against the decision. If objections are raised the matter shall be voted upon anew at another session of the Federal Cabinet. The execution of the matter against which the Federal Minister of Finance protested must be suspended unless approved by a new vote

and by a majority of all Federal Ministers, with the Minister of Finance or his deputy present and with the Federal Chancellor voting with the majority.
(2) Corresponding rules shall apply in the event that the Federal Minister of Justice or the Federal Minister of the Interior have raised objections against the draft of a law or regulation or against a measure of the Federal Cabinet on the grounds of incompatibility with existing laws.

The Federal Ministers Act sets forth the conditions for holding office in the cabinet. The provisions of the Act deal with the tenure, discharge, financial emoluments, and retirement benefits of cabinet members. They also lay down rules designed to avoid conflicts of interest between membership in the cabinet and outside activities.

Document 5

FEDERAL MINISTERS ACT *(BUNDESMINISTERGESETZ)*
Source: BGBl.I, 1953, 407, as amended up to and including 19 July 1968

. . .

Art. 1
The members of the Federal Cabinet have, in accordance with this Act, a public law tenure relationship with the Federation.

. . .

Art. 4
A member of the Federal Cabinet may not simultaneously be a member of a Land cabinet.

Art. 5
(1) Members of the Federal Cabinet may not in addition to their office occupy any other salaried position, nor undertake any business or profession. Neither may they belong during their term of office to the management, board of trustees, or board of directors of a profit-making enterprise nor act as a paid arbiter nor render out-of-court expert opinions. The Bundestag may allow exceptions to the prohibition of membership on a board of trustees or a board of directors.

. . .

Art. 6
(1) The members of the Federal Cabinet shall, even after termination of their tenure, be obliged to maintain secrecy regarding matters learned by virtue of their office. This shall not apply to notifications in the course of office business nor to facts which are publicly known or which according to their significance no longer require secrecy.

. . .

Art. 18

(1) A Federal civil servant or Federal judge appointed a member of the Federal Cabinet shall vacate his office as civil servant or judge at the beginning of his tenure. For the duration of his membership the rights and duties resulting from the service condition shall be suspended, except the duty of official secrecy and the prohibition against acceptance of rewards and gifts ... .

(2) Upon termination of his tenure as member of the Federal Cabinet a civil servant or judge shall, unless assigned with his consent to another position within three months, be put at the expiration of this time on the retired list and shall receive the pension which he would have earned on the basis of his former service, with the time of his tenure as member of the Federal Cabinet added.

. . .

The office of parliamentary state secretary (see also Ch.7), to be distinguished from the permanent under-secretaries of state of the various ministerial bureaucracies, was introduced in 1967. The parliamentary state secretaries help the ministers run their departments, defend their records in parliament, and maintain contact with the public. The document which follows describes their legal status.

Document 6

PARLIAMENTARY UNDER SECRETARIES ACT *(PARLA-MENTARISCHE STAATSSEKRETÄRE)*

Source: BGBl., I, 1967, 396

. . .

Section 1
(1) Parliamentary State Secretaries can be assigned to assist members of the Federal Government. They must be members of the Bundestag.
(2) Parliamentary State Secretaries support the members of the Federal Government to whom they are assigned in the fulfillment of government business.
(3) Under the terms of this law Parliamentary State Secretaries in their official capacity are entitled to 'public law status' within the Federation.

Section 2
Parliamentary State Secretaries are appointed by the Federal President. In consultation with the Federal minister for whom the Parliamentary State Secretary will work, the chancellor makes a nomination to the Federal President.

. . .

Section 4
Parliamentary State Secretaries can be dismissed at any time. They can also resign at any time. The chancellor will propose the dismissal to the Federal President in consultation with the Federal minister concerned. The official position of a Parliamentary State Secretary terminates with the ending of the official

position ... of the responsible member of the Federal Government. It also ends when the Parliamentary State Secretary leaves Parliament, but not with the ending of the legislative period of the Bundestag (Art. 39, 1.2, Basic Law).

. . .

Section 8
At the suggestion of the chancellor and with the agreement of the Federal Minister responsible, the Federal President may give a Parliamentary State Secretary the right to carry the title of 'Minister of State' for the duration of his office or for the carrying out of a particular task.

. . .

ELECTION OF THE FEDERAL PRESIDENT

The Federal President is not elected directly by popular vote as in the Weimar Republic or the United States, but by a specially constituted *ad hoc* convention *(Bundesversammlung)* in accordance both with the Basic Law (Doc.7a) and the Presidential Election Act (Doc.7b).

Document 7a

BASIC LAW

Art. 54: Election by the Federal Convention

(1) The Federal President shall be elected, without debate, by the Federal Convention *(Bundesversammlung)*. Every German shall be eligible who is entitled to vote for Bundestag candidates and has attained the age of forty years.

(2) The term of office of the Federal President shall be five years. Re-election for a consecutive term shall be permitted only once.

(3) The Federal Convention shall consist of the members of the Bundestag and an equal number of members elected by the diets of the Länder according to the principles of proportional representation.

(4) The Federal Convention shall meet not later than thirty days before the expiration of the term of office of the Federal President or, in the case of premature termination, not later than thirty days after that date. It shall be convened by the President of the Bundestag.

(5) After the expiration of a legislative term, the period specified in the first sentence of paragraph (4) of this Article shall begin with the first meeting of the Bundestag.

(6) The person receiving the votes of the majority of the members of the Federal Convention shall be elected. If such majority is not obtained by any candidate in two ballots, the candidate who receives the largest number of votes in the next ballot shall be elected.

(7) Details shall be regulated by a federal law.

Document 7b

PRESIDENTIAL ELECTION ACT
Source: BGBl.I, 1959, 230
Transl.: Official

I: The Federal Convention

. . .

Art. 1

The President of the Bundestag shall determine the place and date of the convening of the Federal Convention.

Art. 2

(1) The Federal Cabinet shall make a timely determination of how many members the various Länder legislatures shall have to elect ... .

Art. 4

(1) The Land legislatures shall elect the members to which their Land is entitled on the basis of nominating lists. The provisions of the Standing Orders of the particular Land legislature shall apply accordingly.
(2) Each member of the Land legislature shall have one vote.
(3) If several nominating lists are submitted, seats shall be apportioned on the basis of the number accruing to each on the basis of the d'Hondt system of the highest average ...

II: Election of the Federal President

Art. 8

The President of the Bundestag shall preside over the sessions and activities of the Federal Convention. The Standing Orders of the Bundestag shall be appropriately applied to the activities of the Convention unless the Federal Convention enacts its own Standing Orders.

Art. 9

(1) Any member of the Federal Convention may make nominations for the election of a Federal President in writing to the President of the Bundestag. New nominations may be made at the second and third ballots. Nominations may contain only information necessary for the designation of the nominee; a written statement of consent by the nominee is to be attached.
(2) The Executive Committee *[Sitzungsvorstand]* shall scrutinize the nominations for their conformity with the legal requirements. The Federal Convention shall decide on the rejection of a nomination.
(3) Votes shall be cast with covered ballot sheets. Ballot sheets which name anyone other than a proper nominee shall be invalid.
(4) The President of the Bundestag shall inform the person who is elected of his election and shall invite him to state within two days whether he accepts

the election. If the elected person does not give his statement within this time, he will be deemed to have declined his election.

(5) The President of the Bundestag shall declare the Federal Convention adjourned after the person elected has accepted his election.

Art. 10

The term of office of the Federal President shall begin with the expiration of the term of his predecessor, but not before the receipt by the President of the Bundestag of his statement of acceptance.

. . .

The office of president is potentially an important symbol of national unity. Standing above partisan political conflict, the president has the opportunity to play an important educative role in the Federal Republic. He can use ceremonial occasions to his advantage by stressing the liberal constitutional values underlying German democracy. The right kind of person might even serve as the moral conscience of the nation. Richard von Weizsäcker, like Gustav Heinemann and Theodor Heuss, played precisely this role during his tenure of office. Weizsäcker never ceased to remind Germans of their moral responsibility to redress the past by committing themselves to the creation of a living democracy infused with the values of individual freedom and social justice. The following extracts are from President Weizsäcker's address celebrating the reunification of Germany (Doc.8a); his address on the fortieth anniversary of the end of the Second World War (Doc.8b) and his successor's—Roman Herzog's—speech in Warsaw on the fiftieth anniversary of the uprising in the Polish capital against the German army (Doc.8c).

Document 8a

ADDRESS BY PRESIDENT WEIZSÄCKER ON 3 OCTOBER 1990

Source: *The Unification of Germany: A Documentation*, pp. 153–161.
Transl.: Official

The preamble to our constitution, which is now valid for all Germans, expresses the quintessence of what is uppermost in our minds today: We have achieved the unity and freedom of Germany in free self-determination. We are resolved to serve world peace in a united Europe. In pursuing this aim we are conscious of our responsibility to God and man.

. . .

Massive problems confront us at home and abroad. We do not ignore them. We take the reservations expressed by our neighbors seriously. We also realize how difficult it will be to fulfill the expectations placed in us by all sides. But we will be guided by confidence, not fear and doubt. Decisive for us is our firm determination to see our responsibilities clearly and to face up to them together. That determination gives us the strength to see our day-to-day problems in the perspective of our history and future in Europe.

. . .

Amidst our European neighbors we were destined to remain divided for over forty years. For the one part of the country this proved to be a boon, for the other a burden. But it was, and remains, our common German fate. A fate which embraces the past and the responsibility for its consequences. The SED [Socialist Unity Party] in East Germany tried to decree the country's division [and] thought it sufficient to proclaim the socialist society of the future in order to free itself from the burden of history.

But in the German Democratic Republic the people saw, and felt, it differently. They had to carry a far greater part of the burden of the war than their countrymen in the West and they have always felt that recalling the past with a sense of responsibility would give them the indispensable strength to free themselves for the future ... .

But now that we have our freedom we must prove ourselves worthy of it ... .Although the people in the German Democratic Republic ... made the best of their situation and worked hard ... the magnitude of their problems and the gulf between them and the West became fully clear only during recent months. If we are to close the gap soon we shall not only have to help but also, and above all, to respect one another.

. . .

... Every life has its meaning and its innate dignity. No period in life is in vain, especially if it is marked by hardship. In human terms, the people in the German Democratic Republic achieved something very substantial under the most difficult conditions and we can only hope that it will be part of the substance of the united Germany.

. . .

Priority must now be given to economic and social problems ... .I am confident we shall succeed in filling existing and newly emerging gulfs. We can fuse the constitutional patriotism of the one side with the human solidarity experienced by the other into a powerful whole. We share the will to carry out our great responsibilities as expected by our neighbors.

We realize how much harder life is for other nations at present. History has given us a chance. We must seize it, with confidence and trust.

And joy—we heard it last night—the joy we feel, is a divine spark.

Document 8b

SPEECH BY PRESIDENT RICHARD VON WEIZSÄCKER IN
THE BUNDESTAG ON 8 MAY 1985 DURING THE CERE-
MONY COMMEMORATING THE 40TH ANNIVERSARY OF
THE END OF WAR IN EUROPE AND OF NATIONAL-
SOCIALIST TYRANNY (excerpts)

Source: *Bundespräsidialamt*
Transl.: official

Many nations are today commemorating the date on which World War II
ended in Europe. Every nation is doing so with different feelings, depending on its fate. Be it victory or defeat, liberation from injustice and alien rule
or transition to new dependence, division, new alliances, vast shifts of
power—8 May 1945 is a date of decisive historical importance for Europe.

We Germans are commemorating that date amongst ourselves, as is
indeed necessary. We must find our own standards. We are not assisted in
this task if we or others spare our feelings. We need and we have the
strength to look truth straight in the eye—without embellishment and
without distortion.

For us, the 8th of May is above all a date to remember what people had
to suffer. It is also a date to reflect on the course taken by our history. The
greater honesty we show in commemorating this day, the freer we are to face
the consequences with due responsibility. For us Germans, 8 May is not a
day of celebration. Those who actually witnessed that day in 1945 think back
on highly personal and hence highly different experiences. Some returned
home, others lost their homes. Some were liberated, whilst for others it was
the start of captivity. Many were simply grateful that the bombing at night
and fear had passed and that they had survived. Others felt first and foremost
grief at the complete defeat suffered by their country. Some Germans felt
bitterness about their shattered illusions, whilst others were grateful for the
gift of a new start.

It was difficult to find one's bearing straight away. Uncertainty prevailed
throughout the country. The military capitulation was unconditional, placing our destiny in the hands of our enemies. The past had been terrible,
especially for many of those enemies, too. Would they not make us pay
many times over for what we had done to them? Most Germans had
believed that they were fighting and suffering for the good of their country.
And now it turned out that their efforts were not only in vain and futile, but
had served the inhuman goals of a criminal regime. The feelings of most
people were those of exhaustion, despair and new anxiety. Had one's next
of kin survived? Did a new start from those ruins make sense at all? Looking back, they saw the dark abyss of the past and, looking forward, they saw
an uncertain, dark future.

Yet with every day something became clearer, and this must be stated on
behalf of all of us today: the 8th of May was a day of liberation. It liberated
all of us from the inhumanity and tyranny of the National-Socialist regime.

Nobody will, because of that liberation, forget the grave suffering that only started for many people on 8 May. But we must not regard the end of the war as the cause of flight, expulsion and deprivation of freedom. The cause goes back to the start of the tyranny that brought about war. We must not separate 8 May 1945 from 30 January 1933.

There is truly no reason for us today to participate in victory celebrations. But there is every reason for us to perceive 8 May 1945 as the end of an aberration in German history, an end bearing seeds of hope for a better future.

. . .

At the root of the tyranny was Hitler's immeasurable hatred against our Jewish compatriots. Hitler had never concealed this hatred from the public, but made the entire nation a tool of it. Only a day before his death, on 30 April 1945, he concluded his so-called will with the words: 'Above all, I call upon the leaders of the nation and their followers to observe painstakingly the race laws and to oppose ruthlessly the poisoners of all nations: international Jewry.' Hardly any country has in its history always remained free from blame for war or violence. The genocide of the Jews is, however, unparalleled in history.

The perpetration of this crime was in the hands of a few people. It was concealed from the eyes of the public, but every German was able to experience what his Jewish compatriots had to suffer, ranging from plain apathy and hidden intolerance to outright hatred. Who could remain unsuspecting after the burning of the synagogues, the plundering, the stigmatization with the Star of David, the deprivation of rights, the ceaseless violation of human dignity? Whoever opened his eyes and ears and sought information could not fail to notice that Jews were being deported. The nature and scope of the destruction may have exceeded human imagination, but in reality there was, apart from the crime itself, the attempt by too many people, including those of my generation, who were young and were not involved in planning the events and carrying them out, not to take note of what was happening. There were many ways of not burdening one's conscience, of shunning responsibility, looking away, keeping mum. When the unspeakable truth of the Holocaust then became known at the end of the war, all too many of us claimed that they had not known anything about it or even suspected anything.

There is no such thing as the guilt or innocence of an entire nation. Guilt is, like innocence, not collective, but personal. There is discovered or concealed individual guilt. There is guilt which people acknowledge or deny. Everyone who directly experienced that era should today quietly ask himself about his involvement then.

The vast majority of today's population were either children then or had not been born. They cannot profess a guilt of their own for crimes that they did not commit. No discerning person can expect them to wear a penitential robe simply because they are Germans. But their forefathers have left them a grave legacy. All of us, whether guilty or not, whether old or young, must accept the past. We are all affected by its consequences and liable for it.

. . .

In the wake of the war, old enemies were brought closer together. As early as 1946, the American Secretary of State, James F. Byrnes, called in his memorable Stuttgart address for understanding in Europe and for assistance to the German nation on its way to a free and peaceable future. Innumerable Americans assisted us Germans, who had lost the war, with their own private means so as to heal the wounds of war. Thanks to the vision of the Frenchmen Jean Monnet and Robert Schuman and their cooperation with Konrad Adenauer, the traditional enmity between the French and Germans was buried forever.

A new will and energy to reconstruct Germany surged through the country. Many an old trench was filled in, religious differences and social strains were defused. People set to work in a spirit of partnership.

There was no 'zero hour', but we had the opportunity to make a fresh start. We have used this opportunity as well as we could.

We have put democratic freedom in the place of oppression. Four years after the end of the war, on this 8th of May in 1949, the Parliamentary Council adopted our Basic Law. Transcending party differences, the democrats on the Council gave their answer to war and tyranny in Article 1 of our Constitution: 'The German people acknowledge inviolable and inalienable human rights as the basis of any community, of peace and of justice in the world.' This further significance of 8 May should also be remembered today.

The Federal Republic of Germany has become an internationally respected State. It is one of the most highly developed industrial countries in the world. It knows that its economic strength commits it to share responsibility for the struggle against hunger and need in the world and for social adjustment between nations. For 40 years we have been living in peace and freedom, to which we, through our policy in union with the free nations of the Atlantic Alliance and the European Community, have ourselves rendered a major contribution. The freedom of the individual has never received better protection in Germany than it does today. A comprehensive system of social welfare that can stand comparison with any other ensures the subsistence of the population. Whereas at the end of the war many Germans tried to hide their passports or to exchange them for another one, German nationality today is highly valued.

We certainly have no reason to be arrogant and self-righteous. But we may look back with gratitude on our development over these 40 years, if we use the memory of our own history as a guideline for our future behaviour.

. . .

In this tradition Roman Herzog, the new President as of 1 July 1994, in Warsaw on August 1st 1994 made the following declaration, in his first public appearance abroad at the invitation of the Polish President, Lech Walesa, in commemoration of the 'Warsaw uprising' against the German army fifty years ago.

Document 8c

Source: Presse- und Informationsamt der Bundesregierung, *Bulletin* 3 August 1994

... it is a very moving moment for me to extend my hands today to you across the graves of the people killed in the uprising of Warsaw. As head of state of my country, I am very grateful to you, Mr. President, and the Polish people for this invitation. At the same time I have sympathy for the feelings of those who view my participation with some criticism. To them I extend my feelings of respect.

What we need are reconciliation and understanding, confidence and a spirit of good neighbourliness. These can only develop and thrive further if our people face the horrors of their latest history with absolute candour, without any prejudices and with the courage to face up to the full truth. There we must not add anything or leave anything out, we should not pass over anything in silence and neither should we offset one grievance against another. We should rather act out of the conviction that we need forgiveness and are ourselves prepared to grant such forgiveness.

. . .

In the last forty years the course of European history has experience dramatic changes. The peoples have begun to draw together in a united Europe. No one needs to give up his own national identity, his culture or national history. What we must give up, however, is hostility and hatred as well as a small part of our national egoism. West of the former Iron Curtain this new idea worked wonders.

Today this path is also open to the people of Poland, which, after all, has always been part of Europe and which the Europeans sadly missed for forty years. Within this context Poles and Germans will be able to stretch their hands out to each other in the same way as this has long since been a reality between French and Germans.

Germany, at any rate, will support categorically and persistently and out of the best motives the endeavours of Poland to become a member of the EU and NATO. Indeed, we cannot do anything better for our children and grandchildren.

Today, however, I bow my head before those Poles who fought in the Warsaw uprising as well as before all Polish victims of the war. I beg forgiveness for what Germans did to them.

In October 1982 Helmut Kohl was elected chancellor on a constructive vote of no-confidence. On 6 January 1983, however, the Chancellor called for a vote of confidence, this time planning his own defeat. After losing the confidence vote as planned, the Federal President, pursuant to Chancellor Kohl's request, dissolved Parliament for the purpose of holding new elections. A number of SPD and FDP members of parliament challenged the constitutionality of the dissolution in the Federal Constitutional Court. The extracts below represent the guiding principles of the decision upholding the validity of the dissolution of the Bundestag by the President under Art. 68 of the Basic Law.

Document 9

DECISION OF THE FEDERAL CONSTITUTIONAL COURT ON THE DISSOLUTION OF THE BUNDESTAG, 16 FEBRUARY 1983

Source: Xeroxed copy issued by the Court

IN THE NAME OF THE GERMAN PEOPLE

In the case of a dispute between federal organs concerning the complaint that the Federal President, through his authorization of the dissolution of the 9th German Bundestag of 6 January 1983(BGBl.I,S.l)and his authorization of Federal elections on 6 January 1983 (BGBl.I,S.2) contravened Article 68 Paragraph 1 of the Basic Law and thereby directly endangered the complainants constitutional rights … .

Guiding Principles of the Judgement of the Second Senate of 16 February 1983:

. . .

(2) Ordering the dissolution of the Bundestag according to Article 68 of the Basic Law or refusing to do so involves a basic political decision which rests with the responsible judgement of the Federal President. A decision within the framework of Article 68 Paragraph 1, Sentence 1 of the Basic Law is thus only open to the Federal President when at the time of his decision the constitutional requirements are present.

(3) Article 68 of the Basic Law lays down a chronological sequence of events. Violations of the constitution which occurred in the previous chronological stages affect the areas of decision in which the Federal President finds himself after the Federal Chancellor has proposed the dissolution.

(4) (a) Article 68 Paragraph 1, Sentence 1 of the Basic Law is a constitutional norm, which is responsive to and requires to be given concrete expression.

(b) The authority to give concrete expression to Federal constitutional law belongs not to the Federal Constitutional Court alone, but also to other supreme constitutional organs. In this connection previously delivered judgements, basic decisions, basic principles, and constitutional norms have to be adhered to.

(c) In giving substance to the constitution as the basic legal order a particularly high degree of consensus is necessary in the analysis and assessment of the relevant facts of the case between the supreme constitutional organs concerned under considerations both of constitutional law and of political practice. It is essential that these organs act in such a given situation consistently and with due regard for durability.

(5) Confidence in the sense intended in Article 68 of the Basic Law means, pursuant to the German tradition of constitutional law, the formally manifested present endorsement, through the act of voting by the members of the Bundestag, of the person and substantive programme of the Federal Chancellor.

(6) The Federal Chancellor, who aims to secure the dissolution of the Bundestag in the manner laid down in Article 68 of the Basic Law, should only be allowed to pursue this course when it is no longer politically possible for him to ensure continued governing with the prevailing power constellation of the Bundestag. The power-political constellation of the Bundestag must so impair his capacity to govern that he is not in a position to pursue a meaningful policy endorsed by the continuing confidence of the majority. This is the unwritten substantive constitutional characteristic of Article 68 Paragraph 1, Sentence 1 of the Basic Law.

(7) An interpretation at this point that Article 68 of the Basic Law permits a Federal Chancellor, whose adequate majority in the Bundestag is not in question, to arrange to have the confidence question answered in the negative at a point in time convenient for him with the aim of getting a dissolution of the Bundestag is not justified by the sense of Article 68 of the Basic Law. Similarly difficulties foreseen in carrying out parliamentary business in the current legislative period do not justify a dissolution.

(8) (a) When he proposes to initiate an application with the object of arriving at a dissolution of the Bundestag the Federal Chancellor has to examine whether a situation exists which would no longer make possible the meaningful pursuit of policy with the continuing confidence of the majority.

(b) In examining whether the application and proposal of the Federal Chancellor under Article 68 of the Basic Law is compatible with the constitution the Federal President does not have to rely on other yardsticks; in this respect he has to take account of the competence of the Federal Chancellor to assess and to judge, except if another evaluation which would argue against a dissolution would have to be given clear preference over the evaluative judgement of the Federal Chancellor.

(c) The unanimity of the parties represented in the Bundestag to secure new elections cannot limit the area of the Federal President's discretion; he can, however, see in this a supplementary indication that a dissolution of the Bundestag will have the result of coming closer to Article 68 of the Basic Law than a decision rejecting it.

(9) In Article 68 the Basic Law itself, through the admission of latitude for estimation and judgement, as well as the granting of discretion to the political decisions of three superior constitutional organs, has narrowed down the possibilities of constitutional review farther than in the realm of law making and of normal execution of the law; the Basic Law relies as far as this goes above all on the system of mutual political control and of political balance between the supreme constitutional organs involved as found in Article 68 itself. Only where constitutional criteria for certain political actions have been specifically spelt out in the Constitution can the Federal Constitutional Court determine their violation.

10
The Judiciary
Donald P. Kommers

German legal scholars often describe the Federal Republic as a *Rechtsstaat*, literally translated as a 'law state' or a state based on law. The notion of a state based on law clearly finds its most significant manifestation in the German judiciary whose structure and jurisdiction offer the most extensive legal protection of any judicial system in the world.

Before discussing the judicial system as such, more needs to be said about the tradition of German law associated with the idea of the *Rechtsstaat*.[1]* By the end of the nineteenth century German law had been systematically arranged and unified in several codes which still exist. Criminal law was codified in 1871; civil and criminal procedure in 1877; general private law in 1896; commercial law in 1897. These codifications followed Germany's political unification in 1871, facilitating in turn the unification of the judicial system in 1877. As Fritz Baur has pointed out, codification reflected 'the optimistic belief that all legally relevant human relations could be thus rationally comprehended and constructed'. The codification drive and the nationalistic feeling that propelled it placed a high premium upon the importance of the state in Germany's legal order. Unlike the Anglo-American or common law tradition that emphasized the importance of natural rights possessed by the individual against the state, the German tradition assumed that law and justice could be achieved only within and under the protection of the state.

The primacy of the state in German jurisprudence influenced attitudes toward the traditional role of the courts. This role is suggested by the following propositions which at one time fairly well summarized the German, and largely continental European, theory of law and judicial authority: that the state is the source of all law; that the locus of all lawmaking authority within the state is the sovereign legislature; that law is a closed system of logically arranged and internally coherent rules; that all legal disputes must be resolved by reference to such laws; that courts of law, independent of the legisla-

* Notes for this chapter begin on p. 293.

ture, are the proper agencies for interpreting the law; that the laws must be applied by the courts in strict accordance with the legislature's will; and that in applying the law as written, judges are to insulate themselves from forces, ideas, or even notions of justice located outside the formal structure of law. This mechanistic view of the judicial role was identified with the theory of legal positivism, the dominant school of legal thought in Germany. But this view of the judge's role hardly conformed to reality. In interpreting positive law or in filling gaps in the law, judges invariably perform a creative role and in doing so they exercise judgment, as inevitably they must.

Legal positivists in Germany have long insisted that a state based on law *(Recht)* is the only means of securing individual persons against the arbitrary exercise of power *(Macht)*. Doubtless an important element of constitutional government, the *Rechtsstaat* as traditionally understood in the German context was nevertheless a long way from the Anglo-American notion of constitutionalism. It did not, for example, presuppose parliamentary democracy, as in British theory, or judicial review, as in American theory. The Basic Law took the concept of constitutionalism far beyond the traditional theory of the *Rechtsstaat*. Art. 20, for example, sets up 'a democratic and social federal state' and a parliamentary system of government in which 'all state authority emanates from the people'. Additionally, Art. 20 subjects legislation to the 'constitutional order' and specifies that 'the executive and the judiciary [are] bound by law *and justice'* [italics supplied]. Art. 28 stipulates that the constitutional order in the Länder must also 'conform to the principles of republican, democratic and social government based on the rule of law'. Finally, the Basic Law's section on the administration of justice provides for the judicial review of legislation and other governmental actions, vesting this power exclusively in the Federal Constitutional Court *(Bundesverfassungsgericht)* (Doc.1).

The German judiciary embraces a single nationwide system of courts. It consists of regular courts and four sets of special courts (Doc.2). The regular courts hear ordinary civil and criminal suits as well as cases dealing with commerical law. Separate administrative, labour, social, and tax courts exercise jurisdiction falling into their specialized domains. Like the regular courts, these tribunals are organized into integrated judicial hierarchies. All trial and intermediate appellate courts are state or Land courts, whereas the final court of appeal within each hierarchy is a federal tribunal. Federal statutes lay down the structure, procedure, and authority of these courts. Except for the final courts of appeal at the federal level, however, all the courts are administered, financed, and staffed by the individual states or Länder. Only courts of limited jurisdiction at the lowest level of the judicial hierarchy are one-judge tribunals. All other courts, trial and appellate, function in panels of three, five, or more judges.[2]

The regular courts operate at four levels: District courts *(Amtsgerichte)*, which number about eight hundred, line the bottom of the judicial pyramid. They operate in towns or other limited geographical areas and exercise jurisdiction over minor civil suits and petty criminal offences (punishable by up to two years imprisonment). They also perform many non-judicial tasks such as administering estates, drafting wills and conveyances, keeping registers, appointing guardians, and supervising executors and trustees in bankruptcy. Around one hundred county courts *(Landgerichte)*—the courts of general trial jurisdiction—occupy the next level of the regular judiciary. Within their territorial limits they also serve as final courts of appeal for the local courts. The court of last resort in each Land is the superior court *(Oberlandesgericht)*, although it has original jurisdiction in cases involving high treason and betrayal of the Basic Law. The final court of appeals in the regular judiciary is the Federal Supreme Court *(Bundesgerichtshof)*.

The special courts have a similar structure although in some cases they are organized at two or three levels rather than four. Cases involving labour law, tax law, social-security law, and a wide range of disputes arising out of the relations between citizens and public administrative authorities are initiated in courts of original jurisdiction corresponding to the regular courts. The highest court of appeal in each of these areas is, respectively, the Federal Labour Court *(Bundesarbeitsgericht)*, Federal Tax Court *(Bundesfinanzgericht)*, Federal Social Court *(Bundessozialgericht)*, and the Federal Administrative Court *(Bundesverwaltungsgericht)*. Like the Federal Supreme Court, these federal high courts are headed by a president and divided into senates of five judges each. The Federal Constitutional Court *(Bundesverfassungsgericht)* is the highest court of review for constitutional cases (Doc.5).

By contrast, the judicial system of the German Democratic Republic consisted of a uniform and simplified three-tiered system of courts to hear most civil and criminal cases, and several thousand social courts at the factory and neighbourhood levels to settle minor civil conflicts and to serve as instruments of education and social discipline in petty criminal cases. The social courts were staffed entirely by non-professional or lay judges. Lay judges often sat alongside professional judges in other courts. The GDR's judiciary was subordinated to the regime's political goals and functioned mainly to uphold the principles of 'socialist legality'.[3] (see also Ch.3) With Germany's unification in 1990, however, the old GDR's judiciary was to be wholly reorganized on the model established under the Basic Law

(Doc.6). The administration of justice in Germany is carried out by approximately 19,000 judges (as of 1993), about 14,000 of whom preside over the regular courts. Other legal professionals associated with the courts are some 4,500 public prosecutors. The 45,000 practicing attorneys in the Federal Republic are also regarded as 'organs' of the overall system of justice. But they are not subject to disciplinary action outside their professional associations. Their practice is by law limited to a certain level of the judiciary as well as to certain courts within a given geographical area, depending on the nature of the litigation. Finally, all judges appointed to the bench in the Federal Republic are career appointments (Doc.3). The only exception to this rule is the Federal Constitutional Court whose sixteen judges are chosen for single nonrenewable terms of twelve years (Doc.5). One-half of the justices must be elected by a two-thirds vote of the Bundesrat; the other half is elected by a two-thirds vote of a special Bundestag electoral committee. Judges of all other *federal* courts are elected by a judicial selection committee composed of eleven members of the Bundestag and those Länder ministers whose portfolios relate to the subject-matter jurisdiction of the particular court concerned (Doc.4). All other judges are recruited and appointed by Land ministries of justice.

The following articles of the Basic Law relate to the establishment of the judicial system and the administration of justice. Especially noteworthy is the authority granted to the Federal Constitutional Court to pass on the validity of laws and other official actions. The power of constitutional review was a new departure in German constitutionalism. Like the Basic Law's ban on extraordinary courts, it was instituted to defend constitutional values and to maintain the rule of law.

Document 1

EXTRACTS FROM THE BASIC LAW
Source: Presse und Informationsamt der Bundesregierung

Art. 92
Judicial power shall be vested in the judges; it shall be exercised by the Federal Constitutional Court, by the federal courts provided for in this Basic Law, and by the courts of the Länder.

Art. 93
(1) The Federal Constitutional Court shall decide:

1. On the interpretation of this Basic Law in the event of disputes concerning the extent of the rights and duties of a highest federal organ or of other parties concerned who have been vested with rights of their own by this Basic Law or by rules of procedure of a highest federal organ;

2. in case of differences of opinion or doubts on the formal and material compatibility of federal law or Land law with this Basic Law, or on the compatibility of Land law with other federal law, at the request of the Federal Government, of a Land government, or of one-third of the Bundestag members;

3. in case of differences of opinion of the rights and duties of the Federation and the Länder, particularly in the execution of federal law by the Länder and in the exercise of federal supervision;

4. on other disputes involving public law, between the Federation and the Lander, between different Länder or within a Land, unless recourse to another court exists;

4a. on complaints of unconstitutionality, which may be entered by any person who claims that one of his basic rights or one of his rights under paragraph (4) of Article 20, under Article 33, 38, 101, 103 or 104 has been violated by public authority;

Art. 94

(1) The Federal Constitutional Court shall consist of federal judges and other members. Half of the members of the Federal Constitutional Court shall be elected by the Bundestag and half by the Bundesrat. They may not be members of the Bundestag, the Bundesrat, the Federal Government, nor of any of the corresponding organs of a Land.

(2) The constitution and procedure of the Federal Constitutional Court shall be regulated by a federal law which shall specify in what cases its decisions shall have the force of law ... .

Art. 95

(1) For the purposes of ordinary, administrative, fiscal, labour, and social jurisdiction, the Federation shall establish as highest courts of justice the Federal Court of Justice, the Federal Administrative Court, the Federal Fiscal Court, the Federal Labour Court, and the Federal Social Court.

Art. 97

(1) The judges shall be independent and subject only to the law.

Art. 100

(1) If a court considers unconstitutional a law the validity of which is relevant to its decision, the proceedings shall be stayed, and a decision shall be obtained from the Land court competent for constitutional disputes if the constitution of a Land is held to be violated, or from the Federal Constitutional Court if this Basic law is held to be violated. This shall also apply if this Basic Law is held to be violated by Land law or if a Land law is held to be incompatible with a federal law.

Art. 101

(1) Extraordinary courts shall be inadmissible. No one may be removed from the jurisdiction of his lawful judge.

(2) Courts for special fields may be established only by legislation.

Art. 102

Capital punishment shall be abolished.

Art. 103

(1) In the courts everyone shall be entitled to a hearing in accordance with the law.

(2) An act can be punished only if it was an offence against the law before the act was committed.

(3) No one may be punished for the same act more than once under general penal legislation.

Art. 104

(1) The liberty of the individual may be restricted only by virtue of a formal law and only with due regard to the forms prescribed therein. Detained persons may not be subjected to mental nor to physical ill-treatment.

As noted in the general introduction, federal law lays down the structure and jurisdiction of all courts. The following document relates to the organization of the regular courts *(ordentliche Gerichte)*.

Document 2

THE JUDICIARY ACT *(GERICHTSVERFASSUNGSGESETZ)*

Source: BGBl., 1950, 513, as amended up to and including 9 May 1975

Transl.: Official

I. Jurisdiction

Art. 1

Judicial power shall be exercised by independent courts that are subject only to the law.

. . .

Art. 12

Jurisdiction over ordinary litigation shall be exercised by District Courts *(Amtsgerichte),* County Courts *(Landgerichte),* Superior Courts *(Oberlandesgerichte)* and the Federal Supreme Court *(Bundesgerichtshof).*

Art. 13

The ordinary courts shall have jurisdiction over all civil law controversies and criminal cases over which jurisdiction either is not vested in administrative agencies or administrative courts or for which special courts have not been established or permitted on the basis of regulations of Federal law.

. . .

Art. 16

Extraordinary courts shall be impermissable. No one may be removed from the jurisdiction of his lawful judge.

. . .

III. District Courts *(Amtsgerichte)*

Art. 22

(1) District Courts shall be presided over by single judges.
(2) A District Court judge may simultaneously be a member or director of a superior County Court.

. . .

Art. 23

The jurisdiction of District Courts over civil law controversies shall include, in so far as they have not been assigned to County Courts irrespective of the value of the object in controversy:

1. Controversies over property claims whose sum or monetary value does not exceed five thousand German marks;
2. regardless of the value of the object in controversy: [disputes involving landlord and tenant, public accommodations and travel, support claims, bankruptcy proceedings, etc.]

. . .

Art. 24

(1) In criminal cases District Courts shall have jurisdiction over:
   [1. misdemeanors]
   [2. minor offences]
   [3. major offences]
(2) A District Court may not pronounce a penalty of imprisonment in a penitentiary of more than three years ... .

IV: Lay Judge Courts *(Schöffengerichte)*

Art. 28

Lay Judge Courts shall be created at the District Courts for hearing and decision on criminal cases belonging within the jurisdiction of District Courts and not decided by a District Court judge sitting singly.

Art. 29

(1) Lay Judge Courts shall be composed of a District Judge as chairman and two lay judges *(Schöffen)* ... .

Art. 31

The office of lay judge shall be an honorary office *(Ehrenamt)*. It may be filled only by Germans.

. . .

Art. 36

(1) Municipalities shall compile a nominating list for lay judges every fourth year ... .

. . .

Art. 42

The committee shall by two-thirds majority elect from the corrected nomination list for the next four business years ... the required number of lay judges ...

. . .

V: County Courts *(Landgerichte)*

Art. 59

(1) County Courts shall be composed of a President and the required number of presiding judges and members ... .

Art. 60

Civil and criminal senates shall be established at the County Courts.

. . .

Art. 75

The civil senates shall be composed of three members including the presiding judge [unless otherwise provided by law].

Art. 76

(1) The criminal senates shall, in proceedings other than trials, decide with three members sitting, including the presiding judge.

(2) The criminal senates shall be composed as follows for trials: the presiding judge and two lay judges (minor criminal senate) if an appeal against a district court verdict is involved; and three judges, including the presiding judge, and two lay judges (major criminal senate) in all other cases.

. . .

VIII. Superior Courts *(Oberlandesgerichte)*

Art. 115

Superior Courts shall be composed of a president and the requisite number of senate presidents and judges.

Art. 116

(1) Civil and criminal senates shall be established at the Superior Courts ... .

. . .

Art. 122

(1) The senates of the Superior Courts shall decide with three judges, including the presiding judge, sitting unless the procedural codes provide that a single judge shall decide instead of a senate.

(2) The criminal senates shall be composed of five judges, including the presiding judge, in trials of first instance ... .

IX. Federal Supreme Court *(Bundesgerichtshof)*

Art. 123

The Federal Supreme Court shall have its seat in Karlsruhe.

Art. 124

The Federal Supreme Court shall be composed of a president and the requisite number of senate presidents.

Art. 125

(1) The judges of the Federal Supreme Court shall be chosen by the Federal Minister of Justice together with the Judicial Election Committee, and shall be appointed by the Federal President.
(2) Only persons who have reached the age of thirty-five shall be eligible for election to the Federal Supreme Court.

. . .

Art. 130

(1) Civil and criminal senates shall be established at the Federal Supreme Court. Their number shall be determined by the Federal Minister of Justice.

. . .

Art. 132

(1) A superior senate for civil cases and a superior senate for criminal cases shall be established at the Federal Supreme Court.
(2) Each superior senate shall consist of a president and eight members.
(3) The members and their deputies shall be designated by the presidium of the Federal Supreme Court for terms of two business years.
(4) The joint superior senate shall consist of the presidents and all members of the superior senates.

. . .

Art. 137

The deciding senate may solicit the decision of the superior senate in a question of fundamental importance if in its opinion the growth of the law and the assurance of uniform interpretation require it.

Art. 138

(1) The superior senates and the joint superior senate shall decide without oral proceedings and only on the question of law.

. . .

Art. 139

(1) The senates of the Federal Supreme Court shall decide with five members, including the presiding judge sitting.

(2) The criminal senate shall decide, in first instance other than the trial, with three members, including the presiding judge, sitting.

. . .

X: The Public Prosecutor

Art. 141

A public prosecutor's office shall be established at each court.

Art. 142

(1) The public prosecution's functions shall be exercised:

1. By a Federal Prosecutor-General and one or several Federal Prosecutors, at the Federal Supreme Court 2. by one or several public prosecutors, at the Superior and County Courts; 3. by one of several public prosecutors or prosecutors *(Amtsanwälte)*, at the District Courts.

. . .

Art. 147

The power of supervision and direction shall rest with:

1. the Federal Minister of Justice in regard to the Federal Prosecutor-General and the Federal Prosecutors;
2. the Land justice administration in regard to all prosecutors in a given Land;

. . .

Art. 150

The public prosecution shall be independent of the courts in its official business.

Art. 151

Public prosecutors may not undertake judicial business ...

. . .

Art. 192

(1) In the rendering of decisions only the statutorily determined number of judges may participate.

. . .

Art. 194

(1) The presiding judges shall direct the deliberation, frame the questions and collect the votes.

(2) Disagreements over the subject, the framing and order of the questions or the result of the vote shall be resolved by the court.

. . .

Art. 196

(1) The court shall, unless otherwise provided by law, decide by an absolute majority of votes.

. . .

(3) If in a criminal case more than two opinions are formed on a question other than that of guilt and if none of these opinions commands a majority, then the votes most detrimental to the accused shall be added to the less detrimental votes until the requisite majority results. If two opinions are formed regarding the matter of punishment without either opinion commanding a majority, then the more lenient opinion shall prevail.
. . .

Federal law also regulates the role and status of judges. The following document specifies their qualifications, tenure, and conditions of removal. Judges in Germany are highly trained legal professionals, and once appointed they hold their positions for life (that is, until the age of retirement). Upon the successful completion of their legal training, young law graduates ordinarily choose to enter one of a number of legal callings. If they choose the judiciary they must embark upon a three-year apprenticeship in a court of law. If their stewardship meets with the approval of their superiors in the various state justice ministries, they are awarded judgeships with permanent tenure and security. The typical appointees begin their career at the lowest level of the judiciary. Most remain there for the duration of their careers. Promotion to higher courts usually depends on the recommendation of higher-ranking judges. Only a small percentage of all judges end their careers on the high federal courts of appeal.

Judges in the old GDR were not as highly trained as their counterparts in the west. GDR students wishing to pursue careers in the judiciary would, after careful screening for their political reliability, embarks upon four years of legal education in East Berlin's Humboldt University. Upon the successful completion of a course of studies laden with Marxist-Leninist ideology, they would receive the degree of *Diplomjurist,* thus qualifying them for an appointment to the regular judiciary. Following a short apprenticeship, they would qualify for election to the regular judiciary. Whether GDR judges would continue to occupy their judicial posts was one of the problems arising out of German unity (see also Ch.4). The *Diplomjurist* degree was not up to the standards required of judges in the western Länder. Most GDR judges lost their positions when the two German states united in 1990. Those who compromised themselves politically while serving in the judiciary were permanently barred from regaining their judgeships. Under the Unification Treaty, however, and for a transitional period, GDR judges with the *Diplomjurist* degree, if otherwise qualified, would be eligible for appointment to the judiciary.

Document 3

JUDGES ACT *(DEUTSCHES RICHTERGESETZ)*

Source: BGBl., I, 1961, 1665, as amended up to and including 19 April 1972

. . .

Art. 1

The judicial power shall be exercised by professional judges and by honorary judges.

Art. 2

The provisions of this Act shall apply only to professional judges unless otherwise provided.

Art. 3

The judges shall be in the service of the Federation or of a Land.

Art. 4

(1) A judge may not concurrently exercise the functions of the judiciary and the functions of the legislative or executive power.

. . .

Art. 5

(1) The qualifications for judicial office shall be attained by passing two examinations.

(2) The first examination must be preceded by legal studies of at least three and one-half years at a university. Of this, at least four semesters of the studies must be undertaken at a university within the jurisdiction of this Act.

Art. 5a

(1) Probationary service of at least two years must occur between the first and second examinations. During this time the person must serve as an apprentice to:

1. A regular civil court,
2. a criminal court or state prosecutor's office,
3. an administrative office,
4. an office of a private attorney,
5. at one of the following (by choice):
   (a) one of the offices listed in 1 to 4 above for an additional period
   (b) a Land or federal legislative body
   (c) an administrative, fiscal, labour, or social court
   (d) an office of a notary public
   (e) a trade union or other trade association
   (f) a corporation

. . .

Art. 6

(1) A candidate may not be denied admission to probationary service on the ground that he passed the first examination specified in Article 5 in another

Land within the jurisdiction of this Act. Time served in probationary service in any Land within the jurisdiction of this Act must be credited in every German Land.

Art. 7

Any professor of law with tenure at a university within the jurisdiction of this Act shall possess the qualifications for judicial office.

Art. 9

Only the following may be appointed to judicial office:

1. Germans within the meaning of Article 116 of the Basic Law;
2. Those offering assurance of supporting at all times the free democratic basic order, within the meaning of the Basic Law.
3. Those possessing the qualifications for judicial office (Articles 5 to 7).

Art. 10

(1) Persons who, after acquiring the qualifications for judicial office, have served in judicial office for at least three years may be appointed judges for life.

. . .

Art. 12

(1) Persons who are to serve later as judges for life or as public prosecutors may be appointed probationary judges.

(2) Probationary judges must be appointed judges for life or, as tenured civil servants, as public prosecutors for life, no later than five years after their appointment as probationary judges.

. . .

Art. 14

(1) Civil servants appointed for life or for a term may be appointed acting judges if they are later to serve as judges for life.

. . .

Art. 15

(1) Acting judges shall retain their previous office ...

(3) Judges appointed for life or a term may, without their written consent, be dismissed only on the basis of a final judicial decision.

. . .

Art. 22

(1) Probationary judges may be dismissed at the expiration of the sixth, twelfth, eighteenth or twenty-fourth month after their appointment.

(2) Probationary judges may be dismissed at the expiration of the third or fourth year if they:

1. are unsuited for judicial office; or
2. a judicial election committee denies them entrance into judicial office for life or for a term.

. . .

Art. 23

The provisions relating to the termination of probationary judgeships shall apply to the termination of acting judgeships.

Art. 24

If a German court within the jurisdiction of this Act renders a verdict against a judge involving ... [imprisonment or loss of civil rights] ... the judicial office shall be terminated without further judicial decision ...

Art. 25

The judges shall be independent and subject only to the laws.

. . .

Art. 27

(1) Judges for life and judges for a term must be assigned a judicial position at a specific court.

. . .

Art. 28

(1) Only judges for life may serve as judges at a court, except as otherwise provided by Federal law.

. . .

Art. 29

No more than one probationary judge or one acting judge ... may participate in a court decision ...

Art. 30

Judges for life or judges for a term may, without their written consent, be transferred into another office or be deprived of their office only:

1. pursuant to impeachment proceedings (Article 98 [2], 98 [5] of the Basic Law);
2. pursuant to a formal disciplinary proceeding;
3. in the interest of the administration of justice (Article 31);
4. for changes in court organization (Article 32).

. . .

Art. 36

(1) Judges accepting nominations as candidates for election to membership in the Bundestag or a legislative body of a Land shall be on paid leave beginning on that day, but not earlier than two months before election day, and until two weeks after election day.

. . .

Art. 39

Judges must so conduct themselves in and outside their office, as well as in political activities, in such a manner that confidence in their independence is not threatened.

. . .

Art. 48

(1) Judges for life serving at the high Federal courts shall be retired at the end of the month in which they reach their sixty-eighth year; all other judges at the end of the month in which they reach their sixty-fifth year.

. . .

Art. 49

There shall be established at the Federal courts:

(1) Judges' Councils for participation in general and social matters;
(2) Presidents' Councils for participation in the appointment of judges.

. . .

Art. 61

(1) A special Senate of the Federal Supreme Court shall be established as the Disciplinary Court for judges in Federal service.

. . .

Art. 62

The Disciplinary Court of the Federation is empowered to rule:

(1) on disciplinary matters ...
(2) on transfers [ofjudges] in the interest of the administration of Justice
(3) with regard to judges chosen for life or for a term on
    1. the invalidity of their appointment;
    2. withdrawal of their appointment;
    3. dismissal;
    4. retirement on account of service disability.

. . .

Federal law governs the appointment, tenure, and qualifications of federal judges, namely those judges sitting on the federal courts which constitute, as noted earlier, the highest courts of appeal in certain jurisdictional areas. Currently, there are 141 judges on the Federal Supreme Court, sixty-five on the Federal Administrative Court, forty-four on the Federal Fiscal Court, forty-one on the Federal Social Court, and sixteen on the Federal Constitutional Court. These high federal courts are located in cities other than the capital of the Federal Republic, in part to remove them from Bonn's highly charged political environment.

Document 4

FEDERAL JUDICIAL ELECTION ACT
(RICHTERWAHLGESETZ)

Source: BGBl., 1950, 368–9

For the implementation of Article 95, paragraph 3, and Article 96, paragraph 2, of the Basic Law the Bundestag has enacted the following law:

Art. 1

(1) The judges of the Federal Supreme Court and of the high Federal courts shall be chosen by the appropriate Federal Minister conjointly with the Judicial Election Committee, and shall be appointed by the Federal President.

(2) The Federal Minister of Justice shall participate in the choice of judges to the Federal Supreme Court; the Federal Minister having jurisdiction over the respective subject area shall participate in the choice of judges to other high Federal courts.

Art. 2

The Judicial Election Committee shall be composed of an equal number of ex officio and elected members.

Art. 3

(1) Ex officio members of the Committee electing judges to a high federal court shall be the Land Ministers who have jurisdiction over those lower Land courts of which the Federal court in question is the court of appeal.

(2) The Land Ministers may be represented by deputies only under the same conditions as apply to their being represented in the Land cabinet.

Art. 4

(1) The elected members must be eligible to serve in the Bundestag and must possess legal experience.

. . .

Art. 5

(1) The elected members and their deputies shall be chosen by the Bundestag according to the rules of proportional representation. (2) Each Parliamentary Party may nominate a slate of candidates. On the basis of the total votes cast for each slate the number of members elected from each slate shall be computed, on the basis of the d'Hondt system of the highest average. Members and their deputies shall be elected in the order in which their names appear on the slate of candidates.

. . .

Art. 8

(1) The Federal Minister of Justice shall convene the Judicial Election Committee.

. . .

Art. 9

(1) The appropriate Federal Minister or his deputy in the cabinet shall preside. He shall have no vote.
(2) Meetings shall not be public.
. . .

Art. 10

(1) The appropriate Federal Minister and the members of the Judicial Election Committee may nominate persons to be chosen as Federal judges.
(2) The appropriate Federal Minister shall present to the Judicial Election Committee the personnel records of persons nominated for judicial office.
. . .

Art. 11

The Judicial Election Committee shall examine whether a candidate for judicial office possesses the professional and personal qualifications for the office.
. . .

Art. 12

(1) The Judicial Election Committee shall decide by secret ballot by a majority of the votes cast.
. . .

———

Judicial review is a relatively new development in German constitutional history. Postwar German leaders were of the opinion that in the light of Germany's authoritarian and totalitarian past, traditional parliamentary and judicial institutions were insufficient to safeguard the new liberal democratic order. So they created a national constitutional tribunal to supervise the judiciary's interpretation of constitutional norms, to enforce a consistent reading of the Constitution on the other branches of government, and to protect the basic liberties of German citizens. In addition, and with the exception of Schleswig-Holstein, each western Land has established a constitutional court to resolve state constitutional disputes arising under its constitution. (Land constitutional courts are in the process of being established in the new eastern Länder.) If a state elects not to establish its own constitutional court, questions arising its constitution are then referred for decision to the Federal Constitutional Court.

Thus the old positivistic belief that separated the realm of law from the realm of politics has been abandoned in Germany, together with the idea that justice could automatically be achieved through the mechanical application of general laws enacted by the legislature. The Federal Constitutional Court, unlike the United States Supreme Court, is a specialized tribunal with exclusive jurisdiction to decide constitutional questions under the Basic Law.[4] (see also Ch.12) An important structural feature of the Court is its division into two chambers, or panels, which have exclusive memberships and exclusive jurisdiction over specified constitutional disputes. The organization, jurisdiction, and internal procedures of the Federal Constitutional Court are elaborated in great detail by the following statute.

Document 5

FEDERAL CONSTITUTIONAL COURT ACT (BUNDESVERFASSUNGSGERICHTSGESETZ)

Source: BGBl., I,1985, 2229.

I: Constitution and Competency of the Federal Constitutional Court

Art. 1

(1) The Federal Constitutional Court shall be a federal court of justice independent of all other constitutional bodies.

(2) The seat of the Federal Constitutional Court shall be at Karlsruhe.

Art. 2

(1) The Federal Constitutional Court shall consist of two panels.

(2) Eight judges shall be elected to each panel.

(3) Three judges of each panel shall be elected from among the judges of the highest federal courts of justice. Only judges who have served at least three years with a highest old federal court of justice shall be elected.

Art. 3

(1) The judges must have reached the age of forty, be eligible for election to the Bundestag, and have stated in writing that they are willing to become a member of the Federal Constitutional Court.

(2) They must be qualified to exercise the functions of a judge pursuant to the Law on German Judges.

(3) They may not be members of the Bundestag, the Bundesrat, the Federal Government, nor of any of the corresponding bodies of a Land. On their appointment they shall cease to be members of such bodies.

(4) The functions of a judge shall preclude any other professional occupation save that of a professor of law at a German institution of higher education. The functions of a judge of the Federal Constitutional Court shall take precedence over the functions of such professor.

Art. 4

(1) The term of office of the judges shall be twelve years, not extending beyond retirement age.

(2) Immediate or subsequent re-election of judges shall not be permissible.

(3) Retirement age shall be the end of the month in which a judge reaches the age of sixty-eight.

(4) Upon expiration of his term of office a judge shall continue to perform his functions until a successor is appointed.

Art. 5

(1) Half of the judges of each panel shall be elected by the Bundestag and the other half by the Bundesrat. Of those to be selected from among the judges of the highest federal courts of justice one shall be elected by one of the electoral organs and two by the other, and of the remaining judges three shall be elected by one body and two by the other.

. . .

Art. 6

(1) The judges to be selected by the Bundestag shall be elected indirectly.

(2) The Bundestag shall elect twelve of its members as electors according to the rules of proportional representation. Each parliamentary group may submit a list of twelve candidates. The number of candidates elected on each list shall be calculated from the total number of votes cast for each list in accordance with the d'Hondt method. The members shall be elected in the sequence in which their names appear on the list. If an elector retires or is unable to perform his functions, he shall be replaced by the next candidate on the same list.

(3) The eldest elector shall immediately with one week's notice convene a meeting of the electors for the purpose of electing the judges and shall chair the meeting which shall continue until all of them have been elected.

(4) The members of the electoral committee are obliged to maintain secrecy about the personal circumstances of candidates which become known to them as a result of their activities in the committee as well as about discussions thereon in the committee and the voting.

(5) To be elected, a judge shall require at least eight votes.

Art. 7

The judges to be selected by the Bundesrat shall be elected with two-thirds of the votes of the Bundesrat.

Art. 7a

(1) If a successor is not elected in accordance with the provisions of Art. 6 above within two months of the expiration of a judge's term of office or his early retirement, the eldest elector shall immediately request the Federal Constitutional Court to propose candidates.

(2) The plenum of the Federal Constitutional Court shall decide with a simple majority on whom to propose as a candidate. If only one judge needs to be elected, the Federal Constitutional Court shall propose three candidates: if several judges are to be elected simultaneously, the Federal Constitutional Court shall propose twice as many candidates as the number of judges to be elected. Art. 16 (2) below shall apply mutatis mutandis.

(3) If the judge is to be elected by the Bundesrat, paragraphs 1 and 2 above shall apply save that the eldest elector shall be replaced by the President of the Bundesrat or his deputy.

(4) The right of the electoral body to elect a person not proposed by the Federal Constitutional Court shall remain unaffected.

Art. 8

(1) The Federal Minister of Justice shall draw up a list of all federal judges meeting the requirements of Art. 3 (1) and (2) above.

(2) The Federal Minister of Justice shall keep another list in which he shall enter all the candidates who are proposed for the post of judge of the Federal Constitutional Court by a parliamentary group of the Bundestag, the Federal Government or a Land government and who meet the requirements of Art. 3 (1) and (2) above.

(3) The lists shall be continually updated and be forwarded to the Presidents of the Bundestag and Bundesrat at least one week before an election.

Art. 9

(1) The Bundestag and the Bundesrat shall alternately elect the President of the Federal Constitutional Court and his deputy. The deputy shall be elected from the panel of which the President is not a member.

(2) At the first election the Bundestag shall elect the President and the Bundesrat his deputy.

(3) The provisions of Arts. 6 and 7 above shall apply *mutatis mutandis*.

Art. 10

The Federal President shall appoint the judges elected.

Art. 11

(1) On assuming office the judges of the Federal Constitutional Court shall take the following oath before the Federal President:

'I swear that as an impartial judge I shall at all times faithfully observe the Basic Law of the Federal Republic of Germany and conscientiously perform my judicial duties towards others. So help me God!'

(2) If a judge belongs to a religious denomination whose members are permitted by law to use a different form of affirmation, he may do so.

(3) The oath may be taken without the religious affirmation.

Art. 12

The judges of the Federal Constitutional Court may ask to be released from service at any time. The Federal President shall pronounce such release.

Art. 13

The Federal Constitutional Court shall decide in the cases determined by the Basic Law, to wit:

  1. on the forfeiture of basic rights (Art. 18 of the Basic Law);
  2. on the unconstitutionality of parties (Art. 21 [2] of the Basic Law);
  3. on complaints against decisions of the Bundestag relating to the validity

of an election or to the acquisition or loss of a deputy's seat in the Bundestag (Art. 41 [2] of the Basic Law);

4. on the impeachment of the Federal President by the Bundestag or the Bundesrat (Art. 61 of the Basic Law);

5. on the interpretation of the Basic Law in the event of disputes concerning the extent of the rights and duties of a highest federal organ or of other parties concerned who have been vested with rights of their own by the Basic Law or by rules of procedure of a highest federal organ (Art. 93 [1] [1] of the Basic Law);

6 in case of differences of opinion or doubts on the formal and material compatibility of federal law or Land law with the Basic Law, or on the compatibility of Land law with other federal law, at the request of the Federal Government, of a Land government, or of one third of the Bundestag members (Art. 93 [1] [2] of the Basic Law);

7. in case of differences of opinion on the rights and duties of the Federation and the Lander, particularly in the execution of federal law by the Lander and in the exercise of federal supervision (Art. 93 [1] [3] and Art. 84 [4], second sentence, of the Basic Law);

8. on other disputes involving public law, between the Federation and the Lander, between different Lander or within a Land, unless recourse to another court exists (Art. 93 [1] [4] of the Basic Law);

8a. on complaints of unconstitutionality (Art. 93 [1] [4a] and [4b] of the Basic Law);

9. on the impeachment of federal and Land judges (Art. 98 [2] and [5] of the Basic Law);

10. on constitutional disputes within a Land if such decision is assigned to the Federal Constitutional Court by Land legislation (Art. 99 of the Basic Law);

11. on the compatibility of a federal or Land law with the Basic Law or the compatibility of a Land law or other Land right with a federal law, when such decision is requested by a court (Art. 100 [1] of the Basic Law);

12. in case of doubt whether a rule of public international law is an integral part of federal law and whether such rule creates rights and duties for the individual, when such decision is requested by a court (Art. 100 [2] of the Basic Law);

13. if the constitutional court of a Land, in interpreting the Basic Law, intends to deviate from a decision of the Federal Constitutional Court or of the constitutional court of another Land, when such decision is requested by that constitutional court (Art. 100 [3] of the Basic Law);

14. in case of differences of opinion on the continuance of law as federal law (Art. 126 of the Basic Law);

15. in such other cases as are assigned to it by federal legislation (Art. 93 [2] of the Basic Law).

Art. 14

(1) The First Panel of the Federal Constitutional Court shall be competent for legal review proceedings (Art. 13 [6] and [11] above) in which mainly a legal provision is claimed to be incompatible with basic rights or with rights

under Arts. 33, 101, 103 and 104 of the Basic Law, as well as for complaints of unconstitutionality with the exception of such complaints pursuant to Art. 91 below and those in the domain of electoral law.

(2) The Second Panel of the Federal Constitutional Court shall be competent for the cases stated in Art. 13 (1) to (5), (7) to (9), (12) and (14) above, as well as for legal review proceedings and complaints of unconstitutionality not assigned to the First Panel.

(3) In the cases stated in Article 13 (10) and (13) above the competency of the panels shall be governed by the provisions of paragraphs 1 and 2 above.

. . .

Art. 15

(1) The President of the Federal Constitutional Court and his deputy shall preside over their respective panels. The eldest judges present on each panel shall act as their deputies.

. . .

Art. 16

(1) If, in a point of law, a panel intends to deviate from the legal opinion contained in a decision by the other panel, the plenum of the Federal Constitutional Court shall decide on the matter.

(2) It has a quorum if two thirds of the judges of each panel are present.

II. General Procedural Provisions

. . .

Art. 22

(1) The parties may be represented at any stage of the proceedings by an attorney registered with a German court or a professor of law at a German institution of higher education; in the oral pleadings before the Federal Constitutional Court they must be represented in this manner. Legislative bodies and parts thereof which are vested with rights of their own by virtue of their statutes or rules of procedure may, in addition, be represented by their members. The Federation, the Länder and their constitutional organs may also be represented by their officials provided that they are qualified to exercise the functions of a judge or are qualified for higher administrative service by having passed the prescribed state examinations. The Federal Constitutional Court may also permit another person to act as counsel for a party.

. . .

Art. 25

(1) In the absence of provisions to the contrary, the Federal Constitutional Court shall decide on the basis of oral pleadings, unless all parties expressly waive them.

(2) Decisions pursuant to oral pleadings shall be issued as judgments, and decisions without oral pleadings as orders.

(3) Partial and interim decisions shall be permissible.

(4) The decisions shall be issued 'in the name of the people'.

Art. 26

(1) The Federal Constitutional Court shall take evidence as needed to establish the truth. It may charge a member of the court with this outside the oral pleadings or ask another court to do so with regard to specific acts and persons.

(2) If so decided by a majority of two-thirds of the votes of the court the obtainment of individual documents may be dispensed with where their use would be detrimental to national security.

Art. 27

All courts and administrative authorities shall afford the Federal Constitutional Court legal and administrative assistance. They shall submit files and documents to it via their highest authority.

. . .

Art. 30

(1) The Federal Constitutional Court shall decide in secret deliberations on the basis of its independent conviction resulting from the pleadings and the taking of evidence. The decision shall be drawn up in writing together with the reasons and signed by the participating judges. If oral pleadings have been held, it shall be proclaimed publicly together with the main reasons at a date announced during the pleadings and lying within three months of their termination. The date for the proclamation of the decision may be deferred by an order of the Federal Constitutional Court; in such case, the three-month time-limit may be exceeded.

(2) If, during the deliberations, a judge holds a dissenting view on the decision or the reasons, he may have it recorded in a separate opinion: the separate opinion shall be appended to the decision. In their decisions the panels may state the number of votes for and against. The details shall be laid down in rules of procedure adopted by the plenum of the Federal Constitutional Court.

(3) All decisions shall be forwarded to the parties.

. . .

The Treaty of Unity and related documents included provisions for the reorganization of the judicial system in the five new Länder. All the courts of the old GDR were to be phased out and a new system based on the West German model phased in as soon as practicable. Currently around 200 regular district courts have been established in the eastern Länder. Other courts, including the specialized public law courts, are in the process of being established. The following treaty provisions deal with the creation and status of courts and judicial decisions in the new Länder.

Document 6a

TREATY OF 18 MAY 1990

Source: The Unification of Germany in 1990. A Documentation. 13-29

Article 6 (Recourse to the Courts)

. . .

(2) The German Democratic Republic shall guarantee recourse to the courts, including recourse for provisional court protection. In the absence of special courts for public law disputes, special arbitration courts shall be set up at ordinary courts. Jurisdiction for such disputes shall be concentrated at specific regional and district courts.

General Guidelines

1. The law of the German Democratic Republic will be modelled on the principles of a free, democratic federal and social order governed by the rule of law and be guided by the legal regime of the European Communities.

2. Regulations which commit individuals or state institutions, including ... the judiciary, to a socialist system of law, a socialist body politic, ... a socialist sense of justice, socialist convictions, the convictions of individual groups or parties, socialist morality, or comparable notions, will no longer be applied ... .

Judicial System

1. Regulations providing for the participation of collectives, social organs, trade unions, works, social prosecutors and defenders in the judicial system and their right to be informed about proceedings will no longer be applied; ...

2. Regulations on cooperation between the courts and local representations of the people and other organs, the duty of judges to inform the latter, as well as criticism of the courts will no longer be applied.

Document 6b

TREATY OF 31 AUGUST 1990 (TREATY OF UNITY)

Source: Ibid. 71-91

Article 13 (Administration of Justice)

(1) Administrative bodies and other institutions serving the purposes of public administration or the administration of justice in the territory specified in Article 3 of this Treaty [i.e., the five new *Länder*] shall pass under the authority of the government of the Land in which they are located. Institutions whose sphere of activities transcends the boundaries of a Land shall come under the joint responsibility of the Länder concerned. Where institutions consist of several branches each of which is in a position to carry out its activities independently, the branches shall come under the responsibility of

the government of the respective Land in which they are located. The Land government shall be responsible for the transfer or winding-up ... .

Article 18 (Continued Validity of Court Decisions)

1. Decisions handed down by the courts of the German Democratic Republic before the accession took effect shall retain their validity and may be executed in conformity with the law put into force according to Article 8 of this Treaty ... .This law shall be taken as the yardstick when checking the compatibility of decisions and their execution with the principles of the rule of law ... .

2. ... . [P]ersons sentenced by criminal courts of the German Democratic Republic are granted by this treaty a right of their own to seek the quashing of final decisions through the courts.

Notes

1. See Ernst-Wolfgang Böckenförde, 'The Origin and Development of the Concept of *Rechtsstaat'*, in Böckenförde, *State, Society and Liberty* (Oxford: Berg, 1991), 47–70.
2. This survey of the judicial system relies heavily on Nigel Foster, *German Law & Legal System* (London: Blackstone Press Limited, 1993), 31-45.
3. An excellent treatment of the old GDR's judiciary is included in Daniel John Meador, *Impressions of Law in East Germany* (Charlottesville: University Press of Virginia, 1986), 117–139.
4. Donald P. Kommers, *The Federal Constitutional Court* (Washington, D.C.: American Institute for Contemporary German Studies, John Hopkins University, 1994).

11
Basic Rights and Constitutional Review

Donald P. Kommers

The Basic Law includes an impressive charter of fundamental rights and freedoms (Doc.1). Such a charter of rights was also included in the Weimar Constitution. But there the relevant articles were not given the priority which they enjoy under the Basic Law of the Federal Republic. The Basic Law starts off with the charter of rights and makes certain that they cannot, as was possible in Weimar, be subjected to amendments as far as their 'substance' is concerned. The rights specifically guaranteed reflect the dominant influence both of the Social and Christian Democratic Parties in the Parliamentary Council *(Parlamentarischer Rat)* as well as Germany's experience with totalitarian government. One manifestation of socialist influence is the limitation on the right to property; under Art. 15, for example, natural resources, land, and the means of production may be transferred to public ownership. A manifestation of Christian influence is the basic right conferred upon parents to have their children receive religious education in public (state) schools in accordance with their religious views and the incorporation into the Basic Law of certain provisions of the Weimar Constitution concerning the public rights of religious organizations.

Apart from these and related provisions, the charter of rights also guarantees all of the fundamental freedoms against the state—so-called negative freedoms—traditionally associated with western liberal democracies. These include freedom of speech, press, religious belief, association, and movement. Included in the Basic Rights charter are also guarantees of the right to property, the right to choose a trade or occupation, the right to marry and raise a family, the right to equality between the sexes, and the right to refuse military service for reasons of conscience. These basic liberties are defined as 'inalienable human rights', constituting 'the basis of every community, of peace and justice in the world'. Another distinctive feature of the Basic Law, distinguishing it from the constitutional provisions of other liberal democracies, is the right to asylum granted to foreign persons who fear persecution on political grounds (Art. 16).

In addition, as the Federal Constitutional Court has ruled, the Basic Law establishes a value-oriented constitutional order based on human dignity. Art. 1 proclaims: 'The dignity of man shall be inviolable. To respect and protect it shall be the duty of all state authority.' Human dignity, according to the Constitutional Court, is the foundation stone of all fundamental rights and liberties. Indeed, under the terms of Art. 79 of the Basic Law, Art. 1 is beyond the amendatory power of Parliament. By the same token, Art. 19 (2), attaches a preferred status to fundamental rights by specifying that 'the essential content of a basic right [may not be] encroached upon'.

On the other hand, while obliging the state to respect human dignity and individual rights, the charter of freedoms predicates these rights upon the observance of certain principles of political obligation. Thus, every person has the right to the free development of his personality so long as 'he does not violate the rights of others or offend against the constitutional order or the moral code' (Art. 2 [1]). Freedom of expression is 'limited by the provisions of the general laws, provisions of law for the protection of youth, and by the right to inviolability of personal honour' (Art. 5 [2]). Freedom to teach 'does not absolve from loyalty to the Constitution' (Art. 5 [3]). All Germans have the right to associate, but activities 'directed against the constitutional order or the concept of international understanding are prohibited' (Art. 9). Moreover, freedoms of expression, press, teaching, assembly, and association may be forfeited if used 'to combat the free democratic basic order' (Art. 18).

Just as the Basic Law has absolutized Art. 1, it also renders certain principles of governance beyond Parliament's amendatory power. As we have seen, a number of these system values are identified in the charter of rights itself. But these values, against which the exercise of basic rights is often weighed, are also found in a number of other constitutional provisions. For example, Art. 20, which like Art. 1 cannot be changed under the terms of Art. 79, defines the Federal Republic as a 'democratic and social federal state'. In addition, the Basic Law sets up a *representative* democracy. The Constitution affirms the principle of popular sovereignty but according to Art. 20 (2), the people are to rule 'through elections and voting and by specific organs of the legislature, the executive power, and the judiciary'. According to the prevailing opinion among constitutional lawyers, such a democracy prohibits the use of popular referenda and plebiscites for purposes of law-making.

Article 21 also includes the principle of a 'fighting democracy'. While guaranteeing the right of political parties freely to 'form the political will of the people', it cautions that 'parties which, by reason of their aims or the behaviour of their adherents, seek to impair or abolish the free democratic basic order or to endanger the existence of the Federal Republic of Germany, shall be unconstitutional.' Such provisions spring from the abiding conviction of the founders, who drafted the Basic Law against the background of Weimar's democracy and Hitler's dictatorship, that a democracy is not an unarmed society, and that it has the right to dissolve organizations and to prohibit activities aimed at the destruction of republican and democratic (the so-called 'free democratic basic order' or *freiheitlich-demokratische Grundordnung*') government so long as the rule of law is thereby observed and protected.

German reunification would place a strain on some of these provisions and result in calls for major constitutional revision. After all, the addition of 16 million people changed the profile and character of the German nation. For many people, Germany had taken on a new identity, raising questions about the 'fit' between the Basic Law and the new Germany. Events in 1990 were moving too fast, however, for the adoption of a new all-German Constitution. Actually, GDR voters themselves dictated the stride of history. They chose immediate reunification and largely on West German terms. When the GDR united with the West under the accession clause of Article 23, the Basic Law extended its reach to all of Germany (see also Ch.4).

Nevertheless, forging unity within the framework of the Basic Law required some constitutional surgery to reflect the realities of a changed Germany. Out of consideration for East Germany's vital interests, the Unity Treaty amended the Basic Law in several particulars. For present purposes, the most important of these changes was the creation of a new article 143. In short, the new article allowed the eastern Länder to deviate from the terms of the Basic Law for a limited period in those areas where compliance with it would be impossible under existing social and economic conditions or inflict considerable hardship on former GDR residents. The new article had important implications for certain basic rights, especially with regard to abortion policy.

On the matter of abortion, the Unity Treaty permitted the eastern Länder to follow a policy in conflict with the Basic Law as interpreted by the Federal Constitutional Court. GDR policy had legalized abortion on demand during the first trimester of pregnancy, whereas prevailing West German policy, following a decision of the Federal Constitutional Court, obligated the state to protect the fetus at all stages of pregnancy unless an abortion was warranted for certified reasons specified by law (Doc.5a). East and West Germany would be allowed to follow their respective laws on abortion pending the adoption of an all-German abortion policy. Certain West German groups allied themselves with East German leaders in securing this temporary arrangement. Under the terms of the Unity Treaty, parliament was obligated to enact a new all-German policy on abortion by the end of 1992, which they did in 1993 (Doc.5b).

Equally important for present purposes is Article 5 of the Unity Treaty, which committed the contracting parties to recommend 'to the legislative bodies of the united Germany that within two years they should deal with the questions regarding amendments or additions to the Basic Law as raised in connection with German unification.' These questions included the matter of introducing state objectives into the Basic Law as well as submitting the Basic Law itself to a popular referendum.

In accord with these treaty provisions, the new all-German parliament established a Joint Commission on Constitutional Reform composed of 64 members, 32 from the Bundestag and 32 from the Bundesrat (see also Ch.4). In the ensuing two-and-a-half years the Commission considered hundreds of proposals for constitutional revision, many of them dealing with basic rights, including proposals to introduce plebiscites and referenda at the federal level, to confer the right of resident aliens to vote in local elections, and to allow the people, as suggested in the previous paragraph, to ratify the Basic Law as a whole in a popular referendum. Proposals for introducing state goals into the Basic law—e.g., obligating the state to protect minorities, to foster a clean environment, and to guarantee the right to employment—were also considered. The goal of environmental protection was the only one of these proposals to win the Commission's support. The one change in the Basic Law to receive parliamentary approval during this period of constitutional debate and reform were the limits placed on the right to asylum (Doc.8a). Whether to change the conditions for acquiring German citizenship was also on the agenda at this time (Doc.8b).

As the material in Chapter 10 indicates, the Federal Constitutional Court serves as a principal guardian of constitutional rights in the Federal Republic. Any person who feels that one of his basic rights has been violated by the state (federal or Land) or any of its agents may lodge, after exhausting all other legal remedies, a constitutional complaint with the Federal Constitutional Court. But Länder and federal governments may also petition the Court, in appropriate cases, to vindicate the basic concepts of the constitutional system. As the constitutional cases in this chapter illustrate, the Court's job is the difficult one of resolving the tension between the rights of the community and individual liberty. The Socialist Reich Party Case presented the Court with its first opportunity to interpret the meaning of the broad terms 'free democratic basic order' and to identify with greater specificity than before those principles that undergird the political system as a whole (Doc.2). The Lüth-Harlan Case (Doc.3) also presented the Court with one of its earliest opportunities to articulate the theory of free speech informing the Basic Law. The Religious Freedom Cases (Doc.4) underscore not only the essential content of free exercise doctrine but also the role of religious bodies in the public life of the Federal Republic. The Abortion Cases of 1975 and 1993 posed a classic conflict between the right of an unborn child to life and the right of a pregnant woman to personal self-realization (Doc.5).

The remaining materials presented in this chapter serve to highlight the conflict between the need for internal security and basic freedoms of speech and political association. The Civil Servant Loyalty Case (Doc.6) is an attempt on the Court's part to reconcile conflicting rights under the Basic Law, among them the right to choose a trade or profession and the corresponding right of equality of access to the civil service. Finally, the Klaas Case implicated the right to privacy under Article 10 of the Basic Law (Doc.7).

The following articles from the Basic Law include most of the important rights and liberties guaranteed to the individual. Several of these rights trace their origin to the Weimar and Frankfurt Constitutions of 1919 and 1848 respectively.

Also included are articles from the Weimar Constitution pertaining to questions of religious freedom that have been incorporated into the Basic Law. The latter are important for a proper understanding of church-state relations in the Federal Republic. Article 137 (6) of the Weimar Constitution provides for a church tax, a practice that would be invalid under the United States Constitution. Interestingly, the old GDR had also provided for a church tax. To preserve this tax the United Treaty provided that '[t]he church tax legislation enacted by the German Democratic Republic in accordance with Annex II shall continue to apply as Land law in the [eastern] Länder.

Because of the importance of the controversy surrounding citizenship and asylum in the aftermath of German unity, we have included the recent amendment to Article 16 (See Doc. 16a). The original version of Article 16 appears in Document 1. Absent from the list of articles below are certain procedural rights guaranteed by the Basic Law, particularly in criminal cases, along with the Constitution's ban on capital punishment. Finally, it should be noted that the Weimar Constitution did not empower the judiciary to enforce basic personal rights against the state. Under the Bonn Constitution, as the documents in Chap. 10 showed, the judiciary is clearly empowered to enforce these rights.

Document 1

EXCERPTS FROM THE BASIC LAW
Source: Presse- und Informationsamt der Bundesregierung

I: Basic Rights

Art. 1

(1) The dignity of man shall be inviolable. To respect and protect it shall be the duty of all state authority.
(2) The German people therefore acknowledge inviolable and inalienable human rights as the basis of every community, of peace and justice in the world.
(3) The following basic rights shall bind the legislature, the executive and the judiciary as directly enforceable law.

Art. 2

(1) Everyone shall have the right to the free development of his personality in so far as he does not violate the rights of others or offend against the constitutional order or the moral code.
(2) Everyone shall have the right to life and to inviolability of his person. The liberty of the individual shall be inviolable. These rights may only be encroached upon pursuant to a law.

Art. 3

(1) All persons shall be equal before the law.
(2) Men and women shall have equal rights.
(3) No one may be prejudiced or favoured because of his sex, his parentage, his race, his language, his homeland and origin, his faith, or his religious or political opinions.
(By an amendment to the Basic Law of September 1994 an additional provision was added 'the state shall promote the effective realization of equality between the sexes and do everything in its power to abolish such discrimination as still exists. A new para was inserted: 'no one may be discriminated against on account of his or her disability')

Art. 4

(1) Freedom of faith, of conscience, and freedom of creed, religious or ideological *(weltanschaulich)*, shall be inviolable.

(2) The undisturbed practice of religion is guaranteed.

. . .

Art. 5

(1) Everyone shall have the right freely to express and disseminate his opinion by speech, writing and pictures and freely to inform himself from generally accessible sources. Freedom of the press and freedom of reporting by means of broadcasts and films are guaranteed. There shall be no censorship.
(2) These rights are subject to limitations in the provisions of general statutes, in statutory provisions for the protection of youth, and in the right to respect for personal honour.

. . .

Art. 6

(1) Marriage and family shall enjoy the special protection of the state.
(2) The care and upbringing of children are a natural right of, and a duty primarily incumbent on, the parents. The national community shall watch over their endeavours in this respect.

. . .

Art. 7

(1) The entire educational system shall be under the supervision of the state.
(2) The persons entitled to bring up a child shall have the right to decide whether it shall receive religious instruction.
(3) Religious instruction shall form part of the ordinary curriculum in state and municipal schools, except in secular *(bekenntnisfrei)* schools ... .

Art. 8

(1) All Germans shall have the right to assemble peaceably and unarmed without prior notification or permission.

. . .

Art. 9

(1) All Germans shall have the right to form associations and societies.

. . .

Art. 12

(1) All Germans shall have the right freely to choose their trade, occupation, or profession, their place of work and their place of training ... .

. . .

Art. 14

(1) Property and the right of inheritance are guaranteed. Their content and limits shall be determined by the laws.

. . .

(3) Expropriation shall be permitted only in the public weal ... .

. . .

Art. 16

(1) No one may be deprived of his German citizenship. Citizenship may be lost only pursuant to a statute, and it may be lost against the will of the person affected only where such person does not become stateless as a result thereof.
(2) No German may be extradited to a foreign country. Persons persecuted on political grounds shall enjoy the right of asylum.

Art. 19

. . .

(4) Should any person's right be violated by public authority, recourse to the court shall be open to him. If jurisdiction is not specified, recourse shall be to the ordinary courts ... .

Appendix to the Basic Law

Art. 135 of the Weimar Constitution

(1) Civil and political rights and duties shall be neither dependent on nor restricted by the exercise of the freedom of religion.
(2) The enjoyment of civil and political rights and eligibility for public office shall be independent of religious creed.
(3) No one shall be bound to disclose his religious convictions ... .

. . .

Art. 137. Weimar Constitution

(1) There shall be no state church.
(2) Freedom of association to form religious bodies is guaranteed ... .

. . .

(5) Religious bodies shall remain corporate bodies under public law in so far as they have been such heretofore ... .
(6) Religious bodies that are corporate bodies under public law shall be entitled to levy taxes in accordance with Land law on the basis of the civil taxation lists.
(7) Associations whose purpose is the cultivation of a philosophical ideology shall have the same status as religious bodies.

. . .

Art. 139. Weimar Constitution

Sunday and the public holidays recognized by the state shall remain under legal protection as days of rest from work and of spiritual edification.

. . .

———

That political parties (see also Ch.8) should be the principal agents of parliamentary representation is one of the tenets of modern German constitutional theory. Art. 21 (1) of the Basic Law provides: 'The political parties shall participate in forming the political will of the people. They can be freely formed. Their internal organization must conform to democratic principles. They must publicly account for the sources of their funds.' Paragraph 2 of the same article, however, makes very clear that totalitarian parties shall not be tolerated. 'Parties which, by reason of their aims or the behaviour of their adherents, seek to impair or abolish the free democratic basic order or to endanger the existence of the Federal Republic of Germany, shall be unconstitutional.' In 1990, the foreign ministers of the two German states used this same language in a joint letter reaffirming the ban on political parties opposed to democracy. The Joint Letter also made clear that '[t]his [principle] also applies to parties and associations with National Socialist aims.'

Under Article 21 (2), the Federal Constitutional Court is the sole agency empowered to declare parties unconstitutional. According to the Federal Constitutional Court Act, however, only the Bundestag, Bundesrat, or Federal Government may petition the Court for an order declaring a party unconstitutional. Up to the present time the Court has declared two parties unconstitutional: the neo-Nazi Socialist Reich Party (Sozialistische Reichspartei) in 1952 and the Communist Party of Germany (Kommunistische Partei Deutschlands) in 1956. In both instances the Federal Government, led by Chancellor Konrad Adenauer, initiated the proceeding before the Federal Constitutional Court.

Document 2

THE SOCIALIST REICH PARTY CASE

Source: *Entscheidungen des Bundesverfassungsgerichts*, Vol. 2, 1952, 1–78
Transl.: Renata Chestnut, in Walter F. Murphy and Joseph Tanenhaus, *Comparative Constitutional Law*, New York, 1977, 602–7

[Political Parties and the Free Democratic Basic Order]

German constitutions following World War I hardly mentioned political parties, although even at that time ... the democratic constitutional life was to a large extent determined by parties. The reasons for this omission are manifold, but in the last analysis, the cause lies in a democratic ideology that refused to recognize groups mediating between the free individual and the will of the entire people composed of the sum of individual wills and represented in parliament by deputies as 'representatives of the entire people' ... The Basic Law abandoned this viewpoint and, more realistically, expressly recognizes parties as agents—even if not the only ones—forming the political will of the people.

. . .

In a free democratic state, as it corresponds to German constitutional development, freedom of association even for associations of a political kind are guaranteed to individual citizens as basic rights. On the other hand, it is part of the nature of every democracy that the supreme power derived from the people is exercised in elections and voting. In the reality of the large modern democratic state, however, this popular will can emerge only through parties as operating political units. Both fundamental ideas lead to the basic conclusion that establishment and activity of political parties must not be restrained.

The framer of the German Constitution was confronted with the question of whether he could fully implement this conclusion or whether he should not rather, enlightened by recent experiences, draw certain limits in this area. He had to consider whether absolute freedom to establish parties on the basis of any political idea should not be limited by principles governing a particular democracy, and whether parties seeking to abolish democracy by using formal democratic means must not be excluded from political processes. In this connection the danger had to be taken into account that the Government might also be tempted to eliminate troublesome opposition parties.

Art. 21 of the Basic Law has tried to master these problems. On the one hand, it establishes the principle that formation of political parties shall be free. On the other hand, it offers a means of preventing activity by 'unconstitutional' parties. To avert the danger of an abuse of this means, Art. 21 authorizes the Federal Constitutional Court to decide the question of unconstitutionality and attempts to determine as far as possible the factual requirements for such a declaration.

According to the constitutional-political decision made by the Basic Law, the essential constitutional order is in the last analysis founded upon the idea that man has an independent value of his own and that freedom and equality are permanent, intrinsic values of national unity. Thus, the basic order is an order heavily laden with values that oppose those of the totalitarian state which ... rejects human dignity, freedom, and equality ... Thus, the free democratic basic order can be defined as an order which excludes any form of tyranny or arbitrariness and represents a governmental system under a rule of law, based upon self-determination of the people as expressed by the will of the existing majority and upon freedom and equality. The fundamental principles of this order include at least: respect for the human rights given concrete form in the Basic Law, in particular for the right of a person to life and free development; popular sovereignty; separation of powers; responsibility of government; lawfulness of administration; independence of the judiciary; the multi-party principle; and equality of opportunities for all political parties.

. . .

The behaviour of the [SRP] party and its members, as do the personnel and organizational relationships between the SRP and the NSDAP, demonstrates that the goal of the SRP is to topple the free democratic basic order.

The very same circles which made it possible for Hitler to lead Germany into the abyss are now again trying to assert their political leadership. They enjoy his means and recommend the same ways that resulted in Germany's being torn apart.

In a very unconcerned manner they declare their approval of Hitler ...

[Conclusion]

The SRP is thus unconstitutional in the sense stipulated in Art. 21, para. 2, of the Basic Law ... The party, therefore, must be dissolved.

The Lüth-Harlan Case is a seminal decision in West German free speech jurisprudence. Harlan was a popular film director under the Nazi regime and best known for producing anti-semitic films. In 1950, several years after he had been acquitted of committing crimes against humanity, he directed a new movie, *Immortal Lover.* Erich Lüth, Hamburg's Public Press Superintendent, called upon film distributors and theatre owners not to show the movie at a German film festival because of Harlan's Nazi past. The film company obtained an injunction from a district court forbidding Lüth to call for a boycott of *Immortal Lover.* The Supreme Court of Hamburg affirmed, whereupon Lüth filed a constitutional complaint with the First Senate of the Federal Constitutional Court, claiming that the injunction violated his rights under Art. 5 of the Basic Law.

Document 3

THE LÜTH-HARLAN CASE

Source: Entscheidungen des Bundesverfassungsgerichts, Vol. 7, 1958, 198–230 *Transl.:* John C. Lane and James K. Pollock, *Source Materials on the Government and Politics of Germany,* Ann Arbor, 1964 (122–3 below); Renata Chestnut, in Murphy and Tanenhaus, ibid. (124 below)

... The fundamental question whether constitutional provisions have an effect in civil law and how this effect must be considered in particular instances is a matter of dispute ... . An extreme position in this controversy is, on the one hand, the thesis that the basic rights are addressed exclusively to the state. On the other hand, there is the opinion that at least some, or at any rate the most important, of these rights are applicable in civil law relations as between anyone. The previous jurisprudence of the Federal Constitutional Court cannot be used in support of either one or the other of these extremes of opinion ... . Nor is there occasion now for the controversy over the so-called 'third person effect' of the basic rights to be discussed in its full scope. The following will suffice for reaching an appropriate decision:

Without doubt the basic rights are above all designed to secure the sphere of individual freedom against invasions by public power *(öffentliche Gewalt);* they are the defensive rights of citizens against the state. This follows from the historical development of the idea of basic rights and from the historical events that led to the inclusion of basic rights in the constitutions of various states.

The basic rights of the Basic Law have a like import. The Basic Law meant to emphasize the priority of the individual and his dignity as against the power of the state by giving the basic rights section first place. It is in accord with this that the legislature permitted the special legal relief for the protection of these rights, the constitutional complaint, only against acts of the public power.

But it is equally true that the Basic Law, which does not constitute a value-free order, erected in its basic rights section an objective order of values and it is precisely here that one finds an expression of the fundamental strengthening of the scope of the basic rights ... This value system, whose core is the freely developing personality and its dignity within the social community must, as a basic constitutional decision, be applicable in all areas of the law; legislation, administration and adjudication receive from it direction and impetus. Thus, it naturally influences also civil law; no civil law provision may be in contradiction to it and each must be interpreted in its spirit ... . Just as new law must be in harmony with the Basic Law's value system, so must existing old law be attuned in its content to this value system; from the latter there flows into it a specific constitutional content which henceforth determines its interpretation. A controversy between private citizens over rights and duties under civil law rules thus influenced by the basic rights remains substantively and procedurally a civil law controversy ... .

While the Federal Constitutional Court is not competent to act as a court of appeals or as a 'super-revisional' body for civil courts, it may neither abstain from a review of their decisions and ignore any mistakings of basic law norms or standards that may possibly be evident to them ... .

... The basic right of free speech, as the most direct expression of the human personality in society, is one of the highest human rights altogether ... . The general laws must be viewed, in regard to their inhibiting effect on the basic right, in the light of the significance of this basic right, and they must be so interpreted that the particular value content of the right ... remains in every case inviolate ... .

Speech as such, i.e. in its purely intellectual effect, is free, but when it impairs a legally protected right of another, a right which is entitled to protection against speech, then this impairment does not become permissible just because it was committed by means of speech. A weighing of interests *(Güterabwägung)* becomes necessary: The right of speech must yield if protected interests of a higher rank would be violated by the exercise of free speech. Whether such overriding interests of others exist must be determined on the basis of all the circumstances of the case ... .

To determine whether an invitation to a boycott ... is contrary to public morals requires that the motives, aim and purpose of the utterances be examined first. It needs to be established, further, that in the pursuit of his aims the petitioner [in the case below] did not exceed the necessary and appropriate limits of impairment of the interests of Harlan and the film company.

... Clearly the motives which prompted the petitioner in his remarks are not contrary to public morals. The petitioner did not pursue his own economic interests ... . [Furthermore] the remarks of the petitioner must be viewed in the context of his general political and cultural concerns ... . The petitioner was legitimized to express his views publicly because of his particularly close connection with all matters of German-Jewish relations ... .

When it is a question of forming public opinion on a question important for the public welfare, then private and particularly economic interests of individuals must generally yield *(zurücktreten)*. These interests do not thereby become unprotected, for the value of the basic right becomes apparent in the very fact that everyone may avail himself of it. Whoever feels himself injured by utterances of another may reply in public himself ... Only in the clash of opinions voiced in equal freedom can public opinion be formed and can the individuals who are addressed form their own opinions ... .

It is beyond question that the state ... could and can proceed against Harlan only within the limits of the laws. But this does not settle anything about what the individual citizen may undertake or say regarding Harlan. What is decisive here is that every individual is the possessor of the same basic rights ... . The argument of the Land Supreme Court of Hamburg ... , that 'since the state does not possess the power [to do certain things], such power can especially not be possessed by individual citizens', is erroneous ... .

The petitioner has appealed out of pure motives to the moral feelings of the affected groups and has asked them to take an irreproachably moral stand. This was not misunderstood in the public mind ... .

The complainant's statements must be seen within the context of his general political and cultural efforts. He was moved by the fear that Harlan's reappearance might—especially in foreign countries—be interpreted to mean that nothing had changed in German cultural life since the National Socialist period.

... These apprehensions concerned a very important issue for the German people.

... Nothing has damaged the German reputation as much as the cruel Nazi persecution of Jews. There exists therefore a crucial interest in assuring the world that the German people have abandoned this attitude and condemn it, not for reasons of political opportunism, but because through an inner conversion they have come to realize its evil.

The complainant's apprehensions were not later rationalizations, but corresponded to the state of affairs as it presented itself to him at that time. This has later been confirmed by, among other things, the fact that the attempt to show the film *Immortal Lover* in Switzerland caused strong protests and even an interpellation in the National Council and an official statement by the Bundesrat ... The film was unanimously rejected not because of its content, but because of Harlan's part in it, and was not shown as a result of these numerous emphatic interventions. In several German cities, too, there were demonstrations against presentation of the film for the same reasons ... .

The District Court considers it permissible that the complainant expressed an opinion about the reappearance of Harlan, but it reprimands him for having exhorted public behaviour. This distinction overlooks the fact that the complainant, if he is permitted to express a negative opinion about Harlan's reappearance, hardly went beyond what was already contained in this value judgment ... .

Because of his especially close personal relation to all that concerned the German-Jewish relationship, the complainant was within his rights to state his view in public. Even at that time he was already known for his efforts towards reestablishing a true inner peace with the Jewish people. He held a leading position in the Society for Christian-Jewish Cooperation; a short time before, he had initiated the campaign 'Peace with Israel' on the radio and in the press ... . It is understandable that he feared all these efforts might be disturbed and thwarted by Harlan's reappearance. But he could also proceed from the assumption that the public expected him especially to make a statement on this matter ... .

The demand that under these circumstances the complainant should nevertheless, out of regard for Harlan's professional interests and the economic interests of the film companies employing him, have refrained from expressing his opinion ... is unjustified.

[Judgment reversed]

The religious provisions of the Basic Law have been interpreted broadly to protect both religious and non-religious belief systems *(Weltanschauungen)*. In addition, the protection of all faiths and beliefs is reinforced by the anti-discrimination clauses of Art. 3 and 33, together with Art. 140, provisions that bar any prejudicial or favoured treatment based on a person's 'faith or his religion or political opinion'. The state's neutrality with respect to religious matters is the central concept behind the Basic Law's church-state provisions (see also Ch.13, Doc.7). The neutrality, however, is one that emphasizes a cooperative rather than a separationist mode of church-state relations. The Weimar articles carried over into the Basic Law confer public corporate status on the major denominations and guarantee self-governing autonomy to 'religious bodies', including their right to own and maintain property for religious, educational, and charitable purposes, an acknowledgement of the importance ascribed by the Constitution to the social role that religion plays in the life of society.

The extracts below are taken from two cases challenging certain applications of the church tax. All wage earners are subject to a church tax ranging between 8 and 10 per cent of their net taxable income. An employee must formally resign his or her church membership—as did 238,000 persons in 1975—to be exempted from the tax. Collected by state revenue officers, these taxes are distributed to the major denominations in amounts proportionate to their total membership. The Federal Constitutional Court has sustained the general validity of the church tax, although it has occasionally invalidated its application to particular persons in situations where the tax has been deemed to infringe religious freedom. The following passages summarize the general theory of religious freedom and church-state relations in West Germany. (see also Ch.13, Doc.7)

Document 4a

CHURCH TAX, I, 1965

Source: Entscheidungen des Bundesverfassungsgerichts, Vol. 18, 1965, 386f.
Vol. 19, 1966, 217ff.

. . .

There can be no state church under the system of church-state relations prescribed by the Basic Law. Every religious community has the right to order and administer its affairs independently within the limits of law applicable to all. Neither the state nor the civic community is permitted to involve itself in the selection of church officials. Churches are institutions endowed with the right of self-determination. Their nature is such as to render them independent of state influence. Thus the state may not interfere in their internal affairs.

Churches are defined by the constitution as corporate bodies under public law (Art. 140 of the Basic Law and Art. 137 of the Weimar Constitution). But their independence is not thereby compromised. This legal characterization does not signify an equality in status to other public law corporations within the organic structure of the state. It is only a recognition of their public status. That status, while higher than that of religious societies organized under private law, does not subordinate the churches to the supreme authority of the state or to close administrative supervision. To the extent that they exercise power conferred by the state, adopt measures beyond their authority as church bodies, or intrude into the domain of the state, they indirectly exercise governmental authority; but in such cases their self-determination is limited ... .

Document 4b

CHURCH TAX, II, 1966

Source: Ibid.

Art. 137, para. 6, of the Weimar Constitution authorizes religious societies organized as corporate bodies under public law to levy taxes 'on the basis of the state's civil tax lists'. The state is obligated to establish the conditions for the levying of such taxes, thus providing for the possibility of their compulsory collection. This sovereign right of tax collection granted by the state is quite different from the process of collecting contributions, which is an internal affair of the church. Pursuant to Art. 137, para. 3 (of the Weimar Constitution), religious societies are able to impose fees and contribution requirements without state interference. The levy of the church tax, on the other hand, is a common affair of both church and state. Here the state makes its own administrative apparatus available to the church for the collection of the tax. State regulation is necessary to administer the tax. For that reason, the levying of the church tax is also subject to judicial review.

. . .

According to Art. 4, para. 1, Art. 3, para. 3, and Art. 33, para. 3 of the Basic Law, together with Art. 136, paras. 1 and 4 and Art. 137, para. 1 of the Weimar Constitution in conjunction with Art. 140 of the Basic Law the state as the home of all citizens is bound by ideological and religious neutrality. The Basic Law prohibits the introduction of official religious forms as well as the granting of any privilege to a religious denomination. This requirement of religious and denominational neutrality means that the state is not permitted to confer on a religious society any sovereign authority over individuals who are not among its members.

Religious societies exercise sovereign authority, however, when pursuant to state law they tax persons who are not among their members .... In the exercise of this authority the state by means of its taxing power is effectively providing financial support for religious societies. This the state may not do when the taxing power reaches persons who do not belong to those religious societies. The churches in their corporate character may only obligate their own members through the power of taxation.

No significance is to be derived from the historical fact that religious societies once held a privileged position under the law. State churches in the sense that they were formally known no longer exist in the light of the prohibition against an official church. Churches no longer have the legal capacity unilaterally to enrol persons, without regard to their wishes, who settle within their territorial jurisdiction. Indeed, the Weimar Constitution had already deprived them of any such territorial control; rather their authority was to extend only to persons within their membership.

In 1975, the Federal Constitutional Court struck down a liberalized abortion law. The Abortion Reform Act, backed by a slim parliamentary majority, provided an abortion would no longer be punished if performed by a licensed physician with the consent of the pregnant woman during the first twelve weeks of pregnancy. The Court declared the statute unconstitutional under the 'human dignity' and 'right to life' clauses of the Basic Law.

Document 5a

THE ABORTION CASE (1975)

Source: Entscheidungen des Bundesverfassungsgerichts, Vol. 39 (1975): 1–95

Headnotes (Leitsätze)

1. The life which is developing itself in the womb of the mother is an independent legal value which enjoys the protection of Constitution. The State's duty to protect [the foetus] not only forbids the state directly to attack developing life, but also requires the state to protect and foster this life.

2. The state has the duty to protect developing life in the womb even against the wishes of the mother.

3. The protection of the life of the child *en ventre sa mere* takes precedence as a matter of principle over the mother's right to self-determination. It does so for the entire period of the pregnancy and must not be called into question for a specific time-span.

4. The legislature may express the legal condemnation of abortion required by the Basic Law through measures other than the threat of punishment. The decisive factor is whether the totality of the measures serving to protect unborn life secures the degree of protection corresponding to the importance of the legal value to be guaranteed. In the extreme case, if the protection required by the constitution cannot be realized in any other manner, the legislature is obligated to employ the criminal law to insure the protection of unborn life.

5. A continuation of a pregnancy is not to be exacted (legally) if an abortion is necessary in order to remove a threat to the pregnant woman's life or the danger of serious damage to her health. Beyond this, the legislature is at liberty to define as non-exactable [i.e. intolerable] other extraordinary burdens upon the pregnant woman, which have a similarly heavy weight, and not to impose criminal sanctions in these cases.

6. The Abortion Reform Act has not met the state's duty adequately to protect the life of the unborn.

OPINION OF THE COURT

1) Article 2 (2) of the Basic Law also protects the life developing itself in the womb of the mother as an intrinsic legal value ... .

b) In construing Article 2 (2) of the Basic Law, one should begin with its language: 'Everyone has a right to life ... '. Life, in the sense of historical existence of a human individual, exists according to definite biological-physiological knowledge, in any case, from the 14th day after conception (nidation, individuation). The process of development which has begun at that point is a continuing process which exhibits no sharp demarcation and does not allow a precise division of the various steps of development of the human life. The process does not end even with birth; the phenomena of consciousness which are specific to the human personality, for example, appear for the first time a rather long time after birth. Therefore, the protection of Article 2 (2) of the Basic Law cannot be limited either to the 'completed' human being after birth or to the child about to be born which is independently capable of living. The right to life is guaranteed to everyone who 'lives'; no distinction can be made here between various stages of the life developing itself before birth, or between unborn and born life. 'Everyone' in the sense of Article 2 (2) of the Basic Law is 'everyone living;' expressed in another way: every life possessing human individuality; 'everyone' also includes the yet unborn human being ... .

. . .

II

1. The duty of the state to protect is comprehensive. It forbids not only—self-evidently—direct state attacks on the life developing itself but also requires the state to take a position protecting and promoting this life, that is to say, it must, above all, preserve it even against illegal attacks by others. It is for the individual areas of the legal order, each according to its special function, to effectuate

this requirement. The degree of seriousness with which the state must take its obligation to protect increases as the rank of the legal value in question increases in importance within the order of values of the Basic Law, an ultimate value, the particulars of which need not be established; it is the living foundation of human dignity and the prerequisite for all other fundamental rights.

. . .

Document 5b

THE ABORTION CASE (1993)

Source: *Entscheidungen des Bundesverfassungsgerichts*, Vol. 88 (1993): 203–366.

In the 1975 Abortion Case, the Constitutional Court reimposed the criminal penalty on abortions procured at any stage of pregnancy and directed parliament to pass a new law in conformity with the Court's decision. Under the new law, which followed the Court's instructions, abortion would be punishable at all stages of pregnancy except in the presence of certain indications specified by law. In short, an abortion would be legally justified only if necessary (1) to protect the life or health of the mother, (2) to prevent the birth of a seriously defective child, (3) to avoid birth resulting from rape or incest, or (4) to relieve the woman of a severe social hardship. This policy prevailed until German unity. The Unity Treaty required parliament to pass a new all-German statute to replace the differing abortion policies of eastern and western Germany. The result was the Pregnancy and Family Assistance Act of 1992.

The new statute represented a hard-fought parliamentary effort to accommodate the interests of east and west. The statute sought to reflect the spirit of the Unity Treaty which directed the all-German parliament to 'ensure [the] better protection of unborn life' and to adopt social policies that would 'provide a better solution' to the problem of pregnant women in distress 'than is the case in either part of Germany at present.' Accordingly, the statute legalized abortion during the first trimester of pregnancy after compulsory counseling and a three-day waiting period. In addition, the statute amended sections of laws dealing with social security, medical insurance, child support, job placement, and welfare assistance to make it easier for women to carry their pregnancies to term if they wished. After the 12th week of pregnancy, an abortion could be legally procured only for special reasons sanctioned by law. In the following extracts, the Federal Constitutional Court also invalidated major portions of the new statute. In doing so, it affirmed the essential core of its 1975 ruling.

OPINION OF THE COURT

The Basic Law requires the state to protect human life. Unborn life is a part of human life and it too is entitled to the protection of the state. The constitution prohibits not only direct violations by the state but it also mandates the state to protect and promote unborn life, that is to say, to protect it from illegal invasion by others ... .

The unborn child is entitled to its right to life independently of acceptance by its mother; this is an elementary and inalienable right which emanates from the dignity of the human being. It is valid independently of any specific religious or philosophical beliefs over which the legal system of a state has no jurisdiction, since it remains neutral toward religion and world views ... .

... The protection of the unborn child against its mother can only be assured when the legislature prohibits her in principle from terminating her pregnancy, thus imposing on her the fundamental legal obligation to carry the child to term. The fundamental ban on abortion and the fundamental duty to carry the child to term are two inseparably connected elements of the constitutionally guaranteed protection.

The constitutional rights of a woman may give rise to situations where it will be necessary in some instances to refrain from imposing such a legal duty ... .It is parliament's duty to define those exceptional situations ... .A balanced approach that would guarantee both the protection of the life of the unborn child as well as a pregnant's woman's right to abortion is not possible because abortion always involves the killing of unborn life ... .

[Yet] there are burdens which demand such a degree of sacrifice of a woman's own existential values that one could no longer expect her to go through with her pregnancy.

[In an extremely complex opinion, the Court went on to declare that abortion could be legally sanctioned for serious medical, eugenic, and criminological reasons. In a departure from its 1975 ruling, however, the Court declared that an abortion procured within the first 12 weeks of pregnancy need not be punished under the criminal code, even though as a matter of principle abortion must be declared illegal. And if the state adopts a time-phase rather than an indications solution to the problem of abortion, it must in turn provide for extensive prolife counseling in a non-intimidating atmosphere and enact supportive social legislation truly and realistically calculated to protect the value of unborn life. Most of the Court's opinion was addressed to the inadequacies of the Pregnancy and Family Assistance Act in this regard. In short, the decision permits abortions to go unpunished in the first 12 weeks of pregnancy, but requires the state to refine its system of compulsory counseling and within a context of care and support, in social life generally as well as in the workplace, which would encourage the woman voluntarily to carry her child to term.]

If ... the legislature adopts a system of counseling [as an alternative to punishment] then the effort to protect unborn life will be essentially preventive and achieved by influencing through counseling a woman who is considering an abortion ... .It will be the state's duty to assure adequate counseling and the state may not shirk its duty by delegating counseling to private organizations, allowing them indiscriminately to impose on women their own religious, philosophical or political agendas ... . [T]he state must not relinquish its control over the administration of the counseling system.

Persons who perform abortions must be excluded from the counseling process. Moreover, it is illegal to integrate institutionally counseling facilities—no matter how organized—into organizations which also perform abortions. Places economically interested in performing abortions must remain separate from [the system of counseling] ...

The state must therefore examine regularly—by way of a statute—the credentials of these facilities; in addition, it must carry out reviews at regular intervals and make certain that the conditions guiding abortion counseling will be heeded. Only after these conditions have been met may a license be continued or renewed.

Since the end of the eighteenth century professional civil servants (see also Ch.12) have enjoyed an esteemed and privileged position in Germany, especially in the former state of Prussia. Art. 33 of the Basic Law carries on this historical tradition. It provides that the 'exercise of state authority as a permanent function shall as a rule be entrusted to members of the public service whose status, service, and loyalty are guaranteed by public law.' Loyalty to the state —not to be confused with an existing government—is of course among the highest principles governing the professional civil service anywhere. Federal and state laws seek to ensure the loyalty of civil servants by requiring, as a condition of entry into the bureaucracy, that they 'defend at all times the free democratic basic order within the spirit of the Basic Law.' Against the background of violent demonstrations by university students together with the renewed determination of radical groups to 'march through the institutions' of the Federal Republic, the federal chancellor and all ten state prime ministers issued, on 28 January 1972, a new loyalty decree setting forth guidelines for the recruitment of civil servants. The first such guidelines went into effect in both Federation and Länder after the outbreak of the Korean War in 1950. They included provisions barring from the public service applicants who have engaged in 'anticonstitutional' activities and permitting the exclusion of persons who were or are members of 'an organization pursuing anticonstitutional goals'. Pursuant to these provisions the Land of Schleswig-Holstein refused to admit a law graduate who had once attended meetings of a radical student group at Kiel University from entering the practical phase of his training in various governmental agencies. He appealed to the courts to vindicate his right to continue his legal training. The Supreme Administrative Court of Schleswig-Holstein referred constitutional questions involved in the case to the Federal Constitutional Court for decision.

Document 6

THE CIVIL SERVANT LOYALTY CASE

Source: *Entscheidungen des Bundesverfassungsgerichts*, Vol. 39, 1975, 334

... Constitutionally, civil servants have the duty of loyalty towards the free democratic state to which they are particularly closely related ... . The democratic state requires a body of civil servants supportive of the existing constitutional order. Civil servants are duty-bound to defend the state in times of crisis by fulfilling the tasks entrusted to them in faithful harmony with the spirit of the constitution along with its system of values and prescriptions. Such loyalty is required of civil servants in the interest of the state's preservation. The realization of this constitutional value in Art. 33, para. 5, of the Basic Law is not opposed to Art. 21, para. 2; Art. 33, para. 5, requires civil servants to support the constitutional order. Art. 21, para. 2, on the other hand, grants to the citizen the freedom to reject the constitutional order and politically to oppose it, so long as he employs permissible means of opposition and operates within a political party that is not prohibited.

The special duties of civil servants have not been imposed to hinder their political activities, but rather to maintain the security of the constitutional state against threats from its civil servants. Without the requirement of political loyalty, civil servants could use their special status and competence for the purpose of altering or subverting the existing constitutional order by means not authorized in the Constitution. It is not a question of discriminating against a civil servant on the grounds of his membership in a political party. Rather, it is one of requiring his loyalty as a state official and insuring that applicants will at all times, with their whole being, stand up for the free democratic basic order. Whether such loyalty can be expected of applicants for the civil service can be determined by their previous activities. Affiliation with or membership in an anti-constitutional party, whether or not it has been declared unconstitutional by the Federal Constitutional court, is an admissible factor in evaluating the credentials of an applicant ... .

. . .

The legal position thus far expounded does not conflict with the fundamental right to freedom of expression ... Owing to his official status [the civil servant] is charged with special duties *vis-à-vis* the state; at the same time, he is a citizen who may assert his fundamental rights against the state. Thus, two basic values of the Basic Law clash within the person of the civil servant: the assurance that the state will be served by an indispensable and reliable body of civil servants who will support the state and affirm the free democratic basic order ... and the fundamental right freely to express one's opinion ... All conduct involving the expression of political opinion is constitutionally protected by Art. 5 of the Basic Law only to the extent that it is compatible with the duty of political loyalty required by the civil servant under Art. 33, para. 5.

. . .

3) According to Art. 3, para. 3, no person may be 'discriminated against or favoured because of ... his political opinions.' ... [Yet] the formal prescription of Art. 3, para. 3, is not absolute. It should be obvious that it is not impermissible to require acknowledgement of a particular creed on the part of a teacher about to be employed at a denominational school, or to give preference to a female for the position of principal at a girl's school, ... Art. 3 prohibits only 'purposeful' discrimination; it does not prohibit favourable or prejudicial treatment based on a different order of intentionality (e.g., rules for the protection of the pregnant mother or for the protection of the constitutional order.) ...

Finally, a constitutional provision should not be interpreted in isolation; on the contrary, it must be interpreted within the context of the Constitution itself. With this understanding, it is simply inconceivable that the constitution which, in the wake of the bitter experience of Weimar's democracy, intended the Federal Republic of Germany to be a strong and valiant democracy also permits the surrender of this state to its enemies under the protection of Art. 3, para. 3, of the Basic Law.

The Klaas Case arose out of Germany's attempt to provide for its internal security against enemies both domestic and foreign, while simultaneously seeking to preserve the liberties of its citizens. When the Constitution was originally adopted Art. 10 contained a simple declaration: 'Privacy of the mail and privacy of posts and telecommunications shall be inviolable. Restrictions may be imposed only pursuant to a law.' In 1968, however, the year the Constitution was amended to include a new and substantial section providing for the defence of the Federal Republic in the event of a serious military threat, Art. 10 was also amended (at the special request of the former occupying powers) to allow the state to interfere with private communications in the interests of protecting the 'free democratic basic order.' Subsequently, the Bundestag passed a law implementing this provision. The law, like the amendment, permitted telephone taps and other interferences with private communications but did not require those under surveillance to be informed of that fact. In addition, the legislature provided for administrative and parliamentary rather than judicial review of this process. The states of Bremen and Hesse challenged the validity of the statute and the amendment before the Second Panel of the Federal Constitutional Court in an abstract judicial review proceeding. It may seem anomalous that the validity of an amendment to the Basic Law could be challenged as unconstitutional. But in a very early case the Constitutional Court hinted *in dicta* that an amendment to the Constitution might itself be unconstitutional if it were to offend a basic principle on which the Constitution as a whole is based. The petitioners seized upon this theory in their argument before the Court.

Document 7

PRIVACY OF COMMUNICATIONS CASE

Source: *Entscheidungen des Bundesverfassungsgerichts*, Vol. 30, 1970, 1
Transl.: Renata Chestnut, in Murphy and Tanenhaus, Ibid., 659–66

JUDGMENT of the Court ...

C.-I ... .

1 ... . a) From the outset, the Basic Law did not unreservedly protect privacy of mails and telecommunications; rather, restrictions were always admissible, but in all cases had to be based on a law ... . In this respect, the newly added sent. 2 of Art. 10, para. 2, does not introduce anything novel ... .

Wherever the Basic Law restricts basic rights, it is always to protect effectively another individual or supra-individual legal interest which has priority ... . The existence of the Federal Republic and its liberal constitutional order are a predominant legal interest for whose effective protection basic rights may, if absolutely necessary, be restricted.

What is really new in the constitutional amendment is ... authorization not to inform the person affected of those restrictions, and to replace recourse to the courts by a review of the case by bodies ... appointed by Parliament. The connection between these special measures and the restrictions ... is clear. Efforts, plans, and measures directed against the constitutional order and against the security and existence of the state are mostly initiated by groups who disguise their work and manoeuver in secret, who are well-organized and rely to a great extent on undisturbed functioning of their communications system. An Office to protect the Constitution can effectively counter such an 'apparatus' only if its measures of surveillance remain secret ... . Even subsequent disclosure ... can furnish forces hostile to the Constitution with clues as to methods of operation and specific areas of observation by the Office for the Protection of the Constitution ... .

b) Constitutional provisions must not be interpreted in isolation, but rather so that they are consistent with the Basic Law's fundamental principles and its system of values [citing a case] ... . In the context of this case, it is especially significant that the Constitution ... has decided in favour of a 'militant democracy' that does not submit to abuse of basic rights for an attack on the liberal order of the state [citing a case]. Enemies of the Constitution must not be allowed to endanger, impair, or destroy the existence of the state while claiming protection of rights granted by the Basic Law (cf. Art. 9, para. 2, Arts. 18 and 21). To protect the Constitution, the Basic Law explicitly provides for an institution, the Office for the Protection of the Constitution (cf. Art. 73, 10, and Art. 87, para. 1). The Basic Law cannot mean to set the constitutionally highest bodies of the state a task and to provide for a special agency for this purpose, while at the same time denying this agency means necessary to fulfill its assigned mission.

. . .

Interpretation of the amendment's substitution of review of administrative action by an agency or agencies appointed by Parliament for protection normally provided by the courts is very important. The principle of the rule of law demands that any statute implementing the amendment must establish agencies and procedures that produce a system of control which, even though the suspect does not participate in the process, functions as an effective equivalent to judicial control.

Accordingly, Art. 10, para. 2, sent. 2, requires that the law which is issued to implement it provides for *one* agency among those appointed by parliament which decides in judicial independence, and can bind all persons who are involved in the preparation, administrative decision making, and execution of the surveillance ... and which can prohibit illegal measures of surveillance. This agency may be established within or outside parliament. It must, however, have sufficient expert and legal knowledge; it must be truly independent; and its members must be irrevocably appointed for a specific period of time. It must be competent to supervise all measures taken by all agencies involved in choosing, preparing, implementing, and supervising encroachment upon the privacy of mails and telecommunications ... . For this purpose, all files relevant to deciding a case must be made available to the agency of control. This control must be a legal control. Art. 10, para. 2, sent. 2, also authorizes creation of a controlling agency that can, for appropriate reasons, order a surveillance discontinued or not exercised, even where legal prerequisites for surveillance are present ... .

. . .

1. The second sentence of Art. 10, para. 2, authorizes the Government to keep secret from a suspect the fact that he is under surveillance. This provision does not violate the dignity of man.

. . .

A regulation or instruction that restricts a citizen's freedom or imposes duties on him does not violate human dignity. Neither does a measure which subjects a citizen, even without his knowledge or consent, to governmental surveillance. Under the circumstances at hand, absence of notification is not an expression of disrespect for a human being and his dignity, but a burden imposed upon a citizen ... to protect the existence of his state and of the free democratic order ... . Possibility of illegal and unconstitutional abuse does not make the rule unconstitutional; in interpreting and assessing a regulation one must rather proceed from the assumption that in a free democracy based on the rule of law it will be applied in a correct and just manner.

. . .

The guarantee of recourse to the courts laid down in Art. 19, para. 4, serves the purpose of legal protection for the individual ... . The essential aspect of this constitutional provision is that legal protection is furnished by a materially and personally independent body, separate from the executive and legislative and therefore neutral ... . If the Constitution is amended so that 'recourse to the courts' is 'replaced by a review of the case by bodies and auxiliary bodies appointed by parliament', then the entire system of legal protection is replaced.

. . .

Furthermore, one cannot infer from the constitutional amendment any tangible limitation on the number of people who may be kept under surveillance. Restrictions on privacy may be ordered in a very general manner, whenever they serve to protect the free democratic basic order or the existence or security of the Federation or a Land ... .

ASYLUM

In the early 1990s, in the aftermath of German unity, the new all-German parliament engaged in a heated debate over the asylum provisions of the Basic Law (Article 16). The debate was prompted by the influx of hundreds of thousands of refugees from the East and other parts of the world, placing a heavy strain on Germany's welfare laws and the administrative apparatus set up to deal with asylum claims. Under Article 16 (2), together with its implementing statute, any person claiming asylum on the ground of a well-founded fear of political persecution, was entitled to have that claim adjudicated, during which time the person claiming the right to asylum would be entitled to free housing and general governmental support. In case of a denial of the asylum claim, the asylee also had the right of appeal to the administrative courts and ultimately to the Federal Constitutional Court.

The debate was enormously important symbolically. The constitutional right to asylum was a powerful expression of Germany's political morality in the light of the nation's Nazi past, and many Germans felt any tampering with Article 16 or any limit on the right to asylum would send the wrong message to a world still mindful of that past. After months of debate, however, parliament left Article 16 (2) untouched but added a new Article 16a to the Basic Law. The purpose behind the new amendment was not to reject the right to asylum but to limit the number of false asylum claims and to accelerate the process of deciding such claims.

The asylum controversy was part of a larger and more extensive debate over immigration and citizenship policy. The influx of over a million refugees between 1990 and 1993 (see also Statistics, Tables 2 and 3) and the presence of millions of permanent foreign residents and their families, many of whom had lived and worked in Germany for decades, triggered demands to amend Germany's immigration and citizenship laws to make it easier for permanent resident aliens to acquire citizenship. Historically, citizenship had been—and still is—tied to the notion of nationhood and the ethnic-cultural identification associated with it.

Some German leaders continued to insist that Germany is not an immigrant country, notwithstanding the presence of millions of immigrants, thus arguing that citizenship should continue to be based on German ethnicity. Others, normatively committed to the reality and desirability of a multicultural society, preferred a broader and more political definition of citizenship. This would mean an immigration policy based on national quotas and similar to laws adopted in the United States and Canada. In the context of high unemployment and numerous acts of violence against foreign residents, the debate has taken on considerable urgency and it continues, without resolution, to this day. The stakes are high, for the debate deals with no less than the question of national identity and the with the kind of society Germans would wish to create as they approach the 21st century. (see also Ch.14, Doc.6)

Document 8a

Source: Gerald L. Neuman, "Buffer Zones Against Regugees: Dublin, Schengen, and the German Asylum Amendment", 33 *Virginia Journal of International Law* (1993): 518–9. The following translation is included with the permission of Gerlad L. Neuman.

ARTICLE 16a

1. The politically persecuted shall enjoy the right of asylum.

2. Paragraph 1 cannot be invoked by those who travel from a member state of the European Communities or a third state in which the application of the Convention Relationing to the Status of Refugees and the [European] Convention for the Protection of Human Rights and Fundamental Freedoms is insured. The states outside the European Communities that satisfy the criteria of sentence 1 shall be designated by a statute, which shall require the concurrence of the Bundesrat. In cases within sentence 1, deportation measures may be enforced despite the pendency of an appeal.

3. States may be designated by a statute, which shall require the concurrence of the Bundesrat, in which, as a result of the legal rules, the application of law and general political conditions, it appears to be guaranteed that neither political persecution nor inhuman or degrading punishment or treatment occurs there. It shall be presumed that an alien from such a state will not be persecuted, so long as he does not present facts that justify the assumption that he will be politically persecuted despite this presumption.

4. A court shall suspend the execution of deportation measures in cases under paragraph 3, and in other cases that are manifestly unfounded or are deemed to be manifestly unfounded, only if there is serious doubt about the legality of the measure; the scope of review can be limited and belated submissions can go unconsidered. The details shall be regulated by a statute.

5. Paragraphs 1 through 4 do not preclude international treaties among member states of the European Communities and with third countries which, subject to observance of the duties arising from the Convention Relating to

the Status of Refugees and the [European] Convention for the Protection of Human Rights and Fundamental Freedoms, whose application in the states parties must be ensured, concern jurisdictional rules for the examination of asylum requests, including the reciprocal recognition of asylum decisions.

CITIZENSHIP

The citizenship clauses of the Basic Law constituted a powerful weapon in the forty-five year-old struggle for German unity. Article 16 (1) declares that no one may be deprived of his German citizenship. But who is a German? Under the terms of Article 116, a German citizen is defined as 'a person who possesses German citizenship or who has been admitted to the territory of the German Reich within the frontiers of 31 December 1937 as a refugee or expellee of German ethnic origin or as a spouse or descendant of such a person.' In the prevailing interpretation of this provision, 'Germans' eligible for immediate citizenship in the Federal Republic included not only those ethnic Germans expelled from the territory of the former Reich, but also Germans living in the GDR. The latter were granted all the rights of German citizenship as soon as they entered the territory of the FRG. Not only did the policy express West Germany's refusal to concede independent nationhood to East Germany; it also encouraged East Germans to flee the regime and take up residence in the FRG. The FRG's policy was based on the proposition that the GDR was not a foreign power separate from Germany.

The Citizenship Case carried the logic of Article 116 one step further. It involved a person who became a naturalized citizen under the laws of the GDR, thus acquiring German nationality by virtue of his citizenship in East Germany. Later he moved to the FRG where his application for immediate citizenship was denied on the ground that the GDR's citizenship statute was incompatible with the FRG's Citizenship and Nationality Act. The Federal Administrative Court upheld the denial, whereupon the complainant petitioned the Federal Constitutional Court for redress. His constitutional complaint argued that under the Court's decision in the Basic Treaty Case, which sustained the constitutionality of a treaty under which both the GDR and FRG recognized each other's status as independent states within the German nation, the FRG's denial of citizenship in his case would interfere with the jurisdictional sovereignty of the GDR, deny the concept of a single German nationality, and thus contravene the principle of German reunification.

Document 8b

THE CITIZENSHIP CASE
Source: *Entscheidungen des Bundesverfassungsgerichts*, Vol. 77 (1987): 137

C.

The constitutional complaint is justified. The decisions challenged infringe the complainant's fundamental rights under Article 16 (1), first sentence of the Basic Law, taken together with Article 116 (1) of the Basic Law, and his entitlement to equal treatment under Article 3 (1) of the Basic Law taken together with the fundamental rights pertaining to Germans.

. . .

... [I]t makes no difference whether the complainant had acquired the citizenship of the German Democratic Republic directly under a statute of the German Democratic Republic or by an individual act of its authorities.

Acquisition of the citizenship of the German Democratic Republic by the complainant meant that he simultaneously acquired German nationality within the meaning of Articles 16 (1) and 116 (1) of the Basic Law. This legal effect did not arise in virtue or on the basis of one of the ways of acquisition in the Citizenship and Nationality Act; the mode whereby the complainant acquired the citizenship of the German Democratic Republic does not have anything corresponding to it in the modes of acquisition in the Citizenship and Nationality Act or other legal rules of the legal system in force in the sovereign territory of the Federal Republic of Germany. However, it follows from the precept of maintenance of the unity of German nationality (Articles 116 [1] and 16 [1] of the Basic Law), which is a normative specification of the reunification precept contained in the Basic Law, that acquisition of the citizenship of the German Democratic Republic is, within the limits of *ordre public,* to be attributed the legal effect for the legal order of the Federal Republic of Germany of acquisition of German nationality.

. . .

Accordingly, the complainant possesses German nationality. The decisions [of the lower courts] contravene his basic right under Article 16 (1) taken together with Article 116 (1) of the Basic Law ... .

12
Federalism: Bund and Länder

R. Taylor Cole†

Updated and edited by C.C. Schweitzer

The legalistic criteria of classical federalism* were present in the West German political system from the beginning, i.e. 1949. Under a rigid constitution like that of the Federal Republic—now of the reunited Germany—the powers are divided between three different levels of government, each of which possesses autonomous powers of decision-making in specific areas: the Federation (Bund), the constituent states (Länder), and local authorities. Though this legalistic classification has been the subject of much controversy in the Federal Republic, and doubts persist as to its appropriateness, the formal federal features of the political system have a continuing importance for policy making, adjudication, and other purposes. On the whole, the West German federal system is based on the principle of 'subsidiarity', that is, problems should be solved where they emerge. Only if problems cannot be solved locally, should a higher level take over. This principle finds its expression above all in articles 30 and 31 of the Basic Law.

Art. 30 Functions of the Länder

The exercise of governmental powers and the discharge of governmental functions shall be incumbent on the Länder insofar as this Basic Law does not otherwise prescribe or permit.

Art. 31. Priority of Federal Law

Federal law shall override Land law ...

(see also below: Federal Legislation)
The local authorities—*Gemeinde, Städte, Kreise*—operate under the administrative surveillance of the Länder, but are otherwise self-governing with their own legislative bodies and heads of administration. The Basic Law contains in its article 28 a federal guarantee:

Article 28

(1) The constitutional order in the Länder must conform to the principles of republican democratic and social government based on the rule of law, within the mean-

---

* The term 'federalism' is used here throughout in the European rather than the North American sense to denote decentralizing rather than centralizing tendencies.

ing of this Basic Law. In each of the Länder, counties (Kreise), and communes (Gemeinden), the people must be represented by a body chosen in general, direct, free, equal, and secret elections. In the communes the assembly of the commune may take the place of an elected body ...

The German federal system can be understood only when viewed in its historical context. For example, the old territorial boundaries of the West German Länder owed as much to the political fiat of the occupying powers after the Second World War as to their evolution in previous centuries. Once the boundaries of the Länder had crystallized the possibility of making changes in them largely disappeared.

Many factors have accelerated the movement in postwar Germany towards centralization of political life and an increasing dominance of the Bund in relation to the Länder. However, two very important institutions in the system operate to monitor the extent to which the balance shifts and indeed on occasion to limit its progress: the Bundesrat and the Federal Constitutional Court.

As defined in the Basic Law, the division of functions between the three levels of government, pertains to three fields:

(1) *Legislation.* In this field the Bund plays a dominant role and, with some exceptions deriving from Länder autonomy such as cultural policy, the interests of the Länder are taken care of by the second chamber in the Bonn parliament, the Bundesrat (Doc.1), which has an important role in the federal legislative process.

(2) *Administration.* Here the main responsibility rests with the Länder. While the Bund has an administrative structure of its own for a limited number of areas such as the execution of foreign and defence policy, most federal laws are executed by Länder administrations. This not only gives the Länder administration discretionary powers, but it also explains why roughly half of the federal laws require the consent of the Bundesrat. Local administrations in the municipalities depend directly on the Länder governments, but they enjoy considerable discretionary powers of their own.

(3) *Finance.* Some taxes or shares of taxes go directly to the municipalities, while other taxes go to the Länder or to the Bund. Some taxes are shared between the three levels. For example, income and corporation taxes are shared in a fixed proportion between the three levels of government, and the value added tax (VAT) is divided between the Bund and the Länder on a ratio which is subject to often highly controversial negotiations. A fixed proportion of the revenue from the VAT goes to the European Community, thus adding a supra-national element to the financial picture (Doc.10g). The municipalities are notoriously weak financially, because they have to provide most public services but have relatively low tax revenues of

their own. In order to secure *uniform living standards* in the Federal Republic (an important objective which is laid down in Art. 72 (2), Art. 106 (3) of the Basic Law), there are arrangements for financial equalization between Bund, Länder and the municipalities (the so-called vertical equalization) and also between 'rich' and 'poor' Länder (the so-called horizontal equalization).

Beyond the formal division of functions between the Bund, the Länder and the local authorities, federalism can also be viewed as a process marked by shifting and flexible relationships between the Bund and its constituent states. The traditional concept of dual federalism, which denotes the classical division of power between the two levels of the central state on the one hand and the constituent states on the other, has been superseded in the Federal Republic by the development towards *cooperative federalism*. Cooperative federalism emphasizes joint programmes and institutionalized forms of cooperation, many of which have their bases not in constitutional provisions, but in various types of fiscal arrangements. These include above all Bund financial assistance, contributions, and grants-in-aid for specific projects. Some of these institutional connections involve new intergovernmental relations between Bund, Länder and local communities and regions. These developments over the years were brought about by amendments to the constitution, particularly in the late 1960s. (see: Joint Tasks of Bund and Länder, Docs.11a-f). Some of the changes were effected by inter state as well as Bund-Länder Treaties and by political conventions creating precedents through political practice in a more anglo-saxon way.

The future of German federalism has been the focus of several official, as well as non-official, reviews in the past years. Among the first was the Troeger Commission, a creation of the Bund and the Länder governments, which submitted a final report on financial reform in 1966. Mention must also be made in this connection of the Commission of Inquiry on Constitutional Reform (the so-called *'Enquete-Kommission für Verfassungsreform'*).[1]* In both official and non-official discussions of the future contours of German federalism there have been at least three separate, though interconnected, paradigms. The first assumes that rapidly increasing centralization is inevitable in German post industrialized society and that the Länder will eventually be recognized as anomalies, useful only as administrative units. In this view, federalism does not reflect, except perhaps formally, the social realities and 'real forces' of the day. A second view, while recognizing that the pulls toward the centre will continue, assumes that these will be accompanied by structural changes

* *Notes for this chapter begin on p. 367.*

that would maintain and might even increase the autonomy of the Länder. With the conclusion of the Maastricht treaty for the European Union another 'level' of government has become of ever increasing importance in this whole connection, i.e. a *semi-supranational European* one. (See Doc.8)

The third paradigm assumes that the existing trend towards centralization is exaggerated. According to this 'theory' there is likely to be a heavier emphasis on coordinating machinery, both vertical (between the Bund and the Länder) and horizontal (between the Länder themselves). The integrity of the Land structure, reflecting the rigidity of boundaries once established, would be safeguarded within limits by the existence of 'federalizers' in the political system. There would thus not be any sudden or fundamental changes in the existing arrangements, but rather a gradual evolution to new types of federal relationships in which the Länder would continue to play an indispensable part.[2]

Two institutions maintain a balance between the Bund and Länder: The Bundesrat and the Federal Constitutional Court (see below and also Ch.10).

BUNDESRAT

The 'Council of the Constituent States' *(Bundesrat)* is, next to the Federal Constitutional Court, the most important institution which helps to preserve a flexible balance between Bund and Länder, as it is a Second Chamber in the whole process of federal legislation next to the Bundestag (see also Ch.7). In the Federal Republic of West Germany the members from Berlin had a special status due to the original four-power agreements on Berlin as a whole (see also Ch.2). Before reunification the Bundesrat had forty-one members with representatives from each Land varying between three and five. After reunification there are now sixty-eight members with representation varying from three to six. Members of the Bundesrat represent the Governments of the Länder and vote as blocs, with, after reunification thirty-five votes providing an absolute majority and forty-six votes a two-thirds majority.

The Bundesrat represents the Länder interest in the full range of federal legislation. In this respect the Bundesrat has assumed an increasingly important role hardly envisaged in 1949.[3]

The result has been an increasingly important use of the Bundesrat's two-fold veto power: a *suspensive* veto, which the Bundesrat can use against any law passed by the Bundestag and which the latter can in the end override by a simple majority[4] and an *absolute* veto against certain bills passed by the Bundestag, which the latter cannot then override. All bills proposed by the Federal Government have to be scrutinized by the Bundesrat first within a certain time limit.[5] An absolute veto can be directed against measures which would seriously affect financial or administrative interests of the Länder, as well as amendments to the constitution which have to be passed by the Bundesrat (as well as the Bundestag) by a two-thirds majority. In case of either a suspensive or an absolute veto against a bill passed by the Bundestag, a special committee of both houses of the German parliament, the so-called joint Mediation Committee *(Vermittlungsausschuß,* see also Ch.7) is called together at the request of either House. In accordance with Art.77 of the Basic Law the Bundesrat can request a meeting within fourteen days after the receipt of the bill from the Bundestag. Composed of an equal number of members of the Bundestag and Bundesrat, the joint committee seeks to resolve differences between the two bodies. On occasion opposition parties to the party or parties forming the government have a majority in the Bundesrat, as they had for some years prior to the defeat of Chancellor Schmidt in October 1982, and again in the early 1990s, this time in the opposite political direction, i.e. versus the Christian Democratic Government of Helmut Kohl from a Social Democratic majority. They can thus influence the political scene and parliamentary process in many—and perhaps even decisive ways. However, the history of Federal legislation in post war Germany shows a high degree of consensus-building by way of compromises arrived at between the Bundestag and the Bundesrat (see Statistics 17).

The constitutional provisions regarding the Bundesrat concern: (1) organisation structure, Arts. 50-53; (2) the procedures by which the Bundesrat is involved in meeting national emergencies, Art. 53a; (3) the involvement of the Bundesrat in federal legislation: Arts. 70 ff (see Doc.6 below); (4) Arts. 83-86 regarding the execution of federal laws and the federal administration (see Doc. 9 below).

Document 1

CONSTITUTIONAL PROVISIONS CONCERNING THE BUNDESRAT (BASIC LAW)

Source: Presse- und Informationsamt der Bundesregierung

Section IV: The Council of Constituent States (Bundesrat)

Art. 50. Function

The Länder shall participate through the Bundesrat in the legislation and administration of the Bund.

Art. 51. Composition

(1) The Bundesrat shall consist of members of the Land governments which appoint and recall them. Other members of such governments may act as substitutes.

(2) Each Land shall have at least three votes Länder with more than two million inhabitants shall have four, Länder with more than six million inhabitants five votes. [See p. 325, ed.]

(3) Each Land may delegate as many members as it has votes. The votes of each Land may be cast only as a block vote and only by members present or their substitutes.

Art. 52. President, Rules of Procedure

(1) The Bundesrat shall elect its President for one year.

(2) The President shall convene the Bundesrat. He must convene it if the members for at least two Länder or the Federal Government so demand.

(3) The Bundesrat shall take its decisions with at least the majority of its votes. It shall draw up its rules of procedure. Its meetings shall be public. The public may be excluded.

(4) Other members of, or persons commissioned by, Land governments may serve on the committees of the Bundesrat.

Art. 53. Participation of the Federal Government

The members of the Federal Government shall have the right, and on demand the duty, to attend the meetings of the Bundesrat and of its committees. They must be heard at any time. The Bundesrat must be currently kept informed by the Federal Government of the conduct of affairs.

Section IVa: The Joint Committee

Art. 53a

(1) Two-thirds of the members of the Joint Committee shall be deputies of the Bundestag and one-third shall be members of the Bundesrat. The Bundestag shall delegate its deputies in proportion to the sizes of its parliamentary groups such deputies must not be members of the Federal Government. Each Land shall be represented by a Bundesrat member of its choice these members shall not be bound by instructions. The establishment of the Joint Committee and its procedures shall be regulated by rules of procedure to be adopted by the Bundestag and requiring the consent of the Bundesrat.

(2) The Federal Government must inform the Joint Committee about its plans in respect of a state of defence. The rights of the Bundestag and its committees under paragraph (1) of Art. 43 shall not be affected by the provision of this paragraph.

. . .

Art. 79. Amendment of the Basic Law

(1) This Basic Law can be amended only by laws which expressly amend or supplement the text thereof. In respect of international treaties the subject of which is a peace settlement, the preparation of a peace settlement, or the

abolition of an occupation regime, or which are designed to serve the defence of the Federal Republic, it shall be sufficient, for the purpose of clarifying that the provisions of this Basic Law do not preclude the conclusion and entry into force of such treaties, to effect a supplementation of the text of this Basic Law confined to such clarification.

(2) Any such law shall require the affirmative veto of two-thirds of the members of the Bundestag and two-thirds of the votes of the Bundesrat.

(3) Amendments of this Basic Law affecting the division of the Federation into Länder, the participation on principle of the Länder in legislation, or the basic principles laid down in Arts. 1 and 20, shall be inadmissible.

As the Rules of Procedure clearly imply, most of the work of the Bundesrat is done in standing committees of which there were fourteen in 1980. In the so-called 'political' committees (Foreign Relations, Defence and Inner German Affairs) the Länder are usually represented by their heads of government or plenipotentiaries, while in the 'technical' committees, the responsible Länder ministers or their representatives serve (i.e. Länder Ministries of Finance on the Bundesrat Finance Committee). The initial stages in the legislative process often involve the relations between Federal ministries and the concerned ministries of the Länder. As Gehard Ziller, one-time Bundesrat Director, commented, there also exist informal means of coordination which work as follows:

'... As a rule, the ministries concerned of the Länder are the first to be informed of the legislative plans of the Federal Government. In accordance with the Rules of Procedure of the Federal ministries, these plans are formulated as rough drafts of bills to be examined by the responsible Länder ministries. These contacts take place as a rule at an informal 'working level' ... . The 'political level' in the Länder ... is informed after the bill has been considered by the Federal Cabinet. After this action by the Federal Cabinet, formal proceedings begin in the Bundesrat ... . The material [the proposed legislation] is printed and is distributed to the Länder. Then the technical departments of the Länder have three weeks to ... study the bill, prepare amendments and supplementary proposals ... . Four weeks after the distribution of the government bill, the committees of the Bundesrat meet. The ministers concerned of the Länder ... now have the opportunity to discuss the proposed law, to ask questions, and to defend their own suggestions ... .'

Document 2

RULES OF PROCEDURE OF THE BUNDESRAT (GESCHÄFTSORDNUNG)

Source: Bundesrat Sekretariat

Art. 1. Members

The governments of the Länder furnish the President of the Bundesrat with names of the members of the Bundesrat, the date of their appointment as members of the Bundesrat and of the Land government and the date on which their membership expires.

Art. 2. Incompatibility of Office

Members of the Bundesrat may not simultaneously be members of the Bundestag.

. . .

Art. 5

(1) The Bundesrat elects without debate one President and three Vice-Presidents from among its members for one year.

. . .

Art. 8. The Presidency

(1) The Presidency consists of the President and the three Vice-Presidents.
(2) On the advice of a Permanent Advisory Council, it prepares the draft budget of the Bundesrat. It makes decisions on the internal affairs of the Bundesrat so long as the power of decision is neither reserved for the Bundesrat as a whole nor incumbent on the President.

. . .

Art. 11. Committees

(1) The Bundesrat establishes standing committees. It may set up additional committees to deal with particular business.
(2) Each of the Länder is represented on every committee by a member of the Bundesrat, another member or a delegate from its government.

. . .

Art. 18. Participation in Debate

(1) The rapporteur of the Mediation Committee and the Under Secretaries of State of the Federal Government may also take part in the discussions of the Bundesrat. Other persons may do so with the permission of the President.
(2) Representatives of the Länder and the Federal government may be called in to assist the members of the Bundesrat and the Federal Government as well as other participants in the discussions.

. . .

Art. 25. Reports

(1) The committees are to make oral reports in the sessions of the Bundesrat

on matters of importance currently under discussion. With the permission of the President an oral report on technical or legal questions may be replaced by a written report ... .

. . .

Art. 30. Voting Rules

(1) According to Arts. 76 to 78 of the Basic Law questions to be put to a vote in legislative proceedings are to be put in such a way that the voting shows conclusively whether the Bundesrat has decided by a majority ... .

. . .

Art. 34. Participation in the Debates of the Bundestag

The Bundesrat may authorize its members to defend its resolutions in the Bundestag and its committees. The committees may make suggestions in this regard.

. . .

Art. 40. Participation and Right to Question

(1) Members of the Bundesrat and delegates of the Land governments who are not members of the committees, as well as representatives of the Federal government may participate in the discussions of the committees and sub-committees, but do not enjoy voting rights.

(2) In session, members of the committees as well as delegates of the Land governments may question the members of the Federal government and its representatives.

. . .

ABSOLUTE VETO POWER

In accordance with the Basic Law the Bundesrat has an absolute veto over some Federal legislation above all in the Field of Federal Finances and the administration of Federal Law if that means the creation of new Länder organisational structures. In most cases a compromise acceptable to the Bundestag is reached, but not always. Otherwise the Bundesrat's veto is a suspensive one and can be overruled by a new vote taken in the Bundesrat with an absolute majority of its members. If, however, the Bundesrat should put in its suspensive vote with a two-thirds majority, then the Bundestag could override this on its side only with a two-thirds majority which was hardly ever a possibility in the history of the Federal Republic of Germany since 1949.[6] The document below gives the official reasons advanced by the Bundesrat in 1976 for rejecting, in accordance with Art.106, (3) of the Basic Law, the proposed increase in the value added tax which would have raised the Bund's percentage of the revenues realized from it. This document illustrates the possibilities the Bundesrat has to protect the financial integrity of the Länder.

(For Parliamentary bills rejected by the Bundesrat see Statistics 17.)

Document 3

DECISION OF THE BUNDESRAT REGARDING THE ACT TO AMEND THE VALUE ADDED TAX AND OTHER ACTS, 6 JUNE 1976

Source: Deutscher Bundesrat, Drucksache 329/76

Decision

In its 435th session of 4 June 1976 the Bundesrat—on the basis of Article 105 Para.3 of the Basic Law—has decided not to approve the act passed by the Bundestag on 13 May 1976 for the following reasons.

Reasons

In its statement on the first submission of the proposed act ... the Bundesrat had already given reasons for its intention not to approve the proposed increase in the value added tax. The objections raised then are upheld.

In addition, interim developments have strengthened doubts regarding the need for the tax increase. According to the latest economic forecasts an increase of tax revenue can be expected; the final budget of the Bund for 1975 has also resulted in a more favourable basis on the expenditure side.

In the opinion of the Bundesrat, therefore, restraints on expenditure and budgetary savings would allow in the medium-term a reduction of the structural deficits of public budgets without resorting to an increase of the value added tax.

This speech on the occasion of the 400th meeting of the Plenum of the Bundesrat suggests the continuing influence of the Bundesrat in the legislative process of the Federal Republic and the importance of the joint Mediation Committee.

Document 4

'THE FEDERAL PRINCIPLE HAS JUSTIFIED ITSELF IN THE BASIC LAW', SPEECH BY BUNDESPRÄSIDENT, KARL CARSTENS, 4 JUNE 1981

Source: Bundesrat Sekretariat

This occasion provides the opportunity to assess the importance of the Bundesrat for our constitutional system and for the well-being and future welfare of our Republic. The founding fathers of the Basic Law decided on a federal framework for our state. This reflected centuries of German constitutional tradition, the approval of the overwhelming majority of the Parliamentary Council, and, above all, the internal orientation of the Germans, who since the beginning of their history have been divided into more or less closely-bound family groups and territories.

Today, thirty-two years after the founding of the Federal Republic, we can be pleased that the federal principle has justified itself. It has been a stabilizing factor, and it has particularly facilitated cultural development.

The Bundesrat has a central role in the federal structure. In it, the Länder jointly participate in the legislative and administrative work of the Bund. They do this not only separately as Länder of the Bund, that is in their autonomous capacities, but they also work together as an organ of the Bund with unified responsibility for the good of the whole.

In the Bundesrat, above all in its committees, the expertise of the Land governments is made available for advice on Bund legislation ... . Their experience in this advisory role on proposed federal legislation is of great value ... .

It is occasionally alleged that important decisions are negated by the Bundesrat—that is, that it pursues a policy of obstruction of policies of the Bund Government and Bundestag. A careful examination of the allegation disproves it ... .

One can, of course, contend that in ... [those] instances where the joint committees had to be activated, compromises became necessary. But, in my opinion, the process of discussion, of negotiation and of compromise is an in dispensable ingredient of the democratic process.

Likewise, as it is unacceptable to view the Bundesrat as an organ of obstruction, so it is inappropriate to consider the differences between the Bundesrat and other Bund organs as primarily the reflection of political partisanship ... . The viewpoints of the Länder as such also have a very significant influence ... . But, in the final decisions ... when there are basic political questions at issue, it is entirely proper that each political party should seek to realize its objectives.

The Bundesrat might also be involved in restructuring the Federal Territory which since 1949 has only happened in very minor cases, apart, of course, from the enlargement of the reunited Germany by what are now known as the 'New Länder'. There are now 16 Länder (million inhabitants in brackets): *Baden-Württemberg* (9.7); *Bayern* (11.3); *Berlin* (3.4); *Brandenburg* (2.6); *Bremen* (0.7); *Hamburg* (1.6); *Hessen* (5.7); *Mecklenburg-Vorpommern* (1.9); *Niedersachsen* (7.3); *Nordrhein-Westfalen* (17.2); *Rheinland-Pfalz* (3.7); *Saarland* (1.1); *Sachsen* (4.8); *Sachsen-Anhalt* (2.9); *Schleswig-Holstein* (2.6); *Thüringen* (2.6).
The theoretically relevant article of the Basic Law here is:

Document 5

ART. 29. Reorganization of the Federal Territory

(1) The federal territory may be reorganized to ensure that the Länder by their size and capacity are able effectively to fulfil the functions incumbent upon them. Due regard shall be given to regional, historical and cultural ties,

economic expediency, regional policy, and the requirements of town and country planning.

(2) Measures for the reorganization of the federal territory shall be introduced by federal laws which shall be subject to confirmation by referendum. The Länder thus affected shall be consulted.

. . .

(7) Other modifications of the territory of the Länder may be effected by state agreements between the Länder concerned or by a federal law with the approval of the Bundesrat if the territory which is to be the subject or reorganization does not have more than 10,000 inhabitants. The details shall be regulated by a federal law requiring the approval of the Bundesrat and the majority of the members of the Bundestag. It must make provision for the affected communes and districts to be heard.

[An amendment to the Basic Law in September 1994 concerning an addition to the above para. 7 laid down that in future the Länder can redraw their common boundaries by state agreements between themselves without regard to the provisions of para 2 above. In such cases the local authorities have to be consulted. Any state agreement under these provisions has to be confirmed by a referendum in each of the Länder concerned ed.]

FEDERAL LEGISLATION IN THE BALANCE BETWEEN
BUND AND LÄNDER

Document 6

CONSTITUTIONAL PROVISIONS

Source: Presse- und Informationsamt der Bundesregierung

Art. 70. Legislation of the Bund and the Länder

(1) The Länder shall have the right to legislate insofar as this Basic Law does not confer legislative power on the Bund.

(2) The division of competence between the Bund and the Länder shall be determined by the provisions of this Basic Law concerning exclusive and concurrent legislative powers.

Art. 71. Exclusive Legislation of the Bund, Definition

In matters within the exclusive legislative power of the Bund the Länder shall have power to legislate only if, and to the extent that, a federal law explicitly so authorizes them.

Art. 72. Concurrent Legislation of the Bund, Definition

(1) In matters within concurrent legislative powers the Länder shall have power to legislate as long as, and to the extent that, the Bund does not exercise its right to legislate.

(2) The Federation shall have the right to legislate in these matters if and to the extent that the need for federal legislation arises in the interests of the country as a whole in order to ensure equal living conditions in the federation or to maintain its legal or economic unity.

(3) A federal law may determine that a Land law can replace federal law if a need for such federal legislation, originally deemed necessary in accordance with para 2, no longer exists.

(The above paras (2) and (3) are here quoted from the amendment of the Basic Law in September 1994 which also provided for a slight change in the text of para 1 above).

Art. 73. Exclusive Legislation, Catalogue

The Bund shall have exclusive power to legislate in the following matters:

1. foreign affairs as well as defence including the protection of the civilian population;
2. citizenship in the Bund;
3. freedom of movement, passport matters, immigration, emigration, and extradition;
4. currency, money and coinage, weights and measures, as well as the determination of standards of time;
5. the unity of the customs and commercial territory, treaties on commerce and on navigation, the freedom of movement of goods, and the exchanges of goods and payments with foreign countries, including customs and other frontier protection;
6. federal railroads and air transport;
7. postal and telecommunication services;
8. the legal status of persons employed by the Bund and by federal corporate bodies under public law;
9. industrial property rights, copyrights and publishers' rights;
10. co-operation of the Bund and the Länder in matters of a) criminal police, b) protection of the free democratic basic order, of the existence and the security of the Bund or of a Land (protection of the constitution), and c) protection against efforts in the federal territory which, by the use of force or actions in preparation for the use of force, endanger the foreign interests of the Federal Republic of Germany, as well as the establishment of a Federal Criminal Police Office and the international control of crime.
11. statistics for federal purposes.

Art. 74. Concurrent Legislation, Catalogue

Concurrent legislative powers shall extend to the following matters:

1. civil law, criminal law and execution of sentences, the organization and procedure of courts, the legal profession, notaries, and legal advice (Rechtsberatung);
2. registration of births, deaths, and marriages;
3. he law of association and assembly;
4. the law relating to residence and establishment of aliens;
4a. the law relating to weapons and explosives;

5. the protection of German cultural treasures against removal abroad;
6. refugee and expellee matters;
7. public welfare;
8. citizenship in the Länder;
9. war damage and reparations;
10. benefits to war-disabled persons and to dependents of those killed in the war as well as assistance to former prisoners of war;
10a. war graves of soldiers, graves of other victims of war and of victims of despotism;
11. the law relating to economic matters (mining, industry, supply of power, crafts, trades, commerce, banking, stock exchanges, and private insurance);
11a. the production and utilization of nuclear energy for peaceful purposes, the construction and operation of installations serving such purposes, protection against hazards arising from the release of nuclear energy or from ionizing radiation, and the disposal of radioactive substances;
12. labour law, including the legal organization of enterprises, protection of workers, employment exchanges and agencies, as well as social insurance, including unemployment insurance;
13. the regulation of educational and training grants and the promotion of scientific research;
14. the law regarding expropriation, to the extent that matters enumerated in Arts. 73 and 74 are concerned;
15. transfer of land, natural resources and means of production to public ownership or other forms of publicly controlled economy;
16. prevention of abuse of economic power;
17. promotion of agricultural and forest production, safeguarding of the supply of food, the importation and exportation of agricultural and forest products, deep sea and coastal fishing, and preservation of the coasts;
18. real estate transactions, land law and matters concerning agricultural leases, as well as housing, settlement and homestead matters;
19. measures against human and animal diseases that are communicable or otherwise endanger public health, admission to the medical profession and to other health occupations or practices, as well as trade in medicines, curatives, narcotics, and poisons;
19a. the economic viability of hospitals and the regulation of hospitalization fees;
20. protection regarding the marketing of food, drink and tobacco, of necessities of life, fodder, agricultural and forest seeds and seedlings, and protection of plants against diseases and pests, as well as the protection of animals;
21. ocean and coastal shipping as well as aids to navigation, inland navigation, meteorological services, sea routes, and inland waterways used for general traffic;
22. road traffic, motor transport, construction and maintenance of long distance highways as well as the collection of charges for the use of public highways by vehicles and the allocation of revenue therefrom;
23. non-federal railroads, except mountain railroads;

24. waste disposal, air purification, and noise abatement.
(By an amendment to the Basic Law of September 1994 points 5 and 8 in the above ennumeration were cancelled while two new points were included: 25: 'state liability' and 26: concerning human artificial insemination, and research in the whole field of genetics and regulations governing organ and tissue transplantation. The original point 5 of the ennumeration was reinserted in art 75 below.)
[A most important additional power of the Federal Government (Bund) is laid down in Article 75 of the Basic Law, ed.]:

Art. 75: General provisions of the Bund, Catalogue

Subject to the conditions laid down in Art. 72 the Bund has the right to enact so-called skeleton or framework provisions (binding the legislation of the Länder) concerning:

1. the legal status of persons in the public service of the Länder, communes, or other corporate bodies under public law, insofar as Art. 74a does not provide otherwise;
1a. the general principles governing higher education;
2. the general legal status of the press (the words 'and the film industry', originally included, were deleted);
3. hunting, nature conservation, and landscape management;
4. land distribution, regional planning, and water regime;
5. matters relating to the registration of changes of residence or domicile (Meldewesen) and to identity cards.

by an amendment to the Basic Law of September 1994 the following point 6 was inserted.

6. the protection of German cultural treasures against removal abroad.

[Two additional points were inserted in this connection by amendment in September 1994 stipulating that 'skeleton provisions shall only in exceptional cases include regulations in detail or of a self-executing nature' and further that 'if the federation enacts skeleton provisions, the Länder are required to enact the necessary land legislation within a period of time deemed appropriate and specified by law ...' ed.]

TWO EXAMPLES FOR THE IMPORTANCE OF SUCH FEDERAL *SKELETON LAWS* WHICH HAVE TO BE IMPLEMENTED BY LÄNDER LEGISLATION

The relations between the Bund and Länder in the execution of the law are also reflected in the legislation regulating the status of the career of professional civil servants *(Beamte)* (see also Ch.11, Doc.6). The civil servants include not only those in the limited areas of administration under exclusive federal control, but also the much larger numbers who are employed by the Länder and local governments and who are also frequently engaged in the execution of federal laws. These include professors, teachers, police officers, tax collectors and many others. These officials are distinguished from the more numerous public employees who occupy positions of governmental authority, but who are legally classified as salaried employees *(Angestellte)* or wage earners *(Arbeiter)*. This three-class system in the German Civil Service has long roots in German history. Differences, once considerable with regard to salaries, social security and pensions, have by now been largely abolished. However, even today, only *Beamte* can perform acts expressing state authority—such as the signing of reports in state schools or signing of birth certificates. Civil servants in the narrower sense traditionally owe a special loyalty to the constitutional order, not to the particular government in power.

Document 7a

FEDERAL CIVIL SERVICE FRAMEWORK ACT 1977 *(BEAMTENRECHTSRAHMENGESETZ)*

Source: BGBl., 6 January 1977, 23ff.

General

Art. 2. Status of the Civil Service

(1) The civil servant is bound to his employer by the terms of his employment and by loyalty.

(2) Only those can be appointed to the civil service who will exercise official functions or such functions which for reasons of state or public security generally cannot be entrusted exclusively to persons whose professional status is subject to private law.

(3) The exercise of official authority is ordinarily to be entrusted to the civil service if permanent functions are involved.

Art. 3. Nature of the Status of the Civil Service

(1) The civil service status can be based on:

1. lifetime appointment if the civil servant is to be permanently employed ... ;
2. term appointment if the civil servant is to be employed in such functions for a specific period;
3. trial appointment if the civil servant must complete a probationary period before future employment on a lifetime basis;
4. temporary appointment if the civil servant (a) must complete a preparatory service, (b) will only be employed incidentally or temporarily for assignments.

. . .

Art. 4. General Personal Requirements

(1) To be appointed to the civil service one must:

1. be a German citizen as defined by Art. 116 of the Basic Law;
2. swear to defend the free and democratic constitutional order as defined by the Basic Law;
3. have the educational background prescribed for this career or, in the absence of such prescription, the standard educational background.

. . .

Termination of the Civil Service Status

Art. 21. Reasons for Termination

(1) The civil service status ends, other than because of death, through:

1. dismissal ... ;
2. loss of the rights of the civil service;
3. removal from service in accordance with disciplinary laws;

. . .

Retirement

Art. 25. Retirement Age

The retirement age for the civil service is to be determined by law. Career civil servants retire after reaching retirement age. The point in time for the beginning of retirement is to be determined by law.

. . .

Art. 34. Members of the Governments of the Länder

It may be determined by law that the civil servant leaves office when he becomes a member of the government of his Land. In this case, it may be further specified that the civil servant who has left office enters into retirement after the end of his term in government. The same holds for any official status which corresponds to the Undersecretary of State as defined by the law governing the legal status of Undersecretaries of State [Staatssekretäre].

. . .

Functions of the Civil Servant

Art. 35. Impartial, Democratic and Political Behaviour

(1) The civil servant serves the whole people, not one party. He must fulfil his duties in an impartial and equitable manner. He must take into consideration the welfare of the general public in the administration of his office. He must defend the free and democratic constitutional order as defined in the Basic Law in every aspect of his behaviour and help preserve it.

(2) In his political activity the civil servant must observe the moderation and discretion which befits his position relative to the general public and out of consideration for the duties of his office.

Art. 36. General Professional Obligations and Behaviour

The civil servant must practice his profession with complete dedication. He must administer his position unselfishly and conscientiously. His behaviour on duty and off must evidence the respect and trust demanded of his profession.

Education, traditionally a recognized reserved field for the Länder, was the subject of attention during the 'reform period' beginning in 1969. In addition to the amended Art. 75, empowering the Bund to enact framework legislation incorporating the 'general principles governing higher education', the amendments passed in 1969/70 (Arts. 91a and 91b) contain important provisions dealing with the facilities for higher education, educational planning in general and the promotion of supra-regional institutions and projects of scientific research.

Impelled by a variety of pressures (the demands for more student capacity, adequate staffing, democratization, rising costs, relevance of programmes to social need, rationalization of administrative and budget arrangements amongst others) as presented in a number of reports, the SPD-FDP coalition government sought after 1970 to implement provisions of Art. 75 through the enactment of a framework law on higher education.

The original drafts of this proposed legislation—passed by the Bundestag in 1975—faced considerable opposition from CDU and CSU ranks, especially in the Bundesrat, which had an absolute veto in the matter due to certain administrative aspects of the framework law. The passage of the resulting compromise was, therefore, delayed until 1976. The new law provided the skeleton confines for the legal guidance of the Land legislators, who were obliged to change their Land university laws in order to implement the legislation. The law established uniform guidelines for internal university organization, student admissions, participation of staff and all other groups in the university community (teaching and research), programmes of study, the planning of integrated universities, inter-university relationships, and other matters. All these reforms changed the traditional structures of German universities as basically established in the nineteenth century. Especially controversial, both within and without the academic community, were the provisions for new modes of participation in the decision-making machinery, doing away, *inter alia,* with the absolute monopoly of Germany's so-called 'chairholders' *(Ordinarien).* Though the reform ethos has been ebbing since the early 1980s, the Hochschulrahmengesetz represents an important milestone in German university development. It also provides a significant illustration of the use of the newly acquired powers of the Bund to restrict the jurisdiction of the Länder over education.

Document 7b

FRAMEWORK ACT FOR HIGHER EDUCATION (*HOCHSCHULRAHMENGESETZ*)

Source: BGBl I, 1976, 185ff, amended several times since
Transl.: Official

Section 1

(1) Reform of higher education shall be a task to be carried out jointly by the institutions of higher education themselves and the competent government authorities.

(2) The higher education system shall be reformed with a view to combining the functions in research, teaching and studies at present performed by different types of institutions of higher education.

(3) The aim of such reform shall in particular be the following:

1. a range of interrelated study courses, phased in coordinated stages with regard to contents, schedule and final qualification in appropriate fields; to the extent that this is compatible with the contents of courses, common study segments or successive courses shall be organized;

2. a structure of courses which will permit the greatest possible transfer of credit for studies performed and examinations passed when a student transfers to another course in the same or a related field of study;

3. a combination of theoretical and practical studies appropriate for each subject;

4. the formulation and implementation of research and teaching programmes of an interdepartmental and interinstitutional nature as well as the concentration of research and teaching subjects, i.e., in coordination with other institutions of research and education and with organizations concerned with the advancement of research;

5. subject-related and interdisciplinary promotion of higher education didactics;

6. effective academic counselling;

7. the optimum use of each institution's facilities;

8. provision of research opportunities for professors at those institutions of higher education where such research opportunities do not exist or are inadequate for the fulfilment of such professors' official duties;

9. coherent planning for the higher education sector as a whole and a balanced provision of institutions of higher education both in regional and supraregional terms.

. . .

Section 9: Study Reform Commissions

(1) In order to promote the reform of studies and examinations and to coordinate and support the reform work already carried out at the individual institutions, study reform commissions shall be set up. Joint study reform commissions shall be established by the Länder for the area of application of the present Act.

(2) The study reform commissions shall be set up by the competent Länder authorities in cooperation with the institutions of higher education concerned.

. . .

Section 31: Central Allocation of Study Places

(1) Study places in courses for which admission quotas have been laid down for several institutions may be allocated by the Central Office set up jointly by the Länder. The decision to allocate places in a particular course of study by means of the procedure of the Central Office must be taken—at the earliest possible point in time—if the Central Office finds that admission quotas have been laid down for the course in question for all State institutions within the purview of this Act, and if it is to be expected that the number of applicants will exceed the total number of available places, unless the decision is left to the institutions themselves on account of the special nature of the admission requirements or the selection criteria for specific courses. Places in a particular course of study shall be allocated by means of the procedure of the Central Office if, according to the facts as registered by the latter, admission quotas have been laid down for the majority of the State institutions within the purview of this Act.

. . .

Section 38: Composition and Voting Rights

(1) The type and the extent of participation as well as the number of members in the composite bodies, committees and other bodies shall depend on the latters' tasks as well as on the qualifications, function, responsibility and involvement of the members of the institution concerned. The proportion of the votes assigned to the different groups (see subsection 2) represented on the composite central bodies and on the departmental councils (Fachbereichsräte) shall be governed by law.

(2) Each of the following shall be represented as a group on the various bodies:

1. professors,
2. students,
3. scientific assistants, artistic assistants and university assistants,
4. other staff members.

. . .

(4) In the case of decisions already affecting research, creative arts projects, teaching or the appointment of professors, the following members of the body concerned shall have the right to vote: the professors, the principal of the institution or a member of the institution's governing board (Leitungsgremium), the university, scientific and artistic assistants, the students and those persons assimilated in status under subsections (2) and (3) of section 36 ... .

(5) Any decisions directly affecting research, creative arts projects and the appointment of professors shall be based not only on the overall majority vote of the whole body but also on that of the professors in that body. If no decision is reached even in the second round of voting, the majority vote of the professors in that body shall suffice for taking the decision concerned. In the case of decisions to be taken on proposals for professional appointments,

the majority within the body shall be entitled to submit an alternative proposal of its own.

. . .

Section 62: Governance of Institutions of Higher Education

(1) Each institution shall have a full-time principal3 elected for a term of
office of at least four years; he shall be solely reponsible for running the institution concerned, maintaining order and exercising authority within the
institution, except where provision for the exercise of these duties by other
person or persons obtain. He shall give an annual account of the fulfilment
of the institution's tasks.

(2) The place of the principal of an institution may be taken by an elected
governing board with at least one full-time member; the senior administrative officer shall be an ex officio member of this body. The provisions of
this Act relating to the composite and other bodies shall not apply to the
governing board.

(3) The principal or the members of the governing board to be determined
by vote shall be elected for a limited term by a composite central body on
the basis of a proposal made by the institution concerned and appointed by
the organ responsible under Land law. Removal from office by vote shall
not be possible.

. . .

Section 64: The Department (Fachbereich)

(1) The department shall be the basic organizational unit of institutions of
higher education; notwithstanding the overall responsibility of the institution and the sphere of competence of the institution's central bodies, the
department shall fulfil the functions of the institution within its own area.
Within the framework of the facility-provision plans, it shall ensure that its
members, its scientific establishments and its operational units can fulfil the
functions incumbent on them.

(2) The organs of the department are the departmental council and the
departmental spokesman (Fachbereichssprecher).

(3) The departmental council shall be responsible for all matters within the
department concerning research and teaching, except for those for which
Land law places responsibility with the departmental spokesman.

. . .

(5) The departmental spokesman shall be elected by the departmental council from among the council's professorial members.

. . .

Document 8

AMENDMENT OF THE BASIC LAW IN 1992 CONCERNING
NEW POWERS OF THE LÄNDER IN THE LEGISLATION OF
THE EUROPEAN UNION AND A NEW STATUS FOR
NATIONALS OF THE EU IN GERMAN LOCAL ELECTIONS
Source: BGBl.1992, I, 2086

1. After article 22 the following article 23 is inserted

Article 23 [old article 23 eliminated since reunification, see p. 103, ed.]

(1) Towards the goal of achieving a united Europe, the Federal Republic of
Germany participates in the development of the European Union, which is
committed to democratic, constitutional, social and federative principles and
to the principle of subsidiarity and also guarantees a protection of basic rights
essentially comparable with this Basic Law. To this end the Federation can
with the consent of the Bundesrat transfer sovereignty by law. For the establishment of the European Union, for amendments to the treaties on which
it is based and for comparable regulations amending or adding to the substance of this Basic Law or facilitating such amendments or additions, Article 79 Par. 2 and 3 apply.

(2) On matters relating to the European Union, the Bundestag cooperates with
the Länder through the Bundesrat. The Federal Government must inform the
Bundestag and the Bundesrat fully and at the earliest possible moment.

(3) The Federal Government gives the Bundestag the opportunity of mak-
ing its views known prior to any participation in the legislative process of the
European Union. The Federal Government takes account of the views of the
Bundestag in negotiations. Details of this are regulated by a law.

(4) The Bundesrat is to participate in federal decision-making process, insofar as it would be authorized to participate in an equivalent national measure,
or insofar as the internal responsibility of the Länder would extend to this.

(5) Insofar as the interests of the Länder are affected in an area for which the
Federation is exclusively responsible, or insofar as the Federation otherwise
has the right of legislation, the Federal Government takes the views of the
Bundesrat into consideration. If, the legislative powers of the Länder, the
establishment of their agencies or their administrative procedures are
affected to any major extend, the views of the Bundesrat on federal decision
making process are to be taken into close consideration; in this connection
the overall responsibility of the Federation is to be upheld. In matters that
may lead to an increase in expenditure or to a reduction in revenue for the
federation, the consent of the Federal Government is needed.

(6) If exclusive legislative powers in the Länder are affected to any major
extent, the exercise of rights vested in the Federal Republic of Germany as a
member state of the European Union, shall be transferred by the Federation
to a representative of the Länder appointed by the Bundesrat. The exercise
of such rights occurs with the participation of and after consultation with the
Federal Government; in this connection the overall responsibility of the Federation is to be upheld.

. . .

3. After Article 28 § 1 sentence 2 the following sentence is inserted:

In local and communal elections, persons holding the nationality of a member state of the European Community are also eligible to vote or stand for election under the terms of European Community law.

THE EXECUTION OF FEDERAL LAW

Considerable attention is given in the Basic Law to administrative matters, especially in Part VIII, 'The Execution of Federal Laws and the Federal Administration'. In accordance with German traditions, the responsibility for the administration of most federal laws belongs to the Länder. While the Länder, of course, execute their own laws, for example, those dealing with education, cultural affairs, police and local government—there is a division of responsibility between the Bund and the Länder for the execution of the federal laws by the civil services of the Bund and Länder. Directly administered by the federal civil service are such matters as the foreign service, armed forces, and postal services. Administered by the Länder acting as agents of the Bund are, in particular, laws relating to federal taxes and federal highways (Auftragsverwaltung); administered by the Länder civil services as 'matters of their own concern' are all those laws which do not fall in the other categories. Where the Länder have autonomy in the administration of federal laws, any exercise of supervision by the Federal Government requires Bundesrat approval. Though the degree of flexibility allowed to the Länder in administration of federal laws varies, it is clear that most federal laws are administered by Land officials. The resulting system is often and properly referred to as one of administrative decentralization.

Document 9

THE EXECUTION OF FEDERAL LAWS AND THE FEDERAL ADMINISTRATION UNDER THE BASIC LAW

Source: Presse- und Informationsamt der Bundesregierung

Art. 83. Execution of Federal Laws by the Länder

The Länder shall execute federal laws as matters of their own concern insofar as this Basic Law does not otherwise provide or permit.

Art. 84. Land Administration and Federal Government Supervision

(1) Where the Länder execute federal laws as matters of their own concern, they shall provide for the establishment of the requisite authorities and the

regulation of administrative procedures insofar as federal laws consented to by the Bundesrat do not otherwise provide.

(2) The Federal Government may, with the consent of the Bundesrat, issue pertinent general administrative rules.

(3) The Federal Government shall exercise supervision to ensure that the Länder execute the federal laws in accordance with applicable law. For this purpose the Federal Government may send commissioners to the highest Land authorities and with their consent or, if such consent is refused, with the consent of the Bundesrat, also to subordinate authorities.

(4) Should any shortcomings which the Federal Government has found to exist in the execution of federal laws in the Länder not be corrected, the Bundesrat shall decide, on the application of the Federal Government or the Land concerned, whether such Land has violated applicable law. The decision of the Bundesrat may be challenged in the Federal Constitutional Court.

(5) With a view to the execution of federal laws, the Federal Government may be authorized by a federal law requiring the consent of the Bundesrat to issue individual instructions for particular cases. They shall be addressed to the highest Land authorities unless the Federal Government considers the matter urgent.

Art. 85. Execution by Länder as Agents of the Bund

(1) Where the Länder execute federal laws as agents of the Bund, the establishment of the requisite authorities shall remain the concern of the Länder except in sofar as federal laws consented to by the Bundesrat otherwise provide.

(2) The Federal Government may, with the consent of the Bundesrat, issue pertinent general administrative rules. It may regulate the uniform training of civil servants (Beamte) and other salaried public employees (Angestellte). The heads of authorities at the intermediate level shall be appointed with its agreement.

(3) The Land authorities shall be subject to the instructions of the appropriate highest federal authorities. Such instructions shall be addressed to the highest Land authorities unless the Federal Government considers the matter urgent. Execution of the instructions shall be ensured by the highest Land authorities.

Art. 86. Direct Federal Administration

Where the Bund executes laws by means of direct federal administration or by federal corporate bodies or institutions under public law, the Federal Government shall, insofar as the law concerned contains no special provision, issue pertinent general administrative rules. The Federal Government shall provide for the establishment of the requisite authorities insofar as the law concerned does not otherwise provide.

DISTRIBUTION OF FINANCES IN THE FEDERAL SYSTEM

The allocation of tasks to the various levels—Bund, Länder, municipalities—requires appropriate economic and financial structures. In

1969 the need to improve fiscal administration and budgetary procedures and to secure a higher degree of uniformity of living standards within the federal territory led to a series of financial reforms effected by means of amendments to the Basic Law. The following Arts. 104a–109 embody the most significant of the provisions in this field.

But even after this reform, one of the major problems remained unsolved; the municipalities have to provide most public services and are responsible for a large proportion of public investment but do not receive adequate funds from the share of public revenue directly accruing to them. This partly explains their growing financial indebtedness.

In addition things have become more complicated by the measures of regional equalization within the mechanisms of the European Community known since 1993 as the European Union (see Doc.106).

Document 10a

PROVISIONS OF THE BASIC LAW ON FINANCIAL EQUALIZATION, FISCAL ADMINISTRATION AND BUDGETARY PROCEDURE

Source: Presse- und Informationsamt der Bundesregierung

Art. 104a. Apportionment of Expenditure, Financial Assistance

(1) The Bund and the Länder shall meet separately the expenditure resulting from the discharge of their respective tasks insofar as this Basic Law does not provide otherwise.

(2) Where the Länder act as agents of the Bund, the Bund shall meet the resulting expenditure.

(3) Federal laws to be executed by the Länder and involving the disbursement of funds may provide that such funds shall be contributed wholly or in part by the Bund. Where any such law provides that the Bund shall meet one-half of the expenditure or more, the Länder shall execute it as agents of the Bund. Where any such law provides that the Länder shall meet one-quarter of the expenditure or more, it shall require the consent of the Bundesrat.

(4) The Bund may grant the Länder financial assistance for particularly important investments by the Länder or communes or associations of communes, provided that such investments are necessary to avert a disturbance of the overall economic equilibrium or to equalize differences of economic capacities within the federal territory or to promote economic growth. Details, especially concerning the kinds of investments to be promoted, shall be regulated by federal legislation requiring the consent of the Bundesrat, or by administrative arrangements based on the federal budget.

(5) The Bund and the Länder shall meet the administrative expenditure incurred by their respective authorities and shall be responsible to each other

for ensuring proper administration. Details shall be regulated by a federal law requiring the consent of the Bundesrat.

Art. 105. Customs Duties, Monopolies, Taxes-Legislation

(1) The Bund shall have exclusive power to legislate on customs matters and fiscal monopolies.

(2) The Bund shall have concurrent power to legislate on all other taxes the revenue from which accrues to it wholly or in part or where the conditions provided for in para. (2) of Art. 72 apply.

(2a) The Länder shall have power to legislate on local excise taxes as long and in sofar as they are not identical with taxes imposed by federal legislation.

(3) Federal laws relating to taxes the receipts from which accrue wholly or in part to the Länder or communes or associations of communes shall require the consent of the Bundesrat.

Art. 106. Apportionment of Tax Revenue

(1) The yield of fiscal monopolies and the revenue from the following taxes shall accrue to the Bund:

1. customs duties,
2. excise taxes insofar as they do not accrue to the Länder pursuant to para. (2) of this Article or jointly to the Bund and the Länder in accordance with paragraph (3) of this Article or to the communes in accordance with paragraph (6) of this Article.
3. the road freight tax,
4. the capital transfer taxes, the insurance tax and the tax on drafts and bills of exchange,
5. non-recurrent levies on property, and contributions imposed for the purpose of implementing the equalization of burdens legislation,
6. income and corporation surtaxes,
7. charges imposed within the framework of the European Communities.

(2) Revenue from the following taxes shall accrue to the Länder:

1. property (net worth) tax,
2. inheritance tax,
3. motor-vehicle tax,
4. such taxes on transactions as do not accrue to the Federation pursuant to para. (1) of this Article or jointly to the Federation and the Länder pursuant to para. (3) of this Article.
5. beer tax,
6. taxes on gambling establishments.

(3) Revenue from income taxes, corporation taxes and turnover taxes shall accrue jointly to the Bund and the Länder (joint taxes) to the extent that the revenue from income tax is not allocated to the communes pursuant to para. (5) of this Article. The Bund and the Länder shall share equally the revenues from income taxes and corporation taxes. The respective shares of the Bund and the Länder in the revenue from turnover tax shall be determined by federal legislation requiring the consent of the Bundesrat. Such determination shall be based on the following principles:

1. The Bund and the Länder shall have an equal claim to coverage from current revenues of their respective necessary expenditures. The extent of such expenditures shall be determined within a system of pluri-annual financial planning;
2. the coverage requirements of the Bund and of the Länder shall be coordinated in such a way that a fair balance is struck, any overburdening of taxpayers precluded, and uniformity of living standards in the federal territory ensured.

(4) The respective shares of the Bund and the Länder in the revenue from the turnover tax shall be apportioned anew whenever the relation of revenues to expenditures in the Bund develops substantially differently from that of the Länder. Where federal legislation imposes additional expenditures on, or withdraws revenue from, the Länder, the additional burden may be compensated by federal grants under federal laws requiring the consent of the Bundesrat, provided such additional burden is limited to a short period. Such laws shall lay down the principles for calculating such grants and distributing them among the Länder.

(5) A share of the revenue from income tax shall accrue to the communes, to be passed on by the Länder to their communes on the basis of income taxes paid by the inhabitants of the latter. Details shall be regulated by a federal law requiring the consent of the Bundesrat. Such law may provide that communes shall assess communal percentages of the communal share.

(6) Revenue from taxes on real property and businesses shall accrue to the communes; revenue from local excise taxes shall accrue to the communes or, as may be provided for by Land legislation, to associations of communes. Communes shall be authorized to assess the communal percentages of taxes on real property and businesses within the framework of existing laws. Where there are no communes in a Land, revenue from taxes on real property and businesses as well as from local excise taxes shall accrue to the Land. The Bund and the Länder may participate, by assessing an impost, in the revenue from the trade tax. Details regarding such impost shall be regulated by a federal law requiring the consent of the Bundesrat. Within the framework of Land legislation, taxes on real property and businesses as well as the communes' share of revenue from income tax may be taken as a basis for calculating the amount of such impost.

(7) An overall percentage, to be determined by Land legislation, of the Land share of total revenue from joint taxes shall accrue to the communes and associations of communes. In all other respects Land legislation shall determine whether and to what extent revenue from Land taxes shall accrue to communes and associations of communes.

(8) If in individual Länder or communes or associations of communes the Bund causes special facilities to be established which directly result in an increase of expenditure of a loss of revenue (special burden) to these Länder or communes or associations of communes, the Bund shall grant the necessary compensation, if and insofar as such Länder or communes or associations of communes cannot reasonably be expected to bear such special burden. In granting such compensation, due account shall be taken of third-party indem-

nities and financial benefits accruing to the Länder or communes or associations of communes concerned as a result of the institution of such facilities.

(9) For the purpose of this Article revenues and expenditures of communes and associations of communes shall be deemed to be Land revenues and expenditures.

Art. 107. Financial Equalization

(1) Revenue from Land taxes and the Land share of revenue from income and corporation taxes shall accrue to the individual Länder to the extent that such taxes are collected by revenue authorities within their respective territories (local revenue). Federal legislation requiring the consent of the Bundesrat may provide in detail for the delimitation as well as the manner and scope of allotment of local revenue from corporation and wage taxes. Legislation may also provide for the delimitation and allotment of local revenue from other taxes. The Land share of revenue from the turnover tax shall accrue to the individual Länder on a per capita basis; federal legislation requiring the consent of the Bundesrat may provide for supplemental shares not exceeding one-quarter of a Land share to be granted to Länder whose per capita revenue from Land taxes and from the income and corporation taxes is below the average of all the Länder combined.

(2) Federal legislation shall ensure a reasonable equalization between financially strong and financially weak Länder, due account being taken of the financial capacity and financial requirements of communes and associations of communes.

Such legislation shall specify the conditions governing equalization claims of Länder entitled to equalization payments and equalization liabilities of Länder owing equalization payments as well as the criteria for determining the amounts of equalization payments. Such legislation may also provide for grants to be made by the Bund from federal funds to financially weak Länder in order to complement the coverage of their general financial requirements (complemental grants).

Art. 108. Fiscal Administration

(1) Customs duties, fiscal monopolies, excise taxes subject to federal legislation, including the excise tax on imports, and charges imposed within the framework of the European Communities, shall be administered by federal revenue authorities. The organization of these authorities shall be regulated by federal legislation. The heads of authorities at the intermediate level shall be appointed in consultation with the respective Land governments.

(2) All other taxes shall be administered by Land revenue authorities. The organization of these authorities and the uniform training of their civil servants may be regulated by federal legislation requiring the consent of the Bundesrat. The heads of authorities at the intermediate level shall be appointed in agreement with the Federal Government.

(3) To the extent that taxes accruing wholly or in part to the Bund are administered by Land revenue authorities, those authorities shall act as agents of the Bund. Paras. (3) and (4) of Art. 85 shall apply, the Federal Minister of Finance being, however, substituted for the Federal Government.

. . .

Art. 109. Separate Budgets for Bund and Länder

(1) The Bund and the Länder shall be autonomous and independent of each other in their fiscal administration.

. . .

TAXES

The percentages of the total tax income from all sources for the period from 1991 to 1994 (estimates for 1993 and 1994) are shown in Doc.9b.

In the constitutional distribution of tax revenues to the Bund, the Länder and the municipalities separate allocations are made from a number of less important taxes. Of the three most productive taxes, the revenues from the corporation and income taxes are divided evenly between the Bund and the Länder, with a legally fixed proportion going to the municipalities. The third, the value added tax, is reexamined regularly. The percentage received by the Bund in 1993 was 63 per cent of the total; as of 1995, the Bund will receive 56 per cent and the Länder 44 per cent; the amounts to be paid to the European Union are met by the Bund.

The primary apportionment of the financial revenue is that between the Bund and the Länder. It is the result of what is known as 'vertical' financial equalization and is reflected in Doc. 9b below. But although in 1969 the apportionment of revenues was reformed, there remained a need for a redistribution among the 'rich' and the 'poor' Länder themselves, termed 'horizontal' financial equalization. Under the auspices of horizontal fiscal equalization, sizable amounts of money were redistributed between the Länder. With unification, all old Länder would have become net-payers into the system, whereas all new Länder would have become net recipients, thus upsetting the financial situation of those old Länder who are maturing. To avoid this, the necessary financial transfers to the new Länder were temporarily effected by a German Unity Fund, financed by the Federal Government and the Länder (see ch.10, Doc.14). Beginning 1995, the new Länder will participate fully in the horizontal fiscal equalization.

The following document gives the percentage of tax revenue accruing to the various levels of the federal system. There is, however, the problem that income tax and value added tax are due to the internal revenue office at the seat of the company. As many firms in the new Länder belong to companies in the old Länder, taxes generated in the new Länder are paid in the old Länder. Consequently, the

originary tax revenue (Table A) gives a somewhat misleading picture
of economic strength; in Table B this distortion is corrected on the
basis of the number of inhabitants.

Document 10b

PERCENTAGE OF TAX REVENUE ANNUALLY ACCRUING
TO THE BUND, LÄNDER, MUNICIPALITIES AND
EUROPEAN COMMUNITY (1991–1994, partly estimates)

Source: Bundesministerium des Finanzen, *Finanzbericht,* 1994, 111

Table A: Before apportionment of income tax and corporate income tax
and **before** the split of value added tax into a West and an East share.

	Share in total tax revenue (%)			
	1991	1992	1993	1994
Tax revenue of the Bund	48.0	48.2	47.6	47.1
Tax revenue of the Länder	34.4	34.3	34.8	34.8
Old Länder	33.2	32.8	33.1	32.9
New Länder	1.3	1.6	1.6	1.9
Tax revenues of municipalities	12.8	12.8	12.7	12.5
Old Länder	12.4	12.2	12.0	11.7
New Länder	0.4	0.6	0.7	0.8
European Community	4.8	4.7	4.9	5.7

Table B: After apportionment of income tax and corporate income tax
and redistribution of value added tax into an East and a West share

	Share in total tax revenue (%)			
	1991	1992	1993	1994
Tax revenue of the Bund	48.0	48.2	47.6	47.1
Tax revenue of the Länder	34.4	34.3	34.8	34.8
Old Länder	31.5	31.1	31.3	31.1
New Länder	2.9	3.2	3.5	3.7
Tax revenues of municipalities	12.8	12.8	12.7	12.5
Old Länder	12.4	12.1	12.0	11.6
New Länder	0.4	0.6	0.7	0.8
European Community	4.8	4.7	4.9	5.7

NEW INTERGOVERNMENTAL RELATIONS—PRACTICAL EXAMPLES

In the course of the years after the Federal Republic was set up with its
Basic Law in 1949 a myriad of shifting intergovernmental relations

emerged involving cooperation between the Länder, the Federal Financing of Länder activities and—since 1969—'joint tasks'. All these provide a multifaceted legal web of increasing complex design governing relationships between Bund and Land, between the Länder, between the Bund and the municipalities, as well as between the Länder and the municipalities and between the municipalities themselves.

Documents 11a-f

DEFINITION OF SO-CALLED 'JOINT TASKS' DEVELOPING CO-OPERATIVE FEDERALISM

Document 11a

THE DEFINITION OF 'JOINT TASKS' ADDED TO THE BASIC LAW IN MAY 1969

Source: Presse- und Informationsamt der Bundesregierung

Art. 91a

(1) The Bund shall participate in the discharge of the following responsibilities of the Länder, provided that such responsibilities are important to society as a whole and that federal participation is necessary for the improvement of living conditions (joint tasks):

1. expansion and construction of institutions of higher education including university clinics;
2. improvement of regional economic structures;
3. improvement of the agrarian structure and of coast preservation.

(2) Joint tasks shall be defined in detail by federal legislation requiring the consent of the Bundesrat. Such legislation should include general principles governing the discharge of joint tasks.

(3) Such legislation shall provide for the procedure and the institutions required for joint overall planning. The inclusion of a project in the overall planning shall require the consent of the Land in which it is to be carried out.

(4) In cases to which items 1 and 2 of para.(1) of this Article apply, the Bund shall meet one-half of the expenditure in each Land. In cases to which item 3 of para.(1) of this Article applies, the Federation shall meet at least one-half of the expenditure, and such proportion shall be the same for all the Länder. Details shall be regulated by legislation. Provision of funds shall be subject to appropriation in the budgets of the Bund and the Länder.

(5) The Federal Government and the Bundesrat shall be informed about the execution of joint tasks, should they so demand.

Art. 91 b. Co-operation of Federation and Länder in Education Planning and in Research

The Bund and the Länder may both, pursuant to agreements, co-operate in educational planning and in promotion of institutions and projects of scientific research of supraregional importance. The apportionment of costs shall be regulated in the pertinent agreements.

After 1945 the Western occupying powers and the Germans alike sought to develop a decentralized police administration. Under the occupation regime the police were organized along zonal lines, with the United States zone achieving the greatest degree of decentralization and local control. When the Basic Law was being developed, the Germans responded to the abuses of the Nazi period by recognizing the police as falling under the reserved power of the Länder. Consequently, in a return to the pre-1933 pattern, there is today no federal police force. Each Land has its own separate force under the direction of its Ministry of the Interior. None the less, the indirect influence and participation of the Bund in police affairs are substantial. The Länder are parties to administrative agreements with the Bund to provide collective action—especially in cases of national emergencies and crises. Land police officers are classified as civil servants and are covered by the Federal Civil Servants Framework Law (Doc.7a). Above all, in the early 1950s, under the impact of the Korean war with its demonstration of the 'clear and present' communist danger, special federal services were created, including the Federal Border Police *(Bundesgrenzschutz)*, the Federal Office for the Protection of the Constitution *(Bundesamt fur Verfassungsschutz)* and the Federal Crime Office *(Bundeskriminalamt)*. As well as the complex Bund-Land relationships, there are agreements covering various relationships between the police forces of the Länder themselves. Police matters thus not only involve Bund-Land but also inter-Land levels of contact under the overall federal umbrella.

In addition to its main responsibilities as a central repository of crime statistics and crime research centre, the Federal Crime Office serves as a coordinating agency for the Länder in nationwide pursuit of criminals.

Document 11b

ACT REGULATING THE ESTABLISHMENT OF THE FEDERAL CRIME OFFICE *(BUNDESKRIMINALAMT)*

Source: BGBl., I, 29 June 1973, 704ff.

Art. 1. Establishment and Function

(1) The Bund establishes a Federal Crime Office for the purpose of procuring cooperation in criminal investigations between the Bund and the Länder. Its function is to pursue any criminal element insofar as it operates, or will potentially operate, internationally or beyond the jurisdiction of a single Land.

(2) The Federal Crime Office is also the national headquarters of the International Police Organization (Interpol) for the Federal Republic of Germany.

Art. 2. Functions in Detail

(1) It is the function of the Federal Crime Office as a central agency to:

1. compile and evaluate all information and data relating to the combating of crime. In this respect it is also the headquarters for the data centre shared by the Federal Government and the Länder;
2. advise the prosecuting authorities of the Federal Government and the Länder immediately of any relevant information and of any connection which it might discover between crimes;
3. maintain the facilities for police records;
4. maintain the facilities necessary for all aspects of criminal investigation and for research on criminal practices, as well as coordinate the cooperation of police in these areas;
5. study crime patterns and compile criminal investigation analyses and statistics based on its findings;
6. conduct research on the development of police practices and on methods of combatting crime;
7. give support to the police of the Länder in the prevention of crime;
8. hold continuing education sessions on special areas of criminal investigation.

At the request of police headquarters, the public prosecutor and the courts, the Federal Crime Office gives expert advice based on police records and criminal practices.

Art. 3. Criminal Investigation Departments of the Länder

(1) To ensure cooperation between the Federal Government and the Länder, the Länder are obliged to maintain Crime Offices for their areas. These centres are to relay to the Federal Crime Office any information or data necessary for it to perform its functions.

Art. 4. Obligation of Notification of the Crime Offices of the Länder

(1) The Land Crime Offices notify the Federal Crime Office of the beginning, the interruption and the termination of a term of imprisonment imposed by the courts.

(2) The same obligation of notification is incumbent on the judicial and administrative authorities vis à vis the Land Crime Offices.

. . .

Art. 6. The Dispatch of Officials to the Police Authorities of the Länder

(1) To assist in criminal prosecutions the Federal Crime Office may dispatch officials to the Länder if so required by the responsible police authorities of the Länder.

(2) The highest Land authority is to be informed immediately.

Art. 7. Central Exercise of Police Functions in Different Länder

(1) If a crime affects more than one Land or if a connection exists with another crime in another Land, and if it is desirable that the functions of the police in regard to criminal prosecutions be carried out from a central location, the Federal Crime Office will inform the Attorney General (Generalstaatsanwalt) and the highest Land authorities in whose areas jurisdiction lies. The Federal Crime Office assigns responsibility in criminal prosecutions to a Land in agreement with the Attorney General and the highest authority of the Land on the understanding that the responsibility will be fully assumed.

(2) The Land Crime Office is responsible for the fulfilment of the responsibility assigned to the Land. The highest Land authority may designate another police authority other than the Land Crime Office as the appropriate agency.

Art. 8. Official Acts of the Executive Officers of the Federal Republic and the Länder

(1) Executive officers must notify the local police authorities immediately of any investigation within their jurisdiction unless there is good reason why this should not be done. Whenever possible local responsible police authorities should be included in the investigation proceedings.

(2) The police authorities of the Land provide information and permit inspection of its records in cases under its jurisdiction to the Federal Crime Office and to the officials dispatched by it ... The same holds true for police officials of the Länder ... .

(3) The locally responsible police authorities furnish personal and practical assistance to the officials of the Federal Crime Office, or in the case of an assignment under Art. 7, para. 1, to officials of another Land who are carrying out an investigation.

. . .

The Federal Office for the Protection of the Constitution, established by federal law in 1950, collects and passes on information to other authorities but has itself no police powers such as the power of arrest. The need to provide for special safeguards for the constitutional order must be viewed against the background of the Nazi seizure of power in 1933 and especially in the light of the division of Germany, with the 'other German state', the German Democratic Republic (GDR), forming the western outpost of Moscow's empire. While the frontier separating the DDR from the Federal Republic was heavily fortified and sealed off to prevent movement from East to West, it was possible for East Germans (and East German agents) to cross the frontier to the West without any visa or other formalities (see Ch.3). There was ample evidence of extensive East German subversive activities in the Federal Republic, including considerable financial assistance to the Moscow-dominated *Deutsche Kommunistische Partei* (DKP) annually.

Since the Länder governments also established similar offices, the cooperation between the Bund and the constituent states had to be laid down in a special agreement, published in excerpts below.

Document 11c

ACT REGULATING THE COOPERATION OF THE FEDERAL GOVERNMENT AND THE LÄNDER IN MATTERS RELATING TO THE PROTECTION OF THE CONSTITUTION *(BUNDESAMT FÜR VERFASSUNGSSCHUTZ, LANDESÄMTER FÜR VERFASSUNGSSCHUTZ)*

Source: Federal Gazette, I, 7 September 1950, 282

Art. 1. Duty of the Bund and the Länder to Cooperate

(1) The Bund and the Länder are obliged to cooperate in matters relating to the protection of the Constitution
(2) Cooperation involves mutual support and assistance.

Art. 2. Federal Office for the Protection of the Constitution

(1) The Federal Government establishes a Federal Office for the Protection of the Constitution as the highest federal authority to realize cooperation between the Federal Government and the Länder. It is placed under the jurisdiction of the Federal Minister of the Interior.
(2) Each Land appoints an authority to deal with matters relating to the protection of the Constitution to implement the cooperation of the Länder with the Federal Government.

Art. 3. Functions of the Federal Office for the Protection of the Constitution

(1) The function of the Federal Office for the Protection of the Constitution and the authorities established under Art. 2, para (2) is the compilation and interpretation of information, intelligence and other data dealing with:

1. efforts which are directed against the stability and security of the Federal Republic or of a Land, or which have as an objective unlawful infringe-

ment on the administrative activities of members of constitutional bodies
of the Federal Republic;

2. threats to security or espionage activities within the scope of this law on
behalf of a foreign power;

3. activities falling within the scope of this law which endanger the foreign
interests of the Federal Republic and which involve the use of force or a
conspiracy to use force.

(2) Further, the Federal Office for the Protection of the Constitution and
the authorities appointed under Art. 2, para. (2), will co-operate in:

1. the investigation of persons who will be entrusted with data, subject matter or information which must be kept secret in the public interest, and of
persons who are believed to have access to or who are capable of gaining
access to such materials;

2. the investigation of persons who are employed or who will be so
employed in sensitive security areas which are essential to life and defense;

3. technical security measures for the protection of data, subject matter or
information which must be kept secret from unauthorized persons.

(3) The Federal Office for the Protection of the Constitution has no police
or supervisory powers. To carry out its duties in accordance with paras. (1)
and (2), it may make use of intelligence service resources. The Office may
not become affiliated with a police authority.

(4) The courts and authorities and the Federal Office for the Protection of
the Constitution cooperate with each other in providing legal and administrative assistance (Art. 35, Basic Law).

Art. 4. Reciprocal Information

(1) The Federal Office for the Protection of the Constitution gives the
authorities established in each Land under Art. 2, para. (2), all data required
by the Land to protect the constitution.

(2) The authorities established in the Länder keep the Federal Office
informed of all those matters relating to the protection of the constitution
which come to their attention and which are important either to the Federal
Republic, to the Länder, or to both.

(3) If an authority other than the supreme Land authority is appointed
under Art. 2, Sec. 2, the supreme Land authority is to be so advised.

Art. 5. Authority to Issue Directives

(1) When an attack on the constitutional order of the Federal Republic is initiated, the Federal Government may issue to the highest Land authorities
directives requiring the cooperation of the Länder with the Federal Republic in the protection of the Constitution.

The Federal Border Police *(Bundesgrenzschutz)*, established in 1951,
had the statutory responsibility to carry out duties on the frontier cross-
ings of the Federal Republic and had to observe, more especially, the
former division line between the two Germanies, sealed off with barbed

wire and electronic and explosive devices by the East German government. As a result of terrorist activities in the 1970s, the Bundesgrenzschutz established a special anti-terrorist unit (the so-called GSG 9 force). Only the Land Bavaria has its own, separate border police force, the Bayrische Grenzschutzpolizei.

Document 11d

LAW CONCERNING THE ORGANIZATION OF THE BAVARIAN LAND POLICE, 10 AUGUST 1976 *(POLIZEIORGANISATIONSGESETZ)*

Source: GVB., 1976, 303ff.

. . .

Art. 4. The Land Police

(1) The Bavarian Land Police has the responsibility within the entire state [*sic*] territory for all tasks incumbent on a police force except when particular local and specialized units ... are responsible.

. . .

Art. 5. The Border Police

(1) The Bavarian Border Police are charged with the protection of the state territory ... . The [border protection] consists of:

1. the surveillance of the borders of the Land,
2. the supervision of the border-crossing traffic including
   (a) the checking of the legal documents required for border crossing,
   (b) criminal investigation emanating outside federal territory,
   (c) the prevention of disturbances and protection against threats and dangers which jeopardize the security of the border territory, within an area of up to 30 km from the frontier.

(2) The State Ministry of the Interior can within the border territory authorize the Border Police to substitute for the Land Police.

. . .

Art. 7. Land Crime Office

(1) The Land Crime Office is the central office in charge of criminal investigations. It is directly subordinate to the State Ministry of the Interior. Furthermore, the Land Crime Office is also the central headquarters for the criminal police within the meaning of the Act for the Creation of the Federal Crime Office, for data processing and data transmission for the police ... .

The Königstein Administrative Agreement of 31 March 1949 provided for the financing of scientific research institutions, including the world famous Max Planck Institutes (especially for the natural sciences). This agreement was subsequently extended several times. It is a good example of early cooperative agreements between the Länder which were arranged outside of the provisions of the Basic Law.

Document 11e

THE KÖNIGSTEIN AGREEMENT OF THE LÄNDER OF THE FEDERAL REPUBLIC OF GERMANY ON THE FINANCING OF SCIENTIFIC RESEARCH FACILITIES, 31 MARCH 1949

Source: Xerox copy, Archiv Kultusministerkonferenz, Bonn

The Länder of Baden, Bavaria, Lower Saxony, North-Rhine-Westfalia, Rhineland-Palatinate, Schleswig-Holstein, Württemberg-Baden, Württemberg Hohenzollern, represented by their Minister Presidents, the Hanseatic city of Hamburg, represented by the Senate, the Free Hanseatic city of Bremen, represented by the President of the Senate, have concluded the following agreement:

Art. 1

Under the terms of this agreement, the signatories undertake to raise jointly the necessary funds for German scientific research facilities whose functions and significance exceed the general sphere of activity of a single Land and whose need for support exceeds the financial capability of a single Land ... .

Art. 2

In order to spend the public funds available for research purposes efficiently and to keep the budgetary accounts straight, the signatories assume that the research facilities to be financed jointly by the Länder are not simultaneously receiving subsidies from the Bund ... .

. . .

Art. 4

The signatories agree that the Länder should be afforded due representation in the Senate of the Max Planck Institute.

Art. 5

The signatories will determine annually the total demands on the funds to be made available by the Länder. They may make the availability of these funds conditional on an appropriate portion of the subsidy requirements of a research facility being covered by the Land in which that research facility has its headquarters.

Art. 6

The sum of the funds to be raised jointly will be assessed for each Land at two thirds based on tax income and one-third based on population. Tax income is increased or reduced relative to the amounts which a Land receives from other Länder or which they pay other Länder within the framework of the general financial settlement.

Art.7

The agreement will run initially for five years. It enters into force on 1 April 1949.

An important example of inter-governmental Länder cooperation is the Standing Conference of the Länder Ministers of Education. This agreement was designed to secure a minimum of uniformity in the educational systems throughout the Bund.

Document 11f

STANDING CONFERENCE OF THE MINISTERS OF EDUCATION, SCIENCE AND CULTURAL AFFAIRS OF THE LÄNDER *(STÄNDIGE KONFERENZ DER KULTUSMINISTER)*

Source: Secretariat of Standing Conference, 1982
Transl.: Secretariat

The Standing Conference is a voluntary body of the ministers (in some cases called senators) in the Länder, including Berlin (West), responsible for education, science and research, and cultural affairs. This institution which, since 1948, has evolved under the shortened name *Kultusministerkonferenz* is not provided for in the constitution. It operates along pragmatic lines, by consultation, mutual information-gathering and discussion. Its function is to deal with 'matters of cultural policy of supraregional importance with the objective to reach common opinions and aims, and representing common interests' (preamble of the standing orders). One of the main tasks of the Standing Conferences is that of co ordination. According to the Basic Law, the legislative body and the government in each Land are responsible for all educational and cultural affairs within the area of the respective territory However, as each Land in the Federal Republic of Germany is a member of the Bund, the activity of one Land is never without influence upon its neighbour; in addition, each Land must be aware of its joint responsibility.

The *plenary* of the Conference consists of the ministers of education, science and cultural affairs of the Länder of the Federal Republic of Germany, including Berlin. It meets at intervals of about eight weeks. Each minister, i.e., each Land, has only one vote. Problems must be discussed as long as it takes to reach a conclusion which is acceptable to all parties concerned. The resolutions of the Conference can only be adopted unanimously. The *ministers' deputies* (senior officials) also meet regularly.

Four major *standing committees* are concerned with the preparation of the decisions to be taken by the plenary:

1. the schools committee

2. the committee on higher education
3. the committee on art and adult education
4. the committee on German, European and International schools abroad

The Conference has also set up various *commissions:* for international affairs, statistics, forecasting and educational economics (i.e., the data commission), and sport. The Länder are represented on the committees and commissions by the officials concerned with these fields of activity. The standing commission for study reform, likewise appointed by the Standing Conference, consists half of representatives of institutions of higher education.

Secretariat

The Standing Conference is served by a Secretariat located at Bonn ... . The Secretariat prepares the plenary, committee and commission meetings and undertakes the evaluation and implementation of the results. It also maintains the flow of information among the education ministries and is a point of contact between them and the federal authorities and other supra-regional institutions, especially as concerns external cultural relations and international and supranational co-operation in the field of educational and cultural policy ... .

THE FEDERAL CONSTITUTIONAL COURT AS PROTECTOR OF LÄNDER RIGHTS

Three examples—Documents 12a-c (see also Ch.10)

The manner in which federalism is protected by the Federal Constitutional Court is illustrated by its 1957 decision on the continuing validity of the Concordat concluded in 1933 between the Hitler government and the Vatican. The Court had to decide whether the treaty-making power of the Reich government exercised in 1933 could, if the treaty were still valid, nullify school legislation of a Land passed in accordance with the provisions of the 1949 Basic Law, which accorded exclusive powers to the states over public instruction. The case, brought on petition of the federal government as plaintiff, was dismissed on the grounds that certain provisions of the constitution, and especially those dealing with the Land powers in educational matters, absolved the Land from abiding by the conflicting Concordat provisions regarding the establishment of public (or state) schools.

Document 12a

CONCORDAT DECISION OF THE FEDERAL CONSTITUTIONAL COURT

Source: Entscheidungen des Bundesverfassungsgerichts, Vol. 6, 1957, 309ff.

A difference of opinion exists between the Land Government of Lower Saxony and the Federal Government over the rights and obligations of the Federal government and the Länder under the Basic Law. The Federal

Constitutional Court decides where such differences exist (Art. 93, para. 1, item 3, Basic Law; Art. 13, item 17, Federal Constitutional Court Law).

According to Art. 68 of the Federal Constitutional Court Law, the petitioner for the Federal Republic in such cases may only be the Federal Government ... . The resolution of the Federal Government was adopted on 9 March 1955 and requested the Federal Constitutional Court to determine whether the Reich Concordat is valid, and whether the Lower Saxony Education Act was compatible with the Reich Concordat.

The Reich Concordat remained in effect under international and domestic law throughout the duration of the National Socialist regime. The repeated and serious violations of the Reich Concordat ... by the National Socialist Government and party agencies did not detract from its legal validity. Rather it gave the injured party the right to withdraw from the contract or to demand its fulfilment. However, the Holy See adhered to the Reich Concordat and in numerous instances, which were climaxed by the Encyclical 'With Deep Anxiety' of 24 March 1937, never ceased protesting against the 'evasion of contract, erosion of contract and finally more or less public breach of contract' by the National Socialist state. In spite of violations of the Concordat and their attacks on the Church and Christianity, the National Socialists never renounced the Concordat or declared it void ... .

During the period of the increasing attack on the Church in the years from 1937–1939, efforts were made by National Socialist party agencies and by government circles to declare certain articles of the Concordat invalid. Later they conspired to nullify the entire agreement. The Reich Government in fact considered issuing a Reich Education Act which would have been incompatible with the education provisions of the Reich Concordat. Nevertheless, this proposal did not progress beyond internal discussion and no notice of cancellation was ever issued ... .

Although the National Socialist regime disregarded the Reich Concordat to an ever increasing degree and the Church regarded it from the beginning as more of a *concordatum defensionis* than a *concordatum amicitiae,* neither party ever questioned its continuing validity.

The Reich Concordat ... did not lose its validity through the collapse of National Socialist tyranny ... .

The Occupation Powers did not abrogate the Reich Concordat. Such action would have had no effect under international law. The Concordat, like other treaties with neutral states, lay outside the unilateral jurisdiction of the Occupation Powers. Decrees of the Occupation Powers could at most have had only domestic application ... .

The continuing validity of the Reich Concordat under international law has resulted in a situation in which the mutual obligations arising from the treaty must be honoured by the treaty partners. Within the purview of the Basic Law, the Federal Republic, that is, constitutionally the Federal Government and the Länder as a whole, is considered to be a party to the Concordat. According to the constitutional law of the Federal Republic, the obligations arising from the education provisions of the Concordat can only be fulfilled by the Länder, since the Federal Government does not possess legislative authority in education matters. The outcome of the present litigation hinges on the question of whether the Federal Government can demand that the Länder comply with the educational provisions [of the Concordat]. This must be answered affirmatively if it is established that the Länder have a constitutional obligation to the Federal Republic to observe those provisions in formulating their education laws.

. . .

As has already been stated, the Basic Law denied the Federal Government legislative and administrative jurisdiction over education matters, assigning this field to the exclusive responsibility of the Länder. It did not thereby ignore the education provisions of the Reich Concordat, but instead left it to the Länder to decide on their own responsibility and with complete freedom how to fashion their education laws in view of the obligations of the Federal Republic to the Reich Concordat under international law. In addition, it did not give the Federal Government the authority constitutionally to interfere in the formulation of objectives in the fulfilment of this task ... .

This treaty was concluded under international law within the competence of the German Reich. The Federal Republic of Germany inherited the obligations arising from this treaty itself since, as a result of her identification with the German Reich, she assumes responsibility for its state treaties under international law. But the Basic Law made available to the Federal government no vehicle by which it could either satisfy the education provisions of the Reich Concordat itself or ensure their observance ... .

[It could be] conjectured that the Basic Law intended to provide the greatest possible insurance that the treaty would be honoured. This conjecture cannot however be sustained where, as here, it is clear that the framers of the Basic Law were not prepared to equip the Federal Government with the necessary means to ensure the fulfilment of the education provisions of the Reich Concordat. The legal consequences flowing from the treaty under international law which binds the Federation rests for its member states exclusively on the provisions of constitutional law ... . This relationship cannot be based on international law.

It is not necessary to determine whether the Federal Republic of Germany is liable for violating the Concordat. Even the liability of the Federal Government under international law cannot change its relation to the Land under constitutional law.

The petition of the Federal Government is unfounded. If the Education Act of Lower Saxony conflicts with the education provision of the Reich Concordat, the rights of the Federal Government vis-a-vis the Land are not violated as a result. Thus it will not be necessary to examine the technical compatibility of the Lower Saxony Education Act with the provisions of the Reich Concordat. The petition of the Federal Government is therefore rejected.

A second case had considerable political undertones and must be read in the light of the intentions and actions of Chancellor Adenauer who was at the time strongly opposed by the SPD-governed

Länder. Adenauer had established by administrative fiat a second television channel (German Television Limited). This action was challenged by all of the Länder with SPD governments as a violation of both their rights over cultural affairs and the principle of federal comity (Bundestreue) in the procedures which the Bonn government had followed. In the court hearings the aggrieved Länder placed reliance on Art. 30 of the Basic Law ('The exercise of governmental powers and the discharge of governmental functions shall be incumbent on the Länder insofar as the Basic Law does not otherwise prescribe or permit') and on Art. 70, para. 1 ('The Länder shall have the right to legislate insofar as the Basic Law does not confer legislative power on the Federation'). The federal government relied chiefly on Art. 73, para. 7, and Art. 87, para. 1, which granted exclusive authority to the federal government to legislate regarding 'postal and telecommunication services' and, as a matter of direct federal administration, to administer 'the federal postal service'.

The case represented the high water mark in the Court's sharp rejection of certain of the federal government's expansionist claims and, while its impact has been modified over time, it still provides a legal bulwark for Länder powers over broadcasting and television. This famous decision led in fact to the setting up of a 'Second German Television' (Zweites Deutsches Fernsehen—ZDF) in 1961 by means of an interstate treaty (Staatsvertrag zwischen den Ländern). On the governing board of the ZDF, however, are represented not only all the Länder and the Bund, but also all political parties with caucuses in parliament and the most important interest groups (see also Ch.13, Doc.11).

Document 12b

'TELEVISION DECISION' OF THE FEDERAL CONSTITUTIONAL COURT

Source: Entscheidungen des Bundesverfassungsgerichts, Vol. 12, 1961, 205ff. (cf. Ch. 11)

As a method of mass communication, the broadcasting system belongs to the same family as the press and film. Art. 5, para. (1) of the Basic Law mentions all three in one line. The legislative competence of the Federal Government is expressly limited to the general legal status of the press and films in Art. 75, item 2 of the Basic Law. The broadcasting system is not mentioned in this Article. Any interpretation which takes into account the context of the provisions of the Basic Law cannot presume that exclusive legislative competence over broadcasting as a whole is vested in the Federal

Government, while for the press and films this competence is limited to the enactment of framework legislation governing legal status.

In defining the legislative competence of the Federal Government and the Länder the Basic Law begins with the concept of Land jurisdiction. The Federal Government has legislative jurisdiction only when expressly granted in the Basic Law (Art. 70, para. 1). Thus, as a rule the legislative competence of the Federal Government can be based only on the express grant of such jurisdiction in the Basic Law. Doubt as to the jurisdiction of the Federal Government must therefore be resolved against its competency, as the Basic Law calls for a strict interpretation of Arts. 73ff.

Added to the above is the fact that the broadcasting system belongs to the cultural sphere. According to fundamental decisions of the Basic Law, insofar as cultural matters can be administered and regulated by the state, ... they fall under the jurisdiction of the Länder, so long as no specific provisions of the Basic Law introduce limits, restrictions or exceptions in favour of the Federal Government. This basic principle of the Basic Law, which is one favouring the federal structure in the interests of an effective division of power, precisely excludes any federal jurisdiction in cultural matters in the absence of any clauses containing exceptions in the Basic Law. No such clause exists ... . The Bund lacks any authority to regulate broadcasting beyond the technical aspects of transmission.

In the German federal state, all constitutional relationships between the state as a whole and its members, as well as the constitutional relationship between Länder, are governed by the unwritten constitutional principle of reciprocal obligation of the Bund and Länder to behave in a pro-federal manner ... . From this the Federal Constitutional Court has developed a number of concrete legal obligations. In connection with the consideration of the constitutionality of the so-called horizontal financial equalization, the Federal Constitutional Court stated: 'By its nature the federal principle establishes not only rights, but also obligations. One such obligation is the duty of the financially stronger Länder to assist the weaker Länder, within certain limits ... .' This constitutional principle can further impose an increased obligation on all participants to cooperate in instances in which the law calls for agreement between the Federal Government and the Länder ... . In the decision to grant Christmas bonuses to public employees the Länder must comply with the principle of federal comity (Bundestreue) and thus take into account the overall financial structure of the Federal Government and the Länder. This restriction resulting from the concept of federal comity is even more applicable in the exercise of legislative authority. If the effects of a law extend beyond the boundaries of a Land, then the Land legislators must take into account the interests of the Federal Government and the other Länder ... . The constitutional principle of the obligation to act in a pro-federal manner can further include the obligation of the Länder to respect treaties of the Federal Republic under international law ... . On the basis of its obligation of federal comity, a Land may be potentially obliged to use its supervisory authority over local government to intervene against communities whose actions are encroaching on matters under expressly federal jurisdiction. As has been indicated, the principle of pro-federal behaviour is also of fundamental importance ... in the area of broadcasting.

The case in question presents an opportunity to develop another aspect of the constitutional obligation to act in a pro-federal manner. Even the procedure and the style of the negotiations necessary in constitutional life between the Federal Republic and its member states and between Länder are subject to the rule of pro-federal behaviour. In the Federal Republic all Länder have the same constitutional status and have the right to the same treatment in dealing with the Federal Government. In seeking a relevant agreement to a constitutional question which involves all of the Länder, the obligation to behave in a pro-federal manner prohibits the Federal Republic from working from the premise of 'divide and conquer'. In other words, the Federal Republic may not take advantage of rifts between Länder by seeking an agreement with some and then pressuring the others to join as well. In negotiations which affect all of the Länder, that principle also prevents the Federal Republic from treating the Länder governments differently according to their political leanings and especially from including in politically decisive discussions only those representatives who are closely connected with politically friendly Länder governments ... . [The procedures followed by the Federal Government in this and other respects] violated the obligation to act in a pro-federal manner ... .

In an unpublished paper on 'The West German Federal System and the Constitutional Court' (1981), Professor Wolfgang Zeidler, the then Vice President of the Court, commented on the role of the Court:

Document 12c

EVALUATION OF DECISIONS BY THE FEDERAL CONSTITUTIONAL COURT RESPECTING FEDERALISM GENERALLY

Source: Federal Constitutional Court

. . .

Decisions of the Federal Constitutional Court have ranged, in the realm of taxation, from the validation of Länder taxes on juke-boxes, pinball machines and other entertainments ... to that of special federal duties on the wine trade or road freight traffic or that on incomes in accordance with the requirements of the economy ... ; from the disallowance of a special local import tax for Helgoland to that of a Land tax on the sale of ice cream ... . Decisions concerning social matters have upheld federal provisions for family allowances, for employers' contributions to employees' pension insurance and for accident insurance ... . In the field of criminal law and public order decisions have covered a variety of subjects, from the assignment to federal or Länder jurisdiction of provisions of Reich laws on explosives and weapons to the denial that existing law on casinos belonged to the federal sphere of competence ... ; from the constitutionality of Land legislation for the expropriation of Hamburg's dikes to confirmation of federal road traffic provisions ... ; from the federal law on the dissemination of literature harmful to young people, to the power to prohibit the importation of films for reasons of public order and security ... .

The importance for the federal system of some of these cases taken individually may appear to be slight. Yet the cumulative effect is substantial. In an examination of these decisions affecting the balance of power between Bund and Länder, ... some differentiation is necessary. As those judgments which went in favour of the Bund were in conformity with the general trend towards the expansion of federal power, they have remained in effect and unchallenged. If this is also true of many decisions in favour of the Länder, the explanation is that many of these decisions concerned relatively minor questions or activities ... . However, other federalist decisions favouring the Länder are more far-reaching in their effects, and it might be expected that some of these would in time be reversed, ignored or eroded. Yet, so far, this has occurred only to a limited extent ... .

Notes

1. The Enquete Kommission published its report in 1976; see Drucksache 7, Deutscher Bundestag, Bonn
2. See also R. Taylor Cole, 'West German Federalism Revisited', *American Journal of Comparative Law,* Spring 1975, 234–36
3. See Philip M. Blair, *Federalism and Judicial Review in West Germany,* Oxford, 1981
4. A two-thirds majority in the Bundestag has never so far been achieved for any one political party. See Statistics 17 for the very small number of bills which did not finally come under Statute Books on account of a final veto by the Bundesrat.
5. The provisions concerning various time limits to be observed in the process of federal legislation were changed by an amendment of September 1994 to article 76 para 2. This i.a. enables the Bundesrat now to make use of a period of up to nine weeks for its scrutinizing of bills in special cases.
6. See footnote 4.

13
Public Opinion: Interest Groups and the Media

Detlev Karsten

In general, interest groups are mediators between the economic and the socio-cultural spheres on the one hand and the political system on the other. The existence and the official recognition of interest groups is characteristic of a pluralistic society; the underlying assumption is that the commonweal can only be reached by taking many different group interests into consideration. In a socialist system like that which existed in the GDR, the common interest is defined by the ruling party-line. There is no room for a formal representation of diverging group interests or for media which express thoughts which deviate from the officially proclaimed views. Consequently, this whole field—insofar as it existed in the GDR—was in one way or the other controlled by the party and the state apparatus; in particular the Stasi (see also Ch.3) watched carefully over all dissenters and non-conformists.*

Reunification meant the transition to a pluralistic system. Not surprisingly, the structures existing in the old Länder were taken over. This change was particularly difficult in the media-sector, because in the GDR this field was fully controlled by the state and the party. Also, most of the media people—at least in high positions—had been staunch supporters of the old system: this, after all, had been a decisive criterion in their recruitment. Moreover, many were actually compromised by or suspected of links with the Stasi. As a result, the personnel for the new beginning came mainly from the old Länder. This also applies to the leading functionaries of all other interest groups. In practice, the western organizations extended their operations to the new Länder, and for the task of organizing their representation in the East, they delegated their own people. All this contributed to the impression occasionally articulated by people in the new Länder that they were colonized. It fits into this picture, that—with the partial exception of the PDS (see also Ch.8)—neither a major organization,

---

* Notes for this chapter begin on p. 396.

nor an important nationwide newspaper or television-station has become the mouthpiece of the people in the new Länder.

This 'state of workers and peasants' (see also Ch.3) did not have free trade unions, either. In fact, the existing unions were part of the state apparatus; they were in Marxist-Leninist terms described as 'transmission belts': their function was to transmit to the workers the decisions of the party and the government. They also organized leisure and recreational activities, such as youth groups and provided holiday facilities, such as guest-houses and hotels in resort areas. Membership was practically compulsory. Again, with reunification, the old structures were dissolved and replaced by the trade-union system of the old FRG.

As in other democratic states, German interest groups pursue their aims by formulating and communicating the viewpoints of their members, although it is not uncommon that the officials develop interests of their own which are not necessarily identical with the interests of the members. In addition to influencing public opinion, interest groups work by feeding information into the political system, by exerting pressure on individual decisionmakers, by direct participation in political processes, e.g. by bringing 'their' representatives into political parties and into administrative positions and parliaments on the local, Länder or federal levels. Occasionally interest groups give support—financial or other—to political parties or individual politicians. Internally, most interest groups—in particular economically motivated groups—perform important functions for their members. They are a source of information and advice especially on matters of economic policy, but also on all kinds of business questions.

Some interest groups entertain close relationships with political parties. Thus, both the CDU/CSU and the FDP enjoy the support of the business community; the CDU/CSU reflect to some extent views of the churches; and the interests of the workers and the labour unions are traditionally represented by the SPD (see also Ch.8).

The overall importance of particular interest groups depends on the interest they represent, on their membership, on their economic strength, on their access to politicians and the media and on the role given to them in the economic and social system. Their influence also depends on whether they act on the local, Länder or federal levels; by now, some are also represented at the level of the European Union.

In the economic field, the most conspicuous interest groups are the various associations of business firms and the trade unions. The trade unions and the employers' associations are especially important because they are the partners in the collective bargaining over wages and other conditions of employment—a field of action which is legally protected against government interference. The employers' associations and the trade unions are represented in most institutions responsible for social policy.

The associations in which firms are organised are described in Doc.1. An interesting feature is the fact that the firms are really represented by three categories of associations:

The Chambers of Industry and Commerce (Industrie- und Handelskammern), which on account of their comprehensive and compulsory membership and due to their public law status cannot pursue particular interests of individual industrial branches.The employers' associations (Arbeitgeberverbände) whose main field is collective bargaining and social policy.The industrial business associations which represent the economic policy interests of their members and which are in fact the real pressure groups. This is particularly true for the powerful Federation of German Industries (Bundesverband der Deutschen Industrie—BDI). An example of the rather outspoken demands which such industrial business associations put to politicians is Doc.2.

The existence of the last two groups has the effect that the first (the employers associations) can remain fairly moderate in their demands and keep a reasonable working relationship with the trade unions, while at the same time industrial business associations and the Federation of German Industries engage in very strong lobbying by expressing interests and opinions which in content and form disqualify them in the eyes of the trade unions as partners in negotiations.

A special feature of the political and social system of post war Germany are the principles along which the trade unions are organized. They are, on the one hand, industrial unions (Industriegewerkschaften), which means that *all* workers of a branch of industry are represented by one union. But they are also unitary unions (Einheitsgewerkschaften), because—at least in theory—they are neutral vis-a-vis political parties and religious denominations. As the industrial union principle implies that basically all employees of a firm belong to the same union, it contributes to a reduction of conflict within firms and in the number of industrial disputes: each employer or employers' association has only one partner in collective bargaining. The unitary trade union is an accomplishment of the post war period. This organizational principle and the ideological neutrality were chosen against the background of negative experiences with professionally organized unions which were also ideologically divided in the Weimar Republic.

The dominant trade union organisation is the Federation of German Trade Unions (Deutscher Gewerkschaftsbund-DGB). The power of the DGB is in a way derived from the power of the individual industrial unions. The Metal Workers' Union (Industriegewerkschaft Metall) occupies a key position in terms of both membership and wealth. About 11 million, or 85 per cent (all figures for 1992) of all organized workers are in unions which belong to the Federation of German Trade Unions which is described in Doc.3. There is also a competing union: the Federation of Christian Trade Unions; its membership is about 315,000, or 2.4 per cent of the total number of workers. In addition there are two organizations which are similar to trade unions: the German Union of Salaried Employees (Deutsche Angestelltengewerkschaft) whose membership was about 580,000 in 1992 and the German Civil Service Federation (Deutscher Beamtenbund) whose membership was about 1.1 million in 1992. Altogether, about 40 per cent of the labour force are organized in all these unions.

As an example of a statement of the unions, Doc.4 gives the trade union view on the issue of lockout. Another important field where the interests and opinions of the employers' federation and the trade unions differ is co-determination at the board level.[1]

An interest group which—in spite of comparatively small membership—is politically quite influential is the German Farmers' Association (Deutscher Bauernverband). As an example, Doc.5 gives its views on the preservation of the family farm.

In addition to these very powerful groups, there are virtually thousands of other organisations covering practically all social activities and interests. These range from automobile associations to sports clubs, from house owners to the associations of refugees, from gardening to literature clubs. Consumer associations, although supported by public funds, have not gained a major significance.

But in addition to these forms of established representation of interests, a new phenomenon—citizens' action groups (Bürgerinitiativen)—has developed during the last decades. Most such citizens' action groups were originally formed to prevent something: the construction of a nuclear power station, the building of a highway through a resort area, the demolition of an old quarter of the town, etc.; very often these citizens' action groups have only local significance. By now, there are thousands of such citizens' action groups. Because of their goals and in particular because of their often uncompromising methods of pursuing these goals—some citizens' action groups do not shy away from violence—these citizens' action groups have developed into a major problem for the administrations and for the politicians. Today, citizens' action groups do not restrict themselves to obstruction, but they try to formulate alternatives of an environmentally healthy, socially just, peaceful, decentralized social and political system with strong citizen participation. Since citizens' action groups have also organized themselves into larger structures, e.g. in the form of associations of citizens' action groups, and as they entertain close relationships with the new Green Party (see also Ch.8) they are considered a threat to the established party structure. Doc.6 gives the views of the Federal Association of Citizens' Action Groups for Environmental Protection *(Bundesverband Bürgerinitiativen Umweltschutz)* on strategic issues.

Both the two dominant churches in Germany, the (Protestant) Evangelical Church in Germany *(Evangelische Kirche in Deutschland)*[2] and the Catholic Church *(Katholische Kirche)* have on occasion appeared as powerful pressure groups. About 85 per cent of the population in the old Länder belongs to these Christian Churches, divided almost equally between Catholic and Protestant. In the new Länder, the share is much lower: about 27 per cent of the population belongs to the Evangelical church and 6 per cent to the Catholic church. The legal position of these two churches is interesting because there is neither a State church nor are the churches merely private associations: the churches have a special status as corporate bodies under public law. There is a church tax which is collected by state revenue offices or local authorities; the churches pay the administrative cost of this service. The churches have a claim to financial allocations from the state which, for example, pays in whole or in part the cost of certain church facilities (e.g. hospitals, old people's homes, etc.). To resign from a church, a member must make a declaration to a state authority. Altogether, the links between the churches and the state are fairly close, a fact which has been criticised for a long time by the Liberal Party, the FDP, with its traditional insistence on a clear separation of state and church (Doc.7) (see also Ch.11).

The churches themselves are important factors in the forming of public opinion. During election campaigns representatives of the Catholic Church in particular have occasionally tried to influence the electorate. Sometimes, on issues of lasting importance, the churches publish their views in memoranda which then typically receive considerable public attention. Two examples are reproduced here: Doc.8 is an excerpt from a memorandum of the lay organisation of the Catholic Church on family policy, and Doc.9 is an excerpt from the 1981 peace memorandum of the Protestant Church.

Until the mid 1980s, the right to broadcast rested exclusively with self-administered corporations under public law. Since then, in response to new technical developments (new terrestrial frequencies, cable and satellite), this exclusively public broadcasting system is being replaced by a dual system in which private companies operate alongside the public law corporations.

The public law corporations are not profit-orientated and most of their revenue derives from license fees rather than from advertising proceeds. For them, the total broadcasting time for commercials is limited to twenty minutes per day on television; there are no commercials on Sundays and public holidays and after 8 p.m. on any normal day. There are eleven independent Länder corporations and two federal broadcasting corporations. These independent corporations cooperate in the Coordinating Association of Broadcasting Corporations governed under Public Law in the Federal Republic of Germany *(Arbeitsgemeinschaft der öffentlich-rechtlichen Rundfunkanstalten der Bundesrepublik Deutschland-ARD)*. In addition, there is a Second German Television *(Zweites Deutsches Fernsehen-ZDF)* which was founded by an inter-state treaty of all Länder. (see also Chs. 10 and 11).

In their programmes the public law broadcasting corporations are obliged to observe political neutrality. Doc.10 is an example of how this obligation is spelled out. To ensure compliance with these and other regulations, broadcasting corporations are controlled by supervisory bodies called broadcasting or television boards. These boards have considerable influence on the activities of the corporation both by providing guidelines for the programmes and by their control over personnel and budget policy. Doc.11 shows how, in the composition of a television board, an attempt is made to arrive at a balanced representation of all interest groups.

Private television stations finance themselves mainly from advertising proceeds. To obtain a license and in their programmes, they have to meet certain requirements which are less stringent than those for the public law corporations. Doc.12 shows the nature of these obligations.

Unlike the supposedly elitist public-law corporations, most private and profit-orientated stations cater to very popular tastes. By now, they have an important share in the market and the public law corporations feel the resulting drain of advertising proceeds. A point of concern is that the private television market is really in the hands of just two powerful media-groups.

In contrast to broadcasting, the printed media are left entirely to private publishers. Here a major problem is the continuing process of concentration of publishing companies. This essentially economically motivated process has resulted in a decline of the total number of publications. Simultaneously the control over the remaining publications is becoming concentrated in fewer hands. This is considered a potential threat to the independent formation of opinion. Attempts legally to guarantee the editorial staff of the various publications independence of the political interest of the owner of the publishing company (commonly referred to as the internal freedom of the press) are important. But the decisive measure to prevent the formation of opinion monopolies seems to be the maintenance of competition between publishing houses, an objective which in 1976 also led to an amendment to Art.23 of the Act against Restraints of Competition6 which specified provisions for merger-control of publishing companies. Doc.13 describes the state of the press.

The Federation of German Industries describes the organisation of business interests.

Document 1

THE ORGANISATION OF BUSINESS INTERESTS

Source: Bundesverband der Deutschen Industrie (Federation of German Industries BDI), *A Good Connection,* Cologne, n.d.(1993)
Transl.: Official

German Industry—Cornerstone of the Economy

Of all western industrialized countries, Germany has the largest industrial sector. From motor vehicles to sugar, it employs over ten million people in 34 branches. In German industry world-renowned large-scale enterprises operate alongside many thriving small and medium-sized businesses. Industry is crucial both to the German economy's performance and its international competitiveness.

. . .

BDI—the Umbrella Organization of German Industry

The BDI is the umbrella organization for a total of 34 industrial trade associations and groups of associations in Germany. Its members represent about 80,000 private industrial enterprises employing over ten million people, a figure that will rise steadily over the next few years as companies in the five new German Länder join the trade associations.

. . .

Multi-level contacts

The BDI represents the economic policy interests of German industry in dealings with parliament, government and the parliamentary opposition, the political parties, the unions and other social groups, the institutions of the European Community as well as many other national and international bodies.

The BDI maintains regional offices in the German Länder and liaison offices in Brussels, Washington and Tokyo.

At national level, the BDI also keeps in close touch with the other umbrella organizations of trade and industry, above all with the Confederation of German Employers' Associations and the Association of German Chambers of Industry and Commerce. In addition, the BDI cooperates with the Institute of German Private Enterprise [an economic research institute, ed.], which is jointly sponsored by trade associations, employers' associations and businesses. On top of this, the BDI is represented in numerous international organizations. Its involvement in European organizations is of key importance today with the advent of the single European market ...

. . .

The BDI and other associations

The hallmark of modern, pluralistic society is its multiplicity of aims and interests. Anyone intent on effectively advancing his ideas, aims and interests must, therefore, join together with others to form interest groups. Enterprises in Germany do this via various associations.

Organized by economic branch, the prime object of *trade associations* is to represent the economic policy interests of their member companies. The umbrella organization of the industrial trade associations is the Federation of German Industries (BDI). The BDI works in concert with other central organizations of trade and industry, with associations of banking and commerce, for example, in the Joint Committee of German Trade and Industry (Gemeinschaftsausschuß der Deutschen Gewerblichen Wirtschaft).

The *employers' associations* represent the socio-political interests of trade and industry in dealings with the unions, the public and the state. Their major concerns are wage and social policy. Their umbrella organization is the Confederation of German Employers' Associations [Bundesvereinigung der Deutschen Arbeitgeberverbände e.V.,ed].

The *chambers of industry and commerce* are self-governing public corporations. Unlike their voluntary membership in the associations, businesses are legally obliged to join the chambers. Their umbrella organization is the Association of German Chambers of Industry and Commerce [Deutscher Industrie- und Handelstag e.V., DIHT, ed].

SERVICES IN THE FOREFRONT

For the associations and their umbrella organizations, services have stepped increasingly to the fore: they advise their member firms in specialized matters and furnish policymakers with a constant flow of information. Often enough, politicians and administrators lack some of the information needed to make sound decisions on government measures. The associations provide expertise and practical experience from trade and industry. Experts from the associations sit on all major ministerial advisory boards and expert committees and they also attend the hearings of parliamentary committees. It has long become accepted practice for the umbrella organizations to be consulted when drafting financial, economic and social legislation. By identifying and focusing member interests and formulating these for submission to policymaking bodies, they facilitate the appraisal of the various strands of argument in the decision-making process.

The industrial business associations are quite outspoken in their political demands. The following excerpts are from the address of Wolf Dieter Kruse, the president of the Association of Textile Industries, to a Press Breakfast given by his organisation on 5 April 1994.

Document 2

BETTER FRAMEWORK CONDITIONS MUST SUPPORT RECOVERY
Source: Textil Pressedienst, 5 April 1994
Transl.: Official

. . .

16. The textile industry needs an economic, competition, tax and social policy that grants the *medium-sized enterprises* a greater freedom of manoeuvre and does not place it at a disadvantage vis-à-vis large enterprises. The state must create sensible *framework conditions* and ensure—both nationally and internationally—fair competition.

17. The burden on enterprises with *social insurance costs* and *other ancillary wage costs* must be reduced. Employment impeding regulations must be eliminated. For *care insurance,* a compensation for employer contributions must be regulated bindingly.

18. *Taxes that are independent* of the earnings of an enterprise must be abolished and taxes on the earnings of the enterprise must be reduced to an internationally comparable level.

19. The *energy costs* in Germany must be lowered considerably and adjusted to the international standard. *Environmental policy* must endeavour to achieve an international harmonisation. In this respect, the gap between the leading position of Germany in comparison to other countries—also in Europe—should not be further increased.

20. Supportive measures by the state for *research* oriented towards practical application are urgently necessary in order to strengthen the innovative potential of small and medium-sized enterprises. The funds for industrial collective research must thus be retrieved.

21. The *East German* textile industry still needs a compensation for location disadvantages in the new Federal States. The sales promotion programme designed as a self-help measure must be resolutely continued.

22. The *European Union* should not be permitted to grant sectoral subsidies for the Community textile and clothing industry. *The Man-Made Fibre Code,* which strictly forbids regional and sectoral subsidies, must be renewed and a comparable code should be negotiated to include the cotton processing, filament weaving and textile finishing industry. Moreover, the textile industry needs a uniform registered design law which does not place it at a disadvantage.

23. *Trade policy* must continue to give flank protection to the textile sector, also subsequent to the conclusion of the GATT-Uruguay-Round. The liberalisation concept embodied in the ten-year *transitional regime* must be realised on a step-by-step basis. Transshipments, false origin declarations, violation of intellectual property rights and copies must be pursued and punished. The improved GATT rights in the area of *anti-dumping* and *anti-subsidy procedures* must be utilised. The announced opening of markets must be realised.

. . .

In the following document, the German Trade Union Federation describes its purposes and its organisational structure. This text does not mention that the German Trade Union Federation also operates an important economic research institute *(Wirtschaftswissenschaftliches Institut der Gewerkschaften).*

Document 3

THE STRUCTURE OF THE GERMAN TRADE UNION FEDERATION

Source: DGB, The German Trade Union Federation, Cologne, 1981, 14–15; updated by the DGB head office in 1994
Transl.: Official

The DGB Constitution

Purpose and tasks of the Federation

The task of the German Trade Union Federation, umbrella organization of sixteen trade unions, is to unify them into an effective unit and to represent their common interests in the fields of general trade union and societal policy, economic and cultural policies.

The Federation and its member unions are democratically structured and—as an essential element of the principle of the unitary union—independent of government, political parties, religious communities, administrations and employers. This party-political independence cannot, however, mean political abstinence. Worker interests have to be represented not only vis-à-vis employers, but also vis-à-vis parliaments, administrations and other institutions in society since these, too, take major decisions affecting the living and working conditions of the dependently employed. In addition to the general set of objectives of working for securing and expanding the social state based on the rule of law and achieving the democratization of the economy, the state and society, this includes the exercising of the right to resist any attempts to overthrow the constitutional order (Art.20, para.4 of the Basic Law).

In addition to the political tasks, the Federation also has a number of organizational ones such as unionist schooling, operation of legal aid services, public relations and coordination of trade union activities. The task and objectives laid down in the Constitution are augmented by a Basic Programme and an Action Programme which provide the further guidelines for trade union activities.

Membership and dues

The following sixteen trade unions are members of the Federation:

Building and Construction Workers' Union
Mine and Energy Workers' Union
Chemical, Paper and Ceramic Workers' Union
Media Workers' Union
German Railway Workers' Union
Education and Sciences Union
Horticultural, Agricultural and Forestry Workers' Union
Commerce, Bank and Insurance Workers' Union
Wood and Plastic Workers' Union
Leather Workers' Union
Metal Workers' Union
Food, Stimulants and Restaurant Workers' Union
Public Service, Transport and Communications Workers' Union
Police Union
German Postal Workers' Union
Textile and Garment Workers' Union

These unions, which have a combined membership of 10.3 million members, are structured according to the industry-union principle, that is 'one industry, one union', grouping wage earners, salaried staff and, where applicable, civil servants of one sector in one union. In contrast to vocational (or craft) trade unions this strengthens worker unity and underlines the common interests. The individual unions are independent in their bargaining and finance policies.

Prerequisite to a trade union's membership of the DGB is its acceptance of and adherence to the Federation's Constitution.

To finance the umbrella organisation the member unions have to pay it 12 per cent of their membership revenues. For support measures and to finance special trade union activities there is a solidarity fund into which DM 0.30 per individual member is paid per quarter.

Structure and organs of the DGB

The German Trade Union Federation covers the territory of the Federal Republic of Germany and parallel to the administrative structure of the state is divided into three levels: Federal *(Bund)*, State *(Landesbezirke)* and County *(Kreise)* districts.

On certain controversial issues, the German Trade Union Federation publishes its opinion.

Document 4

THE TRADE UNIONS' VIEW ON LOCKOUT

Source: DGB, The German Trade Union Federation, Cologne, 1981, 33
Transl.: Official

Industrial disputes

If negotiation and mediation fail, the only option left to the labour side to
obtain a new collective agreement is to take industrial action. Strike, the
joint, organised refusal to work, the ultimate and sharpest trade union
weapon, aims to put pressure on the employers to assert worker interests.

Workers' right to strike is guaranteed under Art.9, Para.3 of the West German constitution, the Basic Law. In contrast to the lock-out, it thus is constitutionally protected.

A strike requires the approval of the executive of the trade union concerned. As a rule, members vote beforehand in a strike ballot. Only if 75 per
cent of the membership vote to down tools does the union leadership call a
strike. Only legitimation by so large a majority creates the basis for successful industrial action.

During the action strikers receive no pay from the employer. Trade union
members of at least three months' standing receive strike support benefit
from their union. Non-unionised workers who strike or are locked out
receive no strike support, nor do they get, say, benefits from the Unemployment Insurance.

West Germany is the only European country where the lock-out plays a
major part in industrial disputes. One can say that it is the European country with the fewest strikes and the most lock-outs. Arguing a questionable
equality of fighting strength, the Federal Labour Court has put the lock-out
weapon in employers' hands. And the entrepreneurs make excessive use of it
with the aim of weakening the trade unions financially. Just one example: in
the Metal Workers' Union 1978 industrial action in the North Württem-
berg/North Baden contractual region it paid out DM 48 million support to
strikers, but more than DM 80 million to members not called out by the
union, but locked out by the employers. By means of the lock-out the
employers try to break the will of the workers by withdrawing the basis of
their livelihood. That violates the fundamentals of human dignity in that
workers are used as mere instruments to raise entrepreneurial profits by the
threat to their livelihood. The fatuous argument that the lock-out was
needed to assure 'fighting parity' is easily refuted. If it were so, there would
also have to be perfect parity between employers and workers if the right to
strike were taken away! On the contrary, the equality of sorts between
employers and workers which only the right to strike established is destroyed
by the lock-out. Only those who would deny the socially weaker position of
wage dependent workers and would subject them to the pay dictate of the
employers can argue in favour of the lock-out.'

The Federal Republic of Germany is a democratic and social federal state,'
says Art. 20, Para.1 of the Basic Law. As long as hundreds of thousands of

workers can be locked out as if it were a matter of course one can seriously doubt this constitutional declaration.

As in most industrial countries, the agricultural sector is shrinking in the Federal Republic of Germany. Particularly endangered by modernisation is the family farm. In the following document, the German Farmers' Association gives its views on the place of the family farm within the common agricultural policy of the European Community.

Document 5

THE GERMAN FARMERS' ASSOCIATION'S VIEWS ON THE FUTURE OF AGRICULTURE

Source: Deutscher Bauernverband, *Der Deutsche Bauernverband zur Fortentwicklung der EG-Agrarpolitik, Schriftenreihe des Deutschen Bauernverbands*, Heft 3, 1980, 51–2

The principles of the German Farmers' Association on agricultural, economic and social policy:

It is the chief aim of the German Farmers' Association to ensure the continuation of an agricultural system where the family farm plays an important role and thus upholds its undeniable economic and ecological advantages. Its aim is also to make sure that those working in agriculture benefit from the general development of incomes. The German Farmers' Association is ready to share the burden of constructive solutions in the further development of a common agricultural policy in as far as they can be carried out uniformly within the European Community and as long as they safeguard the already existing social status of farmers and improve it in line with the rest of the economy. This is justified by, and in keeping with, the policy of equal treatment for all sections of the population. But at the same time the German Farmers' Association can only agree to suggestions which put the fewest limits on the free entrepreneurial decisions of farmers themselves and ensure that their income remains productivity-orientated. It is indispensable that the socio-political achievements brought about by the agricultural community such as the care for, and upkeep of, the landscape should be appropriately rewarded. It is the task of the state's economic and agricultural policies to set up parity of income as laid down in the Agricultural Law of 1955 and in the Treaty of Rome in 1957.

The family farm system is not self-serving; in the long run it serves the interests of the community as a whole:

In comparison with big industrial farms of either the East or the West it has always shown a high capacity to adapt and to produce.

It forms the economic basis of rural areas in many parts of Western Europe. The upholding of a minimum level of population in many areas of the Community would not be possible without the family farm system.

The family farm system maintains many flexible decision-making units in farming and in this way guarantees the best possible provision for the population even in times of crisis.

The family farm system provides for a wide distribution of property which is socio-politically desirable and guarantees independence and self-determination at the place of work. In this way it contributes especially to the preservation of democracy in western Europe as well as to the maintenance of social stability in the European Community.

The family farm system as a family business permits a combination with other forms of employment. One of its hallmarks is its ability to co-exist with full and part-time forms of employment.

A family farm means carrying out the business within the working capacity of the family. In this system there is no place for either farm factories which are not dependent on a particular area or agroindustrial methods of cultivation. The family farm system guarantees the production of food which unquestionably fulfils health standards and guarantees that rural areas will continue to serve as ecological compensators for urban areas.

It must therefore remain the most important common agricultural policy of the European community to maintain and develop the family farm system. Every policy including market, price, foreign trade, social, structural and fiscal policies goes to make up the whole. Decisive statements can only be made after all measures have been considered in relation to each other.

Citizens' action groups are very heterogeneous in many ways. They encounter difficulties in defining their purposes and actions in a way which is acceptable to all members. It is not surprising, therefore, that most documents are provisional and preliminary; very often they are published as drafts. This is also true of the document from which excerpts are reproduced here.

Document 6

CITIZENS' ACTION GROUPS AS SEEN BY THEMSELVES

Source: *Orientierungspapier des Bundesverbandes Bürgerinitiativen Umweltschutz e.B. (BBU)*—draft of September 1977, reproduced in: Volker Hauff (ed.), *Bürgerinitiativen in der Gesellschaft*, Villingen/Schwenningen, 1980, 343–8

Why do citizens' action groups for environmental protection exist?

In the field of environmental protection, citizens' action groups are spontaneously formed where, above all, citizens feel that social developments or state planning measures are encroaching upon their elementary rights. The experience of being helpless in the face of superior economic and political interests induces them to get together with like-minded people to protect their rights. The strength and success of citizens' action groups are still determined by the degree of the citizens' concern about erroneous developments in this society.

Many of us are prepared to offer resistance if a rubbish dump, a motorway or a nuclear power station is being planned right in our front garden, but we return to everyday life whether or not the resistance succeeded. The main thing is to realize that not only our immediate environment but our entire environment is threatened. Only then will the thousand grass roots of single initiatives gradually form a thick green carpet which fundamentally transforms our society and every single one of us.

. . .

What do we want?

We do not merely want to remedy abuses and prevent erroneous developments. On the contrary, we have set ourselves the goal of creating a more just, a freer and a more humane society.

The existing order of society is characterized by the struggle for power, wealth, esteem and knowledge as well as by the fear of powerlessness, poverty, contempt and ignorance. Our society continues to be characterized by the centralization of power, capital, knowledge, etc. We, on the other hand, want to reverse the process of increasing centralization in all areas of society. We want simplification, de-centralization and de-concentration. We want a society in which there is not only the alternative between devouring and being devoured, between winning or perishing; a society in which the antitheses between power and powerlessness, between wealth and poverty are reduced; a society, finally, in which human beings can be human with one another and with nature.

What is our course?

We think we know that an inseparable connection exists between means and aims. This means that peace cannot be attained by war, justice cannot be attained by injustice, and freedom from violence cannot be attained by force. Consequently, we do not only need the outline of an alternative social order; we also need alternative methods of settling and solving conflicts. These methods are constructive work and non-violent action.

Constructive work means the actual building of the new social order, the realization of alternative ways of living in the economy, society, politics and culture in the environment of every individual and of small groups.

Non-violent action means overcoming existing power relations by non cooperation (strike, boycott, etc.), citizens' disobedience (breaking unjust laws) and non-violent confrontations (blocking construction sites, road blockades, sit-ins, work-ins, etc.).

The secret of our success

The work of citizens' action groups has so far been successful because it was possible to agree on a number of common principles (minimum consent) which are:

nonpartisanship,
non-violence,
democratic and decentralized organizational structure.

Nonpartisanship does not mean at all that party members are not allowed to work in citizens' action groups. It merely means that they forego party propaganda whilst working in a group (e.g. distributing pamphlets or brochures marked with the party's name). They are free, however, to present their objective arguments.

Non-violence does not mean passivity or burying one's head in the sand; nor does it mean restricting oneself entirely to legal methods of action. Non-violent, direct actions such as occupying a construction site or blocking an approach road by sitting strikers are absolutely reconcilable with the principle of non-violence. But they should be only applied as a last resort after all the legal possibilities have been exhausted.

Democratic organizational structure means that speakers or delegates are elected and majority decisions are approved as long as they do not offend the individual's conscience.Due to their loose organizational structure, citizens' action groups run the particular danger of their majority decisions being ignored. In order to avoid irreconcilable differences or even splits, crucial votes should whenever possible be avoided. Where important decisions are concerned, the members of the citizens' action groups should keep talking with one another until the large majority agrees.*Decentralized organizational structure* means that every member of a citizens' action group as well as every citizens' action group should be as independent as possible. The strength of citizens' action groups lies in their diversity, activity, spontaneity, imaginativeness and creativity. They live from the interest of *all* members. Regional and national associations should only tackle tasks which can not be managed by local groups.

In our organization we try to avoid the mistakes which have removed the traditional parties and organizations so far from the real needs of the population. The politicians will have to get used to the idea that a popular movement such as the citizens' action groups cannot be filed away in cosily familiar categories. We resist being taken over by established parties, and we also resist the groups that want to misuse us for their own party's goals.

According to these principles, the BBU *[Bundesverband Bürgerinitiativen Umweltschutz:* Federal Association of Citizens' Action Groups for Environmental Protection] does not see itself as a representative 'leading organization' of ecologists either. Due to the decentralized organization, its competence is restricted. Its chief tasks lie in the coordination and establishment of a continuous process of information between the groups. However, the Association can also act independently as a 'citizens' action group on a national level' and express its own opinion.

Citizens' action groups and the Basic Law

Citizens' action groups do not want to take over political power. On the contrary, they want to keep power in control, in the long run even reduce power. Even now there are the first signs of parliaments, supported and challenged by citizens' resistance, actually starting to exercise again their control function over the executive.

The active participation of citizens in political life can only be welcomed in a country which states in its constitution: 'All state authority emanates from the people'. But whoever desires a politically active and interested citizen must allow him the right to participate and add his vote in his working and living environment.

We therefore demand a right of participation and codetermination for the citizen who is directly affected by planning decisions. We demand the right of participation and codetermination for the citizen on all political levels. We demand the expansion or else the introduction of plebiscitarian elements in the Länder constitutions and in the Basic Law.

The liberal tradition calls for a clearcut separation of Church and State (see also Ch.11). In 1974 the Free Democratic Party tried to revive the discussion of this issue by publishing its Church Paper, entitled 'Free Church in a Free State' *(Freie Kirche im Freien Staat)*. There is, however, little chance of a fundamental change in the situation. The thirteen theses of this paper are reproduced here.

Document 7

FREE CHURCH IN A FREE STATE

Source: Günter Verheugen [until 1982 secretary general of the Free Democratic Party] (ed.), *Das Programm der Liberalen*, 2nd. ed., BadenBaden, 1980, 198ff.

1. Churches and ideological communities should make decisions about their own affairs independently of State influences. This requires the State to give up its remaining channels of influence, in particular, with regard to having a share in the regional structuring of the churches, the requirement of the episcopal oath of allegiance to the constitution and its influence on the filling of ecclesiastic offices.
2. The status of 'corporation under public law' is not applicable to religious or ideological groups like the churches because these bodies do not derive their duties from the State. On the other hand, the law regulating associations cannot do justice to the significance of the churches and other large communal bodies. A new law concerning such bodies has therefore to be developed which takes account of their full meaning and public workings. This law should also apply to the churches. Matters concerning religion and ideologies would be taken into consideration within this law.
3. Churches and ideological communities should regulate their membership within the framework of the freedom of religion according to their own laws. In order to leave the church or an ideological community, a declaration of intent addressed to this organization would be required. Every-

body above the age of fifteen should have the right to choose his/her religion, as is true already in most Länder.

4. No one should be obliged to reveal his religious beliefs. This constitutional principle should be respected everywhere and especially in the law of personal status and in public office.

5. The existing church tax should be replaced by the churches' own contributory system. Appropriate discussions with the churches should be taken up concerning the modalities of transition and to set adequate time limits.

6. The constitutional principle of ideological/religious neutrality of the State should be applicable to the Länder constitutions and law, and rules and customs in public life. The religious convictions of individual groups may not be made binding for everyone.Sacred forms and symbols should not be used in the area of public institutions such as courts and state schools. The oath should have a neutral form and those taking it must be allowed to add any formula which accords with their ideology.

7. Already existing state contracts with the churches (church treaties and concordats) are on account of their special character not a suitable means of regulating relations between Church and State. Such treaties should not therefore be renewed. Existing treaties and concordats, in as far as they are still valid, should be terminated by mutual agreement. The subject matter thereof should, as far as this is required, be settled by new laws or separate agreements.

8. Any payments from the State to the churches which are based on a law, a contract or special legal title should be abolished (as provided for by Art. 140 of the Basic Law and Art. 138, para.1 of the Weimar Constitution). Any special privileges concerning tax and payment which the churches or other religious communities enjoy with regard to other public institutions should be terminated.

9. Education, the care of the sick and social welfare should lie within the public domain. The right of independent institutions to be active in these areas should be upheld—although they should not have any privileges. To enable them to render these services independent institutions should receive appropriate state subsidies. Adequate provisions from public funds must be guaranteed to fulfil the need for such institutions which are ideologically neutral and accessible to everyone. Private institutions which receive subsidies from public funds must be accessible to the general public; people of other persuasions must not be subjected to any disadvantages or coercion.

10. The community school which is religiously and ideologically neutral should be the norm for a state school in the entire Federal Republic. Religious instruction is a regular subject according to the existing Constitution. As an alternative, instruction about religion is offered. There should be a free choice between these two subjects. The right to set up and maintain private schools should remain intact.

11. Pastoral care in state institutions such as the Army, the Border Guards and prisons should again become the sole responsibility of the churches. The opportunity of having unrestricted religious care by pastoral work-

ers selected and paid by the churches should be guaranteed. The same right should apply to all religious and ideological communities.

12. Students about to enter the ministry and theology students should have the same rights and duties as other citizens even with regard to military service and conscientious objection.

13. Church representation within public bodies (e.g. broadcasting councils, school committees, youth and social committees, hearings, etc.) should be reexamined having regard to the function of a particular association in a particular area. This principle should also apply to other social groups.

The Catholic Church has always attached particular importance to the family as a foundation element of society. Therefore, it has persistently demanded a governmental policy to protect the traditional family. The following excerpts are from a 1979 declaration of the General Assembly of the Central Committee of German Catholics *(Zentralkomitee der Deutschen Katholiken)*, the lay organization of the Catholic Church.

Document 8

THE CATHOLIC CONCEPT OF FAMILY POLICY

Source: 'Ehe und Familie im Spannungsfeld von personaler Partnerschaft und Institution. Eine Erklärung des Zentralkomitees der Deutschen Katholiken für die Gesellschaftspolitische Diskussion über diese Fragen. Beschlossen von der Vollversammlung des Zentralkomitees der Deutschen Katholiken.' Bonn/Bad Godesberg, 11–12 May 1979

The family finds itself in close mutual interaction with other social groups and processes. The family should be able to expect unlimited support from the forces governing society, not only for the sake of the role it plays in personal human development but also because of the service it renders to society.

The mass media—television, the radio, magazines and the daily press—should paint a realistic picture of the family and its importance in our lives as a whole. Ideological images which are hostile to the family and diminish its work unfairly must be replaced by a more constructively critical representation.

For many families working life imposes unnecessary difficulties. Employers in both the public and private sectors should adapt to the needs of the family and offer part-time jobs or flexible working hours.

In their socio-political dealings concerning the family, political parties should rid themselves of tendencies that are one-sidedly individualistic or collectivist and make as a basis for their social and family policies the more complete vision of marriage and the family. Effective cooperation on political matters concerning the family can only be hampered by thinking which is derived from liberal and Marxist principles.

The statement in the Basic Law on marriage and the family is based on a consensus reached after hard-won experience concerning the dignity of human beings, their freedom and their solidarity. We expect organs of the State, in their practical policies, to implement fully those constitutional provisions which present the personal values of marriage and the family as particularly worthy of being protected.

This constitutional undertaking must continue to be fulfilled in several ways: 1) by a relief from financial burdens; 2) through a social infrastructure which has regard for family interests; 3) special forms of aid for families with particular problems. These matters must be a federal concern as well as the responsibility of the Länder and of the local authorities.

In our opinion the following have precedence at the moment: 1) the lawful safeguarding of the family both as an institution and in its original task of bringing up children; 2) the furthering of the willingness to have children; 3) an extension of support for families with three or more children; 4) a regular index-linked child allowance; 5) the extension of maternity leave; 6) the introduction of a regular allowance for mothers bringing up children. Apart from this, considerable efforts must be made to rebuild a relationship of trust between the home and school.

Through a consistent and continuing development of a systematic family policy an important contribution will be made indirectly to a more balanced structure and development of the population. Of principal importance in this are the means to enable a married woman to decide without difficulty to have children. This would count in those cases too where the woman would like—at least temporarily—to be socially or professionally active.

Just as concrete measures are important so also are the language and spirit in which family problems are dealt with in public discussion. Anyone who in this ignores all human relationships casts doubt on himself in a way that he will hardly be able to overcome. Instead of this a positive readiness is called for, a readiness which is not afraid to make the necessary effort to develop further that which has already proved its worth. Each and every individual is called upon to do this.

In 1981 the Evangelical Church published its Peace Memorandum: 'The Preservation, Promotion and Renewal of Peace'. This paper emphasizes the need for disarmament and détente in a way which then went beyond the official position of the majority of politicians and in this way encouraged and reinforced the 'peace movement'(see also Ch.6 and compare Ch.4).The following excerpt is from the last part of the fifty-eight page memorandum.

Document 9

THE PEACE MEMORANDUM OF THE EVANGELICAL CHURCH

Source: 'The Preservation, Promotion and Renewal of Peace, a Memorandum of the Evangelical Church in Germany.' *EKD-Bulletin,* special issue, 1981 *Transl.:* Official

. . .

3. Strengthening the Desire for Closer Contacts

. . .

a) International Peace Order (Friedensordnung)

The church's task is first and foremost to witness that peace for the world is only found in Jesus Christ. Political witness and the church's political service for peace cannot ignore the fact that any peace order can only be relative and can always be made obsolete.

The prevention of war is an initial step towards peace. But the absence of war does not make for peace. Peace cannot be conceived of as a political state at all; rather it is a process of gradually broadening the base of those social conditions which make up the quality of peace: the refraining from violent solutions to international conflicts, the abolition of hardship and distress, the guaranteeing of freedom and self-determination for all nations, the elimination of racial or social oppression and discrimination, respect for human rights and the protection of natural environmental conditions for life. Such a peace can only be founded on a close interweaving of different interests and a systematic development of solutions which are of such general benefit that they outweigh the unavoidable disadvantages. Such an order would be the transfer of basic concepts of social welfare and the rule of law to the international level, i.e. the attempt to settle inevitable conflicts on the basis of internationally agreed rules. An international peace order must realise the individual and social human rights, include a common approach to security and prevent the imposition of interests by recourse to force; it has to respect the autonomy of nations and promote regional and international cooperation.

A political road to such an order is scarcely within view at the moment, and the projected worldwide peace order, enabling justice and freedom for all, is obviously not feasible at present. It is all the more urgent that the desire for closer contacts be strengthened, that they be neither under-estimated or repudiated, nor themselves mistaken for the further-reaching goals. It is not a question of conserving the present world situation in which peace is so vulnerable. The point is to take steps—however modest—in the direction of an international peace order.

However, the most urgent task is to prevent a war between the two major alliances. Even if opinions differ on whether it can really be prevented, political action must assume that it can, in order to be meaningful. The fact that arms build-up and up-grade continue has altered the nature of the balance and created risks of its own: the possibility of a change of function, to that of triggering off a war instead of guarding against it, is coming into focus more clearly. Since the beginning of the sixties there have thus been efforts towards arms limitation, which must be the first step on the road to disarmament. Most of the expectations in this respect have hitherto been disappointed, however.

The success of such efforts largely depends on the two main power blocs expecting to benefit more from them than from continued arms production. But we are in a situation of heightened confrontation between the superpowers. We Europeans, particularly we Germans, are at present the ones who have the least to gain from a policy of confrontation. It would again restrict the greater room to manoeuvre in the relationship between the two Germanies and reduce the scope for independent political action aimed at a tighter meshing of mutual interests.

Eastern and Western Europe have their own interests, which are not identical with those of the leading powers on either side. On the other hand, Europe is involved in worldwide conflicts of interests from which it cannot extricate itself and which, in a crisis, would rebound on it at the risk of wiping out the achievements of détente. So Europe is bound to be interested in the development of a long-term detente programme involving the superpowers. Even though Europe, specifically the two Germanies, can only play a modest role between the two superpowers, it can contribute to a fresh international perspective. It should not be isolationist, but continually throw its weight into the balance for the sake of peace. Its goal could be to maintain its freedom to seek political strategies aimed at transferring favourable European experience with détente to other world trouble-spots, and encouraging steps in the necessary direction of an international peace order.

In this situation, it is not up to the church to make statements about how such planning could be put into practice. It can however, raise questions for politicians expressing the concerns of many people in the Federal Republic of Germany and their urgent hopes for a new political perspective.

The three major areas for questions are: comprehensive cooperation, typically defensive defence planning and effective disarmament.

b) Towards Comprehensive Cooperation

The present debate highlights control and limitation of arms. These are reasonable and appropriate aims if they are rooted in a broader perspective.

What are the present political chances of a comprehensive cooperative plan being drawn up, involving both the blocs and going beyond arms control and limitation?

Balance cannot be defined solely and satisfactorily in military terms. Moreover, the only promising plans are those taking account of the interests of both power blocs and from which they can both expect to benefit. For these reasons, such an approach would need to include industry, science and technology. The primacy of military confrontation must be replaced by that of political cooperation. This is the only way to reduce the arms production incentive for industry and technological research, and to shift it to other areas of industrial production. Technological and economic constraints are not independent factors: just as they can cut themselves off from politics, and then influence it, different types of policies can also influence the arms industry and give new goals to technology and production.

If military confrontation is to yield to political cooperation, the West must do its best to avoid capitalising on the weak points of the East in such a way as might possibly cause a military reaction. This must certainly not rule out the inclusion of human rights protection in political cooperation.

Such a plan for comprehensive cooperation calls for political imagination which, in turn, needs the latitude of an open political discussion, free of hard lines and insinuation.

c) Towards a Typically Defensive Concept of Armament

What are the chances of stressing the exclusively defensive character of NATO defence, and gradually replacing the weaponry which can also be deployed for purposes of attack? The danger of war can be enhanced by notional threat, and so a defence policy provisionally guaranteeing minimum nuclear deterrence, but emphasising typically defensive weapons, would lessen the danger. This requires the establishing of criteria on what is essential for deterrence and what is superfluous.

There must be a serious discussion in our country and in NATO of this and other alternative defence policies. Here, too, new ways can only be found in a climate of honest public debate.

d) Towards Effective Disarmament

What are the current political prospects for effective arms reduction in the framework of talks on the disturbingly modest objective of cooperative arms control?

In view of the risks entailed by the quantity and quality of existing arsenals, concerned people can only be expected to raise the patience for long-drawn-out arms limitation talks, which have hitherto been only relatively successful, to the extent that they can discern serious intentions and prospects of lessening these risks through effective disarmament.

It is the church's duty to question politicians about ways of breaking the arms production chain, where both sides consider or claim they are reinstating the lost balance. The fact that the striving for parity always means build-up, never reduction, places an intolerable strain on the very concept of balance. Mutual deterrence is provisionally granting scope for political safeguards and if this is not used to break the chain, the time will come when the scandal and risk of the arms race outweighs the effectiveness of the deterrence system.

If calculated unilateral steps can help disarmament talks along, they deserve serious consideration too; we should not be discouraged by the fact that unilateral steps on both sides have not had the effect expected in the past.

Talks on cooperative arms control, arms limitation and disarmament will only be really successful if they aim for agreements also covering foreseeable possibilities of technical advance and systems modernisation.

One way in which the church could strengthen the feeling for rapprochement might be for the Council of the EKD to take the initiative of encouraging the writing of regular expert opinions; on the basis of up-to-date analyses these would make recommendations for possible next steps towards disarmament and political peace orders. In this connection, the Council of the EKD should encourage the continuous flow of reliable news for the general public about basic political developments, dangers to peace, detente and disarmament.

The following quotation is a typical example of how any form of radicalism is banned from a broadcasting corporation.

Document 10

LAW ESTABLISHING THE 'WESTDEUTSCHER RUNDFUNK KÖLN' dated 19 March 1985, in the version of 11 January 1988, last amended on 15 March 1988

Source: Broadcasting Laws, Documents on Politics and Society in the Federal Republic of Germany, Inter Nationes, Bonn 1989, 54–56
Transl.: Official

. . .

Art. 5 Programming Principles

(1) Programmes and news services offered by the WDR *[Westdeutscher Rundfunk Köln]* shall be compatible with the Constitution. The provisions of general laws and regulations for the protection of juveniles and personal honour shall be observed.

(2) In its broadcasts the WDR shall respect and protect the dignity of the individual. It shall seek to enhance respect for the life, freedom and physical integrity, beliefs and opinions of others. The moral and religious convictions of the people shall be respected.

(3) The WDR shall promote international understanding, advocate peace and social justice, defend democratic liberties, help to establish the equality of men and women, and be committed to the truth.

(4) The WDR shall ensure that

1. the diversity of opinions and of ideological, political, scientific and artistic trends are given the widest possible coverage in its programmes,
2. principal social groups in the transmission area are able to present their views in the overall programme,
3. the overall programme is not biased in favour of any one party or group, vested interest, religion or ideology. WDR reports shall allow suitable time for the treatment of controversial issues of general importance. Analytical reports shall comply with the requirement of journalistic fairness. The purpose of reports shall be to provide comprehensive information.

(5) News presentation must be general, independent and objective. Before dissemination the material must be examined with due care as to its content,

origin and truth. Commentaries must be clearly distinct from news and presented as such, together with the name of the author.

. . .

Article 6 Protection of human dignity and minors

(1) Programmes are impermissible if they

    (a) incite to racial hatred or describe cruel or inhuman acts of violence against persons in such a way as to glorify or play down such acts of violence or if they present cruelty or inhumanity in a manner injurious to human dignity ... ,

    (b) glorify war,

    (c) are pornographic (Article 184, Penal Code),

    (d) are obviously inclined to cause serious moral danger to children or adolescents.

(2) Programmes which are likely adversely to affect the physical, spiritual or mental well-being of children or adolescents may not be broadcast unless the operator ensures, by way of the time of broadcast or other means, that children or adolescents in the age groups concerned would not normally see or hear the programmes in question; this may be assumed by the operator for programmes broadcast between 11 p.m. and 6 a.m. Films not released for showing to minors under the age of 16 years in accordance with the terms of the Law on the Protection of Minors in Public may be transmitted only between 10 p.m. and 6 a.m. and films not released for showing to juveniles under the age of 18 years only between 11 p.m. and 6 a.m. and then only if the possible moral danger cannot, all circumstances considered, be regarded as serious.

. . .

The composition of the television board of the Second German Television reflects the attempt to secure a representation of all relevant social groups. There is, however, the difficulty that many representatives of particular social groups are also members of political parties. Therefore, one may speak of an over-representation of party interests in these bodies.

Document 11

REPRESENTATION OF INTEREST GROUPS ON THE
TELEVISION BOARD OF THE 'SECOND GERMAN
TELEVISION'.
as specified in the Inter-state Agreement of 6 June 1961 on the
Establishment of the Public Corporation Zweites Deutsches
Fernsehen (Second German Television, Channel II)

*Source: Broadcasting Laws, Documents on Politics and Society in the Federal
Republic of Germany, Inter Nationes, Bonn 1989, 92/93
Transl.*: Official

Art. 14. Composition of the Television Board

(1) The Tele vision Board shall comprise sixty-six members, namely:

a) one representative of each of the Länder entering into this Treaty, to
be delegated by the respective Land Government;

b) three representatives of the Federation, to be delegated by the Federal
Government;

c) twelve representatives of the political parties in accordance with their
strength of representation in the Bundestag, to be delegated by the
respective party executives;

d) two representatives delegated by the Protestant Church in Germany;

e) two representatives delegated by the Roman Catholic Church in Germany;

f) one representative delegated by the Central Council of Jews in Germany;

g) three representatives of the trades unions;

h) two representatives of the Federation of German Employers' Associations;

i) one representative of the Central Committee of German Agriculture;

k) one representative of the Central Association of German Handicrafts;

l) two representatives of the Federation of German Newspaper Publishers;

m) two representatives of the German Journalists' Association;

n) four representatives of private charity associations, i.e. one each of the
Inner Mission and Relief Organization of the Protestant Church in
Germany; the German Caritas Association (Roman Catholic charity);
the German Red Cross and the Central Committee of German Workers' Charity;

o) four representatives of the main communal associations, i.e. one each
of the Congress of Cities, the Conference of District Councils and the
Conference of Town Councils;

p) one representative of the German Sports Federation;

q) one representative of the Federation of Expellees;

r) ten representatives from the fields of education and training, science
and the arts, as well as one representative each of:

the free professions;
family organizations;
women's associations;
youth associations.

. . .

REGULATIONS FOR PRIVATE TELEVISION AND
BROADCASTING STATIONS

Document 12

INTER-STATE AGREEMENT ON THE RESTRUCTURING
OF BROADCASTING
dated 1–3 April 1987

Source: Broadcasting Laws, Documentation on Politics and Society in the Federal Republic of Germany, Inter Nationes, Bonn 1989, 28–32

. . .

Article 7 Licensing and funding of private broadcasting

(1) Private commercial operators require a license to be able to produce and transmit radio and television programmes. This is issued by the authority responsible under state law.

(2) Private broadcasting operators shall obtain most of their revenue from advertising and payments in return for services.

(3) Advertising may not exceed 20% of daily transmission time.

(4) Advertising shall be clearly distinguishable from the remainder of broadcasting programmes and identified as such. It may not influence the content of the remaining broadcasting programme.

(5) Advertising directed at children or adolescents may not exploit their inexperience.

(6) Television advertising may be disseminated only in blocks; television programmes exceeding 60 minutes in duration may contain advertising inserts once at a pre-announced time ...

. . .

Article 8 Guaranteeing multiplicity of opinion in private broadcasting transmitted throughout the Federal Republic

(1) In general, the content of private commercial broadcasting shall give expression to multiplicity of opinion. Significant political, ideological and social currents and groupings must find expression in the full programmes; attitudes and opinions of minorities shall be fully taken into account ... .

. . .

Article 12 Supervision of private commercial broadcasting

(1) The authority responsible under state law for licensing broadcasting enterprises shall oversee, during the licensing procedure and thereafter, observance of the terms of this Agreement as they apply to private programme operators ... .

In 1978 the Federal Government reported to the Bundestag on the state of the press. Among many other aspects this report deals with the issue of how the freedom of the press is endangered by the process of economic concentration of publishing companies.

Document 13

THE STATE OF THE PRESS *(MEDIENBERICHT)*

Source: *Report of the Federal Government on the State of Press and Broadcasting in the Federal Republic of Germany (1978)*, Deutscher Bundestag, 8th legislative period, Drucksache 8/2264, 67–8

II. Freedom of the Press

. . .

The Federal Government reiterated in the Government Declaration of 16 December 1976 that the private-law character of the press should continue to be upheld in the same way as the public-law character of broadcasting. These are two mutually complementary principles on which the system of the media in the Federal Republic is based. Both organisational solutions must be seen in terms of the aim based in the Constitution that every individual be guaranteed the highest level of freedoms and of possibilities in the media. The individual must have a central place in this from which he should be able to inform himself comprehensively and fully, and to form his own opinion freely and to express it, thereby enabling him to have independently responsible participation in the development of a democratic community.

1. Variety in the Press

Whereas the pluralistic internal structure of broadcasting which is regulated by law is supposed to assure the public of a large number of radio and television programmes, exhibiting in themselves a great diversity, and also of a variety of broadcasting organisations, the diversity of information and opinion in the Press is seen as resulting from entrepreneurial competition and market forces.

Indeed the Federal Constitutional Court based its 1961 ruling on the premise that '… within the German press a relatively large number of publications exist, which are independent and compete with each other according to their inclination, political leanings and in their basic ideological standpoint'. Implicit in this supposition is that the public has a sufficient number of choices. For this reason the maintenance of variety in what the press offers is principally dependent on maintaining those choices.

1.1 General Variety in the Press

The press in the Federal Republic of Germany corresponds essentially to the image of a wealth of choice represented by a multiplicity of different press publications. This is the case as long as this assessment is based on a broad concept of the press which corresponds and is basic to Art. 5 of the Basic Law. This means that all publications which appear periodically and any which do not, and also, apart from daily newspapers, the wide range of magazines of all kinds and so-called local and regional periodicals with an informative content—regardless of their thematic restriction—are taken into consideration.

1.2 Limited variety in the regional/local news press and Sunday newspapers

If, however, one considers just the actual daily press as that part of the press which is important to the formation of opinion, then the present situation does not come up to the ideal of a desirable competitiveness in the newspaper market in the two significant areas of the regional/local daily press and the Sunday newspapers.

There is a wider choice of well-defined independent organs of opinion in the national dailies and weekly periodicals. There, a pluralistic overview both in news and commentary is supplied by a number of independent organs with differing political tendencies and standpoints. These include five national newspapers, three more daily newspapers with a national journalistic reputation, an economic and financial paper which appears when the Stock Exchange is in operation and twelve political weeklies. The national Sunday newspaper market is an exception in that only two publications from the same publisher appear.

. . .

When surveying the landscape of German newspapers one cannot afford to overlook that a growing number of supplementary press publications—even if this varies from region to region—have been able to establish themselves, and these are trying to balance out the gaps in information, mainly concerning local and communal events, which are no longer covered by the dailies and to fill demands for information which have recently arisen. The press of the church, associations and political parties, the so-called 'free newspapers' which serve as sources of information on citizens' action groups, newspapers for different town districts and two magazines, local weeklies and advertising newspapers, publications for school children and for young people and community newspapers—all these contain a multi-layered spectrum of information and opinion which often transcends social and class groupings. The intention of these papers is to supplement information from the dailies and deepen understanding in certain areas of expertise.

1.3 Principles for the conservation of the variety in the press.

The future maintenance of variety in the press, according to the Federal Government, should be specifically based on the idea of the best possible supply of organs of information which are economically and journalistically viable and which, independent of and in competition with each other, provide altogether a greater variety of information and opinion and increase the individual's level of freedom. A concentration into a few market-dominating enterprises, on the other hand, would narrow down the scope of a press which is multistructured in content. Due to the continual concentration of business interests this cannot be prevented in the long run even by measures taken within individual enterprises to ensure a diversity of the publications. At most it can be deferred temporarily in favourable economic conditions. The reasons for this are the same as the ones which apply to the behaviour of enterprises which have a dominant position in the market.

The maintenance of diversity in the Press in the form of an external plurality is therefore absolutely essential. All measures taken within individual publishing houses to ensure diversity within individual publications are therefore no substitute, but rather a concern completely independent thereof.

. . .

Notes

1. Co-determination is documented in Ch. 14, Docs. 5–9
2. The Evangelical Church in Germany comprises: the United Protestant Lutheran Church of Germany, the Protestant Church of the Union and the Reformed Alliance.

14
Economic and Social Policy
Detlev Karsten

The economic system of the Federal Republic of Germany has always been market-oriented, whereas in the German Democratic Republic a socialist system with central planning and a dominance of state ownership of all larger firms was established.* With reunification, the economic system of the Federal Republic of Germany was extended to the new Länder.

In the Federal Republic of Germany, a conscious decision in favour of a market system was taken in 1948 when the planned economy with its fixed prices—the heritage of the war and of the extreme poverty of the post-war period—was abandoned. This economic system of the Federal Republic of Germany can be characterized as basically market-orientated, with strong government intervention mainly for social reasons. The underlying theoretical concept of the economic system was—and to some extent is—the neo-liberal idea of a 'social market economy'. The basic philosophy of this concept is that economic processes should be regulated by market forces rather than by state control. The market forces, however, can only operate to the best advantage if they are harnessed by a legal framework, the most important element of which is a law to protect competition. As the market forces attribute income only to those who also contribute to production, a social policy has to supplement the system. In Germany, the essence of social policy is seen on the one hand in a strategy which secures growth, prosperity and full employment in a situation of stable prices (the latter being considered an instrumental goal both for the functioning of the economy and also a precondition for an effective social policy). This policy is, on the other hand, supplemented by specific welfare measures in support of those who are unable to work, but which also aim at a reduction of economic inequality by helping the economically weaker persons. This mixture of economic and social policy, which also incorporates a legal strengthening of the position of the weaker party in economic conflicts (e.g. the tenant *vis-à-vis* the landlord, the worker *vis-à-vis* the employer), is considered to be conducive to social stability.[1]

---

* *Notes for this chapter begin on p. 426.*

The decision in favour of a market-orientated economic system is now largely accepted as non-controversial between the major political parties (see also Ch.8). This helps to explain the continuity of economic policy regardless of which political parties form the government.

The Basic Law contains few provisions regarding the structure of the economic system. But it does guarantee rights which are necessary for an entrepreneurial system. The most important are:

Art. 2. Rights of Liberty

(1) Everyone shall have the right to the free development of his personality in so far as he does not violate the rights of others or offend against the constitutional order or the moral code.
(2) Everyone shall have the right to life and to inviolability of his person. The liberty of the individual shall be inviolable. These rights may only be encroached upon pursuant to a law.

Art. 9. Freedom of Association

(1) All Germans shall have the right to form associations and societies.
(2) Associations, the purposes or activities of which conflict with criminal laws or which are directed against the constitutional order or the concept of international understanding, are prohibited.
(3) The right to form associations to safeguard and improve working and economic conditions is guaranteed to everyone and to all trades, occupations and professions. Agreements which restrict or seek to impair this right shall be null and void; measures directed to this end shall be illegal ... .

Art. 12. Right to Choose Trade, Occupation or Profession

(1) All Germans shall have the right freely to choose their trade, occupation or profession, their place of work and their place of training. The practice of trades, occupations, and professions may be regulated by or pursuant to a law.
(2) No specific occupation may be imposed on any person except within the framework of a traditional compulsory public service that applies generally and equally to all.
(3) Forced labour may be imposed only on persons deprived of their liberty by court sentence.

Art. 14. Property, Right of Inheritance, Expropriation

(1) Property and the right of inheritance are guaranteed. Their content and limits shall be determined by the laws.
(2) Property imposes duties. Its use should also serve the public weal.
(3) Expropriation shall be permitted only in the public weal. It may be effected only by or pursuant to a law which shall provide for the nature and extent of the compensation. Such compensation shall be determined by establishing an equitable balance between the public interest and the interests of those affected. In case of dispute regarding the amount of compensation, recourse may be had to the ordinary courts.

Art. 15. Socialization

Land, natural resources and means of production may for the purpose of socialization be transferred to public ownership or other forms of publicly controlled economy by a law which shall provide for the nature and extent of compensation. In respect of such compensation the third and fourth sentences of paragraph (3) of Art. 14 shall apply *mutatis mutandis*.

Art. 2 implicitly includes the freedom of economic activity. The independence of the trade unions and employers' associations to determine working conditions through collective bargaining is an element of Art. 9, relating to the freedom of association. Art. 15 which allows socialization of the means of production has not gained a major importance. In Art. 20 (1) and Art. 28 (1) the Basic Law refers to the Federal Republic of Germany as a 'social state', a claim which is interpreted not only as an admonition addressed to the legislature but is also directly relevant for the interpretation of all legal provisions and administrative activities.

It is symptomatic of the general political climate and of the awareness of these issues in the Federal Republic of Germany that a discussion arose as to whether the Basic Law had taken a conscious decision in favour of a specific concept of an economic system, the 'social market economy'. The defenders of this idea tried to raise the 'social market economy' to a constitutional principle. This view was refuted in 1954 when the Federal Constitutional Court ruled that the Basic Law was neutral in regard to the economic system. But, in general, the issue of the economic system—mainly in the form of challenging the conformity or compatibility, with the existing system, of a particular economic or social policy measure—remains an important element of political debate.

The law which is fundamental to the market system is the 'Act against Restraints of Competition' of 1957 with important later amendments (Doc.1).

The recession of the mid-1960s made it apparent that a coordinated economic policy to combat cyclical fluctuations required an effective cooperation of the fiscal authorities of the Federation, the Länder and the municipalities. An attempt to secure this cooperation is the 'Act to Promote Economic Stability and Growth' (Stabilitätsgesetz) of 1967 which largely reflects the then dominant Keynesian view that fiscal policy is the most effective instrument to secure the economic stability (Doc.2). This law was controversial because it introduced a touch of macroeconomic planning into the existing market system and because it brought an element of centralization into a generally decentralized federal system (see also Ch.12). The latter was one of the reasons why the Basic Law was amended at the same time to define the financial autonomy of the Federation and the Länder more clearly:

Art. 109. Separate budgets for Federation and Länder

(1) The Federation and the Länder shall be autonomous and independent of each other in their fiscal administration.

(2) The Federation and the Länder shall take due account in their fiscal administration of the requirements of overall economic equilibrium.

(3) By means of federal legislation requiring the consent of the Bundesrat, principles applicable to both the Federation and the Länder may be established governing budgetary law, responsiveness of the fiscal administration to economic trends, and financial planning to cover several years ahead.

(4) With a view to averting disturbances of the overall economic equilibrium, federal legislation requiring the consent of the Bundesrat may be enacted providing for:

1. maximum amounts, terms and timing of loans to be raised by public administrative entities, whether territorial *(Gebietskörperschaften)* or functional *(Zweckverbände)*, and
2. an obligation on the part of the Federation and the Länder to maintain interest-free deposits in the German Federal Bank (reserves for counter-balancing economic trends).

Authorizations to enact pertinent ordinances having the force of law may be issued only to the Federal Government. Such ordinances shall require the consent of the Bundesrat. They shall be repealed in so far as the Bundestag may demand; details shall be regulated by federal legislation.

Article 72 of the Basic Law, which mainly regulates the powers of the Federation to legislate on matters which also affect the Länder, has gained particular relevance with reunification. It establishes an obligation of the Federal government to bring about 'uniformity of living conditions' in the whole Federation—this is the decisive challenge of reunification, because the new Länder are economically far behind the old Länder.

A particular feature of the German economic system is that the responsibility for monetary policy lies almost exclusively with the central bank, the Deutsche Bundesbank. As Germany has experienced two massive inflations in the course of this century, Germans are particularly sensitive about inflation. In consequence, the Bundesbank has been made an autonomous body which does not have to follow instructions from the Federal Government although it is obliged to support the Government's policy (Doc.3). This autonomy of the Bundesbank restricts the Government's control of monetary policy and has occasionally brought into the open conflicts between the Government, whose first priority is the reduction of unemployment even at the cost of a somewhat higher inflation, and the Bundesbank, whose first priority is the fighting of inflation.

In Germany, the first compulsory social insurance schemes were introduced in 1883. Since then, and especially since the Second World War, the drift has been towards a welfare state. The main reason for this development was the general acceptance of a need for a social policy to support and protect the economically disadvantaged. The present extent of social welfare policy, however, was only reached because of general prosperity, and financial constraints which became apparent in the 1980s and which are sharpened by the financial burdens of reunification may result in far-reaching reforms. The long-lasting prosperity had allowed the financing of social benefits out of public funds, and it had also made possible the burdening of business firms with claims resulting from such legal provisions. Since 1980, an attempt has been made to systematize at least some of the legislative measures in a 'Social Code' (Doc.4). But this picture remains incomplete without reference to other legal provisions as, for example, the general protection of tenants against expulsion, the protection of juvenile workers, of female workers, the guarantee of holidays, the subsidies for the educational system and many other measures of redistribution in favour of the economically weak.

Another important element of German economic life is the highly developed German system of co-determination (workers' participation) in industry. Co-determination was practised informally in the coal, iron and steel industry as early as 1947, and was codified for this sector in 1951 in the 'Act on the Co-determination of Workers in the Supervisory and Management Boards of Enterprises in the Mining Industry and the Iron and Steel Producing Industry'.

Co-determination can be seen as an instrument which improves the economic position of the workers by giving them more rights and more responsibilities in the running of the firm. There is, however, the difficulty that it has a tendency to become co-determination in the interests of the trade unions rather than of the actual workers (which do not necessarily coincide). Since workers' participation is such a specific feature of the German economic system it is dealt with rather more extensively here.[2] Doc.5a is an excerpt from the—essentially non-controversial—Works Constitution Act (*Betriebsverfassungsgesetz*) regulating workers' rights at the shop-floor level. Doc.5b is an excerpt from the Co-determination Act of 1976 which spells out workers' rights of co-determination at the board level. This act was challenged in the Federal Constitutional Court by some firms and employers' federations, and Doc.5c shows their main arguments. Doc.5d gives a general idea of the trade unions' position regarding co-determination. Doc.5e summarizes the relevant decision of the Federal Constitutional Court. The specific issue of co-determination in the coal, iron and steel industry has been omitted here.

An important current and future challenge for the economic and social system of the Federal Republic of Germany is the presence of a large number of foreign workers. At its height in 1976, foreign workers constituted 10 per cent of the labour force, and in 1992, 7.3 per cent of the inhabitants of Germany were foreigners who were also heavily concentrated regionally. Workers from EU countries who have a right to work in any member state constitute only a fraction of the foreign labour force. The real problem is represented by workers from non-EU countries, particularly Turks, who originally were brought to Germany for temporary relief of labour market shortages; they later brought their families, the majority of whom are likely to stay and will thus have to be integrated into German society.[3] There are also considerable numbers of immigrants of German descent from Eastern Europe as well as political refugees and asylum-seekers from other countries. The integration of all these people is a difficult process, especially in times of severe unemployment. The whole issue is politically controversial (Doc.6, see also Ch.8). Other currently controversial issues are the extent of environmental protection and the use of nuclear energy.[4]

The economic and social unification of the two Germanies has two aspects: one is the transformation of a previously socialist economy into a market economy, the other is the integration of two economies with widely divergent levels of economic development. In this process, the whole institutional framework of the Federal Republic of Germany—comprising almost all the legal provisions including the legislation of the European Community and the entire economic system—from one day to the other replaced the old 'socialist' system of the German Democratic Republic. The steps were the Economic and Monetary Union which became effective on 1 July 1990 (Doc.7), which replaced the weak GDR-Mark by the strong Deutschmark of the Federal Republic, and the 'Unification Treaty' which spelled out the terms of the unification which then took place on 3 October 1990 (see als Ch.4, Doc.9). The speed of this process resulted in serious friction; for example, the administrative officials did not even know the new laws and regulations, and very often were totally disconcerted, because they had to take decisions in matters they did not really understand; previously, the highly centralized state apparatus and the party had provided orientation in all important matters.

This unprecedented transition from a centralized state to a federal state and from a socialist to a market economy resulted in many problems and challenges. One was that in the GDR the economic activities, especially industry and agriculture, were organized in very large units, owned either by the state or by cooperatives. This called for two operations: breaking up these large units and privatizing them. Some firms which could not become profitable in the foreseeable future had to be closed down completely. To effect this privatization, a special institution was established: the Treuhandanstalt. Doc.8 describes this institution. The total number of firms to be privatized was about 12,500 and it is expected that its task will be completed by the end of 1993 or early in 1994; then the Treuhandanstalt will be shut down. The activities of the Treuhandanstalt remain controversial.[5] The original intention of rapid privatization overemphasized private profitability, to the detriment of overall economimc and social objectives, such as employment and the needs of structural and regional policy, and had to be changed accordingly. The economic transition was particularly difficult, because—on average—productivity in the GDR was about 30-40 per cent of the level in the Federal Republic of Germany in 1989; the reasons for this were outdated capital equipment, high disguised unemployment and institutional factors which resulted in lack of initiative and low incentives on all levels. The introduction of the strong Deutschmark into this system sharply increased wage-costs without a corresponding increase of productivity. As a consequence, many firms were suddenly no longer competitive; to increase productivity and to restore competitiveness, many workers were dismissed. But even so, a large number of firms never had a chance to recover, because with the often inferior quality of their products they were—because their eastern markets had collapsed—suddenly exposed to the competition on the European market, and the additional demand of the new Länder was often met by existing capacities in the west. Some firms of the previous GDR had no chance of surviving because they could not meet even minimal environmental standards, some had been only viable within the managed trade system of the Council of Mutual Economic Assistance, and some had been highly subsidized.

Consequently, the 'big bang' of the Economic and Monetary Union implied the necessity to restructure the economy on a scale that had not been anticipated by the politicians, although there had been warnings especially from economists. It will also take the new Länder much longer to attain the economic standards of the old Länder than originally envisaged; to date, it is thought that it will take about 15 years to reach 80 per cent of the per capita income of the old Länder. For a long time, the new Länder will depend on massive financial transfers from the old Länder: important challenges are the modernization of infrastructure, the improvement of housing and the rehabilitation of the run-down environment. On top of that, the high unemployment has to be largely financed by the old Länder, and in addition the other social security systems have to be heavily subsidized. This will continue until sufficient new permanent jobs are created; but in spite of strong incentives to encourage industrial investment in the new Länder, the response remains unsatisfactory. There are many reasons for this. Firstly, the West German Economy had surplus capacities, and new capacity in the East was superfluous. Secondly, a law which was formulated as an element of the Unification Treaty established the principle that restitution of property to previous owners or their heirs should have priority over their financial compensation (Doc.9). This principle, on account of the ensuing insecurity regarding ownership, worked as an impediment to investment. Despite modifications designed to speed up investment, uncertainty over ownership of landed property has led to long drawn out disputes damaging economic development.

The financial transfers required from the old to the new Länder can only be estimated; Doc.10 gives such an assessment. There is no question, that many people in the new Länder are disappointed by some of the economic and social consequences of the unification, especially by the resulting high unemployment and by their dependence on such massive transfers from the West, but also by the higher prices—especially rents—of all the goods which previously had been heavily subsidized. And in the old Länder, people feel the burden in the form of higher taxes, higher contributions to the social security institutions and high rates of interest resulting from a mounting public debt.

The 'Act against Restraints of Competition' of 1957 was passed only after sharp political controversies, especially between the 'purist' defenders of the social market economy concept and the representatives of business and industry who claimed that this law was unnecessarily restrictive and would impair the competitiveness of Germany in the international markets. The main elements are: (1) a general prohibition of cartels and similar arrangements with specified exceptions to this rule, (2) control of abuse by firms which hold a market-dominating position, (3) control and prevention of mergers by larger firms. Articles to protect competition are also contained in the EEC Treaty.

The excerpts reproduced here include later amendments.

Document 1

ACT AGAINST RESTRAINTS OF COMPETITION (GESETZ GEGEN WETTBEWERBSBESCHRÄNKUNGEN)

Source: *Gesetz gegen Wettbewerbsbeschränkungen*, BGBl, I, 1980, 1761ff.
Transl.: OECD

Section 1

(1) Agreements made for a common purpose by enterprises or associations of enterprises and decisions of associations of enterprises shall be of no effect, insofar as they are likely to influence, by restraining competition, production or market conditions with respect to trade in goods or commercial services. This shall apply only insofar as this Act does not provide otherwise.

. . .

Section 15

Agreements between enterprises with respect to goods or commercial services relating to markets located within the area of application of this Act shall be null and void, insofar as they restrict a party to them in its freedom to determine prices or terms of business in contracts which it concludes with third parties in regard to the goods supplied, other goods, or commercial services.

. . .

Section 22

(1) An enterprise is market dominating within the meaning of this Act insofar as, in its capacity as a supplier or buyer of a certain type of goods or commercial services:

1. it has no competitor or is not exposed to any substantial competition, or
2. it has a paramount market position in relation to its competitors; for this purpose, in addition to its share of the market, its financial strength, its access to the supply or sales markets for goods or services, its links with other enterprises and the legal or actual barriers to the market entry of other enterprises shall in particular be taken into account.

(2) Two or more enterprises shall also be deemed market dominating insofar as, in regard to a certain type of goods or commercial services, no substantial competition exists between them, for factual reasons, either in general, or in specific markets, and they jointly meet the requirements of subsection (1).

(3) It shall be presumed that:

1. an enterprise is market dominating within the meaning of subsection (1), if it has a market share of at least one-third for a certain type of goods or commercial services; this presumption shall not apply when the enterprise recorded a turnover of less than DM 250 million in the last completed business year;

the conditions specified in subsection (2) are met if, in regard to a certain type of goods or commercial services,

a) three or less enterprises have a combined market share of 50% or over, or
b) five or less enterprises have a combined market share of two-thirds or over this presumption shall not apply, insofar as enterprises are concerned which recorded turnovers of less than DM 100 million in the last completed business year.

As regards the calculation of the market share and turnover, Section 23 (1), sentences 2 to 10 shall apply, as appropriate.

(4) In regard to market dominating enterprises, the cartel authority shall have the powers set out in subsection (5), insofar as these enterprises abuse their dominating position in the market for these or any other goods or commercial services.

An abuse within the meaning of sentence 1 is present, in particular, if a market dominating enterprise as a supplier or buyer of a certain type of goods or commercial services:

1. impairs the competitive possibilities of other enterprises in a manner relevant to competition on the market in the absence of facts justifying such behaviour;
2. demands considerations or other business terms which deviate from those which would result in all probability if effective competition existed; in this context in particular the practices of enterprises on comparable markets characterised by effective competition have to be taken into account;

. . .

(5) If the conditions laid down in subsection (4) are satisfied the cartel authority may prohibit abusive practices by market dominating enterprises and declare agreements to be of no effect; ... Prior to such action, the cartel authority shall request the parties involved to discontinue the abuse to which objection was raised.

Section 23

(1) The merging of enterprises shall immediately be notified to the Federal Cartel Office, if:

1. within the total area of application of this Act or in a substantial part thereof a market share of at least 20% is obtained or increased by the merger or if a participating enterprise has a share of at least 20% in another market, or
2. the participating enterprises together at some date during the completed business year preceding the merger had at least 10,000 employees or recorded a turnover of at least DM 500 million in this period.

Section 24

(1) If it is likely that a market dominating position will be created or strengthened as a result of a merger, the cartel authority shall have the powers specified in the following provisions, unless the participating enterprises prove that the merger will also lead to improvements in the conditions of competition and that these improvements will outweigh the disadvantages of market domination.

(2) If the conditions of subsection (1) are present, the Federal Cartel Office shall prohibit the merger.

In its section 1, the 'Act to Promote Economic Stability and Growth' (Stabilitätsgesetz) of 1967 specifies goals of economic policy. The remaining sections stipulate how the actions of all fiscal authorities are to be coordinated to reach these goals. The following document is a description of this Act by the Deutsche Bundesbank.

Document 2

THE ACT TO PROMOTE STABILITY AND GROWTH (*STABILITÄTSGESETZ*)

Source: Deutsche Bundesbank, *Instruments of Monetary Policy in the Federal Republic of Germany*, Frankfurt, n.d., 6–8

The Act is based on the recognition that in present and future conditions the efficiency of the system of the free market economy can be safeguarded only if it is supplemented by overall control of the major aggregates of the economy. The Act sets up the necessary institutional machinery. It supplements and improves the traditional instruments of short-term economic and monetary policy and hence widens the Federal Government's and the Bundesbank's freedom of action in the economic policy field. The Act is at the same time designed to create the conditions necessary for achieving balanced economic development which, avoiding undue cyclical fluctuations, help to secure adequate economic growth in the longer term too.

Section 1 of the Act defines the general economic policy objectives. All economic and financial policy measures taken by the Federal Government and the Länder must be designed to 'contribute, in the framework of the free market economy, at the same time to price stability, to a high level of employment and to external equilibrium, along with steady and adequate economic growth'. Compliance with these objectives is required not only of the Federal Government and the Länder, but also of the Federal Railways, the Federal Post Office, the ERP Special Fund and the public boards and corporations directly controlled by the Federal Government. The local authorities and local authority associations must also take account of these basic objectives of economic policy in their budget policy.

To safeguard pursuit of these objectives, the Act provides for principles and measures which have sometimes a direct but sometimes only an indirect relevance for monetary policy; examples of the latter type include in particular the provision under the Act for the preparation of a 'subsidy report' at intervals of two years, and for the forward planning of the revenue and expenditure of the Federal Government and the Länder for a period of five years.

The measures laid down in the Act relate to the following four main fields:

(i) *Information*

A definition of the basic aims of economic policy is given in the Act itself.

The annual economic report of the Federal Government, submitted in January, sets out and explains the economic and financial aims envisaged for the current year and the proposed economic and financial policy. The report also contains a statement of the Federal Government's views on the annual opinion on the general economic trends rendered by the Council of Experts.

The report on subsidies, submitted every two years, similarly throws more light on economic and financial policy.

To enable the Government's economic policy and the autonomous decisions of the parties to collective wage agreements to be coordinated, the Federal Government, if a basic objective of economic policy is endangered, makes available target figures for 'concerted action' by the central, regional and local authorities, trade unions and employers' associations. In practice, these target figures are discussed in advance with the parties concerned. The Deutsche Bundesbank also takes part in these discussions.

(ii) *Financial planning*

The Act introduces forward planning, for a period of several years, of the revenue and the expenditure of the Federal Government and the Länder.

(iii) *Co-ordination among the public authorities*

To improve co-ordination of the measures taken by the Federal Government, the Länder and the local authorities in matters of economic and financial policy, the Act introduces elements of co-operative federalism into financial policy, in particular by establishing a Council on Economic Trends, and, more recently, a Financial Planning Council. The Bundesbank may take part in the discussions of either body.

(iv) *Creation of new instruments of short-term economic policy*

These include the provisions for influencing private demand by tax measures and for influencing the public authorities' investment policy, measures to widen the Bundesbank's room for manoeuvre in liquidity policy, provision for anti-cyclical reserves of the Federal Government and the Länder, rules for the borrowing and debt redemption operations of the public authorities, and provisions for the management of the public authorities' demand for credit.

The 1957 'Deutsche Bundesbank Act' specifies the responsibilities of the Bundesbank and its relationship with the Federal Government. In particular, it spells out the autonomy of the central bank.

Document 3

ACT TO ESTABLISH THE CENTRAL BANK *(BUNDESBANKGESETZ)*, 1957

Source: Gesetz über die Deutsche Bundesbank, BGBl., I, 1957, 745

§3 *Duty*

To safeguard the currency, the Deutsche Bundesbank controls the supply of money and credits. It does this by exercising the powers in the field of monetary policy assigned to it by this law. It also provides facilities for internal payment transactions as well as those with foreign countries.

. . .

§12 *Relationship of the Bank to the Federal Government*

Subject to the discharge of its duty, the Deutsche Bundesbank is obliged to support the general economic policy of the Federal Government. In the exercise of the powers assigned to it by this law it is independent of instructions from the Federal Government.

§13 *Cooperation*

(1) The Deutsche Bundesbank shall advise the Federal Government in matters of monetary policy which are of substantial importance and furnish the Federal Government with information at its request.

(2) The members of the Federal Government have the right to participate in the discussions of the Central Bank Council. The Central Bank Council (Zentralbankrat) is the policy-making body of the Bundesbank. They have no right to vote, but may propose motions. If they so request, a decision shall be deferred for up to two weeks.

(3) The Federal Government should invite the President of the Deutsche Bundesbank to take part in its discussions on important matters affecting monetary policy.

. . .

In 1970 a commission was established to codify and systematize social legislation. The first result was the general part of the Social Code which became law in 1976. This Act gives a general impression of the ambitious aims of social policy in the Federal Republic of Germany, although it covers only part of social policy legislation.

Document 4

SOCIAL CODE *(SOZIALGESETZBUCH)*

Source: The Federal Minister of Labour and Social Affairs, *Insurance Code/Social Code (extracts),* Bonn, 1981; BGBl., I, 1975, 3015
Transl.: ILO

Book I. General Part

Division I. Purposes of the Social Code and social rights

1. *Purposes of the Social Code.*

(1) The law declared in the Social Code is intended to provide for social benefits, including social and educational assistance, with the object of making a reality of social justice and social security. Its aim is to contribute to—

ensuring an existence worthy of human beings;

providing equal opportunities for the free development of the personality, especially for young persons;

protecting and encouraging the family;

enabling persons to derive a livelihood through freely chosen activity; and

averting or compensating for special burdens in life, inter alia, by helping persons to help themselves.

(2) The law declared in the Social Code is also intended to contribute to ensuring that the social services and institutions required to achieve the purposes specified in subsection (1) are available at the proper time and on the proper scale.

2. *Social rights.*

(1) The social rights referred to hereinafter serve to achieve the purposes specified in section 1. Claims in connection with such rights may be advanced or derived only in so far as specific provision for the relevant conditions and constituent elements has been made in the special Parts of this Code.

(2) The social rights provided for hereinafter shall be respected in the interpretation of the provisions of this Code and in the exercise of discretionary powers; every effort shall be made in the process to ensure that such rights are implemented to the broadest possible extent.

3. *Training incentives and employment promotion.*

(1) Any person taking part in training corresponding to his inclinations, aptitudes and capacities shall have a right to individual incentives toward such training if the necessary means for the purpose are not otherwise available to him.

(2) Any person taking part, or wishing to take part, in employment shall have a right to—

1. guidance in choosing his form of training and occupation;
2. individual support for his subsequent training (further training and retraining);
3. assistance in obtaining and retaining a suitable job; and

4. financial security in the event of unemployment or the insolvency of his employer.

4. *Social insurance.*

(1) Every person shall have a right of access to social insurance, as provided in this Code.

(2) Any person who is covered by social insurance shall have a right, as part of the statutory sickness, accident and pension insurance schemes, including the farmers' old-age assistance scheme, to—

1. the necessary measures to protect, maintain, improve and restore his health and strength; and
2. financial security in the event of sickness, maternity, reduced earning capacity and old age.

An insured person's survivors shall also have a right to financial security.

5. *Social compensation in the event of injuries to health.*

Any person sustaining injury to his health shall, if the national community, acting in accordance with the principles laid down in the legislation relating to war victims, assumes responsibility for the consequences of the injury so as to compensate him for any special sacrifice or for other reasons, have a right to—

1. the necessary measures to maintain, improve and restore his health and strength; and
2. appropriate financial relief.

The survivors of a person suffering any such injury shall also have a right to appropriate financial relief.

6. *Deduction of family expenditure.*

Any person who provides, or is required to provide, for the maintenance of children shall have a right to a reduction of the resulting financial burdens.

7. *Subsidies for appropriate housing.*

Any person who has to incur expenditure in connection with appropriate housing that he cannot reasonably be expected to incur shall have a right to a subsidy towards his rent or comparable expenditure.

8. *Assistance to youth.*

Every young person shall have a right to an upbringing for the better development of his personality. This right shall be guaranteed by the youth assistance scheme, through benefits for the general encouragement of youth and family upbringing and, in so far as it is not implemented by the parents, through educational assistance.

9. *Social assistance.*

Any person who is not in a position to provide himself with the necessities of life through his own efforts or to help himself in special circumstances and who does not receive sufficient help from any other quarter shall have a right to personal and financial assistance which is in keeping with his special needs, enables him to help himself and take part in the life of the community and ensures that he can lead a life that is worthy of a human being.

10. *Resettlement of handicapped persons.*
Any person who is, or is in danger of becoming, physically, mentally or spiritually handicapped shall have a right to such assistance as he needs to—

1. avert, eliminate or improve his handicap, prevent its aggravation or alleviate its consequences;
2. ensure that he obtains a place in the community, and more particularly in employment, corresponding to his inclinations and abilities.

. . .

The trade unions' demand for co-determination has a long tradition in the Federal Republic of Germany. In 1953, a first Works Constitution Act (Betriebsverfassungsgesetz) regulating co-determination at the shop floor level was passed; in 1972 it was replaced by a new Works Constitution Act. In contrast to co-determination at the board level, co-determination at the shop-floor level is largely non-controversial.

Document 5a

WORKS CONSTITUTION ACT 1972: CO-DETERMINATION AT THE SHOP FLOOR LEVEL

Source: The Federal Minister of Labour and Social Affairs, *Co-determination in the Federal Republic of Germany,* Bonn, 1980, 103; 149–151 BGBl., I, 1972, 13 *Transl.:* ILO

Part I. General provisions

1. Establishment of Works Councils

Works councils shall be elected in all establishments (Betriebe) that normally have five or more permanent employees with voting rights, including three who are eligible.

. . .

87. Right of Co-determination

(1) The works council shall have a right of co-determination in the following matters in so far as they are not prescribed by legislation or collective agreement:

1. matters relating to the order by operation of the establishment and the conduct of employees in the establishment;
2. the commencement and termination of the daily working hours including breaks and the distribution of working hours among the days of the week;
3. any temporary reduction or extension of the hours normally worked in the establishment;
4. the time and place for and the form of payment of remuneration;
5. the establishment of general principles for leave arrangements and the preparation of the leave schedule as well as fixing the time at which the

leave is to be taken by individual employees, if no agreement is reached between the employer and the employees concerned;

6. the introduction and use of technical devices designed to monitor the behaviour or performance of the employees;
7. arrangements for the prevention of employment accidents and occupational diseases and for the protection of health on the basis of legislation or safety regulations;
8. the form, structuring and administration of social services where scope is limited to the establishment, company or combine;
9. the assignment of and notice to vacate accommodation that is rented to employees in view of their employment relationship as well as the general fixing of the conditions for the use of such accommodation;
10. questions related to remuneration arrangements in the establishment, including in particular the establishment of principles of remuneration and the introduction and application of new remuneration methods or modification of existing methods;
11. the fixing of job and bonus rates and comparable performance-related remuneration including cash coefficients (i.e. prices per time unit);
12. principles for suggestion schemes in the establishment.

(2) If no agreement can be reached on a matter covered by the preceding subsection, the conciliation committee shall make a decision. The award of the conciliation committee shall take the place of an agreement between the employer and the works council.

Co-determination at the board level was practised successfully for more than twenty-five years in the coal, iron and steel industry. In spite of this positive experience, the Co-determination Act of 1976 which brought co-determination at the board level to all larger companies was passed only after heated public debate.

Document 5b

ACT RESPECTING WORKERS' CO-DETERMINATION (*GESETZ ÜBER DIE MITBESTIMMUNG DER ARBEITNEHMER*): CO-DETERMINATION AT BOARD LEVEL

Source: The Federal Minister of Labour and Social Affairs, *Co-determination in the Federal Republic of Germany*, Bonn 1980,46,50–1;65–6; BGBl.,1976,1153
Transl.: ILO

1. Undertakings Covered

(1) Subject to the provisions of this Act, workers shall have a right of co-determination in undertakings which:

1. are run in the legal form of a joint-stock company, a company with limited partners holding share capital, a limited liability company, an incorporated cost-book company under mining law or a co-operative; and
2. normally employ over 2,000 workers.

. . .

7. Membership of Supervisory Boards

(1) The supervisory board of an undertaking:

1. normally employing not more than 10,000 workers shall consist of six
   shareholders' members and six workers' members;
2. normally employing more than 10,000 but not more than 20,000 workers
   shall consist of eight shareholders' members and eight workers' members;
3. normally employing more than 20,000 workers shall consist of ten shareholders' members and ten workers' members.

. . .

(2) The workers' members of a supervisory board must include:

1. four workers of the undertaking and two trade union representatives,
   where the board has six workers' members;
2. six workers of the undertaking and two trade union representatives, where
   the board has eight workers' members;
3. seven workers of the undertaking and three trade union representatives,
   where the board has ten workers' members.

. . .

27. Chairmanship of Supervisory Boards

(1) The supervisory board shall elect a chairman and vice-chairman from
among its own number by a majority of two-thirds of the total number of
members of which it is required to be composed.

(2) Where the requisite majority under subsection (1) is not attained during
the election of the chairman or vice-chairman of the supervisory board, a
second vote shall be taken. In this vote the shareholders' members of the
supervisory board shall elect the chairman and the workers' members shall
elect the vice-chairman, in each case by a majority of the votes cast.

. . .

29. Voting

(1) The decisions of the supervisory board shall be taken by a majority of the
votes cast, ...

(2) Where voting in the supervisory board results in a tie and a further vote
on the same subject also results in a tie, the chairman of the board shall have
a casting vote ... . The vice-chairman shall not have a casting vote.

The Co-determination Act of 1976 was strongly criticized by the
business world. Their main objection was that co-determination
might result in more cumbersome decision-making, and thus adversely affect efficiency. Some firms and employers' associations chal-

lenged the legality of the Act in the Federal Constitutional Court. The main arguments of this appeal are summarized here.

Document 5c

THE EMPLOYERS' CRITICISMS OF CO-DETERMINATION AT BOARD LEVEL

Source: The Federal Minister of Labour and Social Affairs, *Co-determination in the Federal Republic of Germany,* Bonn, 1980, 23-4
Transl.: Official

The Constitutional Appeals by the Employers
Constitutional Appeal against the Main Provisions

Even after the German Bundestag passed the new Co-determination Act with an overwhelming majority (including the votes of the Opposition), this did not bring about an end to the constitutional assaults. On 29 June 1977, nine firms and twenty-nine employers' associations lodged an appeal with the Federal Constitutional Court on constitutional grounds against the main provisions of the Co-determination Act.

The employers motivated their constitutional appeals as follows:

- The Co-determination Act contains a provision on the right of employees to an equal say in the supervisory board and this will lead sooner or later to an equal number of employees' and shareholders' representatives in management.
- The provisions of the Co-determination Act and those of the new Works Constitution Act of 1972 mean that the employees' rights will prevail and thus lead to 'supra-parity'.
- Hence, the Co-determination Act infringes the property guarantee contained in Art. 14 of the Basic Law. Shareholders' property is fundamentally affected both in the substance of members' rights as well as in that of their pecuniary rights.
- The Co-determination Act contains elements of an enforced amalgamation between shareholders and employees and thus infringes the free right to form associations and societies pursuant to Art.9, para.1 of the Basic Law.
- Furthermore, the Act infringes entrepreneurial freedom as part of the right freely to choose one's trade, occupation or profession (Art.12 of the Basic Law).
- Finally, the Co-determination Act offends against the right to form associations (Art.9, para.3 of the Basic Law). The employers argued that co-determination in undertakings makes the employers' associations dependent on the opposing side and thus renders the collective wage bargaining system unworkable.
- All things considered, the Co-determination Act results in a reshaping of the structure of the economy and of labour, which would only have been admissible by a law enacted to amend the Constitution.

The 1978 Congress of the German Federation of Trade Unions emphasized the unions' views on co-determination by accepting the following motion.

Document 5d

THE TRADE UNION VIEW OF CO-DETERMINATION

Source: 11th Full Federal Congress of the German Federation of Trade Unions (Deutscher Gewerkschaftsbund-DGB), Hamburg, 1978

Motion No. 17 (adopted)

Concerning co-determination in firms and the economy
The Federal Congress is to adopt the following resolution:

The 11th Full Federal Congress of the DGB renews its demand for co-determination on the part of workers in plants, firms and the economy as a whole as a decisive step towards the democratic restructuring of the economy and society. Co-determination in firms is an essential part of the overall demand for democratizing the economy. The demand for co-determination means not only scope for strong, independent and combative trade unions and acceptance of the principle of free collective bargaining over working and economic conditions, but also supervision of control over the means of production wherever economic power is exercised, i.e. co-determination on the shop-floor through shop stewards, works and staff councils; the right of works' and staff councils to full co-determination in all aspects of management and administration; parity co-determination on the supervisory boards of large firms and concerns; co-determination in the economy as a whole.

The economic crisis has clearly shown that jobs and trainee opportunities and other employee interests are endangered when economic and social development is subordinated to the profit motives of firms. Parity co-determination on the basis of the model practised in the Coal, Iron and Steel Industry is necessary for guarding the rights of employees, supervising investment, protecting employees in cases of rationalization, increasing job safety, improving working conditions, exploiting to the full the rights of works councils and for widening the scope of shop stewards.

The following are essential elements in this:

- Parity on supervisory boards. Employees must be represented in equal numbers and with the same voting rights as shareholders.
- Co-determination through uniform employee representation on supervisory boards. The employee side must not be split by granting special rights to higher grade salaried staff.
- Participation of employee representatives from outside the firm on an equal footing
- Election and removal of employee representatives by the works councils.

– One Labour Director to be a member of the Board with equal rights. He may not be elected to, or removed from, the supervisory board against the wishes of a majority of the employee representatives.

The 1976 Co-determination Act provides on the other hand only for an extension of employee participation on the supervisory boards of certain larger firms. This is a result in particular of:

– Sham-parity on supervisory boards. A genuine equality is prevented by the special representation given to higher-grade salaried staff and by the chairman's double voting rights.
– The splitting of the employee side as a result of the granting of special rights to higher-grade salaried staff.
– The voting procedure which is complicated and also undermines the solidarity of the employee representatives.
– The Labour Director not being safe-guarded according to the model practised in the Coal, Iron and Steel Industry.

The solidarity of all employees, the board's supervisory functions and the uniformity of representation are endangered. The trade unions are called upon to reject these threats to the representation of their interests and at the same time to exploit realistically the opportunities for an improved employee representation provided by the 1976 Co-determination Act.

For this purpose the following are particularly vital:

– Cooperation of all representatives (trade unions, shop-stewards, works and staff councils, employee representatives on supervisory boards).
– Use of additional means of information and argument for improving the work of trade unions and works councils.
– Elaboration and enforcement of demands relating to plants, firms and particular trades.

The trade unions must elucidate their ideas for the minimum rights of employee representation. Among these are:

– Minimum demands for responsibilities on supervisory boards.
– Effective participation in the election of members of the management board. Proposals for information appropriate to co-determination and for the involvement of employee-representatives at the planning stage.
– Preparations for the election, functions and competency of the labour director.
– The division of responsibilities between the employee representatives on the supervisory board.

At the same time it is necessary to link all actions aiming at the full use of the rights of the works council with the potential the trade unions have as a partner in free collective bargaining. This would help to develop and enforce demands of trade union policy on the shop floor. Demands relating to plants and firms must be closely linked to the overall trade union programmes and aims. The demands should draw attention to the firm as a place where social conflicts are argued out and to the diverging interests of labour and capital. They should also involve members and officials in the enforcement of these demands. Spheres of influence might be: jobs and apprenticeships, the social

and personal aspects of coming to terms with rationalization measures, income
guarantees, working conditions, training and further training, information.

Further requirements for making trade union representation effective are:

- The strengthening of the trade unions on the shop-floor, especially through
  increasing union membership; strengthening of the position of shop stewards; trade union support for works and staff councils.
- Extending the range of action of wage policy, especially with regard to
  work place lay-out.
- Pointing to the limitations of the 1976 Co-determination Act and co-
  determination in firms; no taking of responsibility for the decisions reached
  by bodies not sufficiently under the influence of the trade unions.
- Setting up economic and social councils at regional, state and federal level
  as bodies of overall economic co-determination (as demanded by the DGB
  since 1971).

All trade unionists are called upon to defend the co-determination model
of the Coal, Iron and Steel Industry and to fight for its extension to all large-
scale firms and for a reduction in the unilateral control of the entrepreneurs
in firms and the economy as a whole.

In 1979, the Federal Constitutional Court rejected the complaint of
the employers. The main reasons for this decision were given in an
accompanying statement by the Public Relations Office of the Federal Constitutional Court.

Document 5e

THE FEDERAL CONSTITUTIONAL COURT'S JUDGMENT ON THE CO-DETERMINATION ACT

Source: The Federal Minister of Labour and Social Affairs, *Co-determination
in the Federal Republic of Germany,* Bonn, 1980, 38–41. The judgment itself
is to be found in *Entscheidungen des Bundesverfassungsgerichts,* Vol.50,
290ff.

Transl.: Official

Statement by the Public Relations Office of the Federal Constitutional Court

The First Panel of the Federal Constitutional Court today pronounced its
judgment in the two proceedings linked together for a joint hearing and
decision on the Co-determination Act of 4 May 1976.

. . .

(a) To begin with, the decision clarifies the extent of workers' influence in
    undertakings pursuant to the Act, which is taken as the basis for further

examination by the Court. Neither from the legal standpoint nor in any other way connected with the Act is their influence equal to that of the other side or indeed more than equal. Under the statutory provisions, one cannot proceed on the assumption of parity co-determination because of the second vote accorded to the chairman of the supervisory board, who is normally elected by the shareholders, and because of the non-homogeneous composition of the employees' side comprising workers, salaried employees and senior executives. That also holds true if one includes the partially equal rights of co determination for the works council. The basic assumption of the complainants that this non-equal representation in reality conceals a fundamentally equal or even more-than-equal representation, which the legislators actually envisaged or wished to facilitate, does not lead to any other judgment, either. There is nothing to indicate that the material substance of the case, which is fundamentally authoritative for an examination of its constitutionality, and the actual impact of the contested normative provisions are divergent in any way.

(b) There is no certainty about what effect this slightly sub-parity co-determination will produce in future. Particular importance attaches to cooperation in individual firms—a cooperation which the law itself can only facilitate and encourage by providing the machinery. If both sides are willing to engage in loyal cooperation, co-determination for employees will produce a different effect than a situation in which the atmosphere of undertakings is dominated by mutual distrust or even enmity. Another factor which may prove significant is whether there is a willingness outside the undertakings to welcome co-determination in its present form in the interest of these individual enterprises as well as of the economy as a whole. Unlike the complainants, the legislators proceeded on the assumption that the effects envisaged by the Act would actually occur and that they would not involve any disadvantageous consequences for the viability of the individual undertakings and for the economy as a whole. The Federal Constitutional Court could only proceed from another assumption if the prognosis made by the legislators about the future effects of the law did not accord with the requirements of the Constitution. This was not the case, as the legislators had based their opinion on an objective and justifiable assessment of the available material.

The presence of a large number of foreigners in Germany—most of them either originally migrant workers, who with their families seem to be remaining in Germany, or asylum-seekers—has resulted in political problems of all kinds. In July 1993, The Federal Ministry of the Interior published a document, from which the following excerpt is taken.

Document 6

FOREIGN WORKERS AS A CHALLENGE TO POLICY

Source: The Federal Ministry of the Interior, *Survey of the Policy and Law Concerning Foreigners in the Federal Republic of Germany*, Bonn, July 1993, 5–7
Transl.: Official

Basic tenets of the Federal Government's aliens policy

Principles of aliens policy

The aliens policy of the Federal Government aims at

– the **integration** of aliens living legally in our country, particularly recruited foreign workers and their families
– the **restriction** of further immigration from non-EC Member states.

It also includes giving assistance for the **voluntary return** to and re-integration in the home countries.

Aliens living permanently in our country are to be integrated into our economic, social and legal system and may rest assured that they will be given the opportunity to participate to the greatest possible extent and as equal partners in the social life in the Federal Republic of Germany.

This objective, however, can be achieved only if any further immigration from non-EC Member States is consistently restricted.

These positions are in keeping with the long-standing convictions of all parties bearing responsibility within the Federal Government.

With regard to the policy aimed at restricting any further immigration, the Federal Government took, in November 1981 and in February 1982, inter alia, the following decisions:

> 'There is agreement on the fact that the Federal Republic of Germany is neither to be nor to become a country of immigration. The Cabinet is agreed that any further immigration of aliens from non-EC Member States is to be prevented by all legal means.

> . . .

> It is only by applying a consistent and efficient policy of restriction ... that the indispensable commitment of the German population to the integration of aliens can be ensured. This is a prerequisite for safeguarding social peace.'

Integration

Some 47 percent of aliens staying in the Federal Republic of Germany have been living here for ten years or more. Over two in three foreign children and juveniles were born in the Federal Republic of Germany ... .

For these persons there is no convincing alternative to integration (i.e. participation in the economic, social and cultural life in the Federal Republic of Germany).

Integration is facilitated by the legal framework which enables aliens to live under secured conditions as regards their stay and their situation on the labour market ... .

Integration is promoted by the Federation, the Länder, the local authorities but also by social groups (Churches, trade unions, employers, private welfare institutions, clubs) and many other independent groups.

However, integration as a process of adaptation to German conditions also requires some participation of the aliens, who have to accustom themselves above all to the values, norms and ways of living prevailing here. Respect for our culture and the principles of our constitution (separation of State and Church, position of women, religious tolerance), the acquisition of some knowledge of the German language, abandonment of excessive national-religious behaviours and integration into school and professional life (compliance with the obligation to attend school, vocational training also for women, immigration of children at an early stage) are the prerequisites which have to be fulfilled. On the other hand, the aliens living in our country may expect the German population to be tolerant.

. . .

Restrictions

Integration can only be achieved if there are uncompromising restrictions on further immigration from non-EC Member States. Even though aliens stay here for a long period of time or even stay for good, the Federal Republic of Germany does not regard itself as an immigration country, although the recruitment of foreign labour has led many aliens to stay for good. The objective of achieving a successful integration of those aliens who have been living here for a long period, the fact that priority has to be granted to nationals from EC-Member States but also the present situation on the labour market are factors that speak against the idea of tolerating another major influx of immigrants coming to our country as they did in the 1960s and 70s.

. . .

At the same time, the Federal Government has to take further steps against the **abuse of the right to asylum,** which constitutes a form of hidden immigration. In this context, the term 'abuse' is used to describe cases where an individual invokes the provisions applicable in cases of political persecution and does so unjustifiedly from the very start. The Federal Government will continue its efforts both on the national and on the international level, to effectively combat **illegal practices connected with entering, staying and working** in the Federal Republic of Germany ... .

The Treaty on the Establishment of a Monetary, Economic and Social Union, concluded between the Federal Republic of Germany and the German Democratic Republic on 18 May 1990. This Agreement—which took full effect on 1 July 1990—was the decisive step towards political reunification (see also Ch.4).

Document 7

TREATY ON THE ESTABLISHMENT OF A MONETARY, ECONOMIC AND SOCIAL UNION

Source: Presse- und Informationsamt der Bundesregierung, *The Unification of Germany in 1990,* Bonn 1991
Transl.: Official

Article 1

Subject of the Treaty
(1) The Contracting Parties shall establish a Monetary, Economic and Social Union.
(2) Starting on 1 July 1990 the Contracting Parties shall constitute a Monetary Union comprising a unified currency area and with the Deutsche Mark as the common currency. The Deutsche Bundesbank shall be the central bank in this currency area. The liabilities and claims expressed in Mark of the German Democratic Republic shall be converted into Deutsche Mark in accordance with this Treaty.
(3) The basis of the Economic Union shall be the social market economy as the common economic system of the two Contracting Parties. It shall be determined particularly by private ownership, competition, free pricing and, as a basic principle, complete freedom of movement of labour, capital, goods and services; this shall not preclude the legal admission of special forms of ownership providing for the participation of public authorities or other legal entities in trade and commerce as long as private legal entities are not subject to discrimination. It shall take into account the requirements of environmental protection.
(4) The Social Union together with the Monetary and Economic Union shall form one entity. It shall be characterized in particular by a system of labour law that corresponds to the social market economy and a comprehensive system of social security based on merit and social justice.
[The principles of the Monetary Union are specified in Art.10, Para.5]:

Article 10

. . .

(5) To achieve the aims described in paragraphs 1 to 4 above, the contracting Parties shall, in accordance with the provisions laid down in Annex I, agree on the following principles for Monetary Union:

   – With effect from 1 July 1990 the Deutsche Mark shall be introduced as currency in the German Democratic Republic. The banknotes issued by the Deutsche Bundesbank and denominated in Deutsche Mark, and the federal coins issued by the Federal Republic of Germany and denominated in Deutsche Mark or Pfennig, shall be sole legal tender from 1 July 1990.
   – Wages, salaries, grants, pensions, rents and leases as well as other recurring payments shall be converted at a rate of one to one.

– All other claims and liabilities denominated in Mark of the German Democratic Republic shall be converted to Deutsche Mark at the rate of two to one.
– The conversion of banknotes and coins denominated in Mark of the German Democratic Republic shall only be possible for persons or agencies domiciled in the German Democratic Republic via accounts with financial institutions in the German Democratic Republic into which the cash amounts to be converted may be paid.
– Deposits with financial institutions held by individuals domiciled in the German Democratic Republic shall be converted upon application at a rate of one to one up to certain limits, there being a differentiation according to the age of the beneficiaries.
– Special regulations shall apply to deposits of persons domiciled outside the German Democratic Republic.
– Action shall be taken against abuse.

. . .

The *Treuhandanstalt* was established before reunification by a law passed by the last GDR Parliament on 17 June 1990. Its main objective was to reduce the economic activities of the state by privatizing state enterprises to allow the transition to a social market economy (see also Ch.4). The following excerpt from a Treuhandanstalt report describes its work.

Document 8

THE TREUHANDANSTALT

Source: Treuhandanstalt, Abteilung Öffentlichkeitsarbeit, *The Chance of the 90's: Investing in Eastern Germany*, Berlin, n.d., 9

The Treuhandanstalt

The Treuhandanstalt is the most significant new institution created to manage the economic unification of Germany. In its short but turbulent history it has grown from nothing to an organisation with 3,000 staff split between the Berlin Head Quarters and 15 regional offices throughout east Germany. Its principal aim since June 1990 has been the swift privatisation of eastern German industry plus 25bn sq metres of real estate, 17.2bn sq metres of farmland and 19.6bn sq metres of forest. But the Treuhand was actually conceived in March 1990 by East Germany's last semi-communist government and has since lived with three governments and three changes of structure.

. . .

On June 17 a Trusteeship was passed by eastern Germany's shortlived democratic government which transferred all state owned enterprises and property to the Treuhandanstalt and laid-down that on the day of economic and currency union (July 1st) all enterprises should be converted into West German-style corporations (either limited liability GmbHs or stock companies AGs).

. . .

Since June 1990 the organisations' objectives have been to privatise—principally through 100 per cent sales—to restructure (with a view to privatising) or to close the companies in its control when necessary. Additionally the Treuhandanstalt has been charged with breaking up the larger combines, so that instead of the original 8,000 industrial companies it now owns about 10,000 despite having sold 3,000 (July 1991).

. . .

Treuhandanstalt executives were initially side-tracked into keeping the shell-shocked eastern German companies afloat. A total of DM 20bn in liquidity credit was handed out in the first three months after currency union merely to ensure that the companies could pay their wages.

. . .

The privatisation figure, only a couple of hundred at the end of 1990, began to rise sharply at the beginning of 1991. In March the Government responded with a new package of interventionist measures, known as 'Upswing East'. At the same time the Treuhandanstalt placed great public emphasis on the restructuring of those companies which could not be quickly privatised and intensified closer cooperation with the five east German Länder (states).

. . .

The strategy remained the same:

   # to privatise wherever possible
   # to restructure companies with a view to later privatisation
   # to close companies who have no chance of surviving in a market economy.

As an element of the Unification Treaty, a law on the 'Regulation of open Property issues' was negotiated. The following provision of this law is highly controversial.

Document 9

RESTITUTION BEFORE COMPENSATION

Source: Gesetz zur Regelung offener Vermögensfragen vom 23.9.1990, BGBl. II, 1159
Transl.: Official

Act on the Settlement of Open Property Questions

Chapter I
General Provisions

Section 1
Scope of Application

(1) This Act shall settle pecuniary claims to assets which

(a) were expropriated without compensation and transferred into public ownership;
(b) were expropriated with less compensation being paid than that to which citizens of the former German Democratic Republic were entitled;
(c) were sold to third parties by state administrators or, after their transfer into public ownership, by the authorized agents;
(d) were transferred into public ownership on the basis of the decision taken by the Presidium of the Council of Ministers on 9 February 1972 and of related provisions.

(2) Moreover, this Act shall apply to developed real estate and buildings which, on account of rents insufficient to cover the costs and the resulting insolvency, were transferred into public ownership on the basis of expropriation, relinquishment of ownership, a donation or disclaimer of an inheritance.
(3) This Act shall also apply to claims to assets and rights of use acquired by means of dishonest practices, e.g. abuse of power, corruption, coercion or deceit on the part of the purchaser, government agencies or third parties.

. . .

Section 2
Definition

(1) For the purposes of this Act, parties entitled to submit a claim shall be natural and legal persons whose assets are affected by measures pursuant to Section 1 as well as their legal successors.

. . .

Chapter II
Return of assets

Section 3
Principle

(1) Assets which were subject to the measures pursuant to Section 1 and were transferred into public ownership or sold to third parties shall be

returned to the claimants upon application, where this is not ruled out by
this Act. The decision on such return shall lie with the agency responsible.
. . .

In order to even out the economic disparities between the old and
the new Länder, funds and taxes raised in the old Länder are spent in
the new Länder. The volume of these transfers required can only be
estimated.

The following excerpt is taken from a publication of the Director
of the well renowned Institut for Weltwirtschaft, Kiel, who is also a
member of the Council of Economic Advisors.

Document 10

FINANCIAL TRANSFERS REQUIRED

Source: Horst Siebert, *The Big Bang with the Big Brother, German Unification
in Its Third Year,* Kiel Discussion Papers No. 211, Institut für Weltwirtschaft
Kiel, May 1993, p. 10/11:

. . .

Unification was also a shock to the German economy as a whole. Germany
after unification is characterized by a high capital demand, with capital being
needed to replace the capital stock in eastern Germany and to finance public consumption transfers. At the same time, there is an excess supply of
labour, with 3.5 million officially unemployed and 2.5 million in the secondary labour market.

Another basic condition in Germany is the need for governmental transfers, which are running at 150 billion DM per year. In addition, German fiscal policy has to finance the interest payments on the additional debt burden,
which roughly calculated is 30 billion DM ... . All in all, Germany will have
to finance 180 billion DM per year (6 percent of GNP). There are three
options: (1) Increasing the debt, (2) reducing expenditures while shifting
public expenditures to eastern Germany, or (3) increasing taxation.

. . .

It is estimated that the Treuhand will accumulate a debt of 250 billion DM
by 1994. The Credit Processing Fund *(Kreditabwicklungsfonds),* which
manages the liabilities of the former GDR and covers the differential conversion rates for the debt of socialist firms and for individual savings, will
have to be taken over by the federal government. It is estimated that a debt
of 140 billion DM will have been accumulated by the fund. The German
Unity Fund, funded by the federal government and the *Länder,* will have
accumulated 95 billion DM at the end of 1994. The debt of the public
housing sector will be 50 billion DM.

The debt of the total public sector, which amounted to 929 billion DM
in 1989, will have reached 1.9 trillion DM by 1994. Thus, public debt will

double within five years. In relative terms, the ratio of public debt to GNP will rise from 41 percent in 1989 to 58 percent in 1994 ... . Public expenditures relative to GNP will rise from 45 percent in 1989 to over 52 percent in 1994 ... .

The risk for the future is that the budget deficit will have a strong impact on economic policy ... . Financing expenditures may raise either interest rates or taxes, and this will choke off investment. The most serious danger is that the financial constraints will develop into a severe burden for the western German economy, which has to finance the transfers to eastern Germany. This could trigger a vicious circle in which the problems of the east eventually influence the efficiency of the west.

In the solidarity pact of March 1993, an attempt was made to integrate the eastern German *Länder* into Germany's horizontal transfer system among the *Länder (Finanzausgleich)* and to allocate the financing of the transfers to the different federal layers of government ... .

Notes

1. The small number of industrial stoppages is an indicator of relatively peaceful labour relations; see Statistics, Table 9.
2. Cf. Volker R. Berghahn / Detlev Karsten, *Industrial Relations in West Germany*, Oxford etc. 1987.
3. Foreigners acquire the right of permanent residence in the Federal Republic of Germany after five to eight years, and may be granted German nationality after about ten years. Special regulations apply to workers from EU-countries.
4. There are 16 nuclear plants in Germany which in 1992 contributed about one third to the total production of electricity.
5. Jan Priewe, 'Die Folgen der schnellen Privatisierung der Treuhandanstalt, Eine vorläufige Schlußbilanz', *Aus Politik und Zeitgeschichte*, Beilage zur Wochenzeitung Das Parlament, B43-44/94, 28 Oktober 1994, 21–30.

Statistical Tables

Table 1 Population 1991 by age group

Age group	Germany		old Länder		new Länder and Berlin	
	1000	%	1000	%	1000	%
all	80,275	100	64,485	100	15,790	100
Below 15	13,600	17	10,560	16	3,040	19
15–40	29,621	37	24,029	37	5,592	35
40–65	25,521	31	20,530	32	4,991	32
Above 65	12,033	15	9,866	15	2,167	14

Source: Statistisches Jahrbuch 1993, 66

In December 1993, about 8 per cent of the resident population were foreigners; important individual groups were workers with their families from EC-countries (1.5 million) and from Turkey (1.9 million).

Source: Bundesministerium für Arbeit und Sozialordnung, *Ausländer-Daten*, Mai 1994, 2

Table 2 Expellees and immigrants of German descent after 1950 (the term expellees usually refers to those Germans who were forced to leave the German territories as they existed before the outbreak of the Second World War, i.e. in 1949 incorporated into Poland and into the former Soviet Union)

Country of origin	1950–1970	1971–1991	1992	1993
USSR (former)	22,493	528,078	195,576	207,347
Poland	408,425	1,003,892	17,742	5,431
CSSR (former)	80,796	23,435	460	134
Hungary	8,732	12,158	354	37
Rumania	26,267	359,387	16,146	5,811
Yugoslavia (former)	79,992	9,526	207	120
Other areas	2,600	436	15	3
TOTAL	629,305	1,936,904	230,500	218,883

Source: Federal Ministry of the Interior, Bonn 1994

Table 3 The number of asylum-seekers in the Federal Republic of Germany has developed as follows:

Year	Asylum-seekers	Proportion from the former Eastern bloc or Eastern Europe
1983	19,737	4,651 = 23.56%
1984	35,278	6,955 = 19.70%
1985	73,832	10,644 = 14.40%
1986	99,650	15,214 = 15.30%
1987	57,379	20,483 = 35.70%
1988	103,076	35,718 = 34.70%
1989	121,318	33,930 = 27.97%
1990	193,063	57,430 = 29.70%
1991	256,112	67,923 = 26.52%
1992	438,191	159,517 = 36.40%
1993 (first six months)	(244,033)	(150,756 = 67.30%)

In 1992, about 65 per cent of all asylum seekers in Western Europe sought refuge in Germany. In the same year, more than 50 per cent of all asylum seekers came from former Yugoslavia and Romania.

Source: The Federal Minister of the Interior, *Survey of the Policy and Law concerning Foreigners in the Federal Republic of Germany,* July 1993, 59

Table 4 Escapees from the German Democratic Republic and East Berlin to the Federal Republic of Germany

	Total	1.People who left GDR with official permission	2.Refugees who left GDR without permission	3.Numbers of 2. who faced lethal obstacles (after 13.8.1961)	Others
1949 to 12.8.1961 (erection of wall)	2,686,942	—	—	—	—
since erection of wall from 13.8.-31.12.1961	51,624	—	51,624	8,507	
1962	21,356	4,615	16,741	5,761	
1963	42,632	29,665	12,967	3,692	
1964	41,876	30,012	11,864	3,155	
1965	29,552	17,666	11,886	2,329	
1966	24,131	15,675	8,456	1,736	
1967	19,573	13,188	6,385	1,203	
1968	16,036	11,134	4,902	1,135	
1969	16,975	11,702	5,273	1,193	
1970	17,519	12,472	5,047	901	
1971	17,408	11,565	5,843	832	
1972	17,164	11,627	5,537	1,245	
1973	15,189	8,667	6,522	1,842	
1974	13,252	7,928	5,324	969	
1975	16,285	10,274	6,011	673	
1976	15,168	10,058	5,110	610	
1977	12,078	8,041	4,037	721	
1978	12,117	8,271	3,846	461	
1979	12,515	9,003	3,512	463	
1980	12,763	8,775	3,107	424	881
1981	15,433	11,093	2,900	288	1.440
1982	13,208	9,113	2,565	283	1.530
1983	11,343	7,729	2,487	228	1.127
1984	40,974	34,982	3,651	192	2.341
1985	24,912	18,752	3,484	160	2,676
1986	26,178	19,982	4,660	210	1,536
1987	18,958	11,459	6,252	288	1,247
1988	39,832	29,033	9,705	590	1,094
Total	616,051	382,481	219,698	40,101	13,872

In 1989 the mass-exodus began mainly via Hungary—prior to the downfall of the wall.

Source: Federal Ministry of the Interior, Bonn 1994

Table 5 Nominal GNP and GDP of East* and West Germany, 1991

	East Germany		West Germany	
	bil. DM	percent	bil. DM	percent
GNP and expenditure items				
Gross national product	193.1	100.0	2,615.2	100.0
Private consumption	196.3	101.6	1,379.1	52.7
Government consumption	90.2	46.7	469.4	17.9
Investment in machinery and equipment	36.0	18.6	263.8	10.1
Construction	36.4	18.9	306.0	11.7
Aggregate domestic demand	361.2	187.0	2,427.3	92.8
Exports	59.2	30.7	1,009.1	38.6
Imports	227.3	117.7	821.1	31.4
Gross domestic product	183.0	—	2,599.3	—
Gross value added by origin				
Gross value added	197.8	100.0	2,498.1	100.0
Agriculture, forestry and fishing	3.3	1.7	32.2	1.3
Manufacturing, energy mining and construction	67.5	34.1	999.8	40.0
Trade, transportation and communication	33.1	16.7	359.2	14.4
Services	47.0	23.8	771.5	30.9
Government, private households and nonprofit organizations	46.8	23.6	335.5	13.4

* Including East Berlin

Source: Horst Siebert, *Five Traps for German Economic Policy,* Kiel Discussion Papers 185/April 1992, 26

Table 6 Average monthly gross income of workers and salaried employees in the new Länder as a percentage of the level of the old Länder, by industry (October 1993)

	Percent
Manufacturing industry of which:	67.9
Male	66.7
Female	75.6
Electricity and other public utilities	68.1
Mining	79.4
Investment goods	63.6
Consumer goods	63.9
Food processing	60.7
Building and construction	76.0
Banking, insurance	70.2
Wholesale trade	62.2
Retail trade	73.4

Source: Wirtschaft und Statistik 5/1994, 391

Table 7 Working time and holidays

In the old FRG the actual weekly working time was 38 hours in 1990. In addition to the high number of public holidays, workers and salaried employees had paid holidays as follows

(figures for 1990)

Holiday Time	Percentage
From 3 to under 4 weeks	1%
From 4 to under 5 weeks	4%
From 5 to under 6 weeks	25%
6 weeks or more	70%

Source: Statistisches Bundesamt, *Datenreport, Zahlen und Fakten über die Bundesrepublik Deutschland,* Bonn, 1992, 155

Table 8 Rates of unemployment, by Länder (average 1993)

	Rate of unemployment (percent)
Old Länder	8.2
Baden-Württemberg	6.3
Bayern	6.4
Berlin (West)	12.3
Bremen	12.4
Hamburg	8.6
Hessen	7.0
Niedersachsen	9.7
Nordrhein-Westfalen	9.6
Rheinland-Pfalz	7.5
Saarland	11.2
Schleswig-Holstein	8.3
New Länder	15.8
Berlin (East)	13.7
Brandenburg	15.3
Mecklenburg-Vorpommern	17.5
Sachsen	14.9
Sachsen-Anhalt	17.2
Thüringen	16.3

Source: Amtliche Nachrichten der Bundesanstalt für Arbeit, Arbeitsstatistik 1993—Jahreszahlen

Table 9 Industrial Stoppages

Working days lost per 1000 employees

	(per year) 1970–1990	1992
Germany	40	61
USA	225	37
GB	435	24
Ireland	579	225
Spain	708	650
Italy	1042	160

Source: Informationsdienst des Instituts der deutschen Wirtschaft, 27 January 1994

Table 10 Provision of private households with selected durable consumer goods (percentages of all households 1993)

Goods	old Länder	new Länder
Private car	74	66
Dish washer	38	3
Micro wave oven	41	15
Washing machine	88	91
Laundry dryer	25	2
TV	95	96
Video recorder	49	36
Personal computer	22	16

Source: Wirtschaft und Statistik 12/1993, 924–928

Table 11 Public Finance

The consolidated budget of all three levels of government (Federal Government, Länder, local authorities) including para-statal institutions mainly of social security, amounted to public expenditure of DM 1150 billion in 1990, which is 47 per cent of the Gross National Product (GNP). The most important items of expenditure were (% of total):

	Percentage
Social security	47.8 %
Education, research and culture	10.5%
Defence	5.0%
Transport and communication	2.8%
Public health, sport and recreation	4.4%
Servicing of public debt	5.5%

In the budget of the Federal Government alone, defence accounted for 12.8 per cent of all expenditure in 1992.

Sources: Statistisches Bundesamt (ed.), *Statistische Jahrbücher 1991–1993;* Statistisches Bundesamt (ed.), *Datenreport,* Bonn, 1983

Table 12 External trade

As an exporter, the Federal Republic of Germany ranks second in the world with about 9 per cent of world exports. Total exports from the Federal Republic amounted to DM 671 billion in 1992 which was 22,5 per cent of the Gross Domestic Product. Total imports amounted to DM 638 billion in the same year. The Federal Republic has had export surpluses since 1955. The surplus is needed to earn the foreign exchange required for the remittances of the large number of foreign workers and for the deficit in tourism. In 1992 tourism resulted in a deficit of DM 40 billion foreign exchange.

Table 12a Exports

The six most important categories of exports were:

	(1992 % of total exports)
Vehicles	18.0
Machinery (except electric machinery)	15.0
Chemicals	12.7
Electric goods (including electric machinery)	11.9
Food and food processing, tobacco products	4.6
Textiles	3.6

The six most important countries of destination of these exports were:

	(1992% of total exports)
France	13.0
Italy	9.3
Netherlands	8.3
Great Britain	7.7
Belgium and Luxemburg	7.4
USA	6.4

All previous Eastern bloc countries together received about 5.6% of all exports; exports to developing countries (without OPEC) accounted for 8.1% of all exports.

Table 12b Imports

The six most important categories of imports were:

	(1992 % of total imports)
Vehicles	10.9
Electric goods	10.2
Chemicals	9.2
Machinery (except electric machinery)	6.8
Food and processed food, tobacco products	6.4
Textiles	5.2

The six most important countries of origin of these imports were:

	(1992 % of total imports)
France	12.0
Netherlands	9.6
Italy	9.2
Belgium and Luxemburg	7.0
Great Britain	6.8
USA	6.6

The Eastern bloc countries together accounted for about 5.5 per cent of all imports. Developing countries (without OPEC) accounted for 8.7 per cent of all imports.

Source: Wirtschaft und Statistik 5 and 6 /1993.

Table 13 Development of the exports of the former GDR/New Länder

(The GDR industry exports were strongly oriented to the former COME-CON countries)

Exports to	1989 (million DM)	1992 (million DM)
former USSR	16,576	5,543
former CSSR	3,814	789
Poland	3,116	524
Hungary	2,597	179
Romania	1,428	77
Bulgaria	1,361	67

Source: Informationsdienst des Instituts der Deutschen Wirtschaft, 1 July 1993

Table 14 Defence expenditure of NATO countries

Country/Currency (million)		YEAR			
		1970	1980	1990	1992
Belgium	B.fr.	37,388	115,754	155,205	132,819
Denmark	D.Kr.	2,967	9,117	16,399	17,129
France	F.Fr.	32,672	111,672	232,801	248,874
Germany	DM	22,573	48,518	68,376	65,536
Greece	Dr.	14,208	96,975	612,344	835,458
Italy	It.(1000)L	1,562	7,643	28,007	30,813
Luxembourg	Lux.fr.	416	1,534	3,233	3,936
Netherlands	DG	3,909	10,476	13,513	13,900
Norway	N.kr.	2,774	8,242	21,251	22,871
Portugal	Esc.	12,538	43,440	267,299	341,904
Spain	Ptas.	—	350,423	922,808	927,852
Turkey	TL	6,399	203,172	13,865,971	42,319,927
Great Britain	£	2,607	11,593	22,413	23,776
NATO-Europe	US$	—	112,255	186,576	195,035
Canada	Ca$	1,999	5,788	13,473	13,111
United States	US$	78,846	138,191	306,170	305,141
North America	US$	81,754	143,141	317,717	315,988
Total NATO	US$	—	255,396	504,293	511,023

Source: NATO Review, Brussels, April 1994

Table 15 Members of the Bundestag by profession

Bundestag Members	Percentage of total members by year		
	1983–87 %	1987–90 %	1990–94 %
Members of the government*	14.3	12.7	10.1
Civil Servants**	31.1	32.2	29.3
Employees in the public sector**	2.3	1.7	6.6
Clergy (prot.)	0.4	0.0	1.4
Employees of political parties and social organizations	13.6	14.0	13.3
Employees in the private sector	8.3	7.9	11.0
self-employed in industry and the professions	25.3	25.1	23.2
Housewives	1.5	2.1	2.1
Wage earners (no specification given)	1.3	2.7	1.7
Total of deputies	100.0%	100.0%	100.0%

* Chancellor, Federal Ministers, Parliamentary Secretaries of State
** See Ch. 12, Doc. 7a

Source: Peter Schindler (ed.), *Datenhandbuch zur Geschichte des Deutschen Bundestages 1983-1991*, Bonn, 1994

Table 16 Bundestag election results, 1949–1994 ('000s)

In this table results are not given for insignificant party affiliations, which generally gained less than one per cent each, so that figures below do not add up to one hundred percent. The only exception was the election of 1949, where such other groups gained, taken together, 6.2 per cent.

a) Total votes gained in the whole country, b) percentage of total votes, c) number of seats, before 1990 excluding deputies of West Berlin, because Berlin was under an especial international status, d) disappeared later from the German system of political parties.

Eligible Turnout % voting	14.8.1949 31.2 mill. 24.5 mill. 78.5			6.3.1953 33.1 mill. 28.5 mill. 85.8			15.9.1957 35.4 mill. 31.1 mill. 87.8			17.9.1961 37.4 mill. 32.8 mill. 87.7		
	a	b	c	a	b	c	a	b	c	a	b	c
CDU/CSU	7,359	31.0	139	12,440	45.2	243	15,008	50.2	270	14,298	45.3	242
SPD	6,935	29.2	131	7,945	28.8	151	9,496	31.8	169	11,427	36.2	190
FDP	2,83	11.9	52	2,628	9.5	48	2,307	7.7	41	4,029	12.8	67
KPD/DKP	1,362	5.7	15	0,607	2.2	—	—	—	—	—	—	—
DP [d]	0,94	4.0	17	0,898	3.3	15	1,007	3.4	17	GPD	2.8	—
BHE [d]	—	—	—	1,614	5.9	27	1,374	4.6	—	0,871		
Centre [d]	0,728	3.1	10	0,217	0.8	2	0,086	0.3	—	—	—	—
Bavaria Party [d]	0,986	4.2	17	0,466	1.7	—	0,168	0.5	—	—	—	—
WAV [d]	0,682	2.9	12	—	—	—	—	—	—	—	—	—
SRP/NPD	0,429	1.8	5	0,296	1.1	—	0,309	1.0	—	0,263	0.8	—
DFU	—	—	—	—	—	—	—	—	—	0,61	1.9	—

Table 16 (continued)

	19.9.1965 38.50mil. 33.4 mil 86.8			28.9.1969 38.7 mil. 33.0 mil. 86.7			19.11.1972 41.4 mil. 37.8 mil. 91.2			3.10.1976 42.0 mil. 38.1 mil. 90.7			5.10.1980 43.2 mil. 38.3 mil. 88.7		
	a	b	c	a	b	c	a	b	c	a	b	c	a	b	c
CDU/CSU	15,524	47.6	245	15,195	46.1	242	16,794	44.8	225	18,397	48.6	244	16,900	44.5	226
SPD	12,813	39.3	202	14,066	42.7	224	17,167	45.9	230	16,099	42.6	213	16,262	42.9	218
FDP	3,097	9.5	49	1,903	5.8	30	3,129	8.4	41	2,995	7.9	39	4,030	10.6	53
KPD/DKP	—	—	—	0,197	0.6	—	0,114	0.3	—	0,141	0.4	—	0,080	0.2	—
GDP	—	—	—	—	—	—	—	—	—	—	—	—	—	—	—
Centre [d]	—	—	—	—	—	—	—	—	—	—	—	—	—	—	—
Bavaria Party [d])	—	—	—	—	—	—	—	—	—	—	—	—	—	—	—
WAV [d]	—	—	—	—	—	—	—	—	—	—	—	—	—	—	—
SRP/NPD	0,664	2.0	—	1,422	4.3	—	0,207	0.6	0,122	0.3	—	0,067	0.2	—	—
DFU [d])	0,434	1.3	—	—	—	—	—	—	—	—	—	—	—	—	—

Table 16 (*continued*) Bundestag election results, 1949–80 ('000s)

	6.3.83 44.08 mill. 39.2 mill. 89.1			25.1.87 45.3 mill. 38.2 mill. 84.3			2.12.90 60.4 mill. 46.9 mill. 77.8			1994 60.4 mill. 47.0 mill. 79.1		
Eligible / Turnout / % voting	a	b	c*	a	b	c*	a	b	c	a	b	c
CDU/CSU	18.9	48.8	244 (+11)	16.7	44.3	223 (+11)	20.3	43.8	319	19.5	41.5	294
SPD	14.8	39.2	193 (+5)	14.0	37.0	186 (+7)	15.5	33.5	239	17.1	36.4	252
FDP	2.7	7.0	34 (+1)	3.4	9.1	46 (+2)	5.1	11.0	79	3.1	6.9	47
Grüne	2.1	5.6	27 (+1)	3.1	8.3	42 (+2)	1.7	3.8	—			
NPD	0.09	0.2	—	0.2	0.6	0.1	0.4	—				
DKP	0.06	0.2	0.2	—	—	—						
PDS	1.1	2.4 0.4	1.2	8**	1.9	3.4	7.3	49				
REP	1.0	2.1	—	0.8		—						

* +11 Berliner MdB

** The parties got seats although they did not gain 5% of the total votes because of special provisions for the former GDR where they got more than 5%. 1994 this will no longer be the case.

Overall source: Presse—und Informationsamt der Bundesregierung, Bulletin in the week following each election 1949, 1953, ff.

Table 17 Progress of Bills introduced in the Parliament of the Federal Republic

Legislative periods	1949-53	1953-57	1957-61	1961-65	1965-69	1969-72	1972-76	1976-80	1980-83	1983-87	1987-90
Bills introduced (total)	805	877	613	635	665	577	670	485	242	522	595
By the Government	472	446	401	378	417	362	461	322	146	280	321
By the Bundestag	301	414	407	245	227	171	136	111	58	183	227
By the Bundesrat	32	17	5	121	21	44	73	52	58	59	47

Bills may be introduced by any of these three bodies. They reach the statute books when passed after a third reading by the Bundestag, after the assent of the Bundesrat (where required) and the final signature by the President. *Ed.*

Bills passed by Parliament

	1949-53	1953-57	1957-61	1961-65	1965-69	1969-72	1972-76	1976-80	1980-83	1983-87	1987-90
Total, of those originating	545	507	424	427	453	335	516	354	139	320	369
Government	392	368	348	329	368	259	427	288	104	237	267
Bundestag	141	132	74	96	76	58	62	39	16	42	68
Bundesrat	12	7	2	2	9	13	17	15	8	32	15
Absolute veto											
by Bundesrat 2*	12	9	6	7	10	3	19	10	4	0	1*
Not enacted, after veto	8	4	2	3	2	1	8	7	2	0	1*

1 * Figures not available

2 * Ch. explains this in detail

Source: Peter Schindler (ed.), *Datenhandbuch zur Geschichte des Deutscher Bundestags 1980–1987* Bonn 1988 and 1983–1991, Bonn, 1994 (translation here slightly adapted, absolute figures given only)

Glossary

(This glossary lists technical terms and abbreviations applied in the political system of Germany which are either untranslatable, and therefore used in this volume in German only, or so uncommon for Anglo-Saxon readers that they need to be explained, or those that are used differently in Britain and the United States.)

Anfrage (pl: Anfragen) = written questions addressed to the government in parliament, usually with many supplementary questions.
Aktuelle Stunde = ad-hoc debate in parliament, put on the agenda on the motion of any one party, lasting an hour.
Art. (= Artikel) = synonymous in German legal text with paragraph (§) or section (US), therefore used interchangeably in this volume.
Beitrittsgebiet = term referring to the former GDR, constituting now the five so-called 'Neue Bundesländer'.
Blockparteien = bloc parties, term used in the GDR for all the then existing parties closely connected with the SED state party.
Bund = Federation, also synonymous with the source of federal power.
Bundesgesetzblatt (BGBl) = Statute Book of federal laws enacted by Parliament.
Bundeskabinett = Bundesregierung = Federal government, synonymous with cabinet.
Bundeskanzler = Federal chancellor.
Bundesminister = Federal minister.
Bundespräsident = Federal president, head of state.
Bundespresseamt = Press and Information Office of the Federal German Government.
Bundesrat = Council of Constituent States (Länder, see *infra* Land).
Bundesrepublik Deutschland = Federal Republic of Germany.
Bundestag, Deutscher = Federal Parliament.
Bundestagspräsident = Speaker.
Bundesverfassungsgericht = Federal Constitutional Court.
Bundesversammlung = Federal Convention, to elect the Federal president.
Bundeswehr = federal armed forces, services.

CDU (Christlich-Demokratische Union) = Christian Democratic Union.

Coalition Government = a term referring to several political parties with a majority in parliament forming governments since 1949 (very topical German terms now: Rot/Grün (SPD/Green Party) or 'Ampel-Koalition' (traffic-light coalition): red/green/yellow, the latter colour denoting the Liberal Party.

CSU (Christlich-Soziale Union) = Christian Social Union, in Bavaria.

Deutsche Demokratische Republik = GDR (German Democratic Republic, East).

DGB (Deutscher Gewerkschaftsbund) = German Trade Union Federation (TUC, AFL/CIO).

DKP (Deutsche Kommunistische Partei) = German Communist Party.

Einheitsvertrag = Treaty of Unity 1990 between the FRG and the GDR.

Evangelische Kirche in Deutschland = German Council of Protestant Churches.

Federalism = Föderalismus, in German terms referring to the principle of confederate states, stressing therefore constitutional powers of the states in contrast to the federal authorities.

Fraktion = caucus (US), parliamentary party (GB) in parliament.

Freiheitlich-demokratische Grundordnung = free democratic constitutional or basic order, a term frequently used in connection with activities which are regarded as threats to this order.

FDP (Freie Demokratische Partei) = Free Democratic Party.

Geschäftsordnung = Standing Orders (GB), Rules (US)—of parliament, but also of other bodies.

Gesamtdeutsch = all-German, referring before 1989 jointly to the Federal Republic and the GDR.

Gesetz = Law, Act or Statute.

Grüne = Party of the Greens, ecological party, merged with the Bündnis 90, formed after the collapse of the GDR.

Grundgesetz = Basic Law, constitution of the Federal Republic.

IM (informeller Mitarbeiter) = unofficial agent of the STASI (see below).

KBW (Kommunistischer Bund Westdeutschlands) = Communist League of West Germany.

KPD (Kommunistische Partei Deutschlands) = Communist Party of Germany originally outlawed in 1956.

Konstruktives Misstrauensvotum = constructive vote of no-confidence (in the Bundestag).

Land (pl: Länder) = federal state (US), e.g. Bavaria.

Legislaturperiode = legislative period (or term).

Ministerpräsident = minister-president = Prime Minister of a Land; in Hamburg, Berlin and Bremen: Bürgermeister (Regierender or First Minister).

Mitbestimmung = co-determination.

NDP (Nationaldemokratische Partei) = National Democratic Party of Germany.

Öffentlicher Dienst = Civil Service (federal, of the Länder and local).

Parlamentarischer Rat = Parliamentary Council = Constituent Assembly to draw up Basic Law 1948/49.

Parlamentarischer Staatssekretär = Parliamentary Secretary of State, deputizing for the minister in parliament, of which he is a member.

Parteitag = Party Congress or Conference = Convention (US).

PDS, Party of Democratic Socialism = Successor of the GDR State Party, SED.

Rechtsstaat = German tradition of government based on due process of law.

Reich = Old German Empire.

Republikaner, Republican Party (Reps) = extreme right-wing party.

Seilschaften = networking of former GDR functionaries.

SPD (Sozialdemokratische Partei Deutschlands) = Social Democratic Party of Germany.

SRP (Sozialistische Reichspartei) = former neo-Nazi party, outlawed in 1952.

Soziale Marktwirtschaft = social market economy.

Ständige Konferenz der Kultusminister = Permanent Conference of the Ministers for Cultural Affairs (and education) of the Länder.

Staatssekretär = (Permanent) Under-Secretary (of State) in a ministry (GB), Assistant Secretary of State (US).

STASI, Staatssicherheitsdienst (Secret Police of the former GDR).

Tagesordnung = Agenda, Order Paper in parliament; also pertaining to the order of business of other bodies.

Treuhandanstalt = Agency established for the privatization of the former state owned industry of the GDR.

Volkskammer = so-called people's chamber, parliament of the GDR.

Two-plus-Four (zwei plus vier) = abbreviation for the signatories of the international agreements on German Unity: the two German states plus the four allied powers of the Second World War.

Select Bibliography

GENERAL WORKS ON THE POLITICAL SYSTEM OF THE
FEDERAL REPUBLIC OF GERMANY

Bark, Dennis L. and Gress, David R., *From Shadow to Substance,
1945–1963* (A History of West Germany, Volume 1), Oxford
1989; Volume 2: *Democracy and its Discontents, 1963–1968,*
Oxford 1989
Childs, David and Johnson, John, *West Germany: Politics and Society,*
London, 1981
Conradt, David P., *The German Polity,* New York, 1978
Fulbrook, Mary, *The Divided Nation. A History of Germany 1918–
1990,* Oxford University Press, 1992
Heidenheimer, Arnold J. and Kommers, Donald P., *The Governments
of Germany,* 4th edn., New York, 1975
Paterson, William E. and Smith, Gordon, *The West German Model.
Perspectives on a Stable State,* London, 1981
Sontheimer, Kurt, *The Government and Politics of West Germany,*
New York, 1973

CHAPTER 1. *The Origins of the Federal Republic of Germany, 1944–1949*

Adenauer, Konrad, *Memoirs 1945–53,* London, 1966
Balfour, Michael, *West Germany,* London, 1968
——, 'Four-Power Control in Germany 1945–1946' in Balfour,
Michael and Mair, John, (eds.) *Four-Power Control in Germany
and Austria 1945–1946. Survey of International Affairs,
1939–1946,* Arnold Toynbee, London, 1956
Edinger, Lewis J., *Kurt Schumacher,* Oxford, 1965
Feis, Herbert, *Between War and Peace. The Potsdam Conference,*
Princeton, 1960
Gimbel, John, *The American Occupation of Germany,* Stanford, 1968
Heidenheimer, Arnold J., *Adenauer and the CDU. The Rise of the
Leader and the Integration of the Party,* The Hague, 1960

Merkl, Peter H., *The Origin of the West German Republic*, New York, 1963

Pridham, Geoffrey, *Christian Democracy in Western Germany. The CDU/CSU in Government and Opposition, 1945–1976*, London, 1977

Smith, Jean Edward, (ed.), *The Papers of General Lucius D. Clay: Germany 1945–1949*, 2 vols., Bloomington, 1974

Wheeler-Bennett, John W. and Nicholls, Anthony, *The Semblance of Peace, The Political Settlement after the Second World War*, London, 1972

Willis, F. Roy, *The French in Germany, 1945–1949*, Stanford, 1962

de Zayas, Alfred, M., *Nemesis at Potsdam, the Anglo-Americans and the Expulsion of the Germans: Background, Execution, Consequences*, London, 1977

CHAPTER 2. *Berlin*

Bowers, Stephen Reed, *The West Berlin Issue in the Era of Superpower Detente: East Germany and the Politics of West Berlin*, Tennessee,1975

Brandt, Willy, *The Ordeal of Coexistence. The Gustav Pollak Lectures at Harvard University*, 1962, Cambridge, Mass., 1963

Catudal, Honoré M. Jr., *The Diplomacy of the Quadripartite Agreement on Berlin. A New Era in East-West Politics*, Berlin, 1978

Clay, Lucius D., *Decision in Germany*, New York, 1950

Davison, W. Phillips, *The Berlin Blockade*, New York, 1958

Mander, John, *Berlin: Hostage for the West*, London, 1962

Schick, Jack M., *The Berlin Crisis, 1958–1962*, Philadelphia, 1971

Slusser, Robert M., *The Berlin Crisis of 1961. Soviet American Relations and the Struggle for Power in the Kremlin, June-November, 1961*, Baltimore, 1973

Smith, Jean Edward, *The Defense of Berlin*, Baltimore, 1963

Speier, Hans, *Divided Berlin. The Anatomy of Soviet Blackmail*, London, 1961

CHAPTER 3. *The Two Germanies*

Bericht der Bundesregierung und Materialien zur Lage der Nation 1972, Bonn, 1972 ff

Bericht der Enquete Kommission '*Aufarbeitung von Geschichte und Folgen der SED-Diktatur in Deutschland*', Deutscher Budestag, 12. Wahlperiode, Drucksache 12/7820

Doeker, Günther, and Brückner, Jens A., (eds.), *The Federal Republic of Germany and the German Democratic Republic in International Relations*, New York, 1979
Garton Ash, Timothy, *In Europe's Name. Germany and the divided continent*, London 1993
Roth, Margit, *Zwei Staaten in Deutschland - Die sozialliberale Deutschlandpolitik und ihre Auswirkungen 1969–1978*, Opladen, 1981
Schierbaum, Hansjürgen, *Intra-German Relations. Development, Problems, Facts*, Munich 1979
Schweitzer, Carl-Christoph, *Die deutsche Nation. Aussagen von Bismarck bis Honecker.* Dokumentation, 2nd edn., Cologne 1979
Turner, Henry Ashby, *Germany from Partition to Reunification*, Yale University Press 1992

CHAPTER 4. *Germany reunited 1989—Her first successful revolution, and a peaceful one*

German Politics, Vo. 3, No 1 April 1994, Journal of the Association for the Study of German Politics, Ilford (Essex)
Hancock, M. Donald, *German Unification, Process and Outcomes*, Westview Press, Boulder Colorado 1994
Jarausch, Konrad, *The Rush to German Unity*, Oxford University Press 1994
Pond, Elizabeth, *Germany's Road to Unification*, Brookings, Washington D.C. 1993

CHAPTER 5. *Foreign Policy*

Deutsch, Karl W., and Edinger, Lewis J., *Germany Rejoins the Powers. Mass Opinion, Interest Groups, and Elites in Contemporary German Foreign Policy*, Stanford, 1959
Fritsch-Bournazel, Renata, *Europe and German Unification*, New York/Oxford, 1992
Garton Ash, Timothy, *In Europe's Name. Germany and the Divided Continent*, London, 1993
Geipel, Gary L. (ed.), *Germany in a New Era*, Indianapolis, 1993
Griffiths, William E., *The Ostpolitik of the Federal Republic of Germany*, Cambridge, Mass., 1978
Hanrieder, Wolfram F. (ed.), *West German Foreign Policy, 1949–1979*, Boulder, 1979
_____, *Germany, America, and Europe. Forty Years of German Foreign Policy*, New Haven, 1989

Kaiser, Karl, and Maul, Hanns, (eds.) *Deutschlands Neue Außenpolitik.* Bd.I Grundlagen, München 1994

Merkl, Peter H., *German Foreign Policies, West and East. On the Threshold of a New European Era,* Santa Barbara, 1974

————, *German Unification in the European Context,* Philadelphia, 1993

Morgan, Roger, *The United States and West Germany, 1945–1973: A Study in Alliance Politics,* London, 1974

Pond, Elizabeth, *Beyond the Wall. Germany's Road to Unification,* Washington, 1993

Richardson, James L., *Germany and the Atlantic Alliance. The Interaction of Strategy and Politics,* Cambridge, Mass., 1966

Smith, Gordon, Paterson, William E., Merkl, Peter H. and Padgett, Stephen,(eds.), *Developments in German Politics,* Durham NC, 1992

Stent, Angela, *From Embargo to Ostpolitik. The Political Economy of West German-Soviet Relations, 1955–1980,* Cambridge, 1981

Szabo, Stephen F., *The Diplomacy of German Unification,* New York, 1992

Whetten, Lawrence L., *Germany's Ostpolitik. Relations between the Federal Republic and the Warsaw Pact Countries,* London, 1971

CHAPTER 6. *Defence Policy and the Armed Forces*

Barth, Peter, (ed.), *Die Bundeswehr in Staat und Gesellschaft,* Munich, 1982

Brauch, H.G., and Kennedy, Robert, (eds.), *Alternative Conventional Defence postures in the European Theatre,* Vol. 2 and 3, Washington 1992/93

Haftendorn, Helga, 'West Germany and the Management of Security Relations: Security Policy under the Conditions of International Interdependence', in *The Foreign Policy of West Germany,* London, 1980, 7–31

Ministry of Defence, (ed.), White Paper, 1979, *The Security of the Federal Republic of Germany and the Development of the Federal Armed Forces,* Bonn, 1979, see also: *Weißbuch 1994 zur Sicherheit der Bundesrepublik Deutschland und zur Lage und Zukunft der Bundeswehr,* ed. Bundesministerium der Verteidigung, Bonn 1994.

von Schubert, Klaus, *Sicherheitspolitik der Bundesrepublik Deutschland. Dokumentation 1945–1977,* 2 vols., Cologne, 1979

Schwarz, Jürgen, (ed.), *Grundlagen und aktuelle Aspekte der deutschen Sicherheitspolitik,* Munich, 1982

CHAPTER 7. *Parliamentary Democracy –The Bundestag*

Braunthal, Gerard, *The West German Legislative Process*, Ithaca, 1972
Burkett, T. and Schnettemeyer, S., *The West German Parliament*, London, 1982
Loewenberg, Gerhard, *Parliament in the West German Political System*, Ithaca, 1966
Schellknecht, Helmut, and Ziller, Gebhard, 'The Parliamentary Institutions in the Federal Republic of Germany', *Constitutional and Parliamentary Information*, 29, Geneva, 1979, 117, 15–24
Schweitzer, Carl-Christoph, *Der Abgeordnete im parlamentarischen Regierungssystem der Bundesrepublik, Deutschland*, Opladen, 1979
Thaysen, Uwe, (ed.), *US Congress and the German Bundestag. Comparisons of Democratic Processes*, Boulder Colorado 1990

CHAPTER 8. *Political Parties*

Balfour, Michael, *West Germany*, revised edn., London, 1982
Burkett, Tony, *Parties and Elections in West Germany. The Search for Stability*, London, 1974
Dalton, Russell J. (ed.), *The New Germany Votes. Unification and the Creation of a New Party System*. Oxford/Providence, R. I. 1993
Fisher, Stephen L., *The Minor Parties of the Federal Republic of Germany. Toward a Comparative Theory of Minor Parties*, The Hague, 1974
Grosser, Alfred, *Germany in our Time. A Political History of the Post-War Years*, London, 1971
Kaack, Heino, *Geschichte und Struktur des Deutschen Parteiensystems*, Opladen, 1971
Kinz, Rainer, et al., *Programme der politischen Parteien in der Bundesrepublik Deutschland*, Munich, 1979
Kitzinger, Uwe, *German Electoral Politics. A Study of the 1957 Campaign*, Oxford, 1960
Padgett, Stephen (ed.), *Parties and Party Systems in the New Germany*, Dartmouth Publishing Co., Aldershot 1993
Pridham, Geoffrey, *Christian Democracy in Western Germany. The CDU/CSU in Government and Opposition, 1945–1976*, London, 1977
Schellenger, Harold K., *The SPD in the Bonn Republic*, The Hague, 1968
Smith, Gordon, *Democracy in Western Germany. Parties and Politics in the Federal Republic*, London, 1979

CHAPTER 9. *Chancellor, Cabinet and President*

Dyson, Kenneth, 'The German Federal Chancellor's Office, *Political Quarterly* (July-September), 45, 364–71
Johnson, Nevil, *Government in the Federal Republic of Germany,* Oxford, 1973
Mayntz, Renate, and Scharpf, Fritz, *Policy-Making in the German Federal Bureaucracy,* Amsterdam, 1975
Merkl, Peter Hans, *Germany, Yesterday and Tomorrow,* New York, 1965
Prittie, Terrence, *Willy Brandt,* New York, 1974
Rausch, H., *Der Bundespräsident,* Munich, 1979
Ridley, F.F., 'Chancellor Government as a Political System and the German Constitution', *Parliamentary Affairs, 19,* February 1966, 446–61

CHAPTER 10. *The Judiciary*

Geck, Wilhelm K., 'The Reform of Legal Education in the Federal Republic of Germany', *American Journal of Comparative Law, 25,* 1977, 86–119
Heyde, Wolfgang, *The Administration of Justice in the Federal Republic of Germany,* Bonn, 1971
Laufer, Heinz, *Verfassungsgerichtsbarkeit und politischer Prozess,* Tübingen, 1968
Leibholz, Gerhard, *Politics and Law,* Leyden, 1965
Kommers, Donald P., *Judicial Politics in West Germany: A Study of the Federal Constitutional Court,* London, 1976
McWhinney, Edward, *Constitutionalism in Germany and the Federal Constitutional Court,* Leyden, 1962
Pakuscher, Ernst K., 'Administrative Law in Germany—Citizen v. State', *American Journal of Comparative Law, 16,* 1968, 309–31
Rheinstein, Max, 'Approach to German Law', *Indiana Law Journal, 34,* 1959, 546–58
Schram, Glenn N., 'The Recruitment of Judges for the West German Federal Courts', *American Journal of Comparative Law, 21,* 1973, 691–711

CHAPTER 11. *Basic Rights and Constitutional Review*

American Council of Germany, *Civil Liberties and the Defense of*

Democracy Against Extremists and Terrorists: A Report on the West German Situation, New York, 1980

Benda, Ernst, 'New Tendencies in the Development of Fundamental Rights in the Federal Republic of Germany', *John Marshall Journal of Practice and Procedure*, 11, 1977, 1–15

Kauper, Paul, and Halberstadt, Rudolf, 'Religion and Education in West Germany: A Survey and an American Perspective', *Valparaiso University Law Review*, 4, 1969, 1–42

Klein, Ekkehart, 'The Principle of Equality and its Protection in the Federal Republic of Germany' in Koopmans, *Constitutional Protection of Equality*, Leyden, 1975

Kommers, Donald P., 'The Jurisprudence of Free Speech in the United States and the Federal Republic of Germany', *Southern California Law Review*, 53, 1980, 654–95.

Krieger, Leonard, *The German Idea of Freedom,*Boston, 1975

Lautner, Gerd, *Die Freiheitliche Demokratische Ordnung,* Athenäum, 1982

Lee, Orlan, and Robertson, T.A., *'Moral Order' and the Criminal Law: Reform Efforts in the United States and West Germany,* The Hague, 1973

Meyer-Teschendorf, Klaus G., *Staat und Kirche in pluralistischen Gemeinwesen,* Tübingen, 1979

CHAPTER 12 *Federalism: Bund and Länder*

Blair, Philip, *Federalism and Judicial Review in West Germany,* Oxford, 1981

Bundesminister für Bildung und Wissenschaft, *Report of the Federal Government on Education 1970; The Federal Government's Concept of Educational Policy,* Bonn, 1970

Cole, R. Taylor, 'Federalism and Universities in West Germany: Recent Trends', *American Journal of Comparative Law*, 21, Winter, 1973, 45–68

____, 'West German Federalism Revisited', *American Journal of Comparative Law*, 23, 1975, 2, 325–36

Hearnden, Arthur, *Education, Culture and Politics in West Germany,* Oxford/Frankfurt, 1976

Jeffery, Charles, (ed.), *Federalism, unification and European integration,* London 1993

Laufer, Heinz, *Das Föderative System der Bundesrepublik Deutschland,* Munich, 1981

Merkl, Peter Hans, 'The Financial Constitution [Finanzverfassung] of West Germany', *American Journal of Comparative Law*, 6, 1957, 327–40

Pinney, Edward L., *Federalism, Bureaucracy and Party Politics in Western Germany: Role of the Bundesrat*, Chapel Hill, 1963

Reuter, Konrad, *Föderalismus. Grundlagen und Wirkungen in der Bundesrepublik Deutschland*, Heidelberg/Hamburg, 1983

CHAPTER 13. *Public Opinion: Interest Groups and the Media*

Claessens, Dieter, et al., *Sozialkunde der Bundesrepublik Deutschland*, new edn., Düsseldorf/Cologne, 1985

Beyme, Klaus, *Interessengruppen in der Demokratie*, 5th edn., Munich, 1980

Guggenberger, Bernd, *Bürgerinitiativen in der Parteiendemokratie*, Stuttgart/Berlin/Cologne/Mainz, 1980

Inter Nationes, *Press Laws*, Documents on Politics and Society in the Federal Republic of Germany, 3rd ed. Bonn 1994

Inter Nationes, *Broadcasting Laws*, Documents on Politics and Society in the Federal Republic of Germany, Bonn 1989

Weber, Jürgen, *Die Interessengruppen im politischen System der Bundesrepublik Deutschland*, Stuttgart/Berlin/Cologne/Mainz, 1977

Braunthal, Gerard, *The Federation of German Industry in Politics*, Ithaca, 1965

CHAPTER 14. *Economic and Social Policy*

Berghahn, Volker R. and Karsten, Detlev, *Industrial Relations in West Germany*, Oxford/Providence, R. I. 1987

Claessens, Dieter, et al., *Sozialkunde der Bundesrepublik Deutschland*, new edn., Düsseldorf/Cologne, 1985

Ghanie Ghaussy, A. and Schäfer, Wolf, (eds.), *The Economics of German Unification*, London / New York 1993

Hallet, Graham, *The Social Economy of West Germany*, London, 1973

Lampert, Heinz, *Die Wirtschafts- und Sozialordnung der Bundesrepublik Deutschland*, 11th edn., Munich, 1992

Leaman, Jeremy, *The Political Economy of West Germany 1945–1985*, Houndmills etc. 1988

Lipschitz, Leslie and McDonald, Donogh, (eds.), *German Unification, Economic Issues, International Monetary Fund Occasional Papers* 75, Washington D.C., December 1990

Owen-Smith, E., *The West German Economy*, London, 1982

Siebert, Horst, *The Big Bang with the Big Brother, German Unification in Its Third Year*, Kiel Discussion Papers No.211, Institut für Weltwirtschaft Kiel, May 1993

Statistisches Bundesamt (ed.), *Datenreport 1992, Zahlen und Fakten über die Bundesrepublik Deutschland*, Bonn 1992

Wünsche, Horst Friedrich (ed.), *Standard Texts on the Social Market Economy*, Stuttgart/New York, 1982

Notes on the Editors

Carl-Christoph Schweitzer

Professor Emeritus of Political Science at the University of Bonn, graduated from Oxford and received his PhD at the University of Freiburg, visiting Professor at the Universities of Oxford, Duke, Toronto and Leipzig. He has written books on contemporary international affairs, European integration and on the problems of parliamentary government, *inter alia: Amerika's Chinesisches Dilemma,* Opladen, 1969; *Die nationalen Parlamente in der Gemeinschaft, ihr schwindender Einfluß in Bonn und Westminster auf die Europagesetzgebung,* Bonn, 1978; *Bremer Bundeswehrkrawalle-Gefahren für unseren Staat und ihre Verschleierung im Streit der Politischen Parteien im parlamentarischen Untersuchungsverfahren,* Baden-Baden, 1980, and *Weltmacht USA: Kontinuität und Wandel ihrer Außenpolitik nach 1945,* Munich, 1983. For five years he was a member of the German Bundestag, where he served on the Committees for Foreign Relations and Defence.

Detlev Karsten

Professor of Economics and the Didactics of Economics at the University of Bonn, he was previously Professor at Stuttgart University (1970–5) and Visiting Professor of Economics in Ethiopia (1964–70). He is the author of *Wirtschaftsordnung und Erfinderrecht,* 1964, and *The Economics of Handicrafts in Traditional Societies,* Munich, 1973, and (together with Volker R. Berghahn) of *Industrial Relations in West Germany,* Oxford etc. 1987; together with C.C. Schweitzer he edited *The Federal Republic of Germany and EC Membership Evaluated,* London 1990. He has written articles on the economics of development, environmental policy and European integration. He has also produced textbooks for schools and teaching material for courses on economics.

Robert Spencer

Professor Emeritus of History, Trinity College, University of Toronto, and former Director of the university's Graduate Centre for International Studies. He has written books and articles on recent and contemporary German and European history, as well as on international relations and Canadian foreign policy. From 1959–1984 he was co-editor of the *International Journal,* the quarterly journal of the Canadian Institute of International Affairs. A specialist in nineteenth- and twentieth-century German history, his publications include co-authoring

Modern German History, 4th ed., London, 1968, and *The Shaping of Postwar Germany*, London, 1960. He has contributed chapters to *Auf der Suche nach der Gestalt Europas*, Bonn, 1990, and *Wiedervereinigung in Mitteleuropa*, Hg. Josef Becker, München, 1992.

R. Taylor Cole (deceased 1991)

James B. Duke Research Professor Emeritus of Political Science and provost of Duke University from 1960 to 1969. He served as president of the American Political Science Association and the Southern Political Science Association and as editor of the *American Political Science Review* and the *Journal of Politics*. He was a member of the American Academy of Arts and Sciences. From 1943 to 1944, he acted as special assistant to the United States minister in Stockholm and, during the early post war period, as consultant to the United States military government in Germany. He was awarded the Medal of Freedom for his contributions during this period. He is the author of *Recognition Policy of the United States since 1901* and *The Canadian Bureaucracy*, co-author of *Responsible Bureaucracy, Government in Wartime Europe and Japan, European Political Systems* and *The Nigerian Political Scene*. He received his AB and MA degrees from the University of Texas and his PhD degree from Harvard University.

Donald P. Kommers

Joseph and Elizabeth Robbie Professor of Government and International Studies at the University of Notre Dame, where he is also a member of the law faculty. He has written numerous books and articles on German law and politics, including *Judicial Politics in Germany*, 1976, *The Constitutional Jurisprudence of the Federal Republic of Germany* (1989), and *Constitutional Politics in Germany* (forthcoming 1995). He was director of the Notre Dame Law School's Center for Civil and Human Rights from 1976 to 1981 and editor of *The Review of Politics* from 1981 to 1994. In 1994 the American Bar Association named him co-winner of its Silver Gavel award for his contribution to a symposium on privacy and the public interest.

Anthony J. Nicholls

Official Fellow and University Lecturer, St. Antony's College, Oxford, he was educated at Merton College, Oxford. The author of *Freedom With Responsibility. The Social Market Economy in Germany, 1918–1963; Weimar and the Rise of Hitler*, co-author (with Sir John Wheeler-Bennett) of *The Semblance of Peace: the Political Settlement after the Second World War* and co-editor (with Erich Matthias) of *German Democracy and the Triumph of Hitler*.

INDEX